from the room.

For
reference

ENCYCLOPEDIA of IDENTITY

ENCYCLOPEDIA OF
IDENTITY

EDITOR
RONALD L. JACKSON II
UNIVERSITY OF ILLINOIS AT URBANA-CHAMPAIGN

CONSULTING EDITOR
MICHAEL A. HOGG
CLAREMONT GRADUATE UNIVERSITY

VOLUME 2

$SAGE | reference

Los Angeles | London | New Delhi
Singapore | Washington DC

For information:

 SAGE Publications, Inc.
2455 Teller Road
Thousand Oaks, California 91320
E-mail: order@sagepub.com

SAGE Publications Ltd.
1 Oliver's Yard
55 City Road
London EC1Y 1SP
United Kingdom

SAGE Publications India Pvt. Ltd.
B 1/I 1 Mohan Cooperative Industrial Area
Mathura Road, New Delhi 110 044
India

SAGE Publications Asia-Pacific Pte. Ltd.
33 Pekin Street #02–01
Far East Square
Singapore 048763

Printed in Mexico

Library of Congress Cataloging-in-Publication Data

Encyclopedia of identity / edited by Ronald L. Jackson.
    p. cm.
Includes bibliographical references and index.
ISBN 978-1-4129-5153-1 (cloth : acid-free paper)
  1. Identity (Philosophical concept) 2. Identity (Psychology) 3. Group identity. I. Jackson, Ronald L., 1970-

BD236.E42 2010
302.5—dc22   2010001777

This book is printed on acid-free paper.

11   12   13   14   10   9   8   7   6   5   4   3   2

Publisher:	Rolf A. Janke
Assistant to the Publisher:	Michele Thompson
Acquisitions Editor:	Todd Armstrong
Developmental Editor:	Carole Maurer
Reference Systems Manager:	Leticia Gutierrez
Reference Systems Coordinator:	Laura Notton
Production Editor:	Carla Freeman
Copy Editors:	Colleen B. Brennan, Robin Gold
Typesetter:	C&M Digitals (P) Ltd.
Proofreaders:	Annie Lubinsky, Sandy Zilka
Indexer:	David Luljak
Cover Designer:	Bryan Fishman
Marketing Manager:	Amberlyn McKay

Contents

List of Entries

Reader's Guide

As you read through the entries, it will be helpful for you to know how to use the Reader's Guide. In fact, you may choose to browse the terms simply by browsing the categories within the Reader's Guide. The Reader's Guide is provided to assist readers in locating articles on related topics. It classifies articles into 15 general topical categories: Art; Class; Culture, Ethnicity, and Race; Developing Identities; Gender, Sex, and Sexuality; Identities in Conflict; Language and Discourse; Living Ethically; Media and Popular Culture; Nationality; Protecting Identity; Relating Across Cultures; Religion; Representations of Identity; and Theories of Identity. Entries may be listed under more than one topic. So, for example, if you are interested in how identities are protected, you would go to the "Protecting Identity" section in the Reader's Guide and then look at the list of headwords that fall within that category. You will see entries such as Agency, Deviance, Face/Facework, Race Performance, Role Identity, Self-Consciousness, and Self-Construal. Then, if you select one—for example, Face/Facework—you can then search for that entry and read a detailed description of what the term means, how it relates to the category, and how it is related to identity.

Art

Aesthetics
Architecture, Sites, and Spaces
Artistic Development and Cognition
Bricolage
Children's Art
Confessional Art
Human Figure, The
Modern Art
Modernity and Postmodernity
Photographic Truth
Renaissance Art
Self-Image
Self-Portraits
Setting
Simulacra
Social Realism
Visualizing Desire

Class

Absolute Poverty
Anomie
Class
Class Identity
Complex Inequality
Consumption
Cultural Capital
Globalization
Hegemony
Immigration
Material Culture
Social Stratification Theory
Status
Third World
World Systems Theory

Culture, Ethnicity, and Race

Agency
Biracial Identity
Class
Class Identity
Code-Switching
Complex Inequality
Critical Race Theory

Culture
Culture, Ethnicity, and Race
Diaspora
Dimensions of Cultural Variability
Diversity
Ethnicity
Group Identity
Hegemony
Race Performance
Racial Contracts
Racial Disloyalty
Society and Social Identity
Status
Whiteness Studies
White Racial Identity
Xenophobia

Developing Identities

Age
Being and Identity
Consciousness
Deindividuation
Development of Identity
Development of Self-Concept
Evolutionary Psychology
Extraordinary Bodies
Generation X and Generation Y
Habitus
Hybridity
Id, Ego, and Superego
Individual
Individual Autonomy
Individuation
Intersubjectivity
Mind-Body Problem
Nigrescence
Person
Personal Identity Versus Self-Identity
Philosophy of Organization and Identity
Reflexive Self or Reflexivity
Saturated Identity
Self
Self-Affirmation Theory
Self-Assessment
Self-Concept
Self-Discrepancy Theory
Self-Efficacy

Self-Enhancement Theory
Self-Esteem
Self-Image
Self-Monitoring
Self-Perception Theory
Self-Portraits
Self-Presentation
Self-Schema
Self-Verification
Socialization
Theory of Mind

Gender, Sex, and Sexuality

Bisexual/Bicurious
Difference/Différance
Embodiment and Body Politics
Gay
Gaze
Gender
Ideal Body, The
Identity Politics
Performativity of Gender
Queer Theory
Scopophilia
Sexual Identity
Sexual Minorities
Velvet Mafia
Visuality
Visualizing Desire
Voice
Voyeurism
Womanism

Identities in Conflict

Accommodation
Acculturation
Adaptation
Bilingualism
Biracial Identity
Clan Identity
Conflict
Corporate Identity
Cultural Contracts Theory
Culture Shock
Double Consciousness
Identification

Identity Change
Identity Diffusion
Identity Negotiation
Identity Salience
Identity Uncertainty
Intercultural Personhood
Mindfulness
Mobilities
Modernity and Postmodernity
Passing
Perceptual Filtering
Philosophy of Mind
Simulacra

Language and Discourse

Ascribed Identity
Avowal
Brachyology
Colonialism
Deconstruction
Dialect
Discourse
English as a Second Language (ESL)
Ethnicity
Etic/Emic
Figures of Speech
Forms of Address
Framing
Hermeneutics
Hyperreality and Simulation
Idiomatic Expressions
Intonation
Invariant *Be*
Labeling
Language
Language Development
Language Loss
Language Variety in Literature
Narratives
Phonological Elements of Identity
Pidgin/Creole
Profanity and Slang
Public Sphere
Rhetoric
Sapir-Whorf Hypothesis
Satire
Semantics

Semiotics
Signification
Structuration
Style/Diction
Symbolism
Tag Question
Trickster Figure

Living Ethically

Antiracism
Corrosion of Character
Cosmopolitanism
Ethical and Cultural Relativism
Ethics of Identity
Eugenicism
Humanitarianism
Identity and Reason
Identity Politics
Liberation Theology
Myths
Narratives
Neoliberalism
Postliberalism
Social Movements
Terror Management Theory
Xenophobia

Media and Popular Culture

Articulation Theory
Consciousness
Consumption
Critical Theory
Cultural Capital
Cultural Studies
Embeddedness/Embedded Identity
Framing
Frankfurt School
Globalization
Material Culture
Media Studies
Mediation
Propaganda
Social Capital
Society of the Spectacle
Spectacle and the Self
Stock Character

Surveillance and the Panopticon
Technology
Values
Visual Culture
Visual Pleasure

Nationality

Citizenship
Civic Identity
Clan Identity
Collective/Social Identity
Collectivism/Individualism
Culture
Diaspora
First Nations
Historicity
Identity and Democracy
Immigration
Memory
Nationalism
Patriotism
Philosophical History of Identity
Political Identity
Sovereignty
State Identity
Terrorism
Third World
Transnationalism
Transworld Identity
War
Worldview

Protecting Identity

Agency
Deviance
Face/Facework
Ontological Insecurity
Personality/Individual Differences
Psychology of Self and Identity
Race Performance
Role Identity
Self-Consciousness
Self-Construal

Relating Across Cultures

Bilingualism
Code-Switching

Double Consciousness
Ethical and Cultural Relativism
Global Village
Immediacy
Impression Management
I-Other Dialectic
Multiculturalism
Nomadology
Pluralism
Political Psychology

Religion

Fundamentalism
Liberation Theology
Modernity and Postmodernity
Mythologies
Pragmatics
Religious Identity
Rituals
Secular Identity
Syncretism
Transcendentalism
Values

Representations of Identity

Archetype
Attribution
Authenticity
Basking in Reflected Glory
Bricolage
Commodity Self
Critical Realism
Cultural Representation
Desire and the Looking-Glass Self
Existentialist Identity Questions
Extraordinary Bodies
Hyperreality and Simulation
Identification
Identity Politics
Intertextuality
Looking-Glass Self
Masking
Material Culture
Mimesis
Minstrelsy
Orientalism
Other, The
Philosophy of Organization and Identity

Race Performance
Self-Presentation
Social Constructionist Approach to Personal
    Identity
Social Constructivist Approach to Political
    Identity
Stereotypes
Subjectivity

Theories of Identity

Afrocentricity
Articulation Theory
Asiacentricity
Black Atlantic
Cognitive Dissonance Theory
Communication Competence
Communication Theory of Identity
Contact Hypothesis
Corporate Identity
Critical Race Theory
Critical Realism
Critical Theory
Cultivation Theory
Cultural Contracts Theory
Enryo-Sasshi Theory
Ethnolinguistic Identity Theory
Eurocentricity

Global Village
Identity Scripts
Immediacy
Interaction Order
Mirror Stage of Identity Development
Modernity and Postmodernity
Optimal Distinctiveness Theory
Organizational Identity
Otherness, History of
Persistence, Termination, and Memory
Phenomenology
Philosophy of Identity
Political Economy
Postliberalism
Pragmatics
Public Sphere
Racial Contracts
Regulatory Focus Theory
Social Comparison Theory
Social Economy
Social Identity Theory
Sociometer Hypothesis
Symbolic Interactionism
Terror Management Theory
Theory of Mind
Third Culture Building
Uncertainty Avoidance
World Systems Theory

NARRATIVES

Questions of identity are some of the most common yet difficult questions that we as humans ask of ourselves and others. One of the ways we make sense of these questions is through the narratives we share with others. These narratives may be personal or impersonal, they may relate to mundane, everyday types of activities or be grander societal narratives that large-scale communities recognize and share. Narrative is often seen as the fundamentally human way of organizing the world and at the very core of who we are as individuals and communities. The concepts of both narrative and identity are approached from a wide variety of perspectives. An entry such as this cannot hope to capture all of these different perspectives and the nuances associated with them. Instead, this entry explains and illustrates some of the basic concepts and ideas associated with narrative identities that are shared in part by a variety of scholars. The entry identifies five essential elements of a narrative and explores links between these narrative elements and ways they connect to identity formation and expression. However, before going further, an example narrative is provided that can be used to illustrate and explain the narrative elements to be discussed and provide a springboard for the related discussion of identity as it pertains to each element. The terms *story/storyteller* and *narrative/narrator* are used interchangeably in this entry, for although some scholars suggest subtle differences, the more common practice is to treat them synonymously.

Example Narrative

When I was young, we moved close to my maternal grandparents. As part of the move, I had the opportunity to start mowing my grandparents' lawn as well as my own. I came home from one of my first times doing this and proudly showed off the five dollars I had made to my mother. I was surprised because my mother was anything but happy. She explained how my grandparents had to live on a fixed income and that we were family and that I should not need to be paid for mowing their lawn. I felt bad both about the fact that I had taken money from my grandparents and that I wouldn't be getting any more money. However, the next week when I tried to politely refuse two or three times, my grandmother finally just stuffed the money in my pocket and told me to scoot. I was not looking forward to having my mom find out that I had again ended up getting money for mowing my grandparents' lawn. She asked about the lawn mowing. I explained to her what happened. To my surprise, she was not upset and even said it was okay. I came to learn that if I tried to refuse the money ("Oh, you don't need to pay me, Grandma. I'm happy to help."), it was okay to eventually take it, but I should never act like it was expected. As I got older it became a kind of game for me to figure out how I could avoid getting paid for the work I did for my grandparents without hurting any feelings. Alas, they won that game more often than I did.

Universal Narrative Elements and Their Connections to Identity

Narrative News and the Avowal of Identity

First, there is a point made or, in other words, news to share. Narratives do not always have to have an obvious moral point or big news; however, there needs to be some discernable purpose (such as to make others laugh, show what a good person you are, or warn someone). This point of the story is inescapably intertwined with the news of the story. The news may be something surprising, informative, enjoyable, or socially noteworthy, thus worth remembering. Some stories are told over and over in the same community because the news has some ongoing value. Typically, what makes something news in this sense is not that it is new, but that it is tied to an event or situation that is unexpected or does not follow the normal pattern of life. If there is no news, the story is seen as pointless. Thus, humans are quite adept at finding a point in narratives that may on the surface appear mundane. The example narrative carries multiple news items, including the potentially contradictory reactions of the mother to the narrator receiving money from the grandparents and the way the narrator came to understand and deal with this type of situation.

One of the more commonly researched forms of narratives is the personal narrative. The narrator herself or himself is a key character in the story (for example, the son in the example narrative). These types of stories can be particularly powerful and persuasive—after all, an unspoken assumption often exists that the person telling the story is the best person to know what happened. This assumption may be questioned because of issues of memory, honesty, and self-presentation. However, regardless of accuracy, these stories play an important role in identity because a major part of the news or the point of the narrative is the avowal of a particular identity by the narrator. Therefore, these stories teach the narrator as well as others who hear these narratives about the narrator by both confirming past ideas and creating new ones.

When narrators tell stories that describe something they did, they frame themselves as being certain types of people, who act and think in certain ways. No single narrative captures all that a person does, thinks, or feels, but a given narrative makes salient thoughts and actions in a way that stakes an identity claim for that person. The narrative thus presents a certain image of who the person is to others and to the narrator himself or herself. These narratives are not simply revealing what exists (though they may be framed as simply doing this), they are creating who the person is. This creative process happens with others and in the mind of the narrator. The stories people tell themselves have great power. Despite other mundane purposes associated with personal stories, these narratives always address the great questions of "Who am I?" and "Who are you?" Because these questions are so fundamental to human life, these types of narratives will always be a fundamental part of our lives.

Context and the Ascription of Identities

The news or point of a story is intimately related to the context (social and physical setting, narrator, audience, etc.) in which it is told. There is no such thing as a narrative told in a vacuum. All stories have a context, even if that context may be referred to as artificial. The story told in the example narrative has been shared in a variety of contexts. Although these contexts are simplified for the needs of this entry, they include family gatherings that entail reminiscing, explicit teaching moments between a parent and a child, and the university classroom as part of a discussion of informal rituals. The point in each of these settings is a little different. In the academic setting, the news relates to the power and taken-for-granted nature of rituals and the subtle values they create and confirm in our lives. The news for the parent–child setting has to do with how to handle certain types of situations involving family relations, money, and appropriate expectations. At the larger family gathering (which may include the participants in the story), the point may be focused on humor or expressions of gratitude for lessons learned. Thus, the second universal aspect of narratives, the existence of a context, is crucially linked to our understanding of the point or news of a story.

The audience aspect of the context in a narrative is particularly important. The narrator of the preceding story would present what happened differently to his mother than he would present the story of the events to his friends, and this would be different from how he would present it to a scholarly audience. This does not necessarily mean that the narrator is being untruthful or deceitful in the telling of the story; rather, it means that the identity he has already created or wishes to create with the various audiences is different. Narratives are relational in nature. Directly or indirectly, one's point or the news item associated with the narrative is conveying an identity. However, the identity is not simply an avowal of personal identity; indeed, many narratives people tell do not involve the person telling the story at all. The narrator tells a story about other people. In doing so, the narrator ascribes to them certain identities.

Ascription in the narrative process refers to the assigning of an identity by the narrator to others. The narrator in this case may be yourself or others, so that a given person is on both the sending and receiving end of these ascribed identities. In the narrative provided, both the mother and the grandma are ascribed certain identities. They are both described in ways that tell listeners about who they are. Humans grow up hearing people give narratives in which they are part of the action. Identity is not simply something we claim, it is also something received from others. One of the key ways this happens is hearing narratives that involve the person. A person does not have to accept what is said, but as people hear many of these narratives, they can have a profound impact on the creation of personal identity and provide one window into the identity others associate with them.

Characters as Identity Templates

A third item is that stories always involve characters acting in some way. The characters, typically human, act and react to the situations they face in ways that provide insight into their identities. The characters do not have to be human, but even nonhuman characters are fused with humanlike identity by the actions and thoughts attributed to them. This allows humans to connect with others and to see themselves through the stories and lives of others. A human may see herself as a professor, a mother, and an Italian. Narratives that involve these types of persons have a similar

ascriptive power in confirming and creating identity as those stories that involve a specific person directly. The types of people referred to here go beyond specific roles and political or familial associations. These can also be associated with perceived traits or social positions, such as hard workers, nice guys, or underdogs.

In the example story, a specific mother, son, and grandmother are referenced, but these are also general types of characters or identities that potentially link the story to all people. Narratives are cumulative in nature; through hearing many stories of mothers, grandmas, and sons, a template is built that allows other humans who may share these social roles to understand what is expected or associated with these types of roles. These expectations or templates can be an important part of our identity and are often referred to as our social identity. These identity templates may be seen as spaces or positions that people can fill. Even though narratives tend to deal with deviations from the norm at some level, they also rely on common expectations associated with these social positions to make a story sensible and believable. Although a person may never directly fit the socially defined role of grandma, that person may still relate to the grandma in the story because of perceived identity characteristics. By relating to the grandma in one aspect, other choices and actions made by the grandma can affect identity issues of the listener. Although this can be carried to the extreme, humans use perceived similarity with others to expect and create other similarities with those same people.

Temporal Sequencing and Identity as Part of a Narrative Whole

A fourth inherent part of a narrative is that there is temporal sequencing involved (often linear). This sequencing provides a sense or reasoning behind the various actions taken in a story. In a narrative, given things happen over time and adjustments and actions can be understood in terms of the sequencing of these events. In this way, stories provide a basic way for humans to make sense of their own lives and the other lives around them. The narrator's efforts in the earlier story to refuse the money he actually wanted is understood in relation to the mother's earlier response to his eager acceptance of the money. The temporal sequencing provides a structure that encourages humans to see the connections between people, situations, and actions. Narratives are not a series of isolated elements: They are a cohesive sequencing of events and people and things that all interconnect together. These connections are the substance of what it means to live a reasonable and meaningful life.

Narratives create a logical space for people to fill, an acceptable range of actions that allows for cohesion and sense even when events threaten the everyday common sense of life. This allows us to deal with what is interesting and hard to understand in a way that gives it structure and makes it manageable and understandable. Although efforts to find the ultimate deep structure of narratives have had mixed results, understanding that narrative itself is a structure that creates connections that can both link and sever social relations provides an important base for understanding why narratives are an essential part of identity. Human identity is embedded in a sequence of events and cannot be fully understood outside of a narrative pattern.

Point of View and Identity in the Telling of a Narrative

The fifth and final element of narratives is a particular perspective or point of view. This is not limited to common literary classifications, such as first person, second person, and so forth, but refers to a broader perspective that is embodied in the persona (or voice created by the narrator to relate the narrative). The narrator is not the persona. A person may narrate a story, such as the example, and yet adopt a different persona in each narration. The persona in one telling may be a selfish person who clearly likes money, but is constrained by annoying social mores. This persona may convey a sense that the process described in the story was silly or hypocritical. In another telling, the persona may be more supportive in nature, someone who can laugh at himself and appreciate the value of relational rituals. A single individual may create multiple personas even when explicitly telling the same narrative. No narrative includes everything that could have been included (the example story could have included much more detail). What content is included, the tone of voice, word choice, and

so on used to relate the narrative (even one just told to ourselves) all suggests a point of view and attitude. There is an explicit or implicit evaluation of the characters and their respective actions in all stories (even when one tries to be neutral). In addition, the existence of a single persona does not mean that narratives are the expression of just one voice. Narratives may be multivoiced through the process of intertextuality (the use of other narrative texts) and through different levels of voice, personal and communal, that are often expressed without conscious forethought.

The point of view revealed by the persona is important in the creation and understanding of the various identities inhabiting a given narrative. However, the persona also provides clues to the identity of the narrator, for, although they are not the same, they are seen as connected. Thus, when researchers and others listen to a narrator, they make assumptions about the identity of the person based on the persona and the way the narrative is expressed. Often, subtle aspects associated with point of view create an identity for someone. One may argue that the narrator is not the dutiful son portrayed in the persona adopted for the narrative above, but to do so would require other narratives.

Final Thoughts

Although the elements of narratives and identity are discussed in separate sections, they are all intertwined. The narrator of the example story may raise eyebrows and indicate with a tone of voice that he was a stereotypical young man who was not too fond of work, but who appreciated money and knew how to play the system to get it. This identity may be used to get laughs and help the person relate to others as just an ordinary guy. The creation of a different persona may allow for the identity of the narrator to be more about obedience, family ties, and a willingness to respect authority. The value of these identities may vary greatly depending on the context in which the narrative is told. Thus, narratives are an important way through which identities are avowed and ascribed, directly or indirectly. Identities, the way people view who they and others are, are created and confirmed in narratives in ways that help us interpret and evaluate ourselves, others, and the world we live in.

There are, of course, other general elements of narratives, such as framing techniques, that may help regulate the production of a story, but the five common elements noted cross cultures and communities in a way that allows us to see the power of narratives in everyday life and the relationship they have with identities (for the purposes of both doing research and living a life). That these elements cut across cultures does not mean that they exist separately from culture in practice. Indeed, cultural knowledge is both drawn upon and (re)created in the news or point of a narrative, the contextual meaning associated with a story, the recognizable characters and identities, the reasonableness of the narrative's sequencing, and the points of view expressed through a persona. Culture, narratives, and identity are inescapably linked together, with each one providing windows to the others.

Bradford 'J' Hall

See also Communication Theory of Identity; Culture; Embeddedness/Embedded Identity

Further Readings

Bakhtin, M. (1981). *The dialogic imagination*. Austin: University of Texas Press.

Brockmeier, J., & Carbaugh, D. (2001). *Narrative and identity: Studies in autobiography, self and culture*. Amsterdam: John Benjamins.

Bruner, J. (1990). *Acts of meaning*. Cambridge, MA: Harvard University Press.

Fisher, W. (1989). *Human communication as narration*. Columbia: University of South Carolina Press.

Hall, B. (2005). *Among cultures: The challenge of communication* (2nd ed.). Belmont, CA: Thomson Wadsworth.

Johnstone, B. (1991). *Stories, community and place*. Bloomington: Indiana University Press.

Labov, W. (1982). Speech actions and reactions in personal narrative. In D. Tannen (Ed.), *Analyzing discourse: Text and talk* (pp. 219–247). Washington, DC: Georgetown University Press.

Polkinghorne, D. (1987). *Narrative knowing and the human sciences*. Albany: SUNY Press.

Straub, J. (Ed.). (2005). *Narration, identity and historical consciousness*. Oxford, UK: Berghahan Books.

Sunwolf, & Frey, L. (2001). Storytelling: The power of narrative communication and interpretation. In W. Robinson & H. Giles (Eds.), *The new handbook of language and social psychology* (pp. 119–135). New York: Wiley.

Tracy, K. (2002). *Everyday talk*. New York: Guilford Press.

NATIONAL

See Patriotism

NATIONALISM

The concept of *nationalism* is embedded in the everyday lives of citizens of modern nation-states. The pride that people feel for national accomplishments, the appeals of politicians to the national interests in justifying policies, and the symbols that nations use for self-identification (e.g., flags, national anthems, and monuments) are omnipresent and help create a national consciousness and national identity among diverse individuals. However, when examined in its historical, political, and social context, nationalism takes on a much more sophisticated, controversial, and ambiguous meaning that goes beyond the romantic view reflected in everyday notions of this concept. Although nationalism was essential to the formation of modern nation-states and can play an important role when societies face times of crisis, it can also lead people to view their nation as beyond reproach, justifying the use of force and violence to deal with real or perceived enemies. This entry provides an overview of various approaches to nationalism, giving special attention to potential negative consequences of extreme nationalism.

Approaches to Nationalism

Academics from a wide variety of disciplines, including history, anthropology, sociology, political science, and cultural theory, have contributed to a large body of literature that explores many issues of nationalism, including definitions, origins, development, and forms. Scholarly interest in the concept of nationalism increased significantly during the 1980s and has continued. Earlier studies focused on European nationalism, but recently there has been more emphasis on non-Western examples, particularly in Asia, Africa, and the Middle East.

Nationalism has been approached from various philosophical perspectives, with considerable debate surrounding these different interpretations. There is general agreement that nationalism is a Western construction or conception that is inextricably linked to the formation of modern nation-states in Europe. This gradual process, spurred by the ideas of the Enlightenment and the French Revolution as well as by the development of new economic structures, involved transforming diverse peoples inhabiting a defined territory into a nation with a single identity.

Scholars usually make a distinction between nations and states. A nation often consists of an ethnic or cultural community, whereas a state is a political entity with a high degree of sovereignty. The sociologist Anthony D. Smith defines a *nation* as a group of people sharing an historic territory; common myths and historical memories; a mass, public culture; a common economy; and common legal rights and duties for all members. A nation signifies a cultural bond, a community of people united by ideology, language, mythology, symbolism, and consciousness. A *state* refers to public institutions that exercise legal and political power within a given territory and require obedience and loyalty from its citizens. The nation-state is a result of a successful nationalist movement; thus, the state has the same political boundaries and homogeneity of the population as the nation.

Social and political scientists have traditionally made a distinction between the Western *civic* model of the nation, which is based on European nation-states, and the non-Western *ethnic* concept of the nation, which is more closely associated with Eastern Europe and Asia. The civic model emphasizes a spatial or territorial conception of homeland, the idea of a legal-political community and equality among its members, and a common civic culture and ideology, whereas the ethnic model stresses common descent, popular mobilization, and vernacular languages, customs, and traditions.

Contemporary scholarship defines the concept of a nation more broadly, combining both civic and ethic categories. In this view, a nation is a cultural group, one that may have a shared origin, with loyalties to a common political state. Individuals' membership in the nation is usually involuntary, though there are instances where individuals choose to be part of a particular nation (e.g., immigration). In the classical form of nationalism, which is concerned with the creation and maintenance of a sovereign state, loyalty to the nation takes precedence over other allegiances, such as regional, local, or kinship ties. In contrast, moderate forms of nationalism are more likely to promote individual rights, creativity, and diversity of communities within the nation. Liberal nationalism, for example, strives to protect cultural communities while promoting liberal universal principles.

Although most scholars today view the nation as a modern creation, some scholars consider it as a timeless phenomenon (primordialist view). Others argue that nations have existed for a long time, though they take different forms at different points in history (perennialist view). Modernist scholars also differ in their interpretation of nation. Although some anti-realist modernists view nations as pure "constructions," others, such as Benedict Anderson, view the modern nation as an "imagined political community." For Anderson, a critical feature of the emergence of a nation is its "community of anonymity." This form of community enables citizens to identify with one another in a shared allegiance to the nation, allowing them to imagine themselves as part of a national culture without having personal contact with the vast majority of members of that community. Anderson emphasizes the role of literacy and print capitalism in this process.

Nationalism: A Positive–Negative Dialectic

Since its advent in the 19th century, nationalism has had an overwhelming impact on human history. In his work *The Wrath of Nations,* William Pfaff shows how in its historical evolution, nationalism has been a relentless, driving sociopolitical force that transcends and overshadows class differences, distinctions between the political ideologies of the right and the left, as well as internal differences in specific policies and strategies within the nation-state. Johann Gottfried Herder and Giuseppe Mazzini spoke of nationalism as a divinely ordained, historical force of liberation, destined to lead humanity to universal justice and global peace. Others have interpreted it as a functional, sociocultural phenomenon that unifies people, sustains the cohesion of the national community, defines and clarifies collective values, and generates loyalty to the larger whole. More recently, nationalism has also been viewed as a legitimate moral and political force securing the rights and independence of people from the onslaught of globalization.

In contrast to those who conceptualize nationalism as a positive force, others view nationalism as subversive and erosive of the human spirit. Nationalism is seen as an intolerant and destructive historical force; a phenomenon that deeply divides nations and societies; an approach to politics that fosters a culture of collective narcissism and exclusivist notions of belonging; a power-driven and self-serving national and international political force that escalates conflicts, precipitating both civil and international wars; and as a worldview that accommodates the use of force/violence as a premium instrument of national politics and that tolerates the loss of human life as a legitimate necessity. Furthermore, nationalism has been viewed as a sinister force that has contributed to the globalization of conflict, while rendering globalization a conflict-proliferating process.

Nationalism may thus be seen as creating a positive–negative dialectic—promoting loyalty and helping unify people across a variety of perspectives into a national community, but at the same time allowing the nation to absolutize its moral authority regarding its freedom, interests, identity, and power. In this sense, nationalism supports a belief that we have "the right" to employ all means, including adversarial and lethal means, in the nation's defense, sustenance, and advancement. Nationalism justifies the expansion of powers to realize the nation's alleged historical destiny. Such a linkage helps explain the frequently perplexing question as to why nationalism has been so appealing and ennobling but simultaneously dangerous and violent.

Nationalism and the Sacredness of the Nation

The idea of *the nation* has a power over people that is perhaps best understood as a derivative of the exaggerated qualities that the nationalist mind elaborates and projects onto the entity referred to as *the nation*. Irrespective of whether they see nationalism as a positive or a negative force, scholars generally acknowledge that in nationalism, the nation is placed on the highest pedestal and viewed as the supreme agency of meaning, collective identity, and moral justification. Eric Hobsbawm critically noted that one of the powerful ways in which nationalism becomes historically established is through its presumption that *the nation* is sacred—an attribute that he likens to a kind of secular equivalent of the church. Smith, an advocate of nationalism, similarly speaks of *the nation* as being a religion surrogate. This assertion can be applied both to nationalisms that have incorporated traditional religion as part of their mental edifice of values (e.g., Serbian, Greek, Hindu, Islamic, Irish Protestant, and Irish Catholic nationalisms) and to secular nationalisms that purport to have expunged traditional religion from their values structures (e.g., Turkish, French, Egyptian, and Syrian nationalisms).

Historically, the attribution of sacredness to the idea of *the nation* has been ritualized in the images of national leaders, in ethnocentric public ceremonies, and in master narratives of national heroic acts that focus on extraordinary achievements and events. These narratives are underscored by a presumed history of national glory, greatness, binding destiny, and even divine election. Centered on an exaggerated notion of *the nation*, nationalist historiography projects a glorified image of *the nation* into a superlative, primal past, transposed by necessity into a compelling, duty-bound present and an infinite, grandiose future. It cultivates a monocentric, narcissistic concept of the nation's life-world, creating a perception of the nation's history that identifies the "good" with one's own nation and the "bad" with that of "the other," particularly of "the enemy other." In so doing, nationalist historiography presents *the nation* as an inerrant, eternal political entity, concealing its historical follies and the crucial fact that the nationalist concept of *the nation* was a historical product of the 19th century.

Such a nationalist approach to nationhood places *the nation* in an untouchable "moral realm," above and beyond question, reproach, and accountability. The concept of national sovereignty and self-determination, usually viewed as the cornerstone of world order and stability, has often been framed and conditioned by nationalism. Such a perspective implies that the "right" to pursue policies, devise strategies, and take actions unilaterally supersedes the requirement for bilateral or multilateral deliberations. From this perspective, the nationalist mind often views even international law as subsidiary and secondary to the status of *the nation*.

Nationalism and Conflict

The most problematic aspect of nationalism at both the national and international levels has been its capacity to link moral reasoning and the use of force and violence, especially in time of conflict. In a unique manner, nationalism has historically grounded the right to use force or violence in the moral rationale that *the nation* is the ultimate collective value and the imperative basis for community, identity, security, and well-being. This configuration of belief and action has made nationalism a strong legitimizer of the use of force and violence throughout modern and much of postmodern history. The most prominent symbols of nationalism, including national anthems, national flags, monuments, and historiographies, disclose symbols and involve narratives of war, revolution, heroics, and the shedding of blood as supreme references of national identity, glory, and honor.

As a result of the capacity of nationalism to "morally" legitimize force and violence in the name of *the nation*, nationalist-minded leaders and followers tend to develop high levels of tolerance for the use of lethal means in dealing with conflicts, particularly in confronting identifiable historical "enemies" of the nation. Nationalists are inclined toward a high level of tolerance for the loss of human life among their own national community as well as among the enemy community. Nationalism presumes *the nation* to be sacred, so the taking and offering of human life to its service at critical moments in history is viewed as legitimate and as a "moral duty." Hence, according to the nationalist mind, though momentarily inconvenient, the offering and taking of human life for the sake of *the nation* is ultimately neither a problematic nor a tragic phenomenon but one of "supreme duty" and altruistic "ultimate sacrifice."

During the periods preceding and following nationalist conflict, the overall political process becomes forged in a manner that structurally links legitimate human needs and interests to nationalist positions. In other words, vital needs such as security, economic well-being, cultural identity, and community become structurally intertwined with nationalist positions derived from notions of moral or cultural superiority, unilateral projections of power and grandiosity, a sense of historical destiny or divine mission, self-serving justice, and a "we-do-as-we-see-fit" narcissism, all of which inevitably function belligerently in relation to "the other." Legitimate human needs thus become absorbed by, and integrated into, the framework of the absolute and uncompromising value of *the nation*.

New Trends and Challenges

The rising phenomenon of globalization, associated with a postmodern world, has posed new challenges to the nationalist concept and organization of the nation-state. Advanced technologies, international trade, energy needs, climate change, electronic media, and international capital markets have rendered national economies structurally interdependent and interlinked to global, complex networks that transcend what any individual nation can manage. This makes the nationalist premise of the nation-state increasingly problematic and perhaps even untenable. To the degree that the tenets of nationalism persist, nationalist approaches to governance will collide with the increasingly interconnected structures of a globalizing world.

Harry Anastasiou and Benjamin J. Broome

See also Conflict; Ethnicity; Globalization; Group Identity; Political Identity; Transnationalism

Further Readings

Alter, P. (1994). *Nationalism* (2nd ed.). London: Hodder Arnold.

Anderson, B. (1995). *Imagined communities: Reflections on the origin and spread of nationalism*. London: Verso.

Deutsch, K. W. (1966). *Nationalism and social communication: An inquiry into the foundations of nationality*. Cambridge: MIT Press.

Gellner, E. (1983). *Nations and nationalism*. Ithaca, NY: Cornell University Press.

Hobsbawm, E. (1990). *Nations and nationalism since 1780: Program, myth, reality*. Cambridge, UK: Cambridge University Press.

Smith, A. D. (1993). *National identity*. Reno: University of Nevada Press.

NEOLIBERALISM

Neoliberalism is a theory of political economy that contends that free market capitalism is the best, and perhaps only justifiable, basis for political organization. Though often associated in the United States with neoconservativism and Republican Party politics, neoliberalism is a separate movement based in the pursuit of individual economic freedom through the protection of private property, the development of free markets, and the sharp limitation of state power. Since the economic crisis of the 1970s, neoliberalism has taken a place of preeminence, not only in the United States and Great Britain but also in the developing economies of Latin America and Asia. As a theory of political economy, neoliberalism has influenced the ways in which people view their understandings of themselves and their obligations to each other. This entry focuses on the neoliberalism's conceptual history, implications for understanding identity, and criticisms.

Conceptual History

As its name suggests, neoliberalism sees itself as standing within the tradition of liberalism. Though today the term *liberal* refers primarily to those on the political left, political theorist John Gray reminds us that liberalism was the defining political ideology of Western culture during the late 18th and 19th centuries. Gray notes that liberalism in its most classic sense—rooted in what he describes as the Enlightenment's individualistic, egalitarian, universalist, and meliorist conception of humanity—saw in the creative capacity of the individual the power to improve the human condition indefinitely, as long as the individual was unencumbered by the artificial constraints of tradition or religion, and the market was left to run its course.

This first statement of the liberal tradition, what is often called *classical liberalism*, did not last. The challenges of industrialization, urbanization, and bureaucratization during the late 19th and early 20th centuries encouraged many—most notably the British economist John Maynard Keynes—to move toward what anthropologist David Harvey calls *embedded liberalism*. Where classical liberalism tended to emphasize what Gray describes as *negative liberty*, in which freedom was understood narrowly as the right to be left alone, embedded liberalism was far more concerned about *positive liberty*, in which freedom was understood in terms of the capacity to participate substantively in public life. As Keynes's economic theories gave a rationale and practical strategy for enabling the development and participation of persons in the market and the broader society, embedded liberalism became increasingly committed to rigorous governmental interventions in the economy, the redistribution of wealth through progressive taxation, and broad social welfare programs.

During the quarter century following the Great Depression and the World War II, Keynesian economics and the welfare state it created were largely unassailable. But for some scholars, embedded liberalism's apparent triumph amounted to a betrayal of the liberal tradition. At the height of World War II, when the intellectual consensus in Britain and the United States saw Nazi Germany as the natural outgrowth of unfettered capitalism, Friedrich A. Hayek's *The Road to Serfdom* made the controversial claim that it was not capitalism but the interventionist posture of the socialist welfare state that was to blame for the rise of German fascism. The Austrian economist's book became an instant classic and influenced an entire generation of intellectuals. By 1962, when U.S. economist Milton Friedman published *Capitalism and Freedom*, what would become the tenets of neoliberalism—the demand for individual economic freedom; the concern about the size, inefficiency, and inordinate expense of the welfare state's constantly expanding bureaucracy; and the belief in the creativity of the free market to meet social needs—were already beginning to be developed.

Keynesian economics' apparent inability to meet the worldwide economic crisis of the 1970s saw this resurgence of classical liberal ideas emerge as a viable alternative to the welfare state. During the decade, Chilean dictator Augusto Pinochet, with the help of Friedman and others, began to implement neoliberal principles, and Hayek and Friedman both received Nobel Prizes for their respective works. With the elections of Margaret Thatcher and Ronald Reagan—the latter helped by a Republican Party coalition of neoliberals and Christian social conservatives that came to be known as *neoconservativism*—neoliberalism became politically dominant in Great Britain and the United States. During its journey to power, neoliberalism gave rise to what Harvey describes as the *financialization* of economic life, in which the focus of economic activity would shift from the production of goods to speculative financial instruments to create new sources of capital. As it encouraged Latin American and Asian economies—particularly China—to implement its principles, neoliberalism simultaneously fostered the *globalization* of commerce, transforming both advanced and developing nations. In the process, Harvey concludes, neoliberalism at the beginning of the 21st century has achieved the same unquestioned status that Keynesian economics enjoyed in the middle of the 20th century.

Implications for the Understanding of Identity

Perhaps the defining implication of neoliberalism lies in its radical rehabilitation of classical liberalism's emphasis on *individualism.* Hayek considered classical liberalism's understanding of the importance and dignity of the individual to have been Western civilization's crowning achievement, and his critique of the welfare state sought to preserve this gift against those who would diminish individuals' abilities to define their lives as they chose. Throughout his *Capitalism and Freedom,* Friedman, too, defined society as a collection of Robinson Crusoes—or, at most, families of Robinson Crusoes—seeking to maximize their life possibilities independently of each other. From a neoliberal perspective, the competitive self-maximization of the rugged individual is understood to be the vital spark of human creativity and progress, and societies are called to protect this spark against those who would seek to stifle it. The primary enemy in this struggle comes from the institutions—perhaps most especially well-meaning

institutions—whose interventions to improve human society diminish the dynamic capacity of individuals to compete and create. As a result, neoliberal individualism often manifests itself as *anti-institutionalism.*

The neoliberal emphasis on creativity and market competition also leads them to see individual freedom primarily in terms of *economic freedom,* with political and civic freedoms as a distant priority. Such freedom demands that individuals be given the ability to participate in the marketplace however they see fit, and that corporations be given the ability to compete unfettered by burdensome regulations or extraneous concerns that would distract them from maximizing returns for their shareholders. Consequently, neoliberals reject any notion of corporate social responsibility or redistributive justice—environmental regulations and social welfare programs, for instance—as both restrictive to individual economic choice and, as Hayek believed, debilitating to the spirit of competition and risk essential to human life. Certainly, many neoliberals also point out that their opposition to such interventions does not mean that they are against such causes as the environment or social welfare but rather that they believe that the expense and inefficiency of governmental intervention would far outweigh any possible benefit. As a result, neoliberals instead seek to minimize governmental intrusion, emphasizing the expansion of individual choice and market competition—through competitive environmental emissions markets to reduce pollution or the privatization of social insurance programs, for instance—to promote economic expansion, a result they believe to be far more effective in the long run.

Finally, the embrace of individualism and economic freedom encourages neoliberals to see the development of an efficient free market as the ultimate goal of any political arrangement. As they seek this goal, neoliberals such as Hayek reject the charge that they desire a return to *laissez faire,* in which a passive state leaves businesses to run amok. Instead, neoliberal political life constantly emphasizes participation in what Gray describes as a *limited state,* in which a constitutional government limits itself to providing only those functions that the market cannot provide on its own, namely, the rule of law, property rights, security and order, and basic infrastructure. Although this understanding of politics falls far short of the planned interventions of the welfare state, neoliberalism recognizes that all of these objectives are significant—and expensive—undertakings that have tremendous consequences in enabling individuals to pursue economic freedom. Furthermore, as libertarian philosopher Robert Nozick argued in *Anarchy, State, and Utopia,* neoliberals often believe that asking anything more of the state presupposes a level of consensus around a particular set of social values that has never existed in human history and would be inherently oppressive to those who do not share such values. Consequently, the minimal state is understood to be both more fiscally responsible and far more respectful of individual liberty.

Critiques

Neoliberalism has wielded a profound influence on contemporary debates on political economy and public policy, and its ideas have proved vital in foregrounding the importance of creating efficient and fiscally sustainable social programs. In addition, neoliberalism's minimalist approach to public policy seems to be a pragmatic response to the moment of postmodernity, in which the decline of guiding metanarratives has fragmented the moral and ethical consensus necessary to undertake large-scale public projects. Yet, since its inception, neoliberalism has sparked tremendous criticism. Harvey catalogues the charges that have been brought against it: that its strategy of globalization, while achieving mixed results in emerging markets, has succeeded primarily in enriching a small number of global elites, that it has had disastrous effects on the environment, and that its financialization of capital markets has promoted irresponsible speculation and costly bailouts. But beyond these practical concerns, critics of the neoliberal perspective have mounted deeper philosophical challenges that correspond to its emphases on individualism, economic freedom, and the limited state.

First, communitarians such as Michael Sandel contend that neoliberalism's emphasis on the individual abstracted from any community ties is a fundamentally untenable anthropology. Communitarians contend that individuals are never as isolated from sustaining social relationships as neoliberalism—or, indeed, liberalism—typically assumes, and that such

disregard for the role of community in shaping individual identity has profound social consequences. Harvey notes that neoliberalism's ideal of rugged, competitive individualism has indeed had problematic effects on the societies and cultures where it has taken root, often forcing neoliberalism to embed itself in conservative or nationalistic frameworks—such as U.S. neoconservatism and Chinese nationalism—to reestablish the social ties that it unravels and respond to the anomie that its economic policies create.

Second, Harvey notes that neoliberalism's emphasis on economic freedom over either political or civil freedom has often led neoliberals to develop troubling relationships with rogue regimes. Friedman's support of the brutal Chilean dictator Pinochet and the easy relationship between neoliberal ideas and a Chinese regime with a questionable human rights record alarm many critics, even if they believe the neoliberal argument that increased economic freedom now will bring increased political and civil freedom later. The development economist and Nobel laureate Amartya Sen contends that such a perspective on international development neglects the real ways that political and civil freedoms have proven essential in creating foundations for economic security, social trust, and the constructive development of values in diverse, developing nations.

Third, and finally, critics of neoliberalism contend that a purely limited state is of limited value in moving disenfranchised persons out of poverty. Following embedded liberalism's emphasis on the importance of empowering persons to engage in public life, Sen argues that, contrary to what neoliberal theory suggests, disenfranchised persons do require a basic amount of social goods to secure and exercise economic freedom. Indeed, the development economist Jeffery Sachs has found that the societies that have done the best for their people are not pure neoliberal states but rather states like the Scandinavian countries that have preserved strong networks of social services. Such findings suggest that although valuable, neoliberalism works best when acting in concert with perspectives that compensate for its deficiencies.

C. T. Maier

See also Globalization; Political Economy; Political Identity

Further Readings

Friedman, M. (2002). *Capitalism and freedom.* Chicago: University of Chicago Press.

Gray, J. (1995). *Liberalism* (2nd ed.). Minneapolis: University of Minnesota Press.

Harvey, D. (2005). *A brief history of neoliberalism.* Oxford, UK: Oxford University Press.

Hayek, F. A. (2007). *The road to serfdom* (B. Caldwell, Ed.). Chicago: University of Chicago Press.

Nozick, R. (1974). *Anarchy, state, and utopia.* New York: Basic Books.

NIGRESCENCE

Nigrescence is a French term meaning "to become Black." This word has become recognized as one of the most popular academic theories concerning identity. Its progenitor William Cross conceived the concept in 1971 to describe an identity process experienced by Black people who undergo a metamorphosis from identification with whiteness to identification with blackness and beyond. The underlying presumption of the multistage paradigm is that people with healthy identities are comfortable in their own skins. Black people who want to be White or identify primarily with whiteness rather than blackness are said to have either internalized a sense of self-hatred or perhaps not have matured enough to immerse oneself in one's own culture. This is not meant to conflate identity and identification. These words are distinct; however, they are connected in that one's cultural self-definition is linked to the degree to which one identifies with one's indigenous culture.

Nigrescence has been nicknamed the "Negro to Black conversion model." It fits within a constellation of identity theories that have proposed that the level of identity maturity is the principal characteristic that determines the extent of identity maintenance. In other words, when one is comfortable with one's self and has a high self-esteem, he or she is more likely to have a higher degree of self-efficacy than is someone who is uncomfortable with one's self. This hypothesis is contestable. Nonetheless, the significance of this body of work is that it centers on how people define themselves on a daily basis and how that affects their lives. This approach establishes a way of understanding how a deculturalized Black individual becomes revitalized and increasingly identifies with self and culture.

This entry first discusses identity theories. Next, it describes the stages of the nigrescence model and criticisms of the model. Lastly, this entry examines the significant methodological advancements to identity research.

Identity Theories

A few years following the advent of Cross's celebrated nigrescence paradigm in 1971, Edwin Nichols decided to place cultures and their consistencies in a theoretical framework that examined cross-cultural differences; as a result, he created one of the first comprehensive worldview publications. He originally called his model the "psychological aspects of cultural differences" model. Presently, it is referred to as the "philosophical aspects of cultural differences" model, and it is used quite frequently for consultation with both public and private industry organizations throughout the world. The amount of worldview publications increased during that decade and the next. In the 1990s, most of the literature on African American identity is dispersed throughout disciplines such as psychology, sociology, and increasingly within communication. Joseph L. White and Thomas A. Parham issued a second edition of their heralded volume titled *The Psychology of Blacks: An Afro-American Perspective.* This comprehensive guide to the Black personality examines "ethnic" identity, its development and maintenance, and worldview, among other issues.

Ethnic identity in psychology is discussed in some texts interchangeably with cultural identity. Yet ethnic identity is seen as a group phenomenon, socially and relationally driven and now understood from a range of disciplinary perspectives. Parham and Janet Helms developed the Black Racial Identity Attitude Scale to address a specifically African American sociopsychological approach to defining the cultural self and thinking through identity stress and coping.

White and Parham discuss, in the vein of an ethnic orientation toward psychological research, coping strategies for a dual identity and social competency measures. The authors claim, "Long before the child can verbalize, he or she is aware of the fact that something is fundamentally wrong in the American society" (p. 45). Although this point may be arguable, several ethnic identity models do propose that identity awareness begins in early to late adolescence. Both Charles Thomas and William Cross offer several distinct models for examining ethnic identity growth among Blacks. The psychological paradigm discussed most in identity literature is Cross's nigrescence model.

Nigrescence Model

Again, Cross's well-known nigrescence theory describes a metamorphosis from Negro to Black, and Black is defined as the optimal psychological stage in which the Black individual comes to identify and appreciate who he or she really is. Persons at this stage do not consciously attempt to imitate another ethnic group's interpretation of reality.

There are four stages to the nigrescence model: pre-encounter, encounter, immersion-emersion, and internalization. The first is the *pre-encounter stage,* which is the identity locale for those who embrace whiteness and devalue blackness. Thomas uses the term *negromachy* to characterize this stage. These persons refuse any link to a collective conscience or Black culture and have never been successfully influenced by Whites or themselves to accept their blackness. The second stage, *encounter,* is the first instance or sequence of events in which the individual is confronted with an unfair situation because of his or her race. Because of the inconsistency of inequity with the American dream buttressed by "liberty and justice for all," the individual is initially shocked, then confronted with the realization that his or her present worldview is inappropriate. A new identity exploration gradually takes place; eventually the decision to maintain a Black identity is made. The third stage, *immersion-emersion,* represents the transformation from the old to the new self. This transition is marked by an extremist viewpoint on Black–White relations. Whites are castigated for almost everything they do, and Blacks are praised. The world is now perceived from a Black–White perspective. Externally, artifacts of Black identity are worn or bought to decorate the home, car, office, and so on. Internally, however, the individual has yet to become secure. *Internalization* is the final stage, in which the individual achieves a sense of self-comfort. Cross

explains that the emotional and defensive disposition is exchanged for a politically acute awareness of other ideologies and a greater understanding of these views. Since 1971, Cross has published an updated version of the model and added internalization-commitment as a final step in the process of nigrescence. This step explores issues of high and low race and culture salience, presuming that those who have matured to this stage are high in race and culture awareness.

Criticisms

White and Parham indicate that their concern for the nigrescence model is in its restricted focus on young adults and adolescents, with little to no regard for identity transitions later in life. White and Parham theorized that identity transformation is a lived experience beginning in adolescence and continuing throughout life. Nigrescence, then, is a cyclical occurrence that exists in early, middle, and late adulthood. "Recycling" of identity stages accounts for the individual moving back and forth between the stages.

Cross and Peony Fhagen-Smith responded to this critique. They modified the nigrescence paradigm so that it accounts for ego identity development. One of the theoretic concerns of the authors relates to the range of identities and cultural ideologies of persons who have matured to the internalization stage. The correlation between self-esteem, ego-identity development, and racial-cultural development greatly improves the nigrescence model. However, it may be possible that African Americans with a high self-esteem will have an enhanced sense of self-valuation resulting from a self-satisfaction and self-comfort with their present perception of their identities. The reformulation of the nigrescence theory significantly contributes to the advancement of identity studies by considering three dimensions of identity. First, the reformulation accounts for multiple realities by considering the divergent ideologies of contemporary conservative leaders. Second, it includes cross-disciplinary research within the reconfiguration. Finally, it theoretically considers the outcome and process-oriented nature of identity throughout an entire life span. Many other studies have since used this new extension to make sense of Black identities in different contexts.

There have been multiple critiques of the nigrescence paradigm over the years. One heuristic contribution Parham provided was to conceptualize "African American cultural identity" as an independent phenomenon, not established as a reactive formation to White oppression. Parham intuits that African American cultural identity is able to stand alone and function without a European American identity to claim and alter it. Many scholars have spoken of a psychohistorical matrix confounded by an I-Other dialectic that has facilitated a link between culture and personality. The id, ego, superego, and culture are components of the matrix that forms self-concept. In the tradition of a universal psychological mandate for all personality formation, the ego is never satisfied. Progress is never achieved, but simply made—the ego must continue making progress, extending its domain.

Identity Research

There have been three primary themes in Black psychological research: inferiority, deficit/deficiency, and multicultural. The inferiority model asserts that hereditary factors render Blacks inferior to Whites. This inescapable predicament stagnates identity. The deficit/deficiency model suggests that race, class, gender, and other sociocultural factors distract societal members from adhering to normative standards of living, defined by the White middle class. These Black persons are "culturally deprived" because of assumed environmental conditions and a resilience to change. The deficiency lies in the inability of Blacks to reconcile their inherent lack of intelligence, sensible language, family structure, and cognitive style. The multicultural approach, the newest trend in psychological research, contends that all languages, behaviors, and worldviews are contextually related and characterized by strengths and limitations. In the 1990s, ethnic identity research is primarily defined with respect to these three approaches within psychological literature.

Several cultural theories have depicted distinguished interpretations of reality. There has been some confusion about which model best measures cultural identity, but A. Kathleen Burlew and Lori R. Smith maintain that each approach is useful depending on the purpose of the research. The existing measures at the time were divided into four categories: developmental, Afrocentric, group-based, and racial stereotyping approaches. Developmental approaches were exemplified by the process-oriented models of Thomas, Cross, and J. Milliones. Milliones developed an instrument used to measure Black consciousness, foreshadowing Cross's nigrescence model by including the respondent's progression through four stages: preconscious, confrontation, internalization, and integration. The "africentric approaches" were typified by James Baldwin's African self-consciousness scale, and the belief systems analysis scale of Linda James Myers. The latter scale was created to provide an optimal worldview, which encouraged mental healthiness among African Americans. It is composed of three constructs: holistic, nonmaterialistic, and communalistic. The Black Group Identification Index is one of several "group" measures identified by Burlew and Smith. J. P. Davidson, a former doctoral student from the University of Maryland, who discovered a strong correlation between Black student identification and participation in extracurricular activities, created this index. Burlew and Smith also mention the Cultural Mistrust Inventory as it relates to "racial stereotype" measures. This instrument was developed to assess the suspiciousness of Blacks toward Whites in workplace organizations. All of the aforementioned measures are significant methodological additions to identity research, yet they are only a few among many. The nigrescence model has been a major model for discussing racial identity and identification. It is also important to note that scholars such as Beverly Vandiver, Peony Fhagen-Smith, Kevin Cokely, and Frank Worrell have significantly advanced this work along with William Cross.

Ronald L. Jackson II

See also Communication Competence; Culture, Ethnicity, and Race; Self-Consciousness; Self-Esteem

Further Readings

Baldwin, J. A. (1980). The psychology of oppression. In M. K. Asante & A. Vandi (Eds.), *Contemporary Black thought*. Beverly Hills, CA: Sage.

Burlew, A. K., & Smith, L.R. (1991). Measures of racial identity: An overview of a proposed framework. *Journal of Black Psychology, 17*(2), 53–71.

Cross, W. E. (1971). The Negro to Black conversion experience: Towards the psychology of Black liberation. *Black World, 20,* 13–27.

Cross, W. E., & Fhagen-Smith, P. (1995). Nigrescence and ego identity development: Accounting for differential Black identity patterns. In P. Pedersen, J. Draguns, W. Lonner, & J. Trimble (Eds.), *Counseling across cultures* (pp. 108–123). Thousand Oaks, CA: Sage.

Milliones, J. (1980). Construction of a Black consciousness measure: Psycho-therapeutic implications. *Psychotherapy Theory Research and Practice, 17*(2), 458–462.

Myers, L. J. (1991). Expanding the psychology of knowledge optimally: The importance of world view revisited. In R. L. Jones (Ed.), *Black psychology* (pp. 15–32). Berkeley, CA: Cobb & Henry.

Thomas, C. W. (1971). (Ed.). *Boys no more: A Black psychologist's view of community.* Beverly Hills, CA: Glencoe Press.

White, J. L., & Parham, T. A. (1990). *The psychology of Blacks: An Afro-American perspective* (2nd ed.). Englewood Cliffs, NJ: Prentice Hall.

Nomadology

Nomadology is a concept concerned with nomadic distribution and the idea of nomad versus nomos. The nomad is shaped by an identity of being that is not connected to or bound by territory. Nomadology permits us to ask questions about the politics of location, the identities of the self and the other, and the relevance of both defined and undefined identities. Although Gilles Deleuze had already discussed this concept in his *Différence et repetition* (Difference and Repetition), it became of great importance in the magnum opus *Mille Plateaux* (A Thousand Plateaus), which he wrote jointly with Félix Guattari. The concept of nomadology, or rather the anti-methodology that it implies, is used more and more within the humanities and the social sciences today, particularly in the more experimental areas of these fields. In the work of Deleuze and Guattari, nomadology is closely connected to other theoretical concepts aimed at converting their philosophy into a form of praxis (think of "schizoanalysis," "rhizomatica," "empiricism," "pragmatism," and "ethology"). In contrast to these other concepts, however, nomadology has particular interest in the political, though the authors also discuss it in terms of art, religion, architecture, and science. This entry discusses nomadology's conceptual framework; describes its companion concept, the war machine; and provides examples of nomadology's use and application.

Conceptual Framework

Nomadology is derived as a reference to the life of the nomad, one whose being does not unfold according to a territory, bound to cities and villages, but who travels and traverses territories, all along the way following the surface of the earth, from well to well, from marketplace to marketplace, and beyond. The nomad is radically opposed to the civilian, the man/woman living within the state. The civilian is coded in three stages: first, man or woman is surrounded by all types of social apparatuses; then, living according to them, he/she becomes the subject of his/her statements ("I," the civilian); finally he/she is empowered accordingly, functioning within all facets of the state as an active part of its machinery.

The nomad is different. The nomad does not live according to codes (neither of the self nor of the space surrounding him or her). Instead of territoriality he practices a de-territorialization, which creates a mobile existence instead of a sedentary life. The nomad is Genghis Kahn, who "didn't understand" the city, which is to say that he was unaffected by the power of the state apparatuses that had encircled him, warding off all forms of organization through which the state needed to work (intending to capture and organize life), and not accepting the power (the status, the property) it had to offer. The nomad is, however, also the terrorist, the vagabond, the outlaw, or actually any type of life capable of resisting the encoding machineries of power.

Yet we need to think the concept of nomadology in an even more abstract manner. For as actualized in the person of the nomad or any other anarchist personality, the concept still breathes an anthropocentrism, which falls short of the conception of Deleuze and Guattari. In the words of its creators, the nomad stands for *a pure becoming*: nomadology maps an ontology of movement. It is not a metaphor (there is nothing "meta" about it), but rather expresses a way of thinking about both the material and the immaterial that is remarkably absent in the history of Western thought. This denies the power of the state from occurring, along with territoriality (or ownership), institutional subjectivities, and other defined identities for that matter. But in the end nomadology prevents *all* fixed states from taking place. Nomadology illuminates the restless margins that hide themselves from any kind of authority. They are akin to the "faceless enemies" George W. Bush referred to when he tried to define whoever was responsible for 9/11.

War Machine

A crucial companion of the concept of nomadology is what Deleuze and Guattari refer to as the "war machine." This concept, taken from Paul Virilio, is external to the nomad but allies with it whenever the nomad clashes with the state. The war machine refers to the constitution of a series of phenomena that in their aggregation produce or fabricate "war"; radical de-stabilization, de-territorialization, de-subjectification, and even de-identification are the outcomes of this alliance. Denuding the military connotations linked to the concept of a "war" entirely, Paul Patton reads the war machine as a machine of metamorphosis, giving us more insight into how this concept should be used and revealing nomadology, with the war machine or machine of metamorphosis as its tool, as an *anti-semiology*, aimed at decoding whatever strategies it is confronted with. The politics of decoding is thus in the end the way in which Deleuze and Guattari use this concept to ward off political codes and codifying machines in general. They question "royal science" as it defines the science and theorize a (non-Kuhnian) nomad science that persists in not being absorbed by its dominant structure. They question optic space as it defines the (visual) arts and theorize a haptic space that stresses close vision allowing the surface of the artwork to be felt. They question striated space as it places a grid on the surface of the earth, coding the built environment but also the sea with its coordinates and its means of measure.

Nomadology, hand in hand with the war machine/machine of metamorphosis that allows it to experiment with all kinds of decodings, thus turns out be a concept at work within all kinds of political phenomena.

Applications

In *Mille Plateaux*, Deleuze and Guattari take their own advice seriously by showing us that the purpose and value of philosophy are external to philosophy itself. Thus, they say that productive insight into what nomadology stands for necessarily exceeds the realm of philosophy, which is precisely what they do with their analysis. Yet their analysis is by no means final. Nomadology is a concept with a much greater potential, as so many publications have already shown us. It is claimed that even the Israeli army, in its attempts to reply to the urban guerrilla warfare of the Palestinians, experiments with the concept's new take on territoriality (an interesting twist of the concept's uses, no doubt much contrary to the original intent of both Deleuze and Guattari). However, a more positive reading of what the concept of nomadology has yet to offer is still indeed possible in the following example.

In the area of postcolonial studies, Patton gives us some interesting thoughts on rethinking nomadology. Staging the so-called "Mabo" case, he sets the concept into contemporary Australian jurisdiction. The lawsuit dealt with the ownership of land on the Murray Islands, and for the first time, the judges agreed on an aboriginal or native right to form part of Australian common law. It meant a revolution in Australian jurisdiction, but more interesting to us, it shows nomadology at work. The influential Privy Council stated in 1919 that indigenous inhabitants were barbarians without settled law, thus refusing the idea that their claims on property were transferable (from Aborigine customary law to the civil code). Indeed, this case shows us that colonialism is about overcoding, about turning land into territory or property, about identifying the self and the other, and about defining *nomads* as those who "do not understand" the strategies that surround them. This case also tells us that it is still seldom, even in our postcolonial times, that these social and cultural codes meet a war machine, or a machine of metamorphosis. Nomadology reveals to us these colonial codes that are still largely intact in the non-Western world. Nomadology shows us how the British organized the Indian caste system according to the way the capitalist system has structured daily life for people all over the world.

Within feminist theory, Rosi Braidotti made use of the concept of nomadology in several of her best-selling books. Deleuze (re-reading de Beauvoir) claimed that there is no such thing as being a woman, a woman is always a becoming-woman, which means that she is marginalized according to the dominant male. Writing from the female perspective then, *is* a nomadology, according to Braidotti, a journey outside the phallogocentric strategies that striate normality and intend to over-code the marginal. Feminist resistance then is not a search for equality, or for a new type of sedentary subjectivity, or for recognition. Rather, it is about the search for a *nomadic subjectivity,* a subjectivity that primarily practices a *not understanding* of the laws of sedentary masculinity and patriarchy. Feminist resistance is about living and writing "the politics of location" that immanently questions the dominant masculine structures that are encountered everywhere. Deleuze and Guattari add to this that becoming-woman is not a tactic limited to the female: it is a necessary transformation for *all* minorities and marginal practices. Even marginalized men, in order to ward off the dominant forces of society, have to enter a state of becoming-woman. In line with Braidotti, it thus makes sense to consider the nomadic subject she proposes a new way of thinking about feminism, and actually a new way to rethink *all* minorities. The nomadic subject is an invitation to all minorities to write a politics of location, an ethnography of everyday life that uncovers all the dominant political structures that turn life into being.

Rick Dolphijn

See also Cultural Studies; Mediation; Self-Consciousness; Self-Esteem

Further Readings

Braidotti, R. (1994). *Nomadic subjects: Embodiment and sexual difference in contemporary feminist theory.* New York: Columbia University Press.

Deleuze, G., & Guattari, F. (1980). *Mille plateaux: Capitalisme et schizophrénie 2. [A thousand plateaus: Capitalism and schizophrenia: Vol. 2].* Paris: Minuit.

Patton, P. (2000). *Deleuze and the political.* London: Routledge.

ONTOLOGICAL INSECURITY

Ontological insecurity refers, in an existential sense, to a person's sense of "being" in the world. An ontologically insecure person does not accept at a fundamental level the reality or existence of things, themselves, and others. In contrast, the ontologically secure person has a stable and unquestioned sense of self and of his or her place in the world in relation to other people and objects. Ontological insecurity is important for understanding identity because it is an essential foundation for a person to achieve a stable sense of self-identity. In an existential sense, if a person does not believe that he or she exists and that other people and objects are real, that person does not have the necessary foundations to develop a stable self-identity. Total ontological insecurity is rare. Most people achieve a general sense of ontological security, a basic acceptance that they and others exist, which enables them to function in day-to-day life.

Central to achieving a sense of ontological security is a belief in the continuity, reliability, and consistency of oneself, other people, and things. Therefore, a person must learn to trust, or develop a generalized sense of trust, in the nature and stability of the social and structural environments they inhabit. This type of generalized trust is established in childhood and maintained through routine. For instance, it is well documented that good parenting engenders children with a sense of trust in others and things; that through consistency

in parenting practices and love, children learn that other people can be trusted; and that through routine, they obtain a sense of the reliability and stability of their social and structural world. People then carry this generalized sense of trust with them into adulthood as protection against existential anxiety throughout their lives. The establishment of flexible (not rigid or obsessive) routines is also important as adults for maintaining a generalized sense of trust. This is at the core of the establishment and maintenance of self-identity. That is not to say that such a generalized trust is ensured and unchanging; research has also shown that accidents or unexpected life events can undermine a person's sense of generalized trust and therefore threaten the person's ontological security.

Ontological security is central to Anthony Giddens's theory of self-identity. He argues that the processes of late modernity and postmodernity have eroded many of the traditions that underpinned trust in the nature and stability of the social and material world (and therefore provided the foundations for ontological security) in premodern societies. Whereas premodern societies were characterized by tradition, religion, and routine with meaning, modern societies are characterized by rapid change and uncertainty in the economy, employment, culture, and the family. Therefore, there are many social and psychosocial threats in modern life, such as instability in work, employment, and family life. A person needs to develop the ability to take for granted most everyday happenings; people who do not can become caught in a perpetual state of anxiety about the future that undermines their ontological security. Therefore, the desire and need to manage these potential threats raise fundamental questions of trust and self-identity for modern individuals.

To manage the insecurity of day-to-day living, individuals employ strategies to achieve and maintain a state of ontological security; one such process is reflexivity. Individuals respond to social change (and the resulting insecurity) by engaging with expert systems and using the information to assess their positions in the social and material worlds they inhabit. By placing themselves in their own fields of view and assessing their positions in the social and material worlds they inhabit, individuals can be assured of their own existence and manage the risks associated with modern life. However, if taken to the extreme, the process of reflection itself can generate anxiety. An ontologically secure person does not need to engage in a process of reflection about most things—he or she is able to trust or accept things as they are. Self-reflexivity and the ability to engage in the process of self-reflexivity are partly structurally determined and vary depending on class, gender, and ethnicity.

The concept of ontological security is important because it suggests that people need more than just their material needs to be met to live happy and fulfilled lives. Ontologically insecure people are unable to develop and maintain a stable self-identity and therefore have trouble negotiating and "fitting in" to the social and structural worlds they inhabit. This can have a profound impact on an individual's well-being, with research indicating that ontological insecurity is associated with poor physical and mental health, offending behavior, housing instability and insecurity, and national conflict.

Belinda Anne Hewitt

See also Being and Identity; Development of Identity; Development of Self-Concept; Existentialist Identity Questions; Modernity and Postmodernity; Reflexive Self or Reflexivity; Self; Self-Consciousness

Further Readings

Giddens, A. (1990). *The consequences of modernity.* Cambridge, UK: Polity Press.

Giddens, A. (1991). The self: Ontological security and existential anxiety. In *Modernity and self-identity: Self and society in the late modern age* (pp. 35–69). Cambridge, UK: Polity Press.

Laing, R. D. (1965). Ontological insecurity. In *The divided self* (pp. 39–61). Harmondsworth, UK: Penguin Books.

Spitzer, S. P. (1978). Ontological insecurity and reflective processes. *Journal of Phenomenological Psychology, 8*(2), 203–217.

Optimal Distinctiveness Theory

"Everyone needs to belong." "Everyone needs to be unique." That both of these statements are true is the basis for the theory of optimal distinctiveness, which helps explain why we join social groups and become so attached to the social categories we are part of. Optimal distinctiveness theory is about social identity—how we come to define ourselves in terms of our social group memberships.

According to the optimal distinctiveness model, social identities derive from a fundamental tension between two competing social needs—the need for inclusion and belonging on the one hand, and a countervailing need for uniqueness and differentiation, on the other hand. People seek social inclusion to alleviate or avoid the isolation, vulnerability, or stigmatization that may arise from being highly individuated. Researchers studying the effects of tokenism and solo status have generally found that individuals are both uncomfortable and cognitively disadvantaged in situations in which they feel too dissimilar from others, or too much like outsiders. Conversely, too much similarity or excessive deindividuation provides no basis for self-definition, and hence, individuals are uncomfortable in situations in which they lack distinctiveness. Being "just a number" in a large, undifferentiated mass of people is just as unpleasant as being too alone.

Because of these opposing social needs, social identities are selected to achieve a balance between needs for inclusion and for differentiation in a given social context. Optimal identities are those that satisfy the need for inclusion *within* one's own group and simultaneously serve the need for differentiation through distinctions *between* one's own group and other groups. In effect, optimal social identities involve *shared distinctiveness*. (Think of adolescents' trends in clothes and hairstyles; teenagers are anxious to be as much like others of their age group as possible, while differentiating themselves from the older generation.) To satisfy both needs, individuals will select group identities that are inclusive enough that they have a sense of being part of a larger collective but exclusive enough that they provide some basis for distinctiveness from others.

Although a theory of group identification, optimal distinctiveness theory has direct implications for self-concept well-being at the individual level. If individuals are motivated to sustain identification with optimally distinct social groups, then the self-concept should be adapted to fit the norms and expectations of such group memberships. Achieving optimal social identities should be associated with a secure and stable self-concept in which one's own characteristics are congruent with being a good and typical group member. Conversely, if optimal identity is challenged or threatened, the individual should react to restore congruence between the self-concept and the group representation. Optimal identity can be restored either by adjusting individual self-concept to be more consistent with the group norms, or by shifting social identification to a group that is more congruent with the self.

Self-stereotyping is one mechanism for matching the self-concept to characteristics that are distinctively representative of particular group memberships. People stereotype themselves and others in terms of salient social categorizations, and this stereotyping leads to an enhanced perceptual similarity between self and one's own group members and an enhanced contrast between one's own group and other groups. Consistent with the assumptions of optimal distinctiveness theory, research has found that members of distinctive minority groups exhibit more self-stereotyping than do members of large majority groups. In addition, people tend to self-stereotype more when the distinctiveness of their group has been challenged.

Optimal identities (belonging to distinctive groups) are also important for achieving and maintaining positive self-worth. Group identity may play a particularly important role in enhancing self-worth and subjective well-being for individuals who have stigmatizing characteristics or belong to disadvantaged social categories. Some of the potential negative effects of belonging to a social minority may be offset by the identity value of secure inclusion in a distinctive social group. Results of survey research have revealed a positive relationship between strength of ethnic identity and self-worth among minority group members, and some experimental studies have demonstrated that self-esteem can be enhanced by being classified in a distinctive, minority social category.

Finally, because distinctive group identities are so important to one's sense of self, people are motivated to maintain group boundaries—to protect the distinctiveness of their groups by enhancing differences with other groups and limiting membership to "people like us." Being restrictive and excluding others from the group may serve an important function for group members. In effect, exclusion may be one way that individuals are able to enhance their own feelings of group inclusion. Those who are the *least* secure in their membership status (e.g., new members of a group or marginalized members) are sometimes the most likely to adhere to the group's standards and discriminate against members of other groups. Ironically, these noncentral group members may be even more likely than are those who truly embody the group attributes to notice and punish others for violating the norms and standards of the group. When given the power, marginal group members may also be more discriminating in determining who should belong in the group and who should be excluded. In experimental studies, it has been demonstrated that when individuals are made to feel that they are marginal (atypical) group members, they become more stringent about requirements for group membership and more likely to exclude strangers from their group. Similarly, when group identity is under threat (e.g., there is a fear of being absorbed or assimilated into some larger group), members tend to become more exclusionary.

Secure inclusion in distinctive groups enhances well-being and motivates positive social behavior. Insecure belonging or threats to the distinctive identity of one's important social groups motivate defensiveness, protection of group boundaries, and other efforts to restore optimal identities.

Marilynn B. Brewer

See also Collective/Social Identity; Group Identity; Social Identity Theory

Further Readings

Brewer, M. B. (1991). The social self: On being the same and different at the same time. *Personality and Social Psychology Bulletin, 17*, 475–482.

Pickett, C. L., Bonner, B. L., & Coleman, J. M. (2002). Motivated self-stereotyping: Heightened assimilation and differentiation needs result in increased levels of positive and negative self-stereotyping. *Journal of Personality and Social Psychology, 82*, 543–562.

Pickett, C. L., & Brewer, M. B. (2001). Assimilation and differentiation needs as motivational determinants of perceived ingroup and outgroup homogeneity. *Journal of Experimental Social Psychology, 37*, 341–348.

ORGANIZATIONAL IDENTITY

Introduced by Stuart Albert and David Whetten, *organizational identity* generally refers to the central and enduring features of an organization that its members believe distinguish it from other organizations and groups. Research on organizational identity is practically and theoretically significant because it can be used to explain organization-specific phenomena, such as organizational leadership, performance, culture, and many other organizational happenings. The need to understand organizational identity and identification transcends disciplinary demarcations by drawing interest from a variety of diverse domains such as social and organizational psychology, management, leadership, sociology, persuasion and communication, corporate relations, and marketing.

Albert and Whetten presented two uses of organizational identity. First, researchers can delineate and describe certain features of organizations. Second, organizational identity is a concept that organizations can use to define themselves. That is, organizations can decide, to a large extent, how they want to be categorized. These uses imply that organizational identity has a certain degree of fluidity, affording the organization some degree of a malleable identity. This can provide organizations with a means to reinvent their identities, replace managers or leaders, or integrate newly acquired companies or departments in a manner that is beneficial, effective, and efficient for the organization. The ability to reinvent an organizational identity is important for many organizations because without this capacity, many organizations would dissolve or find themselves unable to cope with a constantly evolving globalized economy.

This entry first discusses organizational identity's necessary conditions and core attributes. Then this entry explores the importance of organizational identity and the use of metaphors in defining an organization's identity. Finally, this entry details some of the controversies associated with organization identity research.

Conditions for Organizational Identity

Three defining and necessary conditions of organizational identity were presented by Albert and Whetten: (1) the essence or central criteria of the organization, (2) organizational distinctiveness, and (3) temporal continuity. Of these three conditions, the central character and distinctiveness are closely linked. The core attributes of the organization also distinguish it from other organizations. Defining attributes of the organization, however, are fluid in that they have the capacity to change depending on the organization's current purpose, needs, perspectives, products, goals, culture, or salient outgroups. Organization leaders play an important role in embodying the central characteristics of the organization via social identity processes. A leader is defined as an individual or group who has a disproportionate amount of power and influence over a group. Leaders are able to influence a group's agenda, goals, and achievements; thus, leaders can strategically position the group to accentuate commonalities or differences within and between groups to define and distinguish the organization. This allows organizations to define themselves in manners decided by the organization and its members while permitting placement of the organization into multiple categories. Placement in multiple categories provides the organization the possibility of change while not restricting identification to a single category.

Consistent with Henri Tajfel and John Turner's social identity theory, Albert and Whetten argue that the continuity of organizational identity is critical. That is, one's organizational identity must be enduring in addition to being central and distinctive. Through enduring identities, organizations are capable of creating and maintaining roles within and between organizational communities. For example, Google has created many identities for itself, but it is most commonly known as an Internet search company and technological innovator. The extent to which Google's identity is enduring, distinct, and central can be summed up in a brief, two-word sentence: "Google it."

Organizational identities are shaped and maintained through interactions with other organizations (e.g., mergers, negotiations), as well as through within-group socialization processes (i.e., hiring new employees, training programs, organizational goals); therefore, these between- and within-organization processes directly influence the degree to which an organizational identity is enduring. The longer an organization holds a single or small repertoire of identities, the more difficult it becomes for the organization to shift between identities. For example, Apple has become synonymous with stylish, fun, and easy-to-use computers and other electronic products; however, Microsoft is equated with boring, dull, and evil. Both organizations have difficulty shifting their identities to increase their customer base and market base (e.g., Apple suggesting its products can be used by everyone and not just college students). The capacity for an organization to switch identities or assume multiple identities can be a difficult endeavor for well-established organizations.

Importance of Organizational Identity

In addition to its theoretical and scientific importance, organizational identity and identification have practical relevance for how organizations function. It has been suggested that effective organizational leadership, communication, and development could not exist without a perceived sense of organizational identity. Organizational identity also provides a means by which organizations can successfully implement diversity training programs, improve productivity, ensure smooth mergers and acquisitions, effectively manage, and effectively deal with changes between and within the organization. Because of the implications of organizational identity, it is easy to understand how and

why this concept attracts so much attention from researchers in so many different disciplines.

Organizational Identity as a Metaphor

Using metaphors, researchers are able to define an organizational identity based on the underlying dimensional factors of the organization. This approach enables researchers to define and characterize the multiplicity of identities of a single organization by comparing it against at least two other organizations. By using two or more metaphoric comparisons, the organization passes the primary tests of duality (i.e., that the organization has more than one identity). For example, one might ask how Company X is similar to Google (a utilitarian organization) and to the army (a normative organization). This would be an appropriate metaphor for Company X if the metaphor has the capacity to be applied to the organization at narrow and broad levels of comparison; said differently, the metaphor must fit both general and specific comparisons between the organizations under consideration.

When using metaphors, one must compare the organization against practically significant alternative organizations that are diverse, rather than homogeneous. If this critical step is not met, the outcome may provide little to no practical use for researchers or the organization. Determining that an organization has more than one identity, however, might have considerable consequences for the organization. As such, the extended metaphor analysis provides researchers with a scientific explanation for why and how events occur with and between organizations—that is, it supplies researchers with another avenue to understand and make sense of organizational events.

Critiques

Garnering attention from researchers and practitioners alike, organizational identity research has capitalized on its diverse methodological, theoretical, and analytical perspectives. These diverse perspectives have provided a unique and fruitful approach to advance our understanding of organizations (i.e., groups) and their members; however, many issues still need to be resolved by scholars. Attempts for resolution have been debated in special issues of organizational and management journals, as well as in scholarly forums and workshops, devoted specifically to this topic. Incidentally, many of the controversies regarding organizational identity stem from this transdisciplinary impetus, including what research methods are best suited for studying organizational identity, the different measures of identity, the effects of different methods and measures on interpretations of organizational identity, and the theoretical background of organizational identity.

Although the original definition provided by Albert and Whetten is the most commonly used, there is still much debate about a single, accepted definition. Other definitions refer to organizational identity as a shared understanding based on common cognitive structures of organizational members, rather than an identity based on what is explicitly stated by the organization or its members; other researchers integrate organizational culture, performance, marketing, or production into their definition of organizational identity. This disagreement about an acceptable definition of organizational identity primarily results from the epistemological, disciplinary, and ontological backgrounds of researchers. Regardless of the disagreement about the meaning and definition, the importance of understanding organizational identity and identification is less controversial.

Different measures and methods of organizational identity and identification have also caused some difficulties for researchers. The wide range of methodological approaches includes experiments, quasi-experiments, surveys, ethnographies, metaphors, and archival data. These approaches are further complicated by varying the level of analysis from the individual to small groups to large groups. As a result, data analyses can be difficult, therefore, compelling researchers to apply various quantitative, qualitative, and mixed-method approaches to studying organizational identity. Compounded with the lack of consensus regarding the definition of organizational identity, the methodological concerns seem grim. By working together and across disciplinary boundaries, researchers are able to integrate and replicate each other's findings.

The interpretation of organizational identity is also affected by these concerns. Depending on the theoretical or philosophical orientation, organizational identity researchers adopt different frameworks through which they explain similar organizational phenomena. These explanations may be quite comparable, or contradictory. One general theme stemming from theoretical orientations is whether organizational identity is considered a process or a thing. As a process, identity is an entity under constant development, whereas as a thing, it is perceived as a resource or item obtained by the organization. Each approach leads to different interpretations of identity.

Finally, many argue that organizational identity researchers are examining a specific form of social identity, but others argue that organizational identity is a different conceptualization of identity. A seminal article by Blake Ashforth and Fred Mael argued that from a social identity perspective, organizational identity researchers could achieve some consistency of agreement about the definition of organizational identity, as well as provide a rich perspective of organizational behavior. Although a social identity perspective is commonly prescribed by social psychologists, researchers from other disciplines do not seem to agree. However, this area is becoming dominated more by social psychologists, leading this view to be mainstream among organizational identity researchers. This should lead to some consistency and, one hopes, reduce some of the controversy between scholars and practitioners.

David E. Rast III

See also Social Identity Theory

Further Readings

Academy of Management Review. (2000). Special topic forum on organizational identity and identification. *Academy of Management Review, 25,* 13–152.

Albert, S., & Whetten, D. A. (1985). Organizational identity. In L. L. Cummings & B. M. Staw (Eds.), *Research in organizational behavior* (Vol. 7, pp. 263–295). Greenwich, CT: JAI Press.

Ashforth, B. E., & Mael, F. (1989). Social identity theory and the organization. *Academy of Management Review, 14,* 20–39.

British Journal of Management. (2007). Organizational and corporate identity [Special Issue]. *British Journal of Management, 18,* S1–S94.

ORIENTALISM

In his groundbreaking book *Orientalism,* Edward Said systematically studies Western scholarship on and representation of the Near East or the Arab world. Focusing on British, French, and U.S. thinkers and artists since the 19th century, Said argues that rather than pure, objective, and disinterested scholarship and cultural practices, Orientalism aims to discursively subjugate the East. It belongs to the imperial drive to, rephrasing Socrates, "know thy colony" and control it. Said incisively diagnoses Orientalist representations as projecting Western desires onto the Orient, rendering the Other as shadow of the Self. The Orient is thus turned into stereotypes of extremities, or the Western Self's aspirations for beauty and love, such as the Islamic harem or Madame Butterfly, and abject fears, such as barbarism and opium. As a result, the Orientalist formula dictates that the Orient is polarized, emptied of psychological depth and subjectivity. The extremes of Samuel Taylor Coleridge's "A sunny pleasure-dome with caves of ice!" in *Kubla Khan* is split between the demonic and the domestic, with the exotic unfolding in the most predictable manner. The West projects its own neuroses onto the opposing constructs of, among others, Khans and Shangri-las, of the Mongolian horde and the Tibetan religiosity. Inherent in both ends of Orientalist stereotypes are transgressions and taboos that the West must shun otherwise. At a time when science and reason are secularizing the West, the need for myth and what lies beyond reason is displaced onto the Orient. Orientalism, hence, allows the West to articulate its own repressions in the name of representing the East. Thus, the West creates an identity for the Orient based on Western rather than Eastern ideas and notions. This entry focuses on the theoretical framework underlying Said's work, the response to *Orientalism,* and its application in the realm of global capitalism.

Theoretical Framework

The theoretical framework of *Orientalism* derives primarily from Michel Foucault's discourse theory and Antonio Gramsci's concept of hegemony. Foucault inspires Said to cross the distinction between nonpolitical and political knowledge in that Western Orientalists are vested in the maintenance of power over their subject matter of the East. Accordingly, no such thing as true, apolitical knowledge exists. Gramsci, on the other hand, demonstrates that consensus or hegemony can be forged in a civil society without resorting to coercion or violence. Foucauldian discursive power is woven into Gramscian hegemony to buttress Saidian Orientalism.

Reaction

Iconoclastic and controversial, Said's *Orientalism* has been credited by some as having single-handedly inaugurated postcolonialism. Said provides a counter-hegemonic theoretical basis for Western liberals and non-Western academics in search of an alternative to canonical criticism. Many postcolonial scholars build on Said's foundational work: Gayatri Chakravorty Spivak links Said with Jacques Derrida's notion of deconstruction and the subaltern group that argues for the need for strategic essentializing; Homi Bhabha refers to Frantz Fanon's psychoanalysis with Saidian colonial stereotypes when interrogating the ambivalence of nation and narration. Other scholars have taken Said to task for creating yet another totalizing, master narrative. Instead of Orientalism, critics accuse Said of Occidentalizing, to the extent of anti-Western rhetoric from a Western-trained elite of Palestinian descent. Critics cite as an example Said's fervent devotion to the Palestinian cause in *The Question of Palestine,* which Said supporters see as engaged scholarship.

Politics aside, Said does ignore counter-hegemonic voices within the colonies as well as within the Western discourse itself. It has been argued that Said's monolithic *Orientalism* fails to account for, in particular, inner tensions within artistic expressions. A host of scholars have challenged Said from various angles: Aijaz Ahmad from the local conditions in India and from the global theory of Marxism; Lisa Lowe from ethnic studies marked by hybridity and heterogeneity; Dennis Porter from the ambivalent genre of travel writings; and John M. MacKenzie from historicism, among others. That one must contend with *Orientalism* to stake out a territory attests to the centrality of Said's book, its flaws notwithstanding. Any rehearsal of Said's flaws without acknowledging his potential suggests a reactionary position, one that may be in denial of the fundamental power dynamics of knowledge production. After all, Said himself hints at some blind spots of his work. With the caveat that Europe sets itself off against the Orient as an alter ego, Said points away from an antithetical and mutually exclusive relationship between the West and the Orient to a symbiosis, with a sense of self-reflexivity shot through the manifest and hegemonic as well as the subterranean and repressed half. Said in *Culture and Imperialism* elaborates that a cultural archive must not be read unilaterally but bilaterally, aware of both the hegemonic discourse and the repressed, alternative discourse. This suggests a possible symbiotic relationship between the metropolitan and the subaltern because we exist in the relationship between the two, rather than outside it. Just as the imperialist instinct propels the West to study and hence gain control of the Orient, the contrapuntal instinct leads the West to absorb, to identify with, and to *be* the Orient. Scholarship in the new millennium ought to expand Said's work to tease out the cultural complexity Said has intimated.

The defensive reaction against Said is evidenced in the discipline of the other Orient—Far East or East Asia, which is not covered in *Orientalism*, with its focus on the Muslim world and, by extension, the Anglophone and Francophone postcolonial condition. Some in ethnic studies and area studies appear to be in denial regarding the relevance of *Orientalism*. In the former—Asian American studies, for instance—Orientalism resides as much in the mainstream culture against which it defines itself as in the Western cultural heritage it inherits. The White gaze at the Oriental Other invariably taints Asian American representations of Asians and things Asian, as Sheng-mei Ma contends in *The Deathly Embrace: Orientalism and Asian American Identity*. Assuredly, complicated psychology energizes ethnic identity formation: Ethnic writers Orientalize the Other to dissociate themselves from their race and to assimilate into the multiethnic United States. With respect to area studies on East Asia, its genesis in the cold war West is already Orientalist in its grappling with the enemy of Red China. To refute

Orientalism without considering area and ethnic studies' own implication in Orientalist projects is tantamount to late capitalism dismissing Karl Marx's critiques. Indeed, this rejection may signal a self-Orientalizing vigorously repressed in Asian America and in Asia. Ethnic and area studies shun the word and concept of "Orientalism" perhaps because it aptly describes their own impulse and genesis. The millennial, self-empowering ethnic and Asian subjects thus turn away from the 19th-century colonial abjection, oblivious to the neo-colonial traces within globalization.

Orientalism and Global Capitalism

Global capitalism does not inherently decolonize and revolutionalize the human mind. Rather than being undone by transnational cultural flow, old mental constructs and biases may be repackaged in neoliberal, politically correct, culturally sensitive, aesthetically entrancing, and commercially viable new clothes. For example, instead of the Oriental yellow peril and Fu Manchu, global cinema now regales us with Jet Li's arch villain in *Lethal Weapon 4* and *The Mummy: Tomb of the Dragon Emperor*. Instead of Madame Butterfly, Broadway and Hollywood entertain us with *Miss Saigon* and the blue-eyed Zhang Ziyi in *Memoirs of a Geisha*. From Hong Kong gangster films, John Woo extracts and perfects his aesthetics of violence for Hollywood blockbusters. From J-Horror and Tartan Asian Extreme labels, the horrendous Orient is wedded to the hypnotic Orient, reinscribing the polarities inherent in Coleridge. That Jet Li et al. would blithely perform in a way that lends themselves to self-Orientalization, admittedly with certain variations each time, can be seen as signaling the discursive power of Western hegemony. Herein lies the potential of Said's *Orientalism* as a theoretical exit from the omnipresent global capitalism: Said can be applied to read cultural formations far from the Near East in the new millennium, as long as the researcher fine-tunes Said for local conditions.

For example, in the cultural productions from greater China, a contender for world leadership in the 21st century, Western hegemony lingers. The paragon of China's fifth-generation filmmaking, Zhang Yimou, has long been charged with self-Orientalizing in pursuit of international accolade such as an Academy Award. It can be argued that the spectatorial extravagance in Zhang's historical martial arts fantasies are intensified so much so that the dynastic China becomes the exotic Other parallel to the West's exotic Orient. In *Red Sorghum* early in his career, Zhang drew from the primordial, archetypal rural past of China constructed by root-searching writers such as Mo Yan. Premodern, rural, and non-Han minority China can be seen as serving the same function as the defamiliarizing Orient in Western Orientalism. Although Mo Yan may sincerely believe that his 1987 novel is iconoclastic and revolutionary within the post-Mao literary landscape, to some the textual violence and sexuality, both in English translation and in Zhang's film, confirm the long-held Orientalist stereotypes in the West. The West does not read Mo Yan/Zhang Yimou within the context of Maoist censorship and repression, but within the context of Orientalist representations. As if to compensate for Oriental excesses, Zhang's long career is punctuated by neorealist films of common people struggling against the authority—films such as *The Story of Qiu Ju, Not One Less,* and *Happy Times.* To mitigate the force of Orientalism, cultural practitioners, particularly those with a non-Western background, must weigh, consciously, ethical as well as aesthetic consideration, balancing marketability with concerns for artistic integrity and collective responsibility. China's sixth-generation filmmakers have seemingly rebelled against their predecessors' aesthetics in making realistic and anti-Orientalist films; their films have been endorsed by various international film awards and art house aficionados, but China's domestic viewers do not particularly favor Jia Zhangke, Zhang Yang, Wang Xiaoshuai, Hao Ning, and the like. Some consider it ironic that anti-Orientalist self-representations on the screen resonate more with film connoisseurs abroad than with the masses at home, even though these sixth-generation films are inspired by and depict the quotidian life of the masses.

In *Orientalism,* Said heralds an egalitarian and non-repressive relationship between the Orient and the Occident, without having charted the route to that utopia. However, that cultural balance remains an elusive dream in view of the armed conflicts between the West and Islamic fundamentalism, the socioeconomic cold war between the United States and China, the inequality between Global North and South, and the divide between the haves and the have-nots within any given nation.

Sheng-mei Ma

See also Colonialism; Cosmopolitanism; Culture

Further Readings

Ma, S. (2000). *The deathly embrace: Orientalism and Asian American identity*. Minneapolis: University of Minnesota Press.

Said, E. (1978). *Orientalism*. New York: Pantheon.

OTHER, THE

The Other (which can refer to just one person or a group of people) is directly related to personal identity and how a person defines himself or herself. Typically, the Other is perceived negatively and is deemed different from and less admired or respected than the self. However, the Other can also be a positive disassociation. When a person deems another Other, he or she has decided that their identities are different. The person rendered Other may or may not be aware of the first person's contempt because the process of Othering may be a direct communication, such as a racial slur, or an unspoken disdain for, or avoidance, of the Other. This socially constructed process of Othering requires a sense of self, with either positive or negative elements, or both, and a motivation by the self to categorize and cognitively organize the perceived identities of other individuals and groups of people. This entry discusses the history and process of Othering, along with some examples of ways people are deemed different and thus Othered.

History of Othering

Georg Wilhelm Friedrich Hegel, the German philosopher, is credited with identifying the process of Othering in his depiction of slave–master relationships and the reciprocal, but not necessarily equal, power between them. Edmund Husserl, also of German descent, further developed the idea of Othering, focusing on lived experiences and the standpoints of individuals based on their interaction with distinct, often different, individuals. The process of Othering is linked to power, as described by the French philosopher Michel Foucault, who suggests that behavior and interaction are influenced by power in all relationships. Othering is socially constructed by all parties of a relationship; the negotiation of identity often involves Othering, or noting differences between individuals and groups, to identify what power a person or group has and what power that person or group would prefer to have. Edward Said's theory of Orientalism is directly related to the Othering process. He argues that through colonialism, Western ideas and practices were privileged over those of the East or Arab countries. When deciding that Western beliefs and practices are better, the rest of the world, and specifically foreign cultures, is Othered and deemed less important or influential. Eating the Other, or partaking of and then consuming Othered cultural products, practices, and values is a concept bell hooks discussed in her many writings criticizing the Othering process. More recently, theorist Mark Orbe has investigated power relationships and outlined communication patterns of cocultural, or minority, groups and their communicative responses to being Othered both in interpersonal interactions and as a group member in civic discourse. Orbe's research identifies multiple strategies used to communicate more—or less, depending on the goal of the minority individual or group—effectively, with perceived or obvious Others. His research also broadens the traditional definitions of the Other from merely racial and gender categories to all of the ways in which the self distinguishes itself from Others, including sexual orientation, age, and socioeconomic status.

The Process of Othering

The Other is identified usually as different in appearance, but not always. One can also be rendered less worthy or not normal in ability or by association to Others, such as friends or family. Othering, or the process of identifying an individual or group of people as the Other, marks them as strange, foreign, exotic, or heathen. Usually, these descriptions of Otherness are negative or unfavorable.

Othering is rooted in the concepts of ingroup favoritism and outgroup bias. Ingroup favoritism suggests that a person deemed similar—in multiple ways including appearance, gait, socioeconomic status, and so forth—to the self will be treated well or better than a dissimilar person and will receive some favoritism in interactions or behaviors by the self. The favoritism could be actual or perceived and might be tangible, but usually is not. Conversely, when someone is deemed a member of an outgroup, or unlike the self, that person will be Othered, or treated poorly or worse than someone in the ingroup. Othering is often covert because of the prescribed social requirements of polite behavior and positive communication.

Othering can have multiple resulting behaviors or outcomes. First, the Other may be ignored or rendered invisible by the self. Ralph Ellison's *Invisible Man* initiated research on invisibility of people because of their differences, suggesting that the Black male is rendered invisible and disempowered because of his Othering by White society, which refuses to acknowledge him as a person or his contributions to society. Because discussions about race and racial research often focus on the dualistic approach of White versus Black, other races are often ignored completely or merely mentioned as footnotes. Recent invisibility research, specifically about Asian American invisibility in the workplace, has been conducted by Wei Sun. Research about Othering and the rendering invisible of many people because of intersections of identity are also being conducted. For example, stay-at-home dads can be Othered because of a combination of both their gender and occupation. Additionally, overweight people are often ironically invisible when Othered, but age and attractiveness may also contribute to the self deeming them different, or Other.

Second, if Others are not rendered invisible, they may instead suffer from hypervisibility, wherein differences between the preferred self or group and the deemed deficient individual or group are highlighted. For example, Muslim women who wear headscarves that hide their hair and necks may be Othered because of their definitions and display of modesty. Although a woman wearing a headscarf may not feel her religious practices are the most important layer of her identity, and instead believes her educational level is the most defining layer of her identity, she will likely be hypervisible in the scarf to others and will be deemed an Other.

Essentialism is a result of the hypervisible Othering. Essentialism suggests that all who look or act similarly have similar experiences. Instead of recognizing individual attitudes and actions within groups, all are perceived similarly, or Othered. Muslim women may be Othered, or essentialized, because it is perceived that they all must wear headscarves because of their religious affiliation, when, in reality, some who are devoutly religious do not wear scarves. According to the research of Ronald L. Jackson II, Black males are hypervisible and Othered by essentializing. Black males are often hypersexualized, stigmatized as criminals, and underestimated in education and occupational levels. These labels, all negative, further illustrate the many intersections of identity that lead to Othering, or defining the Other as different from the assumed or actual status quo.

Third, Othering may be enacted and the Other may be made to feel further unwelcome by linguistic collusion. Linguistic collusion may involve code-switching, or changing to a language foreign or unfamiliar to the Other. When two or more individuals want to exclude another from their conversation, using a foreign language, or using words unfamiliar to the Other sends a message of exclusion. Linguistic collusion can also happen when the self addresses the Other, but in a rude or loud or gesture-filled manner that makes the Other, who is deemed an intruder, uncomfortable.

Fourth, the process of Othering can permanently stigmatize individuals or groups. Explanations for stigmatizing and its negative outcomes are outlined by scholar Erving Goffman. City governments and police officials are usually hesitant to identify juvenile delinquents for fear that they will forever be remembered as the child who either caused or was in trouble. Besides behavior that results in Othering, physical appearance or (lack of) ability can stigmatize, too. Members of the deaf community, when using American Sign Language (ASL), are often Othered linguistically and by ability because the perception is that a normal, fully functioning person requires hearing ability.

Fifth, the person may be Othered, but to some degree accepted, as an outsider within. This concept is also sometimes called the Other other, or a person who belongs to, and should act like, an Othered group but does not. Some Others feel this acceptance is an honorary position and are grateful to be accepted by the self in that manner, having their differences overlooked. Additional individuals may find the outsider within perspective limiting and patronizing. Passing is a related concept of the outsider within. While passing, an Other's differences are not noticed or evaluated. The Other operates as if there are no differences, even though they are present and the self's behavior toward the Other would change if he or she was aware of the Other's differences. An example is easily found in sexual orientation. Because of heteronormativity, some closeted gay men who are not overtly effeminate are thought to be straight and they pass as such. Racially, some biracial people are difficult to Other based solely on physical appearance. Sometimes even though a biracial person would be Othered if his or her race were known, the individual does not disclose family ancestry, but instead passes as a member of the preferred race. Finally, passing is often seen in accents and pronunciation of words. Just as actors expend energy to overcome linguistic identifiers that identify their backgrounds, many people practice pronunciations that sound distinctly different from that of their casual interactions to avoid being Othered.

Most persons can recall a critical incident in their lives when they were deemed an Other or told that their behavior, looks, or abilities were different than those of the privileged and preferred. On the playground, when choosing team members for a kickball or baseball game, the perceived weakest, or physically deficient, player is chosen last by the team captain. When playing as a child, some are told that girls do not play with trucks or that boys do not play with dolls. Racially, slurs and epithets are usually yelled as part of a critical incident when someone is Othered. Mocking of language ability or accents is another example of Othering wherein the self discriminates and delineates between normal and expected attributes, traits, and behaviors, and those that are different. Not all of these critical incidents will be as extreme or affecting as Others as the self forms a personal identity. Some may be deeply affected when told they were too young or too old to participate in an event, but less affected by a critical incident Othering them because of race. Others will have the same experience but not remember its impact as a critical incident, or defining moment of their self-identity construction or cognitive categorizing of Others.

Othering does not have to be based on just one physical characteristic of a person or group of people. Communication scholar Brenda J. Allen refers to herself, a Black female, as both twice blessed and doubly oppressed. When she is Othered, both positively and negatively, it is likely that multiple layers of her identity, or intersections of both gender and race, are being evaluated or perceived in the Othering process. Groups of people are Othered in a similar manner. The process of Othering is not always completely negative. For instance, Cinco de Mayo (May 5th in Spanish) commemorates a Mexican war victory over France. Many U.S. citizens enjoy specific Mexican foods and beverages each year on that day, believing they are celebrating Mexican National (independence) Day and will toast and cheer anyone they deem Latino, or Other. However, Othering can definitely be negative. For example, in the United States, one racial slur used against Latinos is "lazy Mexican," regardless of where the person is from. Citizens of Brazil, Paraguay, or Puerto Rico are just as likely to be called "lazy Mexican" as is a Mexican national or Mexican American. The Latinos' phenotype, or skin tone, facial features, and hair color all likely influence the slur and perception of difference or Other as it does positively in the Cinco de Mayo example. Also, accents are just as likely to result in them being rendered Other, as are their occupations or perceived educational levels and socioeconomic status.

Otherness: Defining Differences

Accent and pronunciation lead to Othering. There is no quicker way to decide someone is foreign than to hear his or her pronunciation of words. One need not be of a foreign nationality, though, to be the Other based on accent and pronunciation. In many areas of the United States, local pronunciations of street, city, and landmark names are unexpected by outsiders and expose the outsider when he or she speaks. The pronunciation of the state of Oregon provides an example, as does the city of Coeur d'Alene, Idaho, and the Gila Valley in Arizona. Accent and pronunciation are also closely tied to geographical biases. Despite everyone in the United States having an accent, some are thought to evoke more intelligence or credibility. For example, the Midwest accent is most typically used by television and radio reporters and is thought to be the preferred accent of the United States. Accents that are believed to express less intelligence or educational background include the southern drawl and the iconic accent from Bronx, New York. Individuals who speak in these accents are quickly—and negatively—identified as Others. A notable exception to the Othering based on accent is the Boston, Massachusetts, accent. Even though it is especially distinct and unique, speaking in the accent usually does not result in being negatively identified as an Other.

In the United States, youth and ability are highly prized. Conversely, age and a loss of agility are despised and deemed Other. This privileging of youth in the United States is opposite of that in many foreign cultures. In Asia, for example, most national cultures revere age and experience. Filial piety, or respect for family and ancestors, are important concepts to the structure of societal interactions.

In recent years in the United States, there have been many conflicts in workplaces caused by Othering practices. New employees, who are typically young and comfortable using technologies to accomplish work tasks, are rendered Other by their older colleagues who value hard work and a focus on task accomplishment. The younger employees are deemed Other and less likely to show devotion to the job, specific tasks, or their coworkers. Older employees are labeled the Other because they are perceived as being less savvy in using technology at work or fully appreciating the concepts of work-life balance. The Othering makes the older employees less desirable colleagues because they are viewed as unable to adapt to a changing work environment.

Twelve-step programs to overcome addictions to alcohol, drugs, or problematic behaviors are sometimes the topic of jokes. These jokes demonstrate some disdain for the addicted person, who is Othered for his or her inability to control his or her appetite for the problematic substance or action. Because 12-step programs are designed to stop and prevent future deviant behavior, participants by default are deemed Other, or unable to lead normal lives without professional intervention and the support of similarly deviant Others. Others with admitted addictions are Othered and sadly, forever stigmatized. For example, during a single family dinner, a person who has been Othered may be reminded multiple times of his or her Otherness. And, although the reminders of Otherness may be meant well, such as to keep temptations away from the Other, they further stigmatize and remind the Other of his or her deviance.

Physical attractiveness is an important commodity in U.S. society. Attractive people are usually stereotyped as being more friendly or personable than unattractive persons. Unattractive people, conversely, are thought to be less intelligent or capable and are Othered as different from the norm, or perceived physical beauty. Situation comedies and movies are believed to reflect or mirror current societal attitudes and opinions. If this reflection is correct, the preferred body shape and type in U.S. society is a mesomorph, or a v-shaped torso with a small waist, slightly wider hips and an obvious bust or pectoral muscles. Those whose bodies are not mesomorphic are Othered and are perceived to have idiosyncratic or stereotypical personalities. Men or women who are thin are called ectomorphs and are usually thought to be somewhat erratic or nervous and uncomfortable with themselves. Male and female overweight bodies, or endomorphs, are Othered as being jolly, slow, and typically less intelligent. The overweight bodies are usually the object of jokes concerning their size, appetite, slowness, or stupidity, which results in ridicule and often laughter. Height, too, is used to gauge similarity between the self and an Other. Taller men are the preferred prototype and, as such, typically earn more than shorter men and are perceived to have more leadership skills and potential than are their shorter counterparts. Women are Othered when they are too tall, too petite, or too short; they are then perceived to be cute and nice.

Occupations and career choices are gendered in the United States. A female who says she works in the health care field is quickly dismissed or Othered as a nurse or physician's assistant, and only rarely immediately identified as a medical doctor. Additionally, the concept of a male nurse, or a male performing tasks that are evaluated as female tasks, causes laughter, especially in media depictions such as the movie *Meet the Parents*.

In the United States, except for notable exceptions, educational level dictates the career a person has and his or her perceived intelligence. High school graduates are seen more favorably than are those who pass the General Educational Development (GED) exams. Those without a high school diploma are Othered, as are persons who do not graduate from college. Having more education typically translates to the perception of increased cognitive abilities and accomplishment. Although more and more colleges and universities are offering online courses and degrees, graduates of residential college programs are still more respected than are those who graduated from online degree programs, who are Othered, or deemed as having a less rigorous or engaging academic experience.

Ethnicity is another way in which people are deemed different, or Othered. Ethnic Othering prescribes who is a member of the ingroup, and will therefore likely be favored, compared with outgroup members, who will likely encounter bias. Some suggest that only by Othering are cultural traditions and practices continued from generation to generation. Holiday celebrations and traditions, such as the spring celebration of No Ruz by Persian Americans, are delineated as different than are holidays that most U.S. citizens celebrate, and worthy of Othering. Yet, if No Ruz is not celebrated within the Persian American community, it will be forgotten quickly. Japanese Americans were Othered by the U.S. government following the attack on Pearl Harbor and were forcibly moved to internment camps. Their extreme Othering suggested the Japanese Americans were not capable of having a sole allegiance to the U.S. government, based on intersections of their identity including family and heritage and physical appearance. Concerning ethnicity and Othering, consider March 17th, or St. Patrick's Day, which is celebrated across the United States, even by those who are not of Irish heritage. This example is interesting because although Irish Americans are now the third largest ethnic group in the United States (following British and German Americans), they were once overwhelmingly despised by the U.S. population. Although Irish Americans were once negatively Othered in U.S. history, they now are Othered positively.

A person can be Othered because of his or her family and heritage. In the United States, jokes and media depictions of Italian Americans often refer to familial ties to the Mafia or criminal activity. Othering resulting from family affiliation is typically the product of multiple intersections of identity, including ethnicity and spiritual beliefs or religious practices. For instance, families who are hesitant to use medical advice and medicine and instead rely more specifically on prayer or meditation for healing are deemed different, and Other. The family practices and faith may be specific to a religious sect, or an adaptation of a religion. The intersections of identity can contribute to their Othering.

Contrary to family, a person chooses whom he or she refers to as friends. The choice of some friends can lead a person to be Othered because those friends represent different social groups than the self believes the Other should be involved with. High school social groups and alliances are often depicted in U.S. movies. The popular students are usually the cheerleaders and athletes. Unpopular Others include academic club members and staff members of the school newspapers. Though it may seem that the popular students are the only ones describing the unpopular students as Other, this goes both directions. The popular students are often labeled negatively, also as Other.

Although the words *gender* and *sex* are often used interchangeably, *sex* usually refers to biological, genetic, and anatomical issues. Gender represents societal and familial socialization concerning appropriate behaviors, communication patterns, and pursuits. Because males and females are specifically socialized concerning appropriate behavior, Othering is often the result of deviant gender(ed) behavior. Young girls are often told to sit like ladies. Young boys are told to not throw like girls or cry like babies. Not adhering to specifically taught gender roles renders one either invisible or hypervisible and Othered. When filling out most surveys, there is always a demographic question labeled *sex* or *gender*. Usually male is listed first and female is juxtaposed as Other, which has been the focus and fight of feminists for many years. The goal of feminism is that women will not be recognized as a second choice, or less than their male counterparts. The feminist movement seeks equal rights for women that are mandated by the law and seen in practice in homes, schools, and workplaces. To further explain how

Othering is a process of multiple layers of identity, the womanism movement criticizes the feminism movement as being solely concerned with the rights and opportunities of White women. Women of color in the womanism movement suggest they are being Othered as less important or less regarded and respected compared with men, when compared with White women. In the socially constructed process of Othering, many intersections of identity are perceived. Further Othering is experienced by some who are intersexed because of the two, limiting gender categories of male and female. Intersexed individuals have both male and female sexual organs and feel Othered when they are rendered invisible and not acknowledged.

Geographical location and background can lead to Othering. In global geography, practices of the West, meaning North America, are often portrayed as correct, or good, and contrary practices, particularly those in the Southern hemisphere, as different, or Other. The phrase "West versus the rest" further demonstrates how ideas and practices emanating from the United States are adopted or imposed worldwide, based on Said's research on Orientalism. Within the United States, the North versus South Othering is consistent with that of the world. The South is typically Othered as backward or slow to accept change, whereas the North is progressive and plentiful. Within cities, similar geographical-based biases can affect perceptions and provide Othering to its inhabitants. The city of South Tucson, the south and west sides of Chicago, and southeast Washington, D.C., all provide perceptions of crime and lack of opportunities, or Other.

Nationality, or country of origin, is information used to determine Others. Depending on the passport a person has, he or she will be deemed Other, or different from the preferred. Othering resulting from nationality is rooted in colonialism and the suggestion that practices that are decided to be negatively primitive should be discontinued and progressive practices pursued. Nationality and country of origin are also described, or Othered, in common language, such as referring to places as third world countries. The term *developing nations* may or may not be less pejorative.

A person's smell can render him or her as Other. A person with poor hygiene or bad body odor is immediately labeled homeless, which suggests anyone with a home would prefer to carry no body odor. A person's smell, or olfactory signature, is determined by his or her diet and body chemistry. Those who smell different are labeled Other. The Othering that is by smell is influenced culturally. People who eat a lot of curry typically emit an odor different from those on diets of pasta and breads. A Korean word, *norinae,* which means "White person smell" was used to describe the new, distinct smell of the U.S. military personnel in South Korea after the Korean War. The soldiers were deemed Other by the local Koreans, whose olfactic signatures were strongly influenced by the kimchi (fermented cabbage) in their diets.

Physiological impairments, such as a loss of hearing, or deafness, and blindness, provide opportunities to Other. Because *normal* is defined as having five senses, those who cannot hear or cannot see are deemed deficient and Other. There is a real frustration within the deaf community, though, concerning the portrayal of deafness as a deficiency. With new technologies, some deaf people can choose to undergo surgery and acquire a cochlear implant, which enables them to hear. Many members of the deaf community resist the surgery, though, suggesting that getting the implant reinforces the notion of a negative Other who cannot hear. Instead, deaf people prefer to be Othered positively, suggesting their other senses are heightened because they cannot hear.

Race is usually the first attribute noticed in deeming someone an Other. Obvious and easily recognizable differences in phenotype, facial features, and skin tone suggest that race is salient to Othering. Many recent researchers, including Thomas Nakayama, have investigated "whiteness" or the White race as relating to the preferred, or status quo. All other races are then compared with the White race, or Othered. Scholars have also focused specifically on members of the White race as not having race, or as having an absence of racial attitudes or attributes. For instance, labeling those who are not White "persons of color" seems to further the idea that Whites are not of color and are the *preferred* Other. The state of Hawai'i is an interesting place to study because many races share the islands and no one race is a majority.

Children, teens, and adults have reported sexual orientation as a form of Othering. Heterosexuality is deemed correct or normal by many, and sexualities that are different are negatively Othered.

When children, teens, or adults are asked about being bullied in school, extracurricular activities, or even on the street, they often point to sexual slurs as one way in which they were intimidated or coerced. Bullying language directed toward males often includes suggestions that the Other is gay or is effeminate, which further embeds the idea of heteronormativity, or that heterosexuality is normal and correct. Females can also be Othered because of sexual orientation. Although men are often deemed invisible, or less than men because of their non-heterosexuality, lesbians are often hypervisible in U.S. culture and revered as straight male fantasies, if they are attractive. Lesbians, who are Othered as being butch, or masculine, are also Othered, but in a negative manner. Notable in this manner of Othering is Elissa Foster's research that challenges the notion of heteronormativity, suggesting educators need to reflexively evaluate their teaching practices and change how they present sexual orientations and relationships to their students.

Others can be labeled as Other because of their socioeconomic status or social class. In India, the caste system dictates the social position and opportunities of a person based on family and ancestry. Although the United States has no formalized caste system, many suggest there is a system in the United States based on socioeconomic status that renders as Others those without ample monetary means or social influence. Although U.S. society emphasizes the concept of the American dream wherein anyone can accomplish anything if he or she works hard enough and follows the advice of the common adage to "pick yourself up by your bootstraps." Those of lower socioeconomic status, who have yet to achieve academically and do not yet have monetary means, are labeled Other. For examples of this concept, one can read biographical information about famous government and business officials. Typically, their biographies indicate that they began life with few resources but worked hard and have accomplished a lot. Now as a successful person, he or she may be Othered, though, as an outsider-within, who is less entitled to his or her current riches. Although socioeconomic status Othering is typically negative, it sometimes is used in a positive manner by the Other. The Other may want to use the Othering as proof that he or she is capable of accomplishing a lot, especially because socioeconomic status was transcended by diligent efforts.

Othering resulting from spiritual beliefs or religious practices has existed in the United States since the founding of the country. The earliest U.S. settlers sought religious freedom, and ironically quickly Othered people in North America whose spiritual beliefs differed from their own. Notably, Native American reverence for the Mother Earth and Great Spirit were labeled blasphemous and Othered. Following September 11, 2001, it was difficult to be a practicing Sikh in the United States. Although the Sikh religion is not affiliated with Islam—the religion of many of the September 11th hijackers—Sikh men, because they wear turbans, were thought to be of the Muslim faith and were Othered. The Othering against anyone Muslim, especially men, or anyone perceived to be Muslim or possibly engendering empathy with the hijackers' views, was intense and sometimes dangerous. One Sikh man was killed in Arizona because he was Othered to be a Muslim who supported or encouraged the hijackings. Differing spiritual beliefs and religious practices are difficult for many to rectify because they feel they personally have the truth or are worshipping the one, true God. All others who practice religious rites and those who have no religious or spiritual affiliation are deemed Other, or unbelievers.

Andrew J. Critchfield

See also Culture; Diversity

Further Readings

Allen, B. J. (2004). *Difference matters: Communicating social identity.* Long Grove, IL: Waveland Press.

Butler, J. (1993). *Bodies that matter: On the discursive limits of "sex."* New York: Routledge.

Goffman, E. (1963). *Stigma: Notes on the management of spoiled identity.* Englewood Cliffs, NJ: Prentice Hall.

hooks, b. (1992). *Black looks: Race and representation.* Boston: South End Press.

Jackson, R. L., II. (2006). *Scripting the Black masculine body: Identity, discourse, and racial politics in popular media.* Albany: SUNY Press.

Sun, W. (2007). *Minority invisibility: An Asian American experience.* Lanham, MD: University Press of America.

OTHERNESS, HISTORY OF

The concept of "the Other," and the related ideas of "Otherness" and "Othering," arose via a series of interconnected intellectual moments in the West, finding expression in philosophy, social studies, literature, feminism, gender and sexuality studies, race and ethnicity studies, aesthetics, architecture, and the visual arts. These movements are linked to investigations of identity and identification, with the need to find one's own identity or selfhood. An outcome of these searches is that one's self often becomes defined *against* another, a phenomenon that can be called "definition through difference," articulated most clearly in the works of the semiotician and linguist Ferdinand de Saussure. He believes that all identity comes into being in relational structures, or, put another way, that individual entities gain meaning through formally structured oppositions and differences. Something is x, in part because it is not y, and only through the knowledge of the identity of y can we understand the identity of x (as "*not-y*"). In this schema, y is "the Other," the alterity. Today, the designation "the Other" has come to be most commonly used to refer to an individual or group who has been or is being marginalized from another, that is being "othered." This entry presents a historical review of conceptualizations of Otherness.

The 19th-Century Origins

Conceptualizations dealing with Otherness have, from their origins, been in some way intimately related to definitions of *modern* and *modernity*—of humankind's existence and knowledge of self in the modern world. At issue are not only self-identity and identification, but also how to define the identity of the modern world and how to understand the process of identification within it. The Ur-use of the concept of the "Other" is believed to be Georg Wilhelm Friedrich Hegel's master–slave dialectic in *The Phenomenology of the Spirit*. Within Hegel's schema, one can see the basis for the idea of the Other as an issue of selfhood and as an issue of difference. To account for the development of "self-consciousness," as opposed to "consciousness," Hegel describes a mythical encounter between two primordial (or "half") people. Upon becoming aware of an other, a "consciousness" has two choices: it can choose to ignore the like-form in front of it, or it can recognize the Other as a "mirror" of itself and start to assert an identity in contradistinction to that which it confronts—it can put forth its identity as subject "I" against the object with which it is faced. The encounter results in a loss of and slippage within identity: In the recognition of another, a self loses itself, as it recognizes the existence of the other consciousness. At the same time, a self cannot truly see the other self but, rather, sees its own self when looking at the other. For Hegel, this encounter causes alienation, so that a consciousness attempts to resynthesize the self into a whole; it seeks resolution, the domination of its subject—I—over the object, "the Other."

An obverse thought process can be seen in the work of the French modernist poet Jean-Nicolas-Arthur Rimbaud. In a letter of May 15, 1871, to Paul Demeny, one of two now known as the "Letters of the Seer," Rimbaud includes a phrase that has come to be his signature utterance: *je est un autre*. It can be translated in many ways, including *I is someone else, I is an other,* and *I is other.* The phrase has seen myriad interpretations, including the argument that Rimbaud sought to know himself by looking inward at his soul, distancing himself from himself to be able to look at himself. In so doing, he questioned every element of his psyche, believing that the "I" that is left would be the essence of his self. In this way, for Rimbaud, a poet becomes a seer. Rimbaud's formulation has kinship with Hegel's, except that the encounter is interior rather than exterior. Additionally, his fertile phrasing allows for two definitions of the Other, both of which can exist simultaneously—the Other that must be encountered and conquered is within one's self, or the Other and Otherness is a state that one wants to achieve.

Early Developments of the 20th Century

The most immediate inheritors of these conceptualizations are found in 20th-century psychoanalysis and philosophy. Jacques Lacan investigates the Other in psychoanalytic terms, taking as his starting point Sigmund Freud's exploration of the ego. In a series of lectures and writings, Lacan imagines a scenario in which the Other is both interior and exterior to a self. The two main concepts of import

here are his theories of the mirror-stage and of the great Other. Lacan postulates that an infant first sees himself or herself only incompletely, able to view the body only in sections, from his or her eyes. This phenomenon is the pre-mirror stage. At 6 months, the child encounters a mirror and is able to see his or her self as a whole. The child at first perceives the image as a competition, a contrast to the fragmented identity seen up to that point. To resolve this rivalry, the child identifies with the image in the mirror, creating his or her ego identity and giving rise to a feeling of victory or mastery. However, the child also soon perceives the greater mastery of the father and mother, the great Others, whose gazes are all-encompassing. Thus, Otherness in Lacan is both enabling and debilitating.

In *Being and Nothingness: An Essay on Phenomenological Ontology* of 1943, the existentialist philosopher and author Jean-Paul Sartre posits an activation of self-ness that comes into existence via an encounter with the Other, an encounter that again involves the gaze. This encounter is somewhat more positive than the one outlined by Hegel and involves a Saussurian process of identification via difference. For Sartre, a being only becomes aware of itself when it encounters the gaze of an Other. In essence, upon realizing that one is being watched by another, one gains awareness of self. The outside viewer gazes on the being, and in so doing, looks on that person as an object. Realization of one's objectness creates the ability to look at oneself as an object, in something of a Rimbaudian fashion. This phenomenon creates a paradox that Sartre sees but does not resolve. On the one hand, a being learns to recognize itself via that which it is not, and consciousness is predicated on recognition of the outside world and one's difference. On the other hand, the gaze of the Other is recognized as a power over the self, and to challenge it one must attempt to reverse the dynamic and become dominant, become the seer rather than the seen, subject rather than object. Thus, as is true with Hegel, the attempt to know one's self comes about via an exterior encounter.

Simone de Beauvoir, Sartre's morganistic partner in life and thought, works in a similar vein, but she approaches the exterior interaction with the Other from a different direction and addresses the issue of the Otherness of gender. In "Pyrrhus and Cinéas," she explores the idea that the Other is the one who has the freedom—as this self is free *because* of his or her difference. The Other by definition is free from the power of another, and all Others are united by their contingent nature, as one needs to convince another of an idea to create a world of shared values. In *The Second Sex,* de Beauvoir explicates the ways in which the female gender has been placed in a secondary role to that of the male, codified as early as Plato's *Republic.* Here one can see the influence of Hegel's master–slave dialectic because she postulates that it is a construct that woman is the Other (object) to man's primacy (subject). De Beauvoir's stance in *The Second Sex* is not contradictory to the ideas she outlines in *Pyrrhus:* the contingency she describes in *Pyrrhus* provides a path to liberation. With *The Second Sex,* the definition of "the Other" as one who is marginalized in society becomes cemented. De Beauvoir has been criticized, however, as being "heterosexist" because she deals here with gender rather than sexuality. However, she does later address the issue of the Othering of the elderly, in *The Coming of Age.* The complexities of these issues for feminist philosophy were immediately picked up by others, especially theorists influenced by Freud and Lacan, including Luce Irigary and Julia Kristeva, who both criticized and are indebted to de Beauvoir.

The 1970s to the Early 21st Century

The 1970s saw an explosion of scholarship regarding Otherness in race, ethnicity, gender, and sexuality. Of particular note are the works of Linda Nochlin and Edward Said. In 1971, Nochlin produced the germinal work of feminist art history, "Why Have There Been No Great Women Artists?" reprinted in *Women, Art, and Power and Other Essays.* Nochlin addresses the "woman question," revealing that part of the problem lies in the ways the issues have been formulated, the language with which they are composed. She interrogates the issue from all angles, including questioning the idea of "greatness" and the "great artist," and the formulation of the identity of the "woman artist." In 1978, Said ushered in colonial studies with his groundbreaking book *Orientalism.* Examining history, art, and literature, Said argues that the West is invested in depicting the Orient as a feminized Other—irrational, weak, lesser, and secondary—in

essence revisiting the physical colonial act of domination in the intellectual world.

Since the 1970s, a spectacular spectrum of scholars has visited and revisited the issue of the Other, resulting in numerous anthologies of great rigor and scope. In the visual arts, the touchstone exhibition for the exploration of the Other in all its forms is *The Decade Show: Frameworks of Identity in the 1980s,* a joint effort by the Museum of Contemporary Hispanic Art, the New Museum of Contemporary Art, and the Studio Museum of Harlem in New York in 1990. In the 1970s and 1980s, artists and theorists explored the idea of the Other from multiple directions, ranging from investigations or condemnations of the ways that one group can "other" another group to celebrations of one's own Otherness, an embracing of the identities of difference. The philosopher and artist Adrian Piper has had a particularly fascinating oeuvre. As a woman of both Black and White heritage and a Kantian scholar, Piper has probed the issue from the point of view of both popular culture and philosophical inquiry, and has been able to address Otherness as one who is part of two different cultures, who occupies a shifting space that can be both liminal and central. Her oeuvre spans the heydays of identity politics and liberation movements of the 1970s and the multiculturalism of the 1980s, as well as the developments of the late 20th and early 21st centuries, in which attention has increasingly been turned to the limits to and paradoxes inherent in the idea of the "Other." In the first place, the Other is by definition relative, that is to say, what is "other" to one person or group is the familiar, recognizable identity of another, and vice versa. Likewise, to celebrate one's "Otherness" can also in some ways be a reinforcement of difference and distinction, a self-ghettoization. Thus, such scholars as bell hooks, Mary McLeod, and Gayatri Chakravorty Spivak have investigated the "space" of Otherness, a space both literal and psychic.

In like fashion, to accept the dynamic of the "Other" is to accept a binary schema, with two results. First, one group will always and only be defined against another, and, more insidious, there is only room for *two* groups. Latino/a scholars have long complained that in a Black–White schema, there is no place for another Other; the same is true for other groups, including those of

Asian origin and Native Americans. Additionally, a binary schema runs the risk of creating a hegemonic Other, in which one determinant is given precedent over all others. For instance, if race is the criterion of Otherness, then socioeconomic issues can remain unconsidered within a group of a racial Other. Thus, recently scholarship has also turned to examining ways around the binary schema, as seen in Wendy Brown's *States of Injury: Power and Freedom in Later Modernity* and Anthony Kwame Appiah's *Cosmopolitanism: Ethics in a World of Strangers.*

In part, these shifts in approaches are related to the advent of the "post-s"—in particular, the postmodern, the poststructuralist, the postcolonial, the postfeminist, and the post-Black. The final term is one coined by curator Thelma Golden and artist Glenn Ligon, explored in the 2001 Studio Museum of Harlem exhibition *Freestyle,* and the term and the exhibition are together an extremely clear example of such a shift. The *Freestyle* artists were chosen because each, in some way, creates art that both is predicated on Black identity and also goes beyond it, so that blackness is not *the* signifier or source of power, but *one* signifier among many. Ewa Lajer-Burcharth articulates a similar issue regarding gender and video art in her essay "Duchess of Nothing," in *Women Artists at the Millennium.* Lajer-Burcharth discusses the video art created by Pipilotti Rist and Sam Taylor-Wood, works that interrogate the issue of the male gaze and the female Other; again, for Lajer-Burcharth, this issue is not *the* issue but one of many. In some ways, this reframing is the legacy of the postmodern Other, rather than that of the modern.

The Other and the Modern

Although the Other came into existence in and through modern culture, the obverse is also true: the "modern" and "modernity" were in part born from the creation and use of Otherness. Definition through difference is at the core of the modern identity. A paradigmatic example is that of the so-called inception of modern art, Pablo Picasso's *Les Demoiselles d'Avignon.* The "modernity" of this canvas is linked both to the avant-garde work of his immediate western predecessors—the impressionists and postimpressionists—and to Picasso's use of forms from outside the Western tradition—Oceanic

and African masks. To Picasso and his contemporaries, these masks were primitive forms that they could appropriate and reinvent in a Western context. These appropriative acts are quintessentially related to Otherness: Picasso uses these outside forms to create a "new" and different identity in relation to the Western art that came before his, and his appropriation relegates these forms to Otherness, signaling their identity as primitive, as less whole, less powerful, and less full.

These masks and cultures are Othered a second time by a 1984 exhibition at the Museum of Modern Art in New York, *"Primitivism" in 20th-Century Art: Affinity of the Tribal and the Modern,* curated by William Rubin. As Hal Foster records in "The 'Primitive' Unconscious of Modern Art, or White Skin Black Masks," the exhibition reinforced this stereotype: Modern Western art is intentional, sophisticated, individual, and deliberate, but non-Western African and Oceanic art is tribal, primitive, and lacking in individual identity. Faith Ringgold addresses this issue in her work *The French Collection Part I; #7: Picasso's Studio,* 1991 Here, she reinserts an active Black female model into Picasso's creative process of *Les Demoiselles d'Avignon* and reappropriates his appropriative image into her work. She places it on a quilt, which is both a feminine space and a traditional African American medium. Ringgold reinserts the past, precedent, and tradition that are lost when modern artists such as Picasso "borrow" from African sculpture and find their "inspiration" from the figure of a woman. Her work *Picasso's Studio* is both an illustration of the act of Othering and an image of how to take back one's Otherness.

Otherness and Early Modernity

Ironically, the act of Othering that has been the least understood is that of the creation of the early modern era—the invention of the Renaissance *against* the late medieval, the so-called gothic. For scholarship, this act of Othering has been treated as less laden or personal, partly because of its temporal distance from us. Unlike modern and contemporary Otherness, there is no living medieval being with a voice to speak out against this act, yet the issues are the same. Italian Renaissance humanists conceived of it (and themselves) as newly rational, defined against the irrational medieval age.

The late medieval was deemed "Gothic" or "barbaric" from the 15th century on, and in the late 18th and 19th centuries, its art came to be known as the work of the "Italian primitives." With the Renaissance as positive exemplar, Heinrich Wöfflin codified the definition by difference and Otherness of art history in his 1915 *Principles of Art History*, creating a schema of binary identification. Only recently has Marvin Trachtenberg proposed a term not predicated on Otherness but on self-identification: the *medieval modern*. In addition, throughout scholarship on the late medieval and early modern periods, there remains a tendency to make assessments according to criteria of norms and standards versus anomalies and deviations: that which is not the norm becomes an Other. Thus, the issue of the Other has reached the level of the "post-Other" in some fields and in some scholarship, but there remain many examples in which the issue has been barely investigated, and perhaps not even yet identified.

Mia Reinoso Genoni

See also Architecture, Sites, and Spaces; Renaissance Art

Further Readings

Armstrong, C. M., & Zegher, C. D. (Eds.). (2006). *Women artists at the millennium*. Cambridge: MIT Press.

Blake, N., Rinder, L., & Scholder, A. (1995). *In a different light: Visual culture, sexual identity, queer practice*. San Francisco: City Lights Books.

Foster, H. (1985). The "primitive" unconscious of modern art, or White skin Black masks. In *Recodings: Art, spectacle, cultural politics* (pp. 181–210, 228–233). Port Townsend, WA: Bay Press.

Genoni, M. R. (2009). *Vedere e 'ntendere:* Word and image as persuasion in Filarete's *Architettonico Libro*. *Arte lombarda*, tbd. Available at http://www.vponline.it/riviste/666112/2009/1/5/acquista

Golden, T. (Ed.). (2001). *Freestyle*. New York: Studio Museum in Harlem.

Hassan, S., & Dadi, I. (Eds.). (2001). *Unpacking Europe: Towards a critical reading*. Rotterdam, the Netherlands: Museum Boijmans Van Beuningen, NAi.

Peraza, N., Tucker, M., & Conwill, K. H. (1990). *The decade show: Frameworks of identity in the 1980s*. New York: Museum of Contemporary Hispanic Art, New Museum of Contemporary Art, and Studio Museum of Harlem.

Philippou, S. (2004). The primitive as an instrument of subversion in twentieth-century Brazilian cultural practice. *Arq, 8*(3–4), 285–298.

Shotwell, A. (2007). Shame in alterities: Adrian Piper, intersubjectivity, and the racial formation of identity. In S. Horstkotte & E. Peeren (Eds.), *The shock of the Other: Situating alterity*. Amsterdam: Rodopi.

Trachtenberg, M. (2000). Suger's miracles, Branner's Bourges: Reflections on "Gothic architecture" as medieval modernism. *Gesta, 39*(2), 183–205.

PASSING

Passing refers to the act of deception in which individuals use their inherent appearance and/or learned ability in the pretense of infiltrating a socioeconomic or an ethnic population to which they do not belong but of which they are assumed to be part. Historically, the connotation is usually in reference to fair-skinned African American individuals who purposely misrepresent themselves to the public as White. Although rare, there are cases where this definition does apply to other social and ethnic groups who also conceal or abandon their true identity to assume another.

The infiltrator's purpose usually is to achieve personal and material advantages or escape being persecuted because of racial discrimination. Many passers engaged in this practice as a means of gaining employment or advancing their careers. Others did so to gain access to racially exclusive retail and eating establishments. Some individuals passed to experience the euphoria of interacting with Whites. Passing is the means by which individuals who are classified internally or externally as part of a discriminated group are able to penetrate socioeconomic barriers and interact with a more privileged social circle.

In some cases, the passers, only partially African American (genetically speaking), are victims of their parents' deception, causing the individuals to believe themselves to be White. Before learning the truth of their ethnic heritage, these persons were living under a mistaken identity of sorts. Those who were aware of their mixed heritage but consciously continued the deception either through direct actions or the omission of their racial heritage were considered to be passing. This is the working definition for the purposes of this entry.

This entry first presents some personal accounts of and details legal proceedings related to passing. Next, the opinions of African Americans and supporters of racial equality with regard to passing are discussed. Last, literary representations of passing are described and whether the practice continues today is examined.

Personal Accounts

Personal accounts of passing include the testimony of Gregory Howard Williams, product of a White mother and fair-skinned Black man who pretended to be White. History implies that Williams's mother was aware of the deception, but Gregory and his younger brother were not. They lived their lives believing themselves to be White Americans living in the racially segregated state of Virginia. Williams's parents divorced when he was 10 years of age, and that was when he learned his father's racial identity. Similar to many other individuals facing this truth, Williams's initial response was shock and rejection of his newfound heritage. Until this point, he was misinformed. However, when he became aware of his racial identity and still identified himself as White, even only on occasion, Williams was passing.

As stated, the typical passers used their assumed whiteness to escape slavery and discriminatory practices. In keeping with this more common purpose was the case of Ellen Craft, the product of a sexual relationship between a slave owner and his slave mistress in the early 1800s. In 1848, Craft and her husband, also a slave, traveled by train, boat, and carriage for 4 days fleeing slavery in Macon, Georgia, in search of freedom in Philadelphia, Pennsylvania. What made Craft's story more remarkable than most was that she passed herself off as a White man, traveling with a Black servant (her husband).

In a third case, Walter White, a light-skinned, blue-eyed male, used his ability to pass for White to report, through firsthand accounts, racially discriminatory practices to the entire country. Between 1920 and 1955, White assumed the identity of a White male and traveled the southern states of the United States to conduct investigations on lynchings. White's immediate family all reportedly possessed Caucasian features but suffered persecution because they, at the insistence of White's father, chose to identify themselves as African Americans. The family's home was the intended target of a lynch mob. The mob was deterred by the Whites' and their Black neighbors' proven ability to defend themselves.

Events such as these influenced White's decision to become a leader of the civil rights movement and a member of the National Association for the Advancement of Colored People. His principal method was to investigate the crimes against Blacks and publicly expose them to the entire country in hopes of generating more sympathy and possibly changing U.S. opinion. Ironically, during one of his trips in 1919, White's true identity and purpose were exposed. He managed to board a train back to safety where a White conductor reportedly stated to him that Whites were on the lookout for a "yellow nigger" passing for White. The conductor failed to realize that he was addressing the "yellow nigger" in question.

Another example of personal accounts of passing is quite arguably one of the most historically notable. A number of the children born to the union of Thomas Jefferson and his Black mistress, Sally Hemmings, reportedly "shed" their African American ethnic heritage. In the 1820s, their daughters, Beverly and Harriet Hemmings, assumed the identity of White women and escaped slavery. Their brothers Eston and Madison, despite having been emancipated according to the terms of Jefferson's will, eventually left Virginia after their mother's death. They moved to Ohio where they each married women of similar complexion and mixed racial heritage. The two brothers were assumed to be White, but their conscious decision to pass appears historically inconclusive at that point.

Ironically, under Virginia law, they were considered White, but White Americans who knew of their admixture of colored blood regarded them as Negroes and treated them according to the racial practices of the day. As a result, Eston, who grew increasingly aggravated at being barred from the local judicial, political, and educational systems, relocated his family to Madison, Wisconsin, where he assumed the named Eston H. Jefferson and "became" a White man. Although some of Sally Hemmings's descendants followed Madison's example and openly acknowledged their mixed heritage, others chose to pass and gain entry into all-White regiments of the Civil War or married into prosperous White families.

Legal Issues

The issue of passing was the subject of several legal proceedings in U.S. courts. One of the most controversial and highly publicized examples was a lawsuit in 1924, *Rhinelander v. Jones*. Alice Jones was the daughter of a middle-class White mother and a mixed-race father. Leonard Kip Rhinelander was a "pure" White man born to a wealthy and esteemed family in New York. Allegedly, Rhinelander and Jones were in a romantic relationship, during which time the former was fully aware of Jones's mixed ancestry. The two married, and because of his family's status in society, the union was well announced. At that point, the Rhinelander family learned of Jones's mixed ancestry and persuaded Rhinelander to annul the union soon after the wedding. Rhinelander, perhaps out of fear of losing his multimillion-dollar inheritance, caved in to his family's demands. He initially declared that Jones, in an attempt to deceive him, identified herself as a White woman.

During the proceedings, which focused on defining Jones's "true race" moreso than her alleged deception, Rhinelander later contradicted himself by claiming that Jones deceived him by concealing her heritage. Jones's attorneys logically argued that Rhinelander could not have been ignorant of Jones's admixture because of their sexual relationship that began before their marriage. Jones presented correspondence between the two as evidence. In an unprecedented and shocking move, Jones's attorneys persuaded her to partially disrobe exclusively before an all-White male jury, revealing her upper back, breast, and upper legs for the purpose of presenting aspects of her physical appearance that were supposed proof of her mixed ethnicity. The jury was also reminded that Rhinelander had ample opportunity to observe and examine her entire body, which successfully proved that Rhinelander must have been aware of Jones's ethnic identity. The court found in favor of Jones, ruling that Rhinelander's claims for an annulment were invalid. The couple legally separated in 1930.

Rhinelander v. Jones served as a prime example of the mass paranoia some Whites exhibited at the prospect of interaction with "invisible Blacks." There was a fear of unintentional marriage and further contamination of the White bloodline. The growing multitude of slaves who used their fair complexions to escape their owners, and Blacks who passed to gain access to "White America" enraged White segregationists. The result was increasingly strict enforcement of Jim Crow laws in many state governments to create even more severe punishment for passers.

Organizations such as the Anglo Saxon Clubs of America were formed to preserve White dominance and racial segregation in the United States. The club's members in the state of Virginia were known for their attempts to identify passers and create legislation that further defined race and put more restrictions on interracial marriage. Before 1910, a person was considered Black if he or she was quantified as at least one-fourth African American in the state of Virginia. Between 1910 and 1924, this limit was reduced to one-sixteenth partly because of the vigorous labor of the Anglo Saxon Club. Finally in 1924, the state defined "White" as any person in possession of no other blood except Caucasian in any traceable amount. This was a slight variation of the one-drop rule, which stated that any individual with a proven or even suggested African ancestry, regardless of the amount of admixture, was considered to be African American.

Ironically, the apprehension of many state leaders who feared that they and their families might become re-categorized as colored caused them to include the descendants of Pocahontas and John Rolfe, and anyone with one-sixteenth of Native American blood, in the legal definition of marriage. The club vehemently opposed this portion of the legislation on the grounds that it permitted Negro Indians to marry Whites and further diminish the already endangered "pure White" population. Their objections, however, were given little consideration.

African American Opinion

Supporters of White supremacy are not alone in their negative opinions regarding the practice of passing. Many African Americans and other defenders of racial equality have often expressed distaste for the act citing two main arguments: (1) passing goes against Black solidarity, and (2) passing poses a threat to those involved.

Passing, although a voluntary action that may or may not be taken for the most noble of reasons, robs individuals and their progeny of their racial identity. In many instances, the truth is revealed at the most inopportune instance. This causes the progeny and others a great deal of psychological and emotional trauma as a new identity is abruptly forced on them. In an effort to maintain the deception, one usually has to sever all ties to the African American community and abandon the most important ties of family and friendship. Shedding one's identity for the purposes of assuming another makes the already incomplete lineage of African Americans even more convoluted. Perhaps the most compelling argument against passing is the notion that it further diminishes potential support for the arduous cause of uplifting the African American.

Literature

The real-life tradition of miscegenation and the resulting phenomenon of passing were both depicted in the realm of literature. Numerous works of both fiction and nonfiction were derived from interviews, historical incidents, and even the personal accounts of the writers themselves. These works illustrate various opinions, often starkly opposed to each other.

Iola Leroy, written by Frances E. W. Harper, deals with the conflict of passing versus Black solidarity. The novel's primary protagonist, Iola, is the child of a White slave master and fair-skinned slave who the former emancipates and takes as his wife. Three children were born to their union—Iola, Harry, and Grace, all of whom are light-complexioned and able to pass. At the father's insistence, the children are brought up believing themselves and their mother to be White. Iola and Harry are sent from their southern plantation home to be educated in the North. When Mr. Leroy dies, the children learn of their mixed racial heritage and the result is emotional and psychological trauma that even manifests itself in the form of physical sickness. Iola travels home in an attempt to see her father before he dies and is sold into slavery along with her mother. Shortly thereafter, Iola is freed because of the Civil War and the Emancipation Proclamation. While Iola is working as a Union Army nurse, a White doctor who is fully aware of her ethnicity proposes to her. Harper presents Iola's choice as more than just to accept or deny a marriage proposal but her decision to stand with or abandon African American people and their struggles. Iola declines the offer twice during the novel and devotes her life to reuniting her family and uplifting African Americans.

Iola's brother, Harry, leaves school on recovering from the knowledge of his mixed heritage and decides to join the Union Army, where he is presented with the opportunity to join a White unit because of his fair skin. He, like Iola, chooses to identify with Blacks and take up the cause of equality even after the war's end. Throughout the novel, several characters are confronted with the same prospect of passing, and they unanimously illustrate Harper's notion of Black solidarity over personal gain.

James Weldon Johnson's *The Autobiography of an Ex-Colored Man* presents another aspect of passing by depicting a protagonist who chooses to pass. Johnson's unnamed protagonist initially eschews his ability to pass. The ex-colored man at the least comprehends the notion of Black solidarity. He witnesses a lynching and succumbs to a fear for his own survival. His sense of self-preservation is coupled with a sense of shame and self-loathing as he considers the socioeconomic standing in which his inherent identity places him. The protagonist ultimately sheds his true self and assumes the identity of a White man. He marries a White woman under this usurped persona and eventually becomes quite wealthy. Ironically, in the novel's end, he encounters Black activists and on self-examination judges himself to be insignificant in comparison with those who have spent their lives striving for racial equality. He regards his life's accomplishments as worthless in contrast to the unrealized labor of individuals such as Booker T. Washington. Johnson presents just one type of loss the passer experiences.

Louise Burleigh, an avid supporter of White supremacy, attempted to further publicize the fear of many about the possible union of uninformed Whites and demonized passing Blacks in a short story titled "Dark Cloud." In this unpublished narrative, the character Alicia Fairchild and her daughter travel from New England to the South to attend her mother-in-law's funeral. At this point, Alicia learns that her mother-in-law is Black, making her own husband and daughter African American as well. Enraged, the protagonist kills her husband and locks her daughter in a burning church. The author justifies the murders by illustrating Fairchild's determination that she has been defiled in a manner similar to rape.

One of the most popular and more modern literary depictions of passing is Nella Larsen's *Passing.* In this 1920s narrative, Larsen presents the dual sides of the practice by providing two best friends, both light-complexioned females. One chooses to identify herself as Black and the other decides to pass. Through these characters, the author presents at least three major notions: (1) even though some Blacks disagree with passing, Black solidarity should ensure that they will not expose a passer; (2) maintaining deception creates anxiety for the passer; (3) the exposed passer may encounter life-threatening dangers.

Continuing Practice and Evolution

Despite the abolishment of slavery and many efforts made at enforcing racial equality, the practice of passing persists, but it has evolved beyond the historical connotation of Blacks pretending to be White. The term *passing* now incorporates various ethnic and social groups such as Jews, gays, and lesbians, all of whom pass to avoid religious persecution, to enter into the armed forces, or for other reasons similar to those of African Americans. In the case of Blacks, those who choose to identify themselves as multiracial for the purposes of the census, applications for education, and employment are also passing. The debate regarding the merits of passing in all its myriad forms and interpretations continues as well.

Eddie Seron Pierce

See also Biracial Identity; Culture; Culture, Ethnicity, and Race; Ethnicity; White Racial Identity

Further Readings

Behan, B. C. (2008). Leonard "Kip" Rhinelander trial. *The Black past: Remembered and reclaimed.* Retrieved October 10, 2008, from http://www.blackpast .org/?q=aah/leonard-kip-rhinelander-trial-1925

Davis, J. F. (2001). *Who is Black? One nation's definition.* University Park: Pennsylvania State University Press.

Fabi, G. M. (2004). *Passing and the rise of the African American novel.* Chicago: University of Illinois Press.

Harper, F. E. W. (1990). *Iola Leroy: Three classic African American novels* (pp. 225–463). New York: Vintage Books.

Johnson, J. W. (1995). *The autobiography of an ex-colored man.* New York: Dover.

Kennedy, R. (2001). Racial passing. *Ohio State Law Journal, 62,* 1145.

Larsen, N. (1986). *Quicksand and passing.* New Brunswick, NJ: Rutgers University Press.

Russell, K., Wilson, M., & Hall, R. (1993). *The color complex: The politics of skin color among African Americans.* New York: Doubleday.

Sollars, W. (1997). *Neither Black nor White yet both: Thematic explorations of interracial literature.* Cambridge, MA: Harvard University Press.

PATRIOTISM

The term *patriotism* is derived from the Greek word πατρίς (*patris*), which means father, and *patria*, which means fatherland or home country. So the word *patriotism* is used to represent a positive link to one's own nation or fatherland and love for one's home country or own people.

In this definition, patriotism is a positive aspect of national identity. In cultural terms, patriotism identifies distinctive aspects of the nation such as its ethnic, cultural, political, and historical features. Constitutional patriotism stands for loyalty to a democratic constitution with international ethical and political rules. These rules are based in Western legal traditions that respect the central dignity of human beings and thus refer to human rights that are recognized universally. The "hip-hip-hooray-patriotism," however, that sees other countries and peoples as inferior, and one's own country as most important or superior, is considered a negative type of patriotism.

From a historical point of view, in the first instance patriotism was a political development. In central Europe, patriotism evolved from ideologies of liberalism and nationalism of the bourgeoisie or emerging middle class and was regarded as revolutionary. At that time the bourgeoisie sought to establish a national state with a democratic constitution by criticizing feudalism. However, the meaning and the use of the concept changed over time, increasingly becoming a serious, deeply rooted, earnest engagement for the well-being of the community. As a concept linked to democracy, or the reign of the people, patriotism—understood as positive nationalism by most people—became a constitutional and real feature of most European states only after the American Revolution in 1776 and the French revolution in 1789. Before this, patriotism was only an idea, discussed by intellectual elites, and there were many historical setbacks to its establishment. Later, during the Napoleonic wars, patriotism became known as a political idea in bourgeois circles in other European countries as the liberal and democratic ideals of the French revolution—liberty, equality, fraternity—spread. From the middle of the 19th century, the term *patriotism* was increasingly connected with *nationalism* and *chauvinism*, terms that mean the belief in the superiority of one's own nation and the resulting devaluation of other nations. Patriotism especially came to imply national superiority after the German unification of 1871 ("the German character will heal the world"). Subsequently, those promoting European fascism and National Socialism used patriotism as a belief system to legitimate their aims and military objectives. After World War II, the government of the Federal Republic of Germany, as a reaction to the ideologies of fascism and National Socialism, distinguished *patriotism* from the negatively connoted *nationalism,* and thus enabled a place for increased feelings for home country that had been lost under nationalistic conceptions of the term.

Now the term *patriotism* has several distinctive meanings. First, *patriotism* expresses the feeling of positive identification with a nation. In this sense, *patriotism* refers to the emotional aspect of national identity. Second, at a macrolevel, societal-level perspective, it describes a desire for high internal cohesion in a democratically constituted society, especially in the United States. Patriotism, in this sense, is expressed by a variety of nation-related rites such as the loyalty oath to the United States (Pledge of Allegiance), the decoration of houses with the national flag, or conferring laws such as Uniting and Strengthening America by Providing Appropriate Tools Required to Intercept and Obstruct Terrorism (USA PATRIOT Act of 2001) that are intended to protect the security of the nation. The third use of the term *patriotism,* seen from the microperspective of the individual, is closely linked to the description of opinions and behavior referring to the nation (ideology). This ideology is different from nationalism and chauvinism in many ways. First, although nationalism and chauvinism imply idealizing one's own nation without criticism ("my country right or wrong") and the belief in the superiority of one's own group, the meaning of patriotism is identification with one's own land and people without putting them above others or implicitly devaluing other people and nations. Second, there is a distinction between patriotism and nationalism with respect to the criteria that are used to define national membership. *Nationalism* as an ideology implies objective rules of membership of the nation, citizenship, as the result of formal criteria such as birthplace. *Patriotism* as an ideology puts more emphasis on subjective criteria such as identification with the nation, and people can be patriotic without formal "membership" (citizenship) of the nation. Third, patriotism differs from nationalism in emphasizing what central characteristics should define the nation as a social group. Although nationalism emphasizes the importance of national history and tradition, patriotism sees the defining elements of nations in the successful accomplishment of democratic principles and human rights.

Fourth, patriotism favors democratic principles in communication between state and citizen whereas nationalism implies authoritarian solutions to achieving political order. Consequently, patriotism as an ideology is more tolerant of foreigners and minorities than is nationalism. Nationalism is a central aspect in ethnocentrism, the belief that one's own racial or ethnic group is superior to the rest. Apart from these differences, the ideologies of patriotism and nationalism also have common elements. Both imply strong national identity, that is, identification with the nation. Both ideologies also become critical of the nation if the national reality does not meet the respective ideological requirements of nationalism and patriotism.

Despite this distinction, however, concepts of patriotism and nationalism are not always sharply and separately formulated. Their use in research literature is often not precise, and the terms frequently overlap. In addition, researchers have not resolved how to empirically assess patriotism and nationalism in reliable and valid ways. Therefore, researchers in many countries disagree about the differences in the definitions of patriotism and nationalism and thus about their effects on history.

Critics of the distinction between patriotism and nationalism also see a danger that right-wing groups might use the concept of patriotism to advance nationalism. For these groups, nationalism is the only "real" patriotism. Another basic problem with definitions of patriotism is that all define the nation as a homogeneous social group. However, forming a group also excludes people, which is potentially discriminatory; thus, even when the concept is understood benignly, as love for the country, an implicit nationalism may also exist. There is also the danger that patriotism as an ideology can be used to privilege certain ideas and values as more supportive of the nation, while denigrating other ideas and as being destructive of the nation or not in the "national interest."

Thomas Blank

See also Citizenship; Ethnicity; Nationalism; State Identity

Further Readings

Bar-Tal, D., & Staub, E. (Eds.). (1997). *Patriotism in the lives of individuals and nations.* Chicago: Nelson-Hall.

Blank, T., & Schmidt, P. (Eds.). (2003). Special issue: National identity in Europe. *Political Psychology* 24(2).

Kosterman, R., & Feshbach, S. (1989). Toward a measure of patriotic and nationalistic attitudes. *Political Psychology, 10*(2), 257–274.

Müller, J.-W. (2007). *Constitutional patriotism.* Princeton, NJ: Princeton University Press.

PERCEPTUAL FILTERING

Perceptual filtering refers to the process of taking in new information and interpreting it according to prior experiences and cultural norms. People use these perceptual filters to help reduce uncertainty about new experiences. As the term suggests, *perceptual filtering* regards people's perceptions, the way people take in and make sense of information, about the social world. These perceptions are filtered through several components of social identity, such as age and gender, that help people decide what they decide to communicate about themselves to others and how they make sense of their everyday experiences. Although perceptual filters provide necessary and useful shortcuts for understanding the vast amounts of information that people expose themselves to everyday, they also form prejudices and biases that can impede the ability to perceive new information on its own merit.

Perception and Everyday Encounters

Perception regards how people look at the world around them and comprises three elements: sensation, organization, and interpretation. *Sensation,* sometimes called *observation,* can be defined as the manner in which people learn something is happening according to information received by one or more of the five senses (sight, sound, touch, taste, and smell). Once the mind observes that something is happening, it organizes the information it receives. The process of organization forms perceptual sets that people use to categorize information for current or future reference. Finally, people interpret the information through mental filters that help them make sense of the world according to their own experiences, values, goals,

and needs. The process of perception occurs when people move through these three steps to take in and evaluate the large amounts of information they are exposed to on a daily basis.

Perceptual filtering is closely tied to the process of communication, which entails encoding information, sending and receiving messages, and decoding information. The process of encoding includes placing the verbal and nonverbal meaning into messages. Sending messages refers to the process of transmitting these messages to others. Receiving messages regards the process of obtaining messages from others. Although sending and receiving messages has often been thought of as a linear process, people do both simultaneously. Finally, people decode information as they receive messages from others and understand them based on their own knowledge and experiences. Perceptual filtering influences how people encode and decode messages when they communicate.

The Process of Filtering

People cannot process the amount of information they receive through their senses, so they develop shortcuts and filters to help them. These filters can comprise numerous factors and experiences that include sex and gender, culture and ethnicity, age, societal status, and function. People become socialized at early ages to interpret the world according to these factors. The filter of sex and gender helps explicate the process of perceptual filtering. Girls are often socialized differently than boys are regarding perceptions of danger, strangers, appropriate behavior, norms, and so forth. This socialization process creates filters to help girls understand how they should make sense of and respond to the world around them. For example, boys may be encouraged to perceive something potentially dangerous, such as a fight, as an opportunity to demonstrate their toughness. Girls, contrarily, may be encouraged to perceive this as something to avoid. This process shapes gendered behavior well into adulthood and influences important life choices, such as career and educational decisions.

Deborah Tannen, who coined the term *genderlects,* examines how females and males develop different communication styles based on how they have been taught to understand their social worlds. She asserts that men interrupt more and tend to be more competitive as they focus on being heard. Women, contrarily, focus on listening and understanding, which causes them to be more polite when they communicate. Tannen's ideas help elucidate how gender forms an important perceptual filter for communicating and understanding social reality.

Biases and Potential Misunderstandings

The process of perceptual filtering makes it possible to understand the world and to communicate to others more quickly and efficiently. Despite the benefits of creating and using perceptual filters, they can also have consequences such as biases and misunderstandings. These consequences can range from slight to severe. For example, someone once stated that she enjoyed hot salsa and asked if another person enjoyed hot salsa as well. The second person stated that he also enjoyed hot salsa and mentioned that cold salsa was not as good. The first person expressed confusion and then stated that she meant hot as in spicy. In this instance, the first person encoded hot to mean spicy, but the second person decoded hot to mean warm. Based on different experiences about how this condiment is served, the two people filtered this information differently.

In this example, the misunderstanding is harmless and even comical. Sometimes, however, perceptual filters can lead to hurtful and damaging outcomes, such as prejudices and stereotypes. Following the previous explication of gender and sex socialization, perceptual filters can create norms that constrain people's construction of reality. Females and males may be encouraged into career paths that do not meet their strengths and skills because of these filters, which affects their perceptions of potential job skills and educational paths. Females may be socialized to filter helping fields and childcare positions as gender appropriate. Males, on the other hand, may be socialized into the natural sciences or athletics. Those that do not adhere to these norms may experience negativity when they interact with others and their choices are perceived according to someone else's perceptual filters. Girls who are natural athletes or excel in the natural sciences may be labeled too strong or masculine. Boys who prefer taking care of children may be labeled too feminine or domestic.

Even though perceptual filters help people make sense of their social worlds, people must take care to acknowledge the potential limitations and consequences of filters. Acknowledging biases and prejudices can help mitigate the effects of misunderstandings and limitations that perceptual filters can place on understanding of social reality.

Cerise L. Glenn

See also Class Identity; Cultural Representation; Gender; Looking-Glass Self

Further Readings

Hickson, M., III, Stacks, D. W., & Moore, N. (2004). *Nonverbal communication: Studies and applications* (4th ed.). Los Angeles: Roxbury.

Tannen, D. (1990). *You just don't understand: Women and men in conversation.* New York: William Morrow.

Tannen, D. (1994). *Gender and discourse.* New York: Oxford University Press.

PERFORMATIVITY OF GENDER

The notion of the *performativity of gender* is concerned with an understanding that, rather than possessing a given gender identity, we are constantly in the process of constructing—performing, *doing*—gender. Gender, in other words, can be seen as being a verb in flux rather than a fixed, essential noun.

This take on gender identity is most strongly associated with Judith Butler. A prolific writer, Butler is the author, for example, of *Gender Trouble: Feminism and the Subversion of Identity; Bodies That Matter: On the Discursive Limits of "Sex"; Excitable Speech: Politics of the Performance; The Psychic Life of Power: Theories of Subjection;* and *Undoing Gender.* A recent book, *Precarious Life,* considers, in the light of September 11, 2001, violence, mourning, and the state of modern United States. However, Butler is most renowned for her contribution to queer theory and her work on gender and identity. Indeed, many scholars propose that Butler has helped establish both queer theory (along with others such as Gayle Rubin and Eve

Sedgwick) and a new theoretical framework for thinking about gender identity and subjectivity. Butler's book, *Gender Trouble,* in particular, has been widely influential.

Troubling Gender

Butler made the case in *Gender Trouble* that feminism had erred by suggesting, both implicitly and explicitly, that "women" were a homogenous group with shared, universally common attributes and concerns. Drawing from a range of theoretical approaches throughout—including Michel Foucault, Sigmund Freud, Georg Wilhelm Friedrich Hegel, Luce Irigaray, Julia Kristeva, Jacques Lacan, Friedrich Nietzsche, and Monique Wittig—Butler argued that this stance led to what she described as a *reification* of gender relations: an unquestioning assumption that we know what we mean when we say "woman" and "man," and the inference that there are only these two genders. Such an attitude, she claimed, closes down possibilities, narrowing the range of identities from which people can choose.

Although feminism had rejected the account that gender is the result of biological destiny, instead, according to Butler, it had erected a constructivist account that masculine and feminine genders are shaped, through the influence of culture, onto the biological givens of the male and female bodies. This in a sense therefore reinstates the same determinism that feminism had sought to surmount: that one is born with a "male" or "female" body and consequently becomes, as a matter of course and with no scope for altering the inevitable, a "man" or "woman," respectively.

Butler instead took the view in *Gender Trouble* (developed in later work such as *Bodies That Matter*) that sex, sexuality, gender, and identity are all located within a matrix of power and discourse that produces and regulates how we understand the terms, among others, *man, woman, masculinity,* and *femininity.* She saw there being a multitude of options through which it is possible to disturb the received understandings of such terms. Gender is variable and fluid, changing for each of us at different times and within different contexts. Being a *woman* is, for Butler, a term that is always in process and becoming. We say "I feel more/less like a man" or "I feel more/less like a woman," which,

Butler suggested, implies that we see our experience of a gendered identity as something that we *achieve,* rather than as a given attribute.

Troubling Sex

Butler deconstructed, through a Foucauldian genealogical approach, the commonsense argument that sex causes gender, which, in turn, causes desire for the other ("opposite") gender. Even if we were to assume the stability of the binary of men and women, Butler argued, it does not necessarily follow that the cultural construction of men and women will exclusively attach itself only to male and female bodies, respectively, and that the one will desire the other. Moreover, she asserted that even the notion of sex (male/female) is as much a cultural construct as gender. Sex, for Butler, is a construct rather than a "fact"; it is a process whereby norms consistently materialize the body. This is achieved through language in that, consistent with the poststructural view that reality can only be understood as being produced through language, there is no such entity as a pure body, only one that is being further formed by the language used to describe or refer to it. The act of articulating sex results in an imposition of cultural norms.

Sex, gender, and desire are each open and, crucially therefore, despite the patriarchal cultural requirement to conform to the heterosexist hegemony, they are subject to choice; the "givens" are open to challenge. Hence, Butler proposed, there is opportunity for subversion, for action that demonstrates that gender is not a binary but a multiple choice. There is, in short, scope for gender trouble.

Performativity

The controversial notion of the *performativity* of gender identity is implicit in the previous discussion. Butler advocated that there is no essential identity behind manifestations of gender. Instead, the reverse is the case: Gender identity is *performed,* constituted by the manifestations themselves. Gender is what we do rather than who we are; it is a verb and not a noun. This applies to everyone, whether or not the gender we perform is conventional. Gender, as something objectively natural, does not exist; it is real to the extent that it is performed. Indeed, for Butler, we do not choose to perform; we choose only what shape our performance will take.

Choice is neither simple nor free. It does not, for Butler, mean that we have the option of deciding each day which sex or gender we will have. Given cultural norms impel us, require us to *cite* them; for us to get by as subjects we have to buy into them. However, given that for norms to survive they have to be constantly reiterated, we are never wholly governed through them; there is scope for potential subversion.

The notion of performativity is a significant component of queer theory, where identity (or, more accurately, identi*ties*) in general is/are the *outcome* of how we perform, rather than our behaviors being the expression of an inner, essential identity. Whatever is challenging of the norm, relating to sex, gender, sexuality, or otherwise, is queer. Implicitly, this suggests that identities can in principle be reinvented through different performances.

Jonathan Wyatt

See also Gender; Queer Theory; Sexual Identity

Further Readings

Butler, J. (1990). *Gender trouble: Feminism and the subversion of identity.* London: Routledge.

Butler, J. (1993). *Bodies that matter: On the discursive limits of "sex."* New York: Routledge.

Butler, J. (1997). *Excitable speech: A politics of the performative.* New York: Routledge.

Butler, J. (1997). *The psychic life of power: Theories of subjection.* Palo Alto, CA: Stanford University Press.

Butler, J. (2004). *Precarious life: The powers of mourning and violence.* New York: Verso.

Butler, J. (2004). *Undoing gender.* New York: Routledge.

PERSISTENCE, TERMINATION, AND MEMORY

Concerning identity, the relationship between *persistence, termination, and memory* emerges from the common experience of continuity and change in the self and in the world. Persistence goes beyond basic consciousness of self-existence to self-reflexive knowledge of personal identity in and through time. We are conscious of present identity and of having been ourselves in the past with an expectation of continuing to be in the future. Memory and termination are past and future boundary conditions; both of which limit cases when considering persistence in personal identity.

Philosophical perspectives provide alternative explanations of persistence, termination, and memory. From an essentialist view, the continuity of identity reflects the essential core of the self—a fixed individual identity that exists beyond time. Essential identity does not change; people play roles and adapt to the external dynamics of time and change. From a strict constructionist view, identity is an artifact of social, cultural, and ideological forces. The self, a complex of constructed subject positions sustained and disrupted by social discourses, is a social identity. Participation in the ideological discourses of society and culture gives identity a semblance of persistence—continuity and coherence of self—when actual conditions of life are dominated by discontinuity and incoherence. Constructionist views point to the memory as an unstable social production and to termination as an inevitable, ongoing feature of past, present, and future identity. From phenomenological perspectives, exploration begins with functional approaches to persistence in identity as a commonplace human experience. For example, people may come to an understanding of persistence by continually revising their personal theories of identity, by their identification with cultural narratives, or by recognizing the ongoing process of navigating personal identity in their lives. During everyday living, people consider questions of persistence and identity, partly because the boundary conditions of memory and termination are inescapable.

This entry introduces persistence, termination, and memory as a dynamic triad in identity, changing the focus of attention from one to the other to better explicate the necessary relationship between them. First, the entry describes the paradox of persistence within the context of memory and termination. Second, the boundary condition of death directs attention toward termination and transitions of temporal identity that challenge persistence and place the paradox in sharper relief. Third, the function and role of memory suggests an enigmatic ground of persistence. The entry concludes with an implication of the paradox of persistence, explaining persistence, termination, and memory together as a riddle of identity.

Persistence: The Paradox of Identity

I am the same person I have always been, yet my identity has definitely changed over time and I expect it to change in the future. In a simple form, this is the paradox of identity. In one sense, I do not feel like a different person; the person I am today bears an unmistakable resemblance to my earliest memories, to accounts from others of my past life, and to records of personal identity that are uniquely mine. This commonsense assumption of persistence corresponds with many philosophical standpoints that declare identity a fiction if entertained without some essential ground. Likewise, the science of genetics can identify me as a unique human being according to my DNA, a specification that suggests an essential biological persistence. Conversely, who I have been, who I am, and who I will become seems less certain, and seems a much more difficult problem than documenting genetic identity. For instance, the psychological necessity theory of persistence posits personal identity as dependent on conditions of psychological viability—a condition of change. Other theories insist on the continuation of identity apart from conventional psychological and medical criteria of personality. Concerning personal identity, therefore, the dynamics of permanence and change constitute the paradox of persistence.

Observing others confirms the paradox of persistence. For instance, an acquaintance of many years may become effectively unrecognizable in appearance and character. The person's name may change, both in practice and in official records. Regular, expected changes in seasons of life can explain many such transformations. Others result from persons purposing to alter their identity. Nevertheless, even a purposeful identity change confirms the stability of identity in another sense; it is an alteration of a unique, distinct identity. If legal records change, they remain records of alteration of one distinct person's identity. The new legal identity belongs to one whose personal identity persists. The idea of someone pretending to be someone or something he or she is not, and has not been, reinforces the paradox of persistence. The permanence of identity and alterations in identity both seem real, even profoundly real. I remember others and see changes, sometimes radical changes, in their identities—but the identities have been altered, not reassigned. I remember who I am and yet can see the same "me" changing.

Behind basic reflections and observations that confirm the paradox of persistence, dramatic questions compound the paradox. The questions, though dramatic, are common. What if I had grown up in a different time, place, culture, and family? Who would I have been? We ask such questions with the expectation that our identity would be different; the interesting question is "how different?"—a question of substance, degree, and process. An even more difficult set of questions concerns how long, and under what conditions, identity *can and will* persist—the questions of termination.

Termination: Identity Transition

If the paradox of persistence is a common, even unifying dynamic of human existence, the reality of death is its dialectic counterpart. No one else can live my life, or lose it, but what it means to lose one's life is contested ground. The capacity to contemplate one's own death is a defining feature of human identity. The inevitability of death forces us to consider what happens to personal identity at death, in death, and after death. Although it is not the purpose of this essay to define death itself, only to consider it functionally, death imposes on humankind and every sentient human person the demands of identity—it constitutes the ultimate limit case of identity. A "limit case" represents a condition in which we have gone as far as we can go within the terms or categories of a theory, a philosophy, or reasoning itself. So, memory and termination define the terms in which we can think about persistence of personal identity.

The present question of personal persistence—who am I?—is transformed into the future question of termination, that is, what will become of me? The terminus of physical death begs the question of termination. For many people, the death of a close family member, a friend, or even a pet forces the issue. As one author has noted, as if it were not enough to have lost the person, one's own identity is shaken to the core. Part of oneself and cherished parts of others closely related to the deceased are lost. Thoughts, emotions, and actions that only the deceased could animate in us depart in their death; therefore, the breadth and depth of our distressed identity can multiply exponentially.

Termination issues also emerge from factors unrelated to literal death. Metaphorical death—fear of temporal losses and anxiety about related death of identity—invites consideration of choice and moments of temporal transition as forms of termination. People make defining choices that shape ordinary life and challenge identity by termination. Choosing one line of work and one job position, choosing to live in one place rather than any other, and choosing to marry or remain single involve termination of potential futures. Changing circumstances, conditions, and seasons of life call identity into question. In more extreme versions, all expressions of personal preference and individual style become associated with identity formation and, by extension, termination.

Death remains the ultimate, future limit case in the paradox of persistence. Empirically, the question of persistence is uncomplicated. Death solves the problem of persistence. For instance, the psychological necessity theory declares the condition of persistence to be cognitive response—brain viability. Persistence ends at the moment of brain death. Philosophy and religion offer an alternative range of accounts, all of which treat brain viability as an overly reductive condition to establish identity. If conditions of human identity include spiritual conditions and various definitions of human souls, then conditions for personal identity supersede brain viability alone. Death unequivocally raises the question of persistence into the future; philosophers and theologians suggest that multiple conditions may exist whereby the personal identity continues beyond physical death, whether through reincarnation, resurrection, or other forms of personal existence.

The issue of persistence is essential to the work of Emmanuel Levinas, who reminds us of the call that we hear continually from those who no longer walk among us. Levinas has an understanding of persistence that is phenomenologically based. The call of the other continues after physical death. The identity of another can continue to direct us when that person is no longer physically among us. This persistence manifests itself in everyday life when a maturing adult utters a statement or reaches for an object only to simultaneously notice and remember that the gesture is repetitive, coming not simply from oneself but from another who no longer is physically present. This phenomenological attentiveness to persistence and call also rests within an understanding of memory that is not simply a turning to the past, but a turning to the present with an ear attentive to an ongoing voice that is no longer empirically present, but phenomenologically active.

Memory: Enigmatic Necessity of Identity

A person cannot contemplate identity beyond the bounds of memory. The structure of memory spontaneously generates a sense of identity and the conditions for the commonsense assumption of persistence. Memory is an internal mental record of our own past. Self-consciousness and memory emerge concurrently. The memory by which we shape identity and discern persistence is not merely personal. Much of what constitutes memory involves the expressed memories of others that become part of a person's own memory. Others tells us who we are, based on collective memory—stories and records from family and friends. We interpret memorable moments, events, and documentary materials concerning our initial development with others. In preliminary terms, this basic form of memory is the fabric of persistence through which identity is fashioned. However, a basic description of personal and communal memory does not yet touch on the contribution of memory to the paradox of persistence.

Memory is profoundly variable. In many elements and details, human memory at its best is unreliable. When people reflect on their own memories, some are distinct, complete, and precise. Others are uncertain, incomplete, and fuzzy. People can discern the specific quality of particular memories—recognizing some as more trustworthy than others. Furthermore, selective memory is a condition that most would recognize as being virtually universal. Together, these factors suggest that competent human memory produces a substantive and definitive memory of the past self, but not necessarily a precise, comprehensive, or entirely certain identity.

Memory constitutes a limit condition for persistence by the intrinsic uncertainties of a "healthy" human memory. Threats to memory make it a limit case for past identity—that is, the question of what identity, if any, persists. As a rule, memory deteriorates with age. A specific injury (e.g., head trauma), or illness (e.g., stroke) can destroy memory. Amnesia—the partial or total death of memory—constitutes the ultimate limit case for persistence in memory. Most simply, if people cannot remember anything about their lives, have they lost their identities? The question includes elements of the debate in termination of persistence linked to brain death. But does a person's identity persist if the person loses specific memories, but retains an active mind?

Like death—the question of future termination—memory raises a set of questions focused on the past. In simpler forms, the questions suggest uncertainties that do not disrupt persistence, but make an unchanging identity more difficult to sustain. Meanwhile, more profound memory loss raises more intense questions concerning persistence of identity. At best, memory is an enigma concerning persistence of identity. It insists on persistence, but cannot provide the kind of reliability that would make persistence of coherent identity demonstrable. The enigmatic nature of memory compromises the ability to construct a coherent, centered identity.

Implications: An Identity Riddle

In his work, *Confessions*, Saint Augustine of Hippo traversed the full spectrum of questions concerning persistence, termination, and memory. He offers an integrated philosophy, psychology, and theology of memory and temporal identity that acknowledges the recalcitrance of persistence while exploring the uncertainties of memory against the backdrop of the certainty of death. His radical commitments to the problems of human temporality and the elusiveness of identity and eternity led him in the narrative of *Confessions* to declare the whole matter of his own identity a conundrum. He said, "and I became a riddle to myself."

The recalcitrance of persistence drives a complex of questions concerning identity. Persistence points toward inscrutable ultimate questions about the conditions for continuation of identity in the future. Compelling memories that are themselves unstable and inclined toward termination form the ground of persistent identity. Therefore, persistence, termination, and memory pose significant questions of identity, but provide no satisfactory answers.

Calvin L. Troup

See also Corrosion of Character; Identity Negotiation; Identity Uncertainty; Memory; Philosophy of Identity; Self-Consciousness; Social Constructionist Approach to Personal Identity

Further Readings

Augustine. (1960). *Confessions of Saint Augustine* (J. K. Ryan, Trans.). New York: Doubleday.

Chandler, M. (2000). Cultural-historical time. *Culture & Psychology, 6*(2), 209–231.

Mackie, D. (1999). Personal identity and dead people. *Philosophical Studies, 95*, 219–242.

PERSON

Person is a concept that has been addressed at length by many philosophers throughout the ages. The question of what it means to be a person has been approached through etymological, religious, analytical, phenomenological, and ontological perspectives. Etymologically, *person* as a human being originated from the Latin word *homo*, which is a technical term rather than a philosophical term. *Homo* denotes a physical man or woman, and it is connected to *humus* or ground as an effort to distinguish human beings from the Roman gods. Scholars are interested in understanding person from more textured philosophical perspectives because this understanding is critical to a comprehensive exploration of identity. The idea of person has been connected to concepts including rationality, intentionality, consciousness, and mind-body relationships. A consideration of these different perspectives provides a panoramic view of the relationship between person and identity.

Form and Matter

From some religious perspectives, a person is a coexistence of both spiritual and material aspects. Theologians consider the idea of person as a coexistent body and soul, which suggests a person is a union of form and matter. From this perspective, one part of the soul, the intellect, elevates the conception of person above all other animals. In this religious framework, a body is not a person and a soul is not a person but the person is constituted in the union of these two essences.

Analytical philosophies distinguished the concept of human being from the concept of a person through an understanding of consciousness. The nature of what constitutes consciousness has been explored from many different perspectives that range from rejecting the existence of consciousness at one end to perspectives that claim there is *only* consciousness, which implies there is no reality apart from whatever "has" consciousness. Some scholars find that to accept the existence of consciousness, human beings must first deny its existence, but other scholars suggest that the process of awareness by which we make decisions is consciousness or the thinking part of being. In this case, *person* is a name for this conscious self. Some more complex philosophies suggest that a person is present and past existence by the consciousness that owns and commits to past actions. Other philosophies from psychological perspectives suggest that the physical embodiment of a corporeal human being can be more than one person if there is more than one consciousness. So, one physical human being can be more than one person if she or he has more than one consciousness. Nevertheless, a person is something, an entity, whose actions are imbued with responsibility. Because of this responsibility, people impose laws on themselves, and this imposition of laws requires some kind of reason.

Form and Being

The question whether a person is a mental or physical entity is considered at length in analytical philosophy. From this perspective, the idea of a person is a unitary being comprising a psychological (mentalistic) and material (physicalistic) foundation. Ontological considerations of person refer to the *anyone*, which is a complete amassment of norms for a community that embraces conformity. These norms determine the behavioral dispositions of nondeviant members of the community who are deemed the conformists. The idea of person involves the ontic notion of conforming. Conforming is the essence of community because persons conform as particular cases or occurrences that make up the larger community. A person is not a whole of *Dasein* (Being) because Dasein cannot be measured as people can be measured. A person is therefore an occurrence or a case of Dasein, which is an expansive phenomenon of individual occurrences.

Persons are primordial institutions, which means there is accountability to the larger institution, and this commitment is a conformist accountability because communities must sustain a pattern of normative behavior. This means that there is an inherent responsibility to the larger picture of existence as a person. Something exists if what (or who) it is tries to understand what (or who) it is, similar to *cogito ergo sum*. This is a reflexive questioning that suggests that having this understanding means knowing one's own ability or potential, *ipso facto*, intentionality. A person is a case of Dasein who exists in the action of engaging intentional acts.

Form and the Other

Other philosophers argue that a person is not in the totality of the individual and physical being but that a person exists in the presence of the face of the other and that presence permits one person to be in some kind of relation with another person. The person is awakened by and for the other person. To further consider person as a presence, phenomenologists suggest that the element that is necessary for a person to exist is the essential action that occurs when one person does something and becomes a presence toward another person. The action or intention that comes out of something incomprehensible and makes a presence to something else is the idea of what constitutes a person.

The idea of a person is most clearly not limited to the totality of individual matter and composition. Thus, philosophically speaking, person can be considered in the following ways: as a coexistent union of form and matter, as consciousness that holds actual or potential decision-making abilities, as a conforming unitary primordial being, as consciousness tied to responsibility, as a case of

Dasein connected to a phenomenological presence of rationality, as intentionality of being, and as a concept embodied in a space where consciousness is constituted through questions. This discussion does not presuppose that these are the only ways in which person has been considered philosophically; however, these are valuable representations of the philosophical frameworks that inescapably consider the idea of the meaning of person.

Annette M. Holba

See also Consciousness; Double Consciousness; Mind-Body Problem; Philosophy of Mind; Psychology of Self and Identity; Reflexive Self or Reflexivity

Further Readings

Aquinas, T. (1999). *On human nature.* Indianapolis, IN: Hackett.

Heidegger, M. (1963). *Being and time* (J. Stambaugh, Trans.). Albany: SUNY Press.

Locke, J. (1995). *An essay concerning human understanding.* Amherst, NY: Prometheus Books.

Strawson, P. F., & Hahn, L. E. (1998). *The philosophy of P. F. Strawson.* Chicago: Open Court.

PERSONAL IDENTITY VERSUS SELF-IDENTITY

The terms *personal identity* and *self-identity* can be traced to ancient Greece and are at the heart of the basic philosophical question: Who am I? Both terms explore what it means to be human, their broad nature allowing them to be engaged through a variety of perspectives that include psychological, philosophical, psychosocial, and narrative. Although the terms are often used interchangeably, C. O. Evans differentiates the terms by referring to *personal identity* as the identity of persons other than ourselves and *self-identity* as being aware of one's own identity. The relationship between personal identity and self-identity is a source of scholarly debate because differentiating between personal and self-identity is a matter of idiosyncrasy for some scholars and a matter of central importance for others. Differentiating between personal identity and self-identity is central to a

discussion on identity in that these terms texture an understanding of identity and how we define our own existence. This entry develops an understanding of personal versus self-identity by differentiating between these terms, explaining the relationship between the two terms, and detailing the implications of personal identity versus self-identity as individuals interact in a social world.

Perspectives on Personal Identity

In *The Rise and Fall of Soul and Self,* Raymond Martin and John Barresi suggest that theories of personal identity can be traced to the 5th century BCE. Even though the idea of personal identity has a rich history, there is no generally agreed-upon definition or any consensus about what constitutes personal identity for scholars. Some identity scholars identify personal identity with individual autonomy, but others believe that values determine one's personal identity.

At the most basic level, *personal identity* can be defined as a self-description of highly specific details and experiences. *Personal identity* can also be defined as a set of traits and characteristics that are assigned to a particular person. Conventional definitions of *personal identity*, such as those offered by scholar Erving Goffman, suggest that personal identity is concerned with what makes an individual distinct from other individuals. When viewed in this way, personal identity is tied to individual autonomy and the values, qualities, attributes, and personality characteristics that make the individual unique. A more philosophical rendering is offered by Peter Unger, who defines personal identity as the philosophy of our own strict survival.

Some of the earliest philosophical questions related to personal identity center on what makes it possible to persist over time and through changes. For example, scholars such as Unger are interested in what is involved when a person survives from the present time to some future time. Another question that has emerged relates to the possibility of establishing a set of criteria or conditions that define personal identity and allow a person to persist from one time to another. A third question that has emerged is whether a list of conditions or characteristics can be used to define a person's personal identity. Differing perspectives have emerged that attempt to address these three similar, yet slightly different, central questions. Scholars differ on what constitutes a personal identity and how the identity persists over time and through changes. For example, scholars disagree whether personal identity should be connected to psychological or bodily criterion and the specific conditions that constitute personal identity. Scholars also disagree about whether there is a sense of consistency over time or whether personal identities are always evolving.

Differing conceptions of personal identity result in a variety of approaches to engaging personal identity, including philosophical, psychological, biological, and narrative. A philosophical approach considers personal identity and conscious experiences as topics of metaphysics. Metaphysics has been defined as any inquiry that raises questions about reality that lie beyond or behind those capable of being tackled by the methods of science. John Locke's theory of personal identity and the connection to metaphysics and psychology offers a foundational philosophical perspective of personal identity. His *Essay Concerning Human Understanding* from 1694 ties personal identity to continuity of consciousness. Locke does not agree that personal identity resides with the soul; rather, he moves to consciousness. Consciousness is what allows the identity of a person to persist over time. Locke also defines *personal identity* in terms of memory. For example, Locke's view of personal identity is tied to the individual's ability to recall experiences from memory. His memory theory of personal identity defines *identity* in terms of linked memories. Personal identity relies on one's ability to recall past experiences.

Scholars who identify with a philosophical approach tend to also tread closely to a psychological approach. According to Unger, a psychological approach to personal identity suggests that the key to a person existing at a future time is that one's present psychology be causally carried forward in time and be much of one's future psychology. Foundational to a psychological approach to personal identity is the work of Derek Parfit. Parfit's theory of personal identity has continued to stir debate since 1970. Parfit is credited with bringing the terms *psychological continuity* and *psychological connectedness* to a psychological approach to personal identity. According to Parfit, psychological continuity is central to both survival and

personal identity. *Psychological continuity* is defined in terms of psychological connectedness in that the overlap of connections gives way to continuity over time. Unger offers the following example to demonstrate the distinction between Parfit's use of psychological continuity and psychological connectedness: People change psychologically from day to day, so there may be little psychological connectedness between myself now and myself 30 years ago. However, there may be psychological continuity between me now and me then because of the overlap of connections that ensure this continuity.

Eric T. Olsen differentiates between a psychological perspective of personal identity and a biological perspective of personal identity. A psychological perspective of personal identity suggests that identity through time persists by connecting current mental capacities, memories, beliefs, and desires to past mental capacities, memories, beliefs, and desires. The crux of Olsen's psychological approach is that persistence consists in psychological continuity. In contrast to this perspective, Olsen also presents a biological perspective that ties persistence to biological continuity. One persists because of the capacity to breathe and circulate one's blood.

A narrative approach to personal identity emphasizes that personal narratives form people's identities. A reciprocal relationship exists between story and identity in that identity influences the story, but it is also informed by the story that is being told. This approach focuses on the stories out of which an individual constructs his or her personal identity. Research suggests that people may construct their stories differently. Rivka Tuval-Mashiach points out one noted difference, suggesting that men and women construct narratives differently. Men's narratives are characterized by clear, defined plots, and their stories tend to be more linear, chronological, continuous, and coherent. In contrast, women's stories tend to be more fragmented and constructed along multiple dimensions. Regardless of how stories are constructed, a narrative approach to personal identity suggests that the story is one's personal identity.

Perspectives on Self-Identity

The term *self-identity* emerged in the 1970s from the academic field of social psychology, and scholars situated in sociology, anthropology, and philosophy takes an interest in the term. Studies on self and identity can be traced to the 1890s with the work of William James and to 1900 with the work of James's student, Mary Whiton Calkins. *Self-identity* refers to the understanding that an individual has of himself or herself. The term also refers to the awareness of one's identity and the set of traits and characteristics that one assigns to oneself. Defining self-identity is not a simple task. There are differing perspectives of self-identity because each scholar who studies self-identity defines the concept differently and has a different understanding of what the concept means. As a result, a multiplicity of definitions and conceptualizations of self-identity exist. Psychologists typically define *self-identity* as a process that begins in infancy. Self-identity can also be described in terms of natural self and environmental self. The *natural self* is the stable, innate self that is preserved over time. For the natural self, there is a consistency in how one reacts to life experiences. *Environmental self* refers to the mental and physical changes that one experiences in addition to experiences in a social world. In addition to a lack of a standard definition of *self-identity*, no standard set of properties exists for defining the concept.

Self-identity can be defined by role identities and personal traits, as well as by social structures. The attributes of a particular society inform the particular role identities for a person. Self-identities are dynamic and can be defined in terms of relationships, affiliations, and attributes. Derek Layder suggests that social, psychological, and emotional qualities constitute self-identity. He also believes that self-identity is tied to control over self and others and that there is flexibility associated with self-identity in that it is not fixed or static. A person's identity can change because of interactions in social situations or because of the individual's own choices. Layder suggests that transformations in self-identity are more gradual and minor changes are more frequent.

A narrative approach to self-identity suggests that individuals can understand and give order to the self and the larger social space through stories. For example, Dora Shu-fang Dien defines self-identity as a life story that is socially constructed and constantly being revised throughout the life span, which provides a sense of continuity despite change. Following this perspective, self-identity is defined as life-story construction. A life story gives meaning and offers a sense of continuity over time.

Relationship Between Personal Identity and Self-Identity

Defining the relationship between *personal identity* and *self-identity* and the extent to which these two concepts are intertwined is a complicated enterprise. Scholars often use these terms interchangeably because scholars do not begin their inquiries into identity studies by differentiating personal identity and self-identity. When the assumptions guiding how the scholar is working with personal identity and self-identity are not publicly disclosed, it is difficult to determine how the scholar is defining the terms. The use of *personal identity* and *self-identity* as interchangeable terms contributes to the difficulty in pointing out the relationship between the two terms. As noted earlier, the relationship between personal identity and self-identity is a source of scholarly debate because differentiating between personal and self-identity is a matter of idiosyncrasy for some scholars and a matter of central importance for others. Additionally, both personal identity and self-identity are dynamic phenomena that are changing throughout people's lives. Presenting the relationship as a static construct would be a misrepresentation of the interplay between personal identity and self-identity.

A starting point for beginning to articulate the relationship between personal identity and self-identity is to consider the term *self*. Personal identity is often seen not in relation to a larger community but in relation to the self. Personal identity is central to the self and can be considered a level of self. Differences in personal identity manifest themselves in the self identities that people create and sustain. As the external environment changes for people, so too will personal identity and self-identity. Personal identity and self-identity each texture the concept of human identity and are central to understanding the human experience. Personal identities and self identities can also be described by their connection to social identities.

Implications in a Social World

A social world creates a larger context from which the concepts of personal identity and self-identity engage questions related to rationality, ethics, and morality. Personal identity and self-identity can be considered social phenomenon. According to Roy F. Baumeister, personal identity is a crucial interface between the private organism and society. Self-identity is also influenced by the interface with the social world. Individuals often define themselves in terms of social connections and their interactions in a social world. Both person and self exist within social environments, so both personal identity and self-identity can be understood in social terms. Both terms are theoretically engaged by social identity theory. Social identity theory, developed by Henri Tajfel and John Turner in 1979, suggests that an individual's identities are formed by interactions with various groups. Whereas personal identity is derived from the individual's unique attributes, social identity is derived by group memberships. Michael Hogg differentiates between the collective or social self and the private self by suggesting that collective or social self is defined by group memberships and that the private self is defined individually.

Questions regarding who one is are often tied to relationships and to finding one's place within a social world through family, community, and religious interactions. For example, Charles Taylor suggests that defining who one is requires a social space. Social interactions influence the development of self-identities. Self-identity emerges in the interplay of a variety of characteristics that exist within the individual and within society. Scholars also suggest that possessing a self-identity is essential for interacting in a social world. This view assumes that the concept of self is an autonomous agent that engages with society.

Not all social identity theorists link personal identity to social identity. Layder views the self as partly independent of social forces but also subject to social influences. At the societal level, cultural values influence the conception of personal identity and self-identity. Cultural values and beliefs influence the interactions between parents and children and guide group activities within a given community.

The increased use of technology and social media networking has changed the way social groups can interact in a public space. The phenomenon raises questions related to developing a self-identity in a virtual community. Individuals identify with particular online communities that are based on professional, recreational, or personal affiliations. Individuals construct identities by participating in blogs, reacting to posted articles, posting topics on message boards or forums, and playing online virtual games. Participants in virtual or online communities participate in computer-mediated communication where interactions over the Internet help shape self-identities. The increased use of technology and social media networking continue to challenge previously held notions related to the relationship between individual and society.

Amanda G. McKendree

See also Psychology of Self and Identity; Social Constructionist Approach to Personal Identity; Social Identity Theory

Further Readings

Goffman, E. (1996). *The presentation of self in everyday life.* New York: Doubleday.

Layder, D. (2004). *Social and personal identity: Understanding yourself.* Thousand Oaks, CA: Sage.

Parfit, D. (1971). Personal identity. *The Philosophical Review, 80,* 3–27.

Perry, J. (Ed.). (1975). *Personal identity.* Berkeley: University of California Press.

Taylor, C. (1989). *Sources of the self: The making of the modern identity.* Cambridge, MA: Harvard University Press.

Unger, P. (1990). *Identity, consciousness, and value.* New York: Oxford University Press.

PERSONALITY/INDIVIDUAL DIFFERENCES

Personality researchers have suggested numerous theories on the structure and organization of personality. These theories are attempts at providing a framework for the study of personality—the important ways people differ in their enduring emotional, interpersonal, attitudinal, and motivational styles. The five-factor model has developed as the most influential personality theory currently used by psychologists and other personality researchers. The study of personality, or more specifically the person, has important implications for the study of social behaviors as well, and interest in the role of personality in people's lives continues to have a profound impact on empirical research and theoretical development. Additionally, it has been suggested that personality traits may play a role in the development of identity. This entry provides an overview of the five-factor model of personality, describes the strategies used to study personality and social behavior, and examines the role of personality and personal identity in social identity theory.

Five-Factor Model

Although personality psychologists do not agree upon a single definition of personality, the most commonly used definitions consider the relatively permanent traits and characteristics that give consistency to an individual's behavior. *Traits* refer to individual factors that consistently influence behavior across time and situations. Even though elaborate theories and classifications were developed and used by researchers suggesting the structure and implications of personality traits, including Sigmund Freud's psychoanalytic theory and Alfred Adler's individual psychology, no overarching theory or classification system was consistently used by personality researchers until the development of the *five-factor model.*

In the 1980s, researchers factor analyzed almost every major personality inventory available, including the commonly used Myers-Briggs Indicator and the Eysenck Personality Inventory. The five-factor model, developed through the factor analyses being conducted, attempted to answer the two burning questions at that time. First, with so many personality inventories being used, each with its own scale, how was a common language to emerge for personality researchers to use? With researchers using different inventories, with different measures, and each having its own unique labels and terms, making comparisons between studies was incredibly difficult. The five-factor model also provided an answer to another pressing question: What is the structure of personality? Researchers were arguing about the number of factors involved

in the structure of personality. Was personality best understood by 3, 5, or even 16 factors? The development of the five-factor model answered both of these questions by providing a common framework for researchers to discuss empirical findings and providing a theory of the structure of personality.

Although the idea of personality consisting of five factors was originally suggested by Lewis Goldberg in the late 1970s, in response to the consistent findings from early factor analyses, the publication of the Revised NEO Personality Inventory by Paul T. Costa Jr. and Robert R. McCrae in 1985 provided the first common taxonomy, a scientific technique for classification, for a five-factor model. Research using the five-factor model, and the Revised NEO Personality Inventory, has found permanence in the five factors with age. That is, people tend to maintain their personality structure throughout their lives. Additionally, cross-cultural research has found the five factors across a variety of cultures. The five factors in this model are extraversion, agreeableness, openness to experience, conscientiousness, and neuroticism.

Extraversion

At the core, *extraversion* refers to the extent to which people prefer to be alone or with others. Individuals who score high on extraversion measures tend to be sociable, talkative, active, and confident. These individuals enjoy interacting with others and take pleasure in attending social gatherings, such as parties. In contrast, people who score low tend to be quiet, reserved, cautious, and tend to lack the energy and excitement associated with those high in extraversion. Individuals scoring low on extroversion measures tend to find enjoyment in spending time alone and may find social gatherings less rewarding. Extraversion has been referred to as *surgency* by several personality researchers. The term *surgency* is a label that is meant to capture the energetic aspect of those who score high on extraversion.

Agreeableness

The agreeableness factor distinguishes compassionate and considerate individuals from more ruthless and adamant individuals. People who score high on measures for agreeableness tend to be trusting, good-natured, generous, and lenient. These individuals tend to have a positive view of human nature and, in social situations, tend to be pleasant and accommodating of others. In contrast, those who score low tend to be stingy, suspicious, critical, and frequently irritable. They tend to have a negative view of human nature, are more likely to compete than cooperate, and tend to be manipulative in their social relationships.

Openness to Experience

Openness to experience differentiates individuals who are attracted to and prefer variety in life from those who prefer the comfort of the familiar and who have a need for closure. Individuals who enjoy novelty and seek out new experiences, whether it is trying a new "exotic" restaurant or traveling in a foreign country without a set agenda, would score high on measures for openness to experience. People who prefer to frequent the same restaurant and enjoy the comfort associated with familiar people, food, and other items would score low on openness to experience measures. High scores on this trait have been linked to the questioning of traditional values, creativity, being imaginative, and being liberal. Low scores are associated with being conventional, down-to-earth, conservative and having low curiosity.

Conscientiousness

Conscientiousness refers to people who are ordered, focused, controlled, self-disciplined, and ambitious. Individuals who score high on conscientiousness tend to be industrious and hardworking. When taken to the extreme, these individuals may be perfectionists, workaholics, and compulsive. In contrast, those who score low tend to be unorganized, lazy, without direction, less ambitious, and less goal-oriented. Recent work has found low conscientiousness to be associated with a more liberal-leaning political orientation and high conscientiousness with a more conservative political orientation. Conscientiousness is less tied to interpersonal behavior than are the other traits. Specifically, conscientiousness is related more to one's own behavior (e.g., clean, desire to work hard, setting goals) than to interactions with others.

Neuroticism

Neuroticism, like conscientiousness, is not as strongly related to interpersonal behaviors as the other factors. This factor deals with the emotional life of people. Individuals who score high on neuroticism tend to be emotional, temperamental, self-conscious, and self-pitying and are more likely to experience stress-related disorders. Moreover, these individuals are more likely to interpret ambiguous situations as threatening and view minor setbacks and frustrations as impossible to overcome. Those who score low on measures of neuroticism are more even-tempered, calm, and less emotional.

Personality and Social Behavior

In a proposition that has guided theory development and research for years in the social sciences, Kurt Lewin claimed behavior is a function of the person and the environment. Thus, behavior is a result of the individual's characteristics (i.e., traits, dispositions, past experiences) and of the characteristics of the situation in which the behavior occurs. Three strategies have been commonly used to study the relationship between personality and social behavior: the dispositional strategy, the interactional strategy, and the situational strategy. These strategies differ in the extent to which they emphasize the importance of personal characteristics and social sources of influence.

The Dispositional Strategy

The dispositional strategy attempts to understand consistencies and regularities in behavior based on stable traits and enduring dispositions that are believed to be located "within" the individual. Empirical work using the dispositional strategy has focused on defining domains of behavior where it is possible to discern regularities over time and across situations. These regularities that manifest themselves across various situations and are not limited to any particular length of time are believed to be components of personality. Research has considered the impact of a wide range of traits on behavior: extraversion, empathy, locus of control, need for approval, authoritarianism, and Machiavellianism.

The main critique of the dispositional strategy is that it gives too much emphasis to the role of the individual and overlooks, or greatly minimizes, the powerful impact of the situation. This critique argues that in certain situations people may behave in unusual and irregular ways. Focusing on just the traits and dispositions of individuals may miss the role of the situation in determining and guiding behavioral decisions.

The Interactional Strategy

The interactional strategy attempts to understand behavior by focusing on the interactive influence of personality (i.e., traits and dispositions of the individual) and features of the situation. This strategy addresses the main critique of the dispositional strategy by considering the influence of the situation in addition to the influence of personal characteristics. Specifically, the interactional strategy considers the traits of individuals and aspects of situations within which regularities and consistencies in behaviors are found. Essential to the interactional strategy is the role of moderating variables in the relationship between personal characteristics and aspects of the situation in determining behavioral decisions. The functional approach to the study of moderation seeks to determine variables that shift the cause of behavior from personal characteristics and traits to aspects of the situation or vice versa. Strong situations, those that provide clear guides for behavior and appear to be structured and clearly defined, may exert a greater influence on the person than dispositions and trait. As a result, characteristics of the situation should guide behaviors more than personal characteristics do. Conversely, weak situations, those that are ambiguous and unstructured, should exert a minimal amount of influence on the individual. Thus, the minimal pressure exerted on individuals in weak situations allows dispositions and traits to guide behavioral decisions.

Although the interactional strategy is often viewed as superior to the dispositional strategy, critiques have been leveled against it as well. For instance, critics have claimed that according to this view the causal link between personality and behavior is always assumed to be unidirectional with behavior unable to influence personality, and that this strategy assumes that personality characteristics and the situation are independent, they do not influence each other, and they are not influenced by

behavior. A bidirectional view of behavior and personality suggests that behavior can influence personality just as personality can influence behavior.

The Situational Strategy

The situational strategy attempts to understand consistencies in social behavior in terms of the settings and social situations in which people live their lives. Compared with the restrictions in experimental studies on the social situations people are placed in and the behavioral options available to the participants, the real-world situations people find themselves in have the ability to be the result of an individual's own choosing. People are able to choose their social situations, so the regularities and consistencies often associated with personality may be the result of situational consistency. Personal traits and dispositions may be reflected in the decision to enter into and remain in certain situations and in the processes by which the situation is influenced by decisions and actions of individuals. Thus, people high in extraversion may seek social situations allowing them to express this trait. In contrast, individuals low in extraversion may seek situations that do not require them to frequently interact with others. People high in openness to experience may choose to enter into situations that allow the expression of this trait, such as joining a book club or joining a local sports team, whereas those low in openness to experience may actively avoid these situations.

The situational strategy reflects the dynamic interaction between personality and the situation. Consequently, the situational strategy is subject to the same criticisms as the interactional strategy. The situational strategy, however, stands apart from the other strategies in its view of the relationship between personality and the situation. To the extent that individuals are able to choose their social situations, people may inadvertently choose the situations that influence their behavior.

Personality, Individuality, and Social Identity Theory

Social identity theory developed as a theory of intergroup relations, providing an explanation for prejudice, discrimination, and conflict and cooperation between groups. According to social identity theory, the self-concept is distinguished between both social identity, defined by specific group memberships, and personality identity, defined in terms of personality, personal attributes, idiosyncrasies, and close personal relationships. Although social identity theory has focused almost exclusively on the influence of social identities, research shows people do feel they are unique, that they have an overall personality system, and that people have a stable sense of who they are as individuals. Despite focusing on social identities, social identity theory is a theory of the self at its core. In particular, by making comparisons between one's own group and other groups, people are able to self-enhance and feel good about themselves and their group. According to social identity theory, making social comparisons between groups—and particularly perceiving our own groups to be better off than other groups and people—increases our self-esteem and makes us feel good. Essential to these comparisons is how we categorize, or classify, our social surroundings into groups.

A development in the 1980s that focused on the role of categorization processes on identification and behavior was referred to as self-categorization theory, or the social identity theory of the group. Categorizing both one's self and others into groups, specifically into ingroups and outgroups, depersonalizes individuals. That is, this process assimilates people to the prototype or stereotypical member of that group and, as a result, depersonalizes the self and others in terms of the self-concept. By categorizing people, the self included, individuals are viewed as group members rather than by their own unique attributes and abilities. Three levels of categorization have been suggested. The superordinate level of categorizing includes categorizing in a large, inclusive group, such as human beings. The intermediate level of categorization focuses on social similarities and differences (e.g., female, male, African American). The subordinate level of classification involves personal self-categorizations. This level of categorization focuses on the unique aspects of the individual, and comparisons are made between other individuals.

Social identity theorists have suggested that people experience different levels of the self, depending on specific contexts and situations. For instance, personality and a sense of individuality

may be a result of the particular level of social comparison being made. When people categorize at the superordinate or intermediate level, intergroup comparisons are made and the focus is on social identities. However, at the superordinate level, comparisons are often made between other species. When one categorizes at the subordinate level, however, comparisons are made between self and others, generating a focus on the unique aspects of the self. Accordingly, this level of categorization highlights the unique aspects of individuals and serves as an impetus for interpersonal comparisons. One critique against this level of categorization as generating a focus on personality is whether this level focuses on self–other distinctions, or whether it actually focuses on intragroup comparisons resting on evaluations of self and other as more or less prototypical group members. Proponents of this argument claim making comparisons based on the perceived group prototype does not involve any unique aspects of individuals—it simply focuses on how well they *match* the prototype for the group.

Justin D. Hackett

See also Perceptual Filtering; Personal Identity Versus Self-Identity; Self

Further Readings

Baumeister, R. F. (1991). *The self in social psychology.* Philadelphia: Psychology Press.

Goldberg, L. R. (1981). Language and individual differences: The search for universals in personality lexicons. In L. Wheeler (Ed.), *Review of personality and social psychology* (Vol. 2). Beverly Hills, CA: Sage.

Hogg, M. A. (2006). Social identity theory. In P. J. Burke (Ed.), *Contemporary social psychological theories* (pp. 111–136). Palo Alto, CA: Stanford University Press.

Leary, M. R., & Tangney, J. P. (2003). *Handbook of social identity.* New York: Guilford Press.

McCrae, R. R., & Costa, P. T. (1987). Validation of the five-factor model of personality across instruments and observers. *Journal of Personality and Social Psychology, 52,* 81–90.

McCrae, R. R., & Costa, P. T. (1996). Toward a new generation of personality theories: Theoretical contexts for the five-factor model of personality. In J. S. Wiggins (Ed.), *The five-factor model of personality: Theoretical perspectives* (pp. 51–87). New York: Guilford Press.

McCrae, R. R., & Costa, P. T. (1997). Personality trait structure as a human universal. *American Psychologist, 52*, 509–516.

Snyder, M., & Cantor, N. (1998). Understanding personality and social behavior: A functional strategy. In D. T. Gilbert, S. T. Fiske, & G. Lindzey (Eds.), *Handbook of social psychology* (Vol. 1, pp. 635–679). New York: McGraw-Hill.

Snyder, M., & Ickes, W. (1985). Personality and social behavior. In G. Lindzey & E. Aronson (Eds.), *Handbook of social psychology: Vol. 2. Special fields and applications* (3rd ed., pp. 883–948). New York: Random House.

Turner, J. C., Hogg, M. A., Oakes, P. J., Reicher, S. D., & Wetherell, M. (1987). *Rediscovering the social group: A self-categorization theory.* Oxford, UK: Blackwell.

PHENOMENOLOGY

Phenomenology opens up new vistas and mines uncharted depths about human experience. Any attempt to come to terms with identity—who the human person was, is, and will become—takes place in the crucible of experience, so it is essential to have an appreciation for phenomenology. This entry exposes the manner in which human experience has been analyzed by foundational figures in the phenomenological tradition.

Definition

Philosopher Robert Sokolowski defines *phenomenology* as the study of human experience and of the way things present themselves to humans in and through such experience. Two corollary points regarding this experiential focus give specificity to this definition, according to Carol Becker, a humanistic psychologist. First, experience is a valid and fruitful source of knowledge. Second, everyday human worlds are valuable sources of knowledge. The intersection of knowledge and experience provides a fitting springboard for contextualizing the rise of the phenomenological movement, most specifically in the tradition of continental philosophy.

Edmund Husserl: Returning to the Things Themselves

Edmund Husserl founded the phenomenological movement. A native Austrian, he held teaching positions in Germany, including the University of Freiburg, where he also chaired the philosophy department. Even though the term *phenomenology* is used by Immanuel Kant and Georg Wilhelm Friedrich Hegel, only with its debut in Husserl's project did phenomenology in the proper sense of the term begin in earnest to exert an influence on contemporary thought. Although Husserl's intellectual formation was initially in the field of mathematics, the setting in which his thought took shape sparked his curiosity to cross disciplinary lines. The emergence of a new psychology and a revival of the theory of knowledge in philosophy influenced Husserl to make phenomenology a science of genuine knowledge. To underscore the operative notion of "genuine" in Husserl's strivings for knowledge within the vagaries of human experience, Rudolf Bernet maintains that the goal of Husserl's phenomenology is to account for the validity ("being-true") of objects on the basis of the way in which they are given in the lived experiences of consciousness.

Eidetic and Transcendental Phenomenology

Human consciousness is the basis for the attainment of any true understanding, so Husserl devised a sophisticated theory to explain its inner workings. Essentially, all consciousness is intentional in that it possesses an inherent directedness—whenever humans are conscious, they are always already conscious of something. Husserl emphasized different aspects of this dynamic throughout his career. Early on, his phenomenology was identified as eidetic, from the Greek *essence,* and this embodied Husserl's mantra to get back to "the things themselves." Martin Jay, who specializes in phenomenological experience, asserts that Husserl set an ambitious goal for himself in attempting to find eternal, essential, ideal truths amid the flux of passing encounters between self and world or self and others.

At a subsequent phase, Husserl's phenomenology became transcendental. He shifted his concerns from the functioning of consciousness that enables the knower to derive the essence of an object of his or her consciousness to the structure of the act in which the knower experiences any object. When the human person experiences something, it can be experienced in a variety of ways—for example, a dime can be used for the toll and it can become a makeshift screwdriver. In each case, the same coin is given a different meaning. The key here is the indispensable role of consciousness. Husserl scholar Steven Crowell contends that Husserl would want the knower to attribute these differences in meaning not solely to the thing itself but to the consciousness that experiences them in these ways because only the conscious act explains why at this moment just these aspects of the object are experienced. Human beings cannot fully anticipate the meaning that an object will have when consciously experienced, nor can they fully explain why it takes the meaning it does, so this dynamic retains a transcendental aspect.

Realistic and Constitutive Phenomenology

Husserl redistributed his attention to ensure that the various functionings of consciousness were exposed, and his earliest students as well as contemporary Husserlians can be distinguished according to the emphasis given to the diverse operations of consciousness—object-oriented or act-oriented. These orientations are expressed, respectively, as realistic or constitutive phenomenology. Johannes Daubert advanced the former in the early 1900s. His gleanings from Husserl's *Logical Investigations* convinced him that Husserl gave primacy to object-oriented phenomenology, which in turn underscores the inextricable entanglement of consciousness and world. Barry Smith, a contemporary realistic phenomenologist, summarizes Daubert's interpretation of Husserl by explaining that consciousness functions in a normal way when it "hits" an object in veridical perception. Consciousness is therefore exhausted in its relation to an object.

The counterpoint to realistic phenomenology is *constitutive phenomenology,* a term Husserl explicates in *Ideas I.* Constitutive analysis focuses on the correlation between constituting consciousness and constituted objects. Although this conveys a sense of balance because the structures of consciousness are reciprocally bound up with the objects of consciousness to constitute a world,

Husserl actually maintains that an asymmetry exists. Steven Crowell explains that Husserl's position is "idealistic," as privileging the subjective pole in the functioning of consciousness to constitute objective worldly being.

The Phenomenological and Natural Attitudes

The processes associated with constitutive phenomenology cultivate the phenomenological attitude. This is in contradistinction to what Husserl dubbed the natural attitude. Fostering a natural attitude leads to a preoccupation with ordinary human living, most specifically to being caught up with the various things in the world. However, the complacency of the natural attitude, which takes for granted the nature of the world and all that it signifies, can be converted to a phenomenological attitude. This process requires a fluency with Husserl-specific conceptualizations—reduction, bracketing (*epoché*), and description.

Turning toward the phenomenological attitude is called the *reduction.* With the Latin root *re-ducere,* reduction is a leading back, a withholding, or a withdrawal. When co-opting the phenomenological attitude, the person *suspends* the taken-for-granted way that the world and everything in it are assumed to be. Husserl uses the term *bracketing* for this suspension because all mundane beliefs about the world and things contained therein are bracketed. *Epoché* is the technical word Husserl uses for bracketing.

The upshot of adopting the phenomenological attitude is the ability to engage in the activity of description in a novel way. Typically, descriptions provide a litany of the features of an object. However, when describing something in the phenomenological attitude, this is not just a matter of relating its properties; rather, it becomes an effort to describe an object in terms of the way it can be experienced.

Martin Heidegger: Human Experience and Being

As innovative as Husserl's undertaking was in developing an intricate mechanism for analyzing consciousness and human experience, it remained heavily idealistic—the individual person as a subject attains a heightened insight into reality through a consciousness purified from all the distractions of routine daily existence. Later, Husserl became interested in issues such as embodiment, sociality, and history, which helped recast his study of human experience in less subjectivistic ways. However, the subsequent phenomenologists inspired by him moved the study of human experience to new levels. Chief among these is Martin Heidegger. While lecturing at the University of Freiburg as a *Privatdozent* in the philosophy department, Heidegger formed a close relationship with Husserl. Heidegger referred to his mentor as the thinker who "opened my eyes." Nonetheless, Heidegger's gaze soon looked askance at many of Husserl's key concepts or beheld them with such radical acuity that he ushered in a new era of phenomenology.

Foremost among Heidegger's revisions was his appropriation of consciousness. According to Charles Siewert, Heidegger maintained that typical studies of consciousness had the built-in tendency to oppose the inner realm of consciousness with the external world. Not wanting to perpetuate such dualistic views of subjective consciousness and the objective reality, the early Heidegger's phenomenology in *Being and Time* was oriented toward a general account of the being of human being or *Dasein*. Because Dasein is always and already in a reciprocal relationship with the world, it is unnecessary to overanalyze how consciousness interacts with the objective world.

Aside from shifting attention away from the inner workings of consciousness, Heidegger's phenomenology also reassigned human experience to a lofty (metaphysical) role. No longer is experience to be reserved for describing how things present themselves to a human person in a particular instance; instead, experience now potentially discloses being itself. Although a bold assertion, it is not without precedent in the context of Heidegger's overall project. Heidegger believed that philosophy since Plato has not effectively thought through the question of the meaning of being, thus afflicting the West with a "forgetfulness of being." This is unconscionable because of the importance and pervasiveness of being for everything that is. Heidegger advanced several approaches to steer philosophy to revisit the question of the meaning of being, including the contention that human experience is linked

with being. The concept *Ereignis* (translated "event") best expresses this interaction. The event-like character of experience enables it to be receptive to being, which in turn fosters a deeper affinity between humanity and being. Experience as event also possesses a passive quality. When humans undergo an experience with something, whether it is a thing, a person, or a god, it is not of their making. Instead, that which is being experienced must be received and submitted to with the ultimate outcome of the encounter as potentially overwhelming and transformative.

Hermeneutical Phenomenology

Although Heidegger's approach to the rapport between human experience and being is sanguine, he also avers that any encounter with being has both reveling and concealing dimensions. Heidegger offers a sobering rejoinder to the realization that being beckons humans in their lived experiences—for as much as there is revelation about the meaning of human experience vis-à-vis being in these encounters, there are also aspects that remain hidden and beyond human grasp at the bidding of being. Thus, there is a need for interpretation of the meaning of these experiential encounters largely because of being's retreat. Because Heidegger issues the call for interpretation, he is credited with inaugurating another branch of phenomenology—hermeneutical phenomenology. It remained the work of others to make hermeneutics known in its own right to the world at large, that is, Heidegger's student Hans Georg Gadamer.

French Phenomenology: Existentialism and Beyond

While broadly acknowledging how Heidegger's linking of human experience and being paved the way for hermeneutical phenomenology, it must also be heeded from a more circumscribed call for interpretation that Heidegger inspired yet another tendency in the phenomenological tradition—existential phenomenology. The human experience with being must be interpreted for that which remains concealed in the encounter, but the human existence (Dasein) itself should also be subjected to a rigorous interpretation in its own right. It was left mainly to a group of French philosophers to elucidate Heidegger's overarching description of human existence as situated freedom. In different ways from one another, Maurice Merleau-Ponty, Jean-Paul Sartre, and Simone de Beauvoir appropriated and extended phenomenological insights as they offered their descriptions of the bodily, interpersonal, and historical contingencies of the human condition.

France has also served as the staging area for more radical interpretations of phenomenology in light of the challenges of postmodernism. Although it is beyond the scope of this entry to trace the rudimentary tenets of these positions, representative thinkers such as Emmanuel Levinas, Michel Foucault, and Jacques Derrida all have been influenced by and, to some degree, defined their work in opposition to, the phenomenologies of Husserl and Heidegger. Some commentators have deemed these figures "post-phenomenological"—thus, a phase of deconstructive phenomenology could be added to the various trends delineated earlier.

Daniel J. Martino

See also Being and Identity; Consciousness; Existentialist Identity Questions; Hermeneutics; Intersubjectivity; Mind-Body Problem; Modernity and Postmodernity; Subjectivity

Further Readings

Critchley, S., & Schroeder, W. R. (Eds.). (1999). *A companion to continental philosophy.* Malden, MA: Blackwell.

Dreyfus, H. L., & Wrathall, M. A. (Eds.). (2006). *A companion to phenomenology and existentialism.* Malden, MA: Blackwell.

Embree, L., et al. (Eds.). (1997). *Encyclopedia of phenomenology.* Dordrecht, the Netherlands: Kluwer Academic.

Moran, D. (2000). *Introduction to phenomenology.* London: Routledge.

Sokolowski, R. (2000). *Introduction to phenomenology.* New York: Cambridge University Press.

Tymieniecka, A.-T. (Ed.). (2002). *Phenomenology worldwide: Foundations, expanding dynamisms, life-engagements: A guide for research and study.* Dordrecht, the Netherlands: Kluwer Academic.

Philosophical History of Identity

The philosophical history of identity in the West begins with the ancient Greeks and carries forth through textured evolutions of philosophical inquiry. Each engagement that follows meets the well-known phrase from Socrates: "To know thyself." Such a commonplace phrase finds constitutive significance that is both varied and, at times, contrasting throughout the historical horizon of the West. The following sections, beginning with the Greeks and ending in postmodernity, reveal not so much the complexity of the term *to know thyself*, but the confounded nature of knowing itself. A philosophical history of identity began perhaps with Socrates' phrase and continues today with that same phrase with multiplicity of paradigmatic differences in the meaning and the understanding of the word *know* and the word *thyself*. The history of identity bespeaks difference, not uniformity.

The Ancient Greeks

Any journey across a field this vast must necessarily be but one possible version that takes shape by way of a particular organizing principle. This section begins by going back—back in the manner fitting in the West to philosophies of anything—to Socrates and Plato. If identity can be understood initially as being related to the ancient Greek notion of philosophy, then all such philosophy is concerned with a way of life. To give this idea its context, the dictum, as famous as it is misunderstood, is that the task of identity is to *know thyself*. For the Greeks, this means not that one is already a fully formed self and identity, hence the Greek desire to understand education; rather, one's identity must never take leave of the acknowledgement that one is not an immortal.

Thus, one's place is in mortality, and to know this is to know something inescapable about one's identity. To be mortal—having to have to die—is the overriding issue in the forming of one's identity. This pressing truth is always linked with his never-ending belief in the transformative power of talk, and for Socrates, education remains the key to understanding one's identity. Using this idea of knowing yourself in its Greek sense, from the start, identity is a way of making one's way in the face of one's mortality, and this concern is what can be a way of seeing the motivation of all subsequent searches in the philosophies of identity. The idea of finitude has exerted a nearly unimaginable power in Western thinking about who and how we are. Furthermore, thinking about identity demands questions concerning who and how we *ought* to be.

A growing concern for the distinction between the *psyche* (soul) and the *soma* (body), and from this to the belief in a this-worldly life and an other-worldly life, began to take shape in Greek thinking (this other-worldly thinking in Plato, of course, has differing versions, see e.g., *Republic, Gorgias, Phaedrus,* and see also the claim in *Phaedo,* "Philosophy is the preparation for death"). Platonism (one is careful not to say *Plato* here) won the day rather than Socrates or other of his heirs (e.g., Diogenes or Epicurus), which makes it possible in the face of knowing one's mortality for a certain Christianization of identity to take hold of Western thinking.

Medieval to the Advent of the Modern

On this trajectory, the next stop is with St. Augustine, by way of the Platonist Philo of Alexandria. Augustine turns his thinking about identity in the face of finitude toward a radical inwardness perhaps not seen before in Western thinking. This sense of inwardness tends at the same time upward toward G-d (this entry observes the Jewish tradition of spelling God as G-d) in light of Augustine's disquieting discovery: "I had become a conundrum to myself" (or in another translation: "I have become a question to myself"). This Christian turn inward and upward (to wit in *Confessions:* "The light was in me, but I was outside myself") places care for the soul so that its fate in the afterlife becomes the way identity gets understood. This became no fleeting way of understanding identity. Through the power of the church in Europe, Western thinking is destined by Augustine's thinking.

With this turn to a monotheistic understanding of G-d understood as a certain and infallible placeholder in thinking, a consequence of a Platonism has remained no matter how secular we believe we have become. Against this Platonized and Christianized backdrop, comes René Descartes. Descartes takes over the idea that the identity of who we are needs, by definition, a certain and unassailable starting point.

From his position of methodological doubt, Descartes begins the now-famous search for at least one certain claim free from all possible doubt no matter how hyperbolic or intense. Through his brilliant, if ultimately flawed, *Meditations,* Descartes believes he has found such certainty in the *cogito,* which leads to his claim: *cogito ergo sum* (I think, therefore I am). The separation of the subject and the object that might well be said to begin with the distinction between body and soul finds its final and lasting stamp in the Cartesian project.

Overturning the notion of identity founded in the claim "know thyself" and further embodied in an entire Greek sense of the *polis* held together by their keen and grounded sense of discourse/rhetoric/education, Descartes completes the Platonization and Christianization of identity, making the self and its identity an asocial enclosed zero-point somehow thought to exist in an objective world of things extended in mathematical space, the objectivity of which is guaranteed by G-d himself. This Cartesian completion, then, accomplished the disastrous move from know thyself as a question of *living* to a question of "What can the self know for certain?" as if epistemological questions matter more than living well. Next, a certain strain of continental philosophy is made up of the various attempts to "un-enclose" this self-contained subject as well as the various attempts to reintegrate identity in the relational social world, in history, and in the various structures of understanding that might lurk within and around us.

Although Immanuel Kant makes his most pressing arguments against Descartes in Kant's famous first *Critique,* the types of thinking that begin in earnest the long process of reintegrating identity into the social world are found in Kant's political philosophy. Although Kant's position places one's identity in contact with reason, he nonetheless also realizes that reason is articulated by persons in association with others. In both "What Is Enlightenment?" and "Idea of Universal History From a Cosmopolitan Point of View," Kant, though not always credited with such, shows that who and how we ought to be is an identity produced by talk and discourse. To place identity in the purview of discourse and talk is already to begin to undo the Cartesian project and reintroduce thinking about identity that concerns itself not with wholly isolated individuals. Such persons are not those who wonder how they shall ever encounter the other; rather, Kant begins with persons with shared identities (which do not simply reproduce the same) who are always already caught up in the social world and ask what they shall do to create an ethical commonwealth.

G. W. F. Hegel claims that one's identity is always tied to the identity of others and how others take us to be furthers the reintegration of identity in the social world. Difference from what is "not-self" leads to one's own identity. This position is epitomized in Hegel's description of the bondsman and servant dialectic in the *Phenomenology of Spirit*. Identity needs difference, and this difference is expressed as meaning by way of the unfolding of social and historical relations. Following Kant, who is the beginning of the undoing of the Platonic, Christian, Cartesian dilemma of identity, Hegel's linking the self and identity to difference, history, and the social makes way for three major thinkers who have followed him to lasting consequences: One to set him right—Karl Marx; one to make a way away from him while appealing to history as genealogy in its usefulness and avoiding its disadvantages—Friedrich Nietzsche; and one to tell a different developmental story that is in its own way historical—Sigmund Freud.

The Modern as a Hermeneutics of Suspicion

What Marx, Nietzsche, and Freud share is a commitment to understanding identity as something we cannot conceive outside history and social relations. The self and its identity, no matter how unencumbered we might pretend them to be, is in its existence made possible by the intricate web of social relations in which it must find itself to undertake any sense of identity at all. Marx also understood this situated notion of identity from the standpoint of discourse and talk, as did Kant, who believed that

language is practical consciousness that arises through interaction with others: Language. Identity for Marx, then, becomes a question of where one finds oneself in the ensemble of social relations, including language, that make up class societies. Beginning from his notion of species being and the alienation one suffers from one's actual identity in the *1844 Manuscripts,* and which it might be said he never abandons, identity is social, historical, and class-based, and brings with it an historical role in the praxial process of liberation.

Nietzsche considers identity of modern persons as a transitional identity by placing identity in terms of the genealogy of selves who must find a way to will higher forms of existence and who must find an answer to what their suffering means after the madman announces the death of G-d. In *Thus Spoke Zarathustra,* Nietzsche argues that the identity created by the history of the West must be overcome, making way for a change that would require the transformation of resentment and guilt fostered by Christianity into the creative-aesthetic remaking of identity. The exhortations to "live dangerously" relative to the status quo and to "give style to one's character" are calls by Nietzsche to a sophisticated type of aesthetics that includes a creative transformation of identity and self as well as culture as a whole.

The death of G-d takes a different path in Freud's psychoanalytic project as determined by his embrace of modern scientific methods. In an attempt to tell a developmental story of how identity is formed in infancy and childhood and how the earliest formations of identity stay with us and shape our struggle with ourselves and others in the taking of adult identities, Freud asks us to face the fact we contain forces of otherness shaping our identity over which we do not have complete control. Thus, identity as a response to relationships with others is configured partly by unconscious forces acting, as it were, on their own. As with Marx and Nietzsche, this loss of control over identity places questions of identity in tension with the forces of otherness, whether the forces of history and class, resentment, or the unconscious.

Departing From the Modern

In his masterpiece *Being and Time,* Martin Heidegger articulates the way to think about identity for the foreseeable future. In this work, he returns to philosophy as a way of life grounded in a certain understanding of Greek insights about who and how we are. In his analytic portrait of *Dasein*, Heidegger shows we must twist away from the still-lingering predicament of Cartesianism and its consequences. We must work through these by returning to an understanding of identity grounded in discourse, being-with-others, and world. Rather than beginning with subjects standing over and against a world of objects, Heidegger's genius is to show one is always who and how one is by way of a primordial set of manifold and significant relations with otherness.

By Heidegger's account, one's identity is grounded in these relations without being determined to a predicable end by them. Dasein is, then, from the standpoint of understanding who it is, always incomplete and, what is more, always incompletable. We cannot, however, mistake our incompletability as a condition that would allow us to say our identities are completely fluid. We cannot take on an identity invented ex nihilo. We are always who and how we are in the web of significance of our being-in-the-world—that is to say, a series of relations given from the start that we cannot wholly transcend. Identity is never wholly fixed nor wholly fluid.

Unlike certain popular existentialists and some poststructuralists repeating Descartes's mistake in their own way, Heidegger does not pass over the beginning. Rather than suggesting we begin as resolute wills standing before choices, he begins at the *there* of our being-in-the-world. We are, before this misconstrual of the will, understandingly attuned to the world and held in this grounded understanding by discourse/talk that is communication in its ontologically broad sense. This is a receptive passivity that allows us to understand that the choices we do make about the authenticity of our living well come from the already disclosed world of our existence, which we nonetheless structure partly by our own accumulated historical understandings. With Heidegger, the understanding of identity becomes inextricably linked to language and being-together-with-one-another. Any sophisticated understanding of identity after Heidegger will have to have an equally sophisticated way of thinking about language, meaning, and interpretation from within

which and from out of which we always already share a (social) world.

Finally, Heidegger's focus in *Being and Time* on death—as the going-to-be of each of us—returns without merely going back to the dictum "know thyself" from the Oracle at Delphi with which we began. Following Heidegger's thought, the next stage of thinking about identity addresses issues such as death, difference, and care. There will be no thinking about these issues in the centuries to come that does not take its opening moves from Heidegger's existential phenomenological project.

Having Passed Through Heidegger

Three thinkers will be noted here, each of whose works, as with all those mentioned throughout, demand intensive study and are some of the most radical works in the post-Heideggerian era.

Michel Foucault's project on the care of the self goes back to a certain classical Greek and Roman thinking that returns questions of identity to understanding philosophy as a way of life and as the embodied care of the self (*The Hermeneutics of the Subject*). Furthermore, Foucault's work can be said to be a radical rethinking of the Nietzschean creative-aesthetic project of identity dealt with earlier, as well as a way to return to talk (fearless speech), communication, and hermeneutics as embodied grounds for the exercise of power and resistance with respect to one's identity (*Care of the Self*).

Luce Irigaray's project is seen in this context as thinking of identity on the grounds of sexual difference. Again with Irigaray, identity is linked to understanding language and communication from the standpoint of sexual difference (see *I Love to You*) and as a radical critique of the Freudian and traditional patriarchal understanding of identities ensconced in the history of Western philosophy. In all such radical feminist projects as Irigaray's, gender and sexuality play a fundamental role in thinking through questions of identity.

Finally, Jacques Derrida's post-Heideggerian project can be said to press the understanding of language and communication to its most radical position to date (e.g., "Signature, Event, Context"). In a rethinking of Marx (*Specters of Marx*) linking it to what Derrida calls the messianic without messianism, identity is linked to the continual coming of the other. Thus, identity is linked in strict ways to questions of politics and ethics. In *The Gift of Death,* Derrida can be said to return us to know thyself understood as a question now of not only our mortality but the responsibility of the mortality of others. This is another way of saying that questions of identity always become questions of ethics and responsibility. Derrida is a philosopher who thinks through death and difference to orient us toward living, toward philosophy as a way of life that must see identity in relation to language and otherness. Socrates might well understand this standing before the Oracle at Delphi and when he is off again, on his way to dialogue with others about what it means to know thyself.

Ramsey Eric Ramsey

See also Language; Self

Further Readings

Descartes, R. (1960). *Discourse on method and meditations* (L. J. Lafleur, Trans.). New York: Macmillan.

Hegel, G. W. F. (1979). *Phenomenology of spirit* (A. V. Miller, Trans.). New York: Oxford University Press.

Heidegger, M. (1962). *Being and time* (J. Macquarrie & E. Robinson, Trans.). New York: Harper & Row.

Kant, I. (1983). *Perpetual peace and other essays* (T. Humphrey, Trans.). Indianapolis, IN: Hackett.

Schrag, C. O. (1997). *The self after postmodernity.* New Haven, CT: Yale University Press.

PHILOSOPHY OF IDENTITY

At whatever level of analysis of most diverse disciplines, from metaphysics through structures of civilization, there appear two encompassing and completely interrelated facets: identity, the fixed or permanent, and the streaming, the flux, the dynamic becoming. Using a variety of cultural phenomena, expressive of identity and change, this entry articulates the logic of this interrelationship. Thus, myths, signs, facts, languages, cultural aims and cultures, egos, and metaphysical and ontological claims are variants that express the basic phenomena of identity and flux and their combinations that can be either thickened or attenuated resulting in field-depth compositions sufficient to encompass both the esoteric and the exoteric modes of communication. What is singular about these compositions is that they allow cross-disciplinary and cross-cultural understanding.

Comparative Worlds

Identity and becoming are not meanings, but provide the "logics" in whose contexts meaningful discourses are composed. The study of societies and cultures, and the disciplines within them, reveals their constant and irrevocable presence. No sociocultural discourses and intersubjective practices are totally structural, revealing only fixed identity, or totally in flux. Social and cultural phenomena suggest that in principle, identities are describable in their essence, whereas flux, also in its essence, cannot be delimited without residua. Flux lends itself only to an approximation, and the latter depends on culturally available means of discourse and intersubjective understanding. There are two pervasive modes of discourse, one suited for identity, the other for dynamics. The former, in the West, exhibits something Platonic-scientific, something "puritan" about it; it is bounded and circumscribed, delimiting a presumed order that can be expressed either theoretically or practically. Changes, in turn, may be understood in a sense of wild immersion in some spontaneous movement of forces whose sense requires one to live through the process. This living through appears in life philosophies. This does not imply a superiority of one over the other mode of expression. In some cultures, identity is deemed to be the ruling factor, but the dynamic is more important in others. Thus, for example, in Bali the most significant decisions are gleaned from cryptic sayings of persons caught in a trance, or rebirth is elicited by a catharsis of a revivalist, or national pride and destiny are invented in a flux of political rhetoric uttered by an actor on television. This allows the introduction of one of the pervasive distinctions between the exoteric discourse, appropriate to identity, and the esoteric, appropriate to becoming.

The relationship and differentiation between identity and change, and their major articulations, can be deciphered in rough outlines. Change and identity can be correlated in a harmonious way (e.g., Chinese Confucianism), arranged in a succession of temporary domination of one over the other (e.g., a tendency in Hinduism), immersed in a hierarchy of powers and controls (e.g., medieval and early modern Europe), or even understood as a battle until one of them is completely annihilated (e.g., Marxian revolutionary theory, and some prophetic and eschatological religions). Some becomings can be regarded as totally dominated by the permanent identity wherein the only solution is a complete escape (e.g., Gnosticism), or, finally, the identity could be conceived as a mere appearance, a maya, veiling a total flux (e.g., Buddhism).

Many characteristics relating identity and becoming can be read from the discursive systems of particular traditions. In Chinese tradition, the identity term *LI* is related to the inner, whereas becoming term *CH'I* designates the external. Thus, becoming is not contained by the identity, as would be the tendency in Western romanticism; rather, identity emanates change. In addition, such terms as *spontaneity* and *life* are associated with the identity term *LI*, the immanent, whereas such terms as *order* and *law* are tied to *CH'I*, flux, the outer. It seems, then, that in the Confucian tradition, identity is natural, one must adhere to it spontaneously, and spontaneity consists of this adherence. In turn, flux, in its purity, is compelled less naturally; in this sense, fits of passion that are outside the normal psyche, or even illness as being either abnormal or artificial, require that spontaneity adhere to identity. Taoists even claim that evil becoming arises solely from artificial human self-assertion.

Other phenomena appear to be of similar scope. Though not encompassing all of the complexities, at least the Taoist, Tantric, Western mystical, and even scientific and Romantic traditions exhibit a tendency of assigning masculine terms or qualities to identity and feminine terms to change. In addition, these traditions tend to regard women as emotionally energetic, religiously and politically subversive and radical, without submitting such radicalism to rational logic of identity. When the masculine is regarded as identical and superior, it is always exposed to the cunning dangers and mysterious traps of the feminine energy, most commonly depicted in erotic terms. The most vivid expressions of this danger are found in monastic cultures that are structurally most rigid and comprise efforts to subdue and transcend the erotic-energetic in a movement toward the totally identical point, usually called divine.

Basic Interpretations of Identity and Change

Various dynamisms are regarded as life-sustaining, even if they do not possess positive value in all cases. Vital drives, eros, and desires that, in the case of Hinduism and Buddhism, are deemed to be the sources of suffering, but in Greek culture, specifically eros, are seen as life infusing and elevating. The vital drives and even eros have been regarded as components of natural spontaneity, or at times as influxes from some transcendent source—a god's love for his children. Moreover, they can be wild, both in natural and supernatural senses, or cultivated in accordance with custom and sociocultural functions.

Dark, disruptive, chaotic, indeed deadly, related to Thanatos, and associated with the libidinal death instinct, is at times regarded as demonic, irresistible, and self-defeating; manifesting itself, in Émile Durkheim's understanding of Faustian impulses and bargains with the demonic region. These dynamisms are associated in the main with the lower region. They intrude into identifiable and polite social order through various openings, such as greed, infidelity, jealousy, and destructive obsession, and if they reach the higher plane, they tend to infuse it with pollution and degradation.

The Ur-becoming, signified as hurricane, vast upheaval of unknown cosmic forces, appears in revolutions and is uncontrollable and spontaneous when manifested in mass movements and charismatic figures. Ur-becoming may appear as ambivalent and can be destructive or revitalizing, or both. This appears in G. W. F. Hegel's as well as Sun Tzu's conceptions of war where spirit is purified from daily and mundane concerns and may appear in its pristine nobility, and in Friedrich Nietzsche's depiction of life that is both destructive and creative. Basically, this prime becoming does not signal any warning concerning the rules of its appearance; if it posts signs, they are designed to constantly deviate toward dissolution of any identity. Any chaos theory is premised on this becoming.

Constructive events are regarded as impulses striving to establish meaningful designs, both for symbolic purposes and for direct human interrelationships. These impulses are exemplified in the constant effort to establish and refine legalistic and moralistic systems, precisely coded modes of behavior—Jesuit discipline, and Confucian designs for ritualized ethics—all considered as cultivations of the human. Such disciplines and rituals may become rigid and lose their dynamic attraction. The impulses assume a variety of designations, ranging from vital, through sensuous and emotional, all the way to spiritualities. There is also an allowance for mutual intersections among these impulses.

Mechanistic designs are constructed to signify an indifferent, lifeless, and simultaneously deterministic cosmos. Such designs range from a meaningless and purposeless clash of forces, operating by attraction or repulsion—whether in Greek atomism, or their conception of a battle among psychic cosmic forces—through modern physics, empiricist associational and behavioral psychology, market forces, and logico-mathematical systems, to such notions as predestination—all containing identifiable and indifferent rules.

Although mainly masculine, and partially monastic, certain energies or dynamisms can become all-pervasive preoccupations to transcend the immediate solicitations of the world, to return to the extra-worldly paternal home, so prevalent in chiliastic and eschatological movements and, in another sense, in the detachment of sciences. Such transcendentalizing is expressed usually by attitudes of uninvolvement or nonparticipation in the states of affairs of one's world. It may be regarded as an external look with an attendant longing for something else, for the source of this transcendence and detachment, regardless whether such source is known or unknown. This preoccupation at times assumes an identification either with something extra-worldly, or with something that is deemed pure and ultimate, such as surrender to the laws of nature or a will of divinities. Dynamics of this type may appear in active rituals of purification that result in the shedding of terrestrial pollutions.

Vitalistic flux, usually expressed in animistic forms, shows various unattached, freely floating forces, capable of entering various objects and phenomena, vivifying them, and departing. These forces dominate ritualistic incantations, where the act becomes the power of the event; the word brings about storms, healing, and destruction; and the mask becomes the enacted entity. Additionally, these forces are present in transubstantiations, where the bread becomes flesh, and the wine blood, where a chant gives rebirth such that the human becomes the enchanted word. This is the magic dynamism where through prayers and appropriate deeds, one becomes identical with the powers of a demon, a divinity, or a totemic animal; this identification stretches all the way to an assumption of names of animals or figures of power. Sports teams have their vital names and parade their mascots, and populations identify themselves with the victorious teams by proclaiming, "We won." It appears in rituals of identification with political, religious, and "pop" culture rituals: one becomes a Nazi, a Muslim, a Jew, a Christian, a Communist, a Republican, a Democrat, a German, an American, or a Hindu and is ready to sacrifice everything for this identity. This awareness is also at the basis of theater, where the actor becomes the enacted role, is absorbed, and disappears into the portrayed character.

Cultures suggest permanent identities, ranging from eternal presence of some ultimate being, through the presumption of changeless laws that pervade all movements, all the way to stable and identifiable changes. We shall decipher some invariants of identities that range across diverse cultures. The first, and well-known, interpretation of identity is a stabilizing and directing container that preserves the flow without escape. It might become an iron cage or a prison house for the becoming within it, leading to the conception of an empty shell of mechanical process devoid of any life and working in accordance with changeless laws. This identity is seen as extrinsic to flow. Hence, if there is flow, it has to be dealt with by artificial technical means. The modern mechanistic universe requires no energy; everything that does not conform to the identifiable laws must be "conditioned" to attain the status of a mechanism—such as behavioral, economic, and social conditioning. This is also expressed in Platonic aim at identifiable forms where flow must conform to and be contained by the "forms." The same can be said of "formal" sciences that can be "applied" to categorize and identify becoming, whether such identities are interpreted objectively or subjectively. An identifiable, ultimate being, who transcends the world, also controls the events from outside.

Identifiable essentialisms are associated with the following phrasings: human nature, gender classifications, racial features, positions within coded rules, such as husband/wife, and hierarchy of ascribed bloodlines, such as aristocrat/serf. More recently, the quest for essential identity assumed the guise of science: DNA codes and genetic composition led to attempts to identify desirable characteristics such as intelligence or physical abilities. Such identities are regarded as created by some divinity, are present in nature, or can be constructed by technical means.

A mediating function of identity is necessary for transmitting the relationships among various dynamisms. Such a design is stable, but not free of distortions. Some fluxes that require such transmission may fall under a designation of being inaccessible by themselves, mysterious, too dangerous, or too blind to relate of their own accord. Immanuel Kant's a priori understanding of logical identity of categories does not equate intelligibility with the empirical. Modern democratic institutions can be seen in this light; all activities are permitted as long as they are under the guidance of identifiable law. Various psychiatric and even sociopolitical theories construct an identifiable ego as a function that must mediate between the forces of id and the requirements of the superego, correlating to the identities of economic classes: lower, middle, and ruling.

A permanent core, a stable axis, is necessary for the flow of impulses and dynamisms. Though permanent, such a core is amorphous and cannot be defined in a limited description. Through Buddha's head or through Christian caritas flow all impulses, but neither one can be ascribed definitive parameters. In Hinduism, all events flow through the ever-present Shakti energies. Through Haiku poetry or Zen practice flow all events without disruption, and the forever-present maternal impulses lead all events to their orgiastic fertility and cold dissolution.

A momentary confluence of impulses and dynamisms yields a cross-section of processes. These cross-sections can shift and require constant analyses: constant demographic shifts, incessant shifts in supplies and distribution of economy, instability of

political power alliances, and even spiritual powers. Such confluences do not have a single core, but rather consist of crisscrossing of numerous processes at various levels and domains. Michel Foucault's incessant social battle, though dynamic, manages to maintain an identifiable society. The confluence of fundamentalist and feminist forces with a common purpose to battle the sexed images of women in mass media represents a major identity syndrome central to the modern understanding. The major identity syndrome is modern understanding of an individual as a cross-section of technical-pragmatic discourses: economic, social, cultural, genetic, biochemical, linguistic, religious, professional, psychological, gender, and age. Such discourses can cross into each other: Identifiable psychological states can be "found" in identifiable genetic codes.

Conjunctions

The relationship between identity and change follows identifiable rules that equally cut across cultural boundaries. The first rule decipherable from the sketches of identity and change shows that change can function to enhance, promote, and maintain identity. Whether one works hard to maintain the same job; whether the king fields an army of knights to maintain the identity of his throne; whether Lucifer, before the fall, acts to ensure the changeless paternal edicts; or whether the working class is pressed for labor power to maintain the ruling position of the owner class—all are engaged in identity-maintaining dynamics.

The second rule shows that change can disrupt identity. The barbarians are breaking down the edifices of the civilized world, Lucifer rebels and establishes a process of corruption of paternal edicts, overproduction and resultant workers strikes and revolts disrupt the self-identity of the capitalist class. Meanwhile, the dissidents are disrupting the identity of the new communist state, and the secular devils in the West are disrupting the identity of Islamic republics. In modern literatures and sciences, the primordial chaos is slowly breaking down all order and identifiable laws of nature, and the women's revolution is disrupting the history of the identity of patriarchal rule.

The third rule shows that identity can suppress becoming and disrupt its dynamics. The despotic-imperial edicts prohibit any deviations, the erotic spontaneities are deflected along the paternal edicts, the passions become mortified by the salvific codes of all brands of fundamentalists, and the Confucian hierarchy suppresses the Taoist spontaneity, the "garden of freedom." The scientific reductionism of all social dynamics to identical mechanical rules, the global standardization of all products to identifiable brands, tends to abolish change.

The fourth rule emerges with permanence as enhancing flow. Democratic institutions, articulated in the Promethean mythology of rebellion, but impossible in the Judeo-Christian and Islamic rebellion, are enhancing change. A constant revolution, leading to the possibility of postmodern surrender of hierarchical, stratified, sublimated, ideologized, and alienated thought results in the claim that all identities across all cultures, whether of individuals, divinities, social norms, or scientific laws, are artificial constructs.

The fifth rule shows that each kind of dynamism can subsume or pervade, overlap with, transform, and find resonances in others. For example, both the vital as well as the erotic can be an impetus toward detachment and transcendence toward an identity, or an attraction to identify with them as expressions of cosmic life and love. Such an identity is an implicit criterion that decides what kind of specific dynamics may be regarded as dangerous, even if the criterion is good, simply because it needs strict controls without which it might transgress its limits and become decadent both by overuse and a lack of use.

The Chinese tradition designates becoming as basically life-sustaining. Although the Taoists stress this life-sustaining flow, they express it in primordial terms of Tao; in contrast, the Confucians regard the primordial becoming as coextensive with civilizing impulses seeking identifiable moral laws. If a destructive force appears, it is relegated totally to human selfishness. Resonances of such impetus can be found in the Platonic tradition where eros is the dynamic impulse toward the transcending, such as truth in itself that can be identified eternally. Most changes are regarded as life-preserving, and the dynamics of life are regarded as a way of preserving some identity from which life itself emanates. In the modern West, Nietzsche's interpretation articulates dynamics as a struggle between the civilizing Apollonian forces creating identities and the life-sustaining Dionysian force that disrupts identities even when it gives life. The two relate in a constant fluctuation across various domains, without exhibiting fixed boundaries. In the medieval and early modern West, the two forces are strictly distinguished, but in Gnosticism, there is a continuous struggle between the life-sustaining becoming and the transcendentalizing impulses with a built-in teleological identity that is destined to be victorious. There appears a general designation of these polar impulses in gender terms. For the most part, the life-preserving, the disruptive and dissolving, and even the primordial flow are regarded as feminine, but the transcendentalizing, the ascetic, the striving, and the search for identity are masculine. One could suggest that no woman would ever invent a monastery, designed to lead to one of the transcendentalizing commitments to pure identity. Although there are apparent movements of one gender into its polar impulses, the feminine seems to be better equipped to know both. Then there is aggression as a primordial and disruptive force, although in modern interpretation it is lauded when it becomes directed toward productive expansion and the creation of identifiable individuals at the head of such expansion. In broad terms, the contemporary West takes for granted that dynamics either create or promote the emergence of their own identity; one reason for the emergence of this identity out of becoming might be that the modern West regards itself as having been born both politically and scientifically out of revolutions that, by their own energy, have overthrown previous social systems with their identifiable forms and have created the radically new.

Various relationships among dynamisms reveal clear outlines of the ways that such relationships require identities. In broad terms, some designs of identity function either to separate or to connect diverse impulses. The caste system in Hinduism is a composition capable of weeding out the impulses of purity and of pointing them toward transcendence, from the disruptive, infectious impulses of pollution. Although the West does not contain a strict caste differentiation, it has devised ways or well-coded programs for exorcising the polluting elements: witch hunts and religious and political fundamentalisms and extremisms. Societal structures in the late Renaissance set up a specific identity for the controlling of change. Yet, these controls are seen to be artificially designed and cease to carry a compelling force. For example, in William Shakespeare's play, *The Tempest,* Prospero keeps both nature, the primordial force of Caliban, and spirits, the defused flow of Ariel, confined temporarily in a magically established identity of an artificial culture—an evanescent design of emerging institutionalized humanism. Here, the problem arises of identifying a fundamental design of a culture that no longer contains a strong identity with sufficient power of interrelating texts and activities. This allows an unlimited diversity of autonomous worlds and phenomena, designed under the rubrics of arbitrary or practical given staying power and the substance of identity through public rhetorical conviction. The resultant conclusions of modernity are obvious in what we now label as postmodernity. How are we to decipher identities in texts, discourses that are designed singularly and purely for rhetorical efficacy? At what levels can such a multitude of contingent identities be related? The problem becomes more complicated when, in light of such an emergence, postmodernity forces the other cultures and the modern West to regard their identities as arbitrary, even backward, outdated, and irrelevant. Indeed, the process is completely reversed: One can invent any anonymous identity through electronic mass media, construct any trajectory of one's life, and enact it in daily masquerades. We are in the age of simulacra identities.

Algis Mickunas

See also Culture; Identity Change; Philosophical History of Identity

Further Readings

Mickunas, A. (1994). Cultural logics and the search for national identities. In L. Embree (Ed.), *Phenomenology of the cultural disciplines* (pp. 140–147). Dordrecht, the Netherlands: Kluwer Academic.

Mickunas, A. (1998). Permanence and flux. In B. Hopkins (Ed.), *Phenomenology: Japanese and American perspectives* (pp. 253–273). Dordrecht, the Netherlands: Kluwer Academic.

Mickunas, A. (2001). Self-identity and its disruption. In B. Hopkins & S. Crowell (Eds.), *The new yearbook for phenomenology and phenomenological research* (Vol. 1, pp. 161–181). Seattle, WA: Noesis Press.

PHILOSOPHY OF MIND

Philosophy of mind is the branch of philosophy concerned specifically with mental phenomena. It deals with questions about the nature of mental phenomena and their place in the causal structure of reality, the mind's connection with action and behavior, and its knowledge of both itself and other minds. Consciousness and subjectivity are also central topics. Philosophy of mind houses philosophy of psychology, which is a consideration of the philosophical foundations of psychology. Topics of analysis include psychological concepts (e.g., belief, desire, and intention), the models and methods employed by psychological inquiry, and the mechanisms posited by psychology as being responsible for different cognitive processes. Increasingly, there tends to be a great deal of overlap between philosophy of mind and philosophy of psychology.

Traditionally an a priori armchair enterprise—characterized most vividly by René Descartes, whose famous thought experiments were conjured while reclining before the fire in his dressing gown—some philosophers now freely use empirical research. It is no longer unusual for philosophers to draw upon literature from cognitive sciences including psychology, neuroscience, linguistics, artificial intelligence, and anthropology. This robust interdisciplinary engagement, coupled with a recent explosion of interest in brain and consciousness research, means that philosophy of mind is one of the most active areas in contemporary philosophy. This entry begins with a brief historical overview of philosophical approaches to mind, then looks at how contemporary philosophers of mind have refocused on questions about subjectivity and identity.

Classical Questions

Thinking philosophically about the mind is by no means an exclusively modern enterprise. Descartes is considered to be the father of modern philosophy of mind. Yet the mind had surely been an object of philosophical interest long before Descartes. Such ancient Greek thinkers as Plato and Aristotle had much to say about the nature of the mind and mental activity; they offer views on perception, memory, and representation. Classical Indian sources such as the Advaita Vedanta school of philosophy and the Buddhist Abhidharma tradition developed rich typologies of mental phenomena, programs for cultivating elevated mental states and self-discipline, and sophisticated attempts to explain how the mind fits into the causal structure of the physical universe. This latter metaphysical concern gives rise to one of the perennial problems of philosophy of mind, East and West: *the mind-body problem.* The mind-body problem concerns the issue of how best to characterize the nature of the mind-body relation. In his *Phaedo,* Plato speaks to this problem by arguing for a kind of *dualism:* that the mind or soul of the individual is substantially distinct from the body because the former is immaterial and eternal but the latter has neither of these properties. Two thousand years later, Descartes argued that mind and body thus have fundamentally distinct natures, which he labeled *substance dualism,* because physical substances (e.g., bodies) are essentially extended in space, and moreover, because mental phenomena (e.g., thoughts, images, memories, and representations) are substances essentially *lacking* extension in space. Descartes was clearly aware that minds are intimately linked to bodies and even posited the pineal gland as the seat of this union. Nevertheless, he insisted (following Plato) that the mind is not reducible to the body and that it can continue to exist after death. To be a human person, according to Descartes, is therefore to be a unique entity endowed with a dual nature consisting of both an extended material body and an unextended immaterial mind. Importantly, however, Descartes insisted (again, following Plato) that the essence of a human person is the mind, or consciousness; the body is peripheral to identity. This assumption has been a common one throughout the history of western philosophy.

Descartes's view faced immediate challenges. The most difficult problem for Cartesian dualism is this: How can a nonspatial, immaterial substance causally interact with a spatially extended, material substance? Given the fundamentally different natures of mind and body, it is difficult to see how the two-way psychophysical *interactionism* Descartes proposed is supposed to occur. Descartes never offered a satisfactory resolution to this problem.

Several of his followers, such as Arnold Geulincx and Nicolas Malebranche, proposed the doctrine of *occasionalism:* the idea that an episode of mind-body interaction (e.g., willing to raise one's left arm and then doing so) is the occasion for God to coordinate sensations and volitions of the immaterial mind with overt actions of the physical body. Mind-body causal interaction is thus a species of divine action, and God the only true causal agent. Gottlieb Leibniz's *parallelism* denied that mind and body interact at all, asserting instead that God is responsible for the preestablished harmony coordinating mental and physical states. According to Leibniz, all substances are programmed at the moment of their creation such that their subsequent states run in perfect harmony with the states of every other substance in the universe. Genuine substance-to-substance causal interaction has no place in this account. Proponents of another kind of dualism, *epiphenomenalism,* deny that mind has any causal efficacy. Instead, they claim that mental states are caused by physical states (such as brain activity), but mental states have no causal effect on physical states; mental activity is like a steam whistle that plays no causal role in the workings of a locomotive, to use the image of Aldous Huxley, a proponent of epiphenomenalism. Critics charge that this is a patent absurdity: Mental states and processes (e.g., being in pain, desiring a cold glass of beer, fearing a wild animal) clearly cause physical behavior (e.g., wincing, opening the refrigerator to retrieve the beer, turning and running for safety).

Despite its philosophical difficulties, Cartesian dualism's severing of the mind from the body, as well as its concomitant prioritizing of mind as the locus of personhood, remained the dominant way of conceptualizing mind and self until the 20th century. Many 20th-century approaches to the mind are direct attempts to challenge this "ghost in the machine" model of mentality, as Gilbert Ryle memorably christened it. But dualism is by no means an abandoned view. Philosopher David Chalmers, who has done much to reinvigorate current interest in consciousness research, defends a brand of *property dualism,* the view that consciousness is not reducible to brain processes or anything else in the physical world but is, rather, an emergent phenomenon—a fundamental property of the universe alongside properties such as mass and space-time.

Contemporary Issues

Despite some prominent defenders, dualism is no longer a widely held view, mainly because of the rise of *materialism* and the influence of both *behaviorism* and *functionalism* in the early to middle parts of the 20th century. Materialism is the view that the mind, like everything else in the universe, is ultimately a physical entity. Behaviorism was a kind of materialist thesis. Proponents rejected Cartesian dualism and the notion of mind as some sort of immaterial substance or interior theater of psychological activity, arguing instead that mental talk could be translated into talk about externally observable behavior and dispositions to behave in certain ways, under certain environmental conditions, without loss of meaning. Behaviorism came in multiple forms; sorting out these views is beyond the scope of this entry. But competing formulations of behaviorism were united by a dismissal of conceiving of mind in terms of its *interiority*, an inner structure purportedly accessible via introspection. Critics, however, balked at the idea of jettisoning the notion of an inner mental life, finding the prospect highly implausible and vulnerable to commonsense objections. For instance, a paralytic incapable of all movement and thus lacking behavioral capacities and dispositions (both necessary conditions for thought and experience, according to the behaviorist) can nevertheless enjoy a rich inner life full of thoughts, desires, and intentions. As philosopher Hilary Putnam noted, highly disciplined "pain-pretenders" can, through sheer acts of will, suppress all pain behavior and thus experience pain internally while lacking the behavioral dispositions to externally express it.

Whereas behaviorists defined mental processes exclusively in terms of environmental inputs and behavioral outputs, functionalism left room for inner mental states within its taxonomy of the mind. For the functionalist, mental states are defined by their causal relations to sensory inputs, other mental states, and behavior outputs. Mind is thus given an abstract characterization; mental states are individuated by their causal-functional role within a cognitive system rather than by their internal constitution. Like *behaviorism*, the term *functionalism* refers to a family of positions, and not one unified view. But functionalists are united by their belief that the nature of mentality is independent of its physical realization; that is, mental states are in principle "multiply realizable" within different physical systems, including, for instance, a digital computer. John Searle's famous "Chinese Room" thought experiment is directed at prospects for artificial intelligence but offers a strong challenge to functionalist theories of mind.

Though behaviorism and functionalism offered ways out of the conundrums of Cartesian metaphysics, their Achilles heel for many critics was that neither had anything to say about consciousness. However, after being neglected during the heyday of behaviorism and functionalism, consciousness and subjectivity have now taken center stage in current philosophy of mind. With this renewed interest in consciousness and subjectivity comes a renewed focus on themes related to identity and selfhood.

Conscious states such as tasting a lemon, viewing a sunset, and suffering from a toothache are mental states that have a distinct phenomenological character. It is "like" something for the subject to be in these states, as Thomas Nagel famously put it. Conscious states thus have a qualitative feel or first-personal mode of givenness that marks them as structurally distinct from nonconscious states. This observation about the phenomenological character of consciousness generates a puzzle: How do first-person conscious states emerge from third-person physical processes in the brain? In other words, how do the experiential riches of subjectivity fit into the impersonal structure of the physical world? This is known as the "hard problem" of consciousness research. Much current debate centers on issues related to this problem.

The term *subjectivity* refers to the phenomenological character of conscious states, but additionally, it captures the way that the ongoing stream of conscious states is unified over time in a relatively continuous and coherent way within a subject's experiential life. *Subjectivity* also captures the way that conscious states are always given *to* or *for* a subject who experiences those states as his or her own—states given to the subject from a privileged perspective on the world. Subjectivity is thus intimately tied to consciousness. Subjectivity is a fundamental feature of human identity: namely, that conscious subjects are first-person perspectives anchored in a world providing content for their experiences. However, human subjects are more than simply the sum total of their conscious states: Humans are storytelling creatures. They weave overlapping narratives that bring intelligibility, order, and meaning to their own and others' experiences. Inspired by phenomenological thinkers such as Edmund Husserl, Martin Heidegger, Jean-Paul Sartre, and Maurice Merleau-Ponty, some individuals working in philosophy of mind have attempted to elucidate these dimensions of consciousness and subjectivity by distinguishing between a core *minimal self* and an extended *narrative self.*

The *minimal self* refers to the primitive core of conscious states that mark them as experientially given to a subject (i.e., a minimal self) with a first-person perspective on the world. Neuroscientist Antonio Damasio and philosophers Shaun Gallagher, Dan Zahavi, and Evan Thompson, among others, have argued for the necessity of such a minimal self for understanding consciousness. For these thinkers, the minimal self is the first-personal mode of givenness or "mineness" character of a given state that individuates that state as belonging exclusively to the subject experiencing "what it's like" to have that state. This self is "minimal" in that it is a purely formal feature of mind. In other words, the minimal self is an invariant structural feature of consciousness that must already be in place for conscious episodes to occur in the first place—a necessary feature of our moment-to-moment conscious states.

In contrast, the *narrative self* refers to the self that emerges over time and within our social engagements. Whereas the minimal self secures the subjective mineness of individual conscious states, the narrative self allows the development of the more comprehensive forms of self-understanding and self-knowledge that humans seem uniquely capable of. Thinkers as diverse as Paul Ricœur, Daniel Dennett, and Alasdair MacIntyre have argued that the identity of the self resides in the stories we tell about ourselves and have told about us. These stories give meaning and direction to our lives, situate our own experiences next to one another, and shape how we understand both ourselves and our relationships with others. Thus, although the minimal self is experientially given within the innermost dimension of consciousness, the narrative self is progressively *constructed* through our ongoing storytelling activities and social engagements. Arguably, however, the minimal self is phenomenologically and ontologically prior to the narrative self. To be a narrative self, one must already be a minimal self capable of having experiences that one can then tell stories about. But narrative activity serves a highly important function: Narrative activity is what inaugurates the minimal self into a more robust form of personhood. To be a person is to be a socially situated subject with a continually constructed narrative identity. Whether one wholly agrees with this distinction or not, the minimal/narrative self-paradigm demonstrates that philosophical considerations of mind have direct bearing on our theorizing about selfhood and identity.

In addition to bracketing explicit questions about the self as peripheral to a "pure" consideration of mind, behaviorists and functionalists also said little about how the animate body shapes mental activity. But times have changed. Recent research programs emphasizing the "4 E's" of mind—its *embodied, embedded, enacted,* and *extended* nature—have played a pivotal role in shaping current debates. These approaches argue that, in contrast to Cartesian dualism, all mental activity is inherently embodied. More strongly, 4E approaches urge that the structures of mind emerge from the structures of embodiment. Research into the nature of mentality must thus account for how mind emerges from different forms of brain-body-world interactions. For mind is fundamentally *embodied* in that thoughts, concepts, representations, and other aspects of our mental life depend on the body's perceptual system, as well as its capacity for environmentally sensitive movement and feeling. This environmentally sensitive movement and feeling is a function of the embodied mind always being *embedded* in and interacting with encompassing biological and social environments. The embodied and embedded mind is *enacted* within the changing forms of its skillful engagements with the biological and social world; in other words, mind is a modality of embodied and embedded action. In addition to such "body friendly" phenomenologists as Sartre and Merleau-Ponty, other prominent embodied thinkers include philosophers and cognitive scientists such as José Luis Bermúdez, Hubert Dreyfus, Antonio Damasio, Gerald Edelman, Shaun Gallagher, Raymond Gibbs Jr., Mark Johnson, and Francisco Varela, all of whom situate the body at the center of our thinking about mind and self.

Perhaps the most contentious aspect of the 4E program is the claim that mind is *extended*. Currently, the extended mind thesis is defended by its principal exponent, Andy Clark. Philosophers such as Susan Hurley, Alva Noë, Richard Menary, Mark Rowlands, and Robert Wilson, among others, also defend variants of the thesis. According to the extended mind thesis, or what is sometimes termed *vehicle externalism*, not all mental processes are located in the head of the subject. Many processes (e.g., remembering a date, working through a complex mathematical problem, or searching for and finding the men's toilet in an unfamiliar restaurant) are essentially world-involving; that is to say, these processes do not occur exclusively in brains but rather spread across brain, body, and parts of the surrounding environment. By exploiting structures and artifacts in the environment (e.g., pencils, paper, computers, signs, and labels), cognitive processes dynamically extend beyond the confines of the skull and are, at times, thus constituted by both neural and nonneural vehicles. Critics such as Fred Adams and Ken Aizawa charge that extended mind proponents commit a *coupling-constitution fallacy*. Adams and Aizawa argue that proponents of the extended mind move directly from observations about different types of causal *couplings* linking brain, body, and world to the stronger, unsupported claim that the units of these couplings somehow together *constitute* an extended cognitive system. Adams and Aizawa point out that just because an object or process X is causally coupled to cognitive process Y, it doesn't follow that object or process X therefore comes to constitute a cognitive process. Despite many strong challenges, the extended mind thesis has garnered much support. Part of this support stems from the way the extended mind thesis offers suggestive ways for thinking through the nature of the self. If the mind is extended beyond the skin and skull of the agent, it seems plausible to think that the self, too, is similarly extended. What does this then mean, exactly? And does an extended or "soft" notion of nonlocalized selfhood require us to rethink our usual conceptions of agency, personal responsibility, and self–other relations? These and other questions will continue to provide fodder for philosophical approaches to the mind.

Joel Krueger

See also Consciousness; Embeddedness/Embedded Identity; Intersubjectivity; Mind-Body Problem; Narratives; Phenomenology; Self; Self-Consciousness; Subjectivity

Further Readings

Anuruddha. (2000). *A comprehensive manual of Abhidhamma: The philosophical psychology of Buddhism* (B. Bodhi, Ed.). Seattle, WA: BPS Pariyatti Editions.

Chalmers, D. (Ed.). (2002). *Philosophy of mind: Classical and contemporary readings*. Oxford, UK: Oxford University Press.

Clark, A., & Chalmers, D. (1998). The extended mind. *Analysis, 58*(1), 7–19.

Descartes, R. (1993). *Meditations on first philosophy* (D. A. Cress, Trans.). Indianapolis, IN: Hackett.

Husserl, E. (1964). *Cartesian meditations* (D. Cairns, Trans.). The Hague, the Netherlands: Martinus Nijhoff.

James, W. (1950). *The principles of psychology* (Vols. 1 & 2). New York: Dover.

Lycan, W. (Ed.). (1999). *Mind and cognition: An anthology*. Malden, MA: Blackwell.

Merleau-Ponty, M. (1962). *Phenomenology of perception* (C. Smith, Trans.). New York: Routledge.

Plato. (1977). *Plato's Phaedo* (G. M. A. Grube, Trans.). Indianapolis, IN: Hackett.

Thompson, E. (2007). *Mind in life: Biology, phenomenology, and the sciences of mind*. Cambridge, MA: Belknap.

Zahavi, D. (2005). *Subjectivity and selfhood: Investigating the first-person perspective*. Cambridge: MIT Press.

PHILOSOPHY OF ORGANIZATION AND IDENTITY

Identity is a vast topic with tremendous significance in both everyday life and academic research.

Like power and rationality, identity is an important center of attention in modern life, even as it begs any sort of definitive definition or formulation. These observations are just as true when one considers applications of identity at the level of or in reference to organizations. That is to say, organizations are just as engaged in the pursuit of identity as are individuals, and this is seen in the domains of advertising, public relations, and marketing as well as in the ways individuals struggle to essentialize organizations as they try to derive meaning from them. In industrialized societies, it has become common both to attribute identities to organizations and to hear organizations speaking about "who they are." The idea of organization's possessing "real identities" is often taken for granted by consultants and managers.

One who speaks of the philosophy of organization and identity is concerned with the principles underlying applications of the concept of identity to organizations and to organizational experience. However, one must at the same time consider how principles can be inferred or derived from social practices in this realm and what difference it makes, practically speaking, to make one or another assumption about an organization's identity (including the ontological existence of an organization's identity). For example, one can conceptualize an organization as having an identity fixed in time or as a temporal frame periodically disclosed in the unfolding of a given organizational story. That organizations today are frequently preoccupied with issues of identity calls for further analysis and a modest suspension of judgment about the notion of organizational identity.

Situating Identity and Organization Historically and Culturally

If contemporary notions of individualized identity arose in the European Renaissance and became fully manifest after the European Enlightenment, then the idea of organizations having identities grew up with the institutionalization of the corporate voice from the appearance of public relations in the 1880s through the emergence of postproduct advertising in the 1920s and then with marketing just after World War II. Business, governmental agencies, and later nonprofits gradually came to concern themselves with things such as public

image, reputation, and even personification. For this reason, corporate paternalism took on a strong symbolic dimension from the late 1880s through World War II, as many corporations in the United States and Western Europe portrayed themselves as caretakers of the public trust and even as "part of your family."

The idea of organizations speaking was not new because we can hark back to the embodiment of organizations and institutions in royalty, clergy, lords, and their various representatives. The Treaty of Westphalia in 1648 accorded a similar status to what is now taken for granted to be a central institution of modern society, the state. Along with according the state rights and responsibilities, a line of legal reasoning from that point to the Universal Declaration of Human Rights of 1948 also implicitly granted the state voice, which can then be embodied or strategically mystified for purposes of the preservation of power. A U.S. Supreme Court ruling in 1886 that created "juristic persons" turned out to be momentous. The personhood granted to corporations at that time has been expanded to include rights of due process and rights of free speech, among others. In this way, the *identity* of an organization is simply assumed in formal as well as informal practices, without any searching examination of the root metaphors of person or even that of the organism.

The Modern Organization as a Source and Resource of Identity

The linkage of the individual self to the organization and its presumed identity was not an acknowledged concern of three major founders of organizational studies: Karl Marx, Émile Durkheim, and Max Weber. None of these theorists operated at the individual level of analysis, nor were they writing during the period when individual attachment to organizations would become as much an issue (especially with the spread of commercial branding) as did the idea of an individual's identity and "identity crisis." Organizational identity and individual identification with the organization was only hinted at in the earliest modern writings on identity by figures such as Sigmund Freud and William James.

In the United States in the 1950s, identity and the organization became something of a public issue with William H. Whyte's best-selling book *The Organization Man,* which criticized bland acquiescence, and with research on such topics as organized persuasion, obedience to authority, and social conformity. Perhaps one of the most important yet seldom-cited studies in the area of organizational identity was social psychologists Manford Kuhn and Thomas McPartland's "Twenty Statements Test," which highlighted that individual citizens were increasingly seeing themselves and their identities as leaning on those of organizations. Critical skepticism toward excesses in individual attachment to organizations and institutions followed in the 1960s and 1970s, channeled to some degree into the consumer activism movement. By the 1990s, however, propelled largely by the success of marketing and its infusion into every domain of contemporary life, organization-based identities moved to the forefront of public consciousness and display as never before. The contagion of branding reached beyond organizations and industries to nations and social issues, as seen in Benetton's controversial ads of the 1980s and 1990s and in the use of focus groups to modify national symbols from Europe to New Zealand.

Key Tensions in the Study of Identity and Organization

A significant tension exists between the granting of an ontological status to an organization's identity—seeing it as standing on its own—and a position that instead views organizational identity as being an epistemological creation or tool to investigate what is seen to be "the organization." The ontological position is appealing to many audiences and becomes the foundation for writings on organizations' essences, hearts, heads, souls, and so on, at least insofar as those metaphors are taken seriously and at least somewhat literally. By contrast, the machine metaphor is probably the single most influential metaphor for organization, but it is not typically inspiring or carried forth in quite the same way as the "living" metaphors. The epistemological perspective on organizational identity has several variants, including the neo-Weberian interpretive position that organizational identities are "real" to the extent that people extend such cherished concepts to organizations. One position in this set would focus on language and images to

suggest that an organization's identity is what is commonly used to represent the organization.

Another important tension exists between economic and political interests that would celebrate themselves publicly and those that would conceal their role in an organization's identity projects. Narrow commercial interests can present themselves as broad public ones within a corporation's formal identity projects but in a manner at odds with the policies of the organization. Relatedly, one should discern when to take seriously a corporation's claim to be "green." The question of *actual or real* interests, however, is not always easy to assess, nor can it be determined in an essentialized way. Therefore, it is important to look at various expressions of an organization, treating those as a large "text" available for interpretation and criticism.

Underrepresented Issues in the Study of Identity and Organization

One of the least talked about yet most important issues yet to be investigated is the importation of certain cultural assumptions into discussions of organizational identities by researchers, consultants, and organizational members themselves. This is true in at least two senses: First, the sorts of identities projected onto organizations by individuals and groups will inevitably carry with them biases of identity held by those persons with respect to gender, race/ethnicity, class, nation, and so on. Second, the projects of identity as constructed and administered by policymakers and managers, such as the recently popular "management of diversity," will often manifest biases toward specific groups and certainly toward conformity in general. These observations represent one important way that research on "difference" can more directly encounter research on organizational identity, where the two areas have tended not to intersect.

Another important area for investigation is the set of challenges posed to the idea of a bounded identity by new media technologies and by network forms of organization. Organizational boundaries have never been completely distinct except in the case of such total institutions as prisons or monasteries, and even then, there are people in roles that span those boundaries. Today, however, one finds challenges to the notion of what an organization "is," especially when one considers such formations as multicephalous social movements, ad hoc coalitions and alliances, and even clandestine organizations (engaged in either socially legitimate or illegitimate activities).

Finally, globalization in various forms exposes the balancing act between attempts at consistently expressing an identity and the adaptation to multiple cultures, situations, and times. The overwhelming emphasis on solidity and consistency in organizational identity places organizations in bind with respect to rapid change and the necessity of speaking in at least somewhat different ways to multiple audiences. In this way, fragmentation and multivocality necessarily become part of the project of identity for an organization, unless the organization is to risk rigidity and, ironically, impermanence.

All of these issues merit further reflection and research.

Implications of Attention to Organization and Identity for Practice

Several important practical issues bear mention here. First is the question of individual investment of the self in an organization to the extent that either that person's identity becomes monolithic or univocal or in a way that grants an organization license for excesses in its own pursuits. The two ends of this single problem are reminders of how a lack of competing voices and therefore resources of identity can limit the decision-making and moral horizons of people at any level of society. Totalitarianism is an obvious instance of what can occur at the level of state; fascism is a case where the state, its people, and their leader may be seen to line up in a perfect kind of embodiment. (It has been suggested that the parallels and differences between the state and the corporation have not received sufficient attention by researchers and practitioners.) Additionally, Hannah Arendt's work in her differentiation of public and private lives provided a buttress against the organization becoming a social totality for the individual; in this case, the realm of the social blurs the distinction between public and private life, curtailing the natural ability of a human being to engage in an natural dialectic in which neither public nor private life solely defines one's communicative engagements.

Second, one should be aware of the practical and material limits of one's own symbolic constructions as one pursues identity projects with, within, and for organizations. The pursuit of identity can be a somewhat closed language-and-image game. The questions of significance for either the organization or society at large are swamped by the attention of corporate communication managers to their own clever manipulation of symbols. Therefore, a degree of playfulness and self-criticism are important to cultivate in the identity business.

Third and finally, organization and identity evokes questions about the roles of organizations in today's world, convoluting organization with person and character, engaging machine metaphors for describing their operation, and nourishing dwellings of creation before clarity of understanding is yet feasible by the creators themselves. If organizations are machines, then what do we do when they are not running well? As is the case with other domains of inquiry, our ability to create is often far ahead of our ability to fully understand our own creations.

George Cheney

See also Corporate Identity; Organizational Identity

Further Readings

Ashforth, B. E., & Mael, F. A. (1996). Organizational identity and strategy as a context for the individual. *Advances in Strategic Management, 13,* 19–64.

Balmer, J. M. T., & Greyser, S. A. (Eds.). (2003). *Revealing the corporation: Perspectives on identity, image, reputation, corporate branding, and corporate level marketing,* London: Routledge.

Cheney, G., & Christensen, L. T. (2001). Organizational identity. Linkages between "internal" and "external" organizational communication. In F. Jablin & L. L. Putnam (Eds.), *The new handbook of organizational communication* (pp. 231–269). Thousand Oaks, CA: Sage.

Christensen, L. T., Morsing, M., & Cheney, G. (2008). *Corporate communications: Convention, complexity and critique.* London: Sage.

Dutton, J. E., & Dukerich, J. M. (1991). Keeping an eye on the mirror: Image and identity in organizational adaptation. *Academy of Management Journal, 34,* 517–554.

Marchand, R. (1998). *Creating the corporate soul: The rise of public relations and corporate imagery in big business.* Berkeley: University of California Press.

Whetten, D. A. (2006). Albert and Whetten revisited: Strengthening the concept of organizational identity. *Journal of Management Inquiry, 15*(3), 219–234.

PHONOLOGICAL ELEMENTS OF IDENTITY

Language consists of multiple levels, including grammatical, lexical, semantic, morphological, syntactical, pragmatic, prosodic, and phonological. The grammatical level of language pertains to unconscious rules of a language related to competence and performance. The lexical level encompasses vocabulary. Semantics relates to meaning in its myriad forms, whereas morphological refers to the smallest meaningful units of language. Examples of these small, meaningful units are the past tense marker, *-ed,* and the third person, singular, present tense marker, *-s.* The syntactical level of language relates to sentence formation rules, and the pragmatic level considers the importance of context and language use. Although the prosodic level reveals the complex features that accompany the production of speech sounds such as pitch and timing, and the phonological level pertains to the general sound system of language.

Different systems contribute to distinctions in speech and speech sounds. The systems are the phonatory, velopharyngeal, lingual, labial, and mandibular. These systems control vocal fold movement to produce sound, nasality, vowel and consonant articulation, lip action, and jaw movement. Phonetic symbols help graphically distinguish the various sounds produced by these speech systems. Representative phonetic symbols follow: (1) /ɔ/, /b ɔI/, *boy;* (2) /ə/, / əbʌv/, *above;* (3) /ɚ/, /dIn ɚ/, *dinner;* (4) /ɛ/, /bɛt/, *bet;* (5)/ʌ/, /kʌp/, *cup;* (6) /œ/, /kœt/, *cat;* (7) /ʊ/, /b ʊk/, *book;* and (8) /θ/, /ti θ/, *teeth.* Many phonetic symbols resemble the regular vowels, a, e, i, o, u. The symbols, however, present phonetic representations of sounds. To illustrate, the /i/ represents the high, front vowel sound in *teeth* rather than the regular vowel "i" reflected in the word *bite.* To describe the /i/ as "high front" indicates where the sound

occurs in the oral cavity as well as tongue, jaw, and lip movement. Vowel sounds are produced without obstruction to airflow in the oral cavity. Consonant sounds are produced with various obstructions to airflow in the oral cavity and may be variously described as interdental, alveolar, fricative, bilabial, stop, and so on. Each term yields information about the place or manner of articulation. Variations in vowel and consonant production contribute to the speaker's identity.

Phonological Variation and Identity

Dialect, age, gender, physical ailments, and numerous other factors influence phonological variation. Both Standard English and Black English possess rules that permit variations in the articulation of sounds. In the context of linguistics, a rule states how an aspect of language operates. Rules are descriptive, not prescriptive. That is, linguistic rules describe what actually occurs when people speak. These rules are not prescriptive like those found in grammar books. Linguistic rules do not judge language use or curb language variation; instead, linguistic rules describe language use and language variation. One such rule relates to consonant cluster reduction. A Black English dialect speaker might pronounce "desk" as /dɛs/ rather than /dɛsk/. The Black English dialect rule permits the final consonant omission when both consonants in a consonant cluster are either voiceless or voiced. Vocal fold vibrations distinguish voiceless and voiced sounds. When speakers produce voiceless sounds, the vocal folds do not vibrate. When speakers produce voiced sounds, the vocal folds vibrate. In /dɛsk/, the /s/ is voiceless and the /k/ is voiceless. Because the dialect rule permits the final consonant deletion, what results is /dɛs/. Although consonant cluster reduction creates an identifiable difference among speakers, this variation is acceptable.

Speakers whose dialects permit consonant cluster reduction in a cluster that forms the grammatical past tense marker, *ed,* also permit consonant cluster reduction in words that do not consist of the past tense marker but are phonologically equivalent. Examples are *guest* and *guessed.* Their phonetic equivalence appears as follows: /gɛst/ and /gɛst/. Certain dialects, however, permit consonant cluster reduction, and the following results: /gɛs/ *guest* and /gɛs/ *guessed.* Because /s/ and /t/ are voiceless consonants, certain dialects permit the final consonant deletion. Likewise, in the words *find* and *fined,* phonetically represented as /faInd/ and /faInd/, the phonological rule permits deletion of the final consonant in a consonant cluster. Because /n/ and /d/ are voiced consonants, this dialect rule permits final consonant deletion resulting in the following phonetic representations: /faIn/ and /faIn/. Interestingly, consonant cluster reduction does not occur in consonant clusters consisting of one voiced and one voiceless consonant. For example, the word *stump* does not permit consonant cluster reduction because the /m/ is voiced and the /p/ is voiceless.

Yet another phonological variation and identifiable difference occurs when speakers produce /d/ for the voiced *th* as in *the.* Specifically, speakers replace the interdental fricative, *th,* with the alveolar stop, /d/. Thus, the words *the, that,* and *those,* sound like *da, dat,* and *dose.* Although stigmatized, this phonological variation occurs in numerous speech communities. As speakers adopt different speech patterns over time, phonological changes occur as well. Still, linguists observe little change in the use of /d/ for voiced *th* when they study the language of speakers over time and in succeeding generations.

Still another phonological variation that reflects identity is *r-deletion* or *r-lessness.* Rather than produce the possessive, plural pronoun, *their,* speakers may produce what sounds like *they.* In this instance, a phonological rule that permits final r-deletion creates what sounds like a grammatical error. Rather than the possessive, plural pronoun, *their,* the speaker produces what sounds like the nominative, plural pronoun, *they,* as in "We went to 'they' house." Such a sound variation veers from the expected sound that results from the presence of *r.* That this variation creates a seeming grammatical error thrusts it into the category of stigmatized language use. This r-deletion rule also occurs in words with medial r as in /bak/ for *bark* and /dak/ for *dark.* Because these sound variations create no seeming grammatical errors, they are considered nonstigmatized. This r-deletion rule operates in several varieties of English such as the "Brooklynese," New England, Black English, and Southern English dialects.

Certain varieties of Southern English include phonological rules that permit changes from /z/ to /d/ and /v/ to /b/ in the environment of nasal sounds. These changes reflect a process called *accommodation.* That is, certain speech sounds modify other speech sounds because of the proximity of sounds in a particular environment. Examples occur in the words *business* /bIznɛs/ and *heaven* /hɛvən/. When the Southern English phonological rule operates, /bIznɛs/ becomes /bIdnɛs/. The fricative /z/ followed by the nasal /n/ produces the stop /d/. Similarly in the word *heaven* /hɛvən/, the schwa /ə/ follows the fricative /v/; however, because the schwa receives minimal syllabic stress, the following nasal sound /n/ still influences /v/, which surprisingly results in /hɛbm/. The alveolar nasal, /n/, changes to the bilabial nasal, /m/, because of the bilabial stop, /b/. The process of accommodation, then, permits changes in speech sounds and exemplifies yet another phonological rule of language that contributes to identity.

Lexical items or vocabulary clearly signal group identity, especially age. For example, older speakers may use the term *icebox* even though the appliance no longer exists. Regarding lexical items and phonological elements, older speakers may retain phonological and grammatical patterns acquired during their youth. Such retentions in speech act as clear identity markers. Furthermore, there is a relationship between age and the use of certain phonological and grammatical variants. Adults, in general, use fewer phonological and grammatical variants, and adolescents use more variants. Peers influence the speech of adolescents. Adolescents naturally adopt phonological and other speech patterns from their peers. Because adolescents use more stigmatized forms in general, this presupposes that they use more stigmatized phonological features.

Gender is also important when considering the phonological elements of identity. Males tend to use more stigmatized forms than do females, thus by extension more phonological variants such as the /d/ for the voiced *th.* Stigmatized forms seem to parallel with maleness or masculinity. Although paradoxical, one might argue for positive values associated with the use of stigmatized forms among males. Interestingly, linguists observe that females possess more awareness of language use and listener attitudes. These factors then contribute to the use of fewer stigmatized forms in general and phonological variants in particular.

In addition to ethnicity, age, and gender, seemingly insignificant aspects of speech, such as paralinguistic features, contribute to phonological variation. Paralinguistic features such as hesitation in speech or vowel lengthening could alter sound production. An example similar to the latter occurs in some southern dialects. Rather than /bɛd/, the speaker says /bɛyəd/ for *bed*. The speaker produces what sounds like a two-syllable, monosyllabic word. Other aspects of speech such as suprasegmental features contribute to phonological variation. An example of a suprasegmental feature is intonation. Pitch, timing, and syllabic stress relate to intonation and therefore phonological variation. Even a physical ailment such as the common cold can contribute to sound variations in speech. Restricted nasal passages alter nasal consonant sounds. For example, the consonant sound, /m/, can be identified by its place and manner of articulation. Its place of articulation is bilabial, whereas its manner of articulation is nasal. Likewise, the consonant sound /b/ can be identified by its place and manner of articulation as bilabial and stop, respectively. Because these consonant sounds share the same place of articulation, /m/ becomes /b/ when the nasal cavity restricts the airflow and thereby alters sounds. Thus, "*my* head aches" sounds like "*by* head aches." These familiar examples show how multiple factors contribute to phonological variation and serve as markers of identity.

Listener Responses and Identity

Social markers in speech signal ethnicity, age, and gender. Such markers often cause listeners to judge the speaker's social status because of stylistic variations in speech. Stylistic variations, as noted earlier, are often phonological. Listeners may associate social status, education, and competence with sound variations that result from r-deletion, consonant cluster reduction, or the proximity of nasal sounds. Certain variations may amuse listeners in that they listen to *how* a speaker says rather than *what* a speaker says. Other phonological variations could elicit disdain and result in discriminatory practices because listeners associate certain variations with certain groups. Although there is nothing inherently wrong with vowel variation, assimilation of sounds, or omission of sounds, the

myths, images, and prejudices related to particular groups elicit listener attitudes. Although all speakers recognize social markers in speech, all do not judge variation. For example, children recognize social markers and variation; however, they do not judge language use. A child might respond to phonological elements in speech by saying, "An 'old man' called about the garage sale." Speech sounds then simply elicit an awareness of age and gender, not judgment.

Phonological elements exemplify yet another way in which language reveals identity. The phonological or sound systems of language have the capacity to reveal ethnicity, age, and gender. Additionally, these sound systems and their variations identify those with different abilities such as deaf speakers, cleft palate speakers, and English as a second language speakers. Difference, however, does not signal deficiency. Individual sounds of language do not naturally possess negative qualities. Based on life experiences and preconceived notions, listeners attribute negative qualities. Listeners determine that individual speech sounds and combinations of sounds are stigmatized; therefore, those who produce particular speech sounds are often deemed socially, educationally, or mentally challenged. Listeners must instead view language through a descriptive lens and with the understanding that phonological elements of identity do not occur haphazardly. Like dialect features, phonological elements are governed by the rules of language.

Jacqueline Imani Bryant

See also Code-Switching; Dialect; English as a Second Language (ESL); Intonation; Invariant *Be*; Semantics

Further Readings

Fromkin, V., & Rodman, R. (1983). *An introduction to language.* New York: Holt, Rinehart & Winston.

Jeremiah, M. A. (2008). Linguistic insights from slave narratives. *CLA Journal, 52*(1), 38–54.

Mackay, I. (1987). *Phonetics: The science of speech production.* Boston: Allyn & Bacon.

Scherer, K. R., & Giles, H. (1979). *Social markers in speech.* Cambridge, UK: Cambridge University Press.

Wolfram, W., & Fasold, R. W. (1974). *The study of social dialects in American English.* Englewood Cliffs, NJ: Prentice Hall.

Wolfram, W., & Schilling-Estes, N. (1998). *American English: Dialects and variation.* Malden, MA: Blackwell.

PHOTOGRAPHIC TRUTH

At the heart of the current discourse on still photography in the digital age remains a concern that the "objective truth" of photographs is threatened as image makers digitally alter images into constructions that bear no relation to the reality from which they were originally taken. It is implied that still photographs deal with objective truth, whereas the digital photograph is freed from such an obligation. If the objective truth is argued to be an obsolete concept, then, by extension, so is the traditional still photograph. But although the critical debate on still photography is far from closed, as a starting point, photographic truth may be understood as a partial and constructed truth, the product of a technical form of mediation originating from and appealing to human subjectivities and therefore as subjective a means of understanding as it is objective.

As new technologies are invented, those enamored with them are often quick to apply Darwinian notions of "the survival of the fittest," prophesying the extinction of existing media. Before accepting that the traditional still photograph is a "less evolved species" than the digital photograph because it is "tied to objective truth," it is necessary to examine whether the still photograph ever represented any kind of objective truth in the first place. Likewise, before labeling still photography an "endangered species" and carting it off to the ready-to-go-extinct pile, it is important to uncover how it is that it ever came to be regarded as "the truth."

When one examines the past for clues to the present, what comes to the surface is a dominant ideology that has narrowed and confined the discussions on still photography from its beginnings. What becomes more apparent is how the still photograph, since its invention, may have never been objective; it may have never been "the truth." Although the still photograph attests to its subject's existence in a way that no preceding pictorial form did before it, existence is not synonymous with truth. Rather, the photograph may have always been a *construction* shaped by a dance of negotiation between objective and subjective processes, convention and invention, nature and culture, reality and illusion. An additional layer of this exploration might even show that the emergence of the digital photograph may have only pushed further the split from reality that the still photograph had already begun. The medium of photography, in both traditional still and digital forms, explores identity through visual representations of the self and others. The concept of photographic truth further textures the extent to which photography constructs, maintains, and challenges notions of identity. Additionally, this concept raises ongoing questions of what photography can reveal about identity.

Early Applications of Photography

Since the appearance in 1826 of the oldest known version of a photograph, Joseph-Nicéphore Niépce's heliograph titled *View From a Window at Gras*, an aura of magic has been attached to photography. To some degree, this has resulted from sensationalistic advertising by the inventors themselves. In this regard, Niépce joined with Louis-Jacques-Mandé Daguerre (who in 1839 published his new photographic process, the *daguerreotype*) to define photography as the spontaneous reproduction of the images of nature received in the camera obscura (a box with a lens used as an aid in Renaissance painting). He concludes that the daguerreotype is not merely an instrument, but a process that allows nature to reproduce itself. Such words are hardly value-neutral; indeed, they actively contributed to the sense of magic connected with the act of photography from the beginning.

This sense of awe regarding photography is apparent in the earliest responses of the public. *La Gazette de France,* in 1839, declared the invention to be so significant that it upsets all scientific theories on light and optics. The public, like the inventors, believed that the daguerreotype was a fixed and everlasting impression that can be *taken away* from the presence of the objects.

U.S. writer Edgar Allan Poe regarded photography to be a miraculous invention, even perhaps the most significant of modern science. Poe was more than fascinated by photography; he became an avid supporter, writing three articles within one year explaining and championing the invention. He believed the photograph to be both absolute truth and supreme perfection.

In addition to celebrating the magical qualities of the invention, early commentators on photography wrote about the superhuman ability of the camera to see and record all things. Lady Elizabeth Eastlake (wife of the English neoclassical painter Sir Charles Eastlake) published articles on photography arguing that the camera was a supreme eyewitness to the objects and events of life. However, she contributed an important concept that has gripped many commentators long thereafter: the idea of the photograph being a trace or impression taken from the real. What is implicit in this idea is the belief that the photograph has taken something from something. What that something taken is and to whom that something-taken-from-something belongs is a question that still instigates debate in contemporary criticism of photography.

In 1859, U.S. writer Oliver Wendell Holmes, like Poe, celebrated the miraculous nature of photography. Holmes, too, believed the photograph to be a perfect mirror that fixes reality. His fascination with photography came from his belief that the negative represents form divorced from matter. And this conviction led him to flagrantly disregard the value of the object being photographed. Holmes admitted that there is only one Colosseum, but added that once we have a negative of it, we can make thousands of copies. His exaltation of form, in his mind, necessitates a debasement of matter. He regarded this as a good thing, something commendable. Holmes then concluded that photographers will hunt objects as cattle, taking their skins, and leaving them to die by the roadside.

Among the themes evident in these early commentaries is the photographer's ability to take and scale off the surface of the real, to be a trace or impression of the real. Another theme is the photographer's superhuman ability to *do* (spontaneous reproduction) and to *know* (supreme eyewitness) things beyond human capacities. Poe even stated that the photograph is more *true* and perfect than the object photographed.

The Unreality of Photography

Writer Fred Ritchin believes that the status of photography as a truthful pictorial form faces a severe threat from digital technology. Because digital images may have no origin other than their computer programs yet maintain the look of the photographic image, he doubts whether photographs will mean anything anymore. Ritchin's worry sounds similar to warnings of early commentators on photography who believed that the invention of photography would mean the death of painting. When a new art technology appears, there are often those who foretell the imminent doom of existing media. Many felt photography would render painting obsolete, but it continues to thrive. What usually happens with the introduction of a new art form is a reassessment of the one from which the new form springs. Great questions emerge. Was the still photograph ever a truthful pictorial form? If not, then why have critics like Ritchin come to believe this? If yes, then what exactly is the traditional still photograph evidence of that the digital photograph is not?

As the discussion of the early responses to photography illustrates, there is little that is new in contemporary responses, which betray a belief in photography's privileged relationship and responsibility to reality. Contemporary critics argue that because the film within a camera reacts to the light reflected by objects, the negative constitutes a kind of proof of the object's existence. The object "must" have been there, it is argued, or else there would be no light reflected from it and no form for the negative to "capture."

It can be pointed out, however, that belief in the *transparency* of photographic representation is a fallacy, fostered by the historical development of artistic perspective in Western civilization. An eye already accustomed to reading paintings and prints according to Renaissance perspective is preconditioned to perceive the photograph as an especially "realistic" means of representation. Participants in a given culture are conditioned to see and decipher an image through the particular conventions created by that culture. Pictorial realism is culturally specific. Styles of representation are invented by a culture to be viewed within that culture. Styles of picturing become so familiar and readable to members of that culture that they seem to be realistic, natural, and the way the world is.

Art theoretician Joel Snyder challenges realist theories of photography by claiming that we have falsely come to believe the photograph to be more natural and more closely tied to the real than is any other convention. Snyder reminds us that cameras themselves were invented to conform to Renaissance painting standards. The camera obscura, or "dark chamber"—which was the earliest form of camera—was in use as early as the 16th century precisely to facilitate the way of picturing developed by Renaissance artists, who traced the mirror image it generated. The photograph shows us what the camera sees, not what we do. The camera itself, the lens, the type of film, and the angle and speed at which an object or person was photographed are just a few factors inventing a picture of the world. Along with many other theorists, Snyder affirms that photography is no more inherently tied to the real than is painting, drawing, or, for that matter, language. Rather, photography is merely another way of constructing, ordering, and communicating meaning. Photography relies just as much on convention as do other media.

Anthropological Applications of Photography

Anthropology's beginnings are closely tied to photography. Early anthropology used photography as a tool to identify and categorize human races, to record visually the physical characteristics of different racial groups. Spurred on by Charles Darwin's theory of natural selection, anthropologists used photographs in anthropometry to measure body mass and skeletal size, which were believed to differ among racial groups. Photography provided the visual information used to classify human races in support of theories of social evolution.

Early anthropologists considered photography to be a truth-revealing mechanism. By 1920, however, photography diminished in importance in anthropology as social organization, which was considered to be less visual, increased in importance. Photographs became marginal, relegated to the process of explanation. Photography was perceived to be a technique that recorded the surface rather than the depth that the anthropologist was required to seek.

This perception seems to haunt anthropology today because it remains primarily a discipline of words. Ethnographic studies seek to provide an analysis of the arrangements and practices of a culture. However, these studies are usually presented in the written mode, even though the fieldwork experience involves many senses, especially sight. Although many ethnographies since the 1920s include photographs relating to the fieldwork, the photographs are included more as illustrations rather than as an analysis of the visual dimensions of culture. Photographs have been peripheral to the principal analysis undertaken in ethnographies. Rather than being used as investigative topics in and of themselves, photographs are treated merely as descriptions or a slide show.

Photographs have been greatly underanalyzed in anthropological work. Generally, a comprehensive written report is accompanied by a handful of photographs used only to illustrate the more serious analysis undertaken by the written text. Anthropologists have not used their photographs as a *way* of doing serious analysis. Instead of using photographic methods as a research technique to investigate, analyze, and critique, the anthropologist photographs to illustrate a finding. The photograph is incidental to the research activity itself and confirms the analysis already accomplished by the written account, rather than as a central research methodology.

One ethnographic study that used photography as a vigorous method of observation and analysis is Gregory Bateson and Margaret Mead's book, *Balinese Character: A Photographic Analysis*. This text embodies an interweaving of both image and word. The photographs are neither illustrations nor descriptions in service of the written analysis— beyond serving as mere resources, the photographs are the *topics* of investigation. After studying and writing about Balinese culture for nearly 10 years, Bateson and Mead added photographs to their analysis. After a 2-year field experience, they made more than 25,000 photographs from which they selected 759 photographs for *Balinese Character*. Bateson and Mead's book offered a new model for integrating words and images. *Balinese Character* remains one of the most exemplary uses of photographic analysis in ethnography today. The photograph was treated as a topic of investigation, as a source of data worthy of analysis, and as a way of *doing* anthropology.

Sociological Applications of Photography

Visual sociology and photography have had a special relationship for quite some time. Like anthropology, visual sociology's beginnings reach back to the 19th century. Between 1896 and 1916, 31 articles using photographs were published in the *American Journal of Sociology*, the then-premier journal of the discipline. These articles explored a range of aspects of U.S. life, such as playgrounds, schools, prisons, housing, and work, from a social problems lens. However, the absence of photographs in the journal after 1916 may be the result of its editors' desire to advance sociology as a science. Today major sociology journals in both Europe and the United States seldom publish articles with photographs. Like anthropology, sociology appears to be a discipline of words, where the serious analysis is *verbally* rather than *visually* communicated, and where the visual data (if there are any) tend to be tables, graphs, and histograms. Sociologists hoping to publish papers with photographic materials have to turn to specialist journals such as *The International Journal of Visual Sociology*.

Being relegated to the fringes of sociology, most visual sociologists sought inspiration from documentary photographers who were examining issues that were being ignored by mainstream sociology. Even though documentary photographers did not employ sociological theories, they offered visual sociologists a more direct visual method for critical inquiry and analysis. Documentary photographers were deeply involved with their subjects, and many sociologists believed it could inform and improve sociological fieldwork greatly.

Presently, as the objectivity of science itself is being questioned by postmodern theories, as is sociology's status as a science, so too are photographs being regarded as problematical and tentative statements rather than reflections of truth. Similarly, ethnography is being seen more and more as partial truth rather than as a complete document. Any text that represents a culture, either verbally or visually, is also considered partial or incomplete, because culture itself is not precisely bounded and continually evolves.

Postmodern ethnography challenges the idea of analysis, moving away from abstraction to the lived world, to the experiences of the ethnographer and the subject. Thus, the type of narrative encouraged by this new ethnography is seated in the point of view, voice, and experience of the author. Sociology modeled its verbal text in the shape of the scientific report with the use of the third person and a devotion to objectivity. Postmodern ethnographies instead suggest alternatives to traditional research models: the first person, and the acknowledgment of the subjectivity of all presentations and re-presentations.

Postmodern forms of ethnography challenge the traditional interaction between subject and researcher, arguing that the resulting text is cooperatively constructed. Redefining the relationship between the researcher and the subject, proponents of the new ethnography promote the collaborative nature of this relationship, the two-way flow of information and meaning from researcher to subject and back again. Photography's constructed, subjective, and mutually constitutive nature lends itself as a methodology to this new ethnography. In turn, new forms of ethnography pose the question of what constitutes data in visual sociology: Is photography a method of collecting data, are photographs the data themselves, or is photography the process of analyzing, interpreting, and making meaning of the data? The new research in both anthropology and sociology attests to the photograph's dynamic ability to do all three of these.

Because sociologists and anthropologists have been reconsidering ways of using the still photograph for quite some time now, their efforts can therefore give us clues as to how the photograph can be redefined. Postmodern sociology and anthropology recognize both the still photograph and the verbal text as partial truths rather than complete documents in the constitution of ethnographic research. What remains of photographic truth in the digital age? What has always been there since photography's invention: a partial truth.

Aphrodite Désirée Navab

See also Mediation; Technology

Further Readings

Ball, M. S., & Smith, G. W. H. (1992). Analyzing visual data. *Qualitative Research Methods Series #24*. London: Sage.

Barrett, T. (1996). *Criticizing photographs: An introduction to understanding images* (2nd ed.). Mountain View, CA: Mayfield.

Bateson, G., & Mead, M. (1942). *Balinese character: A photographic analysis*. New York: New York Academy of Sciences.

Clarke, G. (1997). *The photograph: A visual and cultural history*. Oxford, UK: Oxford University Press.

Edwards, E. (Ed.). (1992). *Anthropology and photography 1860–1920*. New Haven, CT: Yale University Press.

Harper, D. (1998). An argument for visual sociology. In J. Prosser (Ed.), *Image-based research* (pp. 24–41). London: Falmer Press.

Navab, A. D. (2001). Re-picturing photography: A language in the making. *Journal of Aesthetic Education, 35*(1), 69–84.

Ritchin, F. (1990). Photojournalism in the age of computers. In C. Squires (Ed.), *The critical image* (pp. 28–37). Seattle, WA: Bay Press.

Snyder, J., & Walsh, N. A. (1975). Photography, vision, and representation. *Critical Inquiry, 2*(1), 148–169.

Trachtenberg, A. (Ed.). (1980). *Classic essays on photography*. New Haven, CT: Leete's Island Books.

PIDGIN/CREOLE

Pidgins and *creoles* are languages. When speakers of different language bases encounter one another, and multilingualism does not predominate, a language woven of intersecting systems develops to accommodate communication. A pidgin has no native speakers—for all users, the pidgin is a second language. When pidgin is no longer spoken as a second language, but as a first language, it becomes a creole language. For example, a pidgin becomes creolized or nativized when the children of a society begin learning the pidgin as a first language. The different needs of native users, versus those of second language users, catalyze nativization. During this process, grammar and vocabulary expand to fill what gaps may exist in the pidgin.

Pidgins and creoles range continuums with one or more *basilects,* first languages, and an *acrolect,* or target language, at the poles. The features of the basilect are frequently less evident and often dismissed as errors. The *mesolect,* or mid-range of the creole or pidgin, sound much different when approaching the acrolect and basilect poles. Thus, a creole may be mistaken for a dialect of the contributing languages. The creole may grow to resemble one of its input languages so much that it is decreolized and relabeled a dialect. Without careful linguistic analysis, creoles and pidgins can be difficult to identify.

The word *creole* also refers to people. The demographic makeup of creole people differs dramatically across the globe. The word has, historically, referred to Europeans born in the Caribbean, mixed-race people of various ethnic makeups across the African and Latin diaspora, indigenous natives, and imported African slaves.

Little ubiquity exists among creoles, pidgins, and extant or honorary creole societies. Nonetheless, the identities of pidgins and creoles and the culture of their language communities and other creole societies deepen two or more coexisting cultures by uniting them.

Examples

Increasingly, creoles and pidgins are recorded and studied. e-mail, text languages, and blogs have opened access to written representations of informal discourse, allowing greater exposure to creoles and pidgins. Features such as spelling, pronunciation, meaning, implication, mood, level, pitch, tone, and frequency of use are considered. Studying a creole or pidgin can uncover clues about geographic expansion.

Hindi and Urdu provide a family of deeply interrelated creoles. At the formal registers, these languages look different, but the creoles merge to form mutually intelligible mesolect mid-ranges. A speaker of one may be functional in many without learning the other creoles. Documented Australian Aboriginal creoles also share mutually intelligible mid-ranges.

The creoles and pidgins of the slave trade have been deeply researched. Including Kiswahili, other existing African trade pidgins, Caribbean creoles, creoles of the American South and South Sea Islands, these creoles and pidgins have long provided a microcosm for viewing language change in pidgins and creoles. African American English, once a distinct creole, decreolized. In form and function, it is now a dialect of Standard American English.

Hawai'i Creole provides significant studies. This language formed the basis for what seminal creolist Derek Bickerton catalogued as the features of creoles. Recent theorists prove, using Hawai'i Creole English, that creoles are far more complicated than Bickerton hypothesized. Cantonese, Portuguese, Japanese, and Filipino pidgin basilects intersected over many generations to form Hawai'i Creole English. The result is an expressive and colorful language. Bickerton offers some examples: "So da guy bin laik daunpeimen bikas i dono mi," or, "so the guy ant want down payment because he don't know me." In Standard American English: "So, the guy wanted a down payment because he didn't know me." In another example from Bickerton: "Dis gai hia sed daet hi gon get mai vainil" or "This guy here said that he was going to get my vinyl."

Nativization/Creolization

Full exposure to another language has successfully produced fluent speakers of foreign tongues, and children have even greater potential for language acquisition than adults do. Languages resist pressure from "corruption" quite well. Languages, both formally and informally, protect themselves. Language adaptations, multilingualism, bureaucracies, canonical and popular literatures, language academies, schools, and social pressures all contribute to the preservation of languages. The ability to communicate with others satisfies many profound human needs, so it corresponds that a speaker has deep emotional and psychological associations with his or her native tongue. The speaker will take great pride in his or her language and guard it, fiercely. The vocabulary contains his or her history, and the grammar has ordered his or her thoughts. Speakers are much more likely to integrate or resist a foreign language than to abandon a native one.

Given the natural resistance of languages to erosion, the historical circumstances that produce a vastly shared or long-enduring pidgin or creole must be remarkable. Natural languages generate independent of, or with minimal interference from, other languages. In the case of a pidgin, one language has been dramatically reduced and simplified. At least one other has lost viability for communication. Both collapse under opposing pressures and merge. Pidgins and creoles are languages, but the distinctions between these and natural languages reveal profound truths about humanity.

Pidgins do not begin because equally yoked linguists negotiate a common parlance. Intense sociohistorical pressures compel a large number of people to acquire new speech. Often, though not always, colonialism generates the context from which pidgins and creoles derive. Although early research on pidgins and creoles examines a broad survey of mother tongues, including other pidgins and creoles, these correspond, frequently, to English, Portuguese, or French target languages. These tongues represent the parlance of power at the genesis of many pidgins.

A pidgin may be a scant jargon or a complicated language. Often, however, reduction and simplification characterize a pidgin in its nascent state. Second-language acquisition need not result in reduction, simplification, or the creation of a pidgin, but it might. The common historical genesis of colonialism for recorded pidgins and creoles spanning Asia, Africa, Australia, the Americas, and islands across the globe, underscores that the target language was often expressed in reduced and simplified forms—jargons, commands, curses, and slang. With only limited exposure to the foreign speech, using intrinsic logic and the patterns of their native language, speakers approximate the target tongue. A comprehendible pidgin emerges.

An emergent pidgin may not allow for full expression, but if sufficient for communication, the pidgin can become the dominant vernacular of a multilingual populous. The pidgin articulates the concepts, attitudes, objects, and actions of a culture of intersection. The words, accents, tones, pronunciations, and phrasings of that emergent tongue contribute to a culturally specific mélange of expression. One society's pidgin may be more advanced than is the creole of another. Nonetheless, if speakers of the pidgin—a second language, by definition—cannot employ the pidgin to express an idea, they might use their first languages.

Nativization distinguishes pidgins from creoles. A pidgin may not expand, or need to, during nativization; likewise, it is not prerequisite that a pidgin be standardized before nativizing. A population may be required to shift, parent and child, into a proto-pidgin before it has grammatical patterns, predictable pronunciations, or a fixed vocabulary. However, rearing a child with the pidgin as his or her first language obligates adults and youth to partner, creatively, to name the unnamed. Concepts that would have been expressed in the former mother tongue must be integrated into the pidgin or creole. An intricate and enduring pidgin may never creolize. A pidgin may creolize before it is standardized. The resultant creole is no more a language than the former pidgin; it is, however, unlike the pidgin, the native language of a generation.

Misunderstandings

Deepening understanding in the field of creolistics, the study of pidgins and creoles, corrects many false prejudices about creoles, pidgins, and their speakers. Only recently, during the late 1950s and early 1960s, have linguists conceded that pidgins and creoles are legitimate languages. Labeling a pidgin or creole becomes increasingly difficult as languages evolve.

Languages will borrow, must adapt, and do collide. They change to accommodate full expression and resist external language pressure. Common intuition and multilingual influences blur the distinctions between pidgins, creoles, and the input languages.

Speakers often do not know that their speech patterns constitute a creole language. According to their enduring social reality, they simply failed to acquire the acrolect. The influence of the basilect, often a marginalized language, will be mistaken for a series of idiosyncratic errors, rather than patterned language choices, and the speaker dismissed as undereducated or unintelligent.

Creole languages and pidgins may be haunted by their function as languages of submission, further hindering their acceptance. Language learners may be encouraged to adopt the mother tongue of oppressed ancestors, royal lineage, or powerful colonialists. Some may argue that the pidgin or creole vocabulary is too limited, or too few outsiders speak the native tongue. In response to scholarly, critical, and political attitudes, the typical language preservation systems, schools, bureaucrats, and writers, among others, correct, mask, deepen, or otherwise legitimize the pidgin or creole.

Pidgins and creoles face the vulnerability of decreolization. Language pressures may, ultimately, encourage speakers to gravitate toward or actively resist the acrolect. A creole may lose the distinctions that give it autonomy as a language.

Creole People Versus Creole Languages

Though creole people may or may not speak a creole language, many similarities exist. The term *creole*, when referring to people, indicates a racial identity, but the demographic referents differ starkly. The creole identity may shift along a continuum; a person may consider himself or herself less creole than others are. Creole people often bear the stigma of colonialist influences, and this history invokes mixed reactions inside and outside the community.

During the exploration of the Americas, the term *creole* referred to the offspring of Spanish citizens born in the New World. This broadened to encompass all Europeans born there. A noticeable population of biracial slaves emerged in the New World. To differentiate the mixed race slaves from others, the former were dubbed Black creoles. However, not all creole slaves descend from mixed race genealogies. Notably, in the L'Isle de France, as slavery yielded to indentured servitude, native African and locally indigenous slaves were lumped by the term *creole* to distinguish them from the indentured servants emigrating from India. For many, this definition predominates. Just as creole languages differ vastly, so creole people vary.

Few schools teach creole or pidgin languages. Rarely will societies accept them as standard grammars. As a result, creole language groups splinter into those who master the parlance of power and elevate socially, and those who cannot. The threat of decreolization looms. People of creole cultures must often fight for inclusion and acknowledgement or remain isolated and face extinction. If a creole society defines itself independent of its input cultures, members face charges of snobbery, minstrelsy, and separatism, among others.

Creole or pidgin speakers, creole and pidgin language communities, and creole societies represent the efflorescence of a unique identity. A widely adopted pidgin or creole may become an indispensable resource in nurturing the collective growth of multicultural communities.

Jewel Sophia Younge

See also Bilingualism; Biracial Identity; Code-Switching; Dialect; Language; Language Development; Language Loss; Language Variety in Literature

Further Readings

Bickerton, D. (1976). Pidgin and creole studies. *Annual Review of Anthropology, 5,* 169–193.

DeGraff, M. (2002). Relexification: A reevaluation. *Linguistic Anthropology, 44*(4), 321–414.

Deuber, D., & Hinrichs, L. (2007). Dynamics of orthographic standardization in Jamaican creole and Nigerian pidgin. *World Englishes, 26*(1), 22–47.

Diamond, J. (1991). Reinventions of human language. *Natural History, 100*(5), 22–28.

Heath, J. G. (1984). Language contact and language change. *Annual Review of Anthropology, 13,* 367–384.

Jourdan, C. (1991). Pidgins and creoles: The blurring of categories. *Annual Review of Anthropology, 20,* 187–209.

Mufwene, S. (2002). *The ecology of language evolution.* Cambridge, UK: Cambridge University Press.

Ravi, S. (2007). Re-thinking creole identities in 18th-century Isle de France. *Postcolonial Studies, 10*(3), 327–332.

Sebba, M. (1997). *Contact languages: Pidgins and Creoles.* London: Macmillan.

Siegel, J. (2007). Recent evidence against the language bioprogram hypothesis: The pivotal case of Hawai'i Creole. *Studies in Language, 31*(1), 51–88.

PLURALISM

Pluralism is a philosophical perspective that has been embraced by postmodernists, poststructuralists, and pragmatists. From these perspectives, it is acknowledged that there is no one privileged position but instead a plurality of positions or interpretations that exist. Postmodernists argue for a plurality of narratives, poststructuralists argue for polysemy, and pragmatists argue for plurality of language in everyday discourse. This philosophical perspective is a co-creation influenced by many different philosophers creating many pluralisms. The emergence of pluralism as a philosophical perspective can be traced back to English and U.S. philosophers at the end of the 19th century and the beginning of the 20th century who were reacting against the limiting philosophies of monism, or only one, and dualism, or only two. Pluralists oppose the abstract and general aspects of monism and oppose the limited duality of dualism. As a comparison, monism is a philosophy that is of the whole and pluralism is a philosophy that is of the parts. Although this comparison poses more questions of legitimacy to the existence of a real whole, pluralism is a philosophical perspective that opens to and invites investigation of new questions. Pluralism is relevant to our understanding of identity because a multiplicity of identities emerge within the context of pluralism. The interfacing of pluralism and identity account for cultural pluralism and other manifestations of identities that naturally emerge, exist, and compete in the world.

Pluralism and Context

Discourse on pluralism often falls under contextual couplets such as cultural pluralism, democratic pluralism, religious pluralism, moral pluralism, and other social, political, or feminist *frameworks.* Issues within these frameworks have sometimes been considered through binary opposites that identify the tensions inherent in living among and with other human beings. These oppositions include diversity and homogeneity, disunity and unity, and difference and similitude. Pluralism emphasizes the hallmarks of a postmodern structure that includes diversity, multiplicity, and difference.

Cultural pluralism emerged from different and opposing perspectives that privileged dominance, exploitation, and hegemony. Cultural pluralists embrace and respect difference—they do not intend acculturation or assimilation; rather, their aim is for pragmatic and moral engagement between groups of difference to be able to continue and coexist with respect and harmony.

Democratic pluralism, or pluralistic democracy, is a form in which there are descriptive and prescriptive models of pluralism; laissez-faire pluralism is a self-correcting system that provides for competing political agents and bargaining among various interest groups; corporate pluralism describes a system in which monopoly cannot emerge, but there is still a controlling power that is outside of any self-correcting system; and public pluralism is a prescriptive model of pluralism because it is reform oriented and invites and regulates interplay of competing interests in society. Religious or theological pluralism has been interpreted as polytheism, and moral pluralism refers to a plurality of ethical systems that engage interpretive interplay of right and wrong. A broader and cosmological way to think about pluralism includes the idea that it recognizes there is more than one principle at play in the universe.

Beyond the contextual aspects of pluralism, philosophers distinguish between substantival pluralism and attributive pluralism. Substantival pluralists offers a perspective that suggests the world contains numerous things that are incapable of being reduced or transformed into other conditions or to other things. Conversely, the multiplicity in attributive pluralism does not reside in the thing or substance as in the case of substantival pluralism but instead refers to the diversity of attributes and characteristic features that make up the things to be distinct and separate from another. In other words, attributive pluralists find the nature of the pluralism in its properties, but substantival pluralists find the nature of pluralism in the-thing-itself and not dependent upon the properties of the thing.

Implications

Implications of pluralism have been situated within the metaphors of vitality, justice, and understanding. Within these metaphors, truth becomes less important than the daily toil and struggle of human engagement. Inherent in the nature of pluralism is the idea that there is not one pluralism; rather, there are pluralisms, and the rejection of these pluralisms then more often results from a misunderstanding of the nature of the term. Therefore, a stance of pluralism suggests these five aspects. First, pluralism permits engagement in critical discourse and self-implicature. Second, meaning emerges out of pluralism from the engagement of critical inquiries. Third, because systems of pluralism are distinct, there is no complete or absolute knowledge. This framework propels a hermeneutic cycle rather than perpetuating an end. Fourth, engagement of more than one perspective can bring about appropriately sufficient results, and having only one perspective falls short of any adequate response. Fifth, some perspectives are deficient; therefore, multiple perspectives are necessary to provide opportunity for optimum engagement, consideration, and understanding.

Pluralists suggest that there are a variety of potential yet conflicting responses to any given question, and this idea is open to a plurality of visions and versions that do not privilege one over the other. Pluralism can invite skepticism because there may not be a rational basis to prefer one response to another. Therefore, this recognition of alternatives annihilates the maintainability of a given position. Nevertheless, pluralism has been embraced by scholars and philosophers as a descriptive and prescriptive philosophical perspective. Pluralism is derived from a disposition that sees the whole world in continuous fluctuation, divergence, variance, disorder, possibilities, and difference. A pluralistic perspective can be applied to a variety of contexts in which human beings engage other human beings under contentious, competing, and ethical conditions. An inescapable and inevitable conclusion about pluralism is that there is more than one.

Annette M. Holba

See also Difference/Différance; Diversity; Hermeneutics; Modernity and Postmodernity; Pragmatics

Further Readings

Antczak, F. J. (1995). *Rhetoric and pluralism: Legacies of Wayne Booth.* Columbus: The Ohio State University.

Kelso, W. A. (1978). *American democratic theory: Pluralism and its critics.* Westport, CT: Greenwood Press.

Rescher, N. (1993). *Pluralism.* New York: Oxford University Press.

Tumin, M. W., & Plotch, W. (1977). *Pluralism in a democratic society.* New York: Praeger.

Wahl, J. A. (1925). *The pluralist philosophies of England and America.* London: Open Court.

POLITICAL ECONOMY

Political economy refers to that body of economic thought whose rise between the 17th and mid-19th centuries coincided with the rise of capitalism and the modern nation-state and the rise of modern science; political economy was composed of "economy in general" and "the art of government." Economy in general was understood as the art of household management; political economy was understood as the same art applied to the *polis*, or political entity. Before the 17th century, economics was deemed a matter of ethics and politics and after the mid-19th century, a science.

This entry examines political economy and its relevance to identity by considering it in relation to the traditional (antique and medieval) ethical understanding that assumed embedded identity in contrast to the modern, scientific (ethically neutral) that assumes atomic individualism. Political economy encompasses aspects of the traditional (naturalistic, organic, holistic, qualitative, concrete) and the modern (materialistic, mechanistic, atomistic, quantitative, abstract).

Traditional Understanding

Aristotle considers the relation between human beings and the socioeconomic order to be natural and organic—socioeconomic order cannot exist without them; they cannot realize their nature without it. As the only animals with the potential for acquiring language, human beings are by nature "political" (because that potential can be actualized only within the polis as a language-using community) and "rational" (because the potential for reason can be actualized only through language). The polis exists for the sake of the good life facilitated by labor's division (providing more abundantly for the common good) and exchange (holding the polis together through mutual need). Wealth constitutes an adequate stock of products useful for the good life; it is the means sufficient to the end of realizing our rational nature in the exercise of moral and intellectual virtues within the polis—for achieving happiness.

Labor, its division, and exchange are natural. Labor is defined by its concrete end and its product by its end or use. A product's use-value is natural and given; its exchange-value is conventional and problematic because different products and the labors producing them are incommensurable. Defined as they are by different ends (and therefore different qualities), use-value and exchange-value share no natural factor that can be measured to calculate reciprocal proportions for equal exchange (e.g., supposing some common factor found twofold in shoes and fivefold in coats, five pairs of shoes would equal two coats). Exchange-value therefore varies, subject to persuasion.

In primitive exchange, products are bartered; in more advanced markets, money mediates. Over time, exchange of products mediated by money becomes instead exchange of money for more money mediated by products—begging the question, toward what end is a product produced, used (quality being paramount), or exchanged (profit being paramount to quality's detriment). Ultimately, mediating products are dropped and money is bartered for more money still. Thus, money, introduced as a conventional means to facilitate exchange, is itself transformed into an end. Products have natural ends and limits to their consumption and acquisition, as does wealth—that is, whatever constitutes enough for the good life. Money as a means has no end and hence no limit to its acquisition, making its pursuit endless, limitless, irrational, and unnatural.

Modern Understanding

Before the 17th century, argues R. H. Tawney, the socioeconomic order was envisioned as a highly articulated organism within which different members contributed in different ways to the material and spiritual well-being of the whole. Thereafter, socioeconomic order was envisioned as a joint stock company in which the liability of shareholders was limited; an individual entered a contract ensuring rights vested in him by nature but not obligating him to pursue anyone's interests but his own—the doctrine of liberal individualism advanced by Thomas Hobbes, among others.

Contract theories assume a method of explanation typical of modern science—resolution of a complex whole into parts and their recombination in such a way as to (supposedly) reconstitute the whole; thus, resolution of the complex whole of social life into individuals and their recombination by means of a contract. The explanation is mechanistic versus organic (disassembling and reassembling a machine vs. an organism being possible vs. impossible without loss of life) and atomistic versus holistic (the whole being a quantity—i.e., the sum of its parts vs. a quality—i.e., more than the sum of its parts). The explanation is congenial to the genius of modern science (the quantification of nature) and consistent with its tendency toward oversimplification (reduction of complex wholes to their simplest parts—e.g., reduction of natural entities to material ingredients).

The presocial being is by nature individual and nonsocial but liable to be aggressive in the case of perceived threats to life or livelihood. Because such a being is supposed to be linguistic and rational, she determines her best interests require entering a contract limiting her and all others' freedom to diminish the prospects for harm. Within the contract, however, her selfish nature remains unchanged; apparent selflessness is actually selfishness disguised. She proceeds in the market as she would in nature except when constrained by the contract.

According to Alasdair MacIntyre, as far back as Plato self-interest has not been considered a real motive, no such thing being the same in all. Self-interest is an abstraction typical of modern science. If a man is thirsty, he seeks water; if hungry, bread. Only abstractly does he seek pleasure–or more abstractly, self-interest. If he drinks or eats in disregard of others when water and bread are scarce, he acts selfishly; if he refrains in regard for them, he acts selflessly. Only in situations involving incompatible aims in which behavior is competitive or noncompetitive does self-interest or benevolence pertain. Such situations are not paradigmatic. Most relations are reciprocal—friendship is sought not out of self-interest but out of a mutual desire for friendship, and exchange out of mutual need.

The abstract end of self-interest gave way to the supposedly more concrete and measurable pursuit of "pleasure" in the 19th century as the utilitarianism characteristic of modern science and implicit in previous economic thought gives way to an explicit, hedonistic form; with the emergence of a more sophisticated consequentialism in the 20th century, pleasure gave way to the "good"— however it is understood. But so abstract an end requires an equally abstract, universalizable means because no other type could be specified for achieving good defined in whatever ways individuals choose. Money constitutes just such a means. But money increasingly becomes an end in itself given the indeterminate good it serves. All forms of utilitarianism judge an act by quantifying its utility as a means for maximizing a desired consequence. For such purposes, money again proves ideal— maximize money to maximize the consequence of whatever is understood to be good. The path open to thorough mathematization of its matter, economics in imitation of biometrics and quantum physics incorporates statistics and proclaims itself a science.

With means and ends so completely abstracted from life, the distinction between natural and conventional blurs. "Need" is subsumed in "demand," which is ever subject to persuasion. The "individual" becomes a bundle of desires whose "identity" is tied to the stream of "goods" he or she is persuaded to purchase, then discard for something new (disregarding use-values they retain). Thus capitalism's immensely productive machinery is maintained in perpetual motion.

Political Economy

Mercantilism was truly modern in some respects— the state between rival nations was viewed as analogous to the state of nature. Nations were to pursue their interests among rivals, establishing colonies as sources of precious metals plus raw materials to be exported as finished products in exchange for more precious metals—that is, money, the measure of wealth. Adam Smith argued that wealth should be gauged by material goods contributing to the standard of living and that free, rather than restricted, domestic and foreign trade was the best means to such wealth.

Smith was more accepting of physiocracy ("the rule of nature"). Francois Quesnay, a fellow free trader who also rejected money as a measure of wealth, argued wealth arose from production and circulated through the body politic. But he considered agriculture—being natural—the only productive enterprise, and manufacture, commerce, and service—being artificial—sterile shifters of wealth.

Smith believed the most significant feature of economic life was division of labor, the source of productivity and material wealth. Concentrating on one job or function enables workers to become more skillful and imagine improvements more easily. Benefits of labor's division can be seen in the household, but as the market extends to the village and beyond and opportunities for exchange increase, the degree of specialization and productivity increase as well.

Smith, however, warned about the adverse effects of dividing and subdividing labor. He feared that, confined to repetitive tasks involving few operations with no occasion to exert understanding, workers would grow "stupid and ignorant," the rot eventually spreading to moral capacities, both domestic and civil. More materially advanced, they would nonetheless suffer stunted personalities. In this regard, he anticipated the effects of atomized labor associated with interchangeable parts assembled on long production lines; confined to turning out smaller parts or exercising lesser functions divorced from completing larger wholes, workers grow bored and robotic.

When Smith turns to economic motivation, he appears trapped by the moral vocabulary of his time. He escapes somewhat when he rejects prudence (rational self-interest) or benevolence as the basis for social life, arguing instead for "imagination" (the ability to see ourselves in others' situations) and "sympathy" for their actions (the basis for judgment), out of which conscience ("the impartial spectator") develops. Smith, however, appears to offer no alternative to prudence or benevolence in economic life, stressing the former over the latter. But D. D. Raphael argues Smith must be understood in the context of labor's division and mutual dependence—that is, in terms of cooperation.

Given his vocabulary, however, the problem of reconciling competing acts proves pressing. Smith's recourse is the metaphor of "an invisible hand," a religious idiom chosen to convey the phenomenon's incredible character. Though a deist, Smith was predisposed to seeing beneficent order in the natural course of human affairs, says David Raphael, given his early enthusiasm for Stoicism, whose proponents professed belief in harmony (*sympatheia*) within the organism that is nature.

Smith's vocabulary may be modern, but his sympathies are clearly traditional, as are those of Karl Marx. Scott Meikle argues that Marx is basically Aristotelian, his critique of capitalism an extension of Aristotelian economics. Marx accepts the nature/convention distinction leading to incommensurability in exchange. The problem does not exist for Smith and David Ricardo, who blur the distinction and thus bridge the gap between use-value and exchange-value. Ricardo argues the only common factor in different products is labor, the basis for commensurability and the measure of value. Marx counters that for labor to constitute a common factor, natural differences in labors directed toward different ends would have to be homogenized by totally abstracting them from their concrete ends so that their different qualities could be rendered uniformly as quantities of time and money. Such labor for a wage becomes a commodity for exchange, bought for a little, its product sold for more—a medium for monetary gain.

Human beings realize themselves through their labor and its products. Divorced from their natural ends, our labor and our lives may become a means to the end of money, their qualities compromised by the quest for quantity. Then all capacities, says Meikle, become particular applications of a single general capacity—that of enterprise. Thus, we are lost or lose ourselves in the conventional, or the taken-for-granted, alienated from what is natural and valuable in the world.

Richard H. Thames

See also Social Economy

Further Readings

MacIntyre, A. (2007). *After virtue* (3rd ed.). Notre Dame, IN: University of Notre Dame Press.

Meikle, S. (1985). *Essentialism in the thought of Karl Marx.* La Salle, IL: Open Court.

Meikle, S. (1995). *Aristotle's economic thought.* Oxford, UK: Oxford University Press.

Raphael, D. D. (1985). *Adam Smith.* Oxford, UK: Oxford University Press.

Tawney, R. H. (1998). *Religion and the rise of capitalism.* London: Transaction.

Tuck, R. (1989). *Hobbes.* Oxford, UK: Oxford University Press.

POLITICAL IDENTITY

Political identity as a concept frames understanding of political affiliation within a spectrum of ideological categories (Democrats, Republicans, Leftists, Centrists, Pluralists, etc.) or movements (women's movement, civil rights movements, worker's rights movement, etc.). Although preliminary formulations as the modern concept appeared in theoretical work of the 19th and 20th centuries, the term became central to Western scholarship and activism in the tumultuous social-political-cultural transformation of the 1960s and 1970s. This entry offers a comprehensive understanding of the concept of political identity and how the term is used to describe individuals and citizens who identify with a particular (if evolving) understanding of political agency and participation. After offering a social constructivist perspective on identity, this entry explores some typical philosophical frameworks of political identity and offers examples of groups of individuals who struggle over the formulation of a common political identity as part of their consciousness-raising processes.

Breakdown of Solidarity

Because of the breakdown of solidarity amid increasing alienation and individualism, the rise of multiculturalism, and the emergence of concepts like identity politics, some argue that the concept political identity itself should be abandoned because of its uselessness in a postmodern era. *Political identity* is a distinct term that intersects with the concept of *identity politics,* a term that emerged into common usage in the early 1980s. Scholars argued that the conceptualization of identity is threatened by the politics of difference, which is the result of competing and intersecting understandings of political identity. Recent scholars have focused on how constructivism rather than neoliberalism would promote the use of rhetoric and identity labels that would signal to others what type of relationship or treatment certain groups desired for their sense of political identity.

Identity gives groups and individuals a conceptual location from which they can clarify a standpoint, purpose, and capacity for action. Erik Erikson is often the starting point for understanding the social-relational character of identity; he saw identity as both a persistent uniformity within oneself (self-sameness) and a persistent correspondence of some kind of essential character with others. Social identity, understood as a preexisting identity, is often the starting place for understandings of political identity; social and political identities are sometimes developed after an identity crisis, which signals that preexistence of social identity is perhaps tentatively conceived here. As the world of work became more public, the family became more private. Within the concept of political identity, one might bridge the two realms.

Transformational Nature

Political identity is by no means a static concept, even in its earliest inceptions; the transformational nature of political identity has to do with the predetermined understandings of sociological, psychological, and moral identity that we base political choices upon. Although this identity might feel stable, it is being formed, deliberated, and reformed continuously. This process is influenced by many factors, and our multiple roles in society make the process of identification difficult. The evolution of political identity as a concept is tied to the differentiation of public and private spheres. As Jürgen Habermas traces it, a bourgeois public sphere was formed in England, France, and Germany as a forum within which private people gathered to form a public. Identity was formed at the intersection of the institutions of the family, the private (economic and cultural) realm, and the public (the state). A collective political identity emerged through mutual reinforcement from private and public institutions. However, some scholars, especially those focusing on welfare and justice theories, argue that political identity and mobilization (toward social change) emerge from a sense of injustice formed by past political struggles.

Scholars in varying disciplines have weighed in on how to classify identity as a category useful for understanding of this intersection of the interests of self and others. Debate is located around whether social identity initiates politics or politics influence social identity. William Mackenzie stressed the emergence of the popular usage of political identity in academia in the mid-1960s and early 1970s when scholars focused on issues of decolonization, alienation within systems and institutions, and increasing individualism. Habermas, for example, acknowledges the historical and cultural conditions associated with structural differentiation of identity, including the political ramifications of identity affiliations. He explains that social identity is based on class structures and arises from a sense of publicness that forges a public opinion.

Identity and Consciousness

However, Karl Marx felt public opinion was false consciousness and situated political identity as consciousness-raising. Marx felt political identity emerged as an epistemological process based on conflict of goods and conflict of rights. Prominent debate over the origins of political identity began chiefly with Marx and the Marxists that followed him. Marxists feel identity is always a social, collective matter that cannot be conceived without a link to politics, whether understood as given or constructed. Western Marxists emphasized the politics of subjectivity to preserve hope in revolution because that helped individuals develop solidarity through their identification with a particular category of politics. Such scholars tended to think that through consciousness-raising, workers could become materially liberated following cultural liberation; however, the causal relationship and focus of unity within revolution has been disputed by the full spectrum of Marxist perspectives, including post-Marxists. Marx felt that to understand an individual point of view in terms of a political identity, individuals needed to view society as a whole; political identity allowed one to negotiate one's own views of the world with one's position within that world.

Marx notably identified the political identity categories of bourgeois and proletariat, arguing that the identity of the proletariat was unique epistemologically, politically, socially, and historically because the proletariat was a large and growing number of people carrying out functions that supported the structure of capitalism while providing an opportunity to gain material interests; consequently, members of the proletariat wielded increasing power in a democratic age, particularly if they identified with this common consciousness of proletariat political identity. Political identity is culturally situated and bound to everyday life; it is often the product of class politics and its creation and re-creation of material and cultural existence. As Stanley Aronowitz suggests, working-class identities are reproduced in everyday living that demonstrate not just a worldview but a lifeworld perspective of identity.

An individual's understanding of political identity is affected by his or her view of politics and whether we view politics as idealism or action. Marx's view of political identity formation emanated from the view that our political identity is tied to our political ideals and interests. For example, in this view, the working class would be better able to express socialism's ideals with a better understanding of their own material interests. Forming a self-conscious sense of identity helps individuals internalize that with which they relate

while letting go of that which should be externalized, representing a tension between subjectivity and objectivity.

Identity and Multiplicity

Political identity is subject to multilayered understandings and emergent divisions. The duality of identity that can occur as a result of class mobility can result in a personal, psychological struggle with duality that requires a need for balance to maintain some sense of stability. Social construction of identity is challenged and redefined by social movements as well, which challenge and re-create our understandings of identity in relation to economics, politics, culture, race, gender, and ethnicity. Just as identity markers shift as times change, the philosophical and practical underpinnings of political identity shift. As political identity is declared, this identity is tested through its relationship to existing identities formed from existing and previous economic, cultural, and political contexts.

For example, in South African apartheid, colonial rule established a correlation between race and class, and consequently, political identities emerged along a continuum of resistance to that subjugation. In that context, race constituted group identity, and racial segregation as part of official government policy classified racial groups as Caucasian, Asian, colored, and Black to justify capitalist exploitation and control of the minority by the majority. Further delineating the groups was the concept of ethnic group identity, which was used by government to segregate by language, tradition, territory, or politics. Ethnic identity changed as migration and community division occurred; yet ethnic identity is highly accessible but not the most reliable predictor of political identity. Differentiation of political identities was reinforced because it served the powers that be, in this case, the colonial state; individual identities were overtaken by group identities. Then, as Africans were educated in the Western world, African pride was elevated, but subjugation in Africa continued; nationalist movements resisted this subjugation, which resulted in elimination of race as a qualifier of power but left ethnicity as a determinant of privilege. Ethnic tensions have escalated because of competition for state resources. Thus, identity politics emerged from an initial concept of political identity in this specific case of how race, culture, and ethnicity were differentiated.

Another prominent case of the splintering of political identity through identity politics emerged within the U.S. feminist movement. In the general sense, feminists have sought sanctioned political identities within national and regional governance; women sought to be identified as citizens rather than as women, representing the transformation of women's political identity from one rooted in virtue and gender to one of national citizenship and natural rights. Yet deeper divisions about what constituted a woman's political identity arose, based on differing notions of Universalist ideals of equality and individualism and more nationalistic understanding of the political virtues affiliated with being feminine and masculine.

Deeper divisions in women's political identity in the United States resulted when White and Black women were segregated during early slavery days. Class issues created a tension between Black men and women's voting rights and White women's voting rights. White male abolitionists supported the Negro male vote, as did many Black women; however, some educated White women considered their vote as necessary to balance the uneducated Black male vote. Feminist identity politics have emerged as a response to the perceived dominance of White women in the early women's suffrage movement. Rather than assuming we are in a post-feminist era, most third-wave feminism emphasizes the need to negotiate differences across multiple feminist standpoints (often categorized as American Indian, Arab American, Asian American, Black, Chicana, cultural, ecofeminist, electoral, liberal, international, Jewish, Latina, lesbian, Marxist, Puerto Rican, radical, socialist, working-class feminists, and womanists) in the pursuit of social change that benefits women's political identity. Although the politics of identity difference arose to broaden the self-conceptualization of feminism, they proved taxing to the movement's sense of unity; they slowed the pace and fragmented the focus in many ways, yet they also resisted essentialist understandings of political identity.

Elesha L. Ruminski

See also Agency; Group Identity; Identity Politics; Political Psychology; Psychology of Self and Identity; Womanism

Further Readings

Aronowitz, S. (1992). *The politics of identity: Class, culture, social movements.* New York: Routledge.

Dean, K. (Ed.). (1997). *Politics and the ends of identity.* Aldershot, UK: Ashgate.

Escobar, E. J. (1999). *Race, police, and the making of a political identity: Mexican Americans and the Los Angeles police department, 1900–1945.* Los Angeles: University of California Press.

Habermas, J. (1975). *Legitimation crisis.* Boston: Beacon Press.

Mackenzie, W. J. M. (1978). *Political identity.* New York: St. Martin's Press.

Meister, R. (1990). *Political identity: Thinking through Marx.* Cambridge, UK: Blackwell.

Zaeske, S. (2003). *Signatures of citizenship: Petitioning anti-slavery, and women's political identity.* Chapel Hill: University of North Carolina Press.

POLITICAL PSYCHOLOGY

Political psychology is the application of the tools of psychology to the realm of politics. Specifically, political psychology usually takes what is known in this behavioral discipline and attempts to explain the political behavior of various actors or events using scientific method. This is accomplished by establishing or manipulating a set of variables that facilitate the study of the actor or event. There is an International Society of Political Psychology, and a dominant journal specializing in the field: *Political Psychology.*

Political psychology as a distinct field is relatively young. Carolyn Funk and David Sears trace the first formal academic course offered with this subject to 1970. Study of the more general use of known human behaviors in political activity may be as old as any politics: from Shakespeare's skillful crowd control by Marc Antony in *Julius Caesar* written during the 16th century to Gustav Le Bon's *The Crowd* in 1889, where he analyzed the manipulation of the mass movement of General Boulanger in France from 1886 to 1889. During World War II, the U.S. government commissioned several independent studies of Adolph Hitler by established psychologists. Psychological warfare has become a standard of modern security studies. Attempts to influence politics, sometimes referred to as propaganda, has become an equal mainstay of mass movements and wartime enterprises. Indeed, Ho Chi Minh, in his outline for the strategic defeat of the United States in Vietnam, specifically counted on the psychological defeat of the nation's population through the use of political means inserted into the media. In domestic electoral politics, vast sums are amassed and spent on media to gauge, shape, and consolidate political identity. In the realm of political life, the behavior and motivations that are propelled by the identity of the participants have become a key engine "for consolidating political identity" or "for shaping domestic electoral politics."

Theoretical Perspectives

Psychology, as a social science, depends upon empirical as well as normative study to analyze its subject material. Psychologists have tried methodologies to use as tools in generating population sets, mining them for data and analyzing their findings. The experimental quality of psychology—which is to say its ability to postulate and test in quantitative samples—may not always translate well into the analysis of political behavior. Psychology does, however, offer some dazzling insights into decision making, voting choices, national security, and international relations, to name just a few of the applications. Real-time polling in elections may be the most didactic example of this approach. Just as there are powerful schools in psychology, there are also distinct perspectives on interpreting political behavior. David Sears, Leonie Huddy, and Robert Jervis describe such precise areas as being personality theories, behaviorist theories, developmental theory, incentive theories, social cognition, and intergroup relations, among others.

Not all descriptors in political psychology are testable, or even empirically demonstrated with reference to data sets. Yet other inferences abound: biological, gender, and environmental explanations for the development of peoples, the construction of their identity, and their behavior in political processes have devoted followings in contemporary writing. Harold and Margaret Sprout postulate ecological explanations for behavior, whereas Sir Halford Mackinder has written extensively on geopolitical explanations. Graham Allison's seminal study of decision making (*Essence of Decision*)

during the Cuban missile crisis is a wide-ranging use of normative models to explain behavior at the individual, bureaucratic, and organizational levels by analyzing the participation in the processes by individuals. Despite this accessible, normative strength, the discipline of political psychology still maintains substantial measurement tools to generate and evaluate data sets.

Political Behavior and Identity

Implicit in the notion of political activity is that a core personality exists that participates in the world around it. This personality must have values, and these form an identity. From this identity, the political actor interacts with the environment. The identity possesses opinions, attitudes, and emotions that may influence these activities. More importantly, all of these elements are an impetus to form associations—groups—that may reinforce membership with a new social identity in addition to individual identity. This group participation, or membership, can deepen personal identity and values as well as be influenced by what individual members bring to their group. Cognitive processes employed by the individual are important to isolate and study. They are the connectors with the wider environment and are the processes through which the identity that is forming receives input.

Needless to say, identity is an integral object in political motivation and is of keen interest to the political psychologist. Some dominant or charismatic individuals—leaders—can accelerate all of these tendencies, as well as mobilize them for specific purposes. At the core, however, such powerful notions as nationalism, religious sentiment, ethnic or cultural beliefs, and partisan politics are centrally influential in the identity of their members. The political psychologist, therefore, is strongly motivated to understand the formation of any relevant identity because it is a vital rung in the wider understanding of political behavior. Practical demonstrations of this analytic process, for example, would facilitate insight into mass movements, political party affiliation, voting choices and decision making, and ethno-religious identity.

Contemporary Challenges

The past century was replete with powerful demonstrations of mass political movements and international events that shook not just the international system, but humanity's conception of its own moral self. Other trends were heady with dreams of a better, perfectible world. Totalitarian movements such as fascism and communism, nascent nationalism and decolonization, the flowering of a prosperous and numerous middle class, creation of unprecedented international cooperative organizations, and the terrible incidence of genocide all have given political psychologists much to reflect upon. What cognitive processes permitted individuals to form identities that could conceive of such ambitious global projects, or be capable of doing such pernicious deeds? The game theory speculation associated with nuclear competition and the revolution of terrorism in recent years have shown that there are still plenty of challenges to understand regarding individual identification and value formation.

John Sawicki

See also Political Identity; Social Constructivist Approach to Political Identity; Terrorism

Further Readings

Allison, G., & Philip, Z. (1999). *Essence of decision explaining the Cuban missile crisis.* New York: Longman.

Cottam, M., Dietz-Uhler, B., Mastors, E., & Preston, T. (2004). *Introduction to political psychology.* Mahwah, NJ: Lawrence Erlbaum.

Houghton, D. (2008). *Political psychology: Situations, individuals, and cases.* New York: Routledge.

Sears, D., Huddy, L., & Jervis, R. (2003). *Oxford handbook of political psychology.* New York: Oxford University Press.

POSTCOLONIALISM

See Modernity and Postmodernity

POSTLIBERALISM

Postliberalism is an orientation in modern Christian theology characterized by its preoccupation with developing an alternative theological framework from dominant liberal and conservative frameworks and practices. Founded by theologians at the Yale Divinity School in the late 1970s and early 1980s, postliberal theology, as it became known, holds significant connections and distinctions with neoorthodox ways of approaching the relation between theology and culture. Postliberal theology is distinctive in the following ways: (a) truth is determined analogically, or by analogy to the narrative of scripture; (b) doctrine is determined by the primacy of God, or the language of the church being primarily accountable to God; and (c) religious practices are determined by Christocentrism, or the focus on the personhood and teachings of Christ. These distinctions lay the foundation for postliberalism's beliefs about the formation and maintenance of religious and cultural identity.

Origins

A consistent area of inquiry for contemporary theologians has been the realm between conservative and liberal theology. The idea of finding a third theological option between these two frameworks has attracted numerous, and quite different, neoorthodox Christian movements: from the mediating theology of 19th-century Germany supported by such scholars as Isaak Dorner and Friedrich Schmid to Karl Barth's theology of the word and Reinhold Niebuhr's social ethics in the 1940s and 1950s. Most neoorthodox theologies emphasized a similar language, however: the biblical language of sin, the realization of transcendence, and "the primacy of the Word" of God. The neoorthodox movements in modern theology gained recognition and support until the early 1960s when, after many of the leading thinkers such as Barth and Niebuhr passed away, liberal theology emerged in Latin America and began to grow.

The neoorthodox movement did not find its footing again until the mid-1970s and early 1980s. This time, it emerged within the postliberal writings of the Yale Divinity School. The movement's first significant work, Hans Frei's *The Eclipse of Biblical Narrative,* was published in 1974. Providing some of the founding arguments of the postliberal school, Frei's work supported an anti-Enlightenment view to biblical interpretation. Frei critiqued the Enlightenment idea that truth could be found within a universal foundation of knowledge, such as rationality, or that the individual constituted the center of authority and experience. Instead, Frei's theology supported biblical truth as grounded within the living communal experience of scriptural narrative. Instead of liberal or conservative theologies that further emphasized the loss of the biblical narrative as formative to religious life, Frei supported a theological framework that emphasized how Christians make sense of the world around them by relating to and participating within scriptural stories.

George Lindbeck's *The Nature of Doctrine*, published in 1984, further differentiated the mode of thinking between postliberalism and both conservative and liberal frameworks. Lindbeck articulated the dichotomy that dominated modern theology: conservatism and liberalism. Conservative theology relies on the *cognitive-propositional* understanding of the Bible and the world. Conservative theologians, following analytic philosophical frameworks, claim that statements of doctrine within the Bible literally refer to the experience of the world. Consequently, biblical language, and hence claims to reality, should be held as universally valid. Conversely, liberal theologians rely on a more *expressive-experiential* understanding of the Christian faith. Liberal theologians ground their claims to reality on the immediate experience of religious feelings. From this experience, an individual believer is connected to a universal experience of moral value and truth that can be abstracted from the text of the Bible.

By dichotomizing cognitive-propositional conservatism and expressive-experiential liberalism, Lindbeck's work offers postliberalism as a third alternative situated in between these extremes: the *cultural-linguistic* alternative. Postliberal theology supports the claim that religious identities are historically situated and culturally grounded. The scriptural narrative is the source of meaning for the postliberal Christian, shaping how the individual believer understands biblical truth and participates within the collective body of Christ. As such, doctrines should not be understood as universalistic propositions of the nature of reality or as interpretations of an abstracted universal religious experience. Instead, Lindbeck claimed that Christian doctrines are akin to the rules of grammar—a

linguistic experience of describing and making sense of the world that is understood and shared within a particular community. Postliberal theology, then, is often referred to as *narrative theology* because of this cultural and linguistic way of understanding the individual's relation to the world.

Narrative Theology and Identity

The emphasis on narrative in postliberal theology has significant implications for the formation and maintenance of religious and cultural identity. Postliberal theology presupposes that we are born into particular languages with particular ways of looking at the world. As such, our identities are communally and historically shaped. Postliberalism emphasizes the importance of tradition in the shaping and the experiencing of thought, belief, and communally held values.

Both the Christian historical and empirical communities are of vital importance to the shaping of individual and collective identity. The postliberal Christian identifies with a faith that is both lived and learned—faith emerges not solely from the historical reality of biblical truths nor from the abstracted experience of the individual, but instead from the history of a narrative started long before the individual and that continues to offer theoretical and pragmatic import. The identity of the Christian community is derivative of an engagement of the scriptural narrative with the language that helps a given community to make sense of the world.

As such, postliberal theologians believe that the element of narrative is central to the unity of scripture. Biblical narrative needs to remain coherent within the text itself, and it needs to lend cohesiveness with the experience of the reader with the world. This is what postliberal theologians refer to when they claim that truth is to be determined by analogy. A narrative perspective of the Bible allows significant elements of similarity and dissimilarity between the Word and its object, or the text of the Bible and the referent within the world of experience. Simply put, faith in biblical truth is inseparably linked to the communal and individual experience of the world.

Postliberal theology points out that we live within a living community of memory and faith.

Christian identities are shaped by the ability to live the narrative of Christ consistently, ever attentive to the ebb and flow of temporal linguistic existence.

Celeste Grayson Seymour

See also Narratives; Religious Identity

Further Readings

DeHart, P. (2006). *The trial of the witnesses: The rise and fall of postliberal theology.* London: Blackwell.

Dorrien, G. (2001, July 4–11). The origins of postliberalism. *Christian Century*, pp. 16–21.

Hauerwas, S., & Jones, L. G. (1989). *Why narrative? Readings in narrative theology.* Grand Rapids, MI: Eerdmans.

Lindbeck, G. (1984). *The nature of doctrine: Religion and theology in a postliberal age.* Philadelphia: Westminster Press.

POSTSTRUCTURALISM

See Modernity and Postmodernity

PRAGMATICS

The discipline of linguistics is classically divided according to three distinct fields of inquiry. First, there is *syntax:* the study of grammar, or the rules of proper sentence construction. Second, there is *semantics:* the study of meaning, or conceptual content. Third, there is *pragmatics:* the study of language use, or the relationship between speakers and words in social contexts. Both syntax and semantics seek to explicate their respective subject matter without reference to social, cultural, and historical circumstances. Thus, a syntactic or semantic analysis seeks in principle to study the formal or universal features of language. Pragmatics is different in that it pays attention to speakers and the way they use words in socially particular settings to achieve different goals, the kinds of goals that require communicating with others. It has been said that pragmatics is the study of those questions that semantics is ill equipped to answer. For example, how is it possible that a speaker can say one thing, but mean something else, as in the case of sarcasm or a polite hint? Pragmatics examines the social and cultural conventions that permit these and other types of speech phenomena. Among the principal topics of pragmatic inquiry are deixis, presupposition, conversational implicature, and speech acts. Pragmatic inquiry considers the role of context and language use in identity construction and maintenance. Identity of self and other is shaped by speech phenomena as contextualized by social, cultural, and historical forces.

Deixis

The meanings of certain utterances depend on their contexts of use. The deictic elements of an utterance vary with such contexts. Deictic elements are primarily of three types: person, spatial, and temporal. *Person deixis* is itself divided into three subtypes: first person (e.g., "I"), second person (e.g., "you"), and third person (e.g., "she"). Depending on which language one speaks, personal pronouns can be either singular or plural and the use of either depends partly on cultural practice. Thus, in modern English, it is not customary to employ the first person plural pronoun *we* when referring to oneself. There is also no second person plural pronoun in formal English. ("You people" would be an exception in informal English.) On the other hand, in French, as in many other languages, it is customary to employ the second person plural pronoun *vous* when speaking to a person of a higher social status or rank. The use of personal pronouns can thus communicate information not otherwise apparent in the literal form of an utterance.

Person deixis can also be used to send an indirect, but firm, message. A parent, for example, might employ a third-person pronoun when speaking about a child present in the room, as in (1):

(1) Billy can't play until he finishes his homework.

Spatial deixis employs terms such as *this, that, here,* and *there* to indicate physical as well as psychological location and distance. Utterances employing spatial deictic terms might communicate directionality as well as location, as in (2):

(2) Move this box over there.

Alternatively, an utterance might employ the term *there* to identify an abstract entity, as in (3):

(3) Now, there's a great plan.

The term *where*, ordinarily used in reference to a physical location, might also be used to indicate a psychological state of mind, as in (4):

(4) Where are you right now? You seem like you're on another planet.

Spatial deixis communicates information, often quite vital to the meaning of an utterance, which cannot always be extracted by semantic analysis alone.

Temporal deixis employs terms such as *now, then, this,* and *next* to indicate events in the past, present, or future. Certain temporal deictic terms, such as *past*, might refer to a previous unit of time, as in (5).

(5) This past week was exciting.

Temporal deictic terms vary from language to language and idiom to idiom. Phrases such as *in the old days, once upon a time,* and *at some point* are culturally specific and do not have literal parallels in every language. Moreover, certain temporal deictic terms, such as *could* or *would*, are liable to be misinterpreted unless a historical context is made explicit, as in (6a) and (6b).

(6a) I could run a five-minute mile.

(6b) I would watch all of his movies.

Only in the light of a historical context can (6a) and (6b) be interpreted as referring to past conduct.

Presupposition

The meaning of certain utterances hinges on a background of facts and assumptions known by the speaker and the audience. Implicit appeal to this background is known as presupposition. It is possible to extract, or make explicit, a presupposition from an utterance. For example, (1b) may be extracted from (1a):

(1a) Peter changed the tires on his car.

(1b) Peter has a car.

Presuppositions can be of several different types. *Existential presuppositions* assume that a person or thing exists by virtue of a statement made about a person or thing. A statement about the hairstyle of the king of France, for example, presupposes that the king of France exists. *Lexical presuppositions* imply a change in a state of affairs, such that two propositional statements can be used interchangeably. Thus, (2a) and (2b) can be used interchangeably:

(2a) Alice is now awake.

(2b) Alice was sleeping.

Structural presuppositions are assumed by virtue of the form of certain types of sentences. The prime example of such types of sentence is that of a question. A question in the form of (3a) presupposes the content of (3b):

(3a) Why did Peter leave the house?

(3b) Peter left the house.

Nonfactive presuppositions assume that some state of affairs is not the case. Nonfactive presuppositions typically feature terms that indicate a hypothetical scenario. Thus, from (4a), one can infer (4b):

(4a) Kate wishes she didn't have any homework.

(4b) Kate has homework.

Taken together, these presuppositions—existential, lexical, structural, and nonfactive—are classified as *potential presuppositions*, an umbrella category referring to presuppositions that remain inoperative unless activated by conversation.

Cooperation and Conversational Implicature

All conversations require a basic degree of trust between speakers. Without this basic degree of trust, no human community would be able to survive. Often, even between enemies, some degree of trust is evident in conversation. In pragmatics, such trust is referred to as *cooperation*. When speakers accept, wittingly or unwittingly, the presuppositions embedded in each other's utterances, they may be said to be cooperating with one another. For example, if one stranger asks another for the time and is told what time it is, each can be said to assume that the other is familiar with the concept of time. Likewise, consider an exchange between two enemies, in which one utters (1) and the other utters (2).

(1) Where is the money?

(2) I will never tell you where the money is.

Even though the two are enemies, each presupposes that the other is familiar with the concept of money. If such basic and minimal cooperation is required for an intelligible exchange between enemies, it is all the more important in the exchange between friends, family members, and colleagues. The philosopher H. Paul Grice has proposed what he calls the *cooperative principle,* a norm implicit in ordinary conversations: Make your conversational contribution such as is required, at the stage at which it occurs, by the accepted purpose or direction of the talk exchange in which you are engaged. Grice has also proposed a set of maxims grouped under four categories:

1. Quantity
   a. Make your contribution as informative as is required (for the current purposes of the exchange).
   b. Do not make your contribution more informative than is required.
2. Quality
   a. Do not say what you believe to be false.
   b. Do not say that for which you lack adequate evidence.
3. Relevance
   a. Be relevant

4. Manner
   a. Avoid obscurity of expression.
   b. Avoid ambiguity.
   c. Be brief (avoid unnecessary prolixity).
   d. Be orderly.

Related to cooperation is Grice's concept of *conversational implicature.* Often, we mean more than what we say. This additional meaning can be both implicit and intended. This is the case with sarcasm. When one, for example, utters (1), he or she might really mean (2):

(1) I just love hearing my neighbor talk about his endless problems.

(2) I don't like hearing my neighbor talk about his endless problems.

Although the concept of implicature at first seems rather simple and straightforward, it has nonetheless generated considerable controversy and debate among specialists in pragmatics.

Speech Acts

Although utterances convey information, they can also constitute the performance of an act, the type of act that would not be possible if not for the exchange of words between speakers. The concept of a speech act was first formulated by the philosopher J. L. Austin and later further developed and expanded by the philosopher John Searle. Speech-act theory brings to light a wide range of phenomena associated with human speech.

Consider the example of a court trial, during which a lawyer utters the words, "Objection, your Honor." The lawyer would have invoked a standard type of utterance appropriate for those occupying a certain role within a certain institutional setting. The lawyer's utterance would carry weight and force by virtue of his or her institutional status. If, conversely, a member of the audience had similarly uttered, "Objection, your Honor," the literal meaning would be the same, but the utterance would lack force by virtue of the audience member's lack of the requisite institutional status. This type of force is referred to in speech-act theory as *illocutionary force.* Although two utterances might consist of the same words, the pragmatic significance of each depends on the social and institutional context. If, after hearing the lawyer's objection, the judge were to respond by uttering the words, "Objection sustained," the lawyer can be said to have achieved his or her desired result. This would be known as the *perlocutionary effect*. Certain speech acts are aimed at bringing about such effects, though they are not always successful.

Speech acts are not limited to formal institutional settings. They may be performed in casual conversational settings as well. For example, if, in response to a compliment, one were to say, "Why, thank you," one would have performed a speech act. It is common in such exchanges for the complimenting party to acknowledge this expression of gratitude with a supplementary utterance like, "You're welcome." Conversations often feature *performative utterances* such as these, in which there is a conventional order by which such utterances are performed. It would be out of place, for example, to say, "You're welcome," before someone says, "Thank you." When speech acts follow a standard social or cultural conventional order, they are *felicitous*. Those that do not are *infelicitous*.

Speech-act theory has attracted a great deal of attention in the study of law, ethics, literary theory, and cultural studies. In a sense, it represents the cutting edge in the study of pragmatics. Because of its explanatory power and broad appeal, speech-act theory has been adopted by a wide range of thinkers and put to various uses, some more prominent than others. Perhaps the most famous use of speech-act theory has been the *universal pragmatics* of the German philosopher and social theorist Jürgen Habermas. According to Habermas, universal norms embedded within the use of language provide a communicative foundation for a democratic conception of justice.

A similar, albeit far more complex, argument has been made by the U.S. philosopher Robert Brandom. According to Brandom, language use must be understood as an inferential practice. That is, to engage in conversation is to be suitably caught up in the language game of giving and asking for reasons. Brandom's argument has received widespread attention because of his persuasive contention that semantics ought to be collapsed

into pragmatics, a move that has been termed the *use-theory of meaning*.

Jason Hannan

See also Communication Competence; Discourse; Performativity of Gender; Rhetoric; Sapir-Whorf Hypothesis; Semantics; Semiotics

Further Readings

Austin, J. L. (1976). *How to do things with words* (2nd ed., J. O. Urmson & M. Sbisà, Eds.). Oxford, UK: Oxford University Press.

Brandom, R. (1994). *Making it explicit: Reasoning, representing, and discursive commitment.* Cambridge, MA: Harvard University Press.

Grice, H. P. (1975). Logic and conversation. In P. Cole & J. Morgan (Eds.), *Syntax and semantics: Vol. 3. Speech acts.* New York: Academic Press.

Habermas, J. (2001). *On the pragmatics of social interaction: Preliminary studies in the theory of communicative action* (B. Fultner, Trans.). Cambridge: MIT Press.

Levinson, S. C. (1993). *Pragmatics.* Cambridge, UK: Cambridge University Press.

May, J. (1993). *Pragmatics: An introduction.* Malden, MA: Blackwell.

Searle, J. (1969). *Speech acts: An essay in the philosophy of language.* Cambridge, UK: Cambridge University Press.

Yule, G. (1996). *Pragmatics.* Oxford, UK: Oxford University Press.

PROFANITY AND SLANG

Profanity and slang are two derivatives from established lexicons that occur in most known languages. They both originate from subcultures and are often viewed as assertions of the rebellious. *Profanity* includes spoken indecencies and gestures that are considered rude, vulgar, insulting, abusive, and offensive; it includes largely irreverent speech or action that causes the majority of a society's members to feel disturbed. *Slang* refers to words and terms from a subculture of society that assists in the evolution of language by adding to its vocabulary. This lexical adaptation occurs through established words being short-ened, known terms being assigned nontradi-tional definitions, and the incorporation of foreign words. Profanity and slang are both derivatives from existing lexicons and are common in most spoken languages. Profanity and slang reflect iden-tity and the linguistic changes of a society. Language is ever changing through the metamorphosis of its lexicons.

Western profanity has its historical origins in statements made against the church. These state-ments were defined as profane; such declarations were interpreted as being opposed to God, thereby blasphemy. The term *profanity* grew to include words not in favor of the church and God, as well as any avowals that could not be said in church. Religious oaths and swearing were also considered profanity; one was not to swear or promise in the name of God.

This blasphemous swearing of oaths was chiefly used by the lower class of English society and was eventually incorporated into use for lesser situa-tions and personal insults. As the language adapted to fit the lives of the users, blasphemous statements became individual damnations and expletives for emotional states. What was once thought of as the strong language of the rebellious heretic is now overlooked as cursing of the provoked. For exam-ple, the swear phrase *God damn* originally was calling for God's damnation on the speaker's foe. Over time, the phrase became a simple expression of an altered state, "God damn it, the Bears lost." The modern-day usage of profanity occurs more during social interactions between people, than during oaths between God and one person.

Modern profanity appears in agitating phrases and physical motions. These unsettling verbaliza-tions and gestures are often racist, scatological (related to human waste functions), sexist, deroga-tory, and sexual in nature. Profanity in its current form is universally human in nature. The profane renaming of copulation as well as the anatomy employed in the sexual act is worldwide, although individual cultures have different profane names for the act and genitalia.

Profane physical gestures as well as verbal pro-fanity are part of most human languages. One profane gesture appears to cross most social bor-ders: the flipping of the bird. The prone, extended middle finger incites unrest globally. The "finger"

has made its appearance throughout history; the Greeks used it for a phallic symbol in theater. The Romans incorporated it for the same purpose; however, the use spread from the theatre to an emperor who forced citizens to kiss him on his middle finger rather than the back of his hand. In the mid-1600s, the finger was included in sign lan-guage as a severe insult.

Slang's recorded origin began in the lowest social economic caste in England; it was a tabooed deriva-tive from the established British vocabulary. What made and makes slang taboo or considered rebel-lious is the change it brings to established standards of language. The ruling class of England did not want its spoken language altered in any form. To this point, early recorded slang was titled the English Criminal Cant. Many of the subcultures that develop slang were or are on the outside of society's mainstream. For example, U.S. slang sprouts from jazz musicians, rap artists, the free love era of the 1960s, drug culture, gangs, and so forth. Slang is often produced by groups outside of the mainstream of society that are struggling for a voice.

Subcultures often use known terms and assign nontraditional definitions to them. Members of the free love era changed the meaning of the word *dig*. Its customary meaning was to turn up soil. The free love era included understanding as part of its definition; *to dig* meant to understand. Here, an established word took on new significance because of a subculture's usage.

Slang marks membership to a particular subcul-ture. The altered usage and coinage of phrases allow a group to be unique, which is important to subculture identity. The term *homey* was largely used by gang members as a reference to a person living in the same area. The term's formal defini-tion is a characteristic of home. The term *homey* being used only by those of that subculture identi-fied the user as a member. This sharing of an altered language helps bond a subculture.

The spoken slang of a subculture differs greatly from jargon. Jargon consists of terms used in a par-ticular trade such as plumbers or electricians. Slang is also pointedly different from dialect that is based on social, geographical, and regional varieties in language, which include colloquialisms, and it is notably different than slogans that can be linked to marketing campaigns and jingles. In current media, modern slang is incorporated in many ad campaigns and jingles.

Slang is an important part of the evolution of language causing the growth of it lexicons. Through the subculture's usage, slang spirals upward to the mainstream. For example, the word *cool* developed its slang etymology from the subculture of jazz musicians. *Cool,* a word whose denotation refers to temperature, took on the connotation of being reserved and not excitable, and commonly thought of as popular or in style.

Slang has also been used to exclude outsiders from a subculture by changing the meanings and pronunciation of established words; many groups code their language. This coding is particularly common among the drug cultures that may fear police involvement within their group. A frequently used word such as *buzz* takes on an entirely different connotation within the drug culture. The definition changes from the sound made by insect wings to an altered state of consciousness brought on through a narcotic.

Tony Lindsay

See also Dialect; Language Development; Language Loss; Semantics; Style/Diction

Further Readings

Burke, W. J. (1965). *The literature of slang.* Detroit, MI: Gale Research.

Lighter, J. E. (Ed.). (1994). *Historical dictionary of American slang.* New York: Random House.

Major, C. (1990). *Juba to jive: A dictionary of African American slang.* New York: Penguin.

Thorne, T. (1990). *The dictionary of contemporary slang.* New York: Pantheon.

PROPAGANDA

A contemporary reading of the persuasive power of propaganda confronts the deliberate attempt to shape the perceptions, thinking, and behavior of others through a systematic use of language, ritual, and images. The manipulation of perceptions, thinking, and behavior is premeditated to accomplish a purpose—working to shape identities that are inclined to respond favorably to, or in affiliation with, the desired intent of the propagandist. The propagandist's desire to shape identities is inherently political, serving both in the original case and in the modern era to secure and extend a base of power and influence across social arenas.

Originally, however, the term *propaganda* derived from a missionary body called the *Sacra Congregatio de Propaganda Fide* or, the Sacred Congregation for the Propagation of the Faith, established in 1622 by Pope Gregory XV. This body was charged with fostering the spread of the Catholic faith to the New World and with reviving and strengthening the Roman Catholic Church in Europe as a means of countering the threat posed by the success of the Protestant revolution. However, although the origin of our modern usage of the word *propaganda* is derived from a benign missionary effort by a committee of cardinals in service to a religious intent, an important aspect of that intent was to propagate the widespread demonstration of the Catholic identity with all of its accompanying ritual social interaction, liturgical language, ecclesiastical costuming, and ceremonial visuality.

The principal intent of propaganda is to persuade a desired social behavior by influencing the opinions of large numbers of people, either by the omission or obfuscation of information or the fabrication of a useful fiction or misinformation that elicits the desired response. The original proselytizing intent of propaganda is revisited by any secular organization or institution employing similar techniques for manipulating opinion and injecting the memes of particular beliefs through any medium into the thinking of potential acolytes within its sphere of influence. Thus, those who are schooled in the propaganda of a political belief, public policy, or sociocultural norm are also schooled for the purpose of perpetuating a regime of influence.

In the polyglot visual culture of the modern and postmodern eras, the regimes of influence that shape social identities and individual behavior have gone global with propaganda being employed in everything from media product advertisement to political campaigns to Olympics competitions. For example, the intent to caricature one group of people as insignificant, foolish, or dangerous in the eyes of another group of people is often executed by the act of stereotyping. Propagandists may produce their caricatures willingly, as in the malicious stereotypes of identity that were first conceived in the minds of demagogues before being unleashed as propaganda to the embrace of an overzealous or bigoted populace. Or, regimes of influence may produce their caricatures unthinkingly, simply creating en masse the thin experience that a dominant and generally homogenous sociocultural group has had in interfacing with its local minorities. Stereotyped imagery, fraught with omissions about the familiarities to be found in the lives of those being targeted as abnormal, is one means of constituting the power of visual regimes to shape individual and social identities.

Most widespread, albeit with varying themes from one social group to another, is the propaganda of normalcy that cultivates the desirability of a normal identity in the public opinion by systematically stigmatizing alternative behaviors and appearances. Because behavior patterns are fair predictors of future behaviors, the manipulation of public behavior patterns—such as legislated penalties for nonconformity to the U.S. "ugly laws" of the 19th and 20th centuries that made it illegal for persons with deformities to be in public—public school curricula employing stigmatizing narratives and texts, the advertisement of a desirable standard of behavior and appearance and social rewards for adherence to those models, and the segregation of deviants and undesirables into marginalized social arenas, communities, and vocational tracks have served as tools in stabilizing the norms that Western societies continue to hold central.

There are many historical instances around the world of the propagandistic advertisement, legislation, or enforced conformity of a desirable standard behavior and appearance, but perhaps none so common as occurs in the institutionalized common schooling of youngsters. Education is often seen in both the West and the East as an important structure for maintaining a unified national, cultural, and linguistic identity, the sanctity of which is a major pretense of the propaganda of normality. The European child-study movement of the late 19th and early 20th centuries, which extended its sphere of influence to U.S. educational philosophy and practice, first coalesced around the belief that an ideal educational practice could manufacture an ideal citizen and serve as a curative for the ills of society. Scientific beliefs about the development of humans suggested that youngsters grew in stages similar to all other biological organisms; consequently, the psychological development of the young was expected to be a recapitulation of what has come to be understood as an evolutionary model. Science and evolutionary theory were conflated into a propaganda of normality that medicalized certain parts of society as unclean and a near-biological threat to the survival of a unified national, cultural, and linguistic identity. Common schooling was thus intended as a systemized and purifying contravention to the urban influx of children from the laboring and maligned lower classes of society viewed as the implicit carriers of potential depravity and dissolution.

Based on a persistent conceptualization of Native American communities as childlike, the U.S. Congress enacted the Civilization Act in 1819, implementing into policy the propagandistic use of tribal schools as a means of social control intended to further manipulate the destiny of Native Americans and ensure their continued subservience to the homogeneous ideal inherent in a European American national identity. With the same resolve as the Roman Catholic *Sacra Congregatio de Propaganda Fide* centuries earlier, Protestant churches in the United States organized to civilize Native Americans by sending in missionary educators intent on converting Native American tribal groups from "foreigners" and "heathens" to good Christians.

To fundamentally alter the traditions that constituted and supported the authentic demonstration of the varying Native American social identities, events in missionary and tribal schools both performed and ritualized the visual iconology of the dominant Anglo-American culture. Educators forbade the speaking of non-English languages, as well as the wearing of traditional clothing and ceremonial costumes, and forced students to adopt the cultural norms prescribed in a pro-Anglo-American curriculum emphasizing patriotism and fealty to the U.S. government. Once they were replaced by tribal schools, tribal governments raised the flag of the United States. Students were compelled to pledge allegiance to their conquerors and participate in patriotic exercises and celebrations of U.S. national holidays and heroes.

Whether propaganda is aimed at the deliberate omission or obfuscation of the information that once informed identity or at the fabrication of a useful fiction or misinformation that generates the environment for new identity, it must be reckoned with as a formidable tool in the sociopolitical construction of identity.

James Haywood Rolling Jr.

See also Language; Rituals; Socialization

Further Readings

Baker, B. M. (2001). *In perpetual motion: Theories of power, educational history, and the child.* New York: Peter Lang.

Jowett, G. S., & O'Donnell, V. (1999). *Propaganda and persuasion.* Thousand Oaks, CA: Sage.

Nandy, A. (1983). *The intimate enemy: The loss and recovery of self under colonialism.* New York: Oxford University Press.

Spring, J. (2001). *The American school: 1642–2000* (5th ed.). New York: McGraw-Hill.

PSYCHOLOGY OF SELF AND IDENTITY

The study of self and identity has a long and storied history in the field of psychology. William James began the discussion by commenting on the distinctions between the I and Me at the beginning of the field. Since then, the study of self and identity has exploded into one of the more researched topics within psychology. However, the discussion of the self did not begin with the field of psychology; it began long before that time. In the beginning, the self was considered to be a simple and uninteresting concept—people were not much aware of themselves and their thoughts. Over the centuries, people's view of the self has morphed from this basic view into a complex, multifaceted structure that operates at a level that the individual does not always perceive. This evolution of self was made possible by philosophic and technological advances throughout human history that begged to be applied to how people viewed the self.

The self as conceptualized in modern times is capable of much more than simply being a physical being within space, as was once conceived in medieval Europe. As viewed today, the self comprises three aspects, which are linked to a person's ability to assess his or her identity. The first major aspect of the self is *reflexive consciousness.* In the most basic terms, *reflexive consciousness* refers to an individual's ability to be self-aware. Second, the self is capable of being an *interpersonal being* where information of the self is gained from interactions with others. Because people do not exist in a social vacuum, it is important that individuals be able to define who they are with reference to those around them. Finally, the self is capable of *executive functioning.* This is the most complex and least understood of the three aspects but allows the self to act upon the world by expressing choices and decisions that interplay with the world around an individual. These three aspects allow an individual to express his or her identity as expressions of the self.

People are able to express identity based on two primary sources of information: information from within and information beyond. Identity from within is based heavily on the component of the reflexive consciousness within the self. Here, people draw a sense of identity from information about their own beings through mood, self-knowledge, and expectations. Gaining identity from beyond is based heavily on the interpersonal aspect of self where information from others is used to gain information about the self. Of note, because the self is capable of gathering information from others to create an identity, identity can come from interactions with others, or the perception of others, on a one-on-one basis as well as from larger conglomerations of people, such as groups and organizations.

This entry focuses on how aspects of the self allow individuals to take information from multiple sources to create identities. The sources of identity considered here are information within, information from the other, and information from the collective. The information that is provided by these three sources may not always produce a consistent identity between the sources or within any one source. Inconsistencies may arise, so mechanisms to create a coherent sense of self from these potentially differing identities exist. These mechanisms are discussed throughout the entry and in the final portion of the entry.

Individual Self: Identity From the Person

The individual self is responsible for individuals' own beliefs about who they are and their evaluations of these identities. Using information available to the individual, a person can try to understand who he or she is solely on this internal information. Before looking to the rest of the world for useful information about identity, people look inward, at the self, to make their own determinations about the person they are in the world.

To identify with anything, people must first be aware that they are capable of such action. *Self-awareness* is the ability a person has to focus on the self in some manner or another and then to compare it with some standard. Unfortunately, simply becoming aware of the self usually leads to people realizing there is some shortcoming between what they are and the standard of comparison. This creates a great deal of tension in the individual that must somehow be reduced. For example, *self-discrepancy theory* argues that people have three selves that are used for comparative purposes: *actual self, ideal self,* and *ought self.* The actual self is the actual perception of the individual. The ideal self is what the individual wants to be like, and the ought self is something the person should be, usually based on some moral grounding. When actual–ideal and actual–ought discrepancies are made apparent, the individual is driven to reduce the emotional distress caused by these inconsistent self-conceptions. Different emotional responses are likely to occur based on the type of self-discrepancy that is experienced. Regardless of the emotional response, though, this is a negative experience that must be dealt with because people want to maintain a positive sense of self. The *cognitive dissonance theory* states that a person will go through any number of options to reduce tension created by inconsistencies, including changing behavior, changing thoughts, finding alternative information, creating new cognitions, or simply ignoring the inconsistency, though this does not effectively address the issue at hand. Based on this, people are motivated to reduce this uncomfortable tension, which is assisted by seeking *self-knowledge.*

Self-knowledge can be sought from any number of places and is used to create *self-schemata* that help dictate attitudes and behaviors. Self-schemata are generalizations a person holds about the self that come from past experience. These are used to organize and process information about the self so people understand who they are and how they should behave in different social settings. Each self-schema has only a certain piece of information or belief related to it, so different self-schemata can be activated in different situations. Interestingly, the information that is sought to create these self-schemata is not exhaustive. People have a tendency to seek specific types of information about who they are, which are driven by three motives: *appraisal, self-verification,* and *self-enhancement.* Appraisal motives focus on gaining information that is valid and accurate. Self-verification motives lead people to seek information that confirms the beliefs they already hold. Finally, self-enhancement motives direct people toward information that makes the individual seem positive. Based on this motive, favorable new information about the self is sought as is information that disconfirms negative self-knowledge.

Research has shown that a hierarchy exists among these three knowledge-seeking motives that dictates the type of self-knowledge that is actually sought. Though seeking valid and accurate information would seem most useful and beneficial to understanding the self, this is by far the least important type of information sought. The most important information people seem to seek is self-enhancing in nature, followed by self-verifying information. This creates a situation where people are seeking information that is positive or, at least, disconfirming of negative information about the self. This is then maintained because people then seek information that is going to verify what they already believe. If people originally collect information about the self that is self-enhancing, a cycle is created to focus only on this type of information. In essence, people only want to hear information that is positive about the self and deflect negative information. The ability to seek certain types of information rather than others implies the ability to *self-regulate.* This means the self is capable of monitoring its own status at any given moment and acting on the status, if necessary. Essentially, self-regulation gives the self a constantly recycling flow of information that can be acted on in the following process: *test, operate, test, exit.* Basically, the self is capable of recognizing a shortcoming between actual and either ideal or ought, it can attempt to do something to fix this, it can then check to see if the action taken fixed the problem, and it can then either stop if the problem was dealt with or go back to the beginning until a solution is reached. Again, self-regulation allows people to realize if there are discrepancies that may threaten a positive sense of self, which then allows them to seek new information. Fortunately for the sense of self, people have a tendency to seek information that is self-enhancing rather than information that may be accurate.

Considering that people generally seek positive self-knowledge, research has shown that in the United States, people generally do not score below average on scales of *self-esteem*, which is the evaluative measure of the self in terms of ability and worth. This means people generally have a positive evaluation of who they are. It is important to distinguish between the two types of self-esteem that are found in the literature. *Trait self-esteem* represents the general outlook a person holds about his or her self, on average. This is believed to be a relatively stable construct. However, *state self-esteem* tends to fluctuate between situations because it is assessing self-worth and ability on a contingent basis. Discussions of low and high self-esteem, then, are relative in nature on a scale that goes from moderate to high and that normally is assessing trait self-esteem. This is still not an arbitrary distinction because low self-esteem has continually shown negative outcomes on a number of variables compared with those who have relatively higher self-esteem.

A major explanation for the existence of self-esteem comes from the *sociometer hypothesis*. Based on this conception, self-esteem serves as an indicator of social inclusion, with fluctuations indicating an increase or decrease in how likely an individual is be included by others. Lowered self-esteem would drive people to identify and change whatever issue is leading to this decrease in positive self-regard. Generally speaking, the sociometer asserts that self-esteem can be considered analogously to a gas tank meter in a car. Trait self-esteem could be considered the average miles per gallon a car gets during its lifetime. The gauge that fluctuates during a specific drive would be analogous to the state self-esteem of an individual. An alternative explanation, *terror management theory,* asserts that self-esteem developed as a way to buffer against thoughts of mortality. Because people are self-aware, they have the ability to explore the possibility of their own deaths, which is a discomforting feeling. Self-esteem works to reduce these unpleasant feelings. Even though each explanation for the functional purpose of self-esteem is drastically different, both operate within the bounds of the psychology of self and identity; both theories address the issue of reducing discomfort from information that is threatening to the positive self-image.

Regardless the reason for the development of self-esteem, the result is that people seem designed to view the self in a generally positive light. The ability to ruminate on the internal happenings of an individual offers a situation where discomfort may be created because of disconnects between actual self and either ideal or ought self that put pressure on the desire to maintain a positive sense of self. Discomfort may also arise from a shift in self-esteem, which has been argued to be a measure of inclusion or as a buffer against fear of death. This pressure demands the attention of the individual and it somehow must be dealt with, which is where information from other people becomes useful because it may help alleviate this tension if self-enhancing and self-verifying information are sought.

Relational Self: Identity From the Other

Social comparison theory argues that people look to others to gain information about themselves through their abilities and attitudes. Through these comparisons with others, people gain an understanding of their relative standing and whether their abilities and attitudes are acceptable or whether work must be done to bring them into a consonant state. This is an important consideration when looking at self and identity because people gain information from others to understand who they are as persons. Importantly though, people will not simply choose any person to compare with because this could offer potentially damaging information if comparisons with the wrong person are made. Ideally, people seek out others who are similar in ability or belief to make comparisons because the information gathered from this person would be most useful when compared with information from someone who is much better or worse in ability or beliefs. This *relational self* creates identities based on the interpersonal interactions an individual has with others and gathers important information about the self from these interactions.

When considering the role others play regarding self and identity, the issue of *self-presentation* must be considered. Self-presentation is where people will change their attitudes, beliefs, or behaviors to make an impression on another individual. The reason behind this manipulation falls into one of two categories, including *strategic motives* and *expressive motives*. Strategic motives are meant to get others to go along with a certain position or belief the individual holds, which follows the self-verification motive of self-knowledge seeking. In this instance, the individual is concerned with what the other thinks and is attempting to gain some benefit. However, expressive motives focus on presenting an identity that is desirable to the individual in terms of who he or she wants to be or should be in his or her mind. The concern in expressive self-presentation is with the beliefs of the individual, and there is an attempt to get validation of the presented identity from others. Expressive motives of self-presentation operate under the self-enhancement motive of self-knowledge seeking because the individual is attempting to validate an identity he or she holds.

Another important consideration in understanding the influence of others stems from research on *symbolic interactionist theory*. This theory claims that people do not have any understanding of who they are without gaining information from other people. As information begins to gather, people gain a clearer picture of themselves. Unfortunately, the correlation between what others believe about the individual and the individual's own self-beliefs are weak. Again, if people are operating under the belief that they are subjectively good in their own eyes, other people may not see these attitudes, beliefs, and behaviors as such. An outsider could easily view the actions of an individual as negative, even though that individual may see his or her own actions as positive. Also, if a person does see his or her own actions as negative, such as an actual–ideal discrepancy, others may be operating under expressive motives to present themselves as polite so they may not agree that there is a discrepancy. That said, research has shown that there is a strong correlation between the beliefs people have about their selves and what they *believe* other people think of them. In essence, people are making a cohesive picture of who they are in their own minds by believing that others

have similar beliefs about who they are. People are not necessarily seeking valid and accurate information as dictated by the appraisal principle, but rather, they are seeking information that confirms their previous beliefs, which is self-verifying that they are good persons.

Research on the self-fulfilling prophecy supports the view that the person's belief of what the other person thinks is what matters. According to the self-fulfilling prophecy, people's false beliefs can become true by influencing their behaviors. For example, if students think that their teacher hates them, they will act negatively when they interact with that teacher. This causes the teacher to perceive that the students do not like the teacher, who might then reciprocate the negative interaction—thus confirming the students' belief that the teacher does not like them. If the student does poorly in this class, instead of being the fault of the individual, the individual can still believe he or she is smart, and that the problem is the fault of the antagonistic relationship with the teacher. This allows the self to be maintained in a cohesive, positive manner. This phenomenon stresses the importance of people seeking consistency in how they see themselves, and this is generally a positive belief.

Individuals are also capable of taking in information from other people, especially those who are close to them, and using it to their own advantage. For example, people are capable of *basking in reflected glory* (BIRG), where a person will enjoy in the successes and failures of close others, as if these were his or her own. A sense of pride is gained from a close partner when the partner succeeds at something that is not a competitive domain of the two people involved. Interestingly, if the other succeeds at a task that is a competitive domain of the two people, the individual may retreat from being associated with that other because he or she realizes that he or she now looks relatively worse in comparison. This affects the individual's positive sense of who he or she is and acts as a buffer against such feelings. Also, processes such as *downward social comparison* facilitate finding information that maintains a positive self-schema. In downward social comparison, people will look to those who are in a worse situation than their own to make themselves relatively look better.

By being interpersonal creatures, people have the ability to use information from others, factual or believed, to gain a clearer picture of who they are in the world and solidify their positive self-schemata. This shows that the self is not simply a static entity but pulls in information from the world around the self to help make identities that are cohesive with the general worldview of a positive self. Though the power of a relationship, perceived or actual, with another individual is capable of shaping identity, a conglomeration of people also has the power to shape identity.

Collective Self: Identity From the Group

Collections of individuals play an important role in developing identities for an individual. In many instances, people can gain a sense of identity from their groups and organizations because of shared characteristics and interests between members, which is known as the *collective self*. However, there are also those groups that people do not choose to join but are naturally grouped into based on distinguishing characteristics resulting from genetics, phenotype, and region (e.g., race, sex, and nationality), which also are included in the collective self. Regardless of the type of group membership, the collections of people we associate with offer a great deal of information when it comes to self and identity.

When discussing the influence of groups on identity, *culture* is something that is often discussed in research settings because it can be such a pervasive source of influence. Culture can be considered a set of attitudes, beliefs, and behaviors that are transmitted from one generation to the next that dictate the manner in which individuals will approach their world regarding their views of the self and others. Individuals observe the people around them to understand and express the attitudes, beliefs, and behaviors their culture dictates. Culture is something people experience from birth and is constantly experienced based on how others from that culture behave and interact with other people. In an effort to maintain consistency between actual–ought *self-construals*, individuals quickly adopt these practices because it is expected that people within a culture will abide by these rules; not adopting these ideals can have serious negative consequences for the individual, including potential ostracism from the group. Within the psychology literature, cultural considerations tend to focus on the dimension of *independence* versus *interdependence*. Those cultures high in interdependence tend to be classified as *collectivist* in nature, whereas those low in interdependent tendencies are classified as *individualist*. Collectivist cultures tend to have people who value the goals of the group over those of the individual. This creates individuals who have self-construals that are more likely to see their membership in groups, especially kinship groups, as the essence of their identity. In contrast, people from individualist cultures tend to have self-construals that favor the goals of the individual over the group and will see their membership in groups as an expression of their unique individuality. This means that cultures offer different types of identity for individuals within different cultural contexts but put equal pressure to abide by the norms and practices dictated by the self-construal of the culture because it is such a pervasive entity.

From an evolutionary perspective, groups functionally serve the purpose of increasing chances for survival. However, psychologically, *uncertainty identity theory* argues that groups offer a means to reduce uncertainty for an individual because groups offer a clear source of identity by dictating attitudes, beliefs, and behaviors for group members. According to *social identity theory*, people gain a positive sense of self from the groups they identify with because the group allows them to positively distinguish themselves from other relevant groups, which is operating on the self-enhancing motive for individuals. These features have been shown to exist in a vast range of group settings from the completely artificial, using a *minimal groups paradigm*, to those groups that are more natural settings, such as culture and ethnicity. The larger the distinction between the two groups is, the clearer the group identity is for the members, which is known as *optimal distinctiveness theory*. If a group does not provide this distinction that produces a positive sense of self, individuals can choose to either leave the group or focus on some other dimension where a positive distinction can be made between groups.

Self-categorization theory argues that to attain this optimal distinctiveness, groups have a process in place to help members monitor their identity within the group to distinguish whether their attitudes, beliefs, and behaviors are still in line with the group. Through the process of *deperson-alization,* people no longer see themselves as unique individuals but as members of the group that share a fuzzy set of attributes, known as the *prototype,* that define the group identity. This definition is derived from both what the group is and what the group is not. The attitudes, beliefs, and behaviors of the group an individual is a part of define this group (what the group is) but they should also be clearly different from other groups (what the group is not). This clear definition of the group makes it easy to find information that is self-verifying, if the group is important to the individual and shares the group's characteristics.

People within the group are then able to monitor themselves and other group members by comparison with the prototype. By focusing on this prototype, individuals within a group will examine how the attitudes, beliefs, and behaviors they hold and that others hold compare with the prototype. People who do not compare favorably with the prototype are deemed outsiders to the group because they blur the line between the ingroup and outgroup. This is a problem for members within the group because the strong distinction brings about a positive sense of self (self-enhancement in action) and people can easily self-verify if people within the group all share the same characteristics. A lack of a clear distinction creates tension that has to be dealt with, which is why the offending group member may be ostracized so that balance and distinction may be restored. As the group becomes more salient to an individual, the individual's identity becomes more closely tied to the group identity, which leads the individual to be more and more prototypical because losing this source of identity would be threatening because it raises uncertainty.

People are members of multiple groups, which means they can garner identity from these various memberships. *Social identity complexity theory* argues that people are capable of maintaining multiple memberships in diverse groups, which is analogous to having a diversified stock portfolio. From this perspective, the strength of identity with any one group can vary, with some memberships being more or less central to the identity of an individual, much like some stocks are more central to

a portfolio because there is a larger investment with those. Similar to stock portfolios, some people invest in companies that are simply subsidiaries of a larger company whereas others choose to invest in companies that are not at all related to each other. Some people are members of groups that are similar, not requiring much cognitive ability to make sense of these group constellations. However, people can also be members of groups that do not overlap much in their norms and beliefs, which requires more cognitive activity to make sense of such a complex group constellation.

The self benefits from the complex memberships because it is capable of losing group membership without a big an impact on identity because the self comprises multiple group identities that extend across boundaries. Losing membership in a group that is central to identity with low social identity complexity is dangerous because all memberships overlap heavily and all identities are central to an individual's self-concept. Relative to stock portfolios, it is more secure to have investments spread out across differing companies with not too much money invested in any one company because this diversity provides a safety net for invested money. Investing money all in one stock is dangerous because if it suffers, so does all invested money. For social identity complexity, this lack of diversity will have severe consequences for the individual because the individual has lost a defining portion of the self. However, the more diversified group membership is for an individual, the easier it will be to recover from such an impact.

Groups affect the identities people develop by offering clarity to an uncertain world. These memberships dictate attitudes, beliefs, and behaviors that become central aspects of the self as the group membership becomes more important to the individual's identity, allowing a great deal of self-verification and self-enhancement. People are able to derive identity from multiple sources, which can be beneficial to the self because identity is not tied to any one group. However, with individual, relational, and collective inputs for the identity of an individual, the self must have mechanisms in place to help make sense of these inputs to present a cohesive self that is positively valued among the many identities a person may juggle, even in a single day.

Creation of a Positive Self

People have a tendency to attribute their own failures to the circumstance, whereas the failures of others are attributed to the individual. People assume their failures are the fault of some outside force, but the failures of others are their own faults that result from some internal force. Known as the *fundamental attribution error,* this demonstrates the importance of maintaining a positive sense of self and identity. Processes exist that make people look better to themselves and that keep other people relatively lower in the mind, so that the individual can view himself or herself positively.

The individual self is capable of monitoring attitudes, beliefs, and behaviors as well as their inclusion with others, which could be considered a measure of how much people like the individual. If any of these become inconsistent with a positive self-belief, an individual then attempts to return this system to consonance through various methods. The self focuses only on knowledge that casts the individual in a positive light or that deflects the individual from being cast in a negative light. Following this, people will seek information that confirms their own beliefs, which have already been tainted to be mostly positive. Accuracy and validity are afterthoughts in the grand scheme of the types of self-knowledge sought by an individual.

The relational self uses information from others to attain a more accurate picture of the self. However, the information used may not necessarily be accurate and could be completely fictitious if it means that a positive sense of self is maintained. Using the successes of a close other helps to bolster the positive sense of self. However, success in a competitive field puts pressure on the individual to disassociate from that close other because the other's successes make the individual look relatively worse. If individuals cannot benefit from the successes of others, people can benefit from the failures of others. These downward comparisons help the individual seem better and offer further confirmation of the belief that the individual has a positive sense of self.

With groups, the collective self uses membership to garner a positive sense of self by distinguishing the group from other groups on relevant dimensions. Groups not offering this positive identity will either be left or a new level of comparison will be created just so a positive comparison between groups can be made that assist the self-enhancement motives of the individual. Within any group, there are pressures to conform to the norms and practices that define the group and that create distinctions between groups. The specter of actual–ought discrepancies helps individuals abide by the rules of the group so all members can gain the positive identity that comes from the clear distinctions with other groups. Threatening the clear distinctions between groups that are meant to bring about positive sources of identity for group members can be dangerous for an individual. Blurring distinctions has the potential for ostracism, which would increase uncertainty for the individual because positive sources of self are not easy to garner for group members. This operates as a mechanism to maintain group cohesion, which also maintains positive senses of self for the individual group members. Group membership also offers a great deal of self-verification because the incidence of conformity to group norms and ideals creates a more homogenous setting for attitudes, beliefs, and behaviors.

In the end, the psychology of self and identity seems to have one focus: the creation and maintenance of positive self-schemata. Whether identity is derived from internal information about the self, information from other individuals, or from groups, people seem to strive for consistency in the way they present themselves, which tends toward a positive light. The self has many tools to help alleviate any pressures that inconsistent identities could create. These can range from the relatively simple (joining a relatively homogenous group) to the relatively complex and cognitively taxing (seeking self-enhancing and self-verifying information with the intent to deflect negative self-knowledge). Accuracy of information is not as important, especially if the accurate information could be perceived as potentially damaging to the self. Ultimately, whether simple or complex tools are employed, a cohesive, positively evaluated self is typically created that balances the identities from the individual self, relational self, and collective self.

Jason E. Rivera and Zachary P. Hohman

See also Development of Identity; Development of Self-Concept; Group Identity; Identification; Individuation; Self; Self-Schema; Social Identity Theory

Further Readings

Baumeister, R. F. (1998). The self. In D. T. Gilbert, S. T. Fiske, & G. Lindzey (Eds.), *Handbook of social psychology* (4th ed., pp. 680–740). New York: McGraw-Hill.

Baumeister, R. F. (Ed.). (1999). *Key readings in social psychology: The self in social psychology.* Philadelphia: Psychology Press.

Hogg, M. A. (2006). Social identity theory. In P. J. Burke (Ed.), *Contemporary social psychological theories* (pp. 111–136). Palo Alto, CA: Stanford University Press.

Leary, M. R., & Tangney, J. P. (Eds.). (2003). *Handbook of self and identity.* New York: Guilford Press.

Markus, H. R. (1977). Self-schemata and processing information about the self. *Journal of Personality and Social Psychology, 35,* 63–78.

Sedikides, C., & Brewer, M. B. (Eds.). (2001). *Individual self, relational self, collective self.* Philadelphia: Psychology Press.

Tajfel, H., & Turner, J. C. (1979). The social identity theory of intergroup behavior. In S. Worchel & W. G. Austin (Eds.), *Psychology of intergroup relations* (pp. 33–47). Monterey, CA: Brooks/Cole.

Turner, J. C., Hogg, M. A., Oakes, P. J., Reicher, S. D., & Wetherell, M. S. (1987). *Rediscovering the social group: A self-categorization theory.* New York: Blackwell.

PUBLIC SPHERE

A general definition of the *public sphere* is a realm within which individuals discuss the public good. Many scholars insist that a public sphere is a necessary element of democratic society, a realm wherein citizens can freely engage in discourse without interference from the state and its agents. However, *public sphere* is a term that has inspired much debate and multiple, sometimes competing, definitions and applications. Interest in theories of the public sphere was revived in the wake of the cold war and the demise of colonialism. Scholars of democratic theory, social movements, rhetoric, and media studies have turned to theories of the public sphere to explore and explain the dynamic changes in civil societies after the fall of the Berlin Wall, the growth of diasporas, and the continued efforts of marginalized religious, sexual, racial, and gender groups to attain equality in contemporary societies. Many of these explorations investigate the role of public discourse in these phenomena and aim to combat triumphalist narratives of capitalism's victory over other forms of sociality. Writers in search of ways to reinvigorate ideals of citizen participation, equality of opportunity, and multiculturalism in global societies have looked to public sphere theories for inspiration and to highlight concerns, including how the public sphere shapes social identity and how one's participation in the public sphere or in counterpublics shapes and reshapes one's identity.

Habermas and the Revival of Public Sphere Theory

Much of the renewed interest in the public sphere during the last three decades was sparked by Thomas Burger's 1989 translation of Jürgen Habermas's *The Structural Transformation of the Public Sphere*. In this generative volume, Habermas traces the rise of the bourgeois public sphere in the era of the European Enlightenment, and its demise in the modern era. He defines the public sphere as the arena where private persons who gathered outside of the state to discuss matters of public import, including issues concerning the state. These discussions were guided by rational-critical debate norms and required individuals to shed particularities of identity to be recognized as rational speakers. The book sparked a host of responses from scholars in anthologies, special issues of academic journals, and book-length treatises.

Critiques of Habermas

Although many writers found Habermas's thesis and history intriguing and vital, multiple critiques of the work quickly found their way to print. Chief among the concerns raised by scholars and social movement activists was the focus on a bourgeois public, the definitions of rational debate, and the bifurcation of public and private. Many respondents felt his history and theory did not contain sufficient attention to marginalized groups and did not apply to the conditions of the multicultural modern societies of either Europe or the United States. From these concerns came reformulations of Habermas's history of the bourgeois Western public to include concurrent formations of working class, women's, and other publics to account for differences in power and access to resources.

Counterpublics

Many critics of Habermas posit that *counterpublics* exist in opposition to majority publics or a dominant public sphere in an ever-shifting terrain of institutions, identity positions, and media arenas. Indeed, long before the English translation of *The Structural Transformation of the Public Sphere*, Oskar Negt and Alexander Kluge described the emergence of working class publics in tandem with bourgeois publics. In 1992, Nancy Fraser posited a feminist public sphere emerging in opposition to the male-dominated bourgeois public. Simultaneously, Houston Baker Jr., Michael Dawson, and others gathered at the University of Chicago to delineate the contours of a Black counterpublic, pondering the ways in which African Americans created separate and overlapping public spheres in response to slavery and White supremacy. These explorations of multiple publics acknowledge the role of cultural identities in creating speech norms, setting agendas, and defining borders between public and private concerns. Many of these writers cited how multiple forms of speech, including more performative and emotive modes of engagement, could not be excluded from the realm of the public, thereby favoring certain identity groups and norms over others.

Lippman, Dewey, and Arendt

Debates over the utility and limits of Habermas's formulation also inspired many to return to the writings of Walter Lippman, Hannah Arendt, and John Dewey on the form and function of public deliberation, public opinion, and civic action. Some scholars question whether any formulation of the public sphere is emancipatory, concurring with Lippman's conclusion that the public itself is a phantom strategically used by elites to leverage opinion and shape agendas. Others look at Dewey's enthusiasm for the public to be reengineered into a great community as an unattainable ideal in a fast-paced, global society. Likewise, Arendt's vision of public involvement, influenced by ancient Greek articulations of citizenship, is seen as too burdensome and idealized for the modern world. Writers in this vein suggest that earlier so-called golden eras of democratic debate were warped by exclusions based on class, gender, and ethnicity and, upon close study, rarely approached the ideals of rational-critical discourse or consensus building. These historians excavate evidence of the rowdy crowds that attended presidential debates; ribald commentary and satire in newspapers; sensationalized stories of celebrities crowding out more tame updates on debates over railroad expansion; and of the carnivalesque, sometimes violent, atmosphere that accompanied public gatherings meant to tease out public opinion.

Critiques of New Public Sphere Theories

Some critics have raised concerns that a model of multiple publics and counterpublics encourages a fractured vision of civil society and heightens cultural balkanization. Many of these critics lament the lack (or imagine the loss) of a common culture and common arenas to gather the public for debate. Robert Putnam's *Bowling Alone* is often held up as an exemplary description of how U.S. society has lost key institutions of social integration, such as Elks Lodges and bowling leagues, sites that formed community ties and provided opportunities for folks to discuss common issues and interests. Like Dewey's vision of the lost Great Community and Habermas's narrative of decline, works such as *Bowling Alone* imply that a sense of public belonging and spirit has been lost in the midst of ever-multiplying media distractions and identity blocs that keep citizens separated into privatized realms and segregated interest groups.

Diversity and Public Spheres

One major response to the charge of balkanization is that, like Habermas's early formulation of the public sphere, it depends on a nostalgic look back to a golden era where identity politics allegedly did not exist. However, close investigations of eras of seeming homogeneity reveal fissures and disjunctures of identity that allowed undemocratic public spheres to operate without full inclusion of people of color, women, and other marginalized members of society. Similarly, writers point to the implied preference for public discussion to only and always end in consensus and emphasize the importance of dissent to democratic debate. A model of public discourse that does not allow for multiple, overlapping public spheres, proponents argue, is both anemic and antidemocratic, and ignores what Fraser termed the actually existing conditions of civil society.

Emerging Approaches to Public Sphere Theory

Numerous scholars have suggested that the spatial metaphor of the public sphere is both misleading and too limited to adequately describe the agents and activities of the public. In an era of multiplying discursive environments, multinational population flows, and media tools that blur interpersonal and mass media practices, the sphere metaphor seems rather simplistic. Influences from cultural studies, postcolonial studies, and queer theory have provided alternative means for reconceptualizing how the public sphere is considered and described. Arjun Appadurai suggested *scapes* and *fractals* as alternative conceptualizations for the complex interactions between publics and discourses. As multinational capitalism, ethnic diasporas, and labor migrations affect communicative practices and spatial realities, Appadurai posits that global flows within *technoscapes, finanscapes, ideoscapes, mediascapes,* and *ethnoscapes* will alter relationships between individuals, nation-states, and the actions of publics. Others posit that the *network* might be a better way to conceptualize the communicative interactions of publics in a multimedia world of near-instantaneous communication.

Scholars are also concerned that the emphasis on the different identity groups that may form multiple publics may distract from understanding what makes a public a public versus an identifiable demographic segment or a crowd. This has inspired many scholars to focus more on the *how* of being public rather than the *where*. For instance, Michael Warner describes the public as a space that exists by virtue of being addressed. That is, shared social identities, whether national, ethnic, sexual, or religious, are not sufficient to form a public or counterpublic. Rather, people must attend to a public address and recognize themselves as members of the public as they pay attention to a public text, whether an advertisement or a presidential radio address. Warner still acknowledges the existence of counterpublics, but focuses on the participation of its members in responding to an address, attending to a text that marks them as members of a gay or Black or women's counterpublic. Moreover, by attending to those particular public texts, one's participation in the counterpublic shapes and reshapes one's identity. In this spirit, Robert Asen and Daniel Brouwer have recently called on scholars to think in terms of public modalities as a more flexible means to understand public spheres—that is, examining the many ways of being public as a means to escape the limitations of the spatial metaphor and to allow a greater variety of explorations of public activity.

Undoubtedly, scholars will continue to build on current themes in public sphere theory to explore a host of emerging questions regarding citizenship and communication. Recent events in the United States, Iran, and China necessitate studies of public culture and public spheres with an eye toward understanding the interactions between discourse, new media technologies, social identities, and state repression. For example, during the protests after the Iranian presidential election, many have asked whether an Iranian diaspora became a public sphere via cell phone and Twitter technologies. Likewise, the Obama campaign's savvy use of the mass and interpersonal aspects of Internet messaging has been described as a bold new means for connecting disparate citizens into a great community, à la Dewey, and as a means to send tailored messages to diverse groups to manipulate publics into a temporary, powerful voting bloc. As the actually existing circumstances on the ground change, the myriad tools provided by public sphere theorists will be applied to understanding the dynamics of modern communications and identities and their role in shaping civil society.

Catherine R. Squires

See also Civic Identity; Cosmopolitanism; Culture, Ethnicity, and Race; Discourse; Diversity; Hegemony; Identity Uncertainty; Multiculturalism; Rhetoric

Further Readings

Asen, R., & Brouwer, C. (2001). *Counterpublics and the state*. Albany: SUNY Press.

Black Public Sphere Collective. (Eds.). (1995). *The Black public sphere*. Chicago: University of Chicago Press.

Calhoun, C. (Ed.). (1992). *Habermas and the public sphere*. Cambridge: MIT Press.

Gaonkar, D. P. (2002). The forum: Publics and counterpublics. *Quarterly Journal of Speech, 88,* 410–412.

Landes, J. B. (Ed.). (1998). *Feminism, the public and the private*. Oxford, UK: Oxford University Press.

Robbins, B. (Ed.). (1993). *The phantom public sphere*. Minneapolis: University of Minnesota Press.

QUEER THEORY

Queer theory is concerned with the philosophy of difference and marginality, and how language, meaning, and identity can be used for political ends to disempower minority groups. Compared with other branches of philosophy, the name itself is especially resonant—intentionally vulgar and defiant. It simultaneously engages the original meaning of queer as unnatural, counterfeit, or deviant, and the effort by a minority group inspired by gay rights and theory to reclaim a term originally intended to wound and stigmatize. *Queer* is less a name or identification here than an ironic wink at the politics of identification, a verbal taunt meant to reverse attention from those called *queer* to a culture that has so named them.

The origins of queer theory lie at the intersection of postmodernism, feminism, and gay theory, each of which has taken up in its own way problems of difference, identity, and resistance to the dominate culture. Queer theory's immediate roots can be traced to three seminal works by three very different authors: Michel Foucault's *History of Sexuality*, Eve Kosofsky Sedgwick's *Epistemology of the Closet*, and Judith Butler's *Gender Trouble*.

The Problem of Subjectivity

In the *History of Sexuality*, Foucault deconstructs the idea of queer/gay identity. His argument, like those in many of his books, is at once obvious, unsettling, and revelatory. In this work, Foucault distinguished between *sexuality* and *sex*. Sex had been an act, a set of pleasures that one performed. Yet at the beginning of first millennium, the Pauline tradition of Christianity focused on sexual pleasure and its restraint as the fundamental question of a religious morality. To live a moral life meant knowing and controlling one's urges, tendencies, and temptations. Foucault calls this *sexuality* rather than *sex*—sex being something visible and external that one did, *sexuality* being invisible and interior, something within oneself. Sexuality thus made it possible to generate feelings of guilt and sin simply because one dreamed of or desired disfavored pleasures, especially any one of those in an ill-defined category of illegal acts called *sodomy*. One could be guilty of sinfulness at any time or place one's sexuality emerged.

In the middle of the 19th century, with the rise of the medical establishment, psychiatry pathologized desire. Certain desires could now be classified as disease. Patients who suffered from this disease required diagnosis and treatment. An entire taxonomy of desire was created that classified people by their pleasures: the homosexual, the invert, the onanist, the pederast, and so forth—each of whom was not just diseased but a specific kind of person. A new priesthood of psychiatrists arose to help them understand and heal their sexuality to save their mental health. Like religion before them, these priests installed sex as the central issue of psychological health and wellbeing. To know oneself meant to know one's sexuality.

Foucault argued that before the rise of psychiatry in the mid-19th century, the idea that one's social identity was defined by one's desires—the idea of *being* a homosexual—was unknown. Even the ancient Greeks, who were familiar with same-sex acts, had no category for it because they did not *view* pleasure or desire as issues of moral or mental health. The homosexual is an extension of the religio-psychiatric demand that each of us define ourselves by our sexuality. From this perspective, homosexuality is an invention of heterosexuality, and homosexuals are complicit in identifying themselves by their deviation from norms of sexuality that were themselves heterosexual in origin.

Foucault is interested not just in deconstructing homosexuality and identity, but in subjectivity itself; that is, how we come to know and experience ourselves as certain kinds of individuals but not others, how and when these particular selves appear, and whose interests they serve. Although how we experience our sense of self seems a natural fact, inevitable and innocent, it is not. It is the product of specific cultural intentions and aims. In short, subjectivity is political, an extension of political aims.

The Problem of Erasure

The promotion of one kind of identity or meaning inevitably erases or excludes many others. As Foucault more evocatively puts it, in this exercise of power, there is not one silence, but many silences. Sedgwick's *Epistemology of the Closet* takes as its project exposing the erasure of homosexuality in the arts, exposing these silences, and recovering themes that were excluded or hidden.

Western art—especially literature, theater, TV, and movies—has long employed a wide range of gay themes, characters, and plotlines—often created by gay authors, playwrights, and directors—without ever naming them as such. From Marcel Proust to Tennessee Williams, from the character Lakey in *The Group,* to the character Jane Hathaway in *The Beverly Hillbillies,* to a long tradition of sexually ambiguous relentlessly fussy male supporting actors—Edward Everett Horton and Gayle Gordon's bank manager in *I Love Lucy*—there are things that are pervasive, unseen in plain sight, forces that drive emotion and narrative tension, and yet are never spoken of or named.

Sedgwick seeks to expose and abolish this ancient silence—a violent and intentional erasure—and to make it impossible thenceforth. *Epistemology* was the first and the best known of what has become a river of books deconstructing a wide array of social texts in order to read homosexual themes and identities back into them. Authors following Sedgwick's path—and some would argue Sedgwick herself—have sometimes gone overboard, insisting that homosexuality is in everything, finding homosexuality in closets that were likely bare, and reading it into situations and texts on, at best, the slenderest of evidence. Yet the project that *Epistemology* began has exposed whole new layers of meaning in what were thought to be familiar and well-understood texts, opening new areas of interpretation and scholarship while igniting fierce controversies that are unlikely to be settled anytime soon. In doing so, this book has not only recovered an entire history for a marginalized community, but returned homosexuality to its rightful place among the major themes sustaining Western art.

The Problems of Identity

Butler's *Gender Trouble* is the most audacious of the three books. In the first two dozen or so pages, Butler reinvents feminist theory and suggests a path to reinventing feminism itself.

Feminism appears to be founded on the simple, uncontroversial idea of forming a movement to represent and pursue the political interests of women. Yet for Butler, identity is always controversial. First, to preserve any sort of coherence, an identity category must have boundaries. This means some identities applying for inclusion must be refused—as transgender women are today. Others must be expelled, as lesbians and the Lavender Menace were by the National Organization for Women in 1970. To decide who can be included requires judges who are empowered to rule on others, creating hierarchies. A movement created to liberate its members generates new powers over them. Some candidates will fit the normative requirements of the identity less well than others and will suffer further discrimination for it, both inside the category and outside it. Paradoxically, identity boundaries eventually begin to serve an unintended function: They keep members in, and they place some areas off-limits as male. Thus, a movement designed to free women ends up imposing new restrictions of its own on them. Because the category *woman* remains unmarked by other dimensions such as race, class, or sexual orientation, the needs of women of color, lesbians, and others are subordinated to those of middle-class, White, heterosexual women with families.

For all these reasons, Butler considers identity to be permanently troubled, the instrument of regulation and exclusion. When she is invited to write essays as a lesbian theorist, she responds by asking how to write *as a lesbian* when the name itself announces a set of terms she wants to dispute. One of her solutions is not to do away with identity categories, but to leave them permanently open, incomplete, and undefined.

Butler offers a way out of basing our political movements on unstable and ultimately oppressive identity categories. She wants politics to be based on aims, not bodies. This means that, instead of being the foundation for political struggle, our identities are created out of the struggles in which we participate. Butler wants identity to become an effect of politics, rather than its basis. The mobility and incompleteness of identity should not be seen as a threat or hindrance to women's political aims but a crucial feminist goal.

Butler believes that gender should be unfixed as well. It should be mobile, shifting, and incomplete. To *trouble gender* should be a key function of a feminist struggle. This should be uncontroversial because a key tenet of feminism is that gender is *not* fixed and "biology is not destiny." In reality, much of U.S. feminism remains deeply wedded to essentialist notions of womanhood, and Butler's "embrace the contradiction, the problem is really the solution" approach remains highly controversial. Although her ideas have permanently altered feminist theorizing, their effect on organized feminist practice remains negligible.

Limitations

Depending as it does on deconstruction, queer theory is a set of tools for taking things apart, but has little to suggest by way of replacement. Because of its attachment to alterity, queer theory can be reflexively antagonistic toward similarity

and assimilation, a modicum of which is necessary for society to survive. In addition, in their emphasis on insubordination and marginality, queer theorists sometimes equate culture with oppression.

Any kind of organizing must involve power and hierarchy, so queer theory is unable to embrace any kind of organized political response other than general insubordination. Butler's prescription for small, individual acts of gender rebellion is a good example. Although such acts serve the goal of overturning the regulation of binary gender, one wonders if it is a big enough gun for the game at hand. Gender is a large target. Will this system really be destabilized and overthrown by little private acts of mutiny? Moreover, will it be able to combat the kinds of broad social injustice still visited on those who are gender different?

Gay rights and even transgender rights are changing the way the dominant culture understands these rights in their relation to sexual orientation and gender, just as feminism before them permanently altered how many men understand and experience themselves. Perhaps, then, some co-optations can have positive as well as negative effects, and some uses of political power to create subjectivity can be morally defensible.

Unfortunately, moral criteria by which we might approach these questions are exactly what postmodernism cannot provide because its aim is tearing down precisely the sort of Universalist claims to truth that moral systems make. This antipathy is understandable, considering that claims of morality were used to tyrannize, torment, and ultimately pathologize the homosexual.

Yet underneath all this, queer theory is also making its own implied moral claims: that difference and multiplicity are good; that uniformity, societies, and organization are bad; and so on. This contradiction—the truth about the evil of truth and the immorality of morality—is at the heart of queer theory and postmodernism and is—within its own terms—inherently irresolvable. Perhaps its dislike of organization, power, and unanimity explains why queer theory—unlike its antecedents in gay and feminist theory—has not yet produced anything like a coherent social movement. That is understandable, given its aims. Yet, given the importance of those aims and those identities still to be heard from, it is also unfortunate.

Into this vacuum has stepped a host of individual youths who understand themselves as *genderqueer,* who are challenging the boundaries of identity, rejecting simplistic binaries like man/woman, gay/straight, and even Black/White while creating new ways of naming themselves. They are moving beyond the labels by which older movements like gay rights or feminism navigate, and their existence challenges the coherence of the categories on which these movements are based. Indeed, genderqueer youth understand such labels as extensions of the same systems of sexism, racism, and heterosexism they want to combat.

Messy are new identities we cannot name and do not understand, yet which nonetheless create new possibilities and freedoms we never intended. This may be another sort of progress. If so, it is something that queer theorists may applaud.

Riki Wilchins

See also Diversity; Gay; Gender; Sexual Minorities

Further Readings

Butler, J. (1999). *Gender trouble: Feminism and subversion of identity.* London: Routledge.

Foucault, M. (1998). *The history of sexuality* (R. Hurley, Trans.). New York: Penguin.

Sedgwick, E. K. (2008). *Epistemology of the closet.* Berkeley: University of California Press.

RACE

See Culture, Ethnicity, and Race

RACE PERFORMANCE

There are different ways in which to think about performance. One can analyze a performance in the role of the art critic, attending to self-referential aesthetics—the qualities that give form to the work produced, the quality of the performance as it measures against the artistic genre in which it is embedded, and the quality of the performers themselves. Cultural theorists, however, present a different view of performance, one based on the notion of performance as a signifier of cultural and social values, attitudes, beliefs, and behaviors. For example, one can perform race, gender, and other identities through a work of art or through everyday life. In this way, a performance can be read as a cultural text, a site for contestation and negotiation of sociocultural issues such as identity. Another use of performance concerns the ways in which it is used as a theory and research methodology. In this way, performance as an analytical concept implies that cultural phenomena will be seen and analyzed as active, fluid, and potentially transformative rather than passive or fixed. Moreover, a performance implies a context, situational acts that constitute a frame in which something can be named as a performance.

Performance Studies

In the academic field of performance studies, performance is both a subject of study and method of inquiry. Performance studies focuses on the critical analysis of performance and performativity, incorporating theories from the visual and performing arts, anthropology, cultural studies, folklore, philosophy, and sociology. The origin of performance studies has no single narrative; rather, it is constructed of multiple narratives that examine performance as ritual and social drama, performance as a speech act, performance as the presentation of self, and performance as the ongoing process of identity construction.

Whereas performance has traditionally been associated with the theatrical or with entertainment value, performance has been reconceived in more contemporary thought as a means for critical social action and for the study of how people create meaning and reinvent their own experiences in the world. Social gestures such as eating, dressing, dating, greeting, and other everyday social practices have been analyzed, as have cultural activities such as plays, operas, weddings, funerals, joke telling, and other staged or ritualized acts of performance in everyday life. Victor Turner examined these categories as well as that of social drama, which occurs when there is a break or disturbance in an otherwise expected social order. Dwight Conquergood challenged the notion of performance as theater and posited that performance studies involves imagination, inquiry, and intervention, the latter category involving activism and civic struggle for social justice.

Performance conceived as an act of intervention or activism can be seen in the work of many scholars who study elocution, speech, and literature. In his speech-act theory, J.L. Austin argued that action is performed with any utterance. Language does not only describe, it actively does something that makes a difference in the world. Whereas Austin referred to particular moments of speech, his student John R. Searle argued that whenever words are spoken, they become performative. In his critique of speech-act theory, Jacques Derrida suggested that speech acts have a history and that their repetition or reiteration (their repeated use over time) determines the effects of speech because certain meanings and intentions are recognizable through repeated use.

Against this background, the development of a concept called *performativity* can be explored as one of the critical theoretical means of exploring the performance of race identity.

Performativity

Social categories such as race, gender, age, sexuality, and ability can be framed as performative, and according to the specific context, they can be challenged, reconstituted, and transformed. Performativity refers to the ways in which subjectivity (i.e., one's own personal views, experience, or background that can be thought of constituting the self) is constructed through the norms of society yet is also a constant process of reconfiguration within existing social institutions, cultural practices, historical traditions, and power relations according to a specific individual. Performativity denotes a cultural convention that has come to define norms associated with a certain identity category (e.g., gestures, acts, speech associated with racial identity or with gender identity); thus, performativity becomes the manifestation of acts that are associated with certain identities. Identity, however, is never fixed because language, gesture, habits, and other acts are part of a social practice that is interpreted at an individual level; discourses and actions are situated within power relations and remain open for reconfiguration of alternative identities. In her theory of gendered performativity, Judith Butler identifies the concept of reiteration as a performative process that constitutes a subject while also creating a space in which subjectivity can contest and rupture existing

identity categories. Identities are constantly reproduced through repetition: People do not merely perform roles but rather, in the process of repetition, establish and destabilize identity categories such as race. The concept of performativity challenges the notion of race identity as biologically determined and instead suggests race identity is socially configured. This is an important theoretical move because it allows for the possibility of alternative performativities and identities. As a theory, performativity allows for shifts, contradictions, movement, and ruptures within existing identity categories.

Performance and Race

Much in the same way that performance has been reconsidered and reworked as a concept, definitions of race have also been revisited. One contemporary theory of race is critical race theory. Growing out of legal scholarship, critical race theory holds that racism is a normative rather than an aberrant component of U.S. society. Critical race theorists challenge the essentializing categories of race as well as gender and class. Beyond the dichotomous views of race as either culturally or biologically constructed, race is situated within a system of power relations that are deeply embedded in American life. Manning Marable defines racism as a system not only of ignorance but also of exploitation and power that are used to oppress people on the basis of ethnicity, color, culture, and behaviors.

When considered in relation to performance, and specifically to the idea of performativity, race can be understood as an identity category that is not inherent or fixed in an individual or group but rather constructed in, through, and by performances of race norms, behaviors, and traditions that have come to be expected. Individuals may continually challenge these norms, and that is where racial identity becomes a performative category rather than a stable and fixed category.

Theorists have commented on the ways in which performance is a reflexive act—that is, it facilitates an understanding of self and society. Commenting on the cultural construction of blackness, for example, cultural theorist Stuart Hall notes that it is through the ways in which people represent and imagine themselves that individuals come to understand how they are constituted.

Other scholars in the field of Black performance studies have discussed the ways in which performance has historically always been a galvanizing force for Black culture, whether it is through the reinforcement of stereotypes or through the resistance and disruption of such stereotypes through the presentation of new identities.

Examples of Performance in Visual Art

A wide range of artists have explored race identity through art-making practices. Perhaps a challenge to the concept of performance is the fact that many visual art pieces are spatially and visually static as opposed to moving and temporal—qualities that have traditionally marked the performing arts. Performance in visual art refers to the extent to which the subject matter, materials, and context of an artwork represents and, in effect, performs certain issues such as identity in interaction with the viewer. An example can be found in the work of Kara Walker. Through the use of silhouette, an art form directly associated with Victorian art, Walker's artwork explores race, gender, and sexuality by subverting the concept of portrait profile through cutouts of disturbing images that evoke the antebellum South, Black stereotypes, violence, and sexuality. In one of her works, *Darkytown Rebellion,* the artist uses overhead projectors that project colored light onto the ceiling, walls, and floor of the exhibition space, which overlay her posted silhouetted figures. This work is performative in several ways. First, this uncommon, subversive use of silhouette prompts a viewer to consider the new ways in which an artistic medium might perform in new ways and thus call attention to critical issues such as race. Second, as an audience views this particular installation, the viewer's body is cast in shadow by the projector and thus intermingles with the images affixed to the wall. In this way, one's own identity expressed via silhouette moves theatrically among Walker's images of a slavery rebellion.

Another example can be found in the work of Fred Wilson, an African American artist whose installation art challenges traditional museum exhibitions by creating new contexts and thus new meanings for exhibitions. His work challenges the ways in which art is curated and the ways in which curators present historical "truth," accuracy, artistic value, and cultural value. One of his well-known works, titled *Mining the Museum,* reexamined the Maryland Historical Society's artifact collection. In a series of installations, Wilson placed objects together to tell stories that were quite different from those usually presented in museum settings. For example, in *Metalwork 1793–1880,* he juxtaposed silver goblets and pitchers with iron slave shackles by placing them alongside each other. His *Cabinetmaking 1820–1960* presented four parlor chairs facing a wooden whipping post in the shape of a crucifix that was once used at a Maryland jail. These works can be said to be performative in that Wilson calls our attention to the display of objects in a different way. The objects take on a new identity in relation to race in the United States; they call into focus racial identity in the United States.

Creators of performance art, a genre within contemporary visual art, are more consciously concerned with the construct of performance as a means for artistic expression of issues such as identity. Growing out of the 1960s, performance art can be defined as an event that occupies a particular place and period of time, typically using the body as the artistic medium. Often, performance artists critique traditional aesthetics of the visual arts, blurring boundaries between the visual arts and performing arts and between art and everyday life. Notably, performance art allows artists and viewers to question and challenge historical, social, and cultural conventions.

Many performance artists have focused on the performance of race. James Luna, for example, critiques cultural stereotypes of Native Americans in Western museum displays. For his installation "Artifact Piece," Luna placed himself in a glass museum display case, dressed in a loincloth and laying motionless for museum-goers. The labels surrounding the display revealed his name and scars on his body attributed to drinking, thus confronting stereotypical images of the drunken American Indian and parodying images of cultural oppression of Native Americans.

The Performance of Objects

The performance of race continues to be of central concern in performance art, but there is also a history of race performance in painting, installation, sculpture, assemblage, and collage, to name a few.

The aesthetics of a work of art performs a social function. An object is made, sold, constructed, and used, and people imbue an object with meaning based on past experiences, emotions, and desires. Art objects are always in social interaction with the artist and the viewers. As such, objects can perform racial meanings, whether they connote stereotypes or new configurations of racial identity on purpose or unintentionally.

Kimberly Powell

See also Aesthetics; Cultural Studies; Culture, Ethnicity, and Race

Further Readings

Butler, J. (1990). *Gender trouble: Feminism and the subversion of identity*. New York: Routledge.

Butler, J. (1993). *Bodies that matter: On the discursive limits of sex*. New York: Routledge.

Conquergood, D. (2002). Performance studies: Interventions and radical research. *Drama Review, 46*(2), 145–156.

Garoian, C. (1999). *Performing pedagogy: Toward an art of politics*. Albany: SUNY Press.

Johnson, E. P. (2006). Black performance studies. In D. S. Madison & J. Hamera (Eds.), *The SAGE handbook of performance studies* (pp. 446–463). Thousand Oaks, CA: Sage.

Madison, D. S., & Hamera, J. (Eds.). (2006). *The SAGE handbook of performance studies*. Thousand Oaks, CA: Sage.

Schechner, R. (2002). *Performance studies: An introduction*. London: Routledge.

Turner, V. (1986). *The anthropology of performance*. New York: PAJ Books.

RACIAL CONTRACTS

Whereas John Rawls and others, in the 20th-century revival of contractualism, took the hypothetical contracts of John Locke and Immanuel Kant as models and sought to justify norms as the output of imagined choices made in designed situations of deliberation, Charles Mills seeks to recover a different, secondary strand of contractualist theory, one centering on the explanatory potential of non-ideal agreements. Such non-ideal contract theory, of which Jean-Jacques Rousseau's "Second Discourse on Inequality" is *locus classicus* and Carole Pateman's *Sexual Contract* is Mills's chief recent model, is used to explain non-ideal actuality, exposing its immorality according to norms that must be otherwise grounded. Mills says his project rests on three claims: existential—that White supremacy exists; conceptual—that White supremacy is a political system; and methodological—that White supremacy can be helpfully modeled as a contact among Whites.

The racial contract, as Mills proposes it, is political, moral, and epistemological. Mills defines the racial contract as (mostly) informal agreements among people deemed "White" (by shifting criteria) to relegate others (deemed "non-Whites" and subpersons) to inferior moral and civil status, and therein legitimizing the restriction of the normal moral and juridical rules so that they do not fully apply to Whites' interactions with non-Whites and the exploitation of non-Whites' bodies, land, and resources. At the moral and political level, the racial contract's purpose is differentially to privilege Whites by founding a racial polity. In it, all Whites benefit from the racial contract, but only most Whites are signatories/parties to it. Because the racial contract entitles and even requires Whites to govern their dealings with one another by higher standards than those it imposes on their dealings with non-Whites, Mills claims to reveal a *Herrenvolk* (master race) ethics in Kant, G. W. F. Hegel, and others usually said to champion equality. Epistemologically, Mills says the racial contract establishes an inverted epistemology, an epistemology of ignorance, and cognitive dysfunction, which blinds both Whites and non-Whites to the manifestly unjust structures whereby Whites exploit non-Whites. Mills claims that as non-ideal, the racial contract is, or at least approximates, a historical actuality. He thinks it comprises an expropriation contract, which rationalized, for example, taking lands from Native Americans; a slavery contract that purported to justify the chattel enslavement, especially of Africans and Native Americans; and a colonial contract that was used to vindicate the oppression of many Africans, Native Americans, Asians, Pacific Islanders, and others, in their own homelands.

Their agreeing to the racial contract is implicit in Whites' complicity of silence, which Mills thinks is the conceptual, juridical, and normative equivalent of signing. The racial contract is thus fundamentally an exploitation contract. The actual racial contract, unlike the older, imagined social contract, is primarily economic, though it also secures to Whites a host of psychic, social, political, and cultural privileges. For example, the racial contract rationalizes European exceptionalism and entitlement. Its economic structures work independently of individual ill will. The racial contract is also continually being rewritten, with today's de-emphasizing the supposed biological inferiority of non-Whites and stressing their cultural inferiority.

According to Mills, the racial contract "norms" and "races" space by, for example, depicting Africa as a "dark continent," its inhabitants as savage peoples, and Blacks in general as bodily driven by appetites and emotions, in contrast to Whites characterized by rational detachment, reasonableness, and self-control. Thus, political space is not the same as geographic space. Europe, conceived as the only real civilization, can be extended to other parts of the world, but colonists can "go native" by embracing savagery, and returning colonists or imported colonials can infect Europe with outposts of Asian, African, or Native American barbarism. Mills contends that the racial contract also "norms" and "races" individuals. For him, the term *Black American* is an oxymoron because an American is implicitly assumed to be White. So, the racial contract establishes both non-Whites' subpersonhood and White personhood, even as it replaces biological racism with cultural racism across three epochs of White supremacy: the period before White supremacy, that of formal and de jure White supremacy, and more recent de facto White supremacy.

Though the racial contract can mask itself by a pretended self-erasure, it provides the "real" meaning of the modern social contract, which it underwrites. Racial contract constructs its parties, just as those parties construct it, with criteria of who counts as White—criteria that shift over times and from place to place. The racial contract not only constructs some people as Whites but also constructs its victims as Black, Red, Yellow, and, sometimes, different kinds of Browns, all of whom are treated within the racial contract as inferior, as in the U.S. Jim Crow contract.

The racial contract needs and gets enforcement through violence and ideological conditioning. Thinking in terms of the racial contract, police brutality, and lynchings are revealed not as exceptions but parts of the racial contract's enforcement mechanism. Because both Whites and non-Whites must be trained not to notice the many injustices and absurdities embedded in the social system, for it to function smoothly, ideological conditioning operates as part of the racial contract's epistemology of ignorance to depreciate non-Whites' morality, intellect, beauty, cultural achievements, and their very being as humans.

Mills claims certain "naturalized" merits for thinking of recent history within the framework that the racial contract provides. First, the idea of the racial contract tracks the actual moral and political consciousness of (most) White agents. That is, it explains White psychology of brutality toward non-Whites and their subjugation. It also explains how some Whites, for example, John Brown and Bartolomé de las Casas, managed personally to repudiate the racial contract and become noble race-traitors. Second, the racial contract, in Mills's view, has always been implicitly recognized by non-Whites as what they must challenge. Thus, recent standpoint theory within epistemology, forms of cross-racial solidarity among non-Whites uniting against their moral, epistemic, aesthetic, and ontological subordination and slandering can be seen as countermeasures against a perceived but not yet theorized racial contract. Modes of non-White self-assertion, by claiming full personhood or offering cognitive resistance to racial mystification are also illuminated and captured within the idea of the racial contract. Third, Mills holds that the racial contract, as a theory, offers a superior explanation in comparison with that of the supposedly raceless social contract. Within racial contract theory, races are conceived as real existents, but as sociopolitical constructs rather than biological entities. So seen, whiteness is ultimately not a color but a set of power relations, so that Mills maintains that Black, Yellow, or Red people might have been politically White. Indeed, he thinks a Yellow racial contract is revealed in the Japanese supremacism manifest in the empire's rhetoric and conduct just before and during World War II. Tying his approach to critical race theory, Mills insists that the racial contract is a true, accurate metanarrative, repudiating deconstructionist and postmodernist claims that the truth (here, about society) cannot be known or that no justifiable means of investigation can be established.

Critics have objected to Mills's central claims on a variety of grounds. Some think the contractualist tradition, and liberalism more generally, are too stained with the racism of its developers to serve as an effective tool of critique. On the opposite side, some judge Mills too harsh in his criticism of liberalism's major classical and recent thinkers. Critics mindful of Karl Marx have held that Mills underplays the materialist role of the economic in his discussion of race relations. On the opposite side, thinkers more race-centered in their analyses worry Mills overplays the economic in a way that resembles Marxism's dismissal of race as epiphenomenal. It has also been argued that Mills vacillates between treating the racial contract as a historical actuality that causally explains race relations and, quite differently, as an imagined model to frame and organize facts. Does Mills conceive the racial contract as a contribution to social science or to normative political theory? His claims that the racial contract captures everyday Black sociopolitical thought, and that of activists, are among others that have been challenged, as well as his stringent standards for what Whites need to do to opt out of the racial contract.

J. L. A. Garcia

See also Critical Race Theory; Culture, Ethnicity, and Race; White Racial Identity

Further Readings

Garcia, J. L. A. (2001). The racial contract hypothesis. *Philosophia Africana, 4,* 27–42.

Mills, C. (1997). *The racial contract.* Ithaca, NY: Cornell University Press.

Mills, C. (2003). The "racial contract" as methodology. In C. Mills, *From class to race.* Lanham, MD: Rowman & Littlefield.

Pateman, C. (1988). *Sexual contract.* Palo Alto, CA: Stanford University Press.

Pateman, C., & Mills, C. (2007). *Contract and domination.* Cambridge, UK: Polity Press.

Rousseau, J.-J. (1964). Discourse on the origin and foundations of inequality among men. In R. D. Masters (Ed.) & R. D. Masters & J. R. Masters
(Trans.), *The first and second discourses* (pp. 77–181). New York: St. Martin's Press. (Original work published 1755)

Racial Disloyalty

Racial loyalty is conceived (on the model of patriotism) as a steadfast allegiance to one's race and faithfulness in discharging supposed obligations of duty, love, and friendship. It partially answers the questions: What do people owe? and How should people feel about their race, its other members, and their own membership within it? Tommie Shelby cites such loyalty as at the core of Black solidarity, along with trust in other Black people, special affection for them, racial pride, and shared values. Racial disloyalty, therefore, can be defined as the betrayal of this allegiance to one's race.

Demands to demonstrate racial loyalty and, conversely, accusations of disloyalty have been prominent among African Americans, whose socially disadvantaged condition and unjust treatment by Whites have made ingroup solidarity particularly urgent and birthed a variety of colorful and (often cruelly used) pejoratives including "Uncle Tom" (from Harriet Beecher Stowe's eponymous fictional slave), "Oreo" (from the sandwich cookie with a dark chocolate exterior and white cream filling), "house-slave" (from the belief that enslaved domestics were less militant than were field hands), and "Afro-Saxon." Such epithets have implications for the racial identity of those labeled.

Many charges of racial disloyalty over the past half-century have been expressions of hatred and efforts to marginalize, intimidate, and silence intellectual and political outliers. Serious conceptual and ethical inquiry into the content, presuppositions, and truth conditions of racial disloyalty and its norms is rare. Randall Kennedy, in his book *Sellout,* has begun an examination of this discourse, its motivation, assumptions, and problems. This entry further explores Kennedy's work.

Understanding Kennedy's Work on Racial Loyalty and Betrayal

Kennedy asserts every group needs to regulate and police its members. Defection, that is, having some members coerced or enticed into disloyalty by powerful social forces, is antagonistic to a socially disadvantaged group's advancement and even survival. Viewing such anxiety, and consequent attempts at regulation, as inescapable and ineradicable, he suggests epithets and charges of selling out are used to trigger ostracism within the group, making some ingroup members, in effect, into outsiders. Thus, he rejects the counsel of Stephen Carter and others who insist on freedom of discussion and debate in a future rid of charges of racial betrayal, selling out, or other conflicts of interest. Nevertheless, Kennedy is himself concerned that racial discourse wherein Black participants are ruled by fear of being labeled sellouts encourages both self-policing and self-censorship, which stifle and distort needed ingroup discussion and debate. Yet Kennedy proposes that epithets expressing anxiety over the threat of racial defection and betrayal should be used sparingly and that evidence should be both demanded and provided by the group's members.

Kennedy, a law professor, takes a legalistic approach to the problem. Rather than focusing on questions of identity (what someone is)—whether someone is a sellout, an Uncle Tom, an Oreo, or a Trojan Horse—Kennedy's emphasis is on how they act. His project is to determine whether a certain offense has been performed. To this end, he demands defining and specifying the charge (informal), procedures for challenging it and requiring the public presentation and weighing of evidence, high standards for the informal analogue of conviction, and a (perhaps implicit) presumption of innocence for the person accused.

Criticisms of Kennedy's Position

Kennedy's terminology of racial disloyalty may be criticized as problematic. Kennedy defines *sellouts* as those who betray a fundamental principle that one owes allegiance to one's social, cultural, or racial group. He defines *Black racial sellouts*, more particularly, as Blacks who knowingly or with gross negligence do something contrary to the interests of Blacks as a whole, usually for personal gain. The "sellout" is as such "bought off." Selling out must therefore be intentional, self-interested, and materialistic. More pertinently, as Kennedy stresses, the sellout must turn against what is perceived as the welfare of the race as a whole to obtain personal gain. Those who oppose programs of racial preference because they believe such programs are in some way counterproductive for Black people are not selling them out, even if their political judgment turns out to be incorrect.

Similarly, to be what some call an Oreo, a person must reject or neglect one's culture (special racial values, modes of reasoning, beliefs, preferences, customs, styles, etc., supposed to exist "inside"), maintaining only outer racial markers. This presupposes some account of specifically Black beliefs, reasoning processes, norms and values, tastes, preferences, motives, goals, and so forth. However, a critic can object that such presumptions about racial identity are dubious at best, murky in their justification as a guide, and counterproductive politically because they marginalize or exclude some from within the group. Kennedy may be correct that a sort of ostracism for embracing certain positions has a proper place even within a regime of free speech. People should be, for example, made to feel shame for advancing racist or totalitarian (e.g., Nazi) ideologies; that they do constitutes social progress. Black people may also have special moral grounds for detesting slavery and racism, or simplistic majoritarianism, because of the salience of these moral horrors in the lives of their ancestors. Still, to the skeptic, it needs to be better articulated just how the racial group benefits from—let alone, needs—anxiety over defection. (What harm does betrayal do, to which individuals, and under what circumstances?) Moreover, this benefit then needs to be shown to be so great as to justify the loss that individuals suffer from social ostracism, self-censorship, and racial intimidation. Obviously, different acts sometimes deemed betrayals will have different effects, which may not matter unless repeated. Even if a racial group were to cease to exist through cultural assimilation or intermarriage, it would need explanation: just what sort of loss or harm this would be, who would suffer it, and why it would be deemed. Other problems with free resort to the rhetoric of selling out, beyond the debate stifling that Kennedy mentions, may lurk. In this discourse, certain political positions, modes of speech, ways of dressing, or aesthetic preferences can implicitly be elevated as normative for the group, in ways that (a) privilege some subgroups (urban, younger, leftist, etc.) and depreciating others; (b) impose rigid group norms that can undermine the unity and camaraderie within a group, thus undoing the existing ingroup solidarity, the very values that racial disloyalty advocates claim to promote and charge others (or their earlier selves) with compromising; and (c) encourage and perpetuate stereotypes.

Such self-censorship, arguably, harms (sets back the welfare of) both those individuals and the group itself (and perhaps even the wider society), who need such critique. However, undue influence by powerful social forces antagonistic to a group's advancement that is clearly detrimental may partially justify a prima facie liberty to employ such self-censorship tactics. Still, that need seems chiefly to motivate and explain the inclination (or perhaps temptation) within the group to discipline and punish; it remains to be shown whether it authorizes or legitimizes such conduct. Rather, only moral considerations can generate moral responsibilities on those in the group and legitimize coercive measures of policing against them. The critique of racial disloyalty thus needs to be tied to the moral virtues in accord with human nature, to imperatives of reason, to universal human sympathy, or to other sources of moral obligation.

It is not obvious that using racial epithets against some people, even if done with a valid goal and even if legitimate, suffices to make *true* what is said therein. Assertive speech cannot be merely prudentially justified because it makes some claim about how the world is. True claims need to match reality. Kennedy expects that those inside the group will, in effect, come to the defense of those unfairly charged with racial disloyalty (by expecting other group members to challenge those who charge some group member's traitorous actions), but this may be an unrealistic expectation, because it exposes the defenders to the same charges of selling out.

The lesson of these considerations seems to be that charges of selling out should not be accepted without critical scrutiny, and challenges to them need to come from outside the group as well as from within it. As seen, this scrutiny may be subject to the charge of racial disloyalty, as the intentions of those who rise to defend a supposed sellout become the subjects of such suspicions.

This may be further reason to tightly scrutinize such rhetoric by assessing its narrow content, lest charges of selling out become self-protected, immunizing the accusers from scrutiny and critique. From this perspective, if one is to follow Kennedy's advice that the rhetoric of selling out be retained but taken more seriously, then perhaps one should first insist on narrow interpretations of such retained terms, in order to target the search for evidence, facilitate the substantiation of challenges, and preserve a presumption of innocence.

Claims of racial disloyalty need further analysis. If members of socially suppressed racial groups should feel racial loyalty, what sort of "should" judgments are essential, and how might they be justified? The explication can occur along two dimensions or types of modality. First, it can be explicated as a "should" of personal self-interest, group (self-)interest, group self-perfection (or group survival), political advantage consequence, or some moral type. Psychologist Janet Helms and nigrescence theorists hold that racial loyalty, pride, and a sense of belonging may be aspects of a Black person's mental health. Second, within the moral, any "should"-judgment needs to be specified as one of morally virtuous action, of what morally fulfills or realizes the self, of what has or brings intrinsic value, of what is admirable/supererogatory, or of interpersonal duty to the group. Sellouts described by Kennedy know they act against their race's interest, which shows limits to their concern for others of their race. That raises the question of whether they are viciously neglectful, insensitive, or uncaring toward others. Even if there is some responsibility not to avoid defection borne by all or some of those in the group, it needs to be shown when and why that ethic takes precedence over someone's other responsibilities and virtues. The widespread view that a people's race *is* their identity tends to exacerbate this problem.

What Is the Morality of Racial Solidarity?

It can be argued that Kennedy goes too far when he suggests that elite Black law students and graduates owe nothing to Black people (or, what may be different, to the U.S. Black community) and should simply go into whatever parts of the law they find fulfilling. They may reasonably see adopting the goal of racial advancement as one legitimate way of expressing justified gratitude to those forebears who worked and sacrificed in ways from which they have benefitted. Gratitude is owed to those who sacrificed to help people like oneself (e.g., civil rights pioneers who worked to break down barriers that would otherwise still be obstructing people today), and this can take the form of today's beneficiaries adopting the project of Black advancement. In contrast, efforts to ground a moral virtue (or even duty) of racial loyalty, trust, special affection, or pride in appeals to a presumed shared racial identity, or to conceiving a race as a family, may be implausible. An individual's adhering to any of what Shelby posits as Black people's shared values and goals should be justified, one by one, by independent moral considerations.

As noted earlier, for someone to undertake a project that has as its goal to become more (stereo)typically Black, Latina/o, or other, is a dubious project, securing no clear benefit even if successful. Rather, it could be harmful. Shelby suggests that poorer and less privileged Black people may be justified in demanding explicit signs of racial loyalty from the more privileged members of the group and seems to excuse, if not vindicate, anti-White race-baiting by Black demagogues as a response to this scrutiny. However, some may see that as ignoring the vocation and responsibility of intellectual and social leaders to speak truth to power, even those with the power to hurt and marginalize, whether by deploying the street idiom of "Uncle Tom," "Oreo," and "sellout"; talk of being "more Black" or "not Black enough"; or the scholarly discourse of "thick racial identity" and "authenticity." Independent individual judgment is still needed to balance the competing needs of most people. Even taking culture as tradition, a past or currently widespread belief about what benefits Black people cannot be treated as proving such claims true. Empirical fact finding and moral theorizing must be done anew. Many actions that some deem to be forms of selling out, when viewed from another perspective, represent social progress—for example, joining the police force, working in a prosecutor's office, becoming a corporate lawyer—while those who break the law are victimizing other Black people (in their reputation, if not more personally with crimes against others).

Although Kennedy may be correct that we should individually continue to think of genuine racial betrayal as immoral, rather than expecting stable success in raising standards for public "conviction" as such a traitor, there may be grounds that his legal/adversarial model for proceeding is flawed. It could be we may do better, as a practical strategy, to develop a disposition to laugh off such public charges as presumptively empty and politically motivated, thus depriving them of social power and leaving us to rely instead on internal moral compunction against real ingratitude and betrayal.

Many Black people may be expected to have a privileged perspective for seeing through this instinct to coalesce around a Black race or culture. This is potentially rife with multiple logical errors that employ moral and political justification. That is because Black people will often have knowledge and appreciation of how such theories have gone wrong in Black history, even if they have no special (racial) responsibility to acquire, deepen, perpetuate, or spread such knowledge. Still, people of every race have moral ground, rooted in the virtue of compassion and benevolence, to care for the least fortunate; rooted in the needs of comity and the common good, to help the marginalized; and, rooted in the virtue of (especially, reparative) justice, to tend to those who have been victimized.

The Rhetoric of White Racial Disloyalty

Kennedy notes that some White social thinkers take pride in proclaiming themselves "race-traitors" for repudiating and working against White supremacy. These include activists who proclaim themselves "wiggers," that is, young White people who emulate styles and speech patterns (stereo)typically associated with urban Black youth. More serious are scholars involved in the recent academic initiative Whiteness studies—studying historically and geographically variant conceptions and constructions of race, including what some pejoratively call "White trash" studies, which focus on low-income, minimally educated White people. U.S. Senator James Webb's celebratory studies of Scots–Irish people of mountain and rural Mason–Dixon line border states are notable. An earlier phenomenon that can be seen as anticipating Whiteness studies was Norman Mailer's 1957 *Dissent* magazine essay, "The White Negro," which lionized the White hipster as cultural outsider and embodiment of "an American existentialism," adapting what Mailer saw as the status of Blacks in 1950s American society. However, Mailer's appropriation has been decried as just repackaged primitivism about Black people.

Seeing it as more a matter of racial loyalty than disloyalty, Anna Stubblefield suggests that White people should see themselves as a family in such a way as to take responsibility for White racists' misconduct. Racial disloyalty presents many issues and concerns as everyday people grapple with race, regardless of their culture or race. It presumes an allegiance to an ascribed or avowed group just on the basis of being intentionally or unintentionally associated with that social group.

J. L. A. Garcia

See also Authenticity; Critical Race Theory; Patriotism; Whiteness Studies

Further Readings

Appiah, K. A. (1996). Race, culture, and identity: Misunderstood connections. In K. A. Appiah & A. Gutmann (Eds.), *Color conscious: The political reality of race* (pp. 30–105). Princeton, NJ: Princeton University Press.

Baker, H. (2008). *Betrayal: How Black intellectuals have abandoned the ideals of the civil rights era.* New York: Columbia University Press.

Carter, S. (1992). *Reflections of an affirmative action baby.* New York: Basic Books.

Helms, J. (Ed.). (1990). *Black and White racial identity theory.* New York: Praeger.

Kennedy, R. (2008). *Sellout: The politics of racial betrayal.* New York: Pantheon.

Shelby, T. (2006). *We who are dark.* Cambridge, MA: Harvard University Press.

Stubblefield, A. (2005). *Ethics across the color line.* Ithaca, NY: Cornell University Press.

RECOGNITION

See Ethics of Identity; I-Other Dialectic

REFLEXIVE SELF OR REFLEXIVITY

In the study of identity, *reflexivity* refers to the human capability of turning the attention of consciousness back upon itself—being aware of the fact that we are aware, thinking about thinking, or more mundanely, perhaps, providing accounts of our selves. The concept of the reflexive self was developed most extensively by the British sociologist Anthony Giddens in the 1990s, though other prominent social theorists with an interest in identity, such as Margaret Archer, Zygmunt Bauman, and Ulrich Beck, have approached reflexivity in different ways. It has become an important and controversial concept in the contemporary sociology and social psychology of identity, used by Giddens and others to elucidate what are perceived to be changes in the relationship between contemporary social structures and people's intimate sense of self.

Giddens's model of selfhood consists of three components: the unconscious, practical consciousness, and self-reflexivity. The realm of the unconscious is of primary importance for the development of self—identity as it is here where relationships of basic trust are initiated. The experience of trust at an unconscious level in infancy provides the individual with a secure orientation toward the world that protects her or him from engulfment when threats to identity inevitably come. But the ontological demand (i.e., demands associated with people's being and existence in the world) for relative order and constancy in the reality of everyday life cannot be met in infancy or at the level of unconscious trust alone; the routine ability to go on in everyday life without being overwhelmed by uncertainty and anxiety is lodged at the level of practical consciousness—a stock of learned knowledge that has become second nature or taken for granted but is nonetheless potentially available to the reflexive scrutiny. Practical consciousness effectively answers existential questions in the doing of everyday life, without them having to be pored over and contemplated at the level of reflexive awareness. Different cultural contexts and traditions consecrate trust in the coherence of everyday life through any number of possible symbolic answers to the existential questions that underpin experience. The success of practical consciousness in defending the self against overwhelming anxiety thus appears dependent upon the viability of traditions to allow subjectivity a relatively unquestioned passage through the trials of life. The final aspect of self-identity is reflexivity, understood as a universal human capability. Any awareness of self *as a self* of some form or another is, by definition, a reflexive feat. Reflexive awareness is the universal vehicle through which we fully constitute and maintain the identity of a self and sustain awareness of it as a distinct and propertied entity.

Traditional and Posttraditional Societies

Although self-reflexivity is considered ubiquitous in this model, the novelty of recent conceptualizations of reflexivity lie in the claim that it is only in posttraditional societies that the self becomes a genuinely reflexive project. This claim rests, in turn, upon an account of the nature of recent social changes and the impact they have upon Gibbons's tripartite model of self. Giddens's account of social change hinges in part on what is considered to be a decisive break with tradition. It is claimed that traditions once provided people with fairly rigid and temporally constant points through which to navigate a sense of self and thus facilitated self-reflexivity within fairly narrow existential parameters; narrow because much of what might be questioned is effectively answered by the givens of tradition. The prescriptive nature of traditional rituals, routines, and beliefs went largely unquestioned and combined forcibly with the chronic localization of most people's experience to bind one's sense of identity. For Giddens, Beck, and others, this past extends right up until the post–World War II period, before which modernity was in thrall to the traditions it had created or inherited from the Enlightenment, a period and philosophical movement beginning in 18th-century Europe and associated with the rise of rational discourse, scientific thinking, and political ideologies such as republicanism and liberalism. For Giddens, Beck, and others, modernist identities were prescribed by traditional institutions of nationality, class, family, sexuality, and intimacy. Although the Enlightenment was premised upon radical doubt, it is argued that these institutions

continued to structure people's identities in relatively unquestioned ways—functioning just as traditions had done in traditional societies and therefore allowing but limiting the scope of self-reflexivity. Numerous social changes are now argued to have propelled individual's experience of themselves out of the orbit of tradition.

Prominent among these changes are factors commonly associated with late 20th-century and early-21st-century globalization. Rapid technological developments in communication, travel, and finance have led to an increase in the traffic of human activity in its broadest and most varied sense. If the power of tradition in shaping identity lies, as Giddens asserts, from it not being consciously understood *as* tradition, then the increasing exposure of humans to humans with other ideas, behaviors, and collective ways of doing things works against such an understanding of any tradition.

As a consequence of the dynamism of social changes touched upon briefly here, the institutions through which social relations are organized and defined are no longer held in stasis by any unifying external criteria. What replaces stability is a constant, chronic reflexive approach to knowledge and practice. These changes are argued to have a profound impact upon the structure of the self, the upshot of which is an extension of reflexivity at the level of self-identity. In such a world, we find it increasingly difficult to build our life stories according to the taken-for-granted knowledge stocks of practical consciousness previously provided by traditions. Instead, we develop our own narratives, and our accounting for ourselves is marked by a pervasive reflexivity. Theorists differ substantially in considering how such an extension of reflexivity is experienced and what its implications are for the future, but there is a general consensus that individual identities are increasingly marked by self-reflexivity at the expense of taken-for-granted knowledge. As a consequence, ontological security (basic security about the conditions, routines, and circumstances of life and existence) is, at the very least, at risk. At the heart of more nuanced theorization, there is a tendency to view the situation as a *dilemma* for the self. On the one hand, there is a certain liberation and sense of mastery in being able, required even, to have more choice in the way we fashion our relations to others and in developing our own biographical trajectory. On the other hand, such a situation is fraught with anxieties and uncertainties—which may stretch as far as unconscious anxieties over the constancy and permanence of relationships with others—basic trust. For Giddens, at least, the balance is tipped toward the positive, as we can increasingly establish the character of our identity through reflexively made choices, heralding the emergence of "the reflexive project of the self," as it is commonly referred to by Giddens.

Giddens, Beck, and Bauman pursued the conceptualization of reflexivity theoretically rather than empirically. Empirical investigation into the role of reflexivity in contemporary identities has since gained some momentum, however. Numerous studies based on interview data have offered qualified support for the claim that self-reflexivity is a contemporary organizing principle of identities in relation to specific areas such as reincarnation, emotional labor, and television viewing, qualifications based on the persistence of structuring principles such as gender, class, and nationality. Onetime interview studies do not reveal much about changes over time in general, so they cannot inform debates over the supposed extension of reflexivity. Neither can they tell us much about the role of reflexivity in structuring life chances and choices that underpin the realization of "projects of selfhood." Longitudinal studies researchers interested in these issues have tended to view reflexivity as a partial and piecemeal phenomenon, and discussions have been much more ambivalent about the material impact of extended reflexivity, where there is evidence of it, having a transformative effect upon people's lives. A stronger case is made in such studies that social structure still underpins identities in differential ways, feeding into some aspects of the critical reception with which claims of extended self-reflexivity have been greeted.

Critique

Criticism of the conceptualization of heightened self-reflexivity has developed out of a number of concerns stemming from a core issue: the apparent neglect of the contextualized, specific, and situated nature of the construction and maintenance of identity. Critique has centered on the ways in which the reflexive capacities of identity are always

already physically embodied (e.g., habitus) and socially embedded, encouraging a reemphasis on the cultural, material, and affective parameters of identity formation. In assigning an increased perspicuity to the contemporary reflexive self, there is a danger in losing sight of the ways in which reflexivity emerges from a complex interface of socially and culturally stratified (e.g., classed) contexts, dynamic interpersonal relations, and psychodynamics. These contexts shape not only the way choices become reflexively known and acted upon but also the forms of reflexivity through which the self engages with, and is constituted through, social reality.

The structural bases for the differentiation of reflexivity are argued to emerge out of more nuanced symptoms of the very social changes claimed to underpin its universal extension: a decline in collective labor power; the international division of, and competition for, labor; the rise of a workforce with little legal protection; and socially differentiated technological advancement, including surveillance technology. Via these structures, beneficially situated groups and individuals are able to consolidate and create new forms of knowledge and power embedded in cosmopolitanism and embodied in forms of heightened reflexivity, but it is claimed to be a partial reflexivity, not least in terms of the unequal structural base of privilege on which it rests. On the other hand, reflexivity accompanying states of extreme poverty may only bring some the starkness of the paucity of life chances available and the relative prosperity of others, whose lifestyles are made increasingly proximate through aforementioned changes and yet are out of reach. The end result is the critical claim that the conceptualization of extended reflexivity thesis relies on an excessively voluntarist notion of the individual agent.

The concept of reflexivity has been central in reinvigorating debates over the relationship between structure and agency in social theories of identity. It has been particularly useful in addressing specific social changes and, particularly in Giddens's work, remarkably adept as a cornerstone concept in metatheorization of the interrelationship of psychological and social dynamics. Empirical support for the concept has been qualified, and criticism has cast doubt on the universal applicability of the notion of heightened reflexivity as a response to social change. There is still a great deal of potential, however, in tracing the paths of reflexivity as it confronts traditional props of identity, where as a phenomenon its positive transformative power, however elusive, is in some senses and on some occasions welcomed as very real.

Matthew Adams

See also Class; Gender; Habitus; Narratives; Ontological Insecurity; Self; Self-Concept; Self-Consciousness; Society and Social Identity

Further Readings

Adams, M. (2007). *Self and social change.* London: Sage.

Adkins, L. (2003). Reflexivity: Freedom or habit of gender? *Theory, Culture & Society, 20*(6), 21–42.

Alexander, J. (1996). Critical reflections on "reflexive modernization." *Theory, Culture & Society, 13*(4), 133–138.

Beck, U., Giddens, A., & Lash, S. (1994). *Reflexive modernization.* Cambridge, UK: Polity Press.

Giddens, A. (1991). *Modernity and self-identity.* Cambridge, UK: Polity Press.

Giddens, A. (1992). *The transformation of intimacy.* Cambridge, UK: Polity Press.

Plumridge, L., & Thomson, R. (2003). Longitudinal qualitative studies and the reflexive self. *International Journal of Social Research Methodology, 6*(3), 213–222.

Threadgold, S., & Nilan, P. (2009). Reflexivity of contemporary youth, risk and cultural capital. *Current Sociology, 57*(1), 47–68.

REGULATORY FOCUS THEORY

The hedonic principle that people approach pleasure and avoid pain has been the dominant motivational principle for centuries. But is this principle enough? What if there are different ways to approach pleasure and avoid pain, and, if there are, might this tell us something about motivation that is as important as the hedonic principle itself? Regulatory focus theory proposes that there are, indeed, distinct systems for regulating pleasure and pain and these distinct systems create fundamentally different ways of experiencing and dealing with the world. Identity studies interacts with regulatory focus theory through the motivations that underlie selection of particular regulatory focus strategies of an individual or group. The process of identity development is shaped as different choices or different ways to proceed on a task result from differing systems for regulating pleasure and pain.

Regulatory focus theory begins with an evolutionary perspective on motivation. Like other animals, people need both nurturance and security to survive; they need support or nourishment from the environment and they need protection from dangers in the environment. The theory proposes that two distinct regulatory systems have developed to deal with each of these distinct survival concerns. Both systems involve approaching pleasure and avoiding pain, but the type of pleasure and the type of pain experienced in these two systems are different, as are the mechanisms and strategies that underlie the self-regulation. Regulatory focus theory emphasizes the motivational and emotional significance of the differences between these systems in *how* the hedonic principle unfolds.

Regulatory focus theory associates the nurturance motive with the development of *promotion focus* concerns with accomplishment, with fulfilling hopes and aspirations (ideals). It associates the security motive with the development of *prevention focus* concerns with safety, with meeting duties and obligations (oughts). People can succeed or fail to fulfill either their promotion concerns or their prevention focus concerns, but the consequences of success or failure in these two systems are not the same. When people have a promotion focus, they experience cheerfulness-related emotions following success (e.g., happy, joyful) and dejection-related emotions following failure (e.g., sad, discouraged). In contrast, when people have a prevention focus, they experience quiescence-related emotions following success (e.g., calm, relaxed) and agitation-related emotions following failure (e.g., nervous, tense). Individuals with a promotion focus also appraise objects and events along a cheerfulness–dejection dimension more readily than along a quiescence–agitation dimension, whereas the opposite is true for individuals with a prevention focus.

If we think of a current satisfactory state of self-regulation as being neutral or the status quo, signified by 0 (zero), then the promotion and prevention systems can be distinguished in terms of which kind of change from 0 is the predominant concern. The promotion focus system is concerned with creating change from 0 to +1, whereas the prevention focus system is concerned with stopping change from 0 to −1. The promotion system is more concerned with advancement and attainment (gains), whereas the prevention system is more concerned with security and maintenance (non-losses). These different concerns translate into different preferences for which strategies to use when pursuing goals. Individuals with a promotion focus prefer to use *eager* strategies to pursue goals—strategies of advancement (a gain) that move the actor to a more positive state. In contrast, individuals with a prevention focus prefer to use *vigilant* strategies to pursue goals (a non-loss)—strategies of carefulness that stop the actor from moving to a negative state.

This difference in strategic preferences contributes to the regulatory focus difference in emotional experiences from success and failure. When individuals succeed in a promotion focus, it increases their eagerness (experienced as high-intensity joy). In contrast, when individuals succeed in a prevention focus, it reduces their vigilance (experienced as low-intensity calmness). When individuals fail in a promotion focus, it reduces their eagerness (experienced as low-intensity sadness). In contrast, when individuals fail in a prevention focus, it increases their vigilance (experienced as high-intensity nervousness). This regulatory focus difference influences postperformance expectations as well. After success on an initial trial of a task, individuals with a promotion focus raise their expectations for the next trial more than do individuals with a prevention focus because optimism increases eagerness (a promotion fit) but reduces vigilance (a prevention non-fit). After failure on an initial trial, individuals with a prevention focus lower their expectations for the next trial more than do individuals with a promotion focus because defensive pessimism increases vigilance (a prevention fit) but reduces eagerness (a promotion non-fit).

Regulatory focus differences in strategic preferences have significant effects under conditions where there is a conflict between different choices or different ways to proceed on a task. When people are uncertain, they can take a chance and accept something as true, thereby risking an error of commission. Alternatively, they can be cautious and reject something as true. Studies on memory and judgment have found that individuals with a promotion focus are generally more "risky" than those in a prevention focus (as long as the current state is satisfactory). Promotion-focused individuals are more willing than prevention-focused individuals to consider new alternatives under conditions of uncertainty rather than simply sticking with the known (albeit satisfactory) current state of affairs. They are also more creative and are more willing to change and try something new when given the opportunity. The trade-off, however, is that prevention-focused individuals are more committed to their choices and thus stick to them even when obstacles arise.

There is also evidence that promotion-focused individuals emphasize speed more than accuracy, whereas prevention-focused individuals emphasize accuracy more than speed. In addition, promotion-focused individuals are more likely to represent objects and events in a global and abstract manner than in a local and concrete manner, whereas the opposite is true for those with a prevention focus. Other studies have found that the nature of the classic ingroup versus outgroup bias varies by regulatory focus. For individuals with a promotion focus, ingroup members are treated with a positive bias ("promoting us"), but there is little bias regarding outgroup members. In contrast, for individuals with a prevention focus, outgroup members are treated with a negative bias ("preventing them"), but there is little bias regarding ingroup members.

All of these emotional and motivational differences between promotion and prevention are found not only when regulatory focus is a chronic individual difference (a *personality* variable) but also when regulatory focus is a momentary, situationally induced difference (a *situation* variable). Moreover, specific individuals can be chronically high in *both* promotion and prevention, with different situations making either their promotion or prevention dominate. As either a personality or situation variable, regulatory focus affects people's experiences of the world and how they get along within it.

E. Tory Higgins

See also Psychology of Self and Identity; Self; Self-Discrepancy Theory; Self-Perception Theory

Further Readings

Crowe, E., & Higgins, E. T. (1997). Regulatory focus and strategic inclinations: Promotion and prevention in decision making. *Organizational Behavior and Human Decision Processes, 69*, 117–132.

Higgins, E. T. (1998). Promotion and prevention: Regulatory focus as a motivational principle. In M. P. Zanna (Ed.), *Advances in experimental social psychology* (Vol. 30, pp. 1–46). New York: Academic Press.

Shah, J., Higgins, E. T., & Friedman, R. (1998). Performance incentives and means: How regulatory focus influences goal attainment. *Journal of Personality and Social Psychology, 74*, 285–293.

RELIGIOUS IDENTITY

Religious identity describes how a person or group understands, experiences, shapes, and is shaped by the psychological, social, political, and devotional facets of religious belonging or affiliation. There has not yet emerged a unifying theory of religious identity, but the plurality contained within the category has occasioned psychological, sociological, and political, as well as philosophical, theological, and tradition-centered, accounts of religious identity. As objects of academic inquiry, religion and religious practices can be the subject of functional or substantive approaches. Scholars with a functional approach understand religion as performing a social, cultural, psychological, or political function. Those advocating substantive definitions of religion, on the other hand, investigate religion, including beliefs, rituals, and institutions, for the sake of understanding what constitutes religion. Adherents of functional approaches are interested in what religion *does,* whereas adherents of substantive definitions are interested in what religious *is.*

This entry reviews functional approaches to religious identity that examine psychology and identity formation, the sacralization of identity, religious identity among multiple identities, and religious identity and politics. To demonstrate substantive approaches to religious identity, the entry discusses the emergence of secularity as forming Western identity, the negotiation of the universal and particular in religious identity, and religious identity in interreligious dialogue.

Functional Approaches to Religious Identity

The following selection of approaches indicates what religious identity does, whether it alleviates a potential identity crisis, shapes a person's sense of place in social order, or provides resources for responding to political events.

Psychology and Identity Formation

In his theory of the eight stages of psychosocial development, Erik Erikson identified religion as an important resource for identity formation. Each of Erikson's stages is marked by a conflict between a polarity that, when negotiated, results in the person recognizing an attendant virtue. For example, the infant stage is marked by a conflict between trust and mistrust that is resolved in hope, whereas an early childhood stage that shifts between industry and inferiority results in competence. Erikson concluded that in order to negotiate each stage successfully, a person must hold the elements of each polarity in tension, rather than rejecting either.

The fifth stage, fidelity, addresses a person's teenage years, which are lived along a polarity of identity and role confusion. In these years, a person self-consciously asks questions like "Who am I?" "Who do people think I am?" and "How do I fit in?" To successfully negotiate the fifth stage, a person needs to develop an identity that steadfastly coheres to an ideology. Identity and ideology are linked, according to Erikson, for ideology provides a way to make sense of life and a worldview coherent enough to inspire a person's total commitment—or fidelity—and to allay identity confusion. Erikson pointed out that the kind of questions an adolescent typically asks in the fidelity stage (e.g., "Who am I?") often leads to questions about a transcendent, such as "Is there an ultimate arbiter of which identities are authentic?" or "Is there one transcendent meaning that subsumes disparate identities?"

Religion may also provide the source of ideology, a necessary ingredient for adolescent identity construction. Erikson offered Mohandas Gandhi and Martin Luther as two examples of people who underwent identity crises that were finally resolved when religion provided an ideological anchor for identity. Erikson depicted Luther as torn between his father's expectations for him to be a lawyer and his own desire to become a monk. When Luther contravened his earthly father's wishes and joined a monastery, he discovered his identity as the son of the heavenly Father. Similarly, Erikson discussed Gandhi's discovery of Hindu and Jain teaching when he was in his early 20s as providing him with the resources he would use to take a nonviolent stand against colonialism in South Africa and India. Although Erikson comes close to collapsing religion with ideology, he emphasized the capacity of religion to be the object of fidelity and thus an important resource for identity formation.

Sacralization of Identity

In his sociological theory of religious identity, Hans Mol considered identity as a sort of religion. Mol claimed that people have an irrepressible need for a strong and reassuring identity and that religion can meet this need. What all religions have in common, according to Mol, is that they produce and sacralize identity. Mol was careful to point out, however, that not all activities that are identity-producing are also religious. For example, work, play, and daily routines may produce identities, but these are not religious ones.

Identity is a fundamental human need and religion is the institution *par excellence* that helps human beings realize this need. Mol began his investigation of identity by recounting the work of animal behaviorists who define identity as an animal's place in the social order. In this sense, an animal's identity determines his place in the group's hierarchy, which in turn determines his relationship with other animals, responsibility to defend territory, and so on. While human animals are advanced symbol makers who can articulate their place in social order in different ways, they retain a primordial need for identity, which defines their place in the group. At the heart of Mol's conception of the sacralization of identity is a dialectical movement between adaptation and identity, differentiation and integration. To exemplify these dynamics, Mol compared religious identity formation to an oyster absorbing grains of sand, for both must incorporate diverse elements and transform them into something integral.

Mol identified four mechanisms that sacralize identity: objectification, commitment, ritual, and myth. Objectification is a process that puts various elements of worldly existence into an orderly and timeless frame of reference. Commitment refers to the emotional commitment that a person feels as a result of identity. Mol underscored the importance of this emotional experience of attachment as a way to confirm a specific identity against competing claims to meaning. Ritual maximizes order and reinforces bonds between an individual and the community. Ritual can also do the important work of restoring identity when disruptions occur. Myths, as a central feature of religious life, are interpretations of reality and in so being, they have the power to reaffirm social and personal identity. Mol's four mechanisms indicate that religious identity formation is a dynamic process that contributes to a basic human need of articulating a person's place in the social order. Mol did not focus on historical examples in particular religious traditions but anticipated a contemporary understanding of religious identity as emerging from an ongoing process of negotiation.

Religious Identity Among Multiple Identities

According to sociologist Nancy Ammerman, much of turn-of-the-millennium theorizing about identity has ignored religious identity or relegated religion to the margins of mainstream culture, as something that it is shaped in religious institutions or in private. Ammerman theorized religious identity as intertwined with the multiplicity of solidarities and entanglements in which a person necessarily exists, including race, class, sexuality, and ability, among others. Ammerman specified religious identity as the strand of identity that directly or indirectly invokes the coparticipation of sacred others.

Following social theory that addresses the problem of agency and structure in identity formation, Ammerman asked whether religious identity is formed by powerful others, particularly religious institutions, or whether a person is an agent in the creation of his or her own religious identity. The answer, according to Ammerman, is both. Agency describes a person's ability to employ symbolic and material resources that guide patterns of behavior. Agency does not mean a person is free of these patterns, but rather that the person can mobilize them in new or alternative ways. Ammerman confirmed that each social encounter provides the possibility for shaping our identity as we negotiate our multiple entanglements in an ongoing process of revision and innovation.

Religious institutions are most often cited as the structures that play a role in religious identity formation. They provide narratives through which an individual can understand his or her identity, for example, as redeemed, one who has surrendered, or as a member of the Buddha's family. Myths, rituals, shared meals, and music provide material opportunities for a person to confirm and rehearse aspects of his or her religious identity. But Ammerman insisted that religious identity is never simply limited to a religious institution or kept within the confines of the private. Instead, religious narratives and practices appear in mass media, political campaigns, and the workplace, among other locations. The construction of religious identities is a dynamic process, in which a person is shaped by, and shapes, intersecting identities. Religious identity cannot simply be willed by the individual, nor is it available at an unchanging core of a specific religious tradition. Ammerman concluded that religious identity is the result of an ongoing and fluid negotiation of dominant narratives, institutional authority, and individual agency.

Religious Identity and Politics

In his influential 1993 essay "The Clash of Civilizations," Samuel Huntington argued that cold war divisions between West and East no longer had the power to shape international politics. In their place, Huntington posited that so-called civilizational divisions would be the fault lines for future conflicts. Huntington identified eight major civilizations as the broadest level of identification a person can have. Huntington connected civilizations to religion; for example, he identified Islamic, Hindu, Slavic Orthodox, and Western (where it suggests Christian) identities. Huntington famously predicted that the most important fault line was between "the West" and "Islam" and it was along this line that future conflicts would be fought. Huntington's article emerged just before conflict in the Balkans erupted and was cast by some readers as prescient of a new world order: Here on the border between, according to Huntington, the West and Islam was a region that was seemingly ripped apart by civilizational differences.

Nobel Prize–winning economist Amartya Sen disputed that Huntington's civilizational identity was useful to identify a person's political or social commitments. Huntington's civilizational approach reduces a person to one dimension, argued Sen, and misunderstands religious identity as univocal. For example, Islam has adherents all over the world and the meaning of a person's religious identity may differ whether the person lives in Los Angeles, Kuala Lumpur, or Lagos. Huntington's premise that religious identities posit the fault lines between civilizations masks historical communication and collaboration between adherents of different religious traditions. Furthermore, Sen pointed out, each person has multiple identities and the relative importance of a select identity can change depending on the context or the person's priorities in changing circumstances.

Lori Peek offered specific insight into how the salience attached to religious identity can be modified in response to political events. Peek focused on the religious identities of college-age Muslim American students in the United States after September 11, 2001. Peek discovered that the students' sense of religious identity became more important in the wake of growing anti-Muslim sentiment in the United States. She identified three stages of religious identity development: religion as ascribed identity, religion as chosen identity, and religion as declared identity.

Religion as ascribed identity describes the religious identity of the majority of her subjects in their childhoods. Most of Peek's subjects were born into Muslim homes and raised as Muslims. They reported that religious identity was part of their everyday lives and not something on which they reflected often. Some of Peek's subjects reported having been stigmatized as adolescents, and many responded by casting their religious identity aside in an effort to assimilate into mainstream U.S. culture. Once her subjects reached college age, however, they became aware of their ability to choose their own religious identity. A religious identity that had been ascribed from their upbringing and their families' religious practices now was an identity that the majority of her subjects claimed for themselves and became, therefore, a chosen identity.

Peek described that following 9/11, one third of her subjects developed a strong sense of religious identity in response to the crisis. As many Americans did, this group of Peek's subjects turned to their religious identity for reflection and reassurance. In response to rising anti-Muslim sentiment in the United States, many students made an effort to learn more about Islam, which in turn strengthened their sense of religious identity. This group of students declared publicly their religious identity, for example, by wearing Muslim attire. Peek concluded that hers is not a universal model for religious identity formation but that her research points to how individual identity can shift over time. Peek's research indicates how a political crisis can motivate a shift in identity salience, the idea that one kind of identity may become more important than others at a particular time.

Substantive Approaches to Religious Identity

The following selection of substantive approaches indicate what religious identity is—whether it is a transformation into secular identity, a negotiation of the universal and the particular, or a dynamic, syncretic process.

Secularity and Western Identity

Charles Taylor is a philosopher whose expansive oeuvre of writing addresses the historical development of the modern self in the West. In *A Secular Age*, Taylor connected the development of Western identity to negotiation of religious identity. He challenged two extant meanings of secularity, as either the evacuation of any reference to God or the transcendent from our public spaces or as a general withering of religious belief and church attendance. These accounts are not robust enough to describe our current situation, Taylor insisted, for the rise of modernity is not merely a story of loss or subtraction. The organizing question of *A Secular Age* is how it was virtually impossible not to believe in God in the 1500s, whereas in the 21st century, religious identity is one option among many. Taylor proposed a third meaning of secularity that traces the redirection of meaning from transcendence to immanence.

At the heart of Taylor's investigation is the Reform Master Narrative, his moniker for a centuries-long process of reform that occasioned an anthropocentric turn in Christian theology, philosophy, art, and politics. This kind of religious reform and its attendant leveling of social roles prompted a drive to reorder society. A sense that people can sustain the order on their own occasioned secularity. Modern philosophy responded through Kant's articulation of inner sources of morality, signaling a shift from a worldview in which our highest spiritual and moral aspirations pointed to the transcendent to one in which "fullness" is available solely in immanent terms. Western, or secular, identity is, therefore, the result of a redirection of the source of meaning. Whereas Western identity used to be oriented toward transcendence, modernity has occasioned a reorientation toward immanence. There are necessarily shortcomings in Taylor's metanarrative, but his sprawling account of modern identity provided an innovative way of understanding secularity as transformed, rather than forsaken, religious identity.

Religious Identity as a Negotiation of Universal and Particular

A metaphysical distinction between the universal and the particular has shaped Jewish and Christian models of religious identity. This section discusses three examples of how this distinction is negotiated.

A Christian theologian, Miroslav Volf, drew his account of religious identity in part from a passage in Paul's Letter to the Galatians: "There is no longer Jew or Greek, there is no longer slave or free, there is no longer male and female; for all of you are one in Christ Jesus" (Gal. 3:28, *New Revised Standard Version*). According to Volf, this text acknowledges that selves are situated in more than one identity at a time; for example, a person can be both Greek and female or slave and male. Volf developed an account of religious identity to model how reconciliation among different identities is possible, especially in light of the great inhumanities of the 20th century. Volf wrote at the end of a bloody century of battles not only over ideology but also over identities. As he wrote, genocidal policies were undertaken in the name of identity in his native Croatia and neighboring nations in the former Yugoslavia. Volf concluded that for a Christian, identity means a change in loyalty from particular identities to a universal identity in Christ. This kind of religious identity necessitates privileging a transcendental ideal over historical identities, or of the universal over the particular.

Using the same Pauline text, Daniel Boyarin developed a model of religious identity that holds the universal in tension with the particular. As a Jewish scholar of Rabbinical Judaism, Boyarin argued that contemporary Jews have a lot to learn from Paul, an ancient Jew who understood himself as undertaking a Jewish revival. Boyarin read Paul as grappling with questions about identity that are familiar to contemporary readers, such as whether identities are valuable or if they get in the way of universal community. In Paul's claim that in Christ there is "neither Jew or Greek, free or slave, male and female," Boyarin interpreted a radical call for a nonhierarchical, nondifferentiated humanity. Boyarin noted that in the ancient Roman Empire, as remains the case today, community has organized along hierarchies of nationality, class, and gender. Paul recognized these distinctions and advocated that in the community of saints (an ancient term for Jesus's followers), the distinctions no longer mattered.

Boyarin credited Paul with wanting to overcome hierarchies that should have no bearing on a person's membership in community. But Boyarin resisted what he interpreted as Paul's related call for a nondifferentiated humanity, a community where differences between people are no longer valued. Boyarin wanted to maintain the distinctiveness of his Jewish identity, even as he aspired for a community that resists hierarchy. Contra Paul (and Volf), Boyarin insisted that a sense of identity that values a universal equality should also value particularity in the form of national, gender, and religious differences. Boyarin promoted a religious identity that holds the universal promise of equality in tension with a valuation of differences.

Womanist ethicist Stacey Floyd-Thomas similarly maintained a tension between the universal and the particular in religious identity when she attested that traditional universality emerges from reflection on the particularities of African American women's experiences. Drawing from Alice Walker's definition of womanism, Floyd-Thomas explained how womanist ethics asserts a traditional universality in reference to Walker's description of blackness as containing a multiplicity of colors. This kind of Black identity points to the universal by resisting dominant accounts of monochromatic blackness. Walker's emphasis on Black women's moral agency is adopted by womanist ethicists as a guide to resist dominating structures of oppression and to recognize Black foremothers' efforts to do the same.

Floyd-Thomas advocated a diasporic identity as a means to redefine identity away from exclusion and marginalization and toward liberation. She argued that traditional universality is available only through investigations of the particular, in this case through the remembering and chronicling of Black women's experiences of, and resistance to, the social evils of racism, classism, and sexism. Only through contextual, material, and historical investigations of Black women's identities can womanist ethics contribute to the universal task of liberation. It is in the particularities of identities, therefore, that the universal is available.

Religious Identity in Interreligious Dialogue

An ongoing dialogue between Buddhists and Christians provides a syncretic model of religious identity. An exemplary discussant is Thich Nhat Hanh, a Zen Buddhist monk originally from Vietnam. Nhat Hanh operates a monastery and retreat center in France for those who want to learn more about Buddhism. Nhat Hanh not only encourages non-Buddhists to learn and practice the Dharma, or the Buddha's teaching, he also insists that it is important for people to be (re)rooted in their own traditions. According to Nhat Hanh, religious identity is shaped by a person's culture, upbringing, and life journey and should not be hastily abandoned. Instead, a person should become an instrument for compassion and change in the person's own tradition. Nhat Hanh uses rootedness as a metaphor for religious identity, but he suggests that a person may grow roots in more than one tradition. He offers his own religious identity as an example. He grew up and was trained in Zen and so considers the Buddha to be his spiritual ancestor, but years of dialogue and shared practice with Christians has helped him to become rooted in the Christian tradition and to recognize Jesus to be his spiritual ancestor as well. For Nhat Hanh, this religious identity is not contradictory, because he insists that every religious identity necessarily contains a plurality. The historical development of each religious tradition has meant the appropriation of various elements from many different sources.

Buddhist scholar Jeffrey Carlson responded to Nhat Hanh with a theory of religious identity as syncretic. Religious identity is a dynamic process that entails selecting, appropriating, and internalizing elements from a wide array of possibilities, even if a person understands himself or herself as developing his or her religious identity out of the resources of a single tradition. According to Carlson, religious identity is a composite of diverse elements brought together in the midst of cultural and linguistic frames that both limit and make identity possible. To characterize religious identity as syncretic discourages any claim to an unchanging or pure religious identity that represents a distinct tradition's presumed best lights. A syncretic religious identity is attuned to how religious traditions emerge in historical processes that cannot be circumscribed to absent other religious and philosophical roots and ongoing influences. A religious identity that draws sharp distinctions between itself and other religious traditions will likely miss, therefore, the plurality that exists within its own tradition and overlook resources to sustain and strengthen religious identity.

Sarah Azaransky

See also Identity Salience; Political Identity; Psychology of Self and Identity; Syncretism; Womanism

Further Readings

Ammerman, N. T. (2003). Religious identities and religious institutions. In M. Dillon (Ed.), *Handbook of the sociology of religion* (pp. 207–224). New York: Cambridge University Press.

Boyarin, D. (1994). *A radical Jew: Paul and the politics of identity.* Berkeley: University of California Press.

Carlson, J. (2000). Pretending to be Buddhist and Christian: Thich Nhat Hanh and the two truths of religious identity. *Buddhist-Christian Studies, 20,* 115–125.

Erikson, E. (1962). *Young man Luther: A study in psychoanalysis and history.* New York: W. W. Norton.

Floyd-Thomas, S. (2006). *Mining the motherlode: Methods in womanist ethics.* Cleveland, OH: Pilgrim Press.

McCarus, E. (Ed.). (1994). *The development of Arab-American identity.* Ann Arbor: University of Michigan Press.

Mol, H. (1976). *Identity and the sacred: A sketch for a new social-scientific theory of religion.* Oxford, UK: Blackwell.

Nhat Hanh, T. (1995). *Living Buddha, living Christ.* New York: Riverhead Books.

Peek, L. (2005). Becoming Muslim: The development of a religious identity. *Sociology of Religion, 66,* 215–242.

Pinn, A. (2003). *Terror and triumph: The nature of Black religion.* Minneapolis, MN: Augsburg Fortress.

Sen, A. (2002, June). Civilizational imprisonments: How to misunderstand everyone in the world. *New Republic, 226,* 28–33.

Volf, M. (1996). *Exclusion and embrace: A theological exploration of identity, otherness, and reconciliation.* Nashville, TN: Abingdon Press.

RENAISSANCE ART

Renaissance art includes a variety of media and genres, falling into the major categories of painting, sculpture, works on paper, objects, and architecture. The first four categories can be further subdivided into panel painting, frescoes, oil painting, portraits, genre scenes, sculpture-in-the-round (ranging from monumental to miniature), reliefs, altarpieces, coins, drawings, prints, illuminated manuscripts, printed books, tapestries, jewelry, works in bronze, stone, ivory, and wood, and domestic objects such as dinnerware, clocks, and marriage chests (*cassoni*). Architecture in the Renaissance includes sacred buildings—cathedrals, monasteries, churches, and chapels; civic structures—town halls (often called *palazzi* in Italy), piazzas, buildings with courts and prisons, loggias, and bridges; and other secular and domestic architecture—villas, personal houses (also known as *palazzi*), gardens, and grottoes. The Renaissance began as an Italian phenomenon, in which humanists and artists believed they were effecting a "rebirth" of classical Greco-Roman art and life. Thus, many of the art forms (e.g., monumental sculpture) are related to classical counterparts. As the Renaissance spread throughout the Italian peninsula and Europe, it was affected by differing governments and socioreligious movements, local aesthetic traditions, and available material, as well as new technologies. The Italian Renaissance in the northern courts of Mantua and Milan, for instance, differed in many ways from that of the republics of central Italy, whereas the French Renaissance on Fontainebleau cannot be separated from the aspirations of King François I in the 16th century. The identity of the German Renaissance is intimately linked with Johann Gutenberg's mid-15th-century invention of the printing press as well as with the Reformation. The Burgundian Netherlands housed the most important centers for tapestries, and the port city of Venice was affected by developments and traditions in northern and southern Western Europe as well as from the East.

Renaissance and Rebirth

Despite its origins in Italy, the term that we use to describe this period, *Renaissance,* is the French word for "rebirth." The earliest codified usage is believed to be found in the first volume of Honoré de Balzac's *Scenes From Private Life, The Ball at Sceaux* of 1829, and it was subsequently codified in Jules Michelet's *The Renaissance* of 1855 and in Jacob Burckhardt's German work *The Civilization of the Renaissance in Italy* of 1860. The Italian word is *rinascità,* used as early as Giorgio Vasari's account of Renaissance art, *The Lives of the Painters, Sculptors and Architects.* Vasari listed three ages of the Italian Renaissance: first, the earliest stirrings in the works of the late Duecento (1200s) and the Trecento (1300s)—such as that of Cimabue, Giotto, Duccio, and the Pisanos; second, the early mature works of the Quattrocento Renaissance (1400s)—such as that of Brunelleschi, Donatello, Massaccio, Alberti, Verrocchio, and Mantegna; and third, the culmination of the Renaissance in works of the late Quattrocento and early Cinquecento (1500s)—such as that of Leonardo da Vinci, Raphael, Michelangelo, Bramante, Peruzzi, and Vasari himself. This last phase is now known as the High Renaissance, which is followed by Mannerism.

The touchstone for the original concept of a rebirth is Petrarch's 1341 letter to Fra Giovanni Colonna, in which he expressed the sentiment that Rome would enact her own rebirth if she were able to rediscover her true (classical) self. From Petrarch to Vasari, the new humanists conceptualized their rinascità as being a purposeful and successful

break from the medieval art that preceded it. They described this art as being of the *maniera tedesca* (German manner) or the *maniera dei Goti* (Gothic), and the term *Gothic* has been in use ever since, carrying the connotation of being "barbaric" or "uncivilized," as opposed to the classicism reborn of the Renaissance. Scholarship since the Renaissance has essentially accepted the self-definition that these humanists devised. There had been a series of what are now called *renascences,* or brief renaissances of ancient Roman and early Christian classicism throughout the Middle Ages, including the Carolingian *renovatio* of Charlemagne, the 10th-century Ottonian Renaissance, and the so-called Tuscan proto-Renaissance of the 11th and 12th centuries (typified by the church of San Minato al Monte in Florence), not to mention the period now known as the Romanesque, which was, quite literally, Roman-esque. Erwin Panofsky's introduction to his *Studies in Iconology: Humanistic Themes in the Art of the Renaissance* of 1939 reveals the degree to which 20th-century scholars still accepted this humanist self-identity. In this introduction, Panofsky first formulates his famous dictum that although there were examples of classical survivals throughout the Middle Ages in Europe, classical motifs were divorced from classical themes. That is to say, a medieval classical motif was not employed to express classical themes, and when a classical theme was communicated, a nonclassical motif was used. Thus, it is not until the Italian Renaissance that classical theme and motif are reunited, and classicism reborn; all other medieval examples are partial survivals as opposed to revivals. This later concept was later further developed, with some correctives, by Aby Warburg and Georges Didi-Huberman.

Anne-Marie Sankovitch has recently pointed out that the Italian Renaissance is not only based on the idea of a rebirth but specifically on the humanists' belief that they had *successfully* recreated a perfect classicism. The Renaissance narrative of history is thus not predicated just on a break but on the ability to overcome that break. In essence, the Renaissance humanists invented a powerful way to define through difference in a Saussurean fashion. In reality, of course, it is necessary to understand that there are both connections and differences between late medieval and early Renaissance art and culture. It is possible to locate significant sociopolitical shifts that had far-reaching artistic and cultural consequences at the start and end of the Italian Renaissance. Two of the most salient involve Rome. From circa 1305–1378, the papacy left Rome for Avignon, France—the period of the Avignon papacy, which was followed by the Great Schism in the Catholic Church (1378–1414); this religious conflict disrupted Roman influence throughout the Italian peninsula. The Cinquecento saw the Sack of Rome, an attack on the city by the armies of Holy Roman Emperor Charles V in 1527 that devastated the urban fabric and High Renaissance culture, causing the artists and intelligentsia to flee to Venice and elsewhere.

The Italian Renaissance

In the intervening centuries, Florence rose to be the most influential cultural center. In any discussion of the Italian Renaissance, Florence must hold a position of prominence, due to its undeniable importance in the creation and development of Italian Renaissance art, life, and culture. However, it is often taken for granted that because it came to pass that Florence became the birthplace of the Renaissance, this occurrence was *natural* or *inevitable*. Such a conception diminishes our understanding of the Renaissance throughout Italy, both in Florence and in other cities. In the Duecento and Trecento, there were many sociopolitical, cultural, and aesthetic factors in play, with cities and artists experiencing triumphs and reversals of fortunes. For instance, Florence and Siena were urbanistic and aesthetic competitors; in the Duecento and Trecento, they competed in the building of their cathedral complexes and town halls, and the Florentine Giotto's and the Sienese Duccio's pictorial inventions are of equal import. Indeed, if Filippo Brunelleschi had not spectacularly solved the problem of the dome of the Florentine Cathedral, the center of the Renaissance may have been elsewhere.

Also interconnected with the idea of a rebirth are the twin poles of the Italian Renaissance: imitation and invention. Renaissance art is judged by these criteria, to the degree to which a work can be seen to be an imitation of a classical precedent and to be a new and individual invention. These criteria seem to be paradoxical, but they are not, as invention is in part defined by a fidelity to classical ideas, and imitation is in part defined as an ability to act as classical artists did, not necessarily to copy them per se. Further, invention and imitation are the two skills necessary to create art that mimics the principles of the natural world: paintings that employ one-point perspective, sculptures of figures that are of human proportions, buildings whose architectural members are based on the scale and ratio of the human body. Indeed, the motivations behind movements toward such naturalism are complex, going beyond a simple desire for a classical rebirth. Scholars have shown, for instance, that religious shifts created by the emergent mendicant orders, especially the Franciscans, were of great import. St. Francis's teachings affected both buildings and visual arts, as a need arose for accessible buildings in which one could speak to and welcome masses of people, accompanied by a need for imagery that could illustrate stories and theology in vivid and legible ways. These effects were immediately seen in Siena, Florence, Padua, and Assisi. Likewise, in *Dominion of the Eye,* Marvin Trachtenberg has shown that the nascent Florentine republican government, the Commune, was invested in creating an urban fabric that was constructed specifically to order space on a human scale, for purposes of communication and control.

The Renaissance in Northern Europe

The issue of imitation and invention is also integral to any definition of the Renaissance outside the Italian peninsula. One criterion applied is that of humanism and classicism. For France, the use of this criterion is largely accurate. The Renaissance in France can be traced to King François I's explicit desire and purposeful intent to import Italian classicism and humanism in contrast to the lingering court style of the French Gothic. In 1527, he embarked upon a large-scale building campaign in the Île-de-France, and beginning in 1530, he invited a series of Italian artists to Fontainebleau, including Rosso Fiorentino, Primaticcio, Nicolò del Abate, and Cellini. These artists helped influence French-born artists, so that a generation later, Jean Cousin, François Clouet, and Jean Goujon, as well as the architects Philibert de L'Orme and Pierre Lescot, were working in an idiom both

French and classical. If we judge German art by the same standard, the German Renaissance begins with the works of Albrecht Dürer, a humanist-artist who traveled specifically to Italy and who studied Italian prints and humanist ideas. Likewise, in the Netherlands, the classicism of the Renaissance was also introduced primarily via prints, especially those of Raphael, as well as printed architectural treatises, starting with Peiter Coecke van Aelst's publication of a Dutch translation of Serlio's treatise in 1539 in Antwerp, which was followed by Hans Vredeman de Vries's pattern book and editions of Vitruvius and Serlio.

Another criterion that is more helpful for an understanding of the Northern Renaissances of Germany and the Netherlands is a more general conceptualization of the humanist endeavor. Humanism is in part predicated on a belief in the individual, or, as some scholars note, in a privileging of human ideas over divine control and intervention. It is thus possible to find parallels that may not have their roots in classicism but that are nonetheless linked to this exploration of a modern human identity. In this context, it is helpful to examine the genre of portraiture. Certainly the interest in the self-portrait is both strictly classical and also reflects an exploration of the identity of an individual. If we use the interest in, and attention to, portraiture as a detail, then we can locate a Northern Renaissance in the early 15th century, and not only in the 16th century. We are thus able to discuss artists such as Claus Sluter, Jan van Eyck, Robert Campin, Rogier van der Weyden, and Konrad Witz, without losing major figures such as Dürer, who was famous for his self-portraits, or excluding other later artists such as Hans Holbein the Younger, Quentin Metsys, and Joos van Cleve, all known for their portraits. Furthermore, this criterion has the added benefit of revealing critical difference between northern and southern renaissances. In Italy, portraits were primarily profiles, created in imitation of antique coins. In the North, there was a significant interest in the three-quarter view, in which both the profile and the full face are depicted. Thus, we see two portrait traditions, connected by an interest in naturalism and the individual; this way of looking encompasses but is not dependent upon humanism and classicism. This standard also has the benefit of being linked not only to Renaissance narratives, but also with those

detailing art of the North after the Renaissance. In *The Art of Describing: Dutch Art of the Seventeenth Century*, Svetlana Alpers offers an analysis of northern art as one predicated on description rather than representation or narrative, noting that the metaphor in question here is not that of a window (Italian Albertian perspective) but of a mirror, or a map. Overall, then, applying such criteria also allows us to understand the bridge between Renaissance and Reformation ideals. As Stephen Greenblatt has powerfully argued in relation to English culture, in *Renaissance Self-Fashioning: From More to Shakespeare*, during this time, there was a strong belief both in the existence of individual identity and of one's ability to shape one's own identity; these concepts are found in Renaissance and Reformation alike. It is in part for reasons such as this that scholars have argued for the term *early modern* to describe this time period, both in Europe and in the New World.

Beyond the Normative Renaissance

There is a corollary issue that arises in a discussion of identity and identification in and of the Renaissance, and this is the question as to whose Renaissance it is. In defining the Renaissance and Renaissance art, the Otherness of gender, sexuality, religion, and geographical location is critical. Many excellent anthologies on the issue of gender and sexuality in Renaissance art have been published, including *Rewriting the Renaissance: The Discourses of Sexual Difference in Early Modern Europe* and *Picturing Women in Renaissance and Baroque Italy*. From the middle to the end of the 16th century, and beyond, we have knowledge of a number of strong female artists in the Italian and Northern Renaissances, including Sofonisba Anguissola, Lavinia Fontana, Caterina van Hemessen, and Levina Teerlinc, some of whom are discussed by Vasari in his *Lives*. Before the 16th century, there is evidence of strong female patronage of the arts and architecture, by women such as Catherine de' Medici, Isabelle d'Este, Caterina Piccolomini, and numerous other noble women in the North, as well as by now-anonymous women. In terms of religious structures, scholars have studied nuns and abbesses who were patrons, as well as investigated buildings and works of art that were commissioned for them to order their space, life, and beliefs. In addition, female saints, especially the Virgin Mary, were an important facet of Renaissance art, providing exempla for men and women throughout Europe of all socioeconomic strata. The "fallen" women of the Bible, such as Eve and Mary Magdalene, also appeared in Renaissance art, as part of a moralized tale, an eroticized image, or both. Likewise, scholars such as Sarah Blake McHam and Geraldine Johnson have shown how the images and identities of women from mythology and the Bible were co-opted to stand as metaphors of political and personal power and control, especially as monumental sculptures in public spaces; of particular interest is McHam's 2001 article in *Art Bulletin*, "Donatello's Bronze *David* and *Judith* as Metaphors of Medici Rule in Florence." Returning to the issue of portraiture, the role of women is the exploration of identity is paramount. Elizabeth Cropper has investigated the ways in which female beauty has functioned rhetorically. Likewise, in a 1995 article in *Zeitschrift für Kunstgeschichte*, "Looking a Sight: Sixteenth-Century Portraits of Woman Artists," Catherine King has revealed the strategies that were available to female artists in creating self-portraits in which they could both etch out their own identities and work within the recognizable and available portrait conventions. Male homoeroticism in Renaissance art has long been understood and explored, notably in Leonard Barkan's 1991 *Transuming Passion: Ganymede and the Erotics of Humanism*, and recent scholarship has turned its attention to lesbian identities and cross-dressing.

In terms of dealing with cross-currents of Otherness in Europe and beyond, including transatlantic studies, the most critical work to emerge is found in *Reframing the Renaissance: Visual Culture in Europe and Latin America, 1450–1650*. Two essays in particular provide much-needed information with regard to the European interaction with the so-called New World. Cecilia Klein reveals how European writers and artists manipulated the forms and identities of indigenous goddesses to create imagery of domination and control. Dana Leibsohn traces the fascinating clash of traditions that occurred when Europeans commissioned maps from chthonic artists, whose cartographic conventions were neither Cartesian nor Albertian. Likewise, the work of Thomas da Costa Kaufmann and Jonathan B. Reiss provides much-needed information about interactions between Italian artists and other European cultures, as well as issues within Italian society. Kaufmann discusses Italian sculptors working outside of Italy, in areas such as Hungary and Poland, and Reiss addresses the issue of anti-Semitism in Luca Signorelli's *Rule of Antichrist* in the Cappella Nuova of Orvieto Cathedral. Anthony Cutler's analysis of the ways that the European Renaissance defined Byzantine art, and the ways in which modern scholarship has continued to follow these identifications, brings us full circle to the issue of the Renaissance self-identification against the medieval and its ramifications for Renaissance art in the East and the West. As the act of self-identification is quintessentially modern, it may be that the term *early modern art* is a fuller, more evocative descriptor of the art and culture both within and outside and beyond Italy, able to contain the concept of an intentional rebirth as well as other interests in the individual and the natural world.

Mia Reinoso Genoni

See also Architecture, Sites, and Spaces; Other, The

Further Readings

Aikema, B., Brown, B. L., & Nepi Sciré, G. (2000). *Renaissance Venice and the North: Crosscurrents in the time of Bellini, Dürer, and Titian*. New York: Rizzoli.

Baxandall, M. (1971). *Giotto and the orators: Humanist observers of painting in Italy and the discovery of pictorial composition, 1350–1450*. Oxford, UK: Clarendon Press.

Farago, C. J. (Ed.). (1995). *Reframing the Renaissance: Visual culture in Europe and Latin America, 1450–1650*. New Haven, CT: Yale University Press.

Ferguson, M. W., Quilligan, M., & Vickers, N. J. (Eds.). (1986). *Rewriting the Renaissance: The discourses of sexual difference in early modern Europe*. Chicago: University of Chicago Press.

Johnson, G. A., & Matthews Grieco, S. F. (Eds.). (1997). *Picturing women in Renaissance and Baroque Italy*. Cambridge, UK: Cambridge University Press.

McIver, K. A. (2006). *Women, art, and architecture in Northern Italy, 1520–1580: Negotiating power*. Aldershot, UK: Ashgate.

Paoletti, J. T., & Radke, G. M. (2005). *Art in Renaissance Italy* (3rd ed.). London: Laurence King.

Payne, A., Kuttner, A. L., & Smick, R. (2000). *Antiquity and its interpreters.* Cambridge, UK: Cambridge University Press.

Sankovitch, A.-M. (2006, Spring/Autumn). Anachronism and simulation in Renaissance architectural theory. *Res, 49/50,* 189–203.

Snyder, J., Silver, L., & Luttikhuizen, H. (2005). *Northern Renaissance art: Painting, sculpture, the graphic arts from 1350 to 1575* (2nd ed.). Upper Saddle River, NJ: Prentice Hall.

Trachtenberg, M. (1997). *Dominion of the eye: Urbanism, art, and power in early modern Florence.* Cambridge, UK: Cambridge University Press.

Zerner, H. (2003). *Renaissance art in France: The invention of classicism* (D. Dusinberre, S. Wilson, & R. Zerner, Trans.). Paris: Flammarion.

RHETORIC

Rhetoric may be defined as persuasive communication, written or oral, formal or informal; a verbal art or a type of poetics; or an academic discipline concerned with persuasive communication. In his seminal work, *Rhetoric,* Aristotle provided the original, neutral definition of the concept as simply "the available means of persuasion." The content and style of one's rhetoric can help to convey to others information about one's politics, geographic region, nationality, race, socioeconomic status, age, religion, level of education, and other critical aspects of self. Depending on its content, for example, one may be correctly or incorrectly labeled "right-wing," "left-wing," "feminist," "chauvinist," "fundamentalist," and so on. This entry explores various aspects and issues of rhetoric, including appeals and canons, history, verbal art or poetics, performance, varieties, and tropes and schemes.

Appeals and Canons of Rhetoric

In *Rhetoric,* Aristotle outlines three modes or appeals of rhetoric: *logos* (reason), *pathos* (emotion), and *ethos* (ethics). To have maximum persuasiveness, a message or speech must appeal to audience members in each of these three ways; that is, it must be logical and well constructed, it must touch the hearer emotionally, and it must be presented by someone who is ethical (or who at least is believed to be a person of integrity).

The five canons of rhetoric are *inventio* (prewriting), *dispositio* (arrangement), *elocutio* (style), *memoria* (memorization), and *pronuntiatio* (delivery). Inventio involves planning and research to give one's communication substance. Arrangement, selection, and use of words, figures of speech, varied sentence types, and paragraphs for greatest effect are all the purview of dispositio. Style (elocutio) can be formal or informal, depending on the type of audience for which one writes or performs. With respect to memoria, orators often make use of various mnemonic devices to help them memorize material they will perform or execute verbally. Lastly, pronuntiatio (delivery) is key to persuasiveness. A powerfully written message with limp or lukewarm delivery loses much of its effectiveness for an audience.

History

Classical Greek Rhetoric and Its Relationship to African Oratory

Many textbooks begin discussion of rhetoric's history at the 4th and 5th centuries BC with the work of Aristotle, Socrates, and others who highlighted techniques for persuasive argumentation in the courtroom and other settings, and there is debate about the influence of African oratory on Greek rhetoric. The question arises, for instance, as to whether the Greeks *invented* or merely *catalogued* tropes and schemes they learned from African orators. Deborah Sweeney's study of law and rhetoric in ancient Egypt uncovers the use of repetition, parallelism, antithesis, hyperbole, metaphor, and other tropes and schemes. The current intellectual milieu is one of increasing suspicion of revisionist history in textbooks, history that highlights European civilizations and their achievements and overlooks non-Western civilizations and their contributions to rhetoric and other fields.

Certain anthropological and rhetorical sources, by African, African American, and White scholars, suggest that whereas ancient Greeks acknowledged the influence of Egyptians on their culture, later Eurocentric scholars, with their own agenda of establishing and maintaining views of White superiority, sought to diminish, if not outright deny, this African influence. James Berlin and other scholars committed to recovery of a history that fully describes the extensive cultural exchanges that went on between persons of ancient Greece and Egypt suggest, for instance, that Socrates and others studied in Egypt and brought back what they learned to help shape the teaching of rhetoric and other aspects of Greek civilization.

Martin Bernal, Carol Lipson, Roberta Binkley, Jacob Carruthers, Cheikh Anta Diop, Lucy Xing Lu, and others have written extensively on issues related to the Eurocentric slant on the history of rhetoric and the distortion of world history in general. In *Black Athena Writes Back*, Bernal describes the difference between an Aryan model of history, which asserts that Greece was conquered from persons to its north and that there was no philosophy before the Greeks, and an ancient model, which highlights the interchanges between Greece and Egypt. Bernal notes that the ancient model was not doubted until the end of the 18th century, and it was not seriously challenged until the 1820s. He proposes a "revised ancient model," one that acknowledges dual influence on Greece of cultural practices from peoples both to the north and south of that country.

Split of Rhetorical Studies and Composition

Rhetoric also is an academic discipline. Two crucial splits occurred in the early 1900s between the *teaching of oral and written rhetoric* (the history, theory, and practice of persuasive communication) and the *teaching of composition* (basic writing). With regard to the teaching of oral rhetoric (specifically, elocution and debate), such instruction saw a decline for the period 1860 to 1910, then experienced a renaissance beginning in 1914 when the National Association of Academic Teachers of Public Speaking (now the National Communication Association) broke away from the National Council of Teachers of English.

A watershed moment occurred in the early 1900s with respect to written rhetoric instruction when the previous approach to rhetorical studies of continental Europe shifted from a focus on the rhetorical thought and methods of ancient philosophers to focus on technical mechanics of the writing process. Specifically, with the advent in 1907 of Edwin C. Woolley's *Handbook of Composition: A Compendium of Rules*, written rhetorical instruction languished as the handbook era began. Woolley's was the first college-level text of its kind, unapologetically covering every aspect of mechanical correction (spelling, grammar, punctuation, etc.) at a very basic level. Edward P. J. Corbett and Robert J. Connors suggest that it was Cornell University that revived interest in classical rhetoric in the 1920s by establishing a seminar in which students read and discussed the works of Aristotle, Cicero, and Quintilian. As graduates from that program went on to be hired at schools in other parts of the country, renewed interest in rhetoric occurred.

Verbal Rhetoric, Poetics, and Performance

In his work on language and artful verbal structure (poetics), Roman Jakobson outlines six functions of language and identifies the appropriate function of poetics within these. In brief, the constitutive factors of any speech event are as follows: An *addresser* sends a *message* to an *addressee*. To be understood, the message must have a *context*, a *code* or language, and a *contact* (physical channel and psychological connection that allow addresser and addressee to enter and remain in communication). The functions can be diagrammed as follows:

	Referential (Context)	
Emotive (Addresser)	Poetic (Message)	Conative (Addressee)
	Phatic (Contact)	
	Metalingual (Code)	

If we try to relate the diagram to a piece of political rhetoric, such as U.S. Senator Barack

Impassioned Orator	2008 Presidential Election (Democratic National Convention)	National Audience
(Senator Obama)	**Nomination Speech**	(Americans who construe or interpret his message as convincing or not)
	(Message about change he plans to bring to America)	
	TV, Cable, Internet/	
	Relationship Between Obama and "The Public"	
	(Their shared concern over what is good for the country)	
	Standard American English	
	(Polished version, charismatic in its delivery)	

Obama's Nomination Acceptance Speech, given in August 2008 at the Democratic National Convention at the Pepsi Center in Denver, it might look like the the chart above.

Rhetorical Frames and Performance

In his work *Verbal Art as Performance,* scholar Richard Bauman suggests that modern theorists in a variety of disciplines, including anthropology, linguistics, and literature, tend to have a *text-centered* approach to the notion of *verbal art* or *oral literature,* focusing on "special usages or patterning of formal features within texts" (p. 7). Specifically, he notes that theorists such as Roman Jakobson and Edward Stankiewicz focus on the message for its own sake, whereas others, such as William Bascom, are greatly concerned with the way a message is expressed or presented. Still others, like Bohuslav Havránek, suggest that verbal art has to do with maximized, conspicuous use of oratorical devices.

By contrast, Bauman wants to study the nature of performance and distinguish it from other ways of speaking. His approach involves particular attention to Gregory Bateson's notion of the interpretive *frame* or context within which messages are to be understood. In addition to the literal, there are many other types of communicative frames that vary by culture. These include but are not limited to insinuation, joking, imitation, translation, quotation, conversational speech, ceremonial speech, and storytelling (viewed as straight speech in some cultures and as performative speech in others). Bauman recognizes performance as a distinctive frame that involves, among other things, a display of communicative competence, accountability to the audience for which the communication is given, and delivery that heightens enjoyment for hearers of this act of expression. He views performance as constitutive of verbal art or verbal rhetoric.

Performance verbal art types, features, and styles vary from speech community to speech community. Here are two examples from Latino/a rhetoric. Sociolinguistics ethnographer Marcia Farr has done extensive research on the Mexican speech event (or frame) *relajo* ("joking") and the Mexican ranchero speech style known as *franqueza* ("frankness"). Farr defines relajo as a Mexican speech event or oral performance during which normal seriousness is suspended, and individuals can deliberately breach the prevailing code of propriety by which they usually live. Her study of verbal art among Mexicanas in Chicago contains details of an oral performance in which the focus is changing gender roles of Mexican and Mexican American women. Relajo provides a social space in which tensions can be released and those participating can collectively explore community values critically and humorously.

Franqueza, according to Farr, is direct, straightforward, candid language that goes directly to a point. It is the speech of the rancher who owns property and takes a proud, egalitarian stance with landowner bosses of large farm cooperatives. Farr says this contrasts with the *cortesia* or indirect verbal politeness style of speech used by the stereotypical indigenous Mexican Indian, who stands with a bowed head and hat in hand before land bosses.

Varieties of Specialized Rhetoric

Studies abound on specialized varieties of rhetoric. Dell Hymes has chronicled aspects of Native American ethnopoetics. In addition to Farr, Victor Villanueva and Jose Gutiérrez also have detailed elements of Hispanic or Latino/a rhetoric. Ronald L. Jackson II, Elaine Richardson, John Lucaites, Michelle Condit, Richard Riecke, and James Golden are among those who have provided groundbreaking scholarship on African American rhetoric. Gerald Davis, Henry Mitchell, Katie Cannon, Susan Bond, and others have written comprehensively about the Black sermon as a special form of rhetoric. Arla Bernstein, Kristina Horn Sheeler, and others are to be credited for creative, insightful scholarship on women's political rhetoric. Various other scholars have tackled Asian and other types of rhetoric.

As an example of the kind of rhetorical conceptual work available, the work of Maulana Karenga on African rhetoric and its relation to African American rhetoric will be considered briefly. Maulana Karenga outlines four characteristics of African American rhetorical communicative practice, which is rooted in African rhetoric. Specifically, this practice features *rhetoric of community, rhetoric of resistance, rhetoric of reaffirmation,* and *rhetoric of possibility.*

Drawing on the works of Molefi Asante, Shirley Wilson Logan, and others, Karenga describes African American rhetoric as one of *community,* involving communal dialogue and action to bring positive outcomes in the community and the world. The community context, one of historical enslavement and ongoing systematic oppression, has helped to shape a brilliant rhetoric of *resistance,* struggle, and protest. African American rhetoric also is a rhetoric of *reaffirmation.* It is intentional about reaffirming the dignity and divinity of African persons and their rights to freedom, meaningful lives, and the opportunity to share their cultural truth and their contributions to the world in their own ways. Lastly, Karenga characterizes this communicative practice as a rhetoric of *possibility,* which seeks to share, inform, question, explore, and investigate in order to solve problems and maximize human quality of life.

The work of Bauman, Farr, Jackson, Condit, Karenga, and others makes clear that all cultures have a variety of speech events and related interpretive frames, but that the performance frame (which is culture specific) is significant because it emphasizes the idea of competence in speaking in socially acceptable ways for an evaluating audience. Bauman's list of communicative means used for framing in various cultures includes but is not limited to special codes, figurative language, parallelism, special paralinguistic features, special formulae, and a disclaimer of performance.

Special codes can include archaic language ("We the people . . ."), poetic language, and other special linguistic usages. *Figurative language* includes the use of metaphor and other figures of speech. *Parallelism* is the systematic repetition and variation of poetic, phonic, grammatical, and semantic structures. It can help a performer with memorization of a written text or with fluency in delivering a spontaneous, improvised piece. Further, Bauman posits that parallelism is as important for the effectiveness of informal and brief passing utterances as for elaborate, public performances.

Special paralinguistic features are those that typically are not recorded in written texts. These include articulation, speed, accents, and other features of delivery style. In his work on Zuni narrative, Dennis Tedlock has developed conventions for indicating features such as rate, loudness, stress, and pitch contour. "Once upon a time," the opening for a fairy tale, and the common joke introduction, "Did you hear the one about . . . ," are among *special formulae,* which often serve as markers of specific genres.

Finally, another means of announcing performance is the *disclaimer of performance,* or denial of competence. Bauman views such disclaimers as attempts at modesty in settings and situations where self-assertiveness is considered a liability.

Figures of Speech: Tropes and Schemes

In the work *Classical Rhetoric for the Modern Student,* Corbett and Connors describe a figure as a type of speech that is creatively crafted in ways divergent from normal usage. *Tropes* and *schemes* are the two main types of figures. In her work on conversational involvement strategies, Deborah Tannen explains that J. D. Sapir and Paul Friedrich use the term *trope* to refer to figures of speech that operate on meaning. Sapir identifies four master tropes: *metaphor* (speaking of one thing in terms of another), *metonymy* (speaking of a thing in terms of something associated with it), *synecdoche* (a part for the whole), and *irony* (saying the opposite of what one means).

The Greeks cataloged some 250 schemes, or artful patterns or arrangements of words. A few examples follow.

Anaphora—repetition of a word or group of words at the beginning of successive clauses.

> "Now is the time to make real the promises of democracy. Now is the time to rise from the dark and desolate valley of segregation to the sunlit path of racial justice. Now is the time to lift our nation from the quick sands of racial injustice to the solid rock of brotherhood. Now is the time to make justice a reality for all of God's children." (Martin Luther King Jr., "I Have A Dream" speech, 1963).

Antimetabole—repetition of the same words or ideas in transposed order.

> "And so, my fellow Americans: Ask not what your country can do for you—ask what you can do for your country." (John F. Kennedy, Inaugural Address, 1961)

Assonance—the repetition of rhyming sounds in words or phrases.

> "Down with dope! Up with hope!" (Frequently uttered exhortation of civil rights leader Reverend Jesse L. Jackson Sr.)

Parallelism—the systematic repetition and variation of poetic, phonic, grammatical, and semantic structures.

> "My faith in the Constitution *is whole; it is complete; it is total.* I am not going to sit here and be an idle spectator to *the diminution, the subversion, the destruction* of the Constitution." (From the historic Statement on Impeachment, given by the late congresswoman from Texas, Barbara Jordan, during the Nixon impeachment hearings, July 1974)

Polyptoton—repetitive use of words with the same root.

> "That's an im*plausible* solution to a *plausible* dilemma."

Polysyndeton—use of many conjunctions for emphasis.

> "The farmer planted *and* fertilized *and* watered *and* tended *and* ultimately harvested his crops."

Conclusion

Crafting polished persuasive communication involves attention to the various appeals, canons, functions, factors, and frames of rhetoric, as well as concern for one's audience. Rhetoric has many varieties and is culture specific. Its persuasiveness in public as well as private arenas depends ultimately on how well each of these considerations is addressed.

Brenda Eatman Aghahowa

See also Communication Competence; Communication Theory of Identity; Ethnolinguistic Identity Theory; Language

Further Readings

Aghahowa, B. E. (2009). *Grace under fire: Barbara Jordan's rhetoric of Watergate, patriotism, and equality.* Chicago: Third World Press.

Bauman, R. (1984). *Verbal art as performance*. Prospect Heights, IL: Waveland Press.

Binkley, R., & Lipson, C. S. (Eds.). (2004). *Rhetoric before and beyond the Greeks*. Albany: SUNY Press.

Corbett, E. P. J., & Connors, R. J. (1998). *Classical rhetoric for the modern student* (4th ed.). New York: Oxford University Press.

Farr, M. (2008). Essayist literacy and other verbal performances. *Written Communication, 10*(1), 4–38.

Golden, J. L., & Rieke, R. D. (1971). *The rhetoric of Black Americans*. Columbus, OH: Merrill.

Hammerback, J. C., Jensen, R. J., & Gutiérrez, J. A. (1985). *A war of words: Chicano protest in the 1960s and 1970s*. Westport, CT: Greenwood Press.

Hymes, D. (1981). *"In vain I tried to tell you": Essays in Native American ethnopoetics*. Philadelphia: University of Pennsylvania Press.

Jackson, R. L., II, & Richardson, E. B. (2003). *Understanding African American rhetoric: Classical origins to contemporary innovations*. New York: Routledge.

Jakobson, R. (1966). Closing statement: Linguistics and poetics. In T. A. Sebeok (Ed.), *Style in language* (pp. 350–373). Cambridge: MIT Press.

Logan, S. W. (1999). *"We are coming": The persuasive discourse of nineteenth-century Black women*. Carbondale: Southern Illinois University Press.

Tannen, D. (1989). *Talking voices: Repetition, dialogue, and imagery in conversational discourse*. Cambridge, UK: Cambridge University Press.

RITUALS

Rituals are often symbolic and are defined as any customary behavior or routine that may vary by location (e.g., manners of greeting), or as prescribed by religious, spiritual, cultural, or political traditions (e.g., rites related to birth or death). Erik Erikson described identity development as occurring along three clusters: society-inward, person-outward, and an interaction between individual and society. Rituals may be analyzed similarly. On a societal level, rituals have the sociological power of making it possible for people to distinguish between groups. On a personal level, rituals determine group affiliation and detail self-identification. From a developmental perspective, studying engagement with rituals contributes to understanding personal identity development and also illustrates how communities maintain cultural cohesion over time. This entry explores the different forms that rituals may take and discusses mechanisms linking rituals and identity development processes.

Rituals and Ingroup/Outgroup Distinctions

From a sociological perspective, rituals help researchers to distinguish ingroups from outgroups. Early ethnographic research done by Erikson detailed the behaviors and rituals of people native to the United States and differentiated tribes through ritual behavior (e.g., how a particular tribe entered their homes). If a person exhibits familiarity with a ritual characteristic of a particular group, others may identify him or her as a member of the referenced group. If participation in the behavior seems unfamiliar or awkward, group membership may be considered by others as unauthentic. Ritual behavior may demarcate not only major sociological groups (e.g., religious groups, ethnic groups, political factions) but also less structured or more localized social groups (e.g., families, friends and neighborhood groups, office culture). For example, work cultures may define rituals for acknowledging special occasions for employees (e.g., first and last day of employment, birthdays, promotions), and these rituals often are consistent with other aspects of the work environment.

The rituals that distinguish ingroups from outgroups may range in the degree to which they require knowledge or intensity of practice. If rituals require a high degree of technical knowledge and language (e.g., a bar mitzvah or bat mitzvah), participation in them may require more preparation or previous experience. The relatively high levels of knowledge may preclude some people from participating in the ritual. Alternately, other ritual observances may have relatively lower entry points. For example, observance of particular holidays may merely mark national affiliation (e.g., Independence Day). The content and significance of rituals associated with holidays may vary according to local values.

Psychological Meaning of Rituals for the Individual

Whereas rituals are socially defined, the individual often has considerable agency in determining the level of participation. For example, one person may participate in a holiday in a minimal manner, such as recognizing the historical reason for the holiday. Another person may celebrate the holiday more deliberately, perhaps by organizing a holiday parade or commemorative event. The degree to which a person participates may reflect important aspects of the identity process, particularly the identity socialization process (i.e., whether a person has been afforded previous opportunities to participate in such rituals, coupled with how the individual has responded to the opportunities).

On a personal level, rituals may organize and mark key developmental transitions. For example, coming-of-age ceremonies vary considerably in terms of how they are celebrated and how they acknowledge physical, spiritual, and social maturity. Whether the ritual is private and can be observed publicly, such as the donning of hijab for a Muslim girl after her first menses, or public such as in a confirmation ceremony, rituals are often integral to coming-of-age ceremonies. A related public ceremony may mark the entry of a young person into a religious community, as observed in traditions like the baptism of children or the Sacred Thread Ceremony.

Less-prescribed rituals may be connected with nearly every feature of the identity development process. In a Western context structured by formal education, one's professional identity frequently has rituals associated with entry into school (e.g., reciting the Pledge of Allegiance), rituals linked with attending school (e.g., awards ceremonies), and rituals coupled with exiting the educational setting (e.g., graduation ceremonies).

Membership in various social groups requires the knowledge and use of rituals appropriate to that group. The identity development process may, to an extent, be measured by the degree to which a person has not only appropriated but also explored the meaning of the rituals. Such exploration may differentiate between the person who preserves a particular ritual habitually and the person who has knowledge of the historical or symbolic significance of a ritual and implores the ritual not merely in a routine manner but in a way that invokes its deeper symbolic meaning.

Ritual Use, Early Socialization, and Identity Development

The study of rituals and their meanings to individuals may provide important insights into the outcomes and internal processes of identity formation. Sociocultural theoretical perspectives highlight how young children appropriate the values of adult members of their community, in large part, through the shared use of rituals and practices that have particular cultural meaning in context. For example, a young child who participates in preparing a communal ritual meal to mark the bounties of harvest season may orient to the ethnic and religious identity aspects of the identity formation process in a qualitatively different manner than a young child who participates in ritual meals with different religious significance (e.g., a seder) or a communal meal with no religious significance.

Implications for Understanding Identity

The study of rituals in the practiced routines of individuals and communities reveals how significant early experiences may influence later identity development markers. Additionally, studying rituals and what they mean to individuals and communities may provide insights into the content and form of the identity development process.

Mona M. Abo-Zena

See also Collective/Social Identity; Culture; Individual; Religious Identity; Socialization

Further Readings

Erikson, E. (1950). *Childhood and society*. New York: W.W. Norton.

Erikson, E. (1968). *Identity, youth, and crisis*. New York: W.W. Norton.

Rogoff, B. (2003). *The cultural nature of human development*. New York: Oxford University Press.

Schwartz, S. J. (2001). The evolution of Eriksonian and neo-Eriksonian identity theory and research: A review and integration. *Identity: An International Journal of Theory and Research*, 1(1), 7–58.

ROLE IDENTITY

In society, individuals occupy different social positions. These social positions may be as varied as student, parent, criminal, or hockey player. Tied to each social position are roles or expectations that guide people's attitudes and behavior. For example, the roles associated with student may include learning new material, attending and passing courses, and obtaining a degree. The role of parent may involve feeding, clothing, bathing, educating, and emotionally supporting a child. The *meanings* people attribute to themselves while in a role are their *role identities*. For example, the student role identity may mean being academically responsible. The parent role identity may mean being nurturing and loving. Thus, what it *means* to a person to take on the role of student or parent is the role identity. In this entry, role identity is defined and discussed, and how role identities are played out in interaction is reviewed.

Defining a Role Identity

For each *role* a person assumes, there is a corresponding *identity* associated with it. A role identity consists of the internal meanings and interpretations that individuals bring to their roles. There are two dimensions of a role identity: a conventional dimension and an idiosyncratic dimension. The conventional dimension is the meanings most people share with one another about a role based on a common culture. Individuals learn the meanings of a role identity in interaction with others in which others act toward individuals as if they had the identity appropriate to their role behavior. The idiosyncratic dimension of a role identity is the unique meanings that individuals bring to their roles; it is individuals' own understanding of the role as it applies to them. For example, the professor role identity typically entails the meanings of one as "instructor" and "educator." This is the conventional dimension of the professor identity. Some may add to this the idiosyncratic dimension of "friend to students" or "protector of students."

Either one of these meanings is more distinctive and not necessarily shared with others while in the role of professor.

Role identities often contain multiple meanings. Individuals turn to more than one characteristic to describe what the role means to them. Additionally, different individuals may have different meanings for the same role identity. For example, for one person, the student role identity may mean being studious and taking one's coursework seriously, whereas for another, the student role identity may mean being outgoing and having fun with friends at school. When role identity meanings are not held in common, individuals must negotiate the meanings with others who may have a different understanding of that role identity. They may find that they have to compromise as to the role identity meanings they can claim and the behaviors that correspond to those meanings.

Despite the actual meanings of one's role identity, the meanings should be similar to the meanings implied by one's behavior. For example, if the role identity of student involves the meaning of being studious, a student should behave in ways that match this meaning, for example, by attending class, taking notes, completing homework assignments, and passing exams. On the other hand, if the student identity means being sociable, a person's behavior should include spending time with one's friends and going to parties.

The meanings individuals attribute to themselves while in a role become their role identity standard. This role identity standard guides their behavior as they play out their roles in situations. Furthermore, individuals will perceive feedback from others in the situation regarding their role behavior, and the perceived meaning of others' feedback should match the meanings held in their role identity standard. When there is correspondence between the meaning of others' feedback and role identity standard meanings, *identity verification* has occurred and individuals will feel good. However, when there is noncorrespondence between the meaning of others' feedback and role identity standard meanings, role *identity nonverification* has occurred and individuals will feel bad. In turn, they will act to reduce the negative feelings by changing their behaviors, changing their perceptions of others' feedback, or, at a slower pace, changing their identity standard.

For example, a woman may characterize her mother identity as involving meanings of being nurturing and loving. These meanings form her identity standard. She should then act in ways consistent with this, such as engaging in warm, physical and verbal interactions with her child, attending to her child's needs and providing comfort. Others who see this will give her feedback that she will perceive as consistent with her view of herself as nurturing and loving. This verifies her mother identity and she will feel good. However, if she is inattentive and ignores her child's physical and emotional needs, she may perceive that others see her as neglectful and careless. This disconfirms the meanings of her mother identity and she will feel bad. To feel better, she may change what she is doing by becoming more attentive to her child's needs, she may ignore others' disconfirming feedback, or she may change her identity standard meaning and see herself as a neglectful mother.

Role Identity in Interaction

When two people interact, they are relating to each other as persons with specific roles. Interaction is guided by the principle of role reciprocity. The idea is that for every role that is played out in a situation, there is a counterrole to which it is related. For example, the role of "teacher" makes no sense without the role of "student." The teacher's behavior can only be understood in relation to the behavior of a student. The role of a husband cannot exist without a wife to which he relates.

If roles are related to counterroles, then role identities must be related to counteridentities. For example, the employee identity has a corresponding counteridentity of the employer identity. Because each person has a different identity in the situation, there will be different perceptions and actions between individuals. For instance, a person in the student identity will have particular goals, use certain resources, and engage in particular behaviors that may be different but interrelated to the goals, resources, and behaviors of the professor identity. A student may desire to excel in an area of study, use resources such as printed texts, videos, and the computer, and engage in behaviors such as attending lectures, completing homework assignments, and taking exams. Correspondingly,

the professor educates the student in the area of study by providing resources such as books, movies, speakers, and Web-based computer material and will enact actions such as lecturing, stimulating class discussions, and distributing homework exercises and exams. Rather than the student and professor acting alike in their identities, they are acting differently, with each person's perception and action interconnected to the other in the situation.

This interrelatedness of identities and counteridentities is successful in situations when individuals effectively make compromises regarding the different meanings and corresponding behaviors tied to each identity. Individuals have their own interests and goals to fulfill, and these may compete with the interests and goals of others in the situation. People need to cooperate for effective interaction to take place. Each needs to give up some of his or her own meanings tied to a particular identity in favor of another's meanings of that identity. Through these concessions, meanings come to be shared.

Ultimately, everyone in a situation wants to verify their identities. Recall that identity verification means that perceptions of the person in the situation are consistent with the person's identity standard meanings. Lack of identity verification occurs when the perceptions about the person in the situation disconfirms the person's identity standard meanings. Persons attempt to achieve identity verification by engaging in behaviors that will keep the perceived meanings of who they are in a situation consistent with the meanings held in their identity standard. If all goes well for all individuals in the situation, there will be mutual identity verification. However, this may not happen automatically in a situation. Mutual identity verification in a situation often requires cooperative and mutually agreed-upon ways of behaving. Because each person's behavior is not the same as the other in the interaction, given the role identities and counterrole identities of each, individuals' respective actions must reflect this complementarily in a coordinated manner. This coordinated effort might involve individuals modifying their behavior somewhat or altering their identity standard a little in order to accomplish identity verification and facilitate the verification of the other's identity.

To illustrate how noncooperative behaviors can generate problems in identity verification, let us take a student–professor interaction. If George, a student, claims the meaning of "studious" as part of his student identity standard, then we expect him to attend a professor's class and complete the course requirements. If the professor, Dr. White, claims the meaning of "instructor" in the professor identity, we expect him to provide the tools for learning, such as lectures and reading materials, and we expect him to evaluate the student's mastery of course materials through assignments and exams. If George does not attend class or attends class but surfs the Internet on his computer or text-messages his friends on his cell phone, he is not verifying his student identity, and he is not providing the feedback necessary to the professor to verify Dr. White's identity as instructor. Alternatively, if Dr. White does not test George on his knowledge of the course material, then Dr. White is failing to verify his professor identity as well as the identity of his counterpart, the student.

If individuals do not obtain verification for their identities, they will become less satisfied with their roles, and they may withdraw from an interaction. For example, research on the leadership role identity shows that when individuals cannot negotiate in a group the behavior that matches the meaning of the leadership identity, those assuming the leadership role become less satisfied and are less inclined to remain in the group than if they successfully negotiate the appropriate leadership behavior. Other research shows that when husbands and wives successfully negotiate the behavior of each in a marriage, what develops is a strong emotional attachment to the other, commitment to the marriage, and a movement away from a self-focus (an "I") to a global unit (a "We"). Thus, the verification of one's role identity verification is not just a result of one's own action but of one's action in relation to others' actions.

By verifying role identities—that is, behaving in ways consistent with the meanings and expectations associated with role identities—individuals come to have a heightened sense of self-efficacy. They feel competent and effective. As a result of this strong feeling of competence, persons with higher self-efficacy are more likely to engage in difficult behaviors that they have not tried before because they have the expectation that they will successfully carry out those behaviors. Persons who have low levels of self-efficacy are more likely to shy away from problematic situations because they feel that they will fail. Self-efficacy arises from the successful verification of role identities. People with high self-efficacy try more things and thus have the opportunity to learn they are successful. In contrast, because people with low self-efficacy tend not to make the effort, they may not have the opportunity to learn about the things they are good at.

Jan E. Stets

See also Identity Change; Identity Salience; Self-Verification; Symbolic Interactionism

Further Readings

Burke, P. J., & Stets, J. E. (2009). *Identity theory*. New York: Oxford University Press.
McCall, G., & Simmons, J. L. (1978). *Identities and interaction*. New York: Free Press.
Stryker, S. (2002). *Symbolic interactionism: A social structural version*. Caldwell, NJ: Blackburn Press. (Original work published 1980)

S

SACRED

See Secular Identity

SAPIR-WHORF HYPOTHESIS

The Sapir-Whorf hypothesis asserts that humans' use of linguistic communication relates to their specific cultural norms. Edward Sapir developed and published the conceptual framework for this hypothesis in the 1920s. In 1956, Benjamin Lee Whorf published his work developing this hypothesis based on his work using the Hopi and English languages. Sapir and Whorf's ideas have been commonly known as the *Sapir-Whorf hypothesis,* which has also been referred to as *linguistic relativity.* This hypothesis counters notions of universal and objective meaning and use of language. This hypothesis further posits that language frames human expression instead of human expression framing language. In other words, the grammatical structure and function of language shapes human thought processes and the manner in which humans perceive reality. The relevance of the Sapir-Whorf hypothesis for identity formation is that it challenges the commonsense notion that a preexisting identity creates and shapes language; rather, the hypothesis argues that identity is formed and informed by language.

Sapir's Concept of Language and Social Reality

The Sapir-Whorf hypothesis asserts that the function and structure of a culture's language shapes the perception and behavior of those in that culture. Therefore, language use and development is relative to the culture that uses it. Sapir believes that language and behavior mutually influence each other. Language use predisposes choices and interpretations of everyday behavior and interaction. The "real world" is composed of the language structure of cultural groups. Thus, the world cannot exist objectively or in a manner that separates human interaction from cultural linguistic expression. Reality is subjective relative to the development and form of language. Further, language does not merely reflect social reality, it determines it.

Sapir's views are often linked with *determinism,* the notion that human cognition and behavior can be causally linked to prior occurrences. In the instance of language, Sapir argues that linguistic systems determine perceptions of social reality. He further contends that cultural groups of different language systems will operate under different frames of reality for making sense of their social world and their behavior in it. Sapir derived these ideas while a student of Franz Boas, who has often been credited as the founder of anthropology, which is a field closely related to communication and language as it regards human behavior. Boas believes that each language has its own paradigm

651

(worldview) and that language serves as a mediator between humans and their understanding of reality. Like Boas, Sapir asserts that language classifies and categorizes human experiences. Sapir built on the relationship between language and behavior by asserting that language determines human behavior. He believes that this causal relationship between language and behavior is automatic and involuntary. Because of the nature of language and behavior, it may be difficult for people to understand how language causes and frames their actions.

Whorf's Principle of Linguistic Relativity

Sapir's protégé, Benjamin Lee Whorf, developed Sapir's ideas into what he coined the *linguistic relativity principle*. Whorf's linguistic relativity principle has also been referred to as *linguistic relativity* as well as *linguistic determinism*. In *Language, Thought, and Reality,* Whorf explains linguistic relativity as "the forms of a person's thoughts are controlled by inexorable laws of pattern of which he is unconscious. These patterns are the unperceived intricate systematizations of his own language shown readily enough by a candid comparison and contrast with other languages" (p. 252).

Simply phrased, because language shapes reality and multiple language systems exist, multiple realities must exist also. Whorf's notion directly counters the notion of Universalism, which asserts that humans fundamentally share similar perceptions of the world even if they do not share the same language. He contends that different grammar patterns cause people to observe phenomena in multiple ways, thus creating cultural differences because language does not remain the same across all social groups. Language determines the nature of human thought and accounts for many cultural worldviews. Whorf contends that language creates perceptions of social reality, and he further asserts that language is the originator of culture. Because language controls human cognition, it in turn patterns humans' experiences in systematic ways. Language shapes ideas and interactions. Whorf posits that because cognition is an unconscious process, people cannot control their own language. This explains how misinterpretations and misunderstandings occur in intercultural encounters because meanings of different language systems do not converge.

Whorf's Examination of Language Systems

Whorf supported his ideas of linguistic relativity through his research of language systems from different cultures. One of his most renowned research projects examined Native American language systems and what he terms Standard Average European languages. He is most famed for his comparison and analysis of Hopi and English to illustrate his ideas. To argue for linguistic determinism, Whorf examined the constructions of time in each language system. Because speakers of Hopi and English encode time differently, they construct their concepts of time in different manners as well. In English (in addition to other Western languages), time is referred to grammatically as object nouns. It is also described in a linear, logical fashion. Hopi does not regard time in this manner. Instead, time refers to temporal cycles, rather than concrete objects. Therefore, time is not a "thing," but a recurring process. English speakers perceive time as a fact occurring on the continuum of past, present, and future. The phrases "She is running" or "He ran" illustrate linear notions of time. Hopi speakers, on the other hand, focus on whether time is recalled, observed, or expected. For example, the phrase *era wari* refers to someone running as a recalled event, not as an observed event.

Whorf contends that the manner in which English and Hopi systematically frame and regard time causes speakers of these languages to perceive and experience time *according to* these linguistic frames. Hopi speakers regard time as a process resulting in accumulated experiences. Therefore, they spend more time engaging in preparation of an experience. English speakers regard time as an object that orders occurrences. They perceive time as an occurrence that has taken place, is currently taking place, or will take place. Because of this, time as an object can be lost or bought. In Western languages, a person who does not adhere to time correctly can be considered "late" or "early." In some Native American languages, however, there is no word for "late." Linguistic determinism contends that because this word does not exist in a language, this concept cannot exist in the minds of its speakers.

Illustrations in Other Language Systems

Advocates of the Sapir-Whorf hypothesis have examined how Native American and Western language systems affect behavior and perceptions of reality as well. *Diné*, the language of the Navajo, uses vocabulary for colors differently than English does. For example, Diné has two different words for variations of the color black. In English, the language structure recognizes blue and green as distinctive colors. In contrast, Diné uses the same word to refer to both colors. Proponents of the Sapir-Whorf hypothesis contend that since language frames reality, Diné speakers and English speakers perceive these colors differently based on the vocabularies within these distinct languages.

Communication and linguistics scholars have noticed difference in language systems even when there are more cultural similarities. Whorf compared Western languages and Native American languages using English and Hopi as exemplars; however, languages that have more in common also reflect tenets of this hypothesis. For example, Spanish (a Western romance language) and English use formal and informal pronouns differently. Spanish uses *tu* and *usted* for the pronoun *you*. *Tu* is used for informal contexts, whereas *usted* is used for more formal settings. English, however, makes no distinction between informal and formal uses of the pronoun *you*. According to the Sapir-Whorf hypothesis, this difference in language structure affects how speakers of each language construct and interpret reality in terms of the formality and informality of social settings.

Critiques

The Universalist Position

Universalists do not support the Sapir-Whorf hypothesis because they assert that language mirrors reality, not constructs it. As the name suggests, Universalists believe that different language structures may refer to social phenomena in different manners; however, they fundamentally address the same objective, external reality. Some languages make more nuanced distinctions of reality based on its relevance to their particular cultures. For example, Universalists would assert that the differences in colors between Diné and English describe the same reality. The differences suggest a variation of the importance of a certain aspect of reality, not different realities. According to the Universalist position, even though Diné has two words for shades of black and English uses only one, English speakers can modify the word *black* to show distinctions between these shades. The adjectives, *light* and *dark* can make these distinctions. Further, a phrase such as *midnight black* may also be used to refer to a darker shade of black. Language structures possess multiple ways of referring to the same reality, but these distinctions do not affect how people perceive reality—merely how they describe it.

Critiques From Nonverbal Communication

Communication scholars assert that communication comprises both verbal and nonverbal messages. Those studying nonverbal communication believe that language only constitutes part of what people communicate to each other and, therefore, how they respond to and interpret the world around them. Cultural context serves as a useful exemplar of the impact of nonverbal cues in communicative exchanges. Communication scholars generally regard nonverbal cultural context in two categories: low-context communication and high-context communication. Low-context cultures place a higher emphasis on language when communicating. High-context cultures, however, place a higher emphasis on the context and nonverbal cues when communicating. The Sapir-Whorf hypothesis is more applicable in low-context cultures that derive meaning primarily from words. Members of high-context cultures, contrarily, use more nonverbal cues to communicate and derive meaning when interacting with others. Language does not weigh as heavily as a source of information when constructing meaning about the social world.

Functional Relativity: Finding a Middle Ground

The Sapir-Whorf hypothesis, with roots in determinism, directly opposes the Universalist approach, which contends there is one external, objective reality. Functional relativity provides another perspective regarding the relationship between language and culture. Proponents assert that language must be understood in terms of its function in human communication. Functional relativists do not focus on cognition or causality, nor do they contend that one objective reality exists for everyone. Instead, they believe that language exists to achieve understanding of the social world and communicative exchanges between people. Because different social and cultural groups will understand the world in different ways and have various communication needs, scholarship should examine the relationships between language use and goals of particular cultural groups. People purposefully apply language systems to understand their particular social context, so cultures develop distinct and multiple ways of manipulating language to achieve their goals.

Functional relativists do not attempt to predict the relationship between language and culture; rather, they seek to describe its use in selected cultural groups. Language correlates to the values of its users at specific times, so there can be no static objective reality. With a focus on understanding, functional relativism opens the door to learning about the relationship between language and culture without predetermined assumptions about the social world. This approach considers multilingual speakers who have more than one language system in their linguistic repertoires. Further, it addresses language that may not be verbalized, such as American Sign Language, a linguistic system commonly used in deaf communities in the United States. Proponents have also examined cross-cultural exchanges between people of different cultures. Although functional relativity does not adhere to the strong beliefs of the Sapir-Whorf hypothesis or Universalism, it serves as a useful alternative to understand the dynamics of language and culture that both Sapir and Whorf sought to achieve.

Cerise L. Glenn

See also Acculturation; Bilingualism; Code-Switching; Language; Language Development

Further Readings

Gudykunst, E. (Ed.). (2003). *Cross-cultural and intercultural communication*. Thousand Oaks, CA: Sage.

Sapir, E. (1921). *Language: An introduction to the study of speech*. New York: Harcourt Brace.

Sapir, E. (1949). *The selected writings of Edward Sapir in language, culture, and personality*. Berkeley: University of California Press.

Whorf, B. L. (1956). *Language, thought, and reality*. New York: Wiley.

Satire

Satire is considered a literary genre; it is often used in the performing arts; and it is used to highlight human folly, vice, abuse, or shortcomings to affect a change in attitude, action, or belief. Thus, *satire* refers to ridicule or criticism with a moral intention. Commonly, satire is comical although it is not always humorous because the intention is to encourage serious improvement in the lives of the audience. In other words, although satire is often meant to be funny, its purpose is not to merely entertain the audience; the purpose is to specifically condemn the subject by drawing attention to the subject's shortcomings. Most satire seems to glorify the topic being criticized, but the use of satiric elements shows that the satirist actually disapproves of the subject. Satire is now part of mainstream U.S. culture and is often used in popular movies, situational comedies, and newspapers.

Often a satirist employs irony, parody, sarcasm, exaggeration, juxtaposition, caricature, and double entendre to make his or her point about the topic or individual of reproach. *Irony* is an inconsistency between what is said and what is meant. There are three types of irony—dramatic, verbal, and situational. *Parody* is a humorous imitation of a serious work. *Sarcasm* is related to *irony*, in that what is said is the opposite of what is intended. Sarcastic remarks require a second order of interpretation to ascertain the speaker's intention. *Exaggeration* is a rhetorical device that deploys overstatement. *Juxtaposition* is a technique that places two concepts side by side for comparison or contrast. A *caricature* is a description or a portrait that exaggerates or distorts prominent characteristics or attributes of a public figure either for humor or critique. *Double entendre* is language that has more than one meaning; usually, one of the interpretations can be unseemly. However, some satire relies solely on the use of humor without using any other satiric devices such as irony, parody, or double entendre. Humor is often used so that the audience is more likely to receive a message that may otherwise come across as moralistic, but some satire uses no humor at all. Perhaps the message is considered so serious that humor is not deemed appropriate. Furthermore, satiric devices are often used in other genres, so the audience needs to know the purpose of the work to determine if it is satire to avoid misunderstandings. Language is, therefore, critical in a satirical work because it is the crux upon which the clear reception of the message rests.

This entry discusses the role satire plays in identity formation and maturation and in U.S. culture, provides literary and cinematic examples, and presents criticisms of satire.

Role in Identity Formation and Maturation

Satire can be used as an important tool of identity formation and maturation because satire is criticism with moral intention, and moral responsibility is an integral part of a person's identity. A formed personal and social identity are both critical for recognizing and attacking social malaise. Effective satire depends on the moral sensitivity and critical ability of the audience; without either, the audience may not receive the message or may not be aware that a message is being communicated. Without these, the audience cannot enact the desired change. Further, identity is influenced by culture; so satire, which permeates culture, influences the identity formation of many U.S. citizens. Satire pushes boundaries and asks individuals to take stock of the ills of their society and necessary change: change of self, change of alliances, or change within society.

Forms of Satire

Satire has been used in the United States since early in the country's development. Benjamin Franklin is often noted for his use of satire although several other colonists used this tool in encouraging a cultural identity and set of social norms. This genre has also been important in the 20th century, used by authors such as George Orwell to warn European and U.S. societies of the consequences of their actions. Some have commented on how prophetic Orwell's writings have been. Other U.S. satirists include Ambrose Bierce, H. L. Mencken, Washington Irving, P. J. O'Rourke, Ishmael Reed, and Kurt Vonnegut.

Literature

Mark Twain is another well-known U.S. satirist. His novel *The Adventures of Huckleberry Finn* is an example of a satirical U.S. literary work that depicts the ills of society and the need for personal maturation; however, it is also an example of a work that was not readily accepted by its contemporary audience and is still debated for its merits in modern U.S. society. In this novel, Twain addresses the racial tension that was present in the United States before the Civil War. Slavery was integral in the U.S. South, but a careful reading of this text may reveal that Twain uses this work to show how oppression degrades the oppressed and the oppressors. Twain shows that people who were considered good people did not extend sympathy to others who were being mistreated, so Huckleberry Finn, who was abused, questions the moral fabric of the society.

As Huckleberry Finn develops a friendship with Jim, a slave seeking freedom, he begins to assess situations making moral judgments based on his conscience. His decisions were not considered appropriate according to the South's set of cultural mores, but Huck Finn was learning to make decisions based on his own interpretation of right and wrong. Huck becomes the moral antithesis of the culture around him. This work, although it is often interpreted as showing the degraded moral state of a society, also depicts one young man's personal maturation. Huck Finn develops as an independent thinker, one who does not easily conform to the expectations of others. As he grows and experiences and witnesses abuses, Huck balks at the hypocrisy that he sees. *The Adventures of Huckleberry Finn* is considered adolescent fiction, so the protagonist, Huck Finn, can serve as an example for young people who read the novel. As an adolescent boy, Huck is in the same process of developing personal identity and critical thinking abilities as young readers are. However, if the reader does not recognize this work as satire, the example is lost and the book may seem offensive.

Because many people do not read *The Adventures of Huckleberry Finn* as satiric, this work has been considered controversial since its publication in 1885. Initially, the book was considered crude, but as more attention has been focused on race relations in the United States, Twain's treatment of race has become more the center of contention. As this book is vivid and the characters' language depicts vernaculars that were employed during the period, many critics believe that the work glorifies racism of the period while other scholars maintain that the work satirizes racism in the United States. This current controversy can reveal that race is still an unsettled matter in the United States more than 100 years after the publication of this work, but more to the point, it is also an example of how satire is a genre that can be interpreted or misinterpreted by the audience and therefore, accepted or rejected unfairly. Interpretation depends on the audience's knowledge of the author's purpose for writing and his or her intended message.

Another commonly read satire is Jonathan Swift's pamphlet "A Modest Proposal: For Preventing the Children of Poor People in Ireland From Being a Burden to Their Parents or Country, and for Making Them Beneficial to the Public." Swift was not a U.S. satirist, but the pamphlet is considered an important work that is commonly read in the United States as an example of argumentative writing. In this work, the narrator states that poor Irish citizens should sell their children to wealthy people so that the children can be eaten, thereby eradicating poverty. The narrator begins gravely discussing the plight of the poor Irish people and their children who are forced to beg in the streets. The lofty language and serious tone in the beginning of the pamphlet suggest that the narrator is serious about this particular matter, but as one continues to read, the argument presented is so preposterous that it is difficult to imagine people not recognizing Swift's use of metaphor, sarcasm, and irony.

Some scholars think that this work attacks the conditions of Ireland and England's treatment of the Irish while still holding the Irish responsible for not bettering their situation. Other scholars feel that the work underscores the economic structure of the period. Still others feel that the work is more critical of social workers of the period who devise illogical, useless plans to better the living conditions of the less fortunate. Nevertheless, this work forces the reader to look closely at the plight of the Irish and what people or circumstances are responsible for the predicament. Readers of the period may not have readily accepted the message contained in Swift's pamphlet, but perhaps they would have been able to decipher the metaphors and sarcasm employed and, as a result, realize the deplorable conditions of the impoverished. Some, however, may have taken the work as a declaration of the benefits of cannibalism.

Television and Cinema

Many other U.S. satirists have helped shape the U.S. cultural identity. These satirists are more often found in mainstream United States because they employ the use of television and cinema. This U.S. satire usually includes humor, however, and focuses most commonly on social ills or human shortcomings although some satire does specifically target the political arena. Most people are more familiar with the social commentaries because these satires tend to be more prevalent in everyday U.S. life. For example, many of the most-watched or long-running television shows are satirical. It is difficult to watch U.S. television without viewing something that is purely satiric or has elements of satire. *The Simpsons, Reno 911!, South Park, Saturday Night Live,* and *Family Guy* are some contemporary U.S. television shows that condemn aspects of U.S. life. For example, *The Simpsons* and *Family Guy* are both animated shows that center on the lives of middle-class U.S. families, but each has a different focus. *The Simpsons* tends to discuss global issues such as the environment and the entertainment industry, whereas *Family Guy* illustrates the ills of a dysfunctional family and comments on the particular personality flaws in people of various walks of life.

In *Family Guy,* Peter Griffin is the patriarch of the family, but he does not demonstrate the maturity and responsibility typically associated with adults. His wife Lois teaches piano lessons and dotes on their youngest child. The two have three children, each of whom has some mediocre quality or offbeat characteristic. Peter makes fun of their daughter Meg because she is unattractive and unpopular. Their older son Chris is overweight and dull like his father. Stewie, the youngest, is adult-like, speaks with a British accent, and attempts to wreak havoc on humankind. Finally, the family has a dog named Brian who has been personified, walks on two legs, and participates in human conversation. Brian also drinks alcohol and smokes cigarettes; nevertheless, he is considered the family pet. Like other satiric television shows focusing on the U.S. family—*Married With Children,* for example—this television show presents the unrealistic nature of other shows that encourage the myth of the ideal U.S. family, which is believed to contain a husband, wife, 2.5 children, a house, and a dog.

Reno 911! is another popular satirical television show, and it parodies another television show, *Cops. Cops* is considered a serious "reality" show about criminal activity in the United States. *Cops* follows real police officers in their daily routines. *Reno 911!,* however, depicts the experiences of an inept police force in daily encounters. This show pointedly parodies *Cops* and some of the documented experiences of the real-life police officers. *Reno 911!* depicts the absurdity of some criminal behavior but also emphasizes problems inherent in local U.S. law enforcement agencies.

Other contemporary U.S. satire focuses on political events and attitudes. *The Simpsons* and *South Park* are often considered political commentaries, although the political references are often vague and not the focus of the episodes. Other shows such as *The Daily Show With Jon Stewart* and *The Colbert Report* are premised on ridiculing the U.S. political arena as well as critiquing journalistic or media practice in the United States. The *Daily Show* is a fake news show that exposes the shortcomings of broadcast journalism. A spin-off of the *Daily Show,* the *Colbert Report* is a direct parody of conservative news commentators, featuring *Daily Show* alumnus Stephen Colbert. Colbert's character is an arrogant, ignorant, stubborn, and self-righteous ideologue. Colbert's show highlights what can be deemed the extreme nature of some commentators who may seem to misinterpret or exaggerate the actions and statements of political figures. Both shows condemn commentators and public figures for making illogical assessments of political events.

Most satirical U.S. films use humor to ridicule some political event or idea, the entertainment industry, or human folly. These films often rely heavily on parody and usually contain bawdy material. *The Great Dictator,* arguably Charlie Chaplin's most critically acclaimed film, is an example of early cinematic use of satire. In this film, Chaplin mocks Hitler and Nazism. This film bitterly condemned the treatment of the Jews and is still held as an intensely culturally relevant movie. *Blazing Saddles, Clueless, Fight Club, Citizen Ruth,* and *Thank You for Smoking* are examples of more recent U.S. satirical films that draw attention to many U.S. social problems such as racism, sexism advertising ethics, and controversies over family planning, birth control, abortion, and so on. The Wayans family is a more contemporary example of satirical entertainers. This family of actors and producers has made movies and TV shows satirizing the entertainment industry, specifically condemning racism in "blaxploitation" films—movies that rearticulated and extended stereotypes of African Americans as they were marketed to primarily Black audiences.

Criticism

Satire is often misunderstood—many people do not take the message that a satirist expresses seriously. Although many satirists bemoan the misunderstanding, they also commonly complain about the listeners who are offended by the messages that are understood. Often, the satirist will discuss the individuals who approve of jokes or parodies that do not criticize their position or particular experience but who become incensed when the focus is on an event or idea that affects them directly. Some critics say that satire that offends them is in poor taste or crude, as is the case with Twain's *The Adventures of Huckleberry Finn.* Often, however, the reader has simply misunderstood the author's message.

A recent example of controversy over satirical humor is the public outcry over a political cartoon in *The New Yorker* magazine that featured a depiction of President Barack Obama. Because Obama is the first African American president, it was unclear to audiences if the cartoon in question was merely recirculating racist stereotypes, or if the artist was ridiculing Americans who held racist attitudes. This particular cartoon featured then-Senator and Mrs. Obama. They are depicted fist bumping—Mrs. Obama is dressed as a terrorist with a large afro and machine gun, and Mr. Obama wears Muslim attire. In the background are a large picture of Osama bin Laden and a U.S. flag in the fire.

A firestorm of outrage was expressed in response to this drawing, but the cartoonist claims that the reaction to his work was not warranted. The cartoon was intended to deride individuals who made claims about the Obamas being radicals that "palled around with terrorists" in the oft-quoted phrase. However, many people were unsure of the artist's intent. Was he endorsing this view of the Obamas, or was the ridiculous and offensive depiction meant to reveal the preposterous nature of those claims? Despite the cartoonist's explanation and apology, many people were unwilling to view the work as satiric. Thus, there is always a risk that audiences will not interpret material as satirical.

Role in U.S. Culture

U.S. satire is an important tool used to express concerns about various aspects of U.S. life. Much of it has become so commonplace that it is considered humor, but U.S. residents often do not realize that they are being shaped by those they consider simple comedians making them laugh. Personal thoughts and resolves are reaffirmed by satirists who publicly condemn many things that common U.S. residents find reprehensible but do not have the voice or ability to rally against.

Mari A. Johnson

See also Conflict; Culture; Figures of Speech; Idiomatic Expressions; Language; Semantics; Stereotypes

Further Readings

Archbold, W. A. J. (1970). *Twentieth-century essays and addresses.* New York: Books for Libraries Press.

Dryden, J. (1693). A discourse concerning the original and progress of satire. In *The satires of Decimus Junius Juvenalis* (Translated into English verse by Mr. Dryden and several other eminent hands). London: J. Tonson.

Elkin, P. K. (1973). *The Augustan defence of satire.* Oxford, UK: Clarendon Press.

Frederick, K., & Shuttleworth, J. M. (1971). *Satire from Aesop to Buchwald.* New York: Odyssey Press.

Highet, G. (1962). *The anatomy of satire.* Princeton, NJ: Princeton University Press.

Kirk, E. (1980). *Menippean satire: An annotated catalogue of texts and criticism.* New York: Garland Press.

Orwell, G. (2003). *Animal Farm: A fairy story.* New York: Harcourt Brace.

Swift, J. (2001). *Gulliver's travels.* New York: Penguin.

SATURATED IDENTITY

In the last half of the 20th century, people's daily experiences began to be transformed through technological change. *Saturated identity* (also referred to as *saturated self*) refers to the idea that self is increasingly saturated or filled to overflowing by the unceasing stimuli available via technological advancements. Social psychologist Kenneth Gergen coined the term *saturated self* to address the relationship between the individual and his or her social environment, which is technologically dynamic. Identity scholars are interested in the saturated self because this idea points to the multiple possibilities that exist as an individual continuously emerges and reforms one's identity in relationship with others. Although social and informational technologies assault the self through massive stimulation, they also hold the possibility for advancing community over individualism and promoting more meaningful relationships.

Identity: A Normative Product

In shaping one's identity, what a person is really like is a product of the ideological, intellectual, political, economic, and literary forces that construct culture, as well as the historical moment of which one is a part—one's cultural inheritance. At various points in time, different views of the self have dominated social thought. The romanticist conception of self gave rise to a vocabulary of moral feeling, loyalty, and inner joy. The modernist view of personality held the reason and observation manifest in science, government, and business as central to human functioning. Historically, identities were seen as more stable and reliable, created through face-to-face interaction, which enabled a firm sense of self. There was strong agreement on patterns of right and wrong, and one could simply be.

As the modern self began to be pulled in different directions through technology, people experienced an enhanced sense of playing a role and acting a part to achieve various goals. With the emergence of postmodern pluralism came an increasing sensitivity to the social construction of reality. No self exists independently of the relationships and context in which one finds oneself. There is no individual essence(s) to which a person remains true or committed—although one may adhere to romanticist and modern views of the self that are also available as a possibility within postmodernity. Identity is continuously emerging and reformed through relationships with others made possible by cell phones, the Internet, and other emerging technologies. Lived experiences are saturated with textuality and discourse. Popular culture barrages people with images and aspects of potential identities that can be purchased or developed.

Identity: Multiplicity and Fragmentation

A person shapes one's identity by *populating the self* or infusing multiple partial identities. *Multiphrenia* refers to the fragmenting or splitting of the individual into multiple areas of self-investment. Each area of self-investment informs aspects in the creation of self—whether to invest (or not) in athletic, culinary, musical, intellectual, and other pursuits as a means to define oneself. One may experience vertigo thinking about the unlimited possibilities for creating one's identity. A *pastiche personality* emerges because it becomes increasingly difficult to distinguish a core essence(s) to which one will remain true. Compared with a modern sense of self, in postmodernity authenticity becomes frayed and a perception of superficiality emerges. As social saturation occurs, people imitate selected patterns of being that are introduced by others. Each "truth" about one's identity is constructed in a particular moment and true for a specific time within certain relationships. At different times, people foreground selected aspect(s) of their identity, which is at the same time influenced by fragments of other identity practices.

With respect to communication, the saturated self recognizes that words are expressions used by various social groups to represent conventions particular to that group. Different social groups use different vocabularies to reflect their values, politics, and ways of life. These forms of communication become localized to participants in various professional, political, religious, and other social groups. No perspective-free position or final voice speaks beyond the interests of a given community, social group, or even individual. All attempts to tell the truth are constructions of language that are fragments that represent meaning in pluralistic and diffuse ways. Some people find it difficult to make a serious investment in language, which is constantly undergoing change. Diverse social groups use language differently to represent their varied experiential realities.

Identity: Otherness

Technologies of social saturation are central to the contemporary erasure of an individual self. We live in a multiplex that acknowledges the interrelationship of biological, social, and physical worlds. The saturated self is not a dissolution of one's self but a shift to a *relational self*. When people are bombarded by electronic messages and open to unlimited personal relationships, the self as an entity breaks down and a person becomes a relational self—wherein the relationship, rather than the individual, is the center of human action. A stable sense of self is replaced by the reality of relatedness with others. Rather than focusing on personal being, one's role is as a participant in the social process; each person is ever-exploring the overabundance of possibilities associated with the construction and manifestation of oneself within the social sphere. Living in a world saturated by communication technologies intensifies the possibilities for relationships with others and enhances opportunities for people to increase their social connections. Within postmodern pluralism, co-created culture is the center of human functioning.

Pat A. Arneson

See also Development of Identity; Development of Self-Concept; Identity Change; Language; Self-Concept; Society and Social Identity

Further Readings

Gergen, K. J. (1991). *The saturated self: Dilemmas of identity in contemporary life.* New York: Basic Books.

Gergen, K. J. (1994). *Realities and relationships: Soundings in social construction.* Cambridge, MA: Harvard University Press.

Sugiman, T., Gergen, K. J., Wagner, W., & Yamada, Y. (Eds.). (2008). *Meaning in action: Constructions, narratives, and representations.* Tokyo: Springer.

SCOPOPHILIA

Scopophilia is mostly related to Jacques Lacan's notion of the gaze. However, Sigmund Freud first introduced the concept in 1905 in his *Three Essays on the Theory of Sexuality. Scopophilia* refers to the pleasure of looking as well as the pleasure of being looked at. It therefore has both voyeuristic and exhibitionistic, as well as narcissistic, overtones. Freud believed the child's looking is motivated by an inquisitive and curious desire to look at forbidden body parts and functions that foreshadow fantasies concerning phallic (masculine) desire, such as the shocking pleasure of seeing genitalia that establish sexual differences. Children manifest voyeuristic tendencies in their desire to see the private and the forbidden. This applies to heterosexual and homosexual sexual desire. Scopophilia is therefore a pre-Oedipal phase when the child still continues to blur the important distinction between an active pleasure of looking (voyeurism) and the passive pleasure of being looked at (exhibitionism), which become codified, according to Freud, as masculine and feminine respectively during Oedipal development. Classically, according to this view, the active voyeuristic function is distinctly masculine and phallic, whereas the passive exhibitionist view is distinctly feminine and castrating. Scopophilia remains a part of our sexual identity because through it we derive erotic pleasure in either heterosexual or homosexual forms of sexual desire.

The Look of Desire

Lacan linked this scopophilic drive to G. W. F. Hegel's master-slave relationship when developing his theory of the gaze. Lacan demonstrated the dialectical association between the subject and the Other, which he claimed constituted subjectivity. The outside societal gaze, in effect, puts one in the social symbolically constructed "picture." By knowing how one is being put in this picture, how one is situated in it—that is, by the way a subject is being framed by the societal gaze—enables some agency to occur. One can "play" with the expected societal gaze to disturb it performatively and thereby mask identity. This raises the notion of simulacra where identity through camouflage can take place. One can mask or pretend—that is, *feign*—a form of subjectivity precisely to avoid detection by imitating or mimicking the way the social order is "putting one in the picture." Lacan made scopophilia more complex.

Visual and cultural theorists have taken up the notion of scopophilia as constituting a look of desire. Laura Mulvey is credited with initiating a politically feminist agenda into cinematic studies maintaining that the constituted screen that is technologically materialized through various apparatuses (television, cinema, the computer's World Wide Web, camera digitalization, cyber-screens and so on) plays with our scopophilic drive through voyeuristic, exhibitionistic, and narcissistic fantasies that enable desire to wander about in imaginative pleasure. In contrast, *scopophobia* is the fear of being looked or stared at. Spectators love looking at themselves in narcissistic fashion, especially when the images they see of themselves come close to the ego ideal they imaginatively hold as to how they should and do look. The confirming mirror is therefore the scopophilic drive, which assures us that we "love" ourselves in the way we believe we look. Cinema's attention to the human form, in the way cinema anthropomorphizes the image, provides ample opportunity to satisfy our needs for likeness and recognition. When we see other people as objects (as voyeurs), we covet a certain power, and we acquire power in exhibitionism through the desire of being looked at and confirmed as being beautiful and recognizable. Narcissistic scopophilia becomes an act of looking at other people and seeing them as surrogates of oneself. This is a confirmation of self-love. Spectators identify with characters in movies, as well as abjecting others, thus creating a tension between the sense of power they receive from observing others as being separate and different from themselves and the pleasure received in imagining and identifying with characters and people they are looking at.

We can say that reality television, as first developed in the beginning of the 21st century, offers the perfect closed circuit of scopic looking. Reality television presents the perversion of scopophilia in a society of enjoyment and consumerism. During Freud's time, blatant displays of both voyeurism and exhibitionism were policed through social norms, taboos, and rules. Beginning with the society of the spectacle as articulated by Guy Debord, and well into our own screen society of the 21st century, what were considered perverse acts have become commonplace occurrences in celebrity cultures. Women can no longer be so easily looked at as merely sex "objects" by men because women can look back, as do hyper-femme fatales who risk their bodies to be seen, rejecting patriarchy and wielding power as in Rob Marshall's 2002 ironic film *Chicago*. Set in the 1920s, Velma Kelly and Roxie Hart have killed their double-crossing lovers (husband and boyfriend, respectively), yet they continue to vie for stardom on death row through media hype by using their "bodily" talents.

Complexities of Voyeurism

In reality television, spectators are always positioned as active voyeurs having power over the subject they are seeing in containers, on islands, in houses, or in compounds—in short, in any contained identifiable space that is riddled with cameras. This active looking is then perfectly complemented by the passive exhibitionism of the ordinary "real" actors themselves. They are told *not* to play into the camera, for this would disturb the perfect exchange of erotic desire that is established between audience and the pseudo actors who are quite aware that cameras are present.

Another subject position also disrupts this perfect scopophilic circuit and ruins the voyeur's pleasure, making him or her doubt having the power of looking in rather than looking out. This can be illustrated by the reality game show *Joe Schmo* that took its script from the film, *The Truman Show*. The contestant was unaware that actors pretending to be part of a reality show within the *Joe Schmo* show were mislead him. The first season had Matt Kennedy Gould as the "schmo" who thought he was a contestant in a reality game show called *Lap of Luxury*. What Gould did was to follow the rules of the game to the letter, so much so that it became difficult for audience and producers alike to figure out whether he was "in the know.'" Was he intentionally overplaying his part, becoming a

hyper-exhibitionist who was beginning to short circuit the active/passive binary? This led to a hysterical state that spread even to the actors. When Earl ("the Veteran") on the set bonded with Gould, but was then "voted" off the show, Gould psychically broke down and began to openly weep, unable to pull himself together. Was Gould "genuinely" feeling Earl's loss, like the moment when Truman reunites with his father again and begins to shed tears? Or was he faking it? The actors were not sure. They began consoling one another as well. Were they then faking it or genuinely distraught because Gould was distraught? Both voyeurism and exhibitionism perversely collapse into one another with the pleasure of seeing is disrupted because the viewers are left unsure of what they have seen. Even the normative pleasure derived from simply *knowing,* which is what scopophilia makes possible when watching television programs (other than reality series), is cast into doubt here. The producers wanted to stop shooting. Gould's case shows how the power of imitation, in this case over-identification, can be disruptive.

Television is therefore a medium suited to scopophilic intimacy. Trevor Parry-Giles discusses how the political campaigns of presidential candidates in the United States have to play the game of intimate, self-disclosing style that appeals to the voyeurism of some voters and the normative pleasures of scopophilic identification for others. The scopophilic impulse of the spectator-voters has to be properly judged and weighed. Candidates have to exhibit moments of self-disclosure but too much exhibitionist exposure leads to a loss of the sense of the candidate being presidential, as one who is capable of wielding symbolic capital. In other words, intimacy can lead to castration, a sense of impotency and loss of authority. The candidate would be reduced to being just another ordinary schmo—the danger candidates face by making guest appearances on the nightly televised comedy circuit.

Evil Eye

With the emergence of *YouTube* on the Internet, it has become easier to ridicule the pretense that election campaigners are not trying to garner symbolic capital through election promises and slogans. Campaigners become simply ordinary schmos, caught saying outrageous statements, exhibiting outbursts of uncontrollable emotions, or simply caught picking their noses or scratching their derrieres. Therefore, another side of scopophilia is much more sinister; Lacan referred to this as the *evil eye*. The one who is able to totally harness the gaze through his or her look has extraordinary powers. The evil eye is a *fascinum* (spell). A magician or a witch is said to possess a powerful evil eye, albeit sex/gendered differently, that renders the Other into having complete lack or agency; movement is frozen through fascination. Arresting movement or suspending it, like a doe caught in the lights of an automobile, spells death. This is precisely what the perverse subject of the evil eye desires—to keep the Other perfectly passive, in denial, and in disavowal. The evil eye possessing the symbolic gaze is therefore a threat. Even the handheld camera that exposes the politician through the *YouTube* can be said to possess an evil eye of power and explains why the paparazzi are so hated by celebrities who are afraid of being photographed off guard. Consider, for example, a celebrity who is caught in public in various states of undress or "costume malfunctions." Are these intentional acts on the celebrities' part? Or, are they perverse acts of intentional exhibitionism that reward the voyeuristic public that wants to see the celebrities exposed? We may never know. Under the normative circumstances of scopophilic desire, inadvertent exposure of genitalia—the most private of body parts becoming public—truly renders the subject *naked* and *frail* and not *nude,* which still has a sense of agency about it. This is why the pornographic image, it is argued, cannot be so easily rendered as simply as an objectification of a woman's body. The naked-nude distinction rests on the relationship of the way one is seen. This is starkly rendered by women who install cameras in their bathrooms and bedrooms and have paying customers observe them over stream video on the Internet. It is not unusual, however, for these women to tease and infuriate their paying voyeurs by turning a camera off now and again, castrating the Other, and confirming who is controlling and in possession of the gaze. Here the paranoid position of being watched is reversed and controlled. The perverse position of an exhibitionist is not one of feeling naked; on the contrary, it is wanting to be seen in the full desire of the Other, including the gesture of covering up the body when so desired.

Scopophilic nakedness of the evil eye mortifies the body. It exposes the subjects. There is no protection, no mask, and no masquerade to hide from the blinding light of the gaze in possession of the Other. This scopophilic look that captures the gaze cannot be articulated in positive, that is, representational, terms. In other words, it is not possible to specify all the characteristics of identity. When looking, something always escapes. Identification based on the dialectics of negativity—what *is,* is what is *not*—presents the complicated phenomenon of non-representability as informing scopophilia; and this non-representability is, for Lacan, unconscious and not articulable.

jan jagodzinski

See also Gaze; Simulacra; Society of the Spectacle; Visualizing Desire

Further Readings

Debord, G. (1995). *The society of the spectacle.* New York: Zone Books.
Freud, S. (1953–1974). Three essays on the theory of sexuality. In J. Strachey et al. (Eds.), *The standard edition of the complete works of Sigmund Freud* (24 vols., SE 7, pp. 123–243). London: Hogarth Press and the Institute of Psychoanalysis. (Original work published 1905)
Parry-Giles, T. (1996). Political scopophilia, presidential campaigning, and the intimacy of American politics. *Communication Studies, 47,* 191–205.

SECULAR IDENTITY

The concept of *secular identity* was first developed in the mid-19th century to describe a set of beliefs about freedom of religion for the individual in a modern, national state. Secular identity grew with the expanding power and relevance of the state in the life of its citizens in European countries and the United States.

Early scholarly discussion of secular identity was dominated by its connection with the rise of power in the West. The sociologist Max Weber saw the decline in religious identity as marked by the changing social order caused by mass-market economies, industrialization, and universal ideas of citizenship in a state. The sociologist Paul Berger saw the West as predisposed to the rise of a secular identity because of its Judeo-Christian tradition of monotheism and ethical rationalization. For such thinkers, religion was increasingly viewed as less relevant to modern life. Émile Durkheim saw the rise of specialization in government and societal agencies as pushing religion to an ever-decreasing place in the lives of modern people. This view of secular identity is most easily understood by reviewing specific historical instances. The case of Zionism illuminates the new awareness of a changing identity especially well.

With the 20th-century emergence of fundamentalism (or the idea that religious doctrines and practices should be taken literally) in Islam, Christianity, and Judaism, secular-versus-religious debates have become part of an overall global dispute about the role of religion. For the anthropologist Talal Asad, the narratives of modernity have erased the importance of religion for personal identity in the modern nation state. For Asad, continued exercises of power by modernists were attempts to eliminate religion as a competitor. But the debate has reached no conclusion. For every attempt to secularize a population, there is also an example of an effort to place religion back into the discourse of public life. As an example, the recent history of Iran provides a valuable example of the struggle between religious and secular identity in a modern state.

Secular as a Political and Individual Definition: The Case of Zionism

Secular is often defined as a national or political identity. For example, the state of India is officially secular in its orientation. The state does not endorse a particular religion, and its institutions and offices are free from religious control. Secularism, in this context, becomes tied to the idea of national identity and is inseparable from it. The notion of a secular national identity developed along several lines in the 19th and 20th centuries, and often, quite surprisingly, arose from religious contexts. One such secular identity was Zionism.

Traditional religious Judaism was based partly on the assumption that individual Jews would not participate in the larger secular or religious cultures that surrounded them. Jews in Poland in the 18th century, for instance, were viewed primarily as Jews who existed within their own religious community. Jewish identity, as such, was derived from apolitical Jewish religious sources. Jewish identity before the formation of Zionism came from a mix of religious, cultural, and linguistic elements that combined to create a matrix of assumptions. One of the most important assumptions was that Jews would be restored to their homeland of Palestine, or the Land of Israel, by a God-appointed savior who would return Jews to their land and provide them with a Jewish government. This future messianic age would be completely in God's hands and would not be under the control of individual or collective Jews. Before the creation of Zionism, Jewish political identity was submerged in Jewish religious beliefs. Jews could not hasten the coming of the messiah and their return to the Land of Israel and their own government.

During the early- to mid-19th century, several European countries formally emancipated their Jewish citizens. Jews were no longer forced to reside in ghettos, wear distinctive clothing, or engage in certain proscribed trades. But the emancipation of Jews in Western Europe led to an identity crisis among some Jews who began to embrace the new, secular definition of a citizen of a modern state. In what sense was a person a Jew if he or she was now also a full-fledged citizen of a state that gave him or her another national identity? This vexing question, combined with the rise of anti-Semitism in some modern, secular countries, led to the emergence of Zionism.

Zionism from its beginning was conceived as a secular, Jewish alternative to modern European secularism and nationalism. Zionism took the political element latent in Rabbinic Judaism and gave it a place of centrality in an emerging secular outlook: the Land of Israel was the land promised to the Jews, but rather than being brought about by God, their return would be brought about by human activity. Zionist identity was deeply practical, eschewing most, if not all, of the theological elements of Judaism. It took from religious Judaism an abiding sense of the sacredness of the Land of Israel and molded that into a pragmatic program for the settlement of Palestine and the establishment of an independent Jewish state.

Zionism became, in a sense, a new religion of secular Jewish national identity. But Zionism opposed religious Judaism, and most religious Jews were opposed to Zionism in the early days of its existence. Still, Zionism took many of its most potent symbols from religious Judaism. For example, holidays in the Bible that stressed a connection with the Land of Israel were appropriated. The Feast of Shavuot, or the Feast of Weeks, was celebrated with great ceremony among the early agricultural communities in Palestine in the late 19th century because the harvest holiday fit with Zionism's goal of creating a new, secular Jew with a firm, concrete connection to the land. The Jewish religious holiday of Purim also took on new meaning in Zionism. In early Tel-Aviv, which was touted as the first modern Hebrew city, Purim became a vast municipal celebration, when citizens of Tel-Aviv wore costumes and marched in parades. In religious Judaism, Purim is a holiday based on small gatherings of people and the reading of the book of Esther, but for secular Zionism, the holiday became a great celebration of a new, secular identity. As secular Zionism spread and grew, it developed increasingly potent symbols, which enabled it to expand its reach and appeal to Jews who felt left out of the emerging secular nationalism of Europe.

Zionism came to provide an all-around identity for secular Jews in Palestine. Most importantly, Hebrew was revived as a spoken language, which gave Jews a common language of communication for the first time in 2,000 years. Hebrew was roundly endorsed as the language of secular Zionism and became the prime vehicle for the emergence of this new national and secular identity. A robust literature was created in Hebrew as poems, stories, and novels were written and published. Daily newspapers were printed in Hebrew, and all official business of the Jewish community in Palestine had to be conducted in Hebrew. Schools were created in which the primary language of instruction was Hebrew, and schools using other languages either volunteered or were forced to change to Hebrew.

Zionism became one of the most successful secular movements of the modern era. Zionists founded a Jewish state modeled after Western European democracies in Palestine, revived Hebrew as the language of that state, and most importantly, created a new Jew, called an Israeli, who was constructed wholly along nonreligious, secular lines. Zionism created a lasting shift in Jewish identity:

The Israeli citizen could be Jewish without being religious.

The Religious Critique of the Secular: The Case of Iran

Secular identity has been criticized from a religious standpoint almost from the beginning of the concept. Early in its development, secularism—especially in its nationalist, state-sponsored form—was viewed as atheistic, or essentially hostile to the idea of religion. In the West, ideas of human worth and value had been based on religious concepts, so the entire set of assumptions behind secular identity and secularism were viewed as false. In this view, there could be no identity without a religious foundation. Even so, the idea of secularism generally took hold in the West, and the neutrality of secularism was eventually viewed as a self-evident truth: society was a secular space where individuals could work, reside, and play without the systems or structures of organized religion.

Yet, with the spread of European colonialism and after its collapse following World War II, secular identity was increasingly viewed by non-Western cultures as simply another imperial tool of the West. Just like colonialism, secularism and its attitudes were criticized as largely harmful to postcolonial societies in Africa, Asia, and the Middle East.

Nowhere can this be better illustrated than in the case of Iran. In 1979, Islamic religious groups in Iran ousted the shah, or king of Iran. The shah had sought to secularize Iran and install nonreligious institutions in his government. For many Iranians, however, the government of the shah was deeply unpopular and seen as autocratic and oppressive to its people. When religious clerics seized power in Iran in 1979, they immediately set out to dismantle the shah's westernizing program. They imposed Islam in every facet of Iranian life, in a sense seeking to destroy the secular identity that had been created under the auspices of the shah. An Islamic Republic was formed, and elements of Islamic law, or the Shari'a, became the law of Iran.

The Iranian revolution was a change of government, but it was also a profound shift of identity. The leaders of the revolution sought to impose a religious identity on everyone in Iran. Iran's new religious government stripped the country of its secular base, and created a theocracy—a state ruled by religious law. There was an inherent criticism of secular identity in these moves. The Iranian revolutionaries did not see secularism as a neutral concept. For them, secular and Western ideas were equated; thus, the West was responsible for the harsh dictatorial rule of the shah and his supporters in the United States. All the trappings of secular society—such as freedom for women, religious tolerance, a free press, and the rights of religious minorities—were largely viewed as unwanted Western, anti-Islamic imports.

Iran's revolution was part of a greater, overall rejection of secular identity in some developing, non-Western regions of the world. Secular identity, by then long considered a neutral entity providing personal and religious freedom, was now in question. Secular identity was conceived as an imported concept competing with native culture and religion. It was viewed as anything but neutral, and actually as harmful and corrosive to traditional beliefs, religions, customs, and norms. Agreeing with the general reevaluation of the West and its values that took place in postcolonial arts, philosophy, politics, and historical studies, Iranian religious leaders viewed secular identity as yet another Western import.

This assessment has had powerful resonances throughout the world and has led to a great deal of cultural and religious dialogue. What, exactly, is the role of religion in a nation or for an individual? Can there be such a thing as a truly neutral, secular society or a secular self?

Future Directions

Secular identity as a concept has had a profound impact on the modern world, and the strength of its appeal can be seen in such diverse places as India, the United States, South Africa, and Taiwan. The great strides of secularism and secular identity point to a movement which will likely continue to grow in strength despite its critics. Secular identity continues to develop and transform under the pressure of new demands and challenges, and as it broadens its set of definitions, its relevance applies to new groups in new ways.

Eric Maroney

See also Citizenship; Colonialism; Eurocentricity; Fundamentalism; Globalization; Identity and Democracy; Religious Identity; Third World

Further Readings

Almog, O. (2000). *The Sabra: The creation of the new Jew.* Berkeley: University of California Press.

Amstrong, K. (2000). *The battle for God.* New York: Knopf.

Jackobsen, J., & Pellegrini, A. (2008). *Secularisms.* Chapel Hill, NC: Duke University Press.

Keddie, N. (2008). *Modern Iran: Roots and results of revolution.* New Haven, CT: Yale University Press.

Malise, R. (2004). *Fundamentalism: A search for meaning.* Oxford, UK: Oxford University Press.

Wheatcroft, J. (1996). *The controversy of Zion: Jewish nationalism, the Jewish state, and the unresolved Jewish dilemma.* Reading, MA: Addison-Wesley.

SELF

Understanding the constructed nature of social reality, the symbolic dimensions of social processes, the social production of human selves, the shared nature of meanings, and the dynamics entailed in the formation, reinforcement, transformation of the negotiated social order are some of the pivotal issues that students of social psychology have discussed ever since the discipline asserted itself as a viable intellectual enterprise. Among these issues, the discussion of the relationship between self and society has received a disproportional attention. The prominent figures in the field have addressed the issue in different ways while mostly attempting to provide a nuanced view of how individual actions are constituted in social contexts. These scholars have exhibited a strong desire to avoid the pitfalls of social determinism and psychological reductionism. Whereas social determinism focuses on the role of social structural processes in the making of individuals to the extent of disregarding singularity, psychological reductionism considers the individual as the building block of social history without accounting for the role of social forces. Recent social theorists are even clearer regarding the relationship between self and society than were their previous counterparts. In describing the connection between self and society, the preferred expression is "society of selves" instead of "self and society" because the latter implies that self and society are mechanically related to one another where the former acknowledges the reciprocal interconnection between active agents and social situations without glossing over their separation. This entry examines several theories of the self.

Modern Theories of the Self

The U.S. pragmatist George Hebert Mead was the first modern social theorist to clearly spell out a full-fledged theory of the self. In Mead's symbolic interactionist theory, the self is a social construct; yet the self retains its distinctiveness without being outside the context of the social. Selves are responsible for the existence of social activities, but the self exists in the context of social organization only. Following this important precept, Mead was able to provide a luminous view of the self as a process. Three important conclusions follow from this assumption. First, the self as process is an active agent, rather than a passive receptacle, whose nature is determined by unparalleled external social forces. The self reacts with dynamism in as much it is acted upon by processes beyond it. Second, the self, as a process, has the characteristics of being both subject and object to itself. As subject, the self is an agent that is actively involved in acts of reflexivity and communicative action, and as an object to itself, it is the subject of its own analysis. Third, by virtue of its capacity to observe itself as an object, the self adds an important dimension to itself: It is capable of taking the perspective of the other. Through this capacity to be in the shoes of others, individuals retain their identity without being an "I" unto themselves while the social characteristics of the self are asserted and reinforced.

Mead elaborates the latter point by way of a discussion of the bifurcated nature of the self. The self, according to Mead, consists of two inseparable and mutually reinforcing dimensions. He calls these aspects of the self the "I" and the "Me." The I represents the spontaneous and creative facet of the self. The I denotes that the social is not a fully coordinated organization in which individuals merely play a socially prescribed role. The Me represents the social face of the self. Although the I and the Me are interrelated, they remain separate. Except in uncharacteristic circumstances, such as religious fervor or acts of patriotism, in which both temporarily blend, the I and the Me are distinct. Because the self is a social construct, an individual is not born with the two aspects of the self marked for him or her. A good amount of time passes before the two facets of the self are differentiated. This moment of segregation, which is organically linked with the capacity of the self to participate in role-taking processes, comes at a later age.

Mead, accordingly, notes that there are three major steps in the genesis of the self. The first step involves what could be referred to as the *pre-play* stage. At this stage, children mimic the acts of their significant others. Despite taking the role of the other, the child cannot yet take on or see another person's perspective. Here the individual is a member of society by virtue of his or her descent and the social rights that it possesses. Sociologically speaking, however, it is an imminent "self-object" that lacks social characteristics. Hence, the self at this stage is a self only to the degree that it exists within the midst of a society of selves and it has the potential to be a full self. Only in the last stage, the game stage, does a child become a full person in the sense of being able to take the role of multiple others and understand the interconnection that exists between varied roles. Only here is imitation meaningful because it is based on a proper understanding of the subject reproduced. Once a child assumes the role of the "generalized other," he or she is capable of taking the perspective of the community at large—not passively imitating the actions of significant others, but creatively reacting to actions on the basis of understanding broader social processes. But this important stage is reached only after a child passes through the play stage, a stage in which a child takes the role of one concrete other at a time. Role taking at a play stage is limited, for a child lacks the capacity to partake in an abstract imaginative act to see the interconnection between multiple roles.

Quite a few social theorists have managed to reconstruct Mead's theory of the self with some success. Sheldon Stryker and Erving Goffman are among the most important theorists in this regard. The U.S. sociologist Stryker, who is famous for his identity theory, believes that, despite his important contributions to the theory of the self, Mead has not adequately addressed the relationship between social person and social structure. Although Mead contended that an individual can possess multiple selves, and the I and the Me are important dimensions of the self, he never fully extricated himself from the view that the self is an undifferentiated whole. Accordingly, consistent with Mead's point that the self is an active agent that exists in a symbolic universe, and mindful of the intersection between the self and social structure, Stryker provides his own structural version of symbolic interactionism. This structuralist perspective is primarily intended to show the intricate nature of the self because it exists within the perimeters of an increasingly differentiated social system. Self and social structure, however, do not exist in a separate realm; rather, they are two mutually conditioning aspects of the same whole.

In Stryker's structural symbolic interactionist approach of the self, *role theoretic concepts* play a critical role. Roles, as position-related performative expectations, act as important mediators between the social person and social structure. The concept of role, however, has to be stripped of its static connotations before it is synthesized with other symbolic interactionist concepts of the self. Stryker thus notes that roles are not preestablished scripts that are played out by social actors who have no choice but to act accordingly. Although roles are made possible in a relatively structured system of social relations, they are recast as they are played out. The extent to which roles are made depends on the nature of the existing structure. Some social structural conditions are much more open than others are in enabling members of society to perform roles in a creative fashion.

In Stryker's reconstructed notion of the self, a person does not possess more than one self; rather, Stryker notes the existence of multiple interrelated positional designations. He calls these context-dependent designations *identities*. An identity is a "part" within the same self and exists with other counterparts insofar as an individual is actively engaged in a complex social structure. Because actors assume multiple positions and play different roles corresponding to them, they have to prioritize their choices. Here, Stryker introduces the concept of *identity salience*, according to which identities are invoked in a given social situation on the basis of their place in the hierarchy of positional designations. Identity invocation is situational. In a relatively isolated social condition, only the same identity is invoked. But under situations where varied social spaces intersect, there is a good likelihood that multiple identities are brought into play in which an individual is much more committed to some identities than to others. Commitment to an identity largely depends on a person's relationship to a set of individuals with whom he or she interacts on a regular basis.

Goffman, the Canadian American social theorist who described a dramaturgical perspective, was much more specific than Mead was in his description of the self as a social construct. In contrast to Mead, who provided an interiorized view of the self, despite his emphasis on social experience, Goffman sees the self as the dramatic outcome of interactions made possible through the copresence of multiple actors. In describing the nature of the self, Goffman used the metaphor of drama without subscribing to the view that actors are born agents who, on the basis of pre-spelled scripts, make performance possible. The self is also not an organic entity whose potentialities unfold over time. Rather, Goffman sees the self as a dramatic effect instead of being responsible for the existence of dramatic processes. From this perspective, the self is not a social integrated unitary whole existing in its own right. Instead, the self is the result of a joint "ceremonial labor" whose existence is intimately related to the existence of other selves. Nor is the self, although a social element, the result of a generalized social reality. The self is constructed and reconstructed in specific social scenes. More exactly, the self is a performed-character whose fate is either to be credited or discredited.

And so that the self may not be a discredited character, and so that actors can carry on their performances smoothly, they use different techniques, including the techniques of idealization and mystification. In the case of idealization, actors go by the officially subscribed social rules. In instances where their acts contradict these rules, utmost care is taken to hide the act so that it may not be part of the publicly executed transcript. One such example includes secretive consumption, such as consuming alcohol or eating animal products where actors are expected to abide by the principle of ascetic purity. Or, actors may exercise constraint in revealing their wealth to foster the impression that their social status may not be perceived as the result of ascription. However, all idealizations are not carried out in a positive fashion. Actors can be engaged in negative idealization as well. A beggar who pretends that he is too weak to move is acting on the basis of a stereotyped image that may allow him or her to get the desired outcome. Actors do not present the same image to all audiences under all circumstances. They have to be engaged in audience segregation. By so acting, actors make sure that they are presenting themselves in the right manner to the right audience. A politician may be less successful if he or she is engaged in self-presentation of the self to all audiences in the same way; rather, he or she has to highlight certain facts and suppress others to meet the expected demands of a particular audience.

Regulating information to foster a positive impression alone may not bring about the desired outcome. In addition to avoiding acts that disrupt the anticipated definition of the situation, actors have to be involved in regulating their contact with their audiences to avoid ritual contamination. Managing contact with the audience is accomplished through the acts of mystification. To mystify oneself does not mean to be completely extricated from the social scene where the drama is being enacted, for such action renders the actor into a non-actor. Rather, mystification is a balanced form of social distance through which actors create a sense of awe among their audiences. By creating a distance between themselves and their audience, actors get ample time and space to prepare for the forthcoming interaction. Moreover, distance keeps the audience from observing actors at a close range, which could cause performance disruption. Most importantly, social distance prevents actors from revealing "secret mysteries," however minimal they are, that play a critical role in presenting the self positively.

High-Modern/Postmodern Theories of the Self

Contemporary theorists contend that the nature of the self has changed as a result of the major social changes that have taken place recently. Hence, these theorists argue that a reconstructed notion of the self is timely. These social theorists, however, differ regarding the nature of the social change that has occurred. Some contend that a rupture has transpired between the modern and postmodern worlds. Others assert that modernity has not become a bygone era; instead, they note that modernity has asserted itself in a radicalized form rather than leaving the historical space for a qualitatively new social order.

Anthony Giddens, an internationally renowned English sociologist, is one such social theorist who belongs to the second category. He holds the view that we live in what he calls *high modernity,* a global social order in which the salient features of modernity are extended to their ultimate limits. Accordingly, despite some overlaps, his stance on the self is different from the postmodern views of the self. Fundamentally, according to Giddens, the self is now a reflexive agent that is actively involved in the practice of self-construction. To accomplish this, members of the radicalized modernity have to undertake self-observation on a regular basis. Each moment is examined for what it is worth. And in their reflexive engagements, individuals are assisted by experts and expert systems that dominate late modernity. Hence, the self under radicalized modernity can hardly dissociate itself from its autobiographical project in which creative inputs are constantly sought. The project, however, is not limited to a cognitive level. The body is also involved, not as a passive receptacle but as an "action system." In general, the self has not been rendered inconsequential as a result of overwhelming global processes and a good dose of constraining conditions set on it. Rather, despite the enormous influences exerted on it, the radicalized modern self frequently asserts and reconstructs itself, thereby affecting the social processes that condition it.

Conversely, Kenneth Gergen, an U.S. social psychologist who became well-known after proposing an interesting theory of the postmodern self, contends that the change recent Western societies have undergone is so radical that societies have entered a new era and the nature of the self consequently is altered dramatically. The self has now, accordingly, become a "saturated self," a postmodern self much different from selves based on romanticist and modern conceptions that are grounded in the precepts of personal depth, passion, and soul, on the one hand, and reason and rationality, on the other hand. The concomitant results of these conceptions have been, among other things, deeply committed relations, dedicated friendships, and life purposes for the romanticist self and relationships based on rational choice and predictable persona for the modernist self.

The emergence of the postmodern self, according to Gergen, is mainly caused by what he calls *technologies of saturation,* technological transformations that have assumed both low-tech (the railroad, public postal services, the automobile, the telephone, radio broadcasting, motion pictures, printed books) and high-tech (air transportation, television, and electronic communication) forms. The impact of these technologies of saturation on interpersonal relations has resulted in the perseverance of the past and acceleration of the future. In the former case, time and distance have become less threatening elements that jeopardize social relationships. By way of technologies, the cast of characters has increased with the consequences of either creating discomfort from the overburdens of interpersonal contact or creating comfort as a result of the opportunity to maintain relationships with a significant number of people. However, the acceleration of the future entails that the paces of relationships have assumed a faster mode such that interpersonal contacts are carried out almost instantly and in an uninterrupted fashion, leading to an increasing interdependence among individuals. Hence, the "population of the self"—the exposure of the self to varied images, encounters, and opportunities—has undermined commitments to romanticist and modern conceptions of the self. Although the saturated self is well informed in its orientation of the social world and efficient in its undertakings, it is more decentered than were the previous forms of selves. The saturated self is less enduring in its essence and much more subject to reformation and redirection with multiple possibilities of expression.

Alem Kebede

See also Impression Management; Symbolic Interactionism

Further Readings

Bauman, Z. (2004). *Identity: Conversations with Benedetto Vecchi.* Cambridge, UK: Polity Press.

Burkitt, I. (2008). *Social selves: Theories of self and society.* Thousand Oaks, CA: Sage.

Elliott, A. (2008). *Concepts of the self.* Cambridge, UK: Polity Press.

Elliott, A., & Lemert, C. (2006). *The new individualism: The emotional costs of globalization.* London: Routledge.

Gergen, K. (1991). *The saturated self: Dilemmas of identity in contemporary life.* New York: Basic Books.

Giddens, A. (1991). *Modernity and self-identity: Self and society in the late modern age.* Cambridge, UK: Polity Press.

Goffman, E. (1959). *The presentation of self in everyday life.* New York: Anchor Books.

Mead, G. H. (1962). *Mind, self and society: From the standpoint of a social behaviorist.* Chicago: University of Chicago Press. (Original work published 1934)

Stryker, S. (1980). *Symbolic interactionism: A structural version.* Menlo Park, CA: Benjamin/Cummings.

SELF-AFFIRMATION THEORY

Self-affirmation theory asserts that people have a fundamental motivation to maintain self-integrity, that is, a perception of themselves as good, virtuous, and efficacious. Self-affirmation theory examines how people maintain self-integrity when they perceive it to be threatened. The theory posits flexibility in the way the self-system copes with such threats, such that people can respond to threats in one domain by reaffirming self-integrity in another, altogether different domain. Although people may react defensively to information or events that threaten self-integrity, they need not do so if they can secure their self-integrity.

Research and theorizing inspired by self-affirmation theory has led to theoretical advances in social psychology, with wide-ranging implications for how people cope with threats to valued identities. Self-affirmation theory research suggests that defensive resistance to identity-threatening information, group-serving biases, intransigence in social disputes, prejudice and stereotyping, and intellectual under-performance can be understood as arising, in part, from threats to self-integrity and the motivation to protect it. Self-affirmation theory provides a framework for understanding the origins of these problems and points toward some promising interventions to address them.

Background and History

In the late 19th century, the psychologist William James introduced the notion of the *social self*. This notion implied that people care about the way others see them and that their self-worth is based partly on their perceptions of the way others perceive them. As a consequence, an important source of identity and self-integrity involves people's social or group identities and their social roles and relationships with others. How people cope with threats to these social bases of self-worth is a question of historical and contemporary concern in psychology, and one of the central issues addressed by major social psychological theories such as social identity theory.

When an important aspect of the self, such as a social identity, is threatened, people will engage in various adaptations to maintain self-integrity. Some of these adaptations can be termed *defensive* in that they involve denying or distorting the threatening information. Such adaptations may involve rationalizations and even distortions of reality, and can be thus considered defensive in nature. Self-affirmation theory addresses the way people cope with threats to the self—both personal threats, such as those that result from a lack of control or health risk information, and threats to a group or a social identity, such as identification with a sports team, a country, an organization, or a gender or racial group. These identities can constitute important bases of self-worth. Consequently, people will defend against threats to these collective aspects of the self much as they defend against threats to individual or personal aspects of the self.

For example, information that is antagonistic to one's political beliefs may be viewed with skepticism whereas information supporting one's political beliefs may be accepted with little scrutiny. Similarly, when people feel that they could be judged negatively on the basis of a stereotype about their group, they may feel psychologically threatened and as a consequence engage in various adaptations, including avoiding or dis-identifying from the domain in which they feel negatively judged. Positive events that happen to one's group may be thought of as caused by the group itself whereas negative events may be attributed to external factors. Such adaptations can help an individual

maintain self-integrity by reducing the potential threat to a valued identity.

The theory of self-affirmation was first proposed by the social psychologist Claude Steele. A major insight of this theory centers on the notion that although people try to maintain specific self-images and identities (such as "being a good student" or "being a good group member"), that is not their primary motivation. Rather, individuals are motivated to maintain *global* self-integrity—a general perception of their goodness, virtue, and efficacy. There is thus great flexibility in how the self-system responds to threats. If individuals feel relatively positively about themselves in one domain, they will be more willing and able to tolerate threats to self-integrity in other domains. Consequently, when self-affirmed, people can respond to identity-threatening information without resorting to defensive biases.

Self-affirmation theory led to a reinterpretation of classic research findings in cognitive dissonance. In a classic cognitive dissonance study, people are shown to change their attitudes to bring them in line with their past behavior. People led to commit an action that violates a core identity (for example, individuals subtly led to oppose funding for the disabled might feel that they have violated a core value) subsequently change their beliefs to bring them in line with their actions (for instance, they become more opposed to funding for the disabled). Previously, such cognitive dissonance effects had been viewed as evidence of a basic motivation for psychological consistency; people want to see their actions as consistent with their attitudes. However, Steele and colleagues demonstrated that these effects arise, in part, from the motivation to maintain self-integrity. Thus, when people are given an opportunity to affirm their self-integrity in an alternative domain, the rationalization effect disappears. For instance, writing about an important value unrelated to the decision task (such as musical interests) reduced people's tendency to revise their beliefs in light of regrettable past actions.

Contributions of Self-Affirmation Theory

When self-integrity is threatened, according to self-affirmation theory, people need not defensively rationalize or distort reality. Instead, they can reestablish self-integrity through affirmations of alternative domains of self-worth unrelated to the provoking threat. Such *self-affirmations,* by fulfilling the need to protect self-integrity in the face of threat, can enable people to deal with threatening events and information without resorting to defensive biases. Self-affirmations can take the form of reflecting on or expressing overarching values, such as relationships with friends and family, religious values, or reminding oneself of valued identities, such as important group memberships.

Numerous studies demonstrate that individuals are less likely to rationalize, deny, or resist identity-threatening information in one domain if their sense of self-integrity is "affirmed" in other domains. People have been shown to be more open to counter-attitudinal information, and less biased in their evaluations of new and identity-relevant information, if they are first permitted to self-affirm in an unrelated domain, for instance, by reflecting on an important personal value. For example, proponents and opponents of capital punishment proved less critical of scientific evidence contradicting their beliefs regarding the efficacy of the death penalty as a deterrent of would-be murderers if they first wrote an essay on an important value unrelated to their political identity.

Self-affirmation also leads individuals to accept greater responsibility for negative events that happen to their group. When affirmed, winners and losers in a sports competition were less self-serving and group-serving in their attributions for success and failure. That is, those who were affirmed were relatively more willing to lay the blame for their defeats on themselves and their group, and less willing to take credit for their successes.

People are also more open to identity-threatening courses of action—for example, compromising with an adversary in a divisive social-political dispute—when self-affirmed. Pro-choice advocates were more likely to make concessions to a pro-life advocate in a negotiation on abortion policy when they had first been given the opportunity to affirm themselves in an alternative domain of self-worth.

Self-affirmation theory also illuminates the way in which prejudice and stereotyping are forms of self-integrity maintenance. People were less likely to discriminate against a Jewish job candidate, relative to a Catholic one, if they had previously been provided with a self-affirmation. Individuals, it seems, can use a negative stereotype as a cognitively justifiable way of putting other people down, to make the individuals feel better about themselves and their groups. However, if their needs for self-integrity are met in another domain, they have less need to use negative stereotypes.

One of the most important implications of contemporary research on self-affirmation theory involves its demonstration that seemingly small interventions can have large effects, if they are attuned to psychological processes of self-integrity maintenance.

Self-affirmation was used successfully to mitigate the social identity threat arising from being a target of a negative stereotype in school. Previous research had demonstrated that African Americans experience psychological threat when they know that they or fellow group members could be judged in light of a negative racial stereotype, a phenomenon known as stereotype threat, which can undermine performance. A series of field experiments demonstrated that a self-affirmation intervention administered in the context of students' classroom activities improved African American students' end-of-term course grades and thus reduced the racial achievement gap by 40%. Although the affirmed state stemming from a self-affirmation may appear relatively brief, the changes in information processing it prompts can become self-reinforcing or self-sustaining over time.

Intersection of Self-Affirmation and Social Identity Theories

Recent research has integrated self-affirmation and social identity theories to help explicate phenomena of interest to both perspectives. One question centers on the motivational origins of group-serving judgments. Two basic premises of social identity theory are that people are motivated to enhance or maintain self-esteem and that membership in groups constitutes an important part of individuals' self-concept. Consequently, social identity theory predicts that judgments that reflect well on the group will enhance self-esteem; however, reviews of social identity theory suggest mixed support for this self-esteem postulate. The self-affirmation approach, by demonstrating that manipulations that secure an individual's self-integrity can reduce the tendency to make group-serving judgments, has provided important experimental evidence to support the role of the self in motivating group-serving judgments.

A second question centers on the moderating role of identity salience on the effectiveness of self-affirmations on increasing acceptance of identity-threatening information. The centrality of a given identity as a source of self-integrity varies as a function of situational or contextual factors. When a particular social identity is made salient, people are particularly likely to engage in identity-protective strategies, such as defensive information processing of threatening political information. In these situations, self-affirmations are most effective at reducing defensive responses. By contrast, manipulations that make a given identity less salient to the individual reduce the motivational pressure to defend the self. Consequently, affirmations are less effective at reducing bias when the motivation to defend a particular social identity is reduced.

A third area of theoretical overlap between self-affirmation and social identity theories centers on the utility of group affirmations, that is, affirmations of values that are central to one's group. When people affirm their group on values unrelated to a focal threat but central to their group, they are more accepting of threatening group information, particularly when the individuals are highly identified group members. For instance, highly identified sports fans were more likely to acknowledge the role of their favorite team in defeat when they affirmed a value of importance to the group. These findings are consistent with the notion of social creativity proposed in social identity theory, that individuals can cope with threats to their groups by affirming the importance of alternative dimensions of value to their group.

David K. Sherman and Geoffrey L. Cohen

See also Cognitive Dissonance Theory; Psychology of Self and Identity; Self-Image; Social Identity Theory

Further Readings

Cohen, G. L., Garcia, J., Apfel, N., & Master, A. (2006). Reducing the racial achievement gap: A social-psychological intervention. *Science, 313,* 1307–1310.

Cohen, G. L., Sherman, D. K., Bastardi, A., McGoey, M., Hsu, A., & Ross, L. (2007). Bridging the partisan divide: Self-affirmation reduces ideological

closed-mindedness and inflexibility in negotiation. *Journal of Personality and Social Psychology, 93,* 415–430.

Fein, S., & Spencer, S. J. (1997). Prejudice as self-image maintenance: Affirming the self through derogating others. *Journal of Personality and Social Psychology, 73,* 31–44.

Sherman, D. K., & Cohen, G. L. (2006). The psychology of self-defense: Self-affirmation theory. In M. P. Zanna (Ed.), *Advances in experimental social psychology* (Vol. 38, pp. 183–242). San Diego, CA: Academic Press.

Sherman, D. K., Kinias, Z., Major, B., Kim, H. S., & Prenovost, M. A. (2007). The group as a resource: Reducing biased attributions for group success and failure via group-affirmation. *Personality and Social Psychology Bulletin, 33,* 1100–1112.

Steele, C. M. (1988). The psychology of self-affirmation: Sustaining the integrity of the self. In L. Berkowitz (Ed.), *Advances in experimental social psychology* (Vol. 21, pp. 261–302). New York: Academic Press.

SELF-ASSESSMENT

Self-assessment, or the desire to know the truth about oneself, is one of four self-evaluation motives that pervade the study of the self. Self-assessment is characterized by a motivation to accurately evaluate one's self or self-concept. A key feature of this motive that distinguishes it from other self-evaluation motives (i.e., self-enhancement, self-verification, and self-improvement) is that people desire to accurately evaluate themselves, sometimes at the risk of learning information that is negative with respect to their abilities. Individuals engage in self-assessment to reduce uncertainty about their abilities and self-concepts, or put simply, to increase their self-knowledge. An accurate diagnosis of one's abilities allows individuals to feel confident making predictions regarding their world and their place within the world.

People use a variety of tools to increase or acquire self-knowledge. Leon Festinger's 1954 social comparison theory rests on the assumption that people turn to similar others to assess their own abilities and opinions. Specifically, people engage in this comparison process to evaluate the veracity of their opinions and the extent of their abilities in the absence of an objective means of evaluation. For example, students commonly compare exam marks to determine where their individual class performance lies in comparison with other students' marks. The study of self-assessment is often researched within the achievement realm. By definition, achievement implies assessment, thus offering a germane means of studying when and how people choose to engage in self-assessment.

Research in self-assessment has consistently demonstrated that individuals actively seek to engage in activities that provide diagnostic information concerning their abilities. The extent to which people prefer diagnostic tasks depends on their uncertainty with their abilities; thus, individuals seek tasks that provide them with self-knowledge concerning their abilities in an effort to reduce this feeling of uncertainty. Importantly, research on self-assessment has demonstrated that when uncertain of their abilities within a particular domain, people do not actively avoid a task that they believe will provide them with a negative evaluation of their abilities; rather, they seek evaluative and diagnostic practices regardless of how positively or negatively they elucidate their abilities. The veracity of the test of their abilities motivates people to engage in this process of self-assessment, as an accurate ability to know their own abilities increases confidence in people's predictions regarding their capabilities. Along the same lines, people will also engage in a task longer when they believe that the task will diagnose their abilities than when the task cannot provide them with self-knowledge, further highlighting the importance of acquiring self-knowledge regarding one's own abilities.

Though uncertainty about one's abilities may lead most individuals to seek self-assessment, a great deal of literature suggests that self-enhancement may be a competing self-motive. For example, people may compare themselves with less fortunate others, particularly when they feel threatened or are experiencing low self-esteem, in an attempt to self-enhance. The motive for this comparison is not an accurate self-assessment, but rather an attempt to attain or maintain a favorable sense of self. Often, an accurate diagnosis of ability may threaten the self-concept (e.g., in the case of a good student failing his first calculus exam, there is the potential threat to the student perceiving himself as a good

student). Research in both self-assessment and self-enhancement demonstrates that these apparently contradictory motives (i.e., accuracy of self-knowledge vs. enhancement) can be explained by the importance of the ability being assessed. Research comparing these two motives has highlighted that people prefer to engage in diagnostic tasks when they are uncertain regarding their peripheral traits or tasks (i.e., traits and tasks that are not central or important to the self-concept). On the contrary, this same line of research suggests that people tend to avoid diagnostic feedback for central traits and tasks when there is an indication that the feedback will be negative, in an attempt to protect the self-concept (i.e., self-enhancement).

Another important factor that may determine whether one will express a self-enhancement or a self-assessment motive is whether one's performance on the given diagnostic task can be improved in the future. In the case of the good student who deems his grades as important to his self-concept, the poor mark on his calculus exam may indeed lead to a lowered sense of self-adequacy; however, if the student realizes that he can study hard for the next exam to improve his grade, he may indeed continue to engage in self-assessment regarding his calculus abilities. Conversely, if a student believes that there is no way she can improve her calculus abilities (i.e., her calculus ability is fixed, and there is no possible way to change that ability), then the student may seek to avoid feedback from such exams that threaten the part of her self-concept that allows her to perceive herself as a good student. This line of research generally demonstrates that individuals express preference for diagnostic feedback after a success in the given domain, but not after a failure in that domain (i.e., demonstrating a self-enhancement motive). When they believe that they can improve their performance in that domain, particularly when they believe the domain to be important to the self-concept, they tend to express interest in diagnostic feedback.

Self-assessment is an important self-evaluative motive that helps individuals structure and understand their worlds. People engage in assessment processes when they are uncertain of their own abilities or the traits that they possess. Accurate assessment of the self reduces one's subjective sense of self-uncertainty and allows individuals to predict and control their environment, based partly on an accurate understanding of their abilities and capabilities. The extent to which people will engage in and pursue this accurate assessment depends on how central or peripheral the task or trait is that is being assessed, the valence of the expected feedback, and whether one's ability in the given domain is mobile or fixed.

Amber M. Gaffney

See also Self-Concept; Self-Enhancement Theory; Self-Verification

Further Readings

Festinger, L. (1954). A theory of social comparison processes. *Human Relations, 7,* 117–140.

Sedikides, C. (1993). Assessment, enhancement, and verification determinants of self-evaluation processes. *Journal of Personality and Social Psychology, 2,* 317–338.

Sedikides, C., & Strube, M. J. (1997). Self-evaluation: To thine own self be good, to thine own self be sure, to thine own self be true, and to thine own self be better. In M. P. Zanna (Ed.), *Advances in experimental social psychology* (Vol. 29, pp. 209–296). New York: Academic Press.

Trope, Y. (1979). Uncertainty-reducing properties of achievement tasks. *Journal of Social Psychology, 37,* 1505–1518.

Trope, Y., & Ben-Yair, E. (1982). Task construction and persistence as means for self-assessment of abilities. *Journal of Personality and Social Psychology, 4,* 637–645.

SELF-CONCEPT

Self-concept is a topic both well-known and heavily discussed by a number of professionals, including philosophers, psychologists, and educators. In addition, the ideas concerning self-concept have been implemented into various disciplines, such as psychology, sociology, education, and so forth. For example, the famed psychologist Carl Rogers described *self-concept* as the development of self-image and an individual's progress from an undifferentiated self to one fully differentiated. Relative to personality development, self-concept is viewed as being the cognitive or thinking aspect of self.

Self-concept is defined as the general idea people have about themselves; that is, it is a complex and dynamic system of learned beliefs and attitudes that one believes to be true about one's own personal existence. Overall, one's self-concept indicates how an individual sees himself or herself and comprises three major components: *ideal self* (what someone most wants to be), (2) *public self* (the image one thinks others have toward him or her), and (3) *real self* (what one thinks about himself or herself). When a difference exists between these components, it often creates psychological issues, leading individuals toward an unpleasant state of being, that is, anxiety, depression, sadness, and so forth. To maintain a level of mental health, one's public and ideal self need to be companionable with one's real self.

Another way of viewing self-concept is how an individual is aware of his or her behaviors, traits, and other characteristics. The content of the self-concept ranges from episodic memories of behavior and larger self-narratives to specific beliefs about personality traits. The trait self-concept incorporates important dimensions called *self-schemas*, and neurological evidence suggests that processing of information about one's self-concept activates the medial prefrontal cortex. People's self-concepts develop through social feedback, and people often act to try to verify these views, which promote consistency in behavior across different situations. This entry focuses on the development of self-concept and highlights the major theorists that have contributed to our current understanding of it.

Personality Theorists and Self-Concept

The idea of self-concept began when René Descartes wrote *Principles of Philosophy* in 1644, in which he discussed his innermost thoughts regarding doubt. In his opinion, if he doubted, he was thinking, and therefore, he could validate his own existence; thus, his famous *cogito ergo sum* ("I think, therefore I am). Moreover, one's existence depends on his or her self-perception. Sigmund Freud provided new meaning and discussed the significance of the internal mental process, at which point self-concept theory development entered a new stage. Whereas Freud hesitated to view self-concept as a major psychological theory, his daughter Anna experienced no such hesitation. Anna discussed the importance of self-interpretation and ego development, which focused people's attention once again on self-concept.

According to social theorist George Herbert Mead, individuals learn about themselves every day. For example, he believes that when people tell you you're good looking today, this statement becomes part of self-knowledge. He further explains that the primary source through which we learn and develop self-concept is interacting with others. Thus, he concluded that self-concept is affected each day by interacting with others. To understand the significance of self-concept, a person needs awareness concerning the profound implication about how an individual perceives himself or herself; likewise, each person should be aware about how he or she relates and interacts with others.

William James wrote that the "self" is composed of two features: the *I* and the *Me*. The I is the self that thinks, experiences, and acts in the world; it is the self as a *knower*. The Me is the self that is an object in the world; it is the self as *known*. He further stated that the I is much like consciousness, which is a perspective on all of experiences but the Me is about a concept of a person. James further defined *self-concept* as a person's explicit knowledge of his or her own behaviors, traits, and other personal characteristics. He stated that a person's self-concept is an organized body of knowledge that develops from social experiences and has a profound effect on a person's behavior throughout life.

Rogers, the creator of person-centered therapy, brought self-concept theory into the field of psychology and studied it extensively. He viewed self-concept as the way an individual perceives himself or herself in certain images and felt that self-concept development was heavily influenced by individuals' life experiences. As a result, if a child's life experience is negative, the child will likely develop a poor self-concept in adulthood.

At the center of Rogerian therapy is the self, and an individual's consciousness of it. In Rogers' opinion, an individual's self-concept sways how a person looks at himself or herself, as well as his or her environment; thus, the self-concept of an individual who is psychologically healthy is in harmony with what he or she thinks, feels, and acts.

However, it is possible for someone to sustain a self-concept that is diametrically opposed to his or her inner desire to succeed in winning the admiration of one's peers, either in a social or professional setting.

When this situation occurs, it entails the suppression of one's genuine feelings, which ultimately leads a person to feel disconnected from himself or herself, while twisting experiences in such a manner that it is highly unlikely that he or she will ever attain happiness or self-actualization. This gap concerning someone's self-concept and his or her genuine experiences (also known as incongruence) is an unremitting foundation of apprehension and can lead to mental illness. Rogerian therapy posits the idea that when a person has a durable self-concept based on reality, it is adaptable while allowing the individual to tackle new encounters or concepts without experiencing anxiety.

Abraham Maslow, the great humanistic psychologist, stated that to grow as a human being, one had to follow a hierarchy of needs. At the lowest levels, one must have needs met regarding such basic biological processes as thirst, hunger, feeling a modicum of safety in one's life, having a sense of belonging to something, and feeling loved and loving others. Higher than these are the needs an individual has for self-esteem and competence, but at the apex of the hierarchy is self-actualization, which is extremely difficult to reach. Assuming one is born into a middle-to upper-class family in a prosperous country, the acquisition of lower-level needs such as having enough food to eat, feeling safe, and or having a place to live can be a straightforward process; however, it can prove difficult to fulfill the basic human need for love and belongingness. When a person has not had these requisite needs met, his or her personal growth is usually hindered, often leading into a negative self-concept.

Social psychologists stated that self-concept is vital to how each person forms his or her notions of others. This process is called *attribution* explains the origins of our behavior and others; thus, it is highly affected by self-concept. A major emphasis of social learning theory centers on how each individual views himself or herself, especially whether a person feels he or she has affected the environment. Julian B. Rotter stated that the anticipated result of any deed and the worth each person places on that result decide how each person will act in a specific setting. For instance, someone possessing a positive self-concept often feels that he or she will succeed with a given assignment because he or she has the ability to succeed. The reverse is true for someone thinking he or she will fail; that is, a person will fail because he or she lacks the innate ability to be successful.

Freud, the founder of psychoanalysis, stated that when someone is subjugated by an overactive superego (the conscience), the ego (the rational part of our personality) strives for an equilibrium involving the continual battles between the id (the part of our personality that seeks pleasure) and the superego. In other words, a person wants to be able to do things he or she knows is morally wrong, but at the same time, his or her conscience states that he or she should refrain from any illicit behavior because it is immoral. The superego is dominant, so it forces the person to obey, and if the individual gives in to temptation, he or she feels guilty, which in turns leads to a negative self-concept.

Development of Self-Concept

One's self-concept never stops developing; rather, it begins in infancy and lasts for the rest of an individual's life. When a parent or significant other begins to take an interest in the child's development, the child is influenced by the attention and love exhibited, which influences his or her developing self-concept. Quite possibly the most important period in a child's life is the first 2 years. If the child has received a strong psychological foundation, he or she will likely possess a healthy self-concept. The manner in which a parent relates to his or her child on a daily basis is vital for the child's future development. An infant learns to trust others because loving caregivers are there to meet the child's needs. As the child ages, the parents must make sure that the child is allowed to complete more and more tasks on his or her own. As the child grows, so should his or her beliefs regarding his or her ability. The child should come to see that he or she is capable of doing new things, and this attitude will develop over time.

Erik Erikson, the famed Harvard psychologist, believed that each person must successfully conclude the conflict that is inherent in each stage.

How each individual deals with the conflicts can influence greatly his or her self-concept. When we deal with crisis and conflict in a positive manner, our resulting self-concept is often positive, but the reverse is also true; if we deal with conflict negatively, our self-concept is apt to be the same. According to Erikson, individuals experience eight stages throughout their lives that include infancy, toddler, preschool, adolescence, teenage, young adult, middle adult, and senior. Each of these stages is characterized by a set of unique crises. For example, the infancy stage (0 to 12–18 months) is characterized by the crisis of whether we learn to trust others. For the toddler stage (18 months to 3 years), the crisis is whether the child feels he or she is able to investigate his or her surroundings. The preschool stage (3 to 6 years) focuses on the crisis of whether the child feels independent enough to do new things and, likewise, whether he or she feels guilt at trying new things. The adolescence stage (6 years to 12 years) is concerned with the child becoming aware that he or she is different from others. More specifically, the child thinks he or she is capable of doing things on his or her own; the reverse is that the child thinks he or she lacks the wherewithal to attempt new things.

Following the adolescence stage, the teenage stage (12 to 20 years) is characterized by the individual seeking to "know" who he or she is. A successful conclusion leads to greater self-understanding, whereas failing leads to a search for identity. In this stage, problems with alcohol and drugs first appear. During the young adulthood stage (20 to 35 years), an individual feels that he or she is worthy of affection, begins romantic encounters that usually lead to marriage and parenthood. On the other hand, if a person feels that he or she is unlovable, emotional isolation from others is the norm. During the middle adulthood stage (35 to 65 years), the individual will likely lead a life that is full of activity that he or she finds rewarding, if the individual has a positive self-concept. From age 65 years on, individuals experience the senior stage or the final stage of a person's life. If the individual has a positive self-concept, it is likely that he or she will feel integrity; if a person possesses a negative self-concept, the individual probably sees his or her life as a waste of potential.

In addition to the crises that mark each of the eight stages, other factors are vital in the development of self-concept. These factors include age, gender, culture, sexual orientation, appearance, life experiences, emotional maturity, and education. Each of these factors influences how we perceive ourselves and how we perceive others. The myriad experiences a person gains from life are relatively close to how someone views himself or herself, as well as his or her relationship with others.

Self-concept consists of three major characteristics: (1) It is learned, (2) it is organized, and (3) it is dynamic. The first characteristic indicates that a person's self-concept does not come prepackaged in an infant's brain; rather, self-concept is learned over time. In other words, self-concept gradually emerges in the early months of an individual's life, and his or her life experiences shape self-concept. The second characteristic is organization. An individual's basic perception about himself or herself is stable and is unlikely to experience any rapid change, while possessing both consistency and stability. In essence, each individual holds countless perceptions regarding his or her personal existence, and each perception is synchronized with others. Such a stable and organized quality of self-concept is essential and gives consistency to the personality. As a result, researchers agree that self-concept has a relatively stable quality that is characterized by harmony.

The third characteristic is dynamic. As mentioned earlier, self-concept development is a continuous process, and there is a constant assimilation of new ideas and expulsion of old ideas throughout life. The world and the things in it are not just perceived; they are perceived in relation to one's self-concept.

Self-concept may be defined as the way in which a person perceives himself or herself. It can be divided into three primary categories: (1) *personal self-concept:* one's own opinion about one self, such as "I am smart"; (2) *social concept:* one's perception about how he or she is perceived by others in that society, such as "My colleagues think I am attractive"; and (3) *self-ideals:* one's own idea about what one wants to be, such as "I want to be successful."

One critical component affecting an individual's self-concept development is called *referencing,* which includes temporal and social referencing. Temporal referencing occurs when individuals make a self-comparison from an earlier moment in their lives to a later time, and usually takes place in childhood and old age when relatively rapid changes occur because of physical and cognitive transformations. Social referencing occurs when individuals compare their own lives with those of others and tends to occur during adulthood when any change is less noticeable.

Self-concept is organized through a series of different memories. Memories are arranged and organized as highlights of a person's life with memories consisting of specific events, life tasks, memories of people that affect a person, and memories of places. In addition, self-concept can be organized and arranged in an abstract way relative to personality traits, which allows individuals to judge themselves on any number of traits, such as laziness, intelligence, attractiveness, toughness, and so forth.

Each person finds certain unique personality traits especially important for conceptualizing himself or herself. For example, one person might define himself as attractive and another person might emphasize her intelligence and ability to achieve tasks. This phenomenon is called *self-schemas,* which are the traits people use to define themselves.

Cary Stacy Smith and Li-Ching Hung

See also Development of Identity; Development of Self-Concept; Personal Identity Versus Self-Identity

Further Readings

Bushman, B. J., & Baumeister, R. F. (1998). Threatened egotism, narcissism, self-esteem, and direct and displaced aggression: Does self-love or self-hate lead to violence? *Journal of Experimental Social Psychology, 41,* 305–312.

Corey, G. (2001). *Theory and practice of counseling and psychotherapy* (6th ed.). Belmont, CA: Brooks/Cole.

McAdams, D. (1993). *The stories we live by: Personal myths and the making of the self.* New York: William Morrow.

Mead, G. H. (1934). *Mind, self, and society.* Chicago: University of Chicago Press.

Rogers, C. (1980). *A way of being.* Boston: Houghton Mifflin.

SELF-CONSCIOUSNESS

Self-consciousness is a personality trait that involves a heightened sense of self-awareness about personal behavior, appearance, or other attributes of the self. An unpleasant feeling of self-consciousness occurs when one envisions being watched or observed by others, resulting in an overconcern about the impression one is making on others. People tend to differ in the degree to which they are consciously thinking about themselves. Some individuals are more self-conscious than are others and are characterized as high in self-consciousness, whereas some individuals are less self-conscious and are characterized as low in self-consciousness. The level of one's self-consciousness can affect one's identity, behavior, and communication. This entry provides an overview of self-consciousness; describes two dimensions of self-consciousness—public and private; discusses how self-consciousness affects one's identity; and presents philosophical views of self-consciousness.

Overview

The significance of and interest in self-consciousness came from research on the effects of people's behavior and emotion under conditions of an increased sense of awareness about the self and its relationship to surroundings. Early scholarship on self-awareness or self-focused attention showed that directing attention toward oneself provokes a comparison process. This process allows people to judge their behavior against relevant personal standards—goals, attitudes, values, beliefs—and allows them to reflect on how to match their behavior to the standard set by self or society. When people are self-focused, they tend to behave consistently with the standards they set for themselves; when they are not self-focused, they do not place as much emphasis on scrutinizing the self in various situations. Self-consciousness is also associated with self-evaluation. The quality of the self-evaluation, whether positive or negative, is often determined by what one perceives as self-relevant information. For example, those who are overly self-conscious may examine more behaviors (e.g., a look, a comment, a gesture) as being directly related to them, whereas those who are less self-conscious may not evaluate

as many behaviors as being relevant to the self. Scholars developed an interest in the personality trait of self-consciousness when it was discovered that people vary greatly in the degree to which they focus on the self. The degree to which people focus on the self also influences their actions, behaviors, and communication with others.

William James, who was influential in experimental and systematic psychology, made the observation that whenever humans are thinking, they are at the same time aware of themselves and their personal experiences. This observation promoted further discussion on self-consciousness. Researchers looked to the family to understand how a sense of self-consciousness is developed and found that family life provides some of the parameters for self-consciousness. Children come to understand who constitutes their family and use this information to formulate an initial sense of the self. The development of self-consciousness proceeds with the attainment of more experiences outside the family. For example, children start to realize differences when they interact with other children outside the home (e.g., at school, at a friend's house, at the playground). Awareness of the self and one's own personal existence start to shape self-consciousness. Throughout life, people become more conscious of how others, objects, physical features, and events shape their lives. Moreover, people remain conscious of themselves in relationship to people, objects, features, and events. Experience with the world brings about this tension between self-consciousness and people as social entities. This interest in the self and the self in relationship to the other helped develop the research agenda on self-consciousness and led to the development of the self-consciousness scale. The most commonly used measure of self-consciousness is the self-consciousness scale. This scale includes subscales for private and public self-consciousness and for social anxiety. The scale has demonstrated reliability and validity as a means of measuring individual differences in self-consciousness. The scale has been translated into several languages including Chinese, French, German, Brazilian, Dutch, and Turkish. As a result, cross-cultural differences in self-consciousness have been observed. Moreover, the private and public dimensions of self-consciousness may relate differently for other cultures than they do in U.S. samples. These private and public dimensions add to a textured understanding of self-consciousness.

Private and Public Self-Consciousness

Many scholars make a distinction between two components of self-consciousness—private and public. Both of these dimensions refer to cognitive styles. Private self-consciousness is the degree to which people examine their private, inner selves that are not directly open to observation by others—for example, thoughts, feelings, and motives. Public self-consciousness is the degree to which people are aware of public external aspects of themselves that can be observed by others—for example, physical appearance (i.e., weight, clothing, style), overt behaviors, and mannerisms. Research shows that public and private self-consciousness relate to behavior differently. With a focus on private aspects, there is an increase in obedience to personally held standards, whereas a focus on the public aspects of self-consciousness relies on socially held standards. As a result, these dimensions of private and public self-consciousness predict the degree to which people can be influenced by self, others, and society.

Private self-consciousness is related to a clearer understanding of the self, a greater devotion to one's own personal standards, and a higher awareness of stressful situations. Research shows that people high in private self-consciousness direct attention inward, allowing a greater sense of self-awareness. People who are high in private self-consciousness behave more consistently with their own beliefs, values, and attitudes than do people who are low in private self-consciousness. Highly private self-conscious individuals are also less likely to conform to social pressures, erroneous group judgment, and persuasion. Their own perceptions and beliefs are prominent and clear to themselves; as a result, their views tend to persist over the views of others. High levels of private self-consciousness are also associated with a stronger level of independence and autonomy when faced with social demands.

People who are high in private self-consciousness have a heightened tendency to self-reflect, which enhances their understanding of their behaviors and actions, causing less bias in answering questionnaires or reporting on issues where they have

to rate themselves. In addition, privately self-conscious people are said to be more accurate in reporting their behavior and actions and are more likely to dispute inaccurate information that others report about them. When making decisions about the future, highly self-conscious people rely more on their personal standards and experience; consequently, they tend to ponder personal experiences and their implications, causing greater levels of stress. Highly private self-consciousness is also associated with a stronger sense of anxiety, depression, and unease in the company of stressful events because of the tendency to overanalyze. Private self-consciousness does not mean being oblivious to social implications of conduct or being indifferent to the impressions other people form; however, people who have high levels of private self-consciousness are more concerned with personal rather than social factors of identity.

Public self-consciousness is related to a heightened sense of the public aspects of behavior. Individuals who possess high levels of public self-consciousness pay close attention to how they are perceived, evaluated, and judged by others. Public self-consciousness can result in self-monitoring, social anxiety, a stronger sense of embarrassment, worry about one's physique, more blushing, a lack of confidence in social situations, and a greater sensitivity to being shunned by others. High public self-consciousness is correlated with the amount of consideration people devote to their appearance—the importance of make-up, clothing, body weight, and overall style. For example, those who have a high level of public self-consciousness might constantly be worrying about whether they are saying the right thing or dressing appropriately for a particular situation. A main concern of those with high public self-consciousness is making desired impressions with the intention of pleasing others; as a result, they are more likely to give into peer pressure, conform to others' incorrect decisions, and follow the crowd. These individuals are more sensitive to the opinions of others because of fear of possible rejection. Publicly self-conscious individuals may be seen as having a chameleon-type personality in social situations, basing their public conduct on various social contingencies instead of personal conviction. They continually focus on fitting in. Highly public self-consciousness results in individuals who constantly focus on how they think others want them to be, act, and look. The other becomes imperative in how decisions are made.

Scholarship has shown that the private and public dimensions of self-consciousness should be viewed as two distinctive aspects that are weakly correlated rather than two opposite ends of the spectrum. The relationship between high private self-consciousness and high public self-consciousness centers on the presentation and construction of identity. People construct and defend desired identities all the time in social life, although they differ in the particular images that constitute their identity. Private self-consciousness is associated with an identity of authenticity in social settings, whereas public self-consciousness focuses on an identity that promotes a greater sense of presentation and variation. As a result, people who focus on public self-consciousness look toward others for their identity, whereas those high in private self-consciousness look toward their inner self for a desired identity.

Self-Consciousness and Identity

Erik Erikson helped develop the work on the relationship between self-consciousness and identity. Self-consciousness reveals that people are self-aware authors of their own social conduct in which they participate and through which they engage the world. This awareness allows them to shape a desired identity. Through self-consciousness, they are aware of being distinct from the rest of the world and understand that "I" does not exist alone but rather that "I" exists in relationship to others. Self-consciousness involves the ability to make reflective decisions about one's own beliefs and desires, in addition to a sense of embodied agency. As Paul Ricœur noted, people are conscious of being the authors of their own actions, and this awareness often comes from the actions being reflected in the existence of others. Thus, people become aware of themselves through the eyes of others. Through relationships with others, people will modify and reinvent themselves, and by responding to different situations with others, they change themselves and their identity in the process. As a result, intersubjectivity and sociality play an important role in the development of self-consciousness. For example, people are aware of themselves as one among others; this awareness is framed from the perspective of the other. When

people attempt to see themselves as others see them, the result may be a change in or a heightened sense of self-consciousness. The experience with the other is at the same time an experience that involves a self-conscious nature pre-reflectively aware that one is an object for another. This idea is articulated in the work of George Herbert Mead's symbolic interaction theory, which details different images of "I" and "me" with the latter focusing on image construction, in Martin Buber's six dimensions of interplay of images in relational exchanges, and in the Johari window model that uses various quadrants to suggest that parts of the self are open to reflection and sharing information with others and parts of the self are closed and hidden from the self and others. The level of self-consciousness determines how identity is shaped and developed in various situations. Researchers have also linked an excessive focus on self-consciousness and identity confusion. Self-consciousness helps determine a sense of identity and value; however, because self-consciousness depends on social interactions, people may have difficulty understanding their own identities.

Self-consciousness allows people to carefully monitor social situations, imagine the reaction of others, and adapt their behavior to the social context to present a desired identity. Such an identity calls for different sets of self-presentation strategies, relating to either autonomy or conformity. Social psychologists, sociologists, anthropologists, and communication scholars all articulate the idea that people possess multiple perceptions of the self that portray various identities. Whether in the public or private setting, self-consciousness influences how people view or interpret situations and at the same time regulates their involvement in interactions. For example, during an interview, one may have a greater sense of self-consciousness because one is trying to impress a potential employer. One may actively reflect on what "I" should wear, what "I" should say, and how "I" should act during the interview process.

A self-consciousness perspective considers that people have to balance their own perceptions of who they are with what a collective society says they should be. Factors such as social roles, self-concept, self-perception, and self-esteem all influence how people see themselves in relationship to their surroundings. In addition, the judgments people make about themselves are constrained by both social expectations and cultural values. Self-consciousness is contextualized as people try to understand how they appear to others through behaviors and actions. As Edmund Husserl noted, people become aware of themselves specifically as human beings only through intersubjective relations. The idea of self-consciousness has been a subject of a rich and multifaceted discussion within the philosophical community.

Philosophical Views of Self-Consciousness

One view of self-consciousness is that it is considered a reflective structure of the mind that forces people to have a conception of themselves—it is the consciousness of the object, the "self." The mind-body problem, a central metaphysical concept in dealing with "philosophy of the mind," is the problem of whether mental phenomena are physical and, if not, how they are related to physical phenomena. Different philosophers have argued in different ways about the idea of self-consciousness as an object of the self. The answer lies in the practical question of the possibility of reflecting on the unreflected. For example, David Hume believes that people can never catch themselves without a perception or never observe anything but the perception—the subject of thought cannot be thought about as such. Just as the eye cannot see itself, the self cannot be aware of itself as an object; as a result, a subject cannot be an object to itself. Stated a different way, humans can never stand on their own shadow because as the person moves, the shadow moves. Immanuel Kant believed that knowledge of the self as it is in itself is impossible. However, he disagreed with Hume's idea that there is no more to self-consciousness than consciousness of subject-less mental occurrences. Kant believed that consciousness of the self consists in the ability to assign thoughts, expressions, and experiences to oneself.

Another view of self-consciousness consists in the idea of transformation. The self is always changing in consciousness and, as a result, does not attain a final form of completeness or permanence. All objects of experience are constituted as objects of a larger experience, and it would be unsuccessful to discuss them as existing outside this experience. Just as an object possesses and obtains an identity

as an experienced object, so does the self, for which it has its nature and function within a social order. The self is one of many similar selves interacting on each other. The mind of the self is a social affair that involves the realization of life with others. Self-consciousness is real and genuine, but it has its reality within the social order and within the order of nature. One philosophical argument is that it is impossible to think about a certain mental state without thinking about the subject whose mental state it is; self-consciousness is an awareness of the particular state people are in, and therefore their awareness of their conscious state is an awareness of themselves as the subject of those particular mental states.

Self-consciousness has been studied across many disciplines (e.g., anthropology, communication, philosophy, psychology, sociology) with implication for greater understanding of why people do the things they do. Self-consciousness is one area of research that explains the ability to reflect actively and thus increase a sense of self-awareness in various situations. Many studies have been conducted with the self-consciousness scale, resulting in much research that correlates various variables with the public and private dimensions. The public and private dimensions of self-consciousness further explain how people construct their identity in various situations. The idea of self-consciousness and identity are inseparable—people construct and shape their identity through self-consciousness. This identity is continually being shaped by self-perception in relationship to the surrounding world. Moreover, the philosophical implications of understanding self-consciousness play a fundamental role in understanding the self in relationship to consciousness. Self-consciousness is essential to understanding how the self fits into the larger philosophical meaning of one's place in the world.

Leeanne M. Bell

See also Consciousness; Development of Identity; Development of Self-Concept; Intersubjectivity; Philosophy of Mind; Self-Assessment; Self-Concept; Self-Image; Society and Social Identity

Further Readings

Bermúdez, J. L. (1998). *The paradox of self-consciousness*. Cambridge: MIT Press.

Birkmann, K. (2005). Consciousness, self-consciousness, and the modern self. *History of the Human Sciences, 18,* 27–48.

Cohen, A. P. (1994). *Self consciousness: An alternative anthropology of identity.* New York: Routledge.

Fenigstein, A. (1987). On the nature of public and private self-consciousness. *Journal of Personality, 55,* 543–554.

Fenigstein, A., Scheier, M. F., & Buss, A. H. (1975). Public and private self-consciousness: Assessment and theory. *Journal of Consulting and Clinical Psychology, 43,* 522–527.

Manfred, F. (2004). Fragments of a history of the theory of self-consciousness from Kant to Kierkegaard. *Critical Horizons, 5,* 53–136.

Scheier, M. F., & Carver, C. S. (1985). The self-consciousness scale: A revised version for use with general populations. *Journal of Applied Social Psychology, 15,* 687–699.

Schlenker, B. R., & Weigold, M. F. (1990). Self-consciousness and self-presentation: Being autonomous versus appearing autonomous. *Journal of Personality and Social Psychology, 59,* 820–828.

Tani, T. (1998). Inquiry into the I, disclosedness, and self-consciousness: Husserl, Heidegger, Nishida. *Continental Philosophy Review, 31,* 239–253.

Taylor, C. (1989). *The sources of the self: The making of modern identity.* Cambridge, MA: Harvard University Press.

SELF-CONSTRUAL

Since its conception, Hazel Markus and Shinobu Kitayama's self-construal theory has been one of the most popular theoretical frameworks in cross-cultural psychology. Self-construal research primarily focuses on how the individual's self differs across cultures. A *self-construal* can be defined as a constellation of thoughts, feelings, and actions concerning the relationship of the self to others and the self as distinct from others. Self-construals are presumed to mediate the influence of culture. Since Markus and Kitayama introduced the concept of the independent and interdependent self to represent individualist and group-oriented identities, numerous studies have attempted to predict communicative, cognitive, emotional, motivational, and behavioral outcomes associated with the two distinct conceptualizations of self. Many

intercultural scholars were becoming dissatisfied with nationality, broad cultural variability dimensions (e.g., individualism and collectivism), or other forms of crude classification of individuals (such as "Westerners" and "Asians") as a culture proxy for explaining individual behavior. Furthermore, a single paradigm of human functioning (i.e., "individualism") has had a virtual stranglehold within the social sciences in general. Given these criticisms, self-construal research has attracted enthusiastic scholars and has turned into one of the most influential directions in the past decade in cultural research. This entry first describes the cultural differences in self and then discusses the usefulness and criticisms of self-construals.

Cultural Differences in Self

In describing the culture-specific nature of self, Markus and Kitayama suggest that cultural and social groups at any given time are associated with characteristic patterns of sociocultural participation, or, more specifically, with characteristic ways of being a person in the world. Each person is embedded within a variety of sociocultural contexts or cultures (e.g., country, ethnicity, religion, gender, family). Each of these cultural contexts makes some claim on the person and is associated with a set of ideas and practices (i.e., a cultural framework) about how to be a "good" person. Markus and Kitayama refer to these characteristic patterns of sociocultural participation as "selfways." Extending the notion of selfways, Markus and Kitayama delineate two general cultural self-schemata: independent and interdependent. These two images of self were originally conceptualized as reflecting the emphasis on connectedness and relations often found in non-Western cultures ("interdependent self") and the separatedness and uniqueness of the individual ("independent self") stressed in the West.

Whereas the self-system is the complete configuration of self-schemata (e.g., gender, race, religion, social class, and one's developmental history), the independent and interdependent construals of self are among the most general and overarching self-schemata of these in an individual's self-system. Based on an extensive review of cross-cultural literature, Markus and Kitayama argued that these two construals of self influence cognition, emotion, and motivation more powerfully than previously thought.

According to Markus and Kitayama, the main difference between the two self-construals is the belief one holds regarding how the self is related to others. In the independent construal, most representations of the self (i.e., the ways in which an individual thinks of himself or herself) have as their referent the individual's ability, characteristic, attribute, or goal ("I am friendly" or "I am ambitious"). These inner characteristics or traits are the primary regulators of behavior. This view of the self derives from a belief in the wholeness and uniqueness of each person's configuration of internal attributes. The normative imperative of such cultures is to become independent of others and to discover and express one's own unique attributes. Thus, the goals of persons in such cultures are to stand out and to express their own unique characteristics or traits. This orientation has led to an emphasis on the need to pursue personal self-actualization or self-development. Individual weakness, from this cultural perspective, is to be overly dependent on others or to be unassertive. This perspective is rooted in Western philosophical tradition. The ontological goal of this perspective is to highlight the division between the experiencer and what is experienced, in other words, to differentiate the individual from the context.

By contrast, in the interdependent construal, the self is connected to others; the principal components of the self are one's relationships to others. This is not to say that the person with an interdependent view of the self has no conception of internal traits, characteristics, or preferences that are unique to him or her, but rather that these internal, private aspects of the self are not primary forces in directing or guiding behavior. Instead, behavior is more significantly regulated by a desire to maintain harmony and appropriateness in relationships. Within such a construal, the self becomes most meaningful and complete when it is cast in the appropriate social relationship. So one's behavior in a given situation might be a function more of the needs, wishes, and preferences of others than of one's own needs, wishes, or preferences. As a result of this interdependent construal of the self, one may attempt to meet the needs of others and to promote the others' goals. Weakness in this perspective is to be headstrong, unwilling to accommodate the needs of others, or self-centered. The emphasis is on downplaying the division between the experiencer and the object of experience, and it is connection with, rather than separation from, others and the surrounding context that is highlighted.

The distinctions between independent and interdependent construals must be regarded as general tendencies that emerge when the members of the culture are considered as a whole. For instance, even in the United States a theme of interdependence is reflected in the values and activities of many of its cultures. Religious groups, such as the Quakers, explicitly value and promote interdependence, as do many small towns and rural communities. Markus and Kitayama observe that even within highly individualistic Western culture, most people are still much less self-reliant, self-contained, or self-sufficient than the prevailing cultural ideology suggests that they should be. "Independence" and "interdependence" refer to two different orientations toward society and people. But cultures and individuals can balance and develop each of these orientations in many different ways. Thus, although social practices based on these two cultural orientations may differ dramatically, they are not necessarily diametrical antitheses. Nor are their psychological consequences always simple opposites.

Although Markus and Kitayama do not directly link their conceptualization of the self-construals to any culture-level dimensions, they discuss the cultural differences at the individual level under a framework similar to individualism and collectivism. Several cross-cultural studies have reported a link between individualism and collectivism and independent and interdependent self-construals. Self-construals have been used to predict cross-cultural differences in a wide variety of situations, including preferred conversational styles, requesting styles, deception, attribution errors, embarrassment, interactive constraints, conflict strategies, self-esteem, coping, cross-cultural adaptation, depression and social anxiety, five factors of personality, self-esteem, relationship harmony, life satisfaction, acculturation, biculturalism, self-enhancement, and consumer behavior. Recent research has also examined the role of the relational self-construal in social cognition, in the development of closeness in relationships, and in well-being.

Why Self-Construals Are Useful

Historically, cross-cultural researchers have found many cross-cultural differences in individual behaviors and psychological functioning. However, there had been no theoretical framework to explain how culture creates those cultural differences. Then Markus and Kitayama offered their theory, implying that cultures produce specific self-schemata (independent and interdependent self-construals), thereby producing culturally distinct behaviors. This may be the reason self-construal theory has become one of the most influential theories in cross-cultural psychology since the 1990s.

A major benefit of self-construal research is that self-construals or related notions of cultural identity are well suited to identify the nature of identity within an individual who crosses cultural boundaries. Increasing cultural connections, with subsequent hybridization and the emergence of a world system consisting of an interpenetration of the global and the local, increase the complexity of culture. Therefore, there is a pressing need to formulate views of the self-concept that include the newer ideas of multiple or hybrid identities.

Further, the use of broad cultural variability dimensions has been criticized by many authors for its lack of explanatory power. When broad dimensions such as individualism-collectivism or high- versus low-context are invoked to account for cultural differences, it is not clear exactly how or why these differences occur. Although useful in evaluating whether cross-cultural differences exist, they are far less helpful in explaining why culture has an effect. Therefore, a better way to evaluate the effect of culture on behavior is to examine the mediating role of self-construals. To better understand the effect of national culture, it is necessary to identify the psychological variables that distinguish people belonging to different cultures.

Finally, over many years, social scientists have taken for granted the norm of an individualistic, independent self, and many theories in the social sciences are based on this assumption. In the predominant discourse of contemporary Western culture, "self" is equated with the autonomous or self-sufficient individual. Recent research, however, has revealed that substantial variability exists in the self; many theories based on an assumption that the self is independent and separated from

others require revision given the interdependent/relational self-construal.

Critique

Critics have pointed out that Markus and Kitayama's original formulation is misleading because it gives too simplistic a portrayal of how individuals construct their self-construals from their cultural experiences. When Markus and Kitayama introduced the notion of self-construals, they were not clear about the dimensionality of self-construals. Only recently have researchers cautiously started proposing two or more dimensions instead of a single bipolar dimension. Numerous journal articles and books have revealed ever more complexity and subtle issues relating to self-construals. Dimensionality of selves such as independent, relational, interdependent, collective, and many other closely related terms vary markedly between investigators.

Although self-construals are one of the most influential concepts in cross-cultural research, their validity has also been challenged. Some scholars contend that the theory has gained much more prominence than is warranted by the empirical support for it. Further research is needed to test the validity of self-construal theory as well as proposed scales for defining self-construal in ways that can be measured.

Markus and Kitayama introduced the notion of self-construals only in 1991, and self-construal scales were developed even more recently. The scales measuring self-construals may themselves need revision before the validity of self-construal theory can be tested. Establishing validity of the scales is a crucial prerequisite to scientific inquiry and the proper understanding and interpretation of findings. Currently, the validity of the findings of numerous studies in this literature are being seriously debated. Anomalies in the literature warrant a deeper analysis of the current conceptualization of self-construals and the scales employed to measure them.

Accelerated change in the modern world compels us to take cognizance of the dynamic nature of individuals' cultural identity. A contemporary view of self-culture relations suggests that this relationship is more complex than previously assumed, and certainly more complex than a simplistic view of self that pits individual and group needs against each other. Research on cultural identity encourages psychological work that also accounts for hybrid identities. Such identities may be shaped by migration, discrimination, poverty, and minority (e.g., ethnic, racial, or religious) status. There is a need for more fine-grained analyses that capture subtleties such as the heterogeneity and the overlap that exist between and within different cultural communities. The notion of self-construals, although still evolving, may be well suited for this purpose.

Min-Sun Kim

See also Collectivism/Individualism; Self-Schema

Further Readings

Cross, S. E., & Gore, J. (2002). Cultural models of the self. In M. Leary & J. Tangney (Eds.), *Handbook of self and identity* (pp. 536–564). New York: Guilford Press.

Kim, M. S. (2002). *Non-Western perspectives on human communication: Implications for theory and practice.* Thousand Oaks, CA: Sage.

Markus, H., & Kitayama, S. (1991). Culture and the self: Implications for cognition, emotion, and motivation. *Psychological Review, 98,* 224–253.

Matsumoto, D. (1999). Culture and self: An empirical assessment of Markus and Kitayama's theory of independent and interdependent self-construals. *Asian Journal of Social Psychology, 2,* 289–310.

Singelis, T. M. (1994). The measurement of independent and interdependent self- construals. *Personality and Social Psychological Bulletin, 20,* 580–591.

SELF-DISCREPANCY THEORY

Why is it that when people are emotionally overwhelmed by a tragedy or serious setback in their lives, such as the death of their child, the loss of their job, or the break-up of their marriage, some suffer from depression whereas others suffer from anxiety? *Self-discrepancy theory* was developed to find an answer to this question. The answer proposed by self-discrepancy theory is that even when people have the same goal, such as college students wanting a good grade point average (GPA) or older adults wanting a good marriage,

they can vary in how they represent the goal. Some people represent their goals as hopes, wishes, or aspirations—called *ideal* self-guides in self-discrepancy theory. Other individuals represent their goals as beliefs about their duties, responsibilities, or obligations—*ought* self-guides. According to self-discrepancy theory, this difference between pursuing ideals versus oughts explains why people have such different emotional reactions to the same negative life event.

Self-discrepancy theory proposes that people treat what is currently happening in their personal lives as saying something about them now—as representing their *actual selves.* These actual selves are then compared with their ideal or ought self-guides. People suffer emotionally when there is a discrepancy between some aspect of their actual self and one of their self-guides—a *self-discrepancy.* When there is an actual-self discrepancy from a personal ideal, people feel sad, disappointed, discouraged—*dejection-related* emotions that relate to depression. When there is an actual-self discrepancy from a personal ought, people feel nervous, tense, and worried—*agitation-related* emotions that relate to anxiety. Thus, according to self-discrepancy theory, people's emotional vulnerabilities depend on the type of self-guide that motivates their lives—a vulnerability to dejection or depression when ideals dominate and a vulnerability to agitation or anxiety when oughts dominate.

Why are different emotions associated with an actual-ideal discrepancy versus an actual-ought discrepancy? According to self-discrepancy theory, this is because different emotions are associated with different psychological situations that people experience: Success or failure in ideal goal pursuit produce different psychological situations than does success or failure in ought goal pursuit. Specifically, when pursuing ideal goals, people experience success as the presence of a positive outcome (a gain), which is experienced as feeling happy, and they experience failure as the absence of positive outcomes (a non-gain), which is experienced as feeling sad. In contrast, when pursuing ought goals, people experience success as the absence of a negative outcome (a non-loss), which is experienced as feeling relaxed, and they experience failure as the presence of a negative outcome (a loss), which is experienced as feeling nervous.

Self-discrepancy theory also proposes that different kinds of parenting contribute to children developing strong ideal self-guides or strong ought self-guides, and this is because of the different psychological situations involved in the parenting. When children interact with their parents (or other caretakers), the parents respond to them in ways that make the children experience specific kinds of psychological situations. Over time, the children respond to themselves like their parents respond to them, producing the same specific kinds of psychological situations. Over time, this develops into the type of self-guide that is associated with those psychological situations—ideal or ought self-guides.

The kind of parenting that is predicted to create strong *ideals* in children is the combination of *bolstering* (when managing success) and *love withdrawal* (when disciplining failure). Bolstering occurs, for instance, when parents encourage the child to overcome difficulties or set up opportunities for the child to engage in success activities—it creates an experience of the presence of positive outcomes in the child. Love withdrawal occurs, for instance, when parents take away a toy when the child refuses to share it or stop a story when the child is not paying attention—it creates an experience of the absence of positive outcomes in the child.

The kind of parenting that is predicted to create strong *oughts* in children is the combination of *prudence* (when managing success) and *punitive/ critical* (when disciplining failure). Prudence occurs, for instance, when parents train the child to be alert to potential dangers or teach the child to "mind your manners"—this creates an experience of the absence of negative outcomes in the child. Punitive/critical occurs, for instance, when parents yell when the child doesn't listen or criticize when the child makes a mistake—it creates an experience of the presence of negative outcomes.

Self-discrepancy theory also distinguishes between self-guides as a function of whose viewpoint is associated with the self-guide. Self-guides can represent individuals' *own* independent viewpoint about the kind of persons they ideally want or ought to be, such as "What are my goals for myself?" Alternatively, self-guides can represent the viewpoint of a significant *other* about the kind of person this other ideally wants or believes they ought to be, such as "What are my mother's goals for me?" The theory proposes that individuals differ in whether their own self-guides or their significant others' self-guides are the basis for self-regulation and determine emotional vulnerabilities.

Consistent with the predictions of self-discrepancy theory, research with both clinical and nonclinical populations has found that suffering from dejection-depression feelings is more strongly predicted by actual-ideal discrepancies than by actual-ought discrepancies, whereas suffering from agitation-anxiety feelings is more strongly predicted by actual-ought discrepancies than by actual-ideal discrepancies. Moreover, because some individuals have actual-self discrepancies from both their ideal and their ought self-guides, studies have found that one or the other kind of suffering can be temporarily induced by activating (through verbal priming) either an ideal or an ought. When such "priming" occurs, participants whose actual-ideal discrepancy is activated suddenly feel sad and disappointed and fall into a depression-like state of low activity (e.g., talk slower), and participants whose actual-ought discrepancy is activated suddenly feel nervous and worried and fall into an anxiety-like state of high activity (e.g., talk quicker). Studies with U.S. samples have also found that discrepancies from own independent self-guides are a more important determinant of emotional vulnerabilities for males than for females, whereas discrepancies from significant other self-guides are more important for females than for males. Self-discrepancy theory has been used to develop effective therapy interventions for treating depression and anxiety disorders.

E. Tory Higgins

See also Cognitive Dissonance Theory; Self-Concept; Self-Esteem; Self-Perception Theory

Further Readings

Carver, C. S., Lawrence, J. W., & Scheier, M. F. (1999). Self-discrepancies and affect: Introducing the role of feared selves. *Personality and Social Psychology Bulletin, 25*(7), 783–792.

Higgins, E. T. (1987). Self-discrepancy: A theory relating self and affect. *Psychological Review, 94,* 319–340.

Higgins, E. T., Klein, R., & Strauman, T. (1985). Self-concept discrepancy theory: A psychological model for distinguishing among different aspects of depression and anxiety. *Social Cognition, 3,* 51–76.

Self-Efficacy

Albert Bandura's 1997 social learning theory contains the concept of *self-efficacy,* which is the self-perception that one can perform in ways that allow some control over life events. More specifically, self-efficacy determines one's perception that he or she can produce desired results. Self-efficacy forms the foundation of human agency—people's will—and is located in one's self-perception. Self-efficacy can be described in terms of magnitude and generality. Self-efficacy differs in the magnitude of the level of perceived difficulty of the task; the more difficult the task completed, the higher the level of self-efficacy. Accomplishing tasks spurs feelings toward other associated tasks. For those people with higher levels of self-efficacy, when a particular task is achieved, feelings of confidence are generalized to other tasks. Research indicates that children who perform well on math tasks, for example, should efficiently learn new material built on those domains.

Accurate assessment of one's skills is an important component to self-efficacy—there is a developmental component to assessing one's skill. Children are less able to accurately assess their skills than are adults.

Bandura differentiated efficacy expectations from outcome expectations. *Outcome expectancy* is an estimation that a given behavior will lead to a certain outcome, whereas an *efficacy expectation* is the confidence that one can successfully execute the behavior required to accomplish the outcome. The two concepts differ when a person believes that a course of action will produce outcomes (outcome expectation) but is unsure that he or she can complete the task (efficacy expectation). Furthermore, people's expectation of their ability to successfully complete a task determines how much effort and persistence they will devote to accomplish it. Nonetheless, according to Dale Schunk in 1995, high self-efficacy will not influence behavior when people do not value the outcome.

Components of Self-Efficacy

A person's strength of conviction influences self-efficacy. The stronger the perceived self-efficacy, the more effort a person is willing to devote to the task. Those willing to take risks may not always succeed, but they learn from their mistakes and subsequently are more likely to embark on trying more complex tasks. People with low self-efficacy typically are afraid of failing at a task. They either don't risk trying to accomplish what they perceive as difficult or they often give up before succeeding.

Cognitive Thought

Bandura believed that cognitive thought or what he referred to as *self-reflective thought* informs self-efficacy. People interpret their experiences in ways that add to or detract from one's perceived self-efficacy. Bandura identified the type of information people use for this interpretation, including difficulty of the task, level of effort, assistance received, conditions under which the task was performed, emotional and physical state, and perceived improvement over time. A person's biases also play a factor in this interpretation. For example, a person's biased selection of what to remember and what to forget provides data for interpretation.

One's level of perceived self-efficacy influences whether one will focus on opportunity or risk. A person with strong expectations of success will persevere because of established coping strategies despite a previous failing experience. People with a strong perceived self-efficacy are more likely to possess cognitive resourcefulness, be flexible, and effectively manage their environment for continued success. People with lower self-efficacy dwell on what can go wrong.

Motivation

Motivation is another important component to Bandura's social learning theory and is related to self-efficacy. Bandura believed that motivation was often cognitively generated and was affected by casual attributions, outcome expectations, and cognitive goals. Casual attributions means that a person with low perceived self-efficacy will assume that a task was not successful because of his or her low ability whereas a person with high self-efficacy assumes that a task's incompletion resulted from other factors such as insufficient effort and unfavorable circumstances. One's expectation of an outcome influences whether someone will be motivated to pursue the task. People with low self-efficacy will doubt they can succeed and are likely not to pursue the task and think little of the consequences. Therefore, outcome expectation influences implementation. Reflective thought about goals influences what goals to undertake, the amount of effort required, and how long to persevere in attempts to achieve them. People with higher self-efficacy are likely to set motivating goals for themselves and expect favorable outcomes. They strategize about how to overcome obstacles and place responsibility for failures on factors that are controllable.

In describing motivation more precisely, Bandura identified sources that influence self-efficacy. They are described here.

Performance Accomplishments

First titled "performance accomplishments," but later altered to "sources of mastery experiences," Bandura explained that the frequency of a person's accomplishments or failures influenced one's self-efficacy. Perceived frequent failures decreased self-efficacy, whereas increased successes encouraged self-efficacy. Though occasional failures spurred learning from mistakes, the timing, importance, and frequency of failures is important in determining degree of self-efficacy.

Vicarious Experiences

Vicarious sources of self-efficacy include models, both live and symbolic. Parents, caretakers, teachers, and peers become important vicarious models. By watching others, people with a strong perceived sense of self-efficacy believe that they too can succeed. However, watching others fail tends to instill increased self-doubt for those with weak self-efficacy prompting a circular phenomenon of doubt, failure, and more doubt. Research has indicated that providing diverse models of observing the repeated successful completion of tasks by a variety of people increases self-efficacy for those with low self-efficacy.

Social Persuasion

Earlier described by Bandura as "verbal persuasion," social persuasion can influence self-efficacy, but its influence is short lived. Persuasion takes forms other than only through verbal means such as through writing, body language, rewards, awards, and punishment. Experiences that disconfirm social persuasion have a stronger impact on self-efficacy than social persuasion does.

Physical and Emotional States

In his early work, Bandura stressed the emotional influence on self-efficacy, but in his later work, he added the influence of physical factors. People who expect success are not overwhelmed by fear, anxiety, depression, or other arousal states. They are able to reduce negative emotional states, whereas people with low perceived self-efficacy find that more difficult. Their fear of failure begets more fear. People with lower self-efficacy read their tension as a sign of personal deficiency.

Situational Circumstances

Some tasks are more difficult than others are and require more physical and emotional resources to complete. The perceived difficulty of a task influences one's perceived success in accomplishing it, which relates to one's perceived strengths and weaknesses connected to the task.

Application of Aspects of Self-Efficacy

Social learning theory and self-efficacy in particular have been used frequently to guide educational practices, especially in ways to motivate learning from infants to adults. Caregivers early in a child's life pave the way for self-efficacy. Experiences provided by them to enhance curiosity lead to self-mastery, which in turn encourages caregivers to provide additional varied and complex opportunities for self-mastery. According to Dale Schunk and Frank Pajares, environments that offer stimulating exploration through moderate challenges are best able to encourage self-efficacy.

Bandura believed that adults with a low self-efficacy lived in a stressful environment of their own making. Those with higher levels of self-efficacy find means to cope with and manage adversities by transforming threats to achievement. Through cognitive reframing, Bandura believed that people with low levels of self-efficacy could interrupt detrimental thought processes by turning them off. This alters the cause of stress. Depression is of particular concern in relation to self-efficacy. Unfulfilled goals and dreams can lead to a depressive state that can weaken self-efficacy. Depressive states can also weaken social supports. Another avenue in raising levels of self-efficacy is to assist people in selecting environments that nurture their potential. For children and adolescents, schools and peers that contribute to feelings of autonomy and relatedness improve the likelihood of self-efficacy. Examples in schools include less emphasis on competition, more teacher attention to individual progress, and support during school transitions (i.e., moving from elementary school to middle school).

Children and adolescent peer networks greatly influence self-efficacy. According to Schunk and Pajares, academic achievement increases for students in networks where peers are talented academically. However, academic ability groupings in schools can hinder self-efficacy of students who find their academic performance below their peers.

Research addresses the impact of teacher self-efficacy on student achievement. Because teachers with higher levels of self-efficacy predict higher student achievement, efforts in teacher preparation and professional development to ensure teacher self-efficacy is critical.

Bandura observed that prejudicial systems neutralize high levels of self-efficacy. He believed that self-efficacy exceeded academic performance in such environments. In 1997, in response to these environments, Beverly Tatum suggested peer mentoring groups (that she metaphorically referred to as cafeteria tables) and other mentoring programs that offer support and validation to students from others who have had similar experiences. In 2007, Tatum wrote about how racist notions undergirding achievement tests negatively influence the self-efficacy of students of color. She highlighted Shelby Steele's work in stereotype threat that demonstrated how racism and sexism are detrimental to self-efficacy.

Efforts to improve self-efficacy of students cannot overcome under-resourced and ineffective schools. Bandura proposed that collectives as well as individuals possess self-efficacy. Research suggests that paying attention to the self-efficacy of low-performing schools as well as to the individuals in those schools is warranted.

Self-efficacy is often used in career and vocational counseling. In that regard, Vernon Zunker noted that self-efficacy, outcome expectations, and personal goals are the building blocks that determine the course of career development.

Bandura found the concept of self-efficacy easily applicable to people suffering from phobias. He felt that treatment interventions should include modeling with guided participation. Because motivation is often cognitively generated and emotional states can serve as barriers to greater self-efficacy, steps to increase self-efficacy must incorporate managing emotional states. Those with lower levels of self-efficacy consistently worry about crises that rarely come.

Remaining Questions About Self-Efficacy

According to Schunk and Pajares, the generalized impact of self-efficacy is unclear. They also point out that Bandura's emphasis on persistence as a variable of self-efficacy may be problematic because a teacher or parent often imposes environments where children have no choice but to persist.

Because confidence is important to self-efficacy, Schunk and Pajares question whether there is a point at which someone becomes too confident. Though they discourage efforts to decrease students' confidence levels, Schunk and Pajares believe that the impact of overconfidence should be investigated. They also cite questions regarding the cross-cultural validity of self-efficacy.

Bandura lamented problems in measuring self-efficacy in that respondents often offered their hope of succeeding rather than their prediction of whether they would succeed. Research on hope may address this concern.

Jan Arminio

See also Ascribed Identity; Avowal; Identity Change; Self; Self-Concept; Self-Esteem

Further Readings

Bandura, A. (1977). *Social learning theory*. Englewood Cliffs, NJ: Prentice Hall.

Bandura, A. (1997). Social cognitive theory of personality. In L. A. Pervin & O. P. John (Eds.), *Handbook of personality: Theory and research* (2nd ed., pp. 154–196). New York: Guilford Press.

Schunk, D. H. (1995). Self-efficacy and education and instruction. In J. E. Maddux (Ed.), *Self-efficacy, adaption, and adjustment: Theory, research, and applications* (pp. 281–303). New York: Plenum Press.

Schunk, D. H., & Pajares, F. (2005). Competence perceptions and academic functioning. In A. J. Elliot & C. S. Dweck (Eds.), *Handbook of competence and motivation* (pp. 85–104). New York: Guilford Press.

Snyder, C. R., Sympson, S. C., Michael, S. T., & Cheavens, J. (2001). Optimism and hope constructs: Variants on a positive expectancy theme. In E. C. Chang (Ed.), *Optimism & pessimism: Implications for theory, research, and practice.* Washington, DC: American Psychological Association.

Tatum, B. D. (1997). *"Why are all the Black kids sitting together in the cafeteria?" And other conversations about race.* New York: Basic Books.

Tatum, B. D. (2007). *Can we talk about race? And other conversations in an era of school resegregation.* Boston: Beacon Press.

Zunker, V. G. (2006). *Career counseling: A holistic approach* (7th ed.). Belmont, CA: Brooks/Cole.

SELF-ENHANCEMENT THEORY

Self-knowledge is fundamental for developing a sense of the self. Regardless of the accuracy of this self-knowledge, it influences one's perceptions of the self, as well as one's interactions with others. One way of learning about the self is through the evaluations and feedback that one receives from others. *Self-enhancement theory* is based on various personality theories and suggests that people have a basic drive to perceive the self positively and receive positive evaluations from others. One's desire for positive feedback increases if positive evaluations are not received. This theory emphasizes self-enhancement as a basic motive for gathering self-knowledge. The following sections describe self-enhancement theory, provide examples of competing hypotheses for self-evaluation, and present research about the role of enhancement in mental health in different cultures.

Self-Evaluation Motivations

The idea that people want to feel good about themselves is not a unique or unusual concept. Sigmund Freud, a pioneer in the field of psychology, was perhaps one of the first proponents of this idea in the early 1900s. He proposed that people continually strive to achieve pleasure and avoid pain. This drive is called the *pleasure principle,* and it is important especially with respect to young children because of what is considered their selfishness and disregard for others, which allows them to receive basic needs for survival (e.g., crying when hungry). This drive continues over time, where the individual is interested in feeling good about the self and seeking immediate gratification. The same motivation for seeking pleasure was introduced in the drive-reduction theory in the 1940s. Once again, the basic premise was that all behavior is motivated by the desire to seek pleasure that is a result of needs and desires being met. When drive-induced tensions are alleviated, the individual feels pleasure, resulting in an enhancement of the self.

That people want to feel pleasure by thinking positively of themselves and having others express the same regard has been evident in numerous studies within psychology. Self-enhancement theory arose from this basic premise, suggesting that regardless of how a person feels about himself or herself, the person wants others to think positively of him or her. A widely studied phenomenon in social psychology, self-enhancement has been considered a universal motivator. Because an individual cannot directly observe the self, one must look to others to gain self-knowledge that allows one to create beliefs and opinions about the self. Although this knowledge about the self is not always accurate, it still plays an influential role in how one perceives the self.

One way to learn about the self is through interaction and feedback from others. Learning what others think about the self can help reinforce one's self-knowledge. Feedback can be positive or negative and can be consistent or inconsistent with one's self-view. The extent to which people prefer good/bad or (in)consistent self-evaluations has been widely studied. In the 1970s, there were several competing schools of thought on the type of feedback people preferred. Until this time, many "mini-theories" tried to explain the motivational processes affecting self-knowledge. These mini-theories were then categorized into three distinct areas to indicate the type of information preferred from others: accurate information (self-assessment theory), consistent information (self-verification theory), and positive information (self-enhancement theory).

Accurate Feedback

The first motive for self-knowledge is called the appraisal motive, which suggests that people want to receive accurate information about the self. Proposed by Yaacov Trope, self-assessment theory suggests that uncertainty is created when people do not have an objective view of the self. To reduce this aversive state, people seek accurate self-knowledge. One way of gathering accurate information is through diagnostic tests. These tests provide information about one's abilities on a given task. Without extrinsic motivation, the results of these tasks should be able to reduce uncertainty. Research by Trope and colleagues has found that people prefer tasks when they accurately diagnose ability (i.e., tasks high in diagnosticity), regardless of whether such tasks identify failure or success.

Consistent Feedback

A second motive related to self-knowledge involves receiving confirmation about how one sees the self and can be traced to such early symbolic interactionists as Charles Cooley and George Herbert Mead. William Swann called this *self-verification theory,* which suggests that people prefer having others see them as they see themselves. Having this correspondent feedback is important because it allows people to understand responses from others, predict their behavior, and know how to act toward them. For example, if individuals have positive self-concepts, they want others to think positively of them, whereas if they have negative self-concepts, they would prefer to get negative feedback because it is consistent with their self-views.

Preference for consistent feedback can be traced to Prescott Lecky's seminal work on self-consistency theory and other consistency theories from the 1950s such as Fritz Heider's balance theory and Leon Festinger's cognitive dissonance theory. Balance theory proposes that people prefer cognitive consistency and are motivated to achieve psychological balance. Cognitive dissonance theory suggests that when people have contradicting cognitions (defined as attitudes, emotions, beliefs, or values), they are motivated to reduce the negative state of psychological discomfort that such dissonant state produces. To minimize this discomfort, an individual can acquire new thoughts or modify existing thoughts to restore the perception of consistency of cognitions. In interpersonal contexts, a person can change his or her own self-concept, change his or her own actions, or change the relationship with the other person. According to consistency theorists, a person can also choose acquaintances based on consistent self-views. For example, one may only choose to be friends with people who have the same views of the individual that the individual has of himself or herself. According to self-consistency literature, if a person has a negative view of himself or herself, that person would be more receptive to feedback that confirmed his or her view of himself or herself instead of contradicting it.

Many studies have been conducted to test self-verification theory. The research paradigm usually involves measuring self-evaluations of participants and providing them with positive or negative evaluations from their group members. Those with high self-evaluations react more favorably toward group members who provide them with positive evaluations than toward those providing negative evaluations. Participants with low self-evaluations prefer group members who provide negative feedback. Morton Deutsch and Leonard Solomon conducted one of the earliest studies on self-consistency in 1959. In a 2 × 2 experimental design, researchers manipulated self-evaluation and evaluations from others. Participants were told they either succeeded or failed a task, and their partner either wanted to work or not work with them again. Results revealed that participants who were told they succeeded on the task (i.e., had a positive self-evaluation) preferred partners who also gave them positive feedback. Participants who were told they failed the task (i.e., had a negative self-evaluation) preferred partners who gave them negative feedback. Although the study had limitations, it showed that preference for group members was in the direction predicted by self-consistency theories.

Though numerous studies have been conducted to test self-verification motives, critics argue that it is difficult to test the theory because these processes are rare. To test the theory, it is essential to have participants with negative self-views. However, most people have relatively positive self-views, thereby making it difficult to test the theory.

Positive Feedback

Self-enhancement theory suggests that all individuals, regardless of their self-view, prefer to receive positive evaluations from others. This view can be traced to early personality theorists such as Karen Horney, Carl Rogers, and Abraham Tesser. Theorists in this line of research explain that people want to have a high sense of worth. This basic need for self-esteem can be achieved through having others like and respect them. People should respond favorably toward those who provide them positive evaluations of themselves because this feedback fulfills their self-esteem needs. Similarly, they should respond unfavorably toward those who give them negative evaluations. These predictions arose from the social-exchange literature, which suggests that people are attracted to groups that fulfill their needs. Contrary to the self-consistency literature, self-esteem theorists suggested that individuals with low self-esteem respond more favorably toward positive feedback than do those with high self-esteem because those with low self-esteem have a higher need for esteem enhancement. Thus, although everyone prefers positive rather than negative self-evaluations from others, those with low self-esteem prefer it even more than do those with high self-esteem. In 1959, J. E. Ditties conducted one of the earliest experiments on self-esteem, in which participants provided self-reports about self-esteem and either received positive or negative feedback from group members. Results showed that participants with low self-esteem who received negative evaluations were less attracted to the group than when they received positive evaluations.

Comparing Theories

Although extensive empirical support has been found for the three motivations described, they have also been investigated through independent studies. Constantine Sedikides conducted several experiments comparing the three motivations in the self-evaluation process. Participants in these studies were asked to reflect on central or peripheral traits by asking themselves questions that varied in diagnostic ability. The central traits were highly descriptive and important and peripheral traits were low in descriptiveness and importance to the individual. Based on previous findings, the researchers assumed that participants had great self-knowledge and certainty about central traits but not peripheral traits. The study asked participants to reflect on three traits that were central/positive (kind, friendly, and trustworthy), central/negative (unkind, unfriendly, and untrustworthy), peripheral/positive (modest, predictable, and uncomplaining), or peripheral/negative (immodest, unpredictable, and complaining). Results demonstrated that participants confirmed both central and peripheral traits, providing evidence against self-verification theory. Supporting the self-enhancement view, participants confirmed possession of positive traits and disconfirmed possession of negative traits. Participants were also more likely to confirm possessing positive traits when the traits were central versus peripheral, and more likely to disconfirm possessing negative traits when they were central versus peripheral. Pitting self-assessment, self-verification, and self-enhancement motivations against each other, the results from six experiments provided support for the self-enhancement framework (followed by self-verification, then self-assessment), suggesting that enhancement is the most powerful motivation in the self-evaluation process.

Before Sedikides's study, decades of research revealed mixed results, with some studies finding support for one theory over the others. More recently, researchers have attempted to demonstrate that the three theories may be integrated to better explain self-knowledge motivations. J. Sidney Shrauger conducted a literature review to better understand contradicting results about self-knowledge. He found that responses to feedback were measured in two fundamentally different ways: cognitively and affectively. This difference could account for the contradicting results between consistency and enhancement theories. When cognitive reactions to feedback are being studied, people prefer receiving consistent information. If the information is not consistent with the view of the self, it is less accurately recalled and is not perceived as credible. In contrast, the study of emotional responses to feedback (e.g., satisfaction with the evaluation, liking of the evaluator), suggests that people prefer receiving enhancing information. In these studies, people with positive or negative views of the self prefer receiving positive evaluations. Shrauger concluded that people favor getting evaluations that are consistent with the self-view when processing information cognitively. However, emotionally speaking, people prefer to receive enhancing evaluations even if they are inconsistent or distrusted. Though this was an important finding, little research has directly examined cognitive and affective responses to evaluations within the same study. The few that were conducted immediately after Shrauger's review found evidence for the self-enhancement model rather than for the consistency model. William Swann and colleagues later conducted a study where they measured both cognitive and affective reactions to feedback that were consistent or inconsistent with participants' self-view. They found that participants preferred consistent feedback; however, those who received negative feedback were more depressed, hostile, and anxious compared with those who received positive feedback. Consistency of feedback with self-view did not influence these affective responses. Taken together, these findings support Shrauger's hypothesis that preference for feedback may be different depending on cognitive or affective measures.

Self-Enhancement and Mental Health

Self-enhancement motives are studied across numerous contexts, including the mental health domain. Within the mental health field, it is generally accepted that psychologically healthy individuals maintain a realistic view of the self. However, people often have inflated positive illusions of the self. In a review of the literature, Shelley Taylor and Jonathon Brown concluded that people evaluate themselves positively (often unrealistically), have exaggerated illusions of control over their environment, and have unrealistic optimism. Data indicate that people tend to choose positive traits to describe themselves more often than they choose negative traits, positive information about one's personality is more easily recalled than negative information, and positive outcomes are attributed to the self but negative outcomes are not. However, those with low self-esteem or moderate depression have a more balanced view of the self, in which

they acknowledge both good and bad traits and outcomes. This suggests that, contrary to the mental health literature, healthy individuals may not have a realistic view of the self. Taylor and Brown also found that people believe themselves to have more control over events than they actually possess, for instance, over chance events (e.g., gambling). This is not evident among those who are depressed or in a negative mood. The last set of results from Taylor and Brown's review found that people have unrealistically positive views of their future. Individuals tend to believe the future will be better than the present or the past, and that it will result in more positive outcomes for themselves than for their peers. The results, therefore, suggest that self-enhancement may help improve mental health. Indeed, Taylor and Brown indicate that those who enhance self-abilities and attributes may be more caring, have higher work productivity, and are generally happier.

Cultural Differences in Self-Enhancement

People learn about norms and values through socialization. Behaviors deemed appropriate in one culture may not be the same in another culture. To function successfully in a given culture, an individual must learn the cognitive, emotional, and motivational processes that are common and acceptable within that society. In the extensive body of cross-cultural literature, Western cultures are often depicted as being independent and Eastern cultures as interdependent. In Western cultures, people display more concern for their own goals rather than for the goals set out by their ingroups. In addition, people in these cultures pay less attention to the opinions of ingroup members and make decisions based on their own perspectives, rather than on the views of others. Eastern cultures, however, encourage members to base goals and wishes on familial and community desires, thereby displaying interdependent tendencies. Examining employees in the international branches of a large multinational firm, Geert Hofstede found that independence was valued in countries such as the United States, and interdependence was emphasized in countries such as Japan.

The aforementioned research in this review of self-enhancement theory has been primarily conducted in the United States. These studies have provided evidence that self-enhancement—promoting positive aspects of the self—is prevalent and functional in this country. Because individualism is a cultural norm and is thus valued, enhancing the self and emphasizing one's uniqueness is socially valued. Research has shown that these individuals enhance evaluations of themselves, attribute positive outcomes (e.g., success) to the self and negative outcomes to external causes, and overestimate their own positive characteristics. These enhancing behaviors can help the individual function within an individualistic society because the behaviors emphasize uniqueness and independence. Research in other countries, especially Asian countries, has shown that self-enhancement is not highly prevalent and is sometimes completely absent. Shinobu Kitayama, Hazel Rose Marcus, and colleagues have conducted numerous studies examining beliefs and behaviors about the self in various countries and found that people in Eastern cultures rarely make attributions in the same direction as individuals in Western cultures. For example, after reviewing several studies conducted in Japan, the researchers found that positive outcomes were often attributed to luck or chance instead of to the self, and negative outcomes were attributed to a lack of ability or talent. In addition, people were reluctant to indicate their own uniqueness and positive outcomes. These tendencies, though different from those found in the United States, are functional within interdependent societies where dependence and conformity are normative. Kitayama and colleagues put forth a collective constructionist theory of the self, which suggests that psychological processes such as self-enhancement and self-criticism are a result of cultural norms and values. They found that situations in the United States are particularly conducive to enhancement tendencies, where people are likely to engage in self-enhancement. In contrast, situations in Japan are conducive to self-criticism, and Japanese individuals are more likely to engage in self-criticism. Both tendencies are functional and appropriate for the different cultures. These studies demonstrate that the self can be viewed differently in various cultures and contexts, and people act in ways to follow the norms and values of the culture in which they live.

Namrata Mahajan and David E. Rast III

See also Development of Identity; Development of Self-Concept; Psychology of Self and Identity; Self-Assessment; Self-Esteem

Further Readings

Baumeister, R. F. (Ed.). (1999). *The self in social psychology*. Philadelphia: Psychology Press.

Brown, J. D., Collins, R. L., & Schmidt, G. W. (1988). Self-esteem and direct versus indirect forms of self-enhancement. *Journal of Personality and Social Psychology, 55*, 445–453.

Kitayama, S., Markus, H. R., Matsumoto, H., & Norasakkunkit, V. (1997). Individual and collective processes in the construction of the self: Self-enhancement in the United States and self-criticism in Japan. *Journal of Personality and Social Psychology, 72*, 1245–1267.

Sedikides, C. (1993). Assessment, enhancement and verification determinants of the self-evaluation process. *Journal of Personality and Social Psychology, 65*, 317–338.

Shrauger, J. S. (1975). Responses to evaluation as a function of initial self-perceptions. *Psychological Bulletin, 82*, 581–596.

Swann, W. B., Pelham, B. W., & Krull, D. S. (1989). Agreeable fancy or disagreeable truth? Reconciling self-enhancement and self-verification. *Journal of Personality and Social Psychology, 57*, 782–791.

SELF-ESTEEM

Identity is an individual's ability to know himself or herself, and *self-esteem* is the value that an individual places on himself or herself. Self-esteem is a salient component of identity development and maintenance as individuals construct their identity based on interpersonal relationships, group affiliations, and other cultural influences. Some experts think self-esteem is central to human existence from being an innate longing in the subconscious, to a conscious need that must be met by planning, motivation, and determination, all of which influence the thoughts and behaviors of individuals and groups. But just what is self-esteem? And how can something so abstract be measured? And why would one want to measure it? This entry addresses these questions.

What Is Self-Esteem?

Psychologist William James, in his 1890 work *Principles of Psychology*, provides a broad definition for the concept of self-esteem as simply being a person's evaluation of himself or herself. In sum, high self-esteem is a good self-evaluation and low self-esteem is a poor self-evaluation, but that may be too simple. Self-esteem, generally speaking, is a subjective concept because it strongly relates to feelings and perceptions of an individual's self-worth imposed by the self and others. Objectively, self-esteem can be related to how one is evaluated by the self or others in the performance of a particular skill or talent (e.g., a good public speaker + great audience acceptance = high self-esteem versus a poor public speaker + audience rejection = low self-esteem). The meaning of self-esteem can be divided into two components, group and personal, which adds to its complexity of meaning.

The component of group self-esteem refers to how an individual feels about group membership and his or her perceived role and acceptance by the group (e.g., racial or ethnic), and personal self-esteem refers to how an individual feels about himself or herself comprehensively as an individual without regard for group or the approval of others. Trends in the study of self-esteem have gone through three phases—that of human instinct, human need, and motivation—to its current state of wanting to know the reasons why humans are motivated to maintain high levels of self-esteem.

Self-esteem seen as an innate or instinctual concept left many questions unanswered, and many researchers quickly found this perspective useless and moved to the need phase made popular by Abraham Maslow and others. Esteem is generally represented as the fourth level on Maslow's hierarchy of needs and refers to a person's concept of self-worth and need to belong. This need includes such complex and interrelated variables as self-esteem, confidence, achievement, respect of others, and respect by others. Without the esteem need fulfilled, individuals will not reach self-actualization and cannot grow until the esteem need has been fulfilled.

In 1969, however, Nathaniel Branden suggested two additional elements when defining *self-esteem*: first, the ability to cope with the challenges of life, and second, an individual is always worthy of happiness. This view considered that the esteem need would always be met. Branden also believed that the six elements or pillars for healthy self-esteem were (1) living consciously—be aware of what is going on in the world and be willing to understand; (2) self-acceptance—be willing to take ownership for personal thoughts, feelings, and actions; (3) self-responsibility—be part of the solution rather than the problem and each individual is responsible for his or her choices in life; (4) self-assertiveness—be authentic when dealing with others and value humanity even in difficult situations; (5) living purposefully—be able to identify, plan, and organize to reach short-term and long-term goals; and (6) personal integrity—be one who has the ability to keep his or her word (e.g., do what you say and say what you mean).

Self-esteem widely understood to be embedded in an individual's construct of identity, as one determines who he or she is, how one feels about oneself, and how much the feelings others have about him or her influence his or her perceptions of self-worth. This need-based thinking about self-esteem considers two types—global self-esteem and domain-specific self-esteem.

Global self-esteem is an overall value judgment of one's self-worth that is not tied to any specific situation. *Domain-specific* self-esteem is the assessment of one's value in a particular area (e.g., social settings, academic or intellectual ability, or physical prowess). The human need for positive global and domain-specific self-esteem gave way to phase three, that of human motivation and goal setting to reach desired self-esteem goals. The media is filled with books and speakers giving advice about how to build confidence, develop strengths, break bad habits, smile, work well with others, and have the right attitude all to enhance individual self-esteem while achieving personal success. To test and measure self-esteem, various scholars have categorized self-esteem into additional subcategories: (a) contingent self-esteem, which is based on the qualities an individual perceives are needed or things that need to be done or accomplished to be considered a person of value or worth, versus noncontingent self-esteem; (b) explicit self-esteem, which is a conscious and reflective type of self-evaluation, versus implicit self-esteem, which is the ability to unconsciously or without thinking perform self-evaluation; (c) authentic versus false self-esteem;

(d) stable versus unstable self-esteem; (e) global self-esteem versus domain-specific self-esteem; (f) trait self-esteem, which is the result of self-evaluations made over an extended period, versus state self-esteem, which is immediate self-evaluations; and (g) personal self-esteem, the value or worth one has for himself or herself, versus social self-esteem, which is the worth or value that holds the shared self-image for ingroup belonging. The variable elements were used to subcategorize self-esteem to refine research and assist in providing specific definitions of self-esteem in ways that that make it ameliorable to measurement These self-esteem subtypes can be combined with the group and personal components for added specificity in research measurement.

How Does One Measure Self-Esteem and Why?

Humans are inquisitive and often look for answers to explain the behaviors and communicative patterns exhibited by individuals and groups. A specific area of research is related to that of self-esteem and identity. For instance, what role does racial or ethnic identity have on personal or group self-esteem? What happens if one's racial identity creates tension or anxiety in others? And what type of behavior is exhibited that could be interpreted as low self-esteem versus high self-esteem? Can high-self esteem be a coping strategy to deal with the fears expressed by others? These are just some of the questions surrounding self-esteem and identity rather than an exhaustive list. Many theoretical frameworks have been proposed and tested to answer these and many other questions related to self-esteem and cultural identity.

Many sociopsychological theories indicate that individuals are motivated to maintain or enhance feelings of self-esteem, continuity, distinctiveness, belonging, and efficacy in their identities. Most studies using sociopsychological theories indicate that a greater sense of self-esteem is derived from identity elements that provide a positive sense of meaning. This includes individual-, relational-, and group-level identity.

Conceptually, self-esteem is studied through a variety of theoretical perspectives that include social identity theory; sociometer theory, also known as sociometer hypothesis; and terror management theory.

Social Identity Theory

Henry Tajfel and John Turner developed *social identity theory* in 1979 to understand individual and collective behavior based on social group membership and status or classification within the group (e.g., group members engage in intergroup discrimination for higher group status compared with other groups). Self-esteem is one of the concepts or variables that can be assessed using this theory because self-esteem corresponds to perceived worth within the group and perceived worth compared with other groups. An additional assumption is that in addition to the personal self each member has additional selves based on the number of group memberships. Researchers studying identity, prejudice, stereotyping, conflict negotiation, and language have applied this theory.

Sociometer Theory

As a modern theory for the study of self-esteem created by Mark Leary and colleagues in 1999, *sociometer theory* posits that self-esteem is used to monitor an individual's social environment for indicators of low or declining relational value. Self-esteem is then viewed as an internalized representation of societal rejection or acceptance because interpersonal relationships and social acceptance have a higher value. Sociometer theory suggests that people are not motivated to maintain their self-esteem but, rather, seek to increase their relational value and social acceptance by using self-esteem as a gauge of their effectiveness. An application of this theory would be to consider how an individual with low or high self-esteem approaches the decision-making process in a group setting.

Terror Management Theory

Sheldon Solomon, Jeff Greenberg, and Tom Pyszczynski developed *terror management theory* in the 1980s. As a general theoretical framework, terror management theory is used to determine and measure the level that individuals experience and how they handle anxiety in certain situations. However, the main idea of terror management theory is that humans are afraid of death and those with high self-esteem are less afraid of death than are those with low self-esteem. So, what does the fear of death have to do with self-esteem? Terror management theorists posit that individuals seek self-esteem because it provides protection from anxiety or fear of the world. Said another way, when individuals behave in ways that maintain cultural standards of value, self-esteem will be enhanced. As with any theory, some scholars believe that there is not enough evidence to support the correlation between the fear of death and self-esteem. Some have suggested that sociometer theory is better equipped to measure self-esteem in relation to anxiety and the fear of death.

Future Directions

People have an inherent need to belong and feel good about themselves. Individuals are motivated to develop and protect their self-esteem from an early age as evidenced by the "Everybody gets to play and nobody loses rule" in some children's sports and education methods. Self-esteem and identity development are two of the most often studied elements of human behavior across a variety of disciplines, including anthropology, psychology, and human communication studies, and will likely continue to be as scholars continue to question and search for answers to explain human behavior.

Annette D. Madlock

See also Development of Identity; Development of Self-Concept; Social Identity Theory; Sociometer Hypothesis; Terror Management Theory

Further Readings

Branden, N. (1994). *Six pillars of self-esteem.* New York: Bantam.

Hogg, M. A. (2006). Social identity theory. In P. J. Burke (Ed.), *Contemporary social psychological theories* (pp. 111–136). Palo Alto, CA: Stanford University Press.

Leary, M. R. (2004). The function of self-esteem in terror management theory and sociometer theory: Comment on Pyszczynski et al. (2004). *Psychology Bulletin, 130*(3), 478–482.

Pyszczynski, T., Greenberg, J., Solomon, S., Arndt, J., & Schimel, J. (2004). Why do people need self-esteem? A theoretical and empirical review. *Psychology Bulletin, 130*(3), 435–468.

Tajfel, H., & Turner, J. C. (1979). An integrative theory of intergroup conflict. In W. G. Austin & S. Worchel (Eds.), *The social psychology of intergroup relations* (pp. 33–47). Monterey, CA: Brooks/Cole.

SELF-IMAGE

Self-image is more than how one sees one's physical appearance; it is an overlapping of self-concepts from multiple sources and points of view. Self-image is simultaneously how one sees oneself physically and how one interprets one's personality through the lens of one's mood at any given moment; how one sees one's place in relation to the social groups in which he or she participates; how one believes others see him or her both physically and in relation to the social groups in which he or she participates; and how one estimates one's status as a human being as a whole by measuring and re-measuring one self-concept against another. The complexity and mercuriality of self-image reveals that the totality of self-concept has no one form or shape but is a shape-shifting arena of possibilities bounded and overwritten by a palimpsest of self-images making sense of and overwriting our experience of the world over and over again. Self-image, like all images, elicits behavioral and emotional responses toward that imagery, both self-directed responses and responses from others.

An archaeological layering of verbal images and mental images further complicates a reading of the self. As it signifies an aspect of the self-concept or self-schema, a verbal image is a name, the verbal quotient of an idea characterizing one's presence in the world. The verbal attributions that shape self-image may include either surname or the absence of the record of parentage or lineage, national affiliation, social labeling, taxonomic category, stereotype, or other stigmatizing appellations known as name-calling. Although these verbal images may not necessarily be warranted or even apt, once applied, a name, label, category, or stereotype becomes a part of the archaeology of self-imagery, a part of the emerging story.

A mental image of self is a narrative of personal memory, imbricated images of the self held in mind, unconsciously impressed in the recollection of lived experience in our passage through the world. Philosopher David Hume describes the remnants left after memory's dynamic storage process as "faint images" and "decayed sensation." Mental images of the recollected self store information about our experiences and ultimately influence the way we think and how we remember and relate our lives to those of others. Even misremembered or purposely distorted narratives of a lived experience may become a part of the archaeology of self-image.

Each of our self-images is in vertiginous alignment with a deeper archaeology of verbal and mental imagery that constitutes an identity, a multiformational arrangement representative of individual experience that is often also manifested in the visual culture, a construction that recounts a uniquely personal and publicly shared experience. In the visual culture's theater of multiple selves and simultaneous stories, galleries of reinscribed images become sites for newly inaugurated complexities, for freshly enunciated matrices of identity and self-imagery. Thus, at the surface, self-image is both hybridized and interactional, all images contesting for preeminence and position in the constitution of the larger stories of the local experience, the national experience, and the human experience. At the same time, the weight of the archaeology of layered self-imagery means that those self-images that are the most long-lived are also the most foundational and the most difficult to remove or reposition.

According to philosopher Julia Kristeva, any text works by absorbing and destroying at the same time other texts operating in the same arena. Identity can thus be understood as an ongoing interpretation of context-bounded verbal images and mental images, wresting coherence from the contradictory. No self-image is an immutable text, so identity is often rewritten in the diaphanous superimposition of one self-image and another competing self-image, an emergent story improvised while self-images are still being contested.

Research on the brain's processing of visual information offers a useful analogy in how systemic coherence among contesting self-imagery is achieved within an organism as complex as is the human brain. The human brain processes information along parallel pathways. Evidence exists of the abundant parallel and multitrack processing that occurs in similar fashion in many systems within the human brain. For example, memories have often been shown to be reconstructive, the reflection of a confluence between present circumstance and a number of prior experiences.

Increasing evidence indicates that the brain stores its information in temporary functional collections of neurons, or cell assemblies, which are scattered widely across the brain, and in which synaptic electrical firings are synchronized at a given frequency. Moreover, each neuron within an assembly can simultaneously be part of several cell assemblies, each working concurrently to achieve or revive its own uniquely ingrained synaptic semblance. The brain is theorized to contain convergence zones in multiple sensory and motor regions throughout the brain where new sensory fragments can be apprehended and bound to one another to create new experiential sense and to preexisting assemblies of synaptic relationships to augment prior sense. Remembering is said to occur when signals or cues from a convergence zone trigger the simultaneous reactivation and reblending of a constellation of sensory fragments from several distinct brain regions that were once linked together. In essence, we recollect prior sense through a reentrant signaling process that integrates a unified representation as an elaboration of segregated and distributed sensory inputs.

The brain's ability goes beyond mere reconstruction of incoming perceptions of circumstantial data. When we construct a coherent self-image, we order our awareness in keeping with our experience such that the image formed is not necessarily one that others would claim to see in their description of us. The brain routes streams of sensory input to merge with existing tributaries of meaning, attaching data to sense in fluid impressionist brushstrokes rather than Cartesian exactitude.

Daniel C. Dennett theorizes a multiple drafts model of consciousness wherein representations such as self-image arise from the continuous editorial revision of all that we perceive; each draft contributes to the interpretation of other contents, beliefs, or behaviors; each draft is impressed on the memory where it may ultimately decay because of lack of further correlations, is incorporated into subsequent percepts, or is overwritten in part or in entirety. A self-image is thus the result of the brain's editorial liberties.

Hence, identity is a meta-symbol, a by-product of the symbolic systems of verbal and mental imagery by which we construct or re-construct representations of our experience of the world. Personal identity is located within the archaeology of self-imagery, symbols within which we are defined and through which we continually remind ourselves of who we think we are. As a meta-symbol composed of sub-archaeologies of self-imagery, an identity is a living text. Identities are also then intertextual, a system of interrelationships between individual psyche and public memory.

Any given self-image and its oppositional other self-images engage in a form of play, a theater of simultaneity, of mutual clarification, of social performativity. Our self-images are variations in an ongoing and embodied fugue of personal stories; thus, self-imagery remains malleable. Self-image, like memory, can be erased by time or modified as facts are forgotten or misremembered over time. Psychologically, self-image can be contorted by falsehoods or accusations; physiologically, self-image can be invaded by trauma or brain lesion. Self-image can be altogether disconnected from factual experience and either be reinforced by fictional episodes and fantasy, or damaged by acts of stigmatization. Self-image can be recalled by alternative cues and be remembered in emotional keys varying from the discordant to the melodious. An individual's archaeology of self-imagery is a story-in-progress, an improvisation converging to constitute the present sense of personal identity from a plurality of social influences and root stories.

James Haywood Rolling Jr.

See also Development of Identity; Development of Self-Concept; Self-Construal; Self-Esteem

Further Readings

Anderson, W. T. (1997). *The future of the self: Inventing the postmodern person.* New York: Tarcher.

Dennett, D. C. (1991). *Consciousness explained.* Boston: Little, Brown.

Dowling, J. E. (1998). *Creating mind: How the brain works.* New York: W. W. Norton

Edelman, G. (1989). *The remembered present: A biological theory of consciousness.* New York: Basic Books.

Goffman, E. (1963). *Stigma: Notes on the management of spoiled identity.* New York; Simon & Schuster.

Schacter, D. L. (1996). *Searching for memory: The brain, the mind, and the past.* New York: Basic Books.

SELF-MONITORING

Self-monitoring, a concept introduced by Mark Snyder in 1974, refers to individual differences in the extent to which one monitors or controls the outward expression of his or her attitudes, beliefs, and opinions in social situations. According to Snyder's original theory, individuals may control their public expressions or behaviors depending on the importance of accurately presenting their actual or true personal attitudes, beliefs, or opinions weighed against the importance of portraying the proper attitudes, beliefs, and opinions. The concept of self-monitoring is essential in the formation and maintenance of one's social identity.

Self-monitoring can also occur when an individual hides an improper or unpopular response by either acting as if he or she has no reaction at all or by expressing a more socially appropriate response. One example of this form of self-monitoring is in the expression of prejudice. Because overt prejudice is generally looked down upon in today's society, a person will commonly try to mask any sort of expression of prejudicial attitudes. Even though an individual may inwardly feel prejudiced toward another, he or she may outwardly express acceptance of a person of a different race, ethnicity, or sexual orientation. Self-monitoring may occur when an individual actually has no true emotional reaction, but behaves as if he or she does. One instance of this may be when everyone else in a group or setting is outraged by another group, but the individual is not really bothered by the other group. Because a lack of a reaction is not acceptable to those around him or her, the individual has to behave as if he or she is just as angry as everyone else.

The ability to monitor or control behavior does not necessarily encompass all modes of expression. An individual may not be able to control all of the ways that various attitudes and beliefs can be publicly expressed. In other words, individuals can say one thing, but display a contradictory response through nonverbal communication such as through body language.

Although some individuals may differ in their outward expressions of attitudes and beliefs depending on the situation, individuals generally differ in the degree to which they control their behavior in front of others across situations. Those high in self-monitoring are social chameleons in the sense that they adapt to the recognizable norms of appropriate behavior depending on different situations and others present within the social setting. Generally, the behavior of high self-monitors tends to be less consistent across situations and is less likely to reflect the individual's true emotions and beliefs. High self-monitors are also better than low self-monitors at interpreting the body language of others within a social situation and better at recalling information about others in the social setting. Because high self-monitors are motivated to adapt to their social situations, they are more likely to choose situations with clearly defined norms and guidelines that display the behavior of the ideal individual in that setting. For example, a high self-monitor may choose to be a member of a sorority or fraternity—a group with specific norms dictating appropriate behavior.

Low self-monitors, however, display more consistent behavior across situations. This consistency occurs because individuals who are low self-monitors are more likely to express their true opinions and attitudes no matter what differences exist in situations. In this way, unlike those high self-monitors who adapt their behavior according to social cues, low self-monitors look within themselves to determine how to behave. This occurs because low self-monitors generally value being true to their "self." For this reason, attitudes of low self-monitors generally align with their behavior. Because low self-monitors are motivated to express their own opinions, they are more likely to seek situations conducive to open expression whenever possible. One such situation would be various intellectual settings where debate is welcome and even encouraged.

Researchers have conceptualized self-monitoring as an individual difference variable in a diverse range of research areas. Self-monitoring has been found to influence the effect of the perceived norms and behavior of others on changing behavior in persuasion research. In the realm of interpersonal relations research, self-monitoring orientation has been linked to managing relationships, romantic relationship styles, and risky sexual behavior. The role of self-monitoring has also been addressed in relation to leadership styles, prejudice, and creativity to name just a few areas. The influence of self-monitoring has been applied throughout the psychological literature.

Heather T. Stopp

See also Personal Identity Versus Self-Identity; Psychology of Self and Identity; Self-Image

Further Readings

Flynn, F. J., Reagans, R. E., Amanatullah, E. T., & Ames, D. R. (2006). Helping one's way to the top: Self-monitors achieve status by helping others and knowing who helps whom. *Journal of Personality and Social Psychology, 91,* 1123–1137.

Snyder, M. (1979). Self-monitoring processes. In L. Berkowitz (Ed.), *Advances in experimental social psychology* (Vol. 12, pp. 85–128). New York: Academic Press.

Snyder, M., & Gangstead, S. (1982). Choosing social situations: Two investigations of self-monitoring processes. *Journal of Personality and Social Psychology, 43,* 123–135.

Yates, R. A., & Noyes, J. M. (2007). Web site design, self-monitoring style, and consumer preference. *Journal of Applied Social Psychology, 37,* 1341–1362.

SELF-PERCEPTION THEORY

Self-perception theory describes how people form new attitudes and beliefs, including those related to the self, from observing their own behavior. In 1965, Daryl Bem proposed that people deduce their own internal states, like attitudes and emotions via the same processes by which they deduce the internal states and dispositions of others. Specifically, when people attempt to explain the behavior of another individual, they can assume the attitudes, beliefs, and other internal characteristics of the actor by observing the actor's behavior and the external factors that reduce or increase the observed act. By taking an outsider's perspective, people can also deduce their own internal states, including their attitudes, beliefs, emotions, and even self-views, from information provided by their own actions.

The inferences that people make about their own states critically depend upon the external factors perceived to be influencing their behavior in the situation. For example, when observers think that another person's interaction with an object is caused by something external, such as a large reward or pressure from others, observers can reasonably conclude that the behavior does not reflect how the actor thinks or feels about the object. Behavior that is clearly caused by something external to a person does not provide useful information regarding how the person views the issue or about what type of person he or she is. However, behavior that occurs when there is no clear external cause can provide more information about the actor's internal states. Thus, when observers perceive that an actor's behavior was not influenced by external factors such as big rewards or conformity pressures, then observers are likely to conclude that the cause of the observed behavior must be related to the actor's attitudes, values, or beliefs about the object.

Using the same process, if people observe that their own behavior was influenced by external factors, they are reluctant to conclude that their actions say anything about who they are as a person, or anything about their own attitudes or emotions. But when they observe themselves acting without external pressures or other inducements, then people conclude that their behavior was caused by something internal to them, such as an attitude, belief, or even their personality or self-concept. Consequently, people can form a new view of themselves simply by observing that they, and nothing else, were responsible for how they acted in a given situation.

A Rival for Dissonance Theory

Self-perception theory was initially introduced as a rival explanation for the attitude change effects observed in cognitive dissonance experiments. Bem proposed that despite the evidence for attitude change, there was no corroborating evidence that the effects were driven by inconsistency or an aversive state of discomfort. Bem believed self-perception processes, which do not assume that

arousal or a motivation play a role in the attitudes people form, could account for how attitudes follow from discrepant behavior. For example, Bem proposed that in the classic study by Leon Festinger and James Carlsmith, participants who lied about their enjoyment of the boring task for a large reward did not subsequently favor the boring task more because they reasonably concluded that the large reward caused them to tell a lie. In other words, because of the huge reward for lying, no logical assumption could be made about their attitude toward the task. However, participants who lied about the boring task for a small reward subsequently came to like the boring task more because, in their analysis, the only explanation for the lie was that they believed the task was fun. Reasonable conclusions about their own attitudes could be made because there were no clear external reasons for lying about the task. Thus, Bem proposed that participants used their own behavior (the lie about the task) and the relevant external factors (high or low reward to tell the lie) to infer how they personally felt about the task.

Bem further suggested that if self-perception processes were at the heart of dissonance effects, then observers would be able to accurately deduce the attitudes held by actors after they committed a discrepant act. For example, in one study, participants were allowed to observe the $20 and $1 conditions in the Festinger and Carlsmith procedure. As predicted, observers replicated the original effect by reporting that participants who lied about the task for $1 liked the task more compared with participants who lied for $20. Based on a number of "interpersonal simulations" in which observers were able to reproduce the results of a published dissonance experiment, Bem argued that self-perception presented a more parsimonious explanation for how behavior determines attitudes.

The introduction of self-perception as an alternative explanation for dissonance effects caused a lively debate among psychologists about how to interpret the effects of behavior on attitudes. The debate eventually focused on two critical differences between the theories. One was that observers in Bem's interpersonal simulations did not have access to the prior attitudes held by participants in a dissonance experiment. As a result, observers simply assumed that those who would perform a counter-attitudinal act held more positive attitudes toward the issue all along, which is not the same process of inference assumed by self-perception theory. Bem responded to this criticism by suggesting that the interpersonal simulation did reproduce the experience of dissonance because participants were not aware of their initial attitude when they were asked to evaluate their behavior. Several papers from self-perception and dissonance researchers were published to test the "forgetting" hypothesis, but in the end, none were widely accepted as having solved the debate.

The second critical difference between self-perception and dissonance theory concerns the role of arousal and discomfort in how behavior influences attitudes. According to dissonance theory, inconsistency between attitudes and behavior causes an uncomfortable state of arousal that motivates people to change their attitudes. In contrast, self-perception theory assumes that attitudes are formed from assumptions about the cause of behavior and the conditions under which the behavior was performed. Thus, arousal and the motivation to reduce it do not mediate the effect of behavior on attitudes. This difference permits a clear prediction about the conditions under which self-perception and dissonance theory accurately account for how behavior influences attitudes.

Dissonance theory explains the effect of behavior on attitudes when the two are perceived to be discrepant or incongruent with each other. When behavior falls outside of a preferred position, people feel an aversive form of arousal and are motivated to reduce it by bringing their attitudes into line with their behavior. In contrast, self-perception theory explains the effect of behavior on attitudes best when the behavior is perceived to be congruent with a preferred position. Research supports these boundary conditions by showing that arousal mediates attitude change more when a behavior is perceived to fall outside of what people expect of their behavior. Thus, researchers solved the debate about whether self-perception theory accounts for dissonance phenomena by identifying the appropriate conditions under which each theory applies.

Research further shows that people are most likely to infer internal qualities such as attitudes and beliefs from their behavior when preexisting thoughts and feelings are unclear, unimportant, and when cues imply that behavior accurately reflects their existing attitudes. Today, self-perception theory provides an important explanation for how people form new attitudes and beliefs when they do not have much else to go on.

Applying Self-Perception to Social Behavior

Self-perception processes have been applied to understand a wide variety of social behavior, including how people develop attitudes and beliefs about objects, issues, and other people, including romantic partners. Self-perception also helps to explain why people lose their motivation to engage in otherwise enjoyable behavior, why they laugh at a joke, and finally, how they can develop new views of themselves that, under some conditions, cause them to comply with a potentially costly request from a salesperson.

Self-perception theory provides useful insights into the power of intrinsic motivation on behavior. Intrinsic motivation refers to the desire to perform a given behavior simply because it is inherently enjoyable. What happens when people are highly rewarded for a behavior that they perform because it is intrinsically enjoyable? According to self-perception theory, strong external rewards for conducting a behavior reduce the tendency to conclude that the behavior is caused by an internal state. It follows that when actors are highly rewarded for performing an intrinsically enjoyable behavior, they tend to dismiss the role of internal states and conclude that their behavior was caused by the external rewards. As a result, an overjustification effect occurs whereby the external rewards overjustify the act and reduce the intrinsic pleasure of the behavior. Research shows that the overjustification effect can reduce the motivation that students have for learning and that employees exhibit for their work. However, research also indicates that rewards will not undermine intrinsic motivation when they are offered as a reward for excellence and as long as they are not seen as a means for controlling behavior.

Self-perception processes also play a role in the experience of affective states. For example, studies show that when asked to frown or smile while performing a task, people report feeling more angry or happy, and as a result, they recall more negative or positive memories, respectively. Other studies show that when people hold a pen in their teeth to mimic smiling, they think cartoons are more humorous. These findings suggest that, as self-perception theory predicts, people can use their physical expressions as cues to how they feel about an object or stimulus and as cues for what type of information to use in their thinking.

Drawing inferences from behavior can also determine how the influence of others can shape a new view of the self. For example, when people are the target of a social influence attempt, they may deduce a new belief about themselves by observing their reaction to a salesperson's request. Research on the foot-in-the-door social influence technique shows that when people first comply with a small request, they are significantly more likely to comply with a second, more costly target request, compared with when they are only asked to comply with the costly target request. The act of complying with the small initial request causes the actor to conclude that he or she is a helpful person. Consequently, when asked for the second, more costly request, the new view of the self as helpful then increases the desire to comply, partly because thoughts about being helpful are present in one's thinking, and partly because refusing to help would be inconsistent with being a helpful person. The effect of the foot-in-the-door on perceptions of helpfulness suggests that self-perception can play an important role in the formation of the self-concept, especially to the degree that people feel they had free choice to comply and became self-aware when they committed the initial act.

The act of influencing others can also engage self-perception processes that create new views of the self. For example, making rational arguments to persuade another person causes the speaker to perceive himself or herself as more intelligent and friendly, but taking an authoritative approach to persuading others causes the speaker to view himself or herself as more dominant and unfriendly. This suggest that in the absence of other information, portraying oneself in a particular light can lead to new perspectives on the self.

Finally, new research indicates that there are conditions under which people can draw conclusions about their own internal states from observing the behavior of others. To the degree that people share an important social identity, watching others perform an act may be the same as when the self performs the behavior. As a result, people

can deduce what they think and feel from observing the behavior of similar others. The parameters to "vicarious self-perception" processes await future research.

Jeff Stone

See also Cognitive Dissonance Theory

Further Readings

Bem, D. J. (1972). Self-perception theory. In L. Berkowitz (Ed.), *Advances in experimental social psychology* (Vol. 6, pp. 2–62). New York: Academic Press.

Burger, J. M. (1999). The foot-in-the-door compliance procedure: A multiple-process analysis and review. *Personality and Social Psychology Review, 3,* 303–325.

Festinger, L., & Carlsmith, J. M. (1959). Cognitive consequences of forced compliance. *Journal of Abnormal and Social Psychology, 58,* 203–210.

SELF-PORTRAITS

Since the introduction of the mirror in the 15th century, many artists have created independent self-portraits—a portrait that an artist makes using himself or herself as its subject, typically created from a reflection in a mirror. Most painters have painted a self-portrait, and some artists, such as Rembrandt Harmenszoon van Rijn, have intensely practiced this form of self-study throughout their careers. There are generally six types of self-portraits: the self-portrait used as a signature, the self-portrait as a projection of self, the self-portrait as a self-study, the self-portrait as fantasy, the narrative self-portrait, and the metaphorical self-portrait. This entry first places these types in historical context and then discusses the concept of self in relation to self-portraits. Finally, the entry examines the psychological meaning of self-portraits.

History and Types

When and in which culture the first self-portrait appeared is difficult to answer with certainty. Self-portraits painted in burial scenes in ancient

Egyptian temples and pyramids have been discovered as far back as 1365 BCE and can be categorized as self-portraits that function as a signature. However, the self-portrait as a signature was most prevalent during the Middle Ages and the Renaissance period. The emergence of the self-portrait as an independent genre of artistic expression, regardless of the medium, has been attributed to the invention of the flat, nondistorting mirror. The first independent self-portrait (a sketch) or self-portrait as a projection of the self may have been created by Filippino Lippi at the end of 15th century. However, many scholars identify Jean Fouquet's self-portrait (c. 1470) as the earliest surviving example. Even though self-portraits as a projection of self may have begun with Fouquet, artists such as Albrecht Durer who painted several self-portraits reflected the detailed exploration of their own images. Rembrandt is attributed as the first artist to create self-portraits as a study of the self. He created 60 autobiographical self-portraits.

The fourth type of self-portrait attempts to break away from the traditional depiction of the face and attempts to reveal the character of the artist. For example, Gustave Courbet created self-portraits that depicted fantasy by adding an environment to symbolize social status or mental state. The fifth type is the narrative self-portrait, painted by such notable artists as Pablo Picasso and Marc Chagall. Abstractionism led to a shift away from representational painting to painting that allowed colors, shapes, and patterns to represent the inner life of the artist and the world around the artist. This led to the final type, the metaphorical self-portrait pioneered by the abstract expressionists, notably Mark Rothko and Jackson Pollock, who infused their identities into abstract images by conveying their emotions as artists.

The Concept of Self and Self-Portraiture

Since the end of the 15th century, it has become somewhat of an unwritten rule that artists of Western origin paint a self-portrait. Before photography was invented, the portrait was the only means (with the exception of sculpture) for a person to possess an image of himself or herself. Historically, most artists have created at least one self-portrait as a potential memorial. Most artists have sought to present themselves in the best possible light when painting a self-portrait. Whether an artist paints a self-portrait as a projection of self or a self-study, the artist must study his or her own image and consequently explore his or her own persona. For some artists, the self-portrait is cathartic, for others the process is insightful. The self-portrait allows the artist to create characters and myths of himself or herself as the portrait becomes a mask. Despite their vain intentions, self-portraits are still informative. In many self-portraits, the facial features offer limited hints to character. The setting, costume, body language, hands, and overall composition must also be considered. Attributes and symbols are used to reveal the subject's traits and qualities through nonnarrative self-description.

Despite the different types of self-portraits, the question remains, why create a self-portrait in the first place? In a letter to his brother Theo, Vincent Van Gogh suggests that self-portraiture is attractive to an artist because it is a private activity, where pleasing others is not an issue. Some scholars believe that artists created self-portraits to avoid hiring models to sit for them. However, this theory is untenable when closely considered. When considering the motivations of the great masters of self-portraiture, the lack of a model or money to pay a model is often not the case. In fact, Van Gogh ultimately disclosed that although the self-portrait he presented to Paul Gauguin was originally created for lack of a model and to practice painting the human figure, his motives were more significant. In a letter to Gauguin, Van Gogh explains the technical process in creating his self-portrait. However, he goes on to state, "I also exaggerate my personality . . . it has cost me a lot of trouble, yet I shall have to do it all over again if I want to succeed in expressing what I mean" (Gedo, 1999, p. 77).

Artists such as Rembrandt, Paul Cézanne, and Max Beckmann painted so many self-portraits that self-portraiture became an essential part of their oeuvre. For Cézanne, it was possibly a convenience, but for Rembrandt and Beckmann, it was an exploration into self-knowledge.

The idea of fleeting time or mortality could have impelled many artists to create a series of self-portraits. The artist acknowledges the impermanence of existence and attempts to record the change. Perhaps painting a self-portrait is instinctual, an attempt for self-perpetuation. The self-portraiture allows an artist to deal with death by creating an immortal self (the portrait) and is similar to the desire to have a child to carry on one's name. The artist Edvard Munch embodied this belief. Munch immediately created duplicates of any paintings he sold because he was reluctant to sell his paintings and claimed the paintings still belonged to him even after selling them.

When creating a self-portrait, the artist must confront the self, which includes self-interest, self-love, self-evaluation, and self-knowledge. Therefore, likeness or realism is not always the primary goal. Painting a self-portrait can address other concerns, such as spirituality or emotional experience. Beckmann described the idea of the self in self-portraiture in his essay *On My Painting:* "Who am I"? This question haunted Beckmann as he probed deeper and deeper into self-discovery and admittedly played some part in his art. By nature, the dialogue between subject and art is self-referential. The art reflects back to the artist (the subject) and vice versa, which in turn allows us to see a glimpse of the artist's life and personality. The artist confronts himself or herself in mirror image, and re-presents himself or herself on the canvas. The resulting self-image is not just a passing expression of the self, but a lasting object, which can be seen by the creator and others as part of the objective world. The self is essentially objectified.

The common practice in contemporary self-portraiture is for artists to depict their idea of themselves in an effort to answer the question "Who am I?" or to ask the bigger question "Who are we?" In addition to exploring their feelings about themselves, the artists also considered how they fit or do not fit into contemporary society. Common issues explored are sexuality, gender, age, ethnicity, religion, artistic identity, and a broader cultural identity.

Three conditions must be filled to be able to create a self-image. First a sense of self, distinct from other persons' selves must be developed. Second, mastery of a symbolic system must be adequately achieved to enable someone to make communicative representations. Finally, a link must be established between self-awareness and symbolic capacities, so that self-symbolization can occur in visual images. Evidence shows that achievement of these three conditions has been historically late, both for humankind and for the individual. The word *self-portrait* is used to mean a type of effigy, an image created by the artist to represent himself or herself to the contemporary world or to a future audience. Examples of these types of self-portraits are those that were painted as part of altar-paintings or frescoes of the 15th century. As time progressed, the concept of self developed and periods in painting such as the Renaissance changed the way people perceived themselves. As Western culture progressed from the Middle Ages, the Renaissance, romanticism, and so on, concepts such as individual freedom developed. For example, during the romantic age, the experience of the "self" changed into the "person of feeling."

The Psychological Meaning of Self-Portraits

What psychological meaning can self-portraits serve for the artist? Many psychologists, especially those psychoanalytically oriented, have studied famous historic artists' self-portraits in a quest for answers. Van Gogh is considered one of the greatest painters of the 19th century, and it is well-known that his life was tragic, ending in psychosis and suicide. He painted more than 40 self-portraits. The self-portrait acted as a mirror for van Gogh, as a reflection of his mind. His self-portraits reflect his inner conflicts and self-image. Thus, the mirror can portray the ego, superego, self-representations, introjections, and object representations. Self-portraits constitute the best example of psychodynamic theories on the origin of identity by mirroring the level of decline and object relations of the individual.

Jacques Lacan was the first to define the *mirror phase,* an episode in which the infant initially discovers himself or herself in the mirror. For D. W. Winnicott, the mother is the first mirror. By interacting with his or her mother, the infant begins to develop a definition of self. The mirroring experience is responsible for giving the child his or her first sense of identity. The mother and child develop a safe place together called the *transitional space.* At that point, the child who has had good enough caretaking begins to hold in his or her memory a positive image of the mother and internalize this image. When the mirroring experience is distorted, negative, or absent between mother and infant, the child's own existence becomes negated and he or she develops a disturbance in primitive self-feeling.

Egon Schiele, an Austrian artist, produced hundreds of self-portraits throughout his lifetime. Schiele, with other artists, produced a new art form, expressionism. Schiele lived in Vienna at the end of the 19th century, which coincided with the birth of psychoanalysis. His exploration into the depths of his self, primarily through confrontations with his sexuality, is analogous to the concerns of psychoanalysis at that time. He often depicted himself in a castrated, deformed, and mutilated state. Schiele seemed to create self-portraits as a means to objectify and master his problems with identity. Schiele had an unusual relationship to mirrors that may have reflected faulty mirroring experiences during childhood. For example, he never passed a mirror without stopping to scrutinize his reflection. The full-length mirror from which he drew his self-portraits and took with him wherever he went originally belonged to his mother.

Frida Kahlo's self-portraits can also be seen as an attempt at self-consolidation or identity maintenance. For Kahlo, the object of intensive study was herself. After a terrible vehicular accident, which left her permanently crippled at age 18, Kahlo began to paint self-portraits, which she continued to do until her death. Kahlo was preoccupied with her appearance and she surrounded her bed with mirrors. Mirrors of all sizes were placed at varying angles from her bed with a huge one installed on the underside of the canopy. This repeated encounter with her reflection possibly served as a concrete reminder of her existence.

Therefore, a self-portrait can be considered a projection of self or a reflection of the mind. The personality of the artist, which includes the unconscious, is represented in the self-portrait. The self-portrait works as a transitional space that provides a safe area in which to process the feelings associated with emotional distress. Creating a self-portrait may allow the artist to discharge inner emotional tension through a controlled and appropriate artistic outlet. By reproducing aspects of emotional distress in symbolic form, the artist may feel more in control and can master chaotic or disturbing feelings without being overwhelmed.

Self-portraits may also be a means to cope with the impermanence of existence and an attempt to record change. By documenting his or her image over time, the artist recognizes that the environment is changing around the artist and that the artist changes, which is effected by and affects the environment. This endeavor to record change can be understood as an attempt to deal with mortality. The artist acknowledges the impermanence of existence and attempts to record the change. The self-portrait represents the most fundamental desire of humanity, the need for self-perpetuation. The self-portrait allows the artist to cope with death by creating an immortal self (the portrait), similar to having a child to carry on one's name and proof of one's purposeful existence.

Elizabeth A. Patton

See also Self; Self-Concept; Self-Esteem

Further Readings

Bonafoux, P. (1985). *Portraits of the artist: The self-portrait in painting.* New York: Skira/Rizzoli.

Gedo, M. M. (1999). The self-portrait as covert message: The van Gogh–Gauguin exchange. *Annual of Psychoanalysis, 26,* 59–81.

Kelly, S., & Lucie-Smith, E. (1987). *The self-portrait: A modern view.* London: Sarema Press.

Van Meel-Jansen, A. (1993). Images of the self in portrait and autobiography. In G. L. Van Heck, P. Bonaiuto, I. J. Deary, & W. Nowack (Eds.), *Personality psychology in Europe* (pp. 281–303). Tilburg, the Netherlands: Tilburg University Press.

Warick, L. H., & Warick, E. R. (1984). Transitional process and creativity in the life and art of Edvard Munch. *Journal of the American Academy of Psychoanalysis, 12*(3), 413–424.

SELF-PRESENTATION

In our daily lives, we form impressions of people and treat people in a way that is consistent with those impressions. Our selves are constructed, modified, and played in interactions with other people, and it is often in our best interests to influence the impressions that others form of us. *Self-presentation* is the process through which people present a public image of the self to others and attempt to control the impressions that others form of them. Self-presentation helps us obtain the objects we need and value, helps us create and maintain desired identities, and enables our social interactions to run more smoothly.

Most researchers have used the terms *impression management* and *self-presentation* interchangeably, although other researchers have distinguished between them. In general, *impression management* is a broader term than is *self-presentation*; for example, people can manage the impressions of other people and even organizations. For this reason, the term *self-presentation* is generally reserved for instances in which the images that people project are relevant to the self. This entry discusses why and when people engage in self-presentation strategies, along with areas of application and debates associated with self-presentation research.

Why Do People Engage in Self-Presentation?

Roy Baumeister has argued that people engage in self-presentation for two reasons: (1) to please the audience and (2) to construct one's public self. The first motive for self-presentation—to please the audience—is the most common notion of what is involved in self-presentation. That is, other people control desired and valued resources and we obtain these rewards by getting the audience to think favorably of us. Thus, an important motivation for impression management is the attainment of social and material outcomes—conveying the right impression increases the likelihood that one will obtain desired outcomes (e.g., friendship, power, promotion) and avoid undesired outcomes. However, self-presentation behavior is also motivated by a fundamental need to belong, with the result that individuals will present themselves in ways that enhance their belongingness and group membership. A number of strategies might be employed to achieve this end, such as self-promotion (i.e., to persuade others that you are competent), ingratiation (i.e., to persuade others to like you), and exemplification (i.e., to persuade others to see you as a morally respectable individual).

The notion that individuals attempt to please an audience to obtain desired outcomes is a familiar, but somewhat negative, connotation of self-presentation. Self-presentation behavior is often viewed as deceitful and manipulative because people may say and do things they do not really

believe to please the audience and obtain desired outcomes. However, rather than being deceptive and duplicitous, the impressions people try to create are likely to be accurate and honest because people often manage their impressions so that other people will see them as they see themselves. In addition, self-presentation strategies such as intimidation (i.e., persuading others that you are dangerous) or supplication (i.e., persuading others that you are helpless) may appear negative but still enable individuals to achieve their desired goals.

Another motive for self-presentation is *self-construction*. Indeed, early theorists such as Mark Baldwin, Charles Horton Cooley, and George Herbert Mead recognized that the self-concept is constructed during social interaction as actors come to infer personal qualities from the roles they enact and other people's reaction to them. Thus, self-presentation can be used to construct and present particular identities for validation by others and individuals can build the self-concept by presenting certain images to others. Indeed, to claim a particular identity, individuals often need to demonstrate that they have the traits and qualities associated with that identity. For example, gang members need to display delinquent behavior to have the identity validated by other gang members. As a result, self-presentations can have an impact beyond what might seem to be their momentary, local, and often self-serving functions—their influence extends across audiences and situations to shape the actor's public identity and private self-conception.

One by-product of the self-presentation process is that the actor's behavior, which initially may have been intended to create a desired impression on others, may come to influence the self-concept and the way in which individuals view themselves. A number of researchers have demonstrated that self-presentation behavior can be internalized such that behaving in a particular manner can lead to self-concept change where the individual comes to think of himself or herself as the kind of person who engages in that behavior. For example, Dianne Tice asked participants to present themselves as either emotionally stable or responsive or introverted or extroverted in public and private settings and then to rate their emotional stability and introversion at the end of the study. The results demonstrated that participants' ratings came to mirror their self-presentation behavior, especially when the behavior was performed in public.

In addition to the audience pleasing and self-construction motives for self-presentation, Mark Leary has suggested a third reason for self-presentation: emotion regulation. Specifically, he has suggested that an audience's reaction to an individual's attempt at self-presentation, and the individual's perception of the success or failure of their self-presentation attempts, may increase or decrease positive feelings and an individual's self-esteem.

When Do People Engage in Self-Presentation?

People are more likely to engage in self-presentation when they perceive themselves to be in the "public eye." Indeed, the most common procedure for investigating self-presentation is to compare two situations that are identical in all aspects except that some circumstance, such as the actor's behavior, is public in one situation but private in the other situation. If public awareness makes people change their behavior, it is inferred that they are concerned with what their behavior communicates to others. Anonymity, in contrast, is seen to remove people's concern with self-presentation because one's behavior cannot influence the impressions of other people if one is acting anonymously.

We become more concerned with self-presentation when observers can influence whether we achieve our goals (such as when we are observed by a potential employer versus a stranger), when those goals are important to us (such as obtaining our dream job), and when there is a discrepancy between the image we desire to project and the image that the observer holds of us (such as when we believe that the potential employer thinks we are unqualified for the job).

It is also important to consider who the audience is for our self-presentations. Certain audiences may have special value or meaning for constructing particular identities, and we may be more likely to engage in self-presentation to these audiences. For example, we may be more likely to project a positive image as a sociable, attractive person in a room full of potential romantic partners (such as in "speed dating" situations) than in a room of one's family members. In addition, the type of self-presentation will vary as a function of

the audience. For example, Tice and her colleagues have found that people are more likely to be modest in their self-enhancement to an audience of friends but self-enhancing in their self-presentations to an audience of strangers.

Areas of Application

Self-presentation processes have been examined in relation to a number of social psychological phenomena. Research has examined altruistic behavior, finding that donations made in public are dramatically larger than donations made in private. Aggressive behavior is also subject to self-presentation concerns: People are much more likely to display aggressive behavior when the audience is likely to favor aggressive behavior (e.g., a karate instructor) than when the audience is likely to frown upon aggressive behavior (e.g., a pacifist). Conformity, influence, and reactance are major areas of interest in the self-presentation domain. Research has demonstrated that self-presentational concerns mediate and determine how and whether a person responds to external pressures and influence. In general, a person will conform more readily to the opinions and expectations of others when those others are observing her than when they are not (although a desire to be seen as nonconforming or individualistic may produce reactance in public situations). Self-presentation accounts have also been important in the attitude change literature, with some theorists arguing that attitude change via cognitive dissonance can be explained by a desire to present a consistent self. Other phenomena that have been subjected to a self-presentational analysis include attribution, leadership, nonverbal behavior, social facilitation, self-handicapping, social anxiety, personnel selection, and even depression.

Recent research on self-presentation has examined reasons why people may fail at their self-presentation attempts. Not all self-presentation attempts are equally successful—sometimes we succeed at projecting the desired image, but at other times, we fail. Traditional answers provided by self-presentation theorists explained poor self-presentation on a lack of motivation (i.e., not caring about the audience) or a lack of knowledge (i.e., not knowing how to project one's desired image). In recent years, however, Roy Baumeister and Kathleen Vohs have suggested that self-regulation may play a crucial role in self-presentation. Self-presentation, particularly in novel situations or to new audiences, is an effortful process that requires the use of self-regulatory resources. When people must effortfully plan and alter their behavior to convey the desired self-image, success at self-presentation will depend on effective self-regulation.

Debates and Controversies

One criticism of the self-presentation approach is the range of phenomena to which it has been applied. Indeed, it seems that if a phenomenon has a social dimension to it, then the self-presentation approach has been advanced to explain it. Thus, it has been argued that the self-presentation approach provides a ready-made, post hoc account of findings already accounted for by existing theories, and the absence of a formal theoretical structure means that there are no constraints on advocates who want to interpret research findings in terms of a self-presentation perspective.

One debate in the self-presentation literature relates to the idea of private self-presentation—that is, behavior directed at impression management and self-construction in the absence of an audience. Some theorists have argued against the idea that behavior enacted in private has any implications for the self-concept. This unwillingness to acknowledge the role of private self-presentation and private audiences may reflect the way in which public and private self have been conceptualized in much of the self-presentation literature. Traditional accounts of self-presentation have been relatively individualistic in nature, paying little attention to the impact of group memberships on social behavior. Within the field of self-presentation, the public self is varied, controlled, and observed, and the private self exists only for the individual and is immune to the constraints that shape and direct the public self. However, these two extremes ignore the possibility of a collective self—a self created in reference to groups and arising from group membership, but a self that continues to exist and shape behavior, even in private. Recent research within the social identity approach, such as that conducted within the framework of the social identity model of deindividuation effects, has examined the way in which the collective self and social identities can be the focus of self-presentation efforts.

Many analyses of self-presentation have considered impression management in terms of single encounters, often with strangers. However, if one accepts that the audience often consists of members of our social circles and groups, this transforms self-presentation in two ways. First, the repercussions of a single public performance extend far beyond the immediate occasion. Second, displays of behavior contribute to impressions created by numerous such displays over an extended period to create reputations as individuals or group members.

Joanne R. Smith

See also Impression Management; Looking-Glass Self; Self-Concept; Symbolic Interactionism

Further Readings

Baumeister, R. F. (1982). A self-presentational view of social phenomena. *Psychological Bulletin, 91,* 3–26.
Schlenker, B. R. (2003). Self-presentation. In J. P. Tangney & M. R. Leary (Eds.), *Handbook of self and identity* (pp. 492–518). New York: Guilford Press.

SELF-SCHEMA

Self-schema refers to people's self-conceptions, or the ideas and beliefs they have about themselves. As a cognitive-affective structure that organizes information about a concept, or type of stimulus (including representations and relations among those representations), self-schemas are similar to schemas held about others. But differing from schemas about others, this self-knowledge is stored more complexly in separate, context-specific modules. With different contexts, different self-schemas are activated and thus, different aspects of self. As such, self-schemas form a part of individuals' idea of who they are, or their self-concept, based on one's experience.

Schematic Versus Aschematic

Based on Daryl J. Bem's self-perception theory, individuals gain self-knowledge only based on attributions they make about themselves. On dimensions where individuals have clear and well-developed self-conceptions or schemas, they are considered *schematic*; in dimensions where they do not have clear schemas, they are *aschematic*. Schemas are derived from experience and one's interpretation of experiences. According to Hazel Markus, the dimensions where individuals are self-schematic are those that are personally important to the individual, those that individuals think they hold strongly, and those that individuals are sure that the opposite does not stand true. So if a person thinks he or she is athletic, definitely not unathletic or out of shape, and being athletic is important to him or her as part of the self-concept, he or she is schematic on this dimension. If an individual does not care about having an attribute or about the attribute itself, then he or she is considered aschematic for that dimension. An interesting paradox is that in domains in which one is highly self-schematic, or an expert, an individual is likely to form judgments more quickly and more efficiently about information relevant to the self-schema than is a person who is aschematic in that domain, despite having more information to process. This is because self-schematic information is more readily noticed and is overrepresented in one's thought processes, although it is also associated with having a longer processing time. Individuals will also resist information in their environment that is inconsistent with their self-schema, which is related to self-verification.

Schemas vary in their contents and how elaborate they are; some are interrelated but others are discrete. Individuals derive part of their self-concept from their group membership, which is referred to as their *social identity*. The amount of interrelatedness or perceived overlap of social identities by an individual is called *social identity complexity,* as developed by Sonia Roccas and Marilynn Brewer. Along with their descriptive role, self-schemas also provide us with various possible selves, including those we would like to become and others we fear we might become.

Moods

According to Patricia W. Linville, most individuals have complex self-concepts with a moderately sizable amount of discrete self-schemas. Having this assortment helps people buffer the negative effects that one encounters in life by always allowing self-schemas that allow people to draw a sense of fulfillment. However, Carolin Showers suggested that if an individual's self-schemas are too discrete or detached and on extremes (some positive and others negative), external events may lead to extreme mood swings depending on whether the primed self-schemas are negative or positive. Therefore, the more adaptive self-schemas are those that are more integrated because the effects of contexts would be less intense on moods in comparison with those with more compartmentalized self-schemas.

Self-Discrepancy Theory and Regulatory Focus Theory

E. Tory Higgins's self-discrepancy theory suggests that we have three types of self-schemas, namely, the *actual self* (how we are currently), the *ideal self* (how we would like to be), and the *ought self* (how we think we should be). This is an offshoot of Karen Horney's tripartite model (real, actual, and ideal selves). The ideal and ought selves direct our behavior by providing different types of goals; with the ideal self supplying promotional goals (goals to strive for) and the ought self with prevention goals (goals to avoid doing). Differences between the actual and ideal or ought selves are referred to as *self-discrepancies*. These can motivate individuals to act to remedy the discrepancy by engaging in self-regulation, strategies used to modify our behavior to attain ideal or ought standards. However, if one is unsuccessful in resolving discrepancies, negative emotions can be produced. Specifically, actual-ideal discrepancy leads to dejection or depression-type emotions (e.g., sadness, dissatisfaction, disappointment) and actual-ought discrepancy leads to agitation or anxiety-type emotions (e.g., fear, apprehension, threat).

This is further elaborated with the regulatory focus theory in that the two self-regulatory systems, *promotion* and *prevention*, are separate and concerned with different types of goal attaining. The promotion system works with the achievement of an individual's ambitions and expectations, previously defined as an individual's ideals. Promotion-focused individuals use *approach* strategic means to reach their goals and are geared to notice whether positive events are present or absent. While in this promotion focus, individuals are likely to find ways to improve their situations, seek novel challenges, and consider impediments as unique barriers over which to triumph. The prevention system works toward the fulfillment of an individual's duties and obligations, previously defined as an individual's oughts. Prevention-focused individuals use *avoidance strategic means* to reach their goals and are geared to notice whether negative events are present or absent. With this prevention focus, individuals are likely to keep away from new or unfamiliar situations or new people, and to focus on averting failure than on attaining the their best.

Script, Attribution Bias, Self-Esteem, and Aggression

An individual's beliefs about himself or herself may influence aggression by influencing *script* (schema about an event) selection, as self-schemas provide an internal context for where scripts can be evaluated. So when a self-schema is nonaggressive, heightened activation of it decreases likelihood of aggressiveness probably because it filters out potentially aggressive scripts. According to social perception and aggression research by Susan T. Fiske, it has also been posited that hostile *attribution biases* are products of aggressive scripts. Individuals who are aggressive have a tendency to perceive hostility in others even when there is none, thereby displaying a hostile attribution bias. This can lead aggressive individuals to perceive relatively more aggression while observing one-on-one interactions, expecting others to behave in more aggressive manners in hypothetical scenarios. This pattern has also been observed in individuals with greater ingrained beliefs of persecution. With cues being interpreted as hostile over time, they can become an automatic cognitive process.

Self-esteem refers to an individual's self-assessment of self-worth as a static characteristic (trait self-esteem) or situational variance (state self-esteem). Those with inflated or unstable self-esteem are most prone to anger and are most aggressive, especially when their high self-image is threatened. When those with average self-esteem receive

negative evaluations for self-esteem relevant domains, it promotes them to engage in prosocial behavior to counteract the negative evaluation.

Shirley Samson

See also Regulatory Focus Theory; Self-Affirmation Theory; Self-Assessment; Self-Concept; Self-Construal; Self-Discrepancy Theory; Self-Esteem; Self-Image; Self-Perception Theory; Self-Verification; Social Identity Theory

Further Readings

Bem, D. J. (1972). Self-perception theory. In L. Berkowitz (Ed.), *Advances in experimental social psychology* (Vol. 6). New York: Academic Press.

Higgins, E. T. (1987). Self-discrepancy: A theory relating self and affect. *Psychological Review, 94,* 319–340.

Markus, H. (1977). Self-schemata and processing information about the self. *Journal of Personality and Social Psychology, 35,* 63–78.

Roccas, S., & Brewer M. B. (2002). Social identity complexity. *Personality and Social Psychology Review, 6,* 88–106.

Showers, C. (1992). Compartmentalization of positive and negative self-knowledge: Keeping bad apples out of the bunch. *Journal of Personality and Social Psychology, 62,* 1036–1049.

Tajfel, H., & Turner, J. C. (1986). The social identity theory of intergroup behavior. In S. Worchel & W. G. Austin (Eds.), *Psychology of intergroup relations* (2nd ed., pp. 7–24). Chicago: Nelson-Hall.

SELF-VERIFICATION

Self-verification refers to the desire for others to substantiate their thoughts and feelings about their sense of self. Specifically, we seek self-verification to maintain certain views of the self that can provide us with the impression of a coherent identity, a framework for organizing life experiences, and a guide for everyday social interaction. Thus, people want others to confirm the core elements of their self-concept so that these elements may act as a steering wheel, providing continuity and stability, allowing people to navigate the road of social life. Research has uncovered various factors that make self-verification more or less likely to outweigh other motives for self-evaluation.

Self-verification theory advances the idea that individuals feel a basic need to verify the central aspects of their self-concepts. Desires for self-verifying evaluations, or feedback from others that confirms our self concepts, are thought to be motivated by larger needs for certain knowledge of oneself and predictability of one's social behavior. First, self-verifying evaluations can reinforce people's perceptions of psychological consistency by confirming that their self-views and construction of reality are accurate. Second, self-verifying evaluations can provide people with assurance that their social interactions will proceed smoothly and appropriately. Research on the self-assessment process suggests that individuals are motivated to gain verification of their views of themselves, which is both personally and socially beneficial. For example, studies of married couples and roommates have revealed that people favor self-verifying partners, even when they confirm negative self-views. People tend to rate the need for self-knowledge (e.g., "I'd feel more at ease with someone who can judge me for what I am") and predictability of social interaction (e.g., "He knows what he's dealing with, so we might get along better") among their top reasons for preferring a partner who verifies their self-concept over one who does not. Obtaining self-verification from a partner can be beneficial to relationships in that it encourages intimacy, happiness, and commitment.

Research on self-verification processes has revealed that people tend to regard self-verifying evaluations as more convincing and legitimate, compared with feedback that does not seem to confirm self-views. Individuals also tend to pay more attention to, and tend to better remember, evaluations that confirm their self-concept. Evaluations that do not match people's self-views may be threatening in two ways. First, evaluations that are inconsistent with individuals' ideas and beliefs about who they are may cause them to become uncertain about their self-concepts, which conflicts with their need for self-knowledge. Second, people can infer from contrary evaluations that others do not have similar expectations of them, which does not satisfy their need for predictable and smooth social interactions. Further, people who maintain a negative self-concept tend to

desire, seek, and receive self-verification the same way as those who hold positive self-views do. But individuals who see themselves negatively tend to seek different types of feedback. Specifically, those who see themselves in a more positive light are likely to prefer and seek positive evaluations, but others who hold a more negative self-conception tend to desire negative reactions. Such evidence suggests that self-verification motives may supersede self-enhancement motives in the self-evaluation process under certain circumstances.

Depending on the situation, self-verification may be more or less likely than other motives (e.g., self-enhancement) to influence the self-evaluation process. For example, people may be more likely to self-verify when they can pay attention to others' feedback and are not so distracted by the current task that they cannot process others' evaluations of them. When we discover that another sees us in a way that does not verify our self-concept, self-verification is likely to be the most dominant self-evaluation motive. Also, how close or connected we feel to a person can affect the level of self-verification we seek from them. In illustration, studies of intimate partners have revealed that married couples seek more self-verification from each other than do dating couples. People tend to engage in self-verification most when they receive feedback about self-views that are at the core of their identity. Thus, the more central a self-view is to one's self-concept, the more likely he or she is to be motivated to substantiate that view. This idea that the importance of a self-view affects the self-evaluation process is in line with the motives for self-knowledge and predictability of behavior that self-verification theory suggests. If core self-views are at the heart of our identity, when they fail to be verified by another, our sense of coherence or knowledge of who we are is questioned. Consequently, the lack of a strong and stable self-concept can lead to inappropriate social behaviors or misunderstandings and conflicts, like an adolescent who may feel or behave awkwardly in some social situations because his or her identity has yet to be fully forged.

Although substantial evidence indicates that people are motivated to self-verify under the conditions outlined, some individuals do not present such motivations. Just as some individuals who hold themselves in low regard seek positive evaluations from others, some of those who think highly of themselves indicate a desire for distinctly negative reinforcement. Identity researchers suggest that such outcomes result from the multidimensional nature of people's self-concepts. For example, we may hold an overall negative self-concept, but a positive view of ourselves as a student. Such people may seek positive evaluations of their academic ability, while still behaving in ways that demonstrate their low self-regard.

Robert D. Blagg

See also Impression Management; Self-Assessment; Self-Concept; Self-Perception Theory

Further Readings

Swann, W. B., Jr. (1996). *Self-traps: The elusive quest for higher self-esteem.* New York: W. H. Freeman.

Swann, W., Rentfrow, P., & Guinn, J. (2003). Self-verification: The search for coherence. *Handbook of self and identity* (pp. 367–383). New York: Guilford Press.

Swann, W. B., Jr., & Schroeder, D. G. (1995). The search for beauty and truth: A framework for understanding reactions to evaluations. *Personality and Social Psychology Bulletin, 21,* 1307–1318.

SEMANTICS

Language is a mode of communication that can be used in both its oral and written forms to relay meaning. Because language consists of many levels, meaning resides on many levels. Language includes the grammatical, lexical, morphological, phonological, pragmatic, syntactic, and semantic levels. The grammatical level consists of descriptive rather than prescriptive rules of language. All language use adheres to rules whether speakers can articulate those rules or not. The lexical level encompasses the vocabulary of a language. *Morphological* refers to rules of word formation in language. *Phonological* relates to the sounds of language; an aspect of learning a language is learning agreed-upon meanings of sound combinations. *Pragmatics* considers how various contexts influence language use. *Syntax* deals with rules of sentence formation.

Semantics, in general, refers to the system of meanings that includes words, phrases, and sentences. How a person conveys or understands such meanings is part of the complexity of his or her individual and collective identity.

Study of Meaning

Syntax—or rules that regulate the way words are arranged to form sentences, phrases, or any other form of complete thought—contributes to the meaning of the words. Different languages adhere to different syntactical rules. To form sentences according to the syntactical rules of a particular language presents a systematic, orderly arrangement of words that contribute to meaning in a particular language. Semantics is the philosophical and linguistic study of meaning; it is the study of the relationships between words and meanings. Philosophers study the meaning of sentences through the perspectives of reference and truth conditions. An example of reference occurs in the sentence "Biden is vice president of the United States." The word *Biden* and the phrase *vice president of the United States* refer to the same entity, Joe Biden. Truth conditions consider the conditions under which a statement can be deemed true or false. An example of truth conditions is "Gwendolyn Brooks passed away in December 2000." This is true. "Gwendolyn Brooks passed away during the 21st century." This is true. Linguists study the meaning of sentences, phrases, and words through lexical decomposition. Lexical decomposition illuminates the semantic properties of a word in an effort to consider the sense of the word. Semantic properties specify meanings in words. Knowing the meaning of a word means knowing to what it refers. For example, the word *boy* is +male and −adult, whereas the word *man* is +male and +adult. Likewise, *woman* is −male and +adult, and *girl* is −male and −adult. Lexical decomposition provides insight in that it demonstrates the close relationship between *man* and *boy.*

The semanticist pursues the understanding of the word and the object to which the word refers. When one considers the term *semantics* one also considers its ambiguous nature, for the development of various lexicons over time systematically gives "new" meanings to "old" words. Metaphorical meaning in phrases such as *time is money* may also contribute to ambiguity; yet, semantic properties of literal meaning contribute to metaphorical meaning. Semantics is one of the most complex levels of language, for semanticists must ponder what inferences can be legitimately drawn from words, phrases, and sentences while they consider meaning on multiple levels.

Forms of Meaning

Connotation is the associated or secondary meaning of a word or expression in addition to its explicit, core, or primary meaning, which is *denotation*. Interestingly, people often believe that the dictionary definition or explicit meaning of a word more accurately represents the word's meaning than does a person's understanding of a word. The connotative form of meaning maintains its significance in language, regardless. Connotation is a suggested idea or notion. Informative connotation refers to socially agreed-upon, impersonal meanings. Affective connotation refers to the personal feelings that words arouse in people. People generally disregard informative connotations when they are strongly moved to express their views through affective connotations.

Language reveals one's views of the world—that is, language reveals one's perceptions and misconceptions. Other than connotation and denotation, various other forms of language contribute to meaning in language, reveal one's perceptions, and reveal one's identity. For example, figures of speech contribute to meaning in language. Figures of speech include the use of metaphor, simile, idiom, symbol, irony, satire, understatement, hyperbole, metonymy, synecdoche, double entendre, pun, and so forth. Like figures of speech, dialect usage contributes to variations in meanings. Similarly, slang and signification contribute to variations in meanings. Using common words in different ways (lexical), changing pronunciation (phonological), and changing word patterns (syntax) alter meaning (semantics).

Meaning resides in natural language and artificial language. Linguists study meaning in natural, spoken languages. Specialists, such as computer programmers, study and use artificial language. Whether natural or artificial, one derives meaning from the arrangement of words. In natural language, syntactic linguistic rules contribute to the meaningful arrangements of words. Linguists identify these rules of language following in-depth study of natural speech in varieties of languages.

Factors Contributing to Meaning

As noted, language reveals one's views of the world. Understanding how cultural orientation affects language is central to communication. For example, a possible interpretation of the word *home* could be a place of comfort or warmth for one person, but a place of danger and strife for another. Personal perception and emotion are key, despite dictionary definitions and denotations. Differences in cultural orientation often contribute to ambiguity. Words, phrases, and sentences possess ambiguity when they can be interpreted in several ways. For example, "He found the cross on Jackson" could be interpreted in a number of ways depending on one's life experiences and cultural orientation. Consider the following meanings: (1) A long-lost accessory, the cross was found on Jackson (Street or Boulevard). (2) The individual saw the cross, a long-lost accessory, affixed on the lapel of an acquaintance by the name of Jackson. (3) The individual found salvation at this particular location, on this particular street, or in this particular dwelling. Thus, meaning is not fixed.

The meaning of words, phrases, and sentences often depends on the sentiment behind the word. Consider how one's attitude changes when presented with the following words:

nude versus *naked*

wildflower versus *weed*

award versus *gift*

slender versus *skinny*

The word manipulates the perception of the thing described. Note the example *nude* versus *naked*. Both words refer to one's being without clothing; however, the words may elicit different responses. The subtexts and contexts of the words prompt certain responses, a function of the power of language.

Consider also the words *debate* and *dispute*. One might say that the meaning of the words differs significantly or that the meaning is the same.

The word *debate* means a discussion, as of a public question in an assembly, involving opposing viewpoints—for example, *a debate in the Senate on farm price supports*. The word *dispute* means a discussion or an argument. The difference is the suggested emotion behind the words, *debate* generally indicating more positive interaction than *dispute*. Whether written or spoken, words, phrases, and sentences possess something more than suggested and literal meanings. Words possess force. Words possess power.

A significant feature of language is that it changes over time. The perpetual evolutionary development (or deterioration) of language presents a recurrent complexity because its application veers from its intent. Early poetry and prose reflect how language changes over time, semantically, phonologically, grammatically, and lexically. On the lexical level, words can undergo broadening, narrowing, and meaning shifts. Examples of broadening include the word *picture*. During an earlier period, *picture* meant a painting. Today, its meaning has broadened to mean a photo or an electronic image. Another example of lexical broadening occurred in the word *holiday*, which in earlier times meant "holy day," a day of religious significance. Today, *holiday* means a day to commemorate an event, or a day free from the routine of work. Broadening has also occurred with brand names. Although *Kleenex* and *Xerox* are brand names, these words have been broadened to mean any type of facial tissue and any form of photocopy, respectively. An example of lexical narrowing occurred in the word *meat*. In earlier times, *meat* meant food in general. Today, *meat* refers to a specific type of food. Interestingly, the word *girl* once referred to a child, regardless of gender. Another example of narrowing occurred in the word *starve*, which once meant meant "to die." Today, one uses the phrase *to die of hunger*. Informally, one might use hyperbole, a figure of speech, to express hunger by saying "I am starving." An example of meaning shift occurred with the word *silly*. In Old English, *silly* meant happy. In Middle English, it meant naïve; however, in Modern English, it means foolish. The word *knight* has also undergone meaning shift, for its earlier meaning referred to any young person.

Because words influence context and change perspective, this leads one to ponder whether writers consider the inherent power in the meanings of the words they choose. Words can stimulate a "true" assessment of the happenings of the time through the compelling symbolic effects of the words used in written works. Words inevitably trigger programmed perceptions within the brain and change the feelings and judgments of the events described in the written work solely because of the words that are used to describe them. Reader-oriented critics might describe this as a transactional experience. In the transactional experience, words and their meanings possess the power to elicit certain past life and literary experiences of the reader. Because life and literary experiences differ, words and their meanings elicit different experiences for different readers. Identity plays a central role in this transactional experience—an experience that occurs during each reading. As noted earlier, cultural experiences, literary experiences, emotions, and numerous other factors contribute to meaning.

Because semantics relates to the study of the relationship between words and their meanings and the study of how words mean, one must consider how inconsistent elements such as subtexts and contexts influence the meanings of words, phrases, and statements. The context of an utterance contributes to its meaning. A word does not necessarily mean the same thing each time it is used. It must, however, possess some semblance of the same meaning; otherwise, those who speak the same language would fail to communicate. Semantics is yet another level of language that contributes to the complexity of identity.

Christina Robinson

See also Figures of Speech; Idiomatic Expressions; Language; Pragmatics

Further Readings

Crystal, D. (2006). *Words, words, words*. New York: Oxford University Press.

Crystal, D. (2007). *How language works*. New York: Avery.

Francis, C. (2002). "Downstream" effects on the predicate in functional grammar clause derivations. *Journal of Linguistics, 38*(2), 247–278.

Fromkin, V., & Rodman, R. (1983). *Introduction to language*. New York: Holt, Rinehart & Winston.

Hayakawa, S. I. (1978). *Language in thought and action* (4th ed.). New York: Harcourt Brace Jovanovich.

Hipkiss, R. A. (1995). *Semantics: Defining the discipline.* Mahwah, NJ: Lawrence Erlbaum.

Parker, F., & Riley, K. (1994). *Linguistics for non-linguists.* Boston: Allyn & Bacon.

Steinmetz, S. (2008). *Semantic antics: How and why words change meaning.* New York: Random House Reference.

SEMIOTICS

Semiotics refers to the study of signs, their production, use, and meaning. The meanings provided by signs contribute to social identities, and thus, semiotics is often incorporated into studies of identity, communication, and culture. Semiotics covers four areas: semantics, syntactics, pragmatics, and semiosis.

Semantics is the study of the relationship between signs and the things they reference. For instance, one might study the relationship between an object and its name. Charles Morris refers to objects of reference as *designata,* or something designated by a certain sign. For instance, when one thinks of the word *dog,* several things can come to mind, such as a beloved golden retriever, the menacing pit bull that bites, or the evil man that broke a woman's heart by cheating.

Syntactics refers to scholarship that deals with the formal properties of signs and symbols. Specifically, scholars look at the rules that govern how words come together to form phrases and sentences. In other words, syntactics is the study of how signs relate to each other in formal settings. Under syntactics, scholars find interest in how we use words together in particular sentences, phrases, settings, and occasions.

Semiosis refers to the use of signs. Under semiosis, a scholar investigates the ways in which cultural groups produce, use, and assign meaning to signs. *Pragmatics* functions within semiosis because it deals with the practical and natural elements of sign usage. Pragmatics represents the study of how signs affect the people who use them from psychological, biological, and sociological perspectives. For example, under pragmatics, a researcher could

study how using a term directly correlates to a community's cultural production.

Cultural and communication scholars trace the origins of semiotics back to Ferdinand de Saussure, and later, Charles Sanders Peirce. Many consider Saussure the "father" of modern linguistics, specifically in relation to the signified and the signifier. The signified relates to the referent, object, or mental concept. The signifier relates to the sign, or word or phrase, one utters to conjure that mental concept. According to Saussure, the signifiers we assign are arbitrary; there exists no necessary connections between a sign and its meaning. The communicator decides what a particular sign means for his or her audience.

Roland Barthes, a famous philosopher and scholar, found semiotics useful in his studies of bourgeois society. In *Mythologies,* he looked at the symbol of the wine bottle as a signifier, and the act of consuming wine as the signified. The bourgeois class used the wine bottle as a signifier of whatever they wanted it to mean, in this case, a normal and healthy, robust, and relaxing activity. For others not a part of the bourgeois class, wine might signify something unhealthy and expensive.

Peirce founded the school of pragmaticism. He broke semiosis down into action, or influence, that is or involves the cooperation of a sign, and object, and an interpretation. Thus, he caused a shift in the understanding of semiotics because he studied the use of signs rather than Saussure's structure. Peirce deemed the study of the ways in which cultures produced and assigned meanings as important. This understanding of semiotics continues to develop in the field of communication, culture, and identity.

Semiotics is particularly useful for communication and cultural scholars. Cultures form through language. Scholars refer to users of a common language as a *speech community.* Within speech communities, language manifests as discourse, a multifaceted system that incorporates speech sounds, words, and sentences, and provides meaning, values, and social identities to speech communities. Communication and semiotic scholars study discourse, or the systematic pairing of signs and meaning in a particular cultural setting. In critical cultural studies, semiotics is the analysis of how linguistic and nonlinguistic cultural "signs" form systems of meaning. For instance, the peace sign symbolizes antiwar sentiments for some, or a way to say good-bye for others. When a student receives a B grade on an essay, that letter grade symbolizes competency in a subject area. Thus, semiotics represents a critical approach for investigating the construction of meaning in written languages, visual images, and the auditory and visual images of film and television.

There are many popular contemporary studies of semiotics and meaning in cultural settings. In popular culture research, one can study how engagement rings came to represent commitment in relationships. For instance, the tagline "Diamonds Are Forever" gives social significance to the idea of an engagement ring symbolizing commitment. It also highlights the importance of diamond gemstones preferred over other precious stones. It also implies that an engagement is not forever, unless it is brokered with the exchange of a diamond.

Several collections of communication essays use semiotics as their method. One such collection is the *Feminism and Visual Culture Reader,* edited by Amelia Jones. In this text, authors focus on semiotics as method because it allows scholars to look at how images and words are formed, and how those forms affect communication and shared meaning. Other collections include works by Stuart Hall and Paul du Gay.

Amber Johnson

See also Discourse; Pragmatics; Semantics; Signification

Further Readings

Barthes, R. (1957). *Mythologies.* Paris: Edition de Seuil.
Jones, A. (2002). *Feminism and visual culture reader.* London: Routledge.
Saussure, F. de (1986). *Course in general linguistics.* New York: Open Court.

SETTING

A reciprocal relationship exists between language and identity. Language and how people use language change as people adapt to new environments and interact in these new settings. In considering setting and identity, one's identity, in part, depends on current life status, interactions with others, and physical location or setting.

Setting is multifaceted, for it reflects region, social interaction, occupation, and even the arts. Setting is more than location; it encompasses a complex environment surrounding people. It includes language use, interactions with others, and historical and cultural conditions. Just as with characters in the literary realm, setting also includes what people know, own, and experience. This entry discusses the various definitions of *setting* and the ways setting indicates identity.

Definitions

Authors, actors, and artists offer their audiences unique experiences by transporting them from familiar to unfamiliar, and from realistic to imaginary locations. In the literary realm, setting encompasses time (time of day, season, year, era, etc.), place (kitchen, balcony, valley, ocean, desert, etc.), and cultural and historical conditions (war time, enslavement, genocide, etc.). Setting also encompasses what characters know (several languages, family secrets), experience (psychological state, spiritual state), and own (stocks and bonds, a wheelchair). Setting might also be described as the background in which action occurs. When a writer foregrounds setting, that is, when a writer foregrounds the language and customs of a particular place, this literary style is called "local color." Setting, in essence, holds the same significance as character. In many instances, characters become extensions of the setting. The two elements seem to merge. Based on their identities, characters respond to their environments in unique and interesting ways.

In addition to literary definitions, many other definitions of *setting* exist. Consider setting and the computer. The computer allows writers and readers to expand their surroundings. Users can capture and freeze time using digital, still, or video pictures. One can even merge images together to create unique sceneries or backdrops. Inanimate objects gain life through shape, motion, and animation. Technology defines setting through various audio and visual means by allowing light and sound waves to be transmitted into different media with the assistance of electricity. Computer specialists define *setting* as the transference of information from one computer to another using a series of 1s and 0s. The Internet allows messages and images to travel through space through HTML coding and advanced technology.

In the literary and virtual worlds, setting is important. In the literary world, setting is inextricably linked to characters. Characters are verbal representations of human beings. Similar links exist in the virtual world. Both relate to the real world.

Regional Indicators

Geographical boundaries and migration patterns relate to setting and contribute to language variation. Geographical boundaries such as mountains, lakes, rivers, and valleys divide people. When people do not interact with one another, they develop different language patterns. Different language patterns distinguish identities.

When groups verbally interact regularly, each group picks up cues and emulates aspects of the other's language features. Over time, a change called *linguistic convergence* occurs. Linguistic convergence suggests that speakers adjust their speech to that of their addressees. Groups no longer in proximity, and groups that maintain minimal contact with each other, tend to exhibit minimal linguistic convergence. Listeners, then, refer to the differences in language and language varieties as accents. If referring to the southerner, listeners might also use the term *southern drawl*. In actuality, what listeners hear is vowel variation. Listeners identify the southern speaker based on differences in sounds of the language and differences in vocabulary usage. A sound difference unique to the southern U.S. dialect results from monophthongization. Monophthongization results when a speaker produces a one-part vowel rather than a two-part vowel. A two-part vowel is called a *diphthong*. When speakers produce diphthongs, they produce a sound that consists of one vowel sound that glides into another vowel sound. An example of a diphthong occurs in the word *time*. The usual pronunciation is something like "taym." Rather than the two-part vowel, the Southern speaker produces a

lengthened, one-part vowel (monophthongization), and "time" becomes "ta:m." (The colon indicates the lengthening of the vowel.) Even the rhythm and a slower or faster pace influence the sounds of words and can serve as indicators of identity.

In addition to vowel sound changes, listeners recognize differences in vocabulary among speakers from different regions. For example, in some regions, the non-alcoholic beverage is called *pop;* in other regions, it is called *soda*. In still other regions, it is called *soda pop*. In some regions, a front porch is known as a *veranda,* the expressway is called the *highway,* and the sofa is called the *davenport*. Other examples are the chest of drawers and the chifferobe or chifferobe, the faucet and the spigot, and the pail and the bucket. In the southern region of the United States, listeners hear more terms of endearment such as *sweetie pie, honey,* and *darling*. Just as those from other regions recognize these terms of endearment as distinctive markers in southern speech, the southerner recognizes the absence of such terms as distinctive markers in northern speech. Southerners often view the absence of terms of endearment as rude, cold, or inconsiderate. For the southerner, the use of "you-all" rather than the plural "you" is common and might be viewed as redundant or grammatically incorrect by the northerner. Such language variations distinguish one group from another group and serve as indicators of identity. In addition to the sounds of the language and differences in vocabulary identifying southern speakers, behavior in social relationships contributes to identity. For example, the southerner displays more openness toward strangers than do the midwesterner or the northerner. A sense of community and a display of courtesy exist in the South. Setting, then, influences language and behavior.

Social Indicators

Language is culturally and regionally based. The possibility of the average U.S. speaker listening to a classmate, peer, or coworker and distinguishing dialects is minimal. Listeners recognize differences, but they do not necessarily know the linguistic or social reasons for differences. Representative U.S. English dialects include Standard American English, African American English or Ebonics, Southern

African American English, Southern White American English, and Cajun/Creole English. Linguists observe and study natural language use and compare and contrast various words, sounds, and individual speech patterns. They also test and evaluate the results. Many linguists focus on the historical development of social dialects, and others engage in sociolinguistic practices. Sociolinguistics is the study of language in society—the study of language use in its various social contexts. Of interest to the sociolinguist is why people change the ways in which they speak when they move from one setting to another.

Many speakers possess the ability to engage in situational variation or to engage in code-switching as they move from one setting to another. To code-switch entails a change from the use of one language to another, depending on the setting. Bilingual speakers often switch from their native languages to English in a setting that includes native English speakers. In private speech situations, they often switch to their native language. Code-switching also includes changing from the use of one dialect to another, depending on the setting. For example, a speaker might engage in classic African American English when talking with peers in one setting but switch to Standard American English when talking with his employer in another setting. Code-switching is also known to occur within a single speech situation and even within an individual speech act. Speakers consciously and unconsciously select the speech behavior most appropriate for each speech situation or setting. News reporters often discuss the fact that public figures code-switch as they move from one audience to another. Code-switching might entail a change in diction from, for example, formal to informal. Diction reflects the choices speakers make in vocabulary and word order. Formal diction might include polysyllabic words, grammatically complete sentences, and sentences that reflect complex word order. Using formal diction, the speaker might select the word *dine*. Using informal diction, the speaker might choose the phrase *chow down*. Informal diction might also include contractions, sentence fragments, slang, and even profanity. In an attempt to use formal diction and emphasize Standard English, speakers of other dialects tend to engage in hypercorrection.

Hypercorrection extends a particular language feature beyond its normal boundary. For example, speakers engaged in hypercorrection might overly emphasize word endings such as *-ed* and *-ing*. Hypercorrection gives the appearance of elitism.

Changes in language occur as speakers move from one setting or social context to another. When changes occur, they provide cues about the speaker's role in a particular speech situation, the speaker's relationship with others, and the speaker's mood, and, generally, changes in language use reveal information about the speaker's identity.

Jargon

Jargon is technical or specialized language used by particular occupational or social groups and reflects a particular field of knowledge or activity. Jargon users might include chemists, medical doctors, lawyers, computer graphic designers, educators, and even members of sports teams. The use of specialized terms and phrases indicate identity. Speakers generally produce these specialized terms and phrases in specific settings, such as medical offices, chemistry labs, courtrooms, or bowling alleys. Jargon often consists of familiar terms that possess different meanings for specialized groups. For example, bowlers refer to the bowling alley as the "house," and "average" as the highest sanctioned score. *Sanctioned* means to be certified by a state organization. Legal jargon includes root words that appear familiar, but their endings appear unfamiliar. Examples include *trustee, trustor, testate,* and *testator.* Many legal terms derive from Latin forms. Examples include *pro se* and *pro per.* Both terms relate to an individual who represents himself or herself in court. Like many specialized fields, medicine uses jargon in the form of acronyms. Representative terms are CATT, which means crisis assessment and treatment team, and EEG, which means electroencephalogram.

Writers and speakers in specialized fields must consider their settings and audiences when using jargon. If the goal is to reach wide audiences, then writers and speakers must minimize jargon.

Jonnie Simmons-Johnson

See also Code-Switching; Dialect; Figures of Speech; Language; Pragmatics; Semantics; Style/Diction

Further Readings

Hickerson, N. P. (1980). *Linguistic anthropology.* New York: Holt, Rinehart & Winston.

Kennedy, X. J., Gioia, D., & Bauerlein, M. (2009). *Handbook of literary terms.* New York: Pearson/Longman.

Labov, W. (2002, August 2). *Driving forces in linguistic change.* Retrieved June 24, 2009, from University of Pennsylvania Web site: http://www.ling.upenn.edu

Mabele, M. C. (2006). *Linguistic identity.* Retrieved June 24, 2009, from Intertext Syracuse University Writing Program Web site: http://wrt-intertext.syr.edu/XI/linguistic.html

Roberts, E. V. (2008). *Literature: An introduction to reading and writing.* Upper Saddle River, NJ: Pearson Prentice Hall.

Scherer, K. R., & Giles, H. (1979). *Social markers in speech.* Cambridge, UK: Cambridge University Press.

Sterling, P. (2000). *Identity in language: An explosion into the social implications of linguistic variation.* Retrieved June 24, 2009, from Texas A&M University Web site: http://www.tamu.edu/chr/agora/winter2000/sterlilng.pdf

Wolfram, W., & Schilling-Estes, N. (1998). *American English.* Malden, MA: Blackwell.

Sexual Identity

Sexual identity has a least two meanings in the social sciences, both relating to inner convictions or claims about who and what we are. The first meaning refers to the various ways we see ourselves as male or female, and the second defines our sexuality or the kinds of erotic partners we prefer. These inner convictions usually begin with medical designations made about biological sex at birth, based on the appearance of genitalia and presence of certain chromosomes. Children are then raised as girls or boys, and encouraged to accept gender roles or certain mannerisms and behaviors considered appropriate to their biological sex. However, sexual identity is not always consistent with medical designations, physical anatomy, or gender roles.

Sexual identity is difficult to define and measure because it is an inner conviction that could be inconsistent with appearance or overt behavior, because it can change throughout life, and because it does not always reflect the perceptions of others.

A man may be comfortable with his male body, act in a socially appropriate way for his culture, have occasional sex with men, but be married and see himself as a heterosexual. A woman could grow up a tomboy, dress and behave in "masculine" ways, and work in a male-dominated job but know she is a heterosexual woman. A "lipstick" lesbian could wear ultra-feminine clothing and accessories but live with a female partner. Outward expressions of sexual identity can also be altered to suit different social circumstances, or can be radically transformed through sex reassignment procedures.

Most people subconsciously accept social and cultural expectations about sexual or gender-related behavior. Although they may question their degree of masculinity or femininity, they may seldom or never question whether they are male or female. Those who are confused about their sexual identity may disguise these feelings to fit in with social conventions, or become celibate. Alternatively, they may attempt to change societal attitudes, their own external appearance, or their anatomy. Nevertheless, social scientists now argue that individuals can have multiple sexual identities, which may be inconsistent, contradictory, and transitional.

Sex Versus Gender

Historically, biological sex has been considered a dichotomy that can be determined at birth by genitalia and chromosomes. Although a few babies are born with ambiguous genitalia or both male and female anatomy, babies are typically designated as male or female at birth and are expected to grow up accordingly. Some children or adults may undergo sex reassignment or reconstruction surgery if there is a major conflict between what sex they think they are (or want to be) and the medical decision at birth.

In the 19th and early 20th centuries, males and females were thought to be polar opposites with different minds and bodies. Early social theorists argued that biology is destiny and suggested that biological sex led to different dispositions, emotions, and abilities, which explained the "separate spheres" of men and women. Nevertheless, a number of psychoanalysts and psychologists argued that masculine and feminine behavior, as well as heterosexuality and homosexuality, were influenced by biology but resulted more from distinctive life histories.

After the 1950s, more social scientists focused on social learning theory, viewing the newborn child as capable of learning sex-appropriate behavior for either sex if given the right circumstances. The concept of "sex roles" was used to explain how men and women become so different in their behavior. Social scientists argued that children are normally treated differently based on their sex. They are held and cuddled differently by parents, given distinctive toys, and encouraged to develop varying interests and to occupy different sex roles. Social researchers now use the concept of "gender roles" because *sex* is used as a biological concept relating to physical differences, whereas *gender* refers to the socially constructed ways of thinking, looking, and behaving that relate to cultural ideas of masculinity and femininity.

Although there has recently been a resurgence of genetic theories of behavior in science, sociologists continue to focus on the social construction of identity, arguing that people normally create multiple gender and sexual identities. The sociological concept of "doing gender" implies that people express their inner convictions through "performing" certain behavior. These could include girls playing house, women wearing dresses and high heels, or wives accepting responsibility for housework. Males do gender by playing contact sports with other males, pretending to be tough, developing an interest in cars and speed, or performing outdoor housework such as cooking on the barbeque but resisting indoor housework. These performances are sometimes played only for specific audiences and could change in different circumstances. For example, men may acquire various technical skills and regularly fix the car but still ask their wives how to operate the washing machine.

Many cultures polarize gender roles through the ways that children are raised and educated and through etiquette rules, labor force segregation, the division of labor in families, and cultural rituals. This polarization helps shape gender identity but could also reinforce sexual identity and "compulsory heterosexuality."

Sexual Preference

Many researchers now acknowledge that biological sex is a continuum because people vary in their mixture of male and female characteristics. These researchers argue that the development of sexual identity is a psychological process that is shaped from infancy to adulthood by emotional interaction with parents and others. Most adults are clear about whether they are male or female, and most also see themselves as heterosexual. A minority of participants in research projects define themselves as homosexual, bisexual, asexual, intersexed, or transsexual.

Until recently, only heterosexuality was assumed "normal" by governments, professionals and parents in Western countries, although some cultures permitted same-sex relationships and cross-dressing under certain circumstances. Homosexual behavior was generally viewed as deviant and thought to originate from ambiguous genitalia at birth, chromosomal or hormonal abnormalities, or inappropriate gender socialization during childhood. People who were caught engaging in homosexual acts or cross-dressing were treated by authorities as mentally ill or criminalized until well into the 20th century.

Sexual orientation used to be described as an enduring preference but researchers now acknowledge that some people identify as heterosexual, bisexual, or homosexual on different occasions or in different periods of their lives. People might change their sexual identities through lifestyle and associational changes (including hair style, clothing, and association with certain communities), but a few undergo surgical transsexual procedures. Sexual identity does not always match up with biology at birth or even the biological sex of occasional erotic partners.

Much of recent research on sexual identity focuses on gays, lesbians, bisexuals, and transsexuals, including how they "come out" or communicate their sexual identity to others, ways of dealing with discrepancies between identity and lived experience, and sexual practices and relationships. Earlier research on heterosexual identity focused on femininity but much of the current research deals with the development and social organization of masculinity. Some studies have compared the attitudes and lifestyles of same-sex and heterosexual couples, the way they bring up their children, life satisfaction, and patterns of aging. This research suggests that gay couples tend to be less committed and monogamous than lesbian couples do but that both have more egalitarian divisions of labor than do heterosexual couples, especially those that are legally married. However, the family lives of same-sex couples, the outcomes for children they raise, and factors contributing to life satisfaction are similar to those of heterosexuals. Many same-sex couples want to be treated as married couples, and some have taken advantage of new opportunities for marriage or civil unions.

Recent research also discusses the link between sexual identity, sexual performance, and ability to reproduce, finding that parenthood is still used as a rough indicator of maturity, heterosexuality, men's sexual prowess, femininity, mental health, and even moral worth. Those who choose not to reproduce often need to justify their decisions to others in the way that parents do not, and are often seen as immature, sexually incompetent, or hedonistic. Generally, people who choose to live outside heterosexual nuclear families still have greater need to protect their inner convictions from public scrutiny. However, the expectation of heterosexual parenting is less prevalent among younger people.

Social Influences on Sexual Identity

Considerable research concludes that sexual identity is shaped by early emotional interaction with parents but is further modified by sexual experiences, gendered patterns of work and social relations, and identity politics. Sexual identity has also been influenced by improvements in contraception that have separated sex from marriage. New ideas about lifestyle choices and human rights have also encouraged people to live out their inner convictions.

Innovations in surgery and drugs have enabled people to change their bodies as well as their sexual identities, and more people are taking advantage of these procedures. The cosmetic surgery industry has grown rich from people's concerns about sexual identity, enlarging or reducing breasts, reshaping genitalia, and tucking tummies. In addition, new medical procedures have assisted childless people and even postmenopausal women to become parents, and have helped people change from one sex to another through surgery and hormonal treatments.

Advertising and television programs continually encourage us to reshape our images of the desired body and sexual partner. Television programs try to persuade us that changing our appearance will alter our confidence and identity. Grooming products formerly used by women are now promoted for men (including hair removal products and dye), and new products are marketed to improve sexual experience, including those to resolve erectile dysfunction, moisturize vaginas, and make sex fun. Generally, television programs and advertising have normalized sex outside marriage, same-sex lifestyles, transsexual experiences, and medically assisted conception.

Identity politics, designed to change the social meanings of masculinity and femininity or eradicate compulsory heterosexuality, have affected sexual and gender identity. The women's movement of the 1960s and 1970s attempted to redefine femininity and encourage women to become more assertive, to consider the possibility of childfree or lesbian lifestyles, and to strive for education and better jobs. Participants also sought to change attitudes and social organization by lobbying for pay equity, equal rights in marriage, and homemakers' pensions.

Around the same time, the gay rights movement fought to legalize homosexual acts and prevent discrimination against gays and lesbians and, more recently, to encourage gay pride and gain legal protection for same-sex relationships and transsexuals. The men's and father's rights movements have encouraged men to view themselves as caring fathers as well as family breadwinners, to express their emotions, and to improve access to their children after separation. Various religious movements have discouraged or encouraged celibacy.

Over the years, identity politics have changed laws and practices, but they have also transformed assumptions that many people make about sexual preference and gender-related behavior. In addition, these movements provide like-minded communities that encourage people to live their lives according to their inner convictions.

Conclusion

Sexual identity refers to the ways that people see themselves as sexual beings. For most people, their sexual identity, sexual orientation, and gender identity are in agreement, but others experience contradictions and conflicts. Different academic disciplines disagree about the origin of sexual identity. Although sociobiologists and some medical researchers focus on genetic and hormonal factors, social psychologists concentrate on people's unique family histories and psychosexual development. Many sociologists and feminist theorists argue that sexual identity is culturally rather than biologically based.

More opportunities now exist to "create our own biographies" and remake our sexual identities, with more personal freedom and innovations in contraception, surgical procedures and drug treatments, human rights, and laws. However, the development of sexual identity and its exemplification in behavior are still constrained by social forces. Heterosexuality is still considered the dominant and normal sexual orientation by governments, religious institutions, and many individuals. Western culture no longer polarizes gender roles as much, but the socioeconomic status of men and women still differs. These factors may discourage some people from publicly acknowledging contradictions in their sexual identity or living their inner convictions.

Maureen Baker

See also Gender; Sexual Minorities; Society and Social Identity

Further Readings

Diamond, M. (2002). Sex and gender are different: Sexual identity and gender identity are different. *Clinical Child Psychology and Psychiatry, 7,* 320–334.

Tolman, D. L., & Diamond, L. M. (2001). Desegregating sexuality research: Cultural and biological perspectives on gender and desire. *Annual Review of Sex Research, 12,* 33–74.

SEXUAL MINORITIES

Sexual identity is a relatively recent and controversial concept. Common cultural practice and scholarly convention have each developed many of the ways currently used to define and categorize human sexual identity. Some of these focus on *sexual orientation,* defined as a person's gendered preference in the choice of sexual partners. Viewed in this way, an individual could be defined as asexual (having little to no interest in sex, and therefore no need for sexual partners), bisexual (sexual interest in both men and women), gay (preference by a male for male sexual partners), lesbian (preference by a female for female sexual partners), straight (preference by a male for female sexual partners, and for male partners by females), and questioning (still in the process of discerning sexual orientation). Other preferences with respect to choice of sexual partners include necrophilia (desire to have sexual contact with a corpse) and zoophilia, also known as bestiality (desire to have sexual contact with animals).

Another commonly used means of defining sexual identity is through the enumeration of an individual's concurrent sexual partners. Numerical categories of this kind include celibacy (abstinence from sex, and thus no sexual partners); monogamy (sex with only one committed partner); polygamy, of which there are two primary types: polygyny (sex between a male and two or more concurrent and committed female partners) and polyandry (sex between a female and two or more concurrent and committed male partners); and polyamory (sex with multiple partners, with whom one may or may not have committed relationships).

Still another means of defining sexual identity is to do so in terms of an individual's preferences regarding specific sexual foci and practices. There is a wide range of fetishistic interests, also known as paraphilias, which involve eroticizing parts of the human body, manufactured and natural objects, and sensations and situations not normally associated by most people with sex. Examples include erotic interest in such body parts as the ankles or hair, objects such as cigarettes or shoes, and sensations or situations associated with bondage (deriving sexual pleasure from tying others or being tied up), masochism (deriving sexual pleasure from receiving psychological distress and physical pain), fantasy and role play (e.g., discipline, dominance, submission), and sadism (deriving sexual pleasure from imposing psychological distress and physical pain). Fetishes can be as rare—and, from the perspective of the sociosexual mainstream, as disturbing—as such forms of "scat play" as coprophilia (deriving sexual pleasure from playing with or eating feces) and urophilia (deriving sexual pleasure from playing with or drinking urine). Fetishes can also be relatively tame, per normative sociosexual standards, as for example an interest in having sex while dressed as cute, fuzzy animals, or as pirates, sailors, soldiers, Victorian school marms, or their students, and so on.

The broad sexual identity categories briefly outlined—sexual orientation, partner enumeration, and preferred sexual practices—are not mutually exclusive. For example, a woman might define herself as a monogamous lesbian sadist or a man as a polyamorous bisexual. In contrast, some, although not all, of the subcategories within each broader category are mutually exclusive. For example, it is impossible to be simultaneously monogamous and polygamous. At other times, several related sexual categories can be collapsed into an omnibus sexual identity, such as BDSM. The first two letters of this abbreviation, "BD," stands for bondage and discipline (physical restraint and light pain); the middle two letters, "DS," for dominance and submission (fantasy and role-playing); and the last two letters, "SM," for sadism and masochism (heavy pain).

Some sexual identities currently carry a great deal of sociocultural weight, and thus have significant public implications (cultural, legal, social, political, and religious) and personal consequences, as is the case, for example, with gays, lesbians, and straights. Other sexual identities are deemed unimportant or outright ignored by the mainstream. For example, as long as shoe fetishists do not steal or bother others, they are generally permitted to quietly pursue their passion without interference, nor are they typically defined in terms of their sexual preference in the same way that gay men or lesbians are.

Sexual identity is both ascribed and assumed. *Ascription* is the process whereby definitions of sexual identity are imposed on individuals and groups by others. Scientists, medical doctors and psychologists, legislators and lawyers, religious leaders, and others with presumed normative authority define sexual categories into which they conceptually place individuals and groups. Assumption, in contrast, is the process through with which individuals and groups define their sexual identities in their own terms, rather than having identities imposed by others. Thus, at different times during the past century, gay men have

been defined as homosexuals (by pioneering psychologists), as sodomites (by various religious traditions), and as proudly queer (by gay activists). These same men have often defined themselves differently.

A *sexual minority* is made up of those whose shared sexual preferences and practices differ in some significant way from those of the sociosexual mainstream. However, as anthropologists, historians, sexologists, other social scientists, and critical scholars point out, sexual preferences and practices that are regarded as normal in one time and place might well be regarded as strange, and perhaps even undesirable, in another historical and cultural context.

In ancient Greece, for example, it was a common, accepted, and indeed favored practice for a mature man to enter into a mentoring relationship with a pre-pubic boy. This relationship had emotional, intellectual, and sexual dimensions. The latter often included the practice of intercrural (nonpenetrative) intercourse, which for the ancient Greeks typically involved the older male rubbing his penis between the legs of the younger boy. Today, this same pederastic sexual relationship would result in the adult male being arrested, convicted, and imprisoned in accordance with the laws of the United States. The same is true for those who enter into polygamous marital relationships, which are currently prohibited by the laws of most Western countries, but which were fairly common marital arrangements for the ancient Jewish patriarchs and that nation's early kings (for example, according to 1 Kings 11:3, Solomon had 700 wives and 300 concubines). Today, polygyny is still permitted under specially defined conditions (e.g., fair and equal treatment toward, and support of, as many as four wives) by those Islamic countries and peoples that adhere to the traditional Shari'a interpretation of the Qur'an. Given the legal status of polygamy in the United States, such relationships are rare, although they do exist, especially in parts of Utah and the U.S. Southwest. Canada and Mexico also have polygamous communities.

Having briefly defined the terms *sexual identity* and *sexual minority*, this entry outlines practical and theoretical problems associated with defining sexual identity and identifies problems in obtaining accurate demographic data regarding sexual minorities, describes the cultural dimension developed by some sexual minorities, discusses the marginalization and oppression of sexual minorities, notes the occasional social elevation of some sexual minorities, and finally points out the continued relevance of sexual identity as a concept driving social scientific research and critical-cultural critique.

Difficulties in Defining Human Sexual Identity

For most of human history, people were not categorically defined in terms of their sexuality. In the Western world, to the extent that such categorization occurred before the 19th century, it was tied to Judeo-Christian moral concerns, rather than to psychological or social constructs. For example, during the Middle Ages, a person might be labeled an *adulterer, fornicator,* or *sodomite,* but these labels would refer to sins committed and would not be understood as referring to some essential core feature of an individual's identity. (Although in much the same way as habitual thievery would brand a person a *thief,* habitual same-sex relations between a man and other men would brand him as a *sodomite.*) The focus of traditional Judeo-Christian moral concerns regarding sexual behavior was not identity definition, however, but rather the need to differentiate between permitted and prohibited sexual practices. Some practices were expressly forbidden (defined as sins within the Christian tradition). Examples include the commandment forbidding adultery (Exodus 20:14, Deuteronomy 5:18), and the Levitical injunction against male-male sexual intercourse (Leviticus 18:22).

The systematic scientific categorization of human sexual preferences and practices has its origin in work done in the 19th century by pioneers in the field of psychology. The most influential of these scientists was Richard Freiherr von Krafft-Ebing, who authored *Psychopathia Sexualis,* in which he famously coined the terms *sadism* and *masochism.* During this same period, the term *homosexual* originated. Krafft-Ebing, and those who followed him, pathologized sexual behaviors that had once been deemed sinful. In this way, science assumed in the Western world a normative role regarding sexual behavior that had once belonged solely to religion. To these were added other sexual "pathologies," which were sexual preferences and practices that significantly deviated from the norm. This statistically based language reflects the social scientific interest in measuring human attitudes and behaviors, and in designating as mental illness those that deviate too far from the mean.

There is much controversy regarding whether human sexual identity is a product of biology, culture, or both. Disagreement also exists about whether sexual identity is fixed or fluid. In his unfinished magnum opus, the multivolume *Histoire de la sexualité,* French philosopher Michel Foucault argues that human sexuality is fluid, and as such, it is shaped by the changing historical, personal, and sociocultural contexts in which it is experienced and expressed. According to Foucault, these contexts are powerful shaping influences that determine the range and acceptability of sexual options, and the material and other ways in which these options are expressed. This contextual dimension of the expression of human sexuality is reflected in the ancient Greek gay practices and the polygamous marital arrangements discussed previously, and in the adoption of black leather as de rigueur regalia by BDSM practitioners described later in the section on sexual cultures.

Difficulties in Quantifying Human Sexuality

There are logistical and methodological difficulties in obtaining accurate demographic data regarding sexual preferences and practices. Some people are reluctant to provide strangers with honest and open information regarding their sexual preferences, the nature and frequency of their sexual practices, and other intimate information they might regard as personal. For religious and cultural reasons, some might be ashamed to acknowledge what they do, and with whom. Others might be inclined to exaggerate or outright lie about the nature and frequency of their sexual activity. The difficulty in obtaining honest self-report information regarding human sexuality is illustrated by the controversy regarding the accuracy of the information included in Margaret Mead's classic, *Coming of Age in Samoa,* with some scholars suggesting that she had been misled by her informants, whereas others support her findings, and still others suggest the truth about what Mead was actually told might never be known for certain.

The first serious scientific attempt to gather descriptive and statistical data about the sexual attitudes and practices of Americans were the studies of males and females conducted during the 1940s and 1950s by Alfred Charles Kinsey, an Indiana University biologist who turned his attention to humans after having extensively studied gall wasps. The opportunity and snowball sampling techniques used by Kinsey to obtain data regarding the sexual habits of Americans resulted in the inclusion in his study of a disproportionate number of prison inmates, prostitutes, sex offenders, and other groups not representative of the general population. Critics claim this inclusion skewed the statistical results reported by Kinsey. A particularly controversial figure is Kinsey's oft-cited claim that 10% of the general population is homosexual.

A more recent scientific survey of U.S. sexuality was conducted in 1992 by a University of Chicago team of researchers employing the same sophisticated sampling techniques pioneered and perfected by marketing and political pollsters, which the team employed in the hopes of obtaining as accurate a count as possible. The results of this study depict a sociosexual landscape that differs significantly from that charted by Kinsey. Indeed, the team of researchers report that about 3% of those surveyed claimed to have engaged in a same-sex act during 1991, and only 4.5% said they had done so at any point during their lives. The difficulty of obtaining accurate results regarding matters related to human sexuality is illustrated by the percentage of the general population said to be gay by this and other major studies conducted during the past few decades, with a reported low of approximately 2% to a high around 13%. These numerical differences might be explained by the use of different research methodologies, different operational definitions of same-sex attraction and behavior, changing attitudes toward gays and lesbians, and so on. Difficulties occur as well in attempting to gather statistical data about BDSM practitioners, necrophiliacs, polygamists, various fetishists, and the members of other sexual minorities. Thus, although it is usually possible to say that a particular sexual group is in the minority, it is difficult to state decisively what percentage of the general population that group represents.

The Cultural Dimension of Sexual Minorities

Sexual preferences and the practices associated with them, although personal, have sociocultural implications. With a few rare exceptions (e.g., asexuals, solitary masturbators, some object fetishists, those for whom bestiality is their sole source of sexual pleasure), sex requires at least one human partner, and thus the need for a social network that makes meeting and keeping partners possible. Often, however, those whose sexuality differs from the sociosexual mainstream are denied the cultural affirmation, and social networking and support, that members of the mainstream take for granted. In response, some sexual minorities have fostered a sense of community through the creation of alternative cultures that both draw and differ from the dominant sociosexual culture. These cultures can be quite elaborately developed and organized, possessing their own distinctive artifacts, events, historical memory, language, organizations, publications, ritual observances, social practices, symbols, and so forth.

The origin and evolution of the contemporary U.S. BDSM community provides an example of such a culture and illustrates Foucault's claim that sexuality is contextually and socially constructed. This culture first emerged in the wake of World War II, when gay veterans returned home profoundly influenced by their military experiences, which included rigid discipline, strict regimentation, an acknowledged hierarchy, an easy camaraderie among buddies, an almost exclusively male environment, and for some men, their first gay sexual encounter. Some of these gay veterans sought to recreate as civilians aspects of military life they enjoyed while in the service. Many found what they were looking for in the gay motorcycle clubs that emerged in the decade following World War II, notably in Chicago, Los Angeles, and New York. Like the military, these clubs had their rules, rituals, insignia, and so on. In this way, the wearing of black leather biker gear by gay BDSM practitioners emerged as an easily recognizable sign of their sexuality, one that was later adopted by a significant segment of the lesbian and straight BDSM communities. Today, the BDSM community has its own geography (bars, dungeons, leather shops), historical memory (as remembered in books, the Leather Archives and Museum, etc.), language (with its own unique use of such words as *bottom, top, play, toy,* and *scene*), social mores (dungeon etiquette), and many other attributes one associates with a developed and distinctive culture.

The cultures created and maintained by some sexual minorities are deliberately hidden from the scrutiny of the sociosexual mainstream, so that members of that minority are protected from any adverse legal, social, or other unwanted consequences that might occur should their sexual identity be revealed. Such was the largely case with the largely underground U.S. gay and lesbian cultures that existed until the gay liberation movement that emerged in the wake of the 1969 Stonewall riots pushed for and obtained greater public acceptance for, and visibility of, gays and lesbians in contexts ranging from local communities to mass popular culture. Such secrecy is still the case with some sexual minorities. The degree to which a sexual minority values secrecy depends on its acceptance by others. There is, for example, greater gay visibility in urban centers than in rural communities, although this is changing as gays have gained greater acceptance in the United States within and outside urban areas.

Like other groups, sexual minorities have staked their claim to their own space on the Internet, thus extending their cultures into cyberspace. Indeed, without trying, one can easily find Web sites that cater to those with even the most specialized sexual interests. The offerings of such sites are diverse, ranging from educational material to hardcore pornography, from online dating and social networking to the Web pages of clubs and other organizations. Some sites, such as the one maintained by the North American Man/Boy Love Association (NAMBLA), promote a legal and political agenda intended to change laws unfavorable to a particular sexual minority.

Not all sexual minorities have developed their own distinctive cultures. Necrophiliacs, for example, tend to be isolated from one another largely because of the strong social stigma attached to, and the legal prohibitions against, the practice of having sexual relations with human corpses. Nor do necrophiliacs have any incentive to search out others with same sexual proclivities because they have a sexual interest in the dead, not the living. The development of elaborated sexual cultures is

thus a consequence of the establishment of sexual communities, which in turn reflect common needs, shared goals, and the desire for social connection.

The Marginalization and Oppression of Sexual Minorities

Sexual minorities have experienced cultural, legal, political, religious, social, and other forms of marginalization. Such marginalization can have a variety of oppressive consequences for members of sexual minorities, including social ostracization, denial of basic human and legal rights, and even death. Instances of such oppression are numerous throughout history and around the world. The following two examples (one contemporary and one historical) are representative.

During the first decade of the 21st century, in the United States and elsewhere, there has been much spirited debate about whether gays and lesbians should be allowed to enter into legally sanctioned marriages, with all the responsibilities and rights that come with such recognition. The legal status of gay marriage has been fought in the academy, in the courts, in legislatures, in popular culture, and via ballot initiatives. Today, same-sex marriages are legally recognized in some countries, including Canada, South Africa, Spain, and Sweden. In the United States, the legality of such marriages varies by state, and its status is changing rapidly in response to state referenda, new legislation, and court decisions. At the time this entry was written in 2009, gay marriage enjoyed legal recognition in Connecticut, Iowa, Massachusetts, and Vermont, but other states have explicitly rendered such marriage illegal though constitutional amendments and other means. In 2008, a hotly contested battle raged over California's Proposition 8, which would add the following words to that state's constitution: "Only marriage between a man and a woman is valid or recognized in California." Proposition 8 passed, but was challenged in court. In May 2009, the California Supreme Court upheld Proposition 8.

One of the saddest chapters in the history of gays during the last century was the extermination of gays and the decimation of their vibrant culture by the Nazis. Although technically illegal, homosexuality was tolerated in Weimar, Germany, which resulted in a gay golden age immortalized by Christopher Isherwood in *The Berlin Stories* and celebrated by the Broadway musical and film versions of *Cabaret*. This de facto tolerance ended when the Nazis assumed power. Approximately 100,000 gay men were imprisoned by the Nazis in concentration camps under the provisions of the anti-sodomy Paragraph 175 of the German penal code. Some estimate that as many as 60% of those imprisoned gay men died, a mortality rate second only to that of the Jews. Although the Nazis have been consigned to the dustbin of history, gays are still at risk of being the victims of violence and murder. Indeed, such violence is so common that there is a term for it: *gaybashing*. Symptomatic of gaybashing is the case of Matthew Shepherd, a young man who was tortured and killed in Laramie, Wyoming, on October 12, 1998, for no other reason than because he was gay. To date, violent crimes perpetrated against gays and lesbians because of their sexual orientation are still not defined as hate crimes under federal law.

The Social Elevation of Sexual Minorities

Sexual minorities are not always marginalized or oppressed by the societies in which they are situated. Some are tolerated, and some are simply ignored. Occasionally, certain select sexual minorities are accorded special status that sets them apart from, and even places them above, the social mainstream.

An example of the social elevation of a sexual minority is offered by the Two-Spirit people (formerly referred to as *berdaches*, a term that has been largely abandoned because of its perceived pejorative connotation), who are accorded special sexual and social status, and the respect associated with such status, by many Native American tribes and Canadian First Nations. These are "men" who are regarded as belonging to a third gender, neither male nor female but possessing attributes and assuming the roles of both. They are perceived to have special power as a result of this liminal positioning. As a result, they often assume important leadership roles within their communities as conciliators, healers, matchmakers, keepers of communal history and wisdom, tribal leaders, and so on.

Ongoing Implications

Interest in issues related to the concept of sexual identity is an ongoing concern driving research in anthropology, history, psychology, sociology, and many other social sciences. In the humanities, critical-cultural studies—especially the growing body of scholarship and critique that goes by the name of queer theory—continues to explore the cultural, personal, political, religious, and social implications of sexual identity, even as some scholars within that tradition question the legitimacy of defining people in terms of fixed sexual identity. These and other related issues are not merely of academic interest. The continuing debate raging around the legal status of gay marriage is just one indication that the personal and political consequences associated with sexual identity will remain a mainstay of identity politics for years to come. If recent and current trends are any indication, the study of sexual identity promises to be an interesting and fruitful focus of research and scholarship during the first century of the new millennium.

Robert Westerfelhaus and Celeste Lacroix

See also Diversity; Gay; Gender; Queer Theory; Sexual Identity

Further Readings

Baldwin, G., & Bean, J. (1993). *Ties that bind: The SM/leather/fetish erotic style: Issues, commentaries and advice*. Los Angeles: Daedalus.

Foucault, M. (1990). *The history of sexuality: Vol. 1. An introduction*. New York: Random House.

Foucault, M. (1990). *The history of sexuality: Vol. 2. The use of pleasure*. New York: Random House.

Foucault, M. (1990). *The history of sexuality: Vol. 3. The care of the self*. New York: Random House.

Kimmel, M. S., & Plante, R. F. (Eds.). (2004). *Sexualities: Behaviors, identities, society*. Oxford, UK: Oxford University Press.

Kinsey, A. C., Pomeroy, W. B., & Martin, C. E. (1948). *Sexual behavior in the human male*. Philadelphia: W. B. Saunders.

Kinsey, A. C., Pomeroy, W. B., Martin, C. E., & Gebhard, P. (1953). *Sexual behavior in the human female*. Philadelphia: W. B. Saunders.

Krafft-Ebing, R. von. (1998). *Psychopathia sexualis*. New York: Arcade. (Original work published 1886)

Laumann, E. O., Gagnon, J. H., Michael, R. T., & Michaels, S. (1994). *The social organization of sexuality: Sexual practices in the United States.* Chicago: University of Chicago Press.

Laumann, E. O., Michael, R. T., & Kolata, G. (1995). *Sex in America: A definitive study.* New York: Warner.

Mead, M. (2001). *Coming of age in Samoa: A psychological study of primitive youth for Western civilisation.* New York: Harper. (Original work published 1930)

SIGNIFICATION

Signification is the process of using language, directly or indirectly, in a creative and clever way to verbally assault or attack an opponent. The opponent is signified on (i.e., verbally goaded) by the signifier (i.e., the speaker). Signification, or *signifyin'*, as it is called in African American vernacular discourse, requires that a speaker demonstrate a great deal of verbal dexterity to outwit the opponent. Other names that are synonymous or associated with *signifyin'* include *crackin', cappin', jonin', soundin',* and *playing the dozens.* By playing this ritualized type of game, speakers are communicating their cultural identity. This entry explores signification as African American discourse, characteristics of signification, and "Yo Momma" as the quintessential example of signification.

Signification as African American Discourse

Signification is a form of African American discourse. African American discourse is spoken communication by people of African descent such as sermons, speeches, poetry, rap, call and response, and so forth. Molefi Asante's preferred term for African American discourse is *orature,* which is an all-encompassing term for the body of work produced by Africans in the United States. Nevertheless, African American discourse is grounded in a West African oral tradition that recognizes the role of the spoken word in the transmission of culture. In African and African American culture, the beliefs, values, ideals, and knowledge of a people are communicated orally through the spoken word rather than the written code. Through signifyin', African American speakers communicate humor and wit, as well as selfhood and identity.

Nommo

An important concept in African American discourse that affects signification is *nommo.* Nommo is the magical or generative power of the word; it is the spiritual force behind the word. In the African worldview, the spoken word produced by the chief of the village or by the village doctor has the power to heal or effect change in the minds of the audience. The power of the word can cause the audience to emote.

This phenomenon is also true within an African American communication context. An example of this is the wielding of the power of nommo by the preacher in the traditional Black church. At the center of the Black preacher's delivery of the sermon is the presence of nommo. The classic example of the manifestation of nommo in the mind and soul of the Black audience is as follows: After leaving the church, one parishioner says to the other, "Rev sure did preach today. My soul was fed. I don't know what he said, but he sure did sound good." This statement shows that the power of nommo is not just in *what* (content of sermon) is being said, but in *how* the sermon is communicated to the audience.

The magical power of nommo is present in signification as well as in the delivery of a sermon. The centrality of nommo in the delivery of a speaker verbally mocking or jeering an opponent is paramount. Nommo is the generative force that gives the sarcastic or scornful language its sting and is the generative force behind the scornful words that creates tension between opponents that must be relieved through ritualized verbal play but not physical violence. In the end, victory goes to the speaker who can best an opponent with nommo and word play without resorting to physical harm. Whoever throws the first blow loses the game.

In addition to playing a critical role in the speaker's delivery, nommo is also the generative force behind other modes of discourse that are present in signification such as tonal semantics and improvisation. Tonal semantics is the use of the voice to convey meaning, and improvisation is the ability to perform without preparation. Nommo is the force behind the speaker's use of tonal semantics. So, when a speaker retorts with, "Ahhhhhhhhhhhh sh$@," nommo is manifested in the voice and conveys the following meaning: "Man, you done really messed up now, it's on!!" The best example of the power of nommo behind improvisation is the quick retort: "Yo momma!"

Characteristics of Signification

Verbal Dexterity

In addition to the concept of nommo, other characteristics of signification help us further understand the phenomenon. One of those characteristics is verbal dexterity. Verbal dexterity is the ability of a speaker to be skilled or proficient in the use of language. A speaker who is skilled in the use of language will have a keen understanding of code-switching. While under verbal assault, the speaker will quickly switch from the use of pun to a one-liner. Players may name-call, and then switch to the use of tonal semantics to irritate opponents. However, if the speaker's use of the verbal fails, then gamers may attack opponents by using non-verbal hand gestures such as the "middle finger." Signification requires that a speaker be proficient and skilled in the use of style—both verbal and nonverbal.

Participant as Rhetorician and Wordsmith

Another characteristic of signification is participant as rhetorician and wordsmith. Signification requires that participants be skilled in the art of persuasion and the use of style. As rhetoricians, participants rely on the creative use of language to attack their opponents and influence the audience.

Moreover, those who have mastered the art of signifyin' are also skilled in their ability to wield the power of nommo. Having a command of the transformative power of verbal expression is a key attribute of the participant as rhetorician in the ritualized game of signification. Victory goes to the rhetorician who can control the power of nommo the best.

Those *siggin'* are also master wordsmiths. They have a variety of concepts to choose from in their rhetorical tool bags. When engaging their opponents, they rely on the use of one-liners, punning,

obscenities, word play, gestures, tonal semantics, humor, and rhyming. As suggested earlier, when nommo is the force behind the word, the participant is a rhetorical threat to an opponent.

Audience as Participant

The audience as participant is another characteristic of signification. Rarely is signification played in isolation. The game is usually played in the presence of friends, associates, or onlookers. Moreover, the audience can and often does participate in the game. Richard Majors and Janet Mancini Billson suggest that the audience's role in the game is to act as a catalyst by magnifying the insults, egging the participants on or "upping the ante" with their own verbal assaults. For example, an audience participant might up the ante by saying the following: "Dog, you goin' let Mr. Ugly talk about yo momma like dat. You better get on him." Game members are presented with a unique challenge by audience participants. Participants have to engage in a verbal assault with each other, and they must verbally duel with audience members. To do this, a great deal of skill and tact is needed in negotiating and managing the communication interaction between all parties involved. Signification demands that participants multitask while engaging each other in the context of the game.

Cool Pose

Another characteristic of signification involves the notion of cool pose. According to Majors and Billson, *cool pose* is the public persona that African Americans, particularly males, wear to maintain a sense of coolness while under pressure. A cool pose allows Black males to convey a "hardcore" masculine image in the face of other Black males who may attempt to "try" (to confront in a negative way) them on the urban streets of the United States to see how tough they are. African American males often demonstrate the cool pose image through stylish dress, verbal cunning, quick wit, and an aggressive attitude.

Black males and Black females must manage this persona during the playing of the game as a way of maintaining a cool posture in the face of verbal assault. Signifyin' requires that participants not give the impression that they are timid. To be perceived as being weak gives the opponent a chance to attack. While signifyin', participants must manage a "hardcore" persona despite insults about one's mother to demonstrate control of the situation if they want to win.

"Yo Momma!"

A specific type of signification that must be discussed is called *playing the dozens, the dozens,* or if obscenities are involved, *playing the dirty dozens.* "The dozens" has its origins on the slave blocks in New Orleans, Louisiana, during the 19th century, where enslaved Africans who had deformities or were disfigured were sold cheaply by the dozen. To be sold to a slave trader as part of a dozen was degrading and viewed as an insult. Thus, to play the dozens is to make insulting remarks about one's opponent.

As with signification, playing the dozens requires that opponents be skilled in speech. Verbal dexterity, quick thinking, wit, and mental toughness are important attributes to have to be a successful player. Moreover, insults about each other's mothers are commonplace during the playing of the game.

Deconstructing "Yo Momma"

Geneva Smitherman suggests that the most recognized and most common example of *signifyin'* or playing the dozens is *yo momma* or *ask yo (ya) momma.* An example of a "yo momma" joke is as follows: Speaker #1—Man, you are butt-ugly; Speaker #2—Just like yo momma! Another example is this: Speaker #1—Man, what do you want to have next? Speaker #2—Yo momma! As these examples show, "yo momma" is a powerful counter-argument because it is used as a retort. A retort is an insulting or witty statement that turns the words of the speaker back upon himself or herself; it is a quick and creative reply to a charge or accusation.

What makes "yo momma" rhetorical is the word choice of the players. For example, *yo* is a powerful term as slang. Its power lies in its brevity. It is a truncated form of the word *your.* Moreover, *yo* is a much more creative and clever term than *your.* As an exclamation, the term communicates emotion and feeling. *Yo* is also used to show greetings in some speech communities.

Momma is the other term that makes up the stylistic content of the message. *Momma* is the African American vernacular word for mother. And as a result, *momma* has a completely different meaning for African Americans, particularly African American males. In White U.S. culture, mother is the biological female parent. Although this is also true in African American culture, *momma* is also the nonbiological parent who "raised" the African American male and kept him or got him out of trouble. Carlos Morrison and Celnisha Dangerfield posit that "momma" or "the mama complex," which is deeply rooted in African American and hip-hop culture, is symbolic of deep love, strength, and perseverance in the face of adversity, such as "raising" the African American male in an urban society. As a result of the meaning associated with the word, insults marshaled against "momma" are particularly hurtful as well as powerful, and always up the ante of the game.

Signification or signifyin' requires that a speaker demonstrate control over nommo—the generative power of the word to outwit an opponent. Characteristics associated with signification include verbal dexterity, participant as rhetorician and wordsmith, audience as participant, and cool pose. Through signification, participants communicate their cultural identity as African Americans through the telling of "yo momma" jokes. "Yo momma" jokes are the most recognizable type of signifyin' or playing the dozens in the African American community.

Carlos D. Morrison

See also Code-Switching; Dialect; Discourse; Impression Management; Language Variety in Literature; Rhetoric; Trickster Figure

Further Readings

Abrahams, R. D. (1970). *Deep down in the jungle: Negro narrative from the streets of Philadelphia.* Chicago: Aldine.

Asante, M. K. (1998). *The Afrocentric idea.* Philadelphia: Temple University Press.

Baugh, J. (1983). *Black street speech: Its history, structure, and survival.* Austin: University of Texas Press.

Kochaman, T. (1972). *Rappin' and stylin' out: Communication in urban Black America*. Chicago: University of Illinois Press.

Majors, R., & Billson, M. J. (1992). *Cool pose: The dilemmas of Black manhood in America*. New York: Lexington Books.

Smitherman, G. (1977). *Talkin and testifyin: The language of Black America*. Detroit, MI: Wayne State University Press.

SIMULACRA

The notion of the *simulacra* has become a prominent concept in a postmodern digitalized culture as the question of representing reality has become more and more of a contested zone; the belief that a sign can refer to and be exchanged for guaranteed meaning has been challenged. However, the notion of the simulacrum is an historical phenomenon predating our contemporary society, always centering its concerns in the efficacy of the image. Stemming from the Latin root *simulare*, "to make like, to put on an appearance of," simulacra raise the worth of the copy in relation to the original. An image, having internalized its own repetition, begins to question the authority and legitimacy of the original model. In a social order where the reproduction of images and goods has become a standard economic practice, the meaning of simulacra has become crucial when questions emerge concerning the identity of—what is and is not—the genuine article, like the knockoff designer goods sold in various parts of Asia.

Two versions of the concept of simulacra have emerged in postmodernity: one negative—that of Jean Baudrillard—and the other positive—that of Giles Deleuze. Both rethink Plato's initial denouncement of copies as simply deceptive idols that are nothing more than false semblances. The relationship between copy and original for Plato is merely an external relation of similitude, rather than one of intrinsic and essential resemblance as would be the case of Siamese twins for instance. This later relationship is also theorized by Plato as a good copy, an icon that *does* participate in the idea of the original. Each twin, for instance, could iconically participate in the ideal form of man or woman. In contrast, a bad copy can be illustrated in Pliny's account of the battle between the master painters Parrhasius and Zeuxis to capture the realness of life on canvas. The grapes that Zeuxis paints are indeed "real" and are pecked at by birds. However, they have no taste and bear only an external appearance. They do not participate in the original idea of "grape-ness." This entry explores the Baudriallardian simulacra and the Deleuzian simulacra in turn.

Baudrillardian Simulacra

Baudrillard, the scourge of analytic philosophers, presents us with the negative notion of the simulacra by conceiving the simulacrum as the copy of a copy, which then produces an effect of identity whereby the grounding in an original simply drops out. The authentic original no longer serves any purpose. This leads to a hyperreality where it seems the "real" has disappeared, or rather, the referent of the copy can no longer be located or even needs to be located. He identifies the modern means of mechanical reproduction, namely photography and film, as the beginning of this slide toward hyperreality. Baudrillard traces a historical trajectory of the changing reference of the sign that leads to this postmodern condition. He begins with the uncontested representation of the sign as the basic reflection of reality; he then moves through to the sign's emancipation from the feudal world in the Renaissance as a *counterfeit sign*; from there, he moves on to the industrial commodity where signs become unhinged, yet a pretense to reality is maintained, although there is no model of it (e.g., the "original" bottle of Coca-Cola as the "Real thing"); and finally he reaches the emergence of hyperreality of the simulacrum that has no relation to reality whatsoever. In brief, seeing the transformation of the object into a sign in capitalist consumption becomes a simulacrum of the real object. This reduction of reality to sign values means that *the symbolic as the lived character of the world* is lost. The spheres of reproduction (fashion, media, publicity, information and communication networks) become the codes of the simulacra upon which the global processes of capital are founded. Institutionally sanctioned signs of the real are substituted for the real itself, which Baudrillard calls the *simulation model*.

For Baudrillard, the simulacrum is the dominant discourse of postmodernity. Reality has become a product of the sign as a simulacrum of the symbolic. Lived reality is reduced to sign value and sign exchange. Designer capitalism of the simulacra designates, abstracts, and rationalizes a separate sphere that devalues its actual referent. The "real" of the sign is therefore imaginary, a phantasm or "reality-effect" that overrides the symbolic as lived, yet unsignifiable reality. There is no longer any obligation or recourse to any legitimate ground or any presuppositions of resemblance outside simulacra's own immanent effects. Reality is submitted to the repetitions of its codes. The simulation model of the simulacra is judged strictly on its performative value—namely, how well the model operates given that it produces its own heuristic truth that is confirmed through its operation. Because the code of the simulacra answers only to its own functionality, those who control the code can easily fall into a cynicism. Manipulating the code is what the "real" is all about, which has shown to be true with such fraud scandals as Enron and WorldCom that are just tips of these floating global icebergs. Profit margins are to be manipulated to keep up with the market shares to ensure investment and trust in the company. Baudrillard maintains that this loss of the symbolic "scene" results in *obscenity* where the excesses of overexposure, overrepresentation and oversignification fall into an all-too-visible realm, whereby the rule of "disenchanted simulacra" drains desire from reality, presenting us with a hypervisible, pornographic, exhibitionistic, and banal reality to which we have nothing to add. The real is faced not as something living, but as something dead.

Deleuzian Simulacra

Deleuze develops a more positive notion of the simulacra in a surprising way: He recognizes its disruptive powers. The history of the simulacrum is also the history of the image and its reception. The power of the image in the West has long been recognized as a threat to the real (to reality) as being truly demonic, taking hold of the viewer's psyche. Every effort is made to limit its efficacy, to banish this side of it as an "evil demon," and domesticate it as a "good" reflective image. The image as copy participates in or acquires the properties of the represented. However briefly, it

becomes "real." Mimesis therefore transforms the imitational image into the original. The erasure of distinction threatens the original and all the authority associated with it. For instance, anthropologists noted that upon seeing their photographs, aboriginal people felt that their souls (as their imagined double) had been captured and stolen from them. The Judeo-Christian separation of sacred and profane—Christ as God made flesh—enabled a psychic way to subdue this "pagan" belief in the demonic threat of the image by seeing (imaging and imagining) the material world as a deficient reality compared with the purified transcendental sacred realm. The image could no longer attain its "real" idol-like status, but became subject to mediation and reflection. Because of the image's nihilistic power to unground all foundations for truth and falsity, it threatens to overturn ontological and epistemological traditions that ground the West. Deleuze therefore identifies this effect as being positive in the way a model or privileged position is challenged. The simulacrum contains a positive that negates both the original and bad copy, both model and reproduction, thus removing the possibility of distinction between truth and falsity.

For Friedrich Nietzsche, the murder of our transcendent guarantor of meaning, value, and significance (be it God or Science) leads to the nihilism of a cold, empty universe, but the saving grace is a *will to power* associated with his notion of the eternal return. Deleuze latches on to this idea by evoking the "powers of the false" as another name for this *will to power,* which the simulacrum can evoke by producing an effect that subverts the icon and the world of representation. This positive simulation is described in terms of Nietzsche's eternal return. Artists, in this sense, are placed in a privilege position, creating simulacra for the potential of becoming through their will-to-deceive. Artists play with appearances—selecting, correcting, redoubling, and affirming them to produce a "truth affect." Truth itself becomes an appearance. Each repetition does not necessarily lead to sameness but introduces difference by extracting a potential that is already immanent within the representation.

The "power of the false" has no being on its own: It is not grounded in any teleological truth or origin. It is merely an appearance that passes from one repetition to another by becoming other than itself. There is a certain self-enjoyment in such repetitive expression and self-invention. This is not a nihilistic gesture, for it frees the artist from the supposed stable identities and essences that constitute the "true'" world. Through the false, which becomes possible through the creation of images or masks, the powers for transformation of an object, a historical role or a collective institution, begin to emerge. The eternal return that marks a difference is therefore a revelatory procedure, although the narrative is not fully known, it is a thought of the future. Thus, such a notion of the simulacra overcomes the original as well as the good and bad copy as Plato envisioned them in the distance from which they participate in the transcendental ideal forms.

Deleuze's appropriation of Nietzsche overturns Plato and celebrates appearance over any form of idealism. For Nietzsche, there is no image that cannot be subverted by difference and divergence; there is no identity that is so well-grounded that it is not haunted by masks that can virtually exploit the potential that is as yet unactualized—the power to become someone else, assume another role, and so on. An actor can repeat a role only by playing other roles, each repetition being a theatrical space that offers an expression for potential metamorphosis. The experience of repetition of the simulacrum becomes the masked return of difference. The simulacrum's true nature is therefore the potential for variation and displacement that haunt it.

Closeness of the Two Positions

It may well be said that the Baudrillard and Deleuze notions of the simulacra in the end come together in their own mutual ways when maintaining that appearances can be positive for change through imperceptible difference. With Deleuze, this is by appropriating the Nietzschean notion of the eternal return and the "powers of false." For Baudrillard, it becomes the order of *seduction* as a way of mastering the realm of appearances in a game of signs, creating a symbolic relationship with other participants or witnesses, with the order of appearances or with the world itself. Baudrillard pits an "enchanted simulation" against the "disenchanted simulacrum" that hegemonically rules the

order of truth. The former turns the "evil forces" of appearance against the order of truth. Further, Baudrillard also rejected any simple empirical methodology. This would be an impossibility given his characterization of hyperreality. Hence, he too advocated a theory of the false, maintaining that theory should not be true, but should provoke antagonistic opposition of its own making. Such a position follows the creative use of philosophy Deleuze advocated bringing both positions close to one another when it comes to the affirmation of simulacra.

jan jagodzinski

See also Gaze; Scopophilia; Visualizing Desire

Further Readings

Baudrillard, J. (1994). *Simulacra and simulation.* Ann Arbor: University of Michigan Press.

Deleuze, G. (1983). Plato and the simulacrum. *October, 27,* 45–56.

Deleuze, G. (1994). *Difference and repetition* (P. Patton, Trans.). London: Athlone Press.

Merrin, W. (2005). *Baudrillard and the media: A critical introduction.* Cambridge, UK: Polity Press.

Zurbrugg, N. (Ed.). (1997). *Jean Baudrillard: Art and artefact.* London: Sage.

SOCIAL CAPITAL

Social capital is a popular interdisciplinary concept, and yet its origin, meaning, use, and value are highly contested. To begin with, many attribute the origin of social capital to either U.S. political scientist Robert Putnam or French sociologist Pierre Bourdieu. In his renowned text *Bowling Alone: The Collapse and Revival of American Community,* however, Putnam credits the term *social capital* to scholars that long preceded his time, including Lyda J. Hanifan, Yves Dubé, J. E. Howes, D. L. McQueen, Jane Jacobs, Glenn Loury, Pierre Bourdieu, and James Coleman. Although the term *social capital* was used far before the works of Putnam and even Bourdieu, Bourdieu is most often accredited with bringing the term into use in the field of sociology. One's identity status influences one's social capital, whether social capital is conceived in terms of what social organizations or networks one is allowed to join, or how one can function within these groups.

The Meanings of Social Capital

The meaning of social capital varies depending on the approach of authors using the term in their work. Just recently via a thorough review of sociological research, Gregory M. Fulkerson and Gretchen H. Thompson identified two overarching positions in the conceptual debate: (1) normative social capitalists and (2) resource social capitalists. Normative social capitalists fall in alignment with the works of Coleman, who conceptualized social capital with strong regard to social organization at the macrolevels of community and civil society. Strongly influenced by Coleman, this position on social capital is thought to underscore community development, engagement, and action. In essence, by having a shared stake in social capital, community members and communities work together for mutual benefit. In 1988, Coleman described social capital as a means for actors (individuals or corporations) to control certain resources and share a vested interest in those resources. In this context, social capital is considered a valuable and productive entity. Coleman also described social capital as depending on trust and obligations held among actors; for Coleman forms of social capital include but are not limited to information that facilitates potential action, cultural norms, and joint obligations and expectations.

Expanding Coleman's conceptualization, Robert Putnam, Robert Leonardi, and Raffaella Y. Nanetti highlight elements of social capital that play an exceptionally strong role in civically engaged communities, including trust, values, norms of reciprocity, and networks. Operating from this perspective, social bonds (i.e., social capital) are instrumental in any given community movement to achieve particular goals or overcome specific struggles. For example, if a community wants to take action against local crime, the presence of social capital is thought to make the process and the outcome of taking action far more productive. In this sense, social capital is likely to influence community livelihood and, by subsequent relation, individual life

opportunity as well. Given the focus on macrocontexts espoused by normative social capitalists, social capital in this sense can also be extended to understanding how states, regions, and even nations collectively operate. In the global sense, these authors also note how the lack of social capital can inhibit a region's ability to effectively contribute to and draw from a dynamic economy.

By comparison, resource social capitalists fall in alignment with the works of Bourdieu who conceptualized social capital as a means to access and distribute power and privilege at the microlevel. The basic premise of Bourdieu's argument was that the structure and functioning of the hierarchical social world cannot be fully understood without considering how capital operates among individuals. Therefore, whereas normative social capitalists take a communal approach toward social capital, resource social capitalists highlight how social capital creates and maintains structures of inequality through individual and subsequently collective access to capital. For Bourdieu, the significance of social capital is rooted in its emphasis on the role of others in the determination of self-worth. As such, individuals with access to social capital belong to groups of people who via relational networks share their capital. Thus, the value of one's social capital depends on the number of connections an individual can secure, along with the capital that each member of a group has. In this context, social capital is endlessly reproduced by social exchange and often via power, protected by gatekeepers to limit who has access. Given the value of social capital, it can be used to barter for and attain additional forms of capital (i.e., cultural or economic) as well. In a similar vein, Alejandro Portes offers three aspects of social capital closely related to Bourdieu's initial conceptualization: (1) social control (i.e., power), (2) family-mediated benefits, and (3) access to nonfamily networks. To offer an additional differentiation between normative social capitalists and resource social capitalists, social capital is an attribute of the individual accrued via small group networks for the latter, whereas for the former, social capital is an attribute of the community itself.

Although Fulkerson and Thompson label and highlight the respective differences between what they term *normative social capitalists* and *resource social capitalists,* definitive lines have not been drawn in the field of sociology or elsewhere. Thus, there are notable similarities between the scholars whose work has fueled the use of social capital as a means to critique individuals at the microlevel or communities at the macrolevel. For example, both Bourdieu and Coleman conceptualized social capital in relation to the shared resources among individuals and families. In addition, both Coleman and Putnam advocated for social capital to be applied in the understanding of larger social communities, social structures, and civic engagement. Furthermore, most authors who rely upon social capital as a means to examine lived experience, social realities, and social organizations agree that social capital greatly affects levels of agency and the quality of life.

Social Capital Remains Contested

Despite numerous scholars who have attempted to refine and clearly conceptualize—and, in many instances, may agree about the meaning of—*social capital,* this term remains highly contested for a variety of different reasons. Disagreements about the origin and meanings of social capital remain, and strong critiques of the value and use of social capital have arisen as well. For example, Portes calls for scholars to resist assuming that social capital has a steadily positive impact on individuals or communities. Hence, group solidarity and social support are not always positive in intent or outcome. In a similar vein, in a book titled *The Rise of the Creative Class: And How It's Transforming Work, Leisure, Community, and Everyday Life,* Richard Florida cautions against "bonding" social capital, which can stymie community innovation when groups become too homogenous and exclusive.

Articulations of Social Capital Beyond Sociology

Social capital has been conceptualized to examine diverse phenomena in several different fields including but not limited to education, politics, economics, urban development, sport, and violence. For example, in the field of education social capital has been applied to student achievement, faculty promotion, and tenure for scholars of color. Social capital has also been used in the realm of politics to evaluate political participation and civic engagement. Taking the economic route, researchers have used social capital to explore economic growth and development in metropolitan areas and poverty as well. Likewise, others have explored social capital in the context of sport as it relates to trust, building community, and civic engagement. Social capital (or the lack thereof) has also been identified by researchers as an important factor in parenting styles, relationships, and family violence. Extending the discussion of social capital further, in *The Dynamics of Violence in Central Africa,* Rene Lemarchand addresses how social capital has played a role in the violent and genocidal conditions in North Kivu.

Additional Forms of Capital

Scholars such as Bourdieu and Coleman theorized additional forms of capital (i.e., economic and cultural/human capital) that work in tandem with social capital. Along with the conceptualization of social capital, Bourdieu also articulated cultural and economic capital. Cultural capital (a similar conceptualization is referred to as "human capital" by Coleman) may exist in three different states: embodied, objectified, or institutionalized. *Embodied cultural capital* refers to personal characteristics housed within an individual such as knowledge or determination. *Objectified cultural capital* takes on material or symbolic form such as talent. *Institutionalized* cultural capital entails an institutional recognition of power such as a degree certification or skill endorsement. By comparison, *economic capital* was defined as that which can immediately be transformed into money and may or may not be institutionalized as property rights. For Bourdieu, all three forms of capital that he proposed (i.e., social, economic, and cultural) are mitigating factors of equality, opportunity, and access. Furthermore, Bourdieu argued that all forms of capital are derived from economic capital and can (under certain conditions) be transformed into economic capital. Generally speaking across multiple works, the forms of capital provide a language to discuss various indications of worth that influence people's lives.

Rachel A. Griffin

See also Civic Identity; Cultural Capital; Culture; Diversity

Further Readings

Bourdieu, P. (1997). The forms of capital. In
N. W. Biggart (Ed.), *Readings in economic sociology*
(pp. 280–291). Malden, MA: Blackwell.

Coleman, J. S. (1993). Social capital in the creation of
human capital. *American Journal of Sociology, 94,*
S95–S120.

Fulkerson, G. M., & Thompson, G. H. (2008). The
evolution of a contested concept: A meta-analysis of
social capital definitions and trends (1988–2006).
Sociological Inquiry, 78(4), 536–557.

Portes, A. (1998). Social capital: Its origins and
applications in modern sociology. *Annual Sociology,*
24(1), 1–24.

Putnam, R. (2002). *Bowling alone: The collapse and
revival of American community.* New York: Simon &
Schuster.

Putnam, R., Leonardi, R., & Nanetti, R. (1993). *Making
democracy work: Civic traditions in modern Italy.*
Princeton, NJ: Princeton University Press.

SOCIAL COMPARISON THEORY

Generally speaking, as one of many theories and concepts dedicated to understanding the self, social comparison theory can be described as a sociological framework that addresses the complex process of self-evaluation to further one's understanding of one's identity. This entry begins with a historical overview and then discusses historical and current understandings and applications of social comparison theory.

Historical Overview

The formal articulation of social comparison theory can be traced back to Leon Festinger who published an article titled "A Theory of Social Comparison Processes" in 1954 that called attention to the ways that self-knowledge and social knowledge are connected. More specifically, people learn and draw conclusions about who they are by comparing themselves with who they perceive other people to be. Festinger's original essay and a subsequent symposium paper titled "Motivation Leading to Social Behavior" placed specific emphasis on how comparison information was used rather than on how comparison information was

acquired. In his original works, Festinger examined how people socially evaluated their opinions and abilities compared with similar others (rather than dissimilar others) when there was a lack of objective information to base comparisons on. He noted that dissimilar others were not used for social comparison to generate accurate information about the self. Likewise, those who were selected for comparison represented similarities along abilities, opinions, and characteristics that were deemed relevant by the person drawing comparisons. At the foundation of Festinger's early work was the assertion that people have the desire to perform well, rather than worse than or even equal to, compared with similar others. Within his theoretical premise, he also highlighted how pressures toward uniformity were relevant as well. In essence, being similar to, in alignment with, or competitive with those held in high regard as representatives of what is good, correct, or appropriate fosters positive perceptions of the self. Essentially, these individuals serve as favorable role models to whom the comparer wants to measure up.

Although Festinger's original essay was relatively overlooked for a number of years and sparked only a minimal amount of scholarly research, social comparison theory resurfaced in 1966 with an issue of the *Journal of Experimental Social Psychology* dedicated to its examination. The first book on social comparison theory titled *Social Comparison Processes: Theoretical and Empirical Perspectives,* edited by social psychologists Jerry Suls and Richard Miller, emerged 11 years after the special issue. Since these two major publications, social comparison theory has become a staple in social psychological research.

Understandings of Social Comparison Theory

At the foundation of social comparison theory is the desire to succeed in implicit or explicit competition with others as a means to engage in identity formation. Reflecting on William James's historical essay on the self, Suls asserts that people engage in social comparison only when the element being compared is salient to their self-definition. Although these two points of emphasis are rooted in Festinger's work, which remains highly acclaimed, social comparison theory has since been extended in many ways. Inspired by his work, researchers have examined the desire for self-enhancement and the desire for self-improvement as motivating factors for individuals to engage in social comparison in addition to Festinger's emphasis on self-evaluation. The roots of social comparison theory also highlight how individuals evaluate their opinions and abilities via social comparison and were substantially extended to include comparisons of affiliation, fear, threat, and emotion by Stanley Schachter in 1959. For example, Schachter's work indicated that social comparisons were used by individuals to ascertain whether their affective responses were appropriate in specific situations. In addition to the inroads made regarding what people tend to compare, research has also indicated that comparisons can be made at the individual level (micro) as personal comparisons or at the group level (macro) as categorical comparisons. When engaging in group comparisons, evaluations may be intragroup (comparisons within a particular group) or intergroup (comparisons between two groups). Researchers have also termed the need for social comparison information as *social comparison orientation*.

The outcomes of social comparison often entail self-judgments, either favorable or unfavorable. People seek comparisons for characteristics, skills, opinions, abilities, and so forth that are salient to them and heavily desire the evaluation to result in a favorable outcome for themselves. However, in the case of a negative comparison outcome in which an individual's result is unfavorable, Brenda Major, Maria Testa, and Wayne H. Bylsma assert that levels of perceived control over the characteristic or ability being socially evaluated in accordance with others will influence self-blame. For example, if someone loses their health insurance because they become unemployed, the amount of self-blame will likely be influenced by the contextual circumstances (e.g., bad economy, being fired, quitting) surrounding their job loss.

Downward and Upward Social Comparisons

Festinger's original work has also led to the differentiation between downward and upward comparisons. Downward comparisons, originating with the work of Tom Wills in 1981, occur when individuals select people to judge themselves against who are likely not to fare well to increase the individuals'

subjective well-being. Wills argues that the likelihood of such comparisons increases when someone perceives threat or is experiencing stress. Individuals engage in downward comparisons to feel better about their abilities, opinions, or social standing. Therefore, people with low levels of self-esteem or self-confidence are more likely to make downward comparisons because comparing one's self with someone who is less fortunate or who is socially positioned as inferior is often used to increase one's sense of well-being, self-esteem, and self-confidence while decreasing one's sense of risk, inadequacy, or vulnerability. In this vein, although a highly contested area of social comparison research, downward comparisons can also be understood as coping mechanisms for personal struggles such as disease, addiction, and destructive behaviors. Beyond Wills's early work, the examination of downward comparisons is often found in research that addresses stereotyping, fear, perceived threat, humor, or scapegoating. Although downward comparisons have been associated with feeling better about oneself, more secure, and experiencing uplifted moods, downward comparisons do not necessarily change social standing, levels of ability, or levels of correctness. Thus, although a person may feel better about himself or herself, the salient characteristic of comparison is likely to remain the same.

In contrast to downward comparisons, upward comparisons entail individuals comparing themselves with someone who embodies a salient aspect of the comparer's identity. For example, if a male youth aspires to be a professional basketball player, then he may evaluate his athletic talents in comparison with an athlete he greatly admires. In this context, although upward comparisons may seem self-defeating, such comparisons can serve as a source of positive inspiration in group affiliation, role models, access to information, and self-improvement. More specifically, upward comparisons can be a source of positive esteem because individuals tend to seek and expect to find markers of congruence between themselves and the admired social other. Therefore, in this example, the male youth may lay claim to the similarities he perceives between himself and his idol; perhaps they come from similar neighborhoods and excel at the same special move on the court. Researchers indicate that upward comparisons in U.S. society are virtually unavoidable and thus arguably forced because members of the upper classes, such as celebrities, are highly visible via social institutions such as the media.

Examination of the Self

Since its inception, social comparison theory has been closely linked with theories of attribution, affiliation, appraisal, reflected appraisal, equity, social identity theory, and self-categorization theory and, perhaps most notably, is quite relevant to Festinger's later work, which generated the theory of cognitive dissonance. In an article titled "Social Comparison Theory: Psychology from the Lost and Found," George R. Goethals positions Festinger's original work and subsequent publications in the myriad of theories and concepts dedicated to understanding the self, including but not limited to self-concept, self-perception, self-attribution, self-awareness, self-schemata, self-esteem, self-appraisal, and self-image. To generate self-understanding via the examination of social comparison, methods used include but are not limited to comparison selection, reaction effects, ratings, narrative, and social comparison records maintained by research participants.

Contemporary Applications of Social Comparison Theory

In recent years, social comparison theory has become far more interdisciplinary. Researchers have extended its reach beyond social psychology to areas such as education, physical appearance, health, and media. For example, in *Bullying in American Schools*, Dorothy L. Espelage and Susan M. Swearer link social comparison theory to the possible reasons why bystanders typically do not intervene in bullying situations. In addition, researchers have addressed the role of social comparison theory in relation to body image, eating disorders, and media representation. See, for example, *Body Image: Understanding Body Dissatisfaction in Men, Women, and Children* by Sarah Grogan and *The Media and Body Image: If Looks Could Kill* by Maggie Wykes and Barrie Gunter. A significant amount of research regarding the relationship between health and social comparison looks particularly at breast cancer and the role of support groups in treatment and the

role of social comparison in decisions regarding the risks of AIDS/HIV and safe sex. Finally, take, for instance *Adolescents, Media and the Law* by Roger Levesque, which specifically highlights the role of social comparison theory relative to the media and adolescent development.

Rachel A. Griffin

See also Cognitive Dissonance Theory; Collective/Social Identity; Self-Affirmation Theory; Self-Image; Social Identity Theory

Further Readings

Festinger, L. (1954). Motivation leading to social behavior. In M. R. Jones (Ed.), *Nebraska symposium on motivation, 1954*. Lincoln: University of Nebraska Press.

Festinger, L. (1954). A theory of social comparison processes. *Human Relations, 7*, 117–140.

Suls, J. (1986). Notes on the occasion of social comparison theory's thirtieth birthday. *Personality and Social Psychology Bulletin, 12*(3), 289–296.

Suls, J., & Miller, R. L. (Eds.). (1977). *Social comparison processes: Theoretical and empirical perspectives.* Washington, DC: Hemisphere.

Suls, J., & Wheeler, L. (2000). A selective history of classic and neo-social comparison theory. In J. Suls & L. Wheeler (Eds.), *Handbook of social comparison: Theory and research* (pp. 3–19). New York: Kluwer Academic/Plenum.

Wills, T. A. (1986). Discussion remarks on social comparison theory. *Personality and Social Psychology Bulletin, 12*(3), 282–288.

SOCIAL CONSTRUCTIONIST APPROACH TO PERSONAL IDENTITY

A *social constructionist* perspective conceives that personal identity is established within the perception of *self* as derived from thoughtful reflection on communicative interactions between oneself and others from the societal environment. With a pragmatic approach and drawing from the work of George Herbert Mead, among others, social constructionists assume that significant communication is coordinated meaning among individuals where each can take the perspective of the other regarding his or her own gestures and symbols. Where this *reflexive objectification* of the self occurs, personal identity is uniquely socialized, and one chooses how to live within society. Identity is not static, but evolves throughout life in ongoing, dynamic social interaction. The conceptual framework of personal identity includes social construction of identity via the generalized other, communication, the *I* and *me* of identity, and the evolution of identity throughout a life span, resulting in an accumulated identity with many roles within a society.

Personal Identity as Socially Constructed

Personal identity is not a priori, but is formed through interactions with the social world. Experiencing the attitudes, values, and beliefs of the social community, known as the *generalized other,* precedes the establishment of one's personal identity with particular and unique attitudes, values, and beliefs. While one interacts within a societal context, one encounters the norms of a given social environment (the generalized other), which can call one to reflect on the perspective of those norms and decide whether to align with them or to function otherwise than social convention.

Encountering the generalized other allows a person to experience who he or she is as a person. From one social context to another, a person elects elements to take on as part of his or her personal identity from a multiplicity of perspectives. Through each encounter with another, an individual reflects on himself or herself as a person and how others view him or her. Other persons' perspectives can be imagined, and adjustment to one's own self is constituted to form a unique and personal identity.

Humans, unlike others in the animal species, are capable of reflecting on their own identities and the impression made upon other humans. In doing so, *objectification of the self* occurs, placing reflexivity as a pragmatic skill of viewing oneself as if from the standpoint of others where one grasps or understands the perspective of the other. In this social interaction, self-realization of identity is processed and a person comes to know who he or she is.

Communication, Play, and Game

Through communicating with significant others, playing, and participating in games, children begin to make sense of who they are. When children are born, their personal identities are not present; as significant symbols and gestures are learned and others communicate with children, identities begin to form. Identities cannot develop without experiencing others through communication and then reflecting upon these social interactions. *Play* is a medium for children's imaginations to use these symbols and gestures while children's capability of taking the role of another develops. So, as children pretend to be firefighters, doctors, or Indiana Jones, they are playing the role of another. With maturity, children begin to organize the various roles they choose to play and how to act within the greater community. The set of rules of how to act within each role is, in a sense, the *game.* Humans are socialized to play the game of life in their respective communities while attaining their own identities within that community with respect to others. The rules of game playing and appropriate interactions with others are established within a societal context, and social norms constitute the generalized other. In games, individuals cooperate with others and learn how to interact effectively by reflecting on perspectives of others, learning to think as others think, and playing the game. In childhood, these actions of communication, play, and games are foundational to identity formation and continue into adulthood. Unlike a chameleon that changes with every new environment, personal identity is anchored in attitudes, beliefs, and values developed over one's youth. Then, with every new social interaction, personal identity evolves as one reflects on new encounters and decides what values, virtues, and characteristics to accept or reject.

Personal Identity as Comprising the *I* and the *Me*

Identity is not just a reflection of the generalized other, but a result of the individual's decision about who he or she will be and the role he or she will play given the attitudes of others. Therefore, personal identity comprises both a *me* and an *I.* The *me* is the part of an individual that accepts the ideas of the social context—the generalized other—and chooses to conform to the accumulation of social norms, patterns, and unconscious opinions of the social environment. The *I* is a person's individuality with his or her own reflection and creative opinion. The *I* of a person's identity reflects on the attitudes of the generalized other, but does not merely accept these attitudes because the *I* is a person's distinctiveness and what sets him or her apart from others. The *me* conforms and plays the game of their social community, whereas the *I* stimulates the creative and novel impulses of the self. The *me* is socially aware of the appropriateness of interactions within each social situation, and the *I* is spontaneous. Together, the combination of *me* and *I* form personal identity where a unique individual dwells and constitutes part of the larger social community.

A person can only come to know his or her distinctiveness by reflecting on past encounters and noticing his or her reactions to the general social norms of the situation. Identity is objectified and comprehended as a temporal historical dimension. In other words, an individual comes to understand himself or herself, his or her identity, by remembering the responses of the *I* to the *me*. A person views his or her past actions and assesses who he or she is—his or her personal identity.

Personal Identity Evolves Over the Life Span and Many Roles Are Played

Personal identity emerges socially and is the product of social interaction; therefore, identity develops over the life span through the process of interacting with others—communicating—in the social world. As adults, individuals have an underlying sense of who they are—a sense that does not change noticeably—unless *epiphanies* are encountered. Epiphanies are social experiences that are so salient that enlightenment or crisis brings about adjustments in how individuals think of themselves. As individuals communicate with others from various contexts and situations, they make reflective assessments of their own identity. All their experiences, beliefs, values, goals, interests, and reflections are accumulative and aid in assessing new social encounters with others where personal identity is confronted. When individuals communicate with others, reflect on these novel interactions, and assess the exchanges according to past experiences, personal identities evolve.

An individual is not confined to interact with only one generalized other; therefore, communication

with various others results in identity continually evolving. A person is not helpless in the process of his or her developing identity; a choice is made to accept or reject changes to one's identity as one interacts with others. The skill of taking the perspective of the other is developed as one communicates, plays games, and reflects on how others view him or her. Social roles in society are learned by observing others and then deciding to accept or reject what is observed. One's identity is a compilation of many roles. As such, one does not change with every passing whim but because humans are flexible and can take the perspective of others, one selects and plays the role that is suitable for the particular situation and moment in history. Situated within the context of the moment, one expresses an identity that is appropriate.

Society and the Social Act

Society is not a collection of static individuals but comprises a whole set of evolving individuals who are in a process of becoming. Individuals within a society learn who they are by participating with others in their social worlds. Society shapes an individual's identity as the person chooses to coordinate with the others within society through the social act.

The social act is the process by which one acts toward an object while perceiving the perspective that others have toward the same object. With this ability, a person is capable of coordinating meaning with others and assessing the perspective of the other toward himself or herself. An individual within the social act finds meaning while realizing the perspective of the other, then decides how to act from this knowing. A social act spans from the simple interaction of two persons (e.g., playing chess or baking cookies) or many together (e.g., constructing a bridge or playing soccer) or the complex interactions of social organizations and communities (e.g., postal service or environmental awareness). A person assesses how others are reacting to his or her own actions and communication and takes the perspective of others regarding what they think. Consequently, an individual changes himself or herself or his or her ideas to conform to a social counterpart, resulting in evolution of personal identity. Key to taking the role of the other is the generation of self-consciousness and knowing one's own personal identity. The notion of social act is key to social construction with the following scholars functioning as exemplars of the interplay between social construction and identity.

Erving Goffman used the scenario that the social actor operates on a stage with props and plays to a particular audience. In this case, the social actor performs on the front stage while interacting with others; however, the actor also can withdraw to a back stage where his or her identity remains out of the view of others. While on stage, each actor performs with other actors in unique ways.

Peter Berger and Thomas Luckmann were the first scholars to coin the term *social construction* with their proposition that knowledge and people's conception of what reality is (i.e., meaning) arises from people interacting with one another over time. Typifications are formed that eventually become habitualized into reciprocal roles played in relation to each other. Meaning and the way people define themselves (personal identity) occurs through a dialectical and reflexive relationship between individuals and society.

Kenneth Gergen refers to the *relational self* as occurring when a person loses his or her own personal identity to seeing the self and his or her identity in terms of the rendezvous with those surrounding them. For the relational self, the traditional view of identity created between the individual and society is replaced with an emphasis on the individual's relationships with others.

Conclusion

Personal identity develops and evolves as an individual internalizes the attitudes of the generalized other and makes them his or her own. This social process occurs through significant communication, play, and the game. The *I* and the *me* live in a dynamic relationship with one another, and identity emerges from the social encounters where ideas of *I* and *me* are negotiated. The *I* restructures the *me* with every ongoing interaction with society. With every interaction, both individual autonomy and social norms are essential for the emerging personal identity. Identity is the by-product of social construction.

Naomi Bell O'Neil

See also Development of Identity; Development of Self-Concept; Face/Facework; Looking-Glass Self; Psychology of Self and Identity; Reflexive Self or Reflexivity; Socialization; Symbolic Interactionism

Further Readings

Berger, P. L., & Luckmann, T. (1966). *The social construction of reality: A treatise in the sociology of knowledge.* New York: Anchor Books.

Gergen, K. (1991). *The saturated self: Dilemmas of identity in contemporary life.* New York: Basic Books.

Goffman, E. (1959). *The presentation of self in everyday life.* New York: Doubleday.

Gubrium, J., & Holstein, J. A. (2000). *The self we live by: Narrative identity in a postmodern world.* New York: Oxford University Press.

James, W. (1948). *Psychology.* Cleveland, OH: World Publishing.

Kelley, E. C. (1977). The fully functioning self. In J. Stewart (Ed.), *Bridges not walls* (pp. 106–117). Reading, MA: Addison-Wesley.

Mead, G. H. (1934). *Mind, self, and society.* Chicago: University of Chicago Press.

SOCIAL CONSTRUCTIVIST APPROACH TO POLITICAL IDENTITY

A *social constructivist* approach to political identity assumes that we create realities—and make these realities meaningful—by way of interaction. We come to know society by interacting with culturally significant others (such as parents, teachers, and doctors), institutions (such as churches, schools, and governments), and symbolic universes (such as capitalism, patriarchy, and Christianity). The approach frames knowledge as learned, situational, and fallible, and, as such, partial, consequential, and sometimes problematic.

Social constructivists attend to the processes in which realities—and knowledge of these realities—are developed by, maintained by, and transmitted to cultural members. Social constructivists focus on the ways in which a group's beliefs, attitudes, and practices metaphorically crystallize into objective, authorless, seemingly natural and seemingly necessary matters of fact. By way of socialization, these matters, consequentially, also come to be perceived of as correct, valuable, normal, and therefore, unquestionable; they become phenomena we must understand and negotiate to be perceived as competent, legitimate cultural members.

A social constructivist approach to identity recognizes that we experience life being particular kinds of people. These kinds often take the form of categories and are kinds both personally chosen and determined by culturally significant others, institutions, and symbolic universes. Categories influence how we interpret ourselves and others, and when we do not enact the appropriate characteristics relevant to the kinds of people we claim or are perceived to be, questioning, conflict, and relational strife can result.

We come to understand ourselves by the categories of people always already present in the culture(s) in which we're immersed, and we learn, via interaction, how to and why we fit particular labels. However, we can never know, definitively and completely, what categories others may demand of us or what kinds of people others will consider us as; we can try to pass as particular kinds of persons but may not succeed or know if we succeeded. And even though we may consider some categories pivotal to our being, this does not mean that others will recognize these categories always and everywhere or that we will forever consider these categories pivotal. A social constructivist approach to identity thus recognizes that identity requires constant care and negotiation, and understands that the kinds of people we claim or are perceived to be can change with context and relationship.

The kinds of people we claim or are perceived to be can influence interpretations of what we say and do, perceptions of our character, and how we are evaluated; who speaks affects what is said and who listens influences who speaks, what is spoken about, and how a speaker and her or his discourse is perceived. These sense-making processes around identity—the interpretations, perceptions, and evaluations that correspond to claiming or being perceived as a particular kind of person—are what make identity political.

Political Implications

From a social constructivist approach, making identity political means asking *what happens when* we claim or are perceived to be a particular kind of person: What material circumstances develop or shift, what assessments are made, what opportunities are gained or lost, what relationships begin or end. It means discerning the consequences and benefits of identifying, or being identified, as belonging to certain categories. It means recognizing that we, as different kinds of people, have different discursive baggage—different histories, prejudices, perspectives. And it means recognizing that when we are marked as a particular kind of person, we can be evaluated based on this kind's baggage as well as on how this baggage is understood.

Consider, for instance, the categories of female and male. When we enter society, culturally significant others, institutions, and symbolic universes classify us as one or the other. We must understand and negotiate these categories to be perceived as competent and legitimate cultural members, and the labels will follow us throughout our existence regardless of what we say or do; we cannot live outside of or uninfluenced by the female-male classificatory system. These categories often seem objective, authorless, seemingly natural, and necessary, and, consequentially, are often perceived as correct, valuable, normal, and unquestionable.

When this happens—when sex is perceived as correct, valuable, normal, and unquestionable—then a person who does not align nicely with the appropriate sex-requirements—the interpretations, perceptions, and evaluations of how persons should be sexed—can experience questioning, conflict, and relational strife as a result. Babies born with characteristics of both sexes may undergo corrective surgery, and persons who do not enact appropriate feminine and masculine behaviors that correspond to their (classified-at-birth) sex may be physically harmed, fired from jobs, forced into traumatic therapeutic situations, or ostracized by friends and family. Such acts are what make sex, as an identity, political.

The act of categorizing also makes interpretations, perceptions, and evaluations of people possible. Categories that are binary (such as female and male) function differently than do categories that are not (such as Catholic, Baptist, and atheist); in binaries, one term is usually privileged over the other. For instance, across many contexts within the United States, feminine traits are inferior to masculine ones; blackness is made inferior to whiteness; Western cultures are discursively defined as better than those considered Eastern;

heterosexuality is framed as a more beneficial identity and preferred type of relationship than homosexuality is; able-bodied-ness is referred to as more valuable and productive and thus better than disabled-ness; and young and youthful qualities are better than old and aged things. Though each term is not necessarily superior or inferior to its binary-other, the terms used to define people can have corresponding logics that influence how people marked by such terms are understood.

The ways in which a category is understood can also facilitate human interpretation, perception, and evaluation. If a category is understood as innate (and, consequently, unable to change), then evaluating a person as good or bad, right or wrong based on her or his identification with this category becomes irrational, particularly because she or he could not choose to be this kind of person (and thus cannot be judged for identifying in this way). Conversely, a person who claims, or is perceived, to be an identity that is understood as innate may negate her or his personal responsibility for engaging in particular acts (that is, if she or he justifies the acts as a result of being a kind of person). Furthermore, if an identity is understood as innate—particularly one rooted in genetics—then medical intervention becomes possible; doctors can find ways to change a person from one kind of (bad) person to another (better, more normal) kind. And eugenics and genocide—both attempts to control the presence of a particular kind(s) of person—are premised on the possibility that the targeted population(s) is connected by blood, by biology.

However, if a category is understood as chosen (and, consequently, conducive to change), the person identifying with this category may be viewed as having made a good or bad, right or wrong choice. A person's responsibility for acts related to being this kind of person also become indisputable. Attempts to medically alter a person's (chosen) identity are futile as well (since the identity lacks genetic roots), and eugenics and genocide are unfathomable in that no shared biology or common blood exist among the undesired population(s); a society can never be cleansed of the identity.

Real-World Example

The following real-world situation illustrates a variety of assumptions about identity as well as

the ways in which identity can work in interaction. It illustrates the importance of and consequences for claiming to be, or being perceived to be, particular kinds of people. It illustrates that identity, though often assumed to be something a person possesses, is something others can influence and decide. And this situation illustrates that identity can change with context and relationship.

In 1952, Christie Littleton was born in San Antonio, Texas. At this time, she was named Lee Cavazos and classified as male. In 1977, she legally changed her name from Lee to Christie Lee. In 1979 and 1980 she underwent sex reassignment surgery, and, in so doing, was able to legally change her birth certificate from "male" to "female." In 1989, she married Jonathan Littleton in Kentucky, a (legal) heterosexual consummation that reinforced Christie's female status (that is, because same-sex marriages were, and are, illegal in the state). In 1996, Jonathon died because of medical error. In 1999, Christie, acting as Jonathon's spouse, filed a malpractice suit against Mark Prange, the doctor responsible for the error. In his defense, Prange argued that Christie was and would always be male because of her original sex-at-birth classification, and, as such, had no right to marry a person of the same sex, and, as such, could not file a suit as Jonathan's (female) spouse. The court ruled in favor of Prange, thus invalidating the once-legal bond between Christie and Jonathan, invalidating a bond often indicative of legitimate commitment and love.

Markers Engaged

The understood innate- or chosen-ness of categories—and humans marked by these categories—becomes political when such understanding influences interpretations, perceptions, and evaluations of people. For instance, the one-drop rule in the United States categorized a person with non-White (primarily African American) ancestry as non-White. Such categorization understood race as innate and rooted in biology. Consequentially, such understanding fueled arguments against interracial marriage, against the relational mixing of blood. Or consider the example of Christie Littleton. Even though Christie changed her name, underwent sex-reassignment surgery, and got married—acts that constituted her as female—understanding sex as innate, as something incapable of change, marked her as male.

A social constructivist approach to political identity treats categories as phenomena with which we must contend, embrace, and use for a variety of purposes. Identity becomes something we can manipulate and use for a variety of social purposes; the approach allows us to learn ways of positioning ourselves as particular kinds of people while distancing ourselves from being marked as something other.

A social constructivist approach to political identity attends to the ways in which identities emerge in unstable, slippery relational processes as well as how these identities, and the humans marked by these identities, are interpreted, perceived, and evaluated.

A social constructivist approach to political identity suggests that we can never know, completely or definitively, the ways in which innate or chosen characteristics of an identity, and the humans marked by this identity, affect interaction. Rather, the approach maintains that, in interaction, we can only *infer* another's innate or chosen characteristics. We cannot test another person's biology or blood to determine who she or he really is nor can we engage in a rigorous, all-inclusive analysis of the processes involved in her or his coming to be a particular kind; all we can ever do is attend to what might happen if and when a person comes across as a certain kind of person at a particular time and place.

A social constructivist approach to political identity recognizes that the people we claim to be, or are perceived to be, matter.

Tony E. Adams

See also Face/Facework; Identity Negotiation; Identity Uncertainty; Masking; Passing; Queer Theory; Social Constructionist Approach to Personal Identity; Society and Social Identity

Further Readings

Adams, T. E. (2005). Speaking for others: Finding the "whos" of discourse. *Soundings, 88*(3–4), 331–345.

Fenstermaker, S., & West, C. (Eds.). (2002). *Doing gender, doing difference: Inequality, power, and institutional change.* New York: Routledge.

Gergen, K. J. (2000). *The saturated self: Dilemmas of identity in contemporary life.* New York: Basic Books.

Goffman, E. (1959). *The presentation of self in everyday life.* New York: Doubleday.

Greenberg, J. A. (2000). When is a man a man, and when is a woman a woman? *Florida Law Review, 52,* 745–768.

Hacking, I. (1990). Making up people. In E. Stein (Ed.), *Forms of desire: Sexual orientation and the social constructionist controversy* (pp. 69–88). New York: Garland Press.

Weeks, J. (1993). Necessary fictions. In J. Murray (Ed.), *Constructing sexualities* (pp. 93–121). Windsor, ON, Canada: Humanities Research Group, University of Windsor.

Yoshino, K. (2007). *Covering: The hidden assault on our civil rights.* New York: Random House.

SOCIAL ECONOMY

The economic, philosophical, and practical relevance of the social economy has been considered across disciplines, cultures, and historical moments. With its origins arguably established thousands of years ago in Chinese dynasties and its contemporary roots often cited vis-à-vis the work of Jean-Jacques Rousseau and Karl Marx, the significance of this interpretive economic framework continues to deepen in the global marketplace of the 21st century. Specifically, as the world's economy experiences unprecedented change and growth the conversation about economics and its relationship to the human condition likewise experiences unprecedented visibility and engagement. More than simply a textbook term, the social economy is being advanced to bring about greater public accountability for the economic enterprise and its impact on people, especially how economic resources shape people's individual and shared sense of identity. The common thread among those researching and actively engaging the social economy in the marketplace is a directive to invest an otherwise scientific discipline with a distinctly human perspective.

Conceptualizing the Social Economy

As a complement to traditional economics, the *social economy* is a term characterizing an approach to the marketplace that focuses on answering questions that traditional economics does not. Social economists aim to resolve discord and debilitating divisions often associated with the development of capitalism. To this end, the social economy is not about monetary capital alone; instead, it is fundamentally concerned with the social and personal dimensions of economic life.

In its broadest sense, understanding what is meant by the social economy is captured in the 18th century writings of Rousseau. His affirmation of the ordinary life whereby an honest and useful trade yields virtuous civic engagement emphasizes the unity between civic and private life in which the common good is evident everywhere. In 1871, J. E. Thorold Rogers made explicit the common good of the social economy as that which permits the greatest regularity for the largest number of people that work and safety might be the hallmarks of collective existence. Writing in 20th century, Marx intensified the idea by arguing for a more critical evaluation of the relationship between production, distribution, exchange, and consumption. His intent was to expose the problems in capitalism, validate the worker, and offer an alternative in socialism. Today, the social economy is represented in many ways, not the least of which is the prominent call for sustainability in every aspect of business and society. The U.S. Environmental Protection Agency defines sustainability as meeting the needs of the present without compromising the ability of future generations to meet their own needs. Sustainability argues for responsibility to all forms of capital—natural, monetary, and human—as essential to guiding today's decisions as well as tomorrow's vision so that all generations receive adequate provision.

Irrespective of the source or solution, the inner workings of the social economy point toward the importance of gaining a deeper understanding of all forms of capital and their impact on the human condition, especially identity formation. At the heart of this undertaking is a careful examination of how resources, or a lack thereof, affect individual and collective existence. Implicit in this concern is a desire to combat exclusion based on socially useful goods by focusing on the multiplication of resources to bridge human social activities with production and reproduction. For example, advocates for connecting a community to local

farmers through a cooperative food establishment argue that it offers sustainable benefits to all participants. Such relationships establish a pattern for cooperative living that supports the local economy while binding the community together around shared values.

Conceptualizing the social economy is, therefore, a task attentive to the human component of economic activity. Beyond the social science of evaluating people through demographic data, the social economy attempts to establish a textured understanding of how people shape and are shaped by the economic forces at work in their lives. The commitment is to nourish a traditional enterprise (economics) with a cooperative, humane, and sustainable way of doing business. The anticipated outcome is that through a more visible engagement of the social economy people will find their place, reconstitute their sense of personal responsibility, and enhance the collective resolve of a community through their social citizenship.

Embedded Social Engagement

Achieving a heightened awareness and engagement of the social economy calls people to recognize their social embeddedness and the universal presuppositions of that existence. Clark Everling explains these presuppositions as the ways in which capital builds a given social space. Capital in any form, but especially monetary capital, affects the nature of personal as well as social transactions. It builds spaces through appropriation, consumption, and accumulation. These social transactions embed people in specific practices, each of which inform the fabric of their experiences and how they form associations with others. What follows is a sense of identity and relation between people that is cultivated partly by certain social expectations established in and through the communicative life of goods.

Within the social economy, this embedded transaction process associates exchange and production as two sides of the same coin. The ideal is a balanced, proportionate relationship between the two indicative of the classical Aristotelian golden mean. When enacted with the appropriate magnitude, exchange is more than monetary; it is embedded in useful values that benefit the individual as well as the collective. Consumption is simply the use of relevant goods associated with the necessities of everyday life.

The competitive capitalist marketplace, however, also supports another twofold relationship of consumption and production. It is argued that this relationship encourages and even glorifies the commoditization of life experiences. Exchange is an exchange of values established by the individual. This form of exchange does not focus on the usefulness of goods. Instead, it elevates a disproportionate relationship between consumption and production in favor of consumption. According to the social economy, such an unbalanced dynamic in favor of consumption edifies autonomous behavior and narrows the community focus to only that which supports the individual's emotive desires. As Alexis de Tocqueville, Alasdair MacIntyre, and Charles Taylor have noted, an emotive turn distances the individual from others, causing a conformity to the self absent any commitment to acknowledge that life is lived in relation—to others, institutions, and so forth.

In sum, the social economy posits that a proportionate relationship between exchange and production lends itself to constructive alliances with the potential for yielding comprehensive benefits. The disproportionate relationship between consumption and production, however, releases the individual from his or her connectedness to a larger social enterprise. Consciousness of one's embeddedness and social responsibility is thus compromised.

Commitment, Connection, and Community

Embedded social engagement is a part of everyday life even though many may not be aware that they are participants in the social economic enterprise. Capital transactions and their subsequent impact on experience and association take place as people adjust to shifts in the commodities exchange, respond with aid to those suffering from natural disasters, support local merchants, or donate their time and talent to people in need. The alterity of the social economy calls for business to elevate social needs in an order that Marx advocated in attending to the use-value of goods over the potential exchange value. This alterity perspective on social economy might inspire a renewed commitment (even priority) to useful goods that benefit

collective existence and the expansion of human life. The desired outcome is to advance greater care and attention toward the human dimension of economic life.

Commitment, connection, and community are drivers of active participation in the social economy; they reflect a textured, threefold emphasis on the role and value of people within this enterprise. Sustainable action requires attentiveness to each, offering a measured, socially concentrated approach to all forms of capital management as they are enacted through appropriation, consumption, and accumulation.

Commitment

The social economy is firmly rooted in commitment. It is committed to a shared space in which social relations are shaped by and depend on other social relations. This commitment constitutes a framework for developing personal and collective identity. It reaffirms the interconnectedness of humanity while recognizing that this bears with it tremendous responsibility to the other.

Whether to one's neighbor or a generation yet to come, the commitment of the social economy demands invested action that reflects an implicit trust. This trust, according to Bruce G. Carruthers and Sarah L. Babb, is derived from interpersonal or interorganizational relationships and networks that are established through the economic sphere. The historical relevance or contractual agreements does not build the potential for this trust. Rather, meeting the expectations and obligations of social relationships establish the ground from which this trust can emerge. Economic coherence is thus a by-product of an interpersonal or interorganizational commitment to goods that extend beyond any one perspective.

Connection

The result of trust is an interconnectedness that makes public the dynamics, constitution, and demands of social relations. This trust addresses a core issue of the social economy: redemption from social exclusion. As mentioned earlier, social exclusion inhibits individual and collective potential for sustainable production and reproduction. Max Weber's conception of "webs of significance," a concept further developed in the work of cultural anthropologist Clifford Geertz, points to a potential source of disconnectedness or exclusion as emergent from culturally transmitted meanings that shape how we interact and the value we ascribe to social interactions. If negative or limiting, these interactions can plague generations and even entire cultures, making it difficult to comprehend the latent potential of embedded persons within those contexts. Likewise, the nature of exclusion can also be considered through June Lapidis's conception of "webs of relationships." To the web metaphor, Lapidis brings a sense of the tension between connectivity and economic needs, making visible the reality that we are affected and even shaped by the goods that inhabit our everyday lives.

Both web metaphors address the root issue of exclusion versus inclusion, suggesting that connectivity is more involved than simple claims of "being green" or making charitable gestures to gain visibility in the moment. Connection is about acknowledging embeddedness in webs whose strands reach into the past and ahead to the future, certain of only one thing: that identity is shaped in relation to others. The social economy presupposes that individual and collective identities are inseparable, that one affects the other. Therefore, the social economy embraces connectivity because it privileges interrelation that aims to meet and sustain the needs of people, not propagate the isolation of emotive, purely consumptive behaviors.

Community

The final driver of social economy posited here is community. Pierre Bourdieu presents a compelling look at the implications of community in the social economy as it is formed around dwelling spaces or habitats. At one time, work and home were located in the same space or local community. The economic infrastructure that made this possible has, however, changed significantly. People are now deployed out of the local community to work. This economic transition creates an increasingly disconnected sense of social relationships. People are gathered together in what is termed a *community,* yet no one knows each other

and their work often exists to benefit areas outside of that local space.

The importance of true community within the social economy is in heterogeneous individuals gathering around a common center or shared community interests that, according to Bourdieu, emerge from working together. What contemporary housing developments and sprawling suburbs lack is a connectedness that affirms interdependency and a collective purpose.

The social economy reclaims community as a central factor in individual and collective identity formation that ultimately shapes the state of the economy. Trust is built in interpersonal and interorganizational sanctuaries from which connection is made possible. Connection creates opportunities for community to form and be sustained in the long run. The community calls the individual into responsibility; the community establishes a sustainable future for generations to come.

S. Alyssa Groom

See also Consumption; Embeddedness/Embedded Identity; Material Culture; Society and Social Identity

Further Readings

Amin, A., Cameron, A., & Hudson, R. (2002). *Placing the social economy.* New York: Routledge.

Bourdieu, P. (2005). *The social structures of the economy* (C. Turner, Trans.). Cambridge, UK: Polity Press.

Carruthers, B. G., & Babb, S. L. (2000). *Economy/society: Markets, meanings, and social structure.* Thousand Oaks, CA: Pine Forge Press.

Everling, C. (1997). *Social economy: The logic of capitalist development.* New York: Routledge.

Lapidis, J. (2004). All the lesbian mothers are coupled, all the single mothers are straight, and all of us are tired: Reflections on being a single lesbian mom. *Feminist Economics, 10*(2), 227–236.

Marx, K. (1976). The economic and philosophical manuscripts of 1844. In *Collected Works* (Vol. 3). New York: International Publishers.

Rousseau, J. J. (1994). *Discourse on political economy and the social contract* (C. Betts, Trans.). Oxford, UK: Oxford University Press.

Taylor, C. (1989). *Sources of the self: The making of the modern identity.* Cambridge, UK: Cambridge University Press.

SOCIAL IDENTITY THEORY

Social identity theory is a social psychological theory that explains how people's conception of who they are (their self-concept) is associated with their membership of social groups and categories, and with group and intergroup behaviors. The theory defines group membership in terms of people's identification, definition, and evaluation of themselves as members of a group (social identity), and specifies cognitive, social interactive and societal processes that interact to produce characteristic group phenomena.

Originating in Britain in the work of Henri Tajfel in the late 1960s and collaboration with John Turner in the 1970s, social identity theory has a number of different but compatible conceptual foci. The two most significant are Tajfel and Turner's social identity theory of intergroup relations and Turner and colleagues' social identity theory of the group, the latter called *self-categorization theory*. Social identity theory has developed to become one of social psychology's most significant and extensively cited analyses of intergroup and group phenomena—in such topics as, for example, prejudice, discrimination, stereotyping, cooperation and competition, conformity, norms, group decision-making, leadership, and deviance.

Within social psychology, social identity theory was predicted on a metatheory that differentiated the behavior of people as group members from individual and interpersonal behaviors and encouraged the development of theory specifically catered to the former.

How People Represent Themselves: Personal and Social Identity

People have a repertoire of different ways to conceive of themselves—they have many different identities that can be classified as personal identities or social identities. *Personal identities* are definitions and evaluations of oneself in terms of idiosyncratic personal attributes (e.g., witty, shy), or personal relationships (e.g., X's friend, Y's spouse). *Social identities* are definitions and evaluations of oneself in terms of the attributes of specific groups one belongs to (e.g., American, Democrat, nurse). Personal identity is tied to the personal self and associated with interpersonal or idiosyncratic individual behaviors; social identity is tied to the collective self and associated with group and intergroup behaviors.

Recently, Marilynn Brewer has argued that in some cultures, particularly more collectivist cultures, social identity rests more on people's networks of relations with one another within a group than on self-definition in shared attributes and is thus associated with the relational self.

How People Represent Groups: Categories and Prototypes

Human groups are social categories that people mentally represent as *prototypes*—complex fuzzy sets of interrelated attributes (behaviors, beliefs, attitudes, customs, dress, and so forth) that capture similarities within groups and differences between groups. Prototypes represent attributes that maximize the group's *entitativity*—the extent to which a group appears to be a distinct and clearly defined entity. Prototypes also maximize *meta-contrast*—the ratio of differences between the group and other groups to differences within the group. One way to think of a group prototype is what comes immediately to mind if, for example, one were to say to you, "French," "Republican" or "terrorist."

Overwhelmingly, we make binary categorizations where one of the categories is the group that we are in, the ingroup. Thus, prototypes capture similarities within the ingroup and accentuate differences between our group and a specific outgroup. Ingroup prototypes can therefore change when one compares one's group with a different outgroup. For this reason, prototypes are context-dependent. Generally speaking, however, group prototypes are not completely context-*determined*—usually a core component is modified or qualified to varying degree by context. If a particular contextual change is enduring, the prototype changes more profoundly and more enduringly.

Categorization and Depersonalization

The process of categorizing someone has predictable consequences. Rather than "seeing" those people as idiosyncratic individuals, you see them through the lens of the prototype of the category you have placed them in—they become *depersonalized*. Depersonalization is not at all the same thing as *dehumanization*—the former refers to a change in the basis of perception, the latter to a perception that someone is not a human being. Prototype-based perception of outgroup members is more commonly called *stereotyping*—you view "them" as being similar to one another and all having outgroup attributes.

You can also depersonalize ingroup members and yourself in exactly the same way. When you categorize yourself, you view yourself in terms of the defining attributes of the ingroup (self-stereotyping), and, because prototypes also describe and prescribe group-appropriate ways to think, feel, and behave, you think, feel and behave group prototypically. Your own behavior conforms to ingroup norms. In this way, self-categorization transforms one's self-conception and produces normative behavior among members of a group.

Depersonalization of self should not be confused with deindividuation—the former describes how self-perception and behavior conforms tightly to group-defining norms, the latter to a loss of responsibility and accountability that is associated with an unsocialized and primitively impulsive self. Stephen Reicher has shown how explanations of crowd behavior that often hinge on deindividuation fail to capture the goal-oriented and social identity-contingent structure of crowd events—a self-categorization–based depersonalization explanation does a better job.

Feelings for Group Members: Social Attraction

Social categorization affects how you feel toward other people. Feelings are governed by how prototypical of the group you think other people are, rather than by personal preferences, friendships, and enmities—liking becomes prototype-based depersonalized *social attraction*. The more ingroup prototypical people are, the more you like them. Furthermore, because within one's group, there is usually agreement over prototypicality, prototypical members are liked by all—they are "popular." Likewise, less prototypical members are "unpopular," and can be marginalized as undesirable deviants. Outgroup members are effectively un-prototypical of the ingroup and so are liked less than are ingroup members.

Social attraction also occurs because our ingroup prototypes are generally more favorable than our outgroup prototypes. We engage in ethnocentrism—evaluating the ingroup more favorably than the outgroup on as many dimensions as possible. Thus, preference for ingroup members over outgroup members and for prototypical ingroup members over non-prototypical ingroup members reflects a bias for the prototypical and the valence asymmetry of ingroup and outgroup prototypes.

Social identity–based liking is also affected by the extent to which a person is seen as threatening the normative integrity of one's group, and thus, the essence of who one is as a group member. According to Dominic Abrams and José Marques's theory of *subjective group dynamics* people who occupy positions that are nonnormative of the ingroup are disliked more if they are ingroup than outgroup members—this is because ingroup deviants are considered "black sheep" who are particularly threatening to social identity.

Intergroup Behavior

As described previously, the tendency for ingroup prototypes to be more favorable than outgroup prototypes represents *ethnocentrism*—the belief that all things ingroup are superior to all things outgroup. Ethnocentrism exists because of the correspondence, through social identity and self-categorization, between how the group is evaluated and how we ourselves are evaluated. Thus, intergroup behavior is a struggle over the relative status or prestige of one's ingroup—a struggle for evaluatively positive ingroup distinctiveness and social identity. Higher-status groups fight to protect their evaluative superiority; lower-status groups struggle to shrug off their social stigma and promote their positivity.

The strategies that groups adopt to manage their identity depend on *subjective belief structures*—members' beliefs about the nature of the relationship between their group and a specific outgroup. Beliefs focus on *status* (what is my group's social standing relative to the outgroup?), *stability* (how stable is this status relationship?), *legitimacy* (how legitimate is this status relationship?), *permeability* (how easy is it for people to change their social identity by "passing" into the outgroup?), and *cognitive alternatives* (is a different intergroup relationship conceivable?).

A *social mobility* belief structure hinges on a belief in permeability, that intergroup boundaries are effectively soft and easy to cross. This causes members of lower-status groups as isolated individuals to dis-identify from their group to try to join and gain acceptance by the higher-status outgroup—they try to "pass." In reality, intergroup boundaries are rarely permeable, but dominant groups often promulgate an ideology of social mobility, and sometimes limited passing because it undermines and prevents collective action by the minority.

A *social change* belief structure hinges on recognition that permeability is actually low; that intergroup boundaries are actually hard and difficult to cross. This causes low-status groups to engage in *social creativity*—behaviors aimed at redefining the social value of their group and its attributes, coupled with attempts to avoid (upward) comparison with higher-status groups and instead engage in (lateral or downward) comparisons with other groups lower in the social pecking order. Dominant groups can sometimes promulgate a social change belief structure that encourages lateral or downward comparisons and competition among subordinate groups—an often effective strategy of "divide and conquer."

Where a social change belief structure is coupled with recognition that the social order is illegitimate, group members can develop *cognitive alternatives* (essentially a critical ideology and road map for the plausible achievement of social change) and engage in *social competition*—direct competition with the outgroup over status, which can range from debate through protest, to revolution and war.

Social Identity Motivations

The group pursuit of positive distinctiveness is reflected in people's desire to have a relatively favorable self-concept, in this case through positive social identity. The *self-esteem hypothesis* draws out this logic—social identity processes are motivated by the individual pursuit of a relatively favorable self-concept, and possibly by the global human pursuit of self-esteem. Research suggests that group membership generally does make people feel good about themselves, even if the group is relatively stigmatized, but feeling good or bad about oneself does not easily predict whether one will actually identify with a group.

Another perspective on social identity motivation is offered by Brewer's *optimal distinctiveness theory*. People are driven by contrasting motives for inclusion and distinctiveness, and strive to reach an optimal balance. Large groups over-satisfy the inclusion motive and small groups over-satisfy the distinctiveness motive. Mid-size groups within larger social aggregates are more likely to be optimally distinctive.

According to Michael Hogg's *uncertainty-identity theory*, there is another basic motivation for social identity processes. People strive to reduce feelings of uncertainty about themselves, their social world, and their place within it—they like to know who they are and how to behave, and who others are and how they might behave. Because social identity ties self-definition and behavior to prototypes that describe and prescribe behavior, it reduces uncertainty about who you are and about how you and others will behave. Some prototypes are better suited to identification-related uncertainty reduction—specifically, prototypes that are simple, unambiguous, and clearly defined. Prototypes like this typically define groups that are highly entitative—distinctive, homogeneous, and clearly structured.

One implication of uncertainty-identity theory is that under conditions of chronic or extreme self-uncertainty (e.g., economic collapse, cultural disintegration, civil war, terrorism or large scale natural disasters, or unemployment, bereavement, divorce, relocation, or adolescence), the motivation to reduce uncertainty is greatly amplified. Under these circumstances, people will identify strongly; having a powerful feeling of belonging and attachment to the group, and a sense of self comprehensively defined by the group—they could be described as zealots, fanatics, or true believers. Furthermore, they will seek to identify with groups that are not merely entitative but extreme—groups that are homogeneous in their attitudes, values, and membership; have inflexible customs and carefully policed boundaries; have orthodox and ideological belief systems; are intolerant and suspicious of outsiders and of internal dissent and criticism; are rigidly and hierarchically structured, often with strong autocratic leadership; and are ethnocentric and narcissistic.

When Does Social Identity Come Into Play?

A social identity comes into play psychologically to govern perceptions, attitudes, feelings, and behavior only when it is psychologically salient. Penelope Oakes has elaborated on Jerome Bruner's 1957 notions of accessibility and fit to describe a set of principles that govern the psychological salience of social identity.

People draw on readily accessible social identities and categorizations (e.g., gender, profession). These are valued, important, and frequently employed aspects of the self-concept (*chronically accessible* in memory), or those that are self-evident and perceptually obvious in the immediate situation (*situationally accessible*). People use accessible identities and categorizations to make sense of their social context. They check how well the categorization accounts for similarities and differences among people (*structural/comparative fit*) and how well the stereotypical properties of the categorization account for people's actual behavior (*normative fit*). People try different categorizations, and the categorization with optimal fit becomes psychologically salient. Although largely an automatic process, salience is influenced by motivations to employ categorizations that favor the ingroup and do not raise self-uncertainty.

Influence Processes in Groups

People in groups adhere to similar standards, have similar attitudes and behave in similar ways. They conform to group norms and behave group prototypically. Self-categorization is the cognitive process responsible for an individual group member behaving prototypically—transforming his or her self-concept and behavior to be identity-consistent.

Because it is critical to know what the context-specific group norm is, people are highly motivated to obtain reliable information about the norm. There are many sources of such information. For example, one can observe fellow members' behavior, or construct a norm that contrasts with the behavior of outgroup members or deviant/marginal ingroup members. However, according to

Turner's *referent informational influence theory*, the most reliable information is usually gleaned from the identity-consistent behavior of people who are known to be generally prototypical members of the group. Members pay close attention to these people and infer from their behavior what is contextually group normative and thus self-defining.

This idea underpins Hogg's *social identity theory of leadership*. In salient groups, prototypical members occupy a leadership role, and prototypical leaders are more effective than are non-prototypical leaders. People look to these people to provide reliable information about their identity as group members. They do this because prototypical leaders are assumed to be "one of us"—highly identified members who are trusted because they are unlikely to behave in ways that do not protect and promote the group. Paradoxically, this trust allows prototypical leaders to actually be normatively innovative, which is a key transformational function of effective leadership. People are prepared to follow their lead even if at first blush the direction they are taking the group looks odd.

Another quite different source of transformative normative information in groups is ingroup criticism. Simply being a nonnormative ingroup member, someone occupying a nonnormative position, invites rejection. However, according to Matthew Hornsey's *intergroup sensitivity effect* and William Crano's *leniency bias*, although people pretty much outright reject *actively* norm-challenging information from outgroup sources, they are much more tolerant of such behavior from ingroup sources. In this way, an ingroup critic (Hornsey) or an active ingroup minority (Crano) can play a role in changing ingroup norms.

Michael A. Hogg

See also Collective/Social Identity; Deindividuation; Identity Salience; Identity Uncertainty; Optimal Distinctiveness Theory

Further Readings

Abrams, D., Hogg, M. A., Hinkle, S., & Otten, S. (2005). The social identity perspective on small groups. In M. S. Poole & A. B. Hollingshead (Eds.), *Theories of small groups: Interdisciplinary perspectives* (pp. 99–137). Thousand Oaks, CA: Sage.

Hogg, M. A. (2003). Social identity. In M. R. Leary & J. P. Tangney (Eds.), *Handbook of self and identity* (pp. 462–479). New York: Guilford Press.

Hogg, M. A. (2005). The social identity perspective. In S. A. Wheelan (Ed.), *The handbook of group research and practice* (pp. 133–157). Thousand Oaks, CA: Sage.

Hogg, M. A. (2006). Social identity theory. In P. J. Burke (Ed.), *Contemporary social psychological theories* (pp. 111–136). Palo Alto, CA: Stanford University Press.

Hogg, M. A., & Abrams, D. (1988). *Social identifications: A social psychology of intergroup relations and group processes.* London: Routledge.

Hogg, M. A., & Abrams, D. (2003). Intergroup behavior and social identity. In M. A. Hogg & J. Cooper (Eds.), *The SAGE handbook of social psychology* (pp. 407–431). London: Sage.

Tajfel, H., & Turner, J. C. (1986). The social identity theory of intergroup behavior. In S. Worchel & W. Austin (Eds.), *Psychology of intergroup relations* (pp. 7–24). Chicago: Nelson-Hall.

Turner, J. C., Hogg, M. A., Oakes, P. J., Reicher, S. D., & Wetherell, M. S. (1987). *Rediscovering the social group: A self-categorization theory.* Oxford, UK: Blackwell.

SOCIALIZATION

Socialization refers to the process through which people learn skills, knowledge, values, motives, and roles appropriate to their position(s) in a social group or society, resulting in a particular identity or identities relevant to that social group or society. Socialization takes place through communicative interaction with others whenever new roles are engaged as part of a group or society. One basic assumption of socialization theory is the internalization of group or social requirements. During socialization, one learns to take on an identity associated with a particular group and perform it in a competent manner.

Disciplinary and Contextual Engagement

The process of socialization involves multiple disciplinary perspectives, including anthropology, communication theory, psychology, social psychology, and sociology, with a common pool of intellectual ancestors (e.g., Erik Erikson, Sigmund Freud, George Herbert Mead). The academic concept of socialization as the relationship of the individual to society or collectives can be traced from its emergence in the late 1800s to current theory and research, including work on self-socialization, moving from a focus on stages tied to biological development to increased focus on the interaction of person and environment through language. Persons are socialized to identities based on their connection to and membership in particular social groups.

Socialization takes place in multiple life contexts, including family socialization, occupational/professional socialization, and organizational socialization. Gender and sex role socialization, language socialization, parental role socialization, political socialization, racial socialization, and consumer socialization tap particular identities drawn from a given domain of social life. Primary socialization refers to family and school socialization, where children learn behaviors appropriate to a particular culture, secondary socialization refers to socialization into particular groups during adulthood (for example, to an organization or occupation), and resocialization refers to learning patterns of behavior different from previously learned ones—for example, joining the military.

From the social collective's perspective, socialization is the individual's adaptation and conformity to role expectations, others' opinions, and the norms and values of the collective. This structuralist/functionalist approach stresses the transmission of group culture. Socialization involves adaptation to the group for which the person will develop an identity. From the individual's perspective, socialization is the development of personal and social identity and associated attitudes and behaviors resulting from social influences. Symbolic interaction is the theoretical tradition of this view. Through interaction with others, one is socialized to norms and rules relevant to identity as a member of a particular gender, race, class, or other group.

Theories of Socialization

Theories of socialization can be organized according to life stage, life span, and life course perspectives. Life stage perspectives (e.g., Sigmund Freud, Jean Piaget, Erik Erikson) focus on a biological basis for socialization. Life span perspectives (e.g., Orville Gilbert Brim and Stanton Wheeler) emphasize the role of both biology and experience. The life course perspective (G. H. Mead, Margaret Mead, Ruth Benedict, and Erik Erikson) highlights the influence of social norms, role prescriptions, and group processes on age-related life transitions. Karl Mannheim suggested that one's generation defines a unique socialization experience.

Much subsequent theoretical work on socialization was a reaction to Freud, who assumed that movement from one stage to another is ordered, basically fixed or invariant, and biological in origin. Most sociological research until the late 1960s and the 1970s emphasized childhood socialization, as did Freud, though its basis was no longer believed to be related to psychosexual stages. Socialization theorists came to recognize the role of environmental influences on the person's movement through stages, along with the shaping influence of communicative interaction on identity formation during the socialization process.

Piaget's cognitive-developmental theory has stages similar to Freud's, but differs in that experience and social interaction are central in movement from one stage to another. Freud considered the social environment as potential interference with the individual's development; he attributed development to maturation, not to interaction, assuming that biology unfolds the individual. Piaget focuses more on the social, collective world than does Freud, as does Lev Vygotsky. Piaget's emphasis is placed on the person as active agent in the socialization process, resonating with the symbolic interactionist tradition as articulated by G. H. Mead and Charles Horton Cooley, which highlighted the influence of social interaction on learning to take on a role particular to a given identity.

G. H. Mead's theory of self in social interaction assumes that socialization takes place through a process of social interaction, emphasizing socialization's social character. Whereas Piaget focuses more on the individual's acting on and adapting information to cognitive structures, Mead focuses on taking on society's attitudes as one's own, a process that accompanies maturation. Taking attitudes and roles of other individuals and of the generalized other constitutes the basic process of socialization. Mead's perspective focused on the life span perspective as an ongoing process and suggested two stages to development of identity. In the first, the self or identity is built through particular attitudes of other people toward self or others. In the second, the person constructs a generalized other from these attitudes.

Anthropologists Margaret Mead and Ruth Benedict dealt with status transitions or passages during the socialization process, unlike Freud, Piaget, or G. H. Mead. Passages from childhood to adolescence to adulthood are significant to identity as a member of a culture. M. Mead and Benedict focused on the extent to which cultures provide continuity or discontinuity for role transitions. Their work provided an important foundation for subsequent theories on the life course and life cycles.

Erikson offered a socialization theory of self in social interaction with eight ages of the human being, emphasizing the life span. Working from the psychoanalytic tradition with the ego as the central psychic structure, he emphasized developmental tasks that human beings must accomplish in stages from childhood through adulthood. Mannheim brought the issue of generations to the forefront, arguing that each generation is socialized differently, providing a standpoint from which to view the world. From this perspective, a generation could be seen as constituting a distinct group with an identity tied to temporal location.

Janie Harden Fritz

See also Gender; Group Identity; Identity Change; Language; Looking-Glass Self; Mirror Stage of Identity Development; Role Identity; Self-Concept; Symbolic Interactionism

Further Readings

Bush, D. M., & Simmons, R. G. (1981). Socialization processes over the life course. In M. Rosenberg & R. H. Turner (Eds.), *Social psychology: Sociological perspectives* (pp. 133–164). New York: Basic Books.

Heinz, W. R. (2002). Self-socialization and post-traditional society. In R. A. Settersten & T. J. Owens (Eds.), *Advances in life course research: New frontiers in socialization* (pp. 41–64). New York: Elsevier.

Luftey, K., & Mortimer, J. T. (2003). Socialization through the life course. In J. Delamater (Ed.), *Handbook of social psychology* (pp. 183–202). New York: Kluwer Academic.

Maccoby, E. (2007). Historical overview of socialization research and theory. In J. E. Grusec & P. D. Hastings (Eds.), *Handbook of socialization: Theory and research* (pp. 13–41). New York: Guilford Press.

Ochs, E. (1993). Constructing social identity: A language socialization perspective. *Research on Language and Social Interaction, 26(3),* 287–306.

SOCIAL MOVEMENTS

Social movements can be defined as socially constructed groups, networks, and organizations that express social and cultural conflict through a reflexively negotiated and contested, permanently evolving collective identity. At times, these conflicts are expressed through highly visible mobilization and engagement with and against the state. At other times, conflict may be expressed in alternative forms of cultural expression and in daily life. In either case, the construction and negotiation of collective identity is central to the definition and work of a movement. This entry draws distinctions between the individual identity quest often associated with social movements and movement collective identity; provides an overview of collective identity as a key process for social movements, highlighting the centrality of conflict to these processes; discusses some of the criticisms of social movements and identity politics; outlines some of the strategic uses of identity in social movements; and suggests some of the paradoxes inherent to collective identity in social movements.

Overview

Social movement identity can be understood across two dimensions. The first is the relationship of the individual to the collective and the impact on individual biography that occurs through the identity quest often associated with joining a social movement. The second is the ongoing process of constructing and maintaining a collective or movement identity. Such an identity is never fixed, but represents the sorts of permanently evolving solidarity networks that, in and of themselves, raise symbolic challenges to the dominant social order. Within these networks also exists a range of multiple, overlapping, and sometimes conflicting individual identities. Social movement actors must negotiate across differences in these identities to create a strategic unity through which to articulate movement claims.

Identity and Biography

Individual identities are often changed in the process of joining a social movement and such movements are understood to play an identity-affirming function for many participants. For many activists, the act of joining a social movement is part of an individual identity quest. Activists often report experiencing new feelings of "belonging" and "recognition" in movement groups and organizations. The conscious and reflexive process of defining an identity that is separate from—or oppositional to—an identity imposed by the dominant social system is the most personal experience of the liberation associated with social movement action. Individuals who identify as belonging to a particular movement can enjoy feelings of solidarity with other activists with whom they share a range of values and aspirations, but with whom they may not otherwise experience personal contact.

An interest in individual identity has also been driven by social movement scholars' attempts to answer what is known as the "free rider" dilemma as it relates to activists' motivation to participate in collective action. Scholars working in the rational tradition of social movement scholarship have struggled to understand why individuals would make the "irrational" choice of engaging in social movement activism when they could instead make the more "rational" decision to "free ride" on the efforts of others, enjoying the collective benefits produced by others but without cost to themselves. The pleasures and rewards associated with identity-quest have been posited as one alternative to material rewards that may motivate individuals to participate in social movement action.

The key difference between an individual identity and a collective identity is the extent to which the latter is a fundamentally political rather than a personal or psychological concept. That is, rather than an individual identity, say, as a lesbian, being based merely in an individual's sexual orientation, a collective identity as a member of the gay and lesbian rights movement is based in the shared understandings among movement participants of the way in which their identities are shaped by common experiences of oppression and resistance that in turn are grounded in their identities. In contrast to the (primarily U.S.-based) rationalist social movement scholars, the constructivist European tradition of social movement scholarship turned their attention to the question of collective identity not as a movement resource or as an explanation for movement participation, but as a process key to the existence of social movements.

Collective Identity

A social movement's collective identity is more than merely an aggregation of individual identities. The identity of a social movement—its collective identity—is not a natural or accidental occurrence. Social movement collective identity is arrived at through an ongoing process of contestation and negotiation and is located in the highly observable realm of action and interaction rather than at the level of individual attitudes or beliefs. Collective identity is based in a perception of a shared status or social relation, usually associated with some form of oppression, marginalization, or injustice. The concept of collective identity is vital to understanding the work of social movements that are engaged in politics beyond institutional transformation because it enables scholars to recognize movement continuity and to identify struggles that occur in culture and everyday life.

The key theorist of social movement collective identity was the late Italian sociologist and psychoanalyst Alberto Melucci. Melucci argued that collective identity should not be understood as a "thing to be studied" or as a fixed and observable social phenomenon. Rather, Melucci suggested that collective identity is a crucial analytical tool for understanding processes that produce a set of reflexively constructed and negotiated definitions regarding the field of opportunities and constraints offered to social movement actors. These processes are not free floating but are constrained by the context and location of social action and involve acts of perception, construction, and negotiation among actors. Understanding the processes of collective identity in this way provides insight into the ways in which social movements determine such issues as membership and activities and agree on the fundamental question of "who they are," while

allowing for the constantly debated and contested nature of these agreements.

Engaging in processes of collective identity allows social movement groups to create the labels by which they define themselves, the barriers by which they determine who is in and who is out, and to work toward common understandings of their goals and strategies. In this sense, collective identities are constantly changing and evolving in response to debate and discussion, and can only exist for as long as movement actors are prepared to engage in their construction. Ultimately, however, that we are able to observe the action of social movements in the form of organizational structures presupposes ongoing processes of collective identity.

Melucci outlines the processes of collective identity as requiring three central factors. First, these processes require the sorts of shared cognitive definitions about the goal and strategies of social action discussed earlier, and an acceptance that these definitions are constructed through interaction and compromise. Second, collective identity requires networks of active relationships, in which norms of organization, leadership, and communication will vary across different movements. Third, these processes necessitate emotional investment by participants, through which individuals are enabled to feel like part of a common unity. Through an ongoing and reflexive engagement with these factors social movements are able to present an empirical unity. However, Melucci also emphasizes that this apparent unity should not be considered as an endpoint or as evidence of the life of a movement. Rather, the processes underlying this presentation of unity are the focus of interest and investigation. Collective identity involves continual reformulation and discussion in groups about the central questions of personal, social, and political action. Continued debate about the factors that Melucci outlines is an indication of a movement's ongoing vitality and relevance.

Conflict and Collective Identity

Contrary to the view that collective identity assumes a homogenous and united movement membership, conflict and disagreement play an important role in processes of collective identity. To many activists, experiences of conflict appear to clash with notions of unity and solidarity that are often deemed essential to successful political practice. For this reason, conflicts themselves are often repressed or smothered. Attempts to repress conflict, however, do not recognize its significance as a creative force in social movement processes of collective identity. Through conflicts regarding differences to do with identity (race, class, sexuality and age), meaning, goals, and strategy, movement actors are able to conceive new forms of social existence and produce new understandings of social, cultural, and political life that have implications beyond the movement itself.

Processes of collective identity provide the space for these conflicts to occur. Further, these conflicts should be seen as both productive and as integral to movement survival, rather than as something to be resolved and put aside. Movements often renew and remake themselves in periods of internal conflict to maintain their relevance in changing political contexts. Even more importantly, however, movement actors have the possibility of imagining and constructing new forms of social existence in the processes of these debates.

Social Movements and Identity Politics

The birth of "identity politics" in the 1960s created a new political paradigm by which identity and liberation became closely linked in the minds of those working for progressive social change. This new view of politics made visible some of the previous assumptions on which the social order rested. Feminists exposed the invisible masculinity inherent in the universal subject, gay and lesbian activists exposed the heteronormativity of this subject, and activists of color exposed the invisible norms of White race privilege in much political thought and action. Those who challenged these assumptions articulated the ways in which dominant identities had been historically and structurally entrenched and universalized. Identity took on a new importance as an organizing principle for movements, and actors were committed in their belief that recognition of their identities would in and of itself provide a challenge to the dominant social order.

By the 1980s, however, identity politics began to be seen as something of a retreat from the broader challenges of social and political reform. As neo-conservatism began to dominate mainstream politics, activists became increasingly disillusioned and pessimistic about the possibilities of social transformation. The new conservatism became dominant in the West, leaving the ideals of the 1960s seeming less and less attainable. During this period, identity politics scholars focused less on social transformation than they did on claims for recognition of a marginalized or victimized identity. With the socialist alternative dismantled along with the Berlin Wall, the struggles for a new model of society seemed to have been lost. In their place emerged competing identity or recognition claims that of themselves did not focus on challenging broader social structures. Critics of this version of identity politics saw it as rejecting the search for a comprehensive solution to social problems in favor of separatism and political goals focused on the well-being of particular groups.

The tension between this approach to identity as struggles for recognition and the older struggles for social justice through a redistribution of resources is articulated in the work of U.S. political philosopher Nancy Fraser. Fraser analyses what she calls the postsocialist condition, which she defines as the absence of a credible, progressive alternative to the current order, marked by a false antithesis between claims for recognition and the need for redistribution. Central to Fraser's argument is the notion that what has essentially been constructed as an either/or choice between, on the one hand, a social politics of class or equality and, on the other hand, a cultural politics of identity or difference is unnecessary and evades the postsocialist tasks of understanding how culture and economy work together to produce injustices. She further argues that developing a critical theory that integrates recognition and redistribution in political claims making is an essential and urgent task. Like other critics of identity politics, Fraser suggests that recognition struggles can function to simplify and concretize group identities with the result that the important struggles within groups are obscured.

Identity as Movement Strategy

Despite the criticism of identity politics as an end in itself, however, social movement identity should not be understood as distinct or separate from movement strategy. Many social movement groups use identities strategically, and a range of other strategic options is meaningful precisely because of the groups with which they are identified. In this sense, identity should not be seen as being at odds with strategy. Rather, processes of collective identity and the making of identity claims can be seen as strategies in and of themselves.

Francesca Polletta and James Jasper have suggested that collective identity processes make a range of strategic contributions to the work of a social movement. In periods where a movement is less publicly visible, collective identity processes maintain a political space for future cycles of movement activity. Identity work is also important for sustaining abeyance structures during periods of limited political opportunities, meaning that identities nurtured within these often-invisible networks contribute to a spillover effect from one movement to another. Broad movement identities such as feminist, pacifist, or anarchist can be preserved in discourse and popular culture as well as in institutions and organizations, thus becoming available for subsequent waves of protest. Further, how successful a movement group or organization is in framing its identities for public consumption affects its ability to recruit new members and supporters, to gain a public hearing, make alliances with other groups, and defuse opposition.

Maintaining a degree of exclusivity in its collective identity can also be an important movement strategy. One possible cost of social movement success, however, is that the collective identity of a movement is transformed into a public good, thereby losing its power to compel participation. This diffusion of a movement's collective identity blurs the boundary between the movement and the general public and allows a more heterogeneous group to attach itself to a movement organization. This can, in turn, contribute to the decline of a movement as the definition and distinctiveness of its collective identity becomes more ambiguous. Although this flow of a movement's discourse into the realms of the public and popular culture is often thought of as success, what can instead occur is a neutralizing of contemporary movements' more radical critiques.

The Paradox of Identity

Identity work is an essential aspect of social movements and collective action. However, as the above sections suggest, it is also inherently paradoxical. Collective identity is both fluid and dynamic in the internal processes by which it is constructed and maintained, as well as fixed and unified in the way that it is presented or performed to the wider public. Collective identity is rooted in history as activists draw on movement identities from earlier periods to nourish contemporary struggle, as well as constantly evolving and changing as a part of the negotiation and debate that are central to processes of collective identity. There is a further paradox to movement collective identity derived from the multiple identities of activists themselves. The unified identity of *feminist, environmentalist,* or *unionist* is inevitably complicated because the feminist might also be a unionist, the environmentalist might also be woman of color, or the unionist might also be a lesbian. At times, these different aspects of activists' identities will conflict, and the carefully constructed unity of the movement will come under enormous pressure.

Knowing who is in and who is out begins the process of creating a movement identity, defining what the struggle is about and determining the strategies that activists will use. Yet, many social movement groups are torn between asserting a clear identity for themselves and deconstructing it, revealing the group's internal diversity and the constructed nature of its public expressions of unity. Where some activists see it as important to expose the internal processes of a movement's collective identity even when those processes involve conflict, others may be concerned that such exposure is a threat to group unity that may diminish the group's legitimacy in the eyes of the public.

In response to these paradoxes, many activists focus on constructing a partial and contingent collective identity. Complicating Melucci's understanding of collective identity as involving shared cognitive definitions of movement goals and strategy, many activists acknowledge that what they share may also be complicated by incommensurable differences. Many activists share a vision of a society characterized by equality among socially and culturally differentiated groups, who are able to respect and affirm one another in their differences. Although the public articulation of a unified collective identity is necessary to achieve that vision, the unity required must be fluid, shifting, and flexible rather than constrained by definition, uniformity, or rigid, impermeable boundaries.

Sarah Maddison

See also Collective/Social Identity; Identity Politics

Further Readings

Fraser, N. (1997). *Justice interruptus: Critical reflections on the "postsocialist" condition.* New York: Routledge.

Goodwin, J., Jasper, J. M., & Polletta, F. (2001). *Passionate politics: Emotions and social movements.* Chicago: University of Chicago Press.

Laraña, E., Johnston, H., & Gusfield, J. R. (Eds.). (1994). *New social movements: From ideology to identity.* Philadelphia: Temple University Press.

Melucci, A. (1995). The process of collective identity. In H. Johnston & B. Klandermans (Eds.), *Social movements and culture.* Minneapolis: University of Minnesota Press.

Melucci, A. (1996). *Challenging codes: Collective action in the information age.* Cambridge, UK: Cambridge University Press.

Melucci, A. (1996). *The playing self: Person and meaning in the planetary society.* Cambridge, UK: Cambridge University Press.

Meyer, D. S., Whittier, N., & Robnett, B. (Eds.). (2002). *Social movements: Identity, culture and the state.* New York: Oxford University Press.

Polletta, F., & Jasper, J. M. (2001). Collective identity and social movements. *Annual Review of Sociology, 27,* 283–305.

Stryker, S., Owens, T. J., & White, R. W. (Eds.). (2000). *Self, identity, and social movements.* Minneapolis: University of Minnesota Press.

SOCIAL REALISM

Social realism was a politically engaged and socially critical form of U.S. painting during the 1930s that called attention to the plight of the working class and the poor. Though it emerged directly from the bleak conditions of the Great Depression, which provoked many artists to emphasize the social function of their work, its origins can be traced to the European movement of realism in the mid-19th century. Artists such as

Gustave Courbet and Jean-François Millet were known for their depictions of peasants who embodied their attitudes toward industrialization and urbanization. Realism as a tool of social critique was also employed in 19th-century Russia and later in the United States with the Ashcan school's depictions of the grim conditions of urban life. For this reason, social realism is sometimes broadly used to refer to these other international movements. In 1930s United States, however, at a time when many artists and critics turned to leftist ideologies, realism was not simply seen as a necessary mode of representation for those committed to socialist and communist politics. It was also tied to a nascent nationalism and growing desire for an aesthetic that had a distinct identity as U.S. art.

Social Role of Artists

This desire to return a social role to artists in the United States manifested itself—by artists and critics alike—in the need for art to be more democratic. The modernist ideal of the artist as a bourgeois individualist, isolated and misunderstood by society, was replaced by one in which the artist was fully integrated into that society. Artists would now work alongside other artists on communal projects, such as murals, and their art would be brought into the public realm, moving beyond the restricted space of the museum and art gallery, and into libraries, schools, hospitals, prisons, and other public institutions. Rejecting contemporary art in the United States as feeble imitations of modern European art, the new ideal was an art created by Americans and for Americans. Epitomized by Pablo Picasso, who in the 1930s was creating increasingly abstract art, modern art was perceived by artists and the public as decadent and bourgeois, far removed from questions of politics and society, and concerned only with its own aesthetic. Moreover, as a foreign influence, it had to be purged in the search for an indigenous U.S. art. Several art critics, including Thomas Craven and Royal Cortissoz were adamantly against modernism, and the artist Thomas Hart Benton, who had been a modernist painter before World War I, turned against it during the Depression. Realism— the opposite of modern art, which was moving increasingly toward abstraction—thus came to be the most appropriate and authentic mode of representation. This rejection of the avant-garde distinguishes social realism from the realism of 19th-century Europe.

These goals lay at the center of Franklin D. Roosevelt's Federal Art Project (FAP), which began in 1935 and ended in 1943. Part of the New Deal, the FAP employed artists as state workers, often collectively, on public projects in return for a standard weekly wage. The commissioned works put into visual form the nationalist and populist rhetoric of Roosevelt's reformist policies, their function was to restore public faith in the government as a unifying source in a moment of political and economic crisis and to offer images of a promised social utopia. Murals such as Philip Guston's *Work and Play* in the lobby of the community room in the Queensbridge Housing Project in New York City, with its images of a family, children playing, musicians and dancers, and workers, were meant to depict the different social roles of a productive society, and its idealization of these roles illustrated the unifying and ordering function of state-sponsored art. Other FAP works, such as Cesare Stea's *Sculptural Relief for the Bower Bay Sewage Disposal Plant* (1936), offered heroic and monumental images of workers, symbolic of the country's efforts to rebuild itself.

Social Realism Versus Socialist Realism and Regionalism

These heroic depictions of workers come closest to the socialist realist iconography of art within the Soviet Union at that time. However, it should be understood that social realism is distinct from its counterpart in the USSR. Whereas the latter was a heroic and monumentalizing style institutionalized by Soviet leader Joseph Stalin in 1934, social realism, though it could encompass this type of iconography, was not limited to it. Thus, social realism could offer images far more varied in subject, ranging from idealizations of workers to pointed critique depicting poverty or racial and social injustice, and as the decade went on, agitating against the growing threat of fascism. Moreover, social realism also had far greater stylistic latitude. In addition to naturalism, which was the only form of representation permitted by Stalin, social realism also included forms of expressionism as well as symbolism.

Nor should social realism be confused with a similar form of U.S. painting in the 1930s, *regionalism*. If regionalist artists also longed for a democratic art integrated into everyday life—and as a result rejected modernism as foreign and elitist—regionalism was determinedly apolitical in content. Instead, in place of heroic workers, lynchings, and other scenes of poverty and injustice, regionalism offered rustic and country views, suffused with a sentiment of nostalgia. The effects of the Depression, both economic and social, were almost always ignored for an idealized vision of a rural past.

Murals

Although the FAP also commissioned sculptures from artists, the predominant form of art created for the organization was the mural. Perceived as an art form both permanent and public, mural painting was hailed by Roosevelt's administration as a vital mode of national expression. Interest in the medium was spurred largely by the Mexican muralists, notably Diego Rivera, José Clemente Orozco, and David Alfaro Siqueiros, who had already begun to garner critical acclaim for their work by the early 1930s. A series of exhibitions on Mexican art, including one by the New York Metropolitan Museum of Art in 1930 and a Rivera retrospective at the New York Museum of Modern Art the following year, along with commissions for these artists within the United States, familiarized the U.S. public with the Mexican muralists and added to their growing popularity. Using their murals to demand social justice, the Mexican artists combined revolutionary imagery of the working class with sympathetic depictions of their country's mistreated and oppressed indigenous ethnic minorities. Their fight against the inequalities of race and class held a strong attraction for leftist artists in the United States who saw in it a model for a politically engaged and aesthetically powerful art that appealed to the masses.

African Americans in particular were drawn to the art of Rivera and others. Many of them held similar political views, and they appreciated the resonance between their fight against racism and the muralists' documentation of the oppression suffered by Mexico's ethnic minorities as well as admiration for those indigenous cultures. Additionally, they could not have failed to take note of the muralists' inclusion of African Americans in their depictions of racial and social injustice in the United States and in their images of revolutionary workers. Thus, it is hardly surprising that several African American artists were strongly influenced by their contact with the Mexican muralists. Charles Alston, for example, often went to see Rivera's *Man at the Crossroads* before it was destroyed; Hale Woodruff apprenticed with Rivera in Mexico in 1936; and both Charles White and John Wilson studied in Mexico in the mid-1940s and early 1950s, respectively. These contacts were all the more important given the limited number of African American artists employed by the FAP.

The U.S. government officials were interested in the Mexican muralists for similar reasons, though they appropriated the idea of the mural and its monumentalizing conventions while eliminating all reference to its revolutionary ideology, replacing it with patriotic content supporting Roosevelt's New Deal administration. Despite the leftist politics of many artists, visual evidence of either socialism or communism often resulted in the censorship or destruction of the works. Murals that were not obvious in their criticism of a capitalist society, such as Diego Rivera's *Detroit Industry* frescoes (1932–1933) at the Detroit Institute of Arts, posed no problems. His *Man at the Crossroads,* however, painted for the Rockefeller Center in New York in 1933 and that included a portrait of Lenin alongside workers to symbolize the possibility of revolution instead of further capitalist development, was painted over when the artist refused to comply with Nelson Rockefeller's demands to eliminate Lenin. The FAP was no less adamant in its desire to maintain the images free from allusions to revolutionary ideology. This was in addition to its requirement that artists paint in a representational, rather than abstract, mode. Any extremists—abstractionists, Mexican partisans, academics—were rooted out and, depending on their compliance with the directives, divided into three categories of "good," "medium," and "bums."

Criticism

If social realism had seemed like the ideal mode of representation for the artist-as-worker to demand justice and equality in the early 1930s, less than 10 years later, it had already fallen out of favor. The rise of fascism in the late 1930s, combined with the revelations about Stalinism in the Soviet Union, led to increasing disillusionment with communism. What little support remained among artists largely collapsed in April 1940 when the American Artists' Congress (AAC), an organization affiliated with communism, voted in support of the USSR's invasion of Finland the previous year. Despite the differences separating social realism from socialist realism, the two became linked in the public mind, associating the former with Stalin's doctrinaire enforcement of the latter as the only acceptable mode of art. Even worse, there were widespread suspicions that the American Communist Party, or even Stalinist communists who had infiltrated the United States, were employing social realism as a tool of propaganda. Once hailed as the embodiment of democracy and social justice, social realism now exemplified totalitarianism and brutality.

Critics also faulted social realism for its inability to effect the social change it promised. By its nature, social realism looked to the past rather than the future in relying on an artistic style that was not modern and, thus, contradicted its claims to a theory of progress in politics. Moreover, by depicting scenes in which everything was recognizable to the viewers, social realism seemed to suggest that the social and political change it promised would not be any different from the current situation. Regionalism fared even worse in the eyes of critics in the early 1940s. Though social realism ultimately seemed entrenched in the past, it at least made the promise, albeit one that remained unfulfilled, of effecting a social utopia. Regionalism, however, made no such claims, and was instead unabashedly nostalgic and sentimental with its depictions of a mythic U.S. past. This had worked well in the previous decade when the nation had been concerned with its economic recovery and establishing a sense of nationalism and pride among its citizens. But with the onset of World War II, the fight for freedom and democracy against the threat of fascism acquired paramount importance. Regionalism's antimodernism and its desire to create a native U.S. art purged of all foreign influences were now seen as fascist attitudes antithetical to the heart of the U.S. project. Democracy in the 1940s was equated with aesthetic freedom.

In the end, artists and critics turned to abstraction as exemplifying U.S. democracy and freedom.

Several artists who had been committed to socialism in the 1930s—including Jackson Pollock, Barnett Newman, and Mark Rothko—became part of abstract expressionism, a U.S. movement in painting that emerged after the war. Their art was completely abstract; with titles often composed only of numbers or colors (when given titles at all), it created the impression that their art was free of any political or social subject matter, and most important of all, any propagandistic elements. Critics discussed the new movement in terms of universality, individuality, freedom, and Americanness, the same terms used to describe U.S. democracy during the cold war.

Isabel Suchanek

See also Collectivism/Individualism; Modernity and Postmodernity; Nationalism; Propaganda

Further Readings

Anreus, A., Linden, D. L., & Weinberg, J. (Eds.). (2006). *The social and the real: Political art of the 1930s in the Western hemisphere*. University Park: Pennsylvania State University Press.

Brown, M. C. (1998). *Socialist realist painting*. New Haven, CT: Yale University Press.

Folgarait, L. (1998). *Mural painting and social revolution in Mexico, 1920–1940: Art of the new order*. Cambridge, UK: Cambridge University Press.

Guilbaut, S. (1983). *How New York stole the idea of modern art: Abstract expressionism, freedom, and the cold war* (A. Goldhammer, Trans.). Chicago: University of Chicago Press.

Harris, J. (1995). *Federal art and national culture: The politics of identity in New Deal America*. Cambridge, UK: Cambridge University Press.

Morgan, S. I. (2004). *Rethinking social realism: African American art and literature, 1930–1953*. Athens: University of Georgia Press.

Whiting, C. (1989). *Antifascism in American art*. New Haven, CT: Yale University Press.

SOCIAL STRATIFICATION THEORY

Drawing on the metaphoric image of strata in rock formations, *social stratification theory* is concerned with understanding the forces that shape and affect the identity and lives of members of particular *strata* of social and cultural systems and groupings through their relationship to other strata within larger social and cultural formations. Moving beyond this geological image, social stratification theory is not simply concerned with the formation of strata, but with the social, cultural, political, psychological, and communicative dynamics by which people's identities are shaped, maintained, resisted, conflicted, changed, and reproduced around the important construct of *differences* between and among important types of social strata. Put simply, social stratification is a group of ideas, theories, and research that is concerned with how differences make, and are made to make, a difference for people within societies in terms of who they are, what they can be, how they are viewed by others, the life-scripts that people perceive are possible for them, and even the structural conflicts (for example, class struggles) with members of other strata. To explain the important specifics of this theory as it relates to identity, this entry explains what social stratification theory assumes about differences that make a difference, how such differences work within the dynamics of social systems, and the relationship of the differences and dynamics of stratification for peoples' identities.

Historical Conditions

Inspiration for earlier versions of social stratification theory came from the study of largely historical exemplars of social and cultural strata. Specifically, examination of feudal societies (primarily European) and their impact on people's lives revealed the importance of largely ordained social class strata on the lives and identities of people. Simply, being born into specific strata was fundamental in shaping one's life. For example, "aristocracy," "tenant farmer," "trader," and "peasant" were significant constructs in structuring social order that was relatively fixed and impermeable, as well as the long-term identities and relationships of people within and between such social strata. Perceptions of self-worth, status, life opportunities—one's place in the world—as well as a host of ways that relationships between such different strata were managed helped show how status, power, class, hierarchy, and the identities of individuals and groups within these strata were organized or stratified. Some branches of social stratification theory approach the relatively fixed or preordained structure of classes and function both as sources of strength and as possible ways of explaining how such feudal societies, in which everyone seemed to know their place, became dominant—even colonial—powers. Some branches of thought about social stratification focused less on hierarchy as a functionally strong characteristic, and more as a source of division and struggle.

Later theoretical permutations of social stratification theory focused on more critical treatments of how feudal and, later, industrial societies affected people's lives. Important anthropological data on more cooperative social and cultural groupings added to the questioning of the functionalist assumptions that feudal order in some societies was a natural, desirable, or even divinely inspired way of organizing strata of people. Interesting too are the ways that ancient feudal structures still permeate and echo through the identities and the relationship between social classes in societies that have long since moved beyond feudal ways of organizing people and institutions. It is possible, for example, to understand current conflicts in some cultures over fox hunting as a reproduction or re-articulation of ancient class tensions between aristocracy and lower classes. Aristocracy appears to be holding onto fox hunting as part of its way of life, and protestors believe it to be a cruel remnant of privilege born of high social status. Although social class is a fundamental construct in social stratification theory, in European societies of this kind, material wealth and class are not necessarily correlated. It is possible to be poor materially and be considered "upper class," and it is possible to be rich materially and be considered lower or middle class. Class is not earned or acquired in the same way that it is in some societies because markers of class may be different from society to society (birth versus earned education or wealth, for example). In many European societies today, it is also much more likely that people can experience mobility between strata such as social class and status. Upward mobility can occur through professional status, and related aspects of taste and consumption habits through which particular aspects of the performance of higher class status are appropriated into people's performances of identities.

Modern Conditions

More recent inspirations for the development of social stratification theory came from modern industrial and colonial examples, experiences, and concepts. Primary among the issues arising from the move from agrarian to industrial modern societies was an increased sensibility to the importance of social class. "Owners," "managers" (middle class) and "labor" (working class) are three of the important strata that emerged through industrialization and remain important dimensions of identity for people as well as places (for example, some towns identify themselves as having a blue-collar identity). In some cultures, "caste" is a particularly fixed and intractable form of class strata where one's identity is closely correlated with one's level of social hierarchy. In terms of social stratification theory, the often stark differences in the lives of people based on their place in the industrial order led to the emergence of more critical theoretic accounts of social structure that were grounded in Marxist schools of thought. These critical approaches attempted to link people's experiences of social class to issues of working conditions, access to ownership and production, and other opportunities with the argument that labor classes not having a connection to the means of production or ownership often resulted in their exploitation and neglect. Access to health care, concerns with public health, and developments in the legal protection of working classes (including child labor laws) can be read as progress in lessening the gaps between the life experiences of those in lower and middle social strata. Concepts such as marginalization and oppression began to take on an explanatory significance in accounting for the experiences of those members of lower strata at the hands of those of higher strata. With the development of mass media in industrialized countries, attention also turned to the role that media play in helping to express a variety of tensions related to stratification. Some have argued, for example, that media have often been complicit in helping to manufacture and diffuse images and assumptions that privilege the upper levels of social strata. For example, a good deal of research in cultural studies suggests that news media often support the status quo regarding social order, and might have a tendency to demonize or discredit the voices and actions of activists and strikers who might be perceived by members of upper levels of social strata to be a threat to social order, and the potential loss of privilege that this would mean to members of upper social strata.

When immigrants from colonies began to relocate to the major industrial nations that had colonized them or, as in the case of the United States, when slaves were freed and society was struggling with the deep change thereafter, this brought race and ethnicity to the fore for researchers as significant sources of social stratification. Coupled with this were changes relating to gender roles in society. Hence, social stratification theory developed beyond social and economic class to embrace notions of status and hierarchy related to race, ethnicity, and gender (particularly the experiences of women in modern societies). Key to understanding identity was an increased sensitivity to ways that class, race, ethnicity, and gender were intimately interrelated and mediated by culture (high culture and popular culture). The 20th century in particular brought changes in assumptions about gender roles and the deconstruction of prevalent gender stereotyping. These changes were often brought about by activists who voiced dissent with the way that women's experiences were often structured in ways that were assumed to be naturally subordinate to men. Questioning the ways that women's lives were structured and stratified by social institutions, including politics, social and public policy, and law, has led to much progress in changing the ways that social stratifications affect the ways opportunities for women are different from (and less than) those for men. Questioning around these issues and implications of stratification continues in the United States and around the world and often takes the form of examining mass media images and portrayals of women. Such issues as how media present and represent issues that should be of priority to women (body type, relationships, domestic work in the home), often indicate that there are subtle ways that identities are still assumed to echo those of times before the women's liberation movement challenged and changed sexism. Social stratification theorists and activists have done much to show how assumptions of gender roles can be linked in often subtle and subliminal ways to social

structures that propagated inequality, and how to change those assumptions and the behavior that spring from them. As a natural extension of the understanding of gender has come more recent activism related to the rights and treatment of gay, lesbian, and transgendered people. Social stratification, it may be argued, is part of the explanation of why such groupings of people outside of the traditional norm have been treated as subordinate to those strata of society that are heterosexual.

Race and Gender

Some have argued that one of the greatest struggles in contemporary U.S. society is the resolution of formerly slave-owner relationships and its interrelationship with class and related issues of fairness and opportunity for African Americans. Significant for social stratification theorists, for example, is an examination of how the previous relationship—one essentially of ownership or property—translates into ways that social strata (class and race) in contemporary society still maintains the reproduction of unequal status and prestige for non-Whites. Research in this vein has explored social and cultural constructions of "whiteness" in terms of how the experiences and identity constructions of White people are often still connected to assumptions of privilege and even superiority. One concern is with how the assumptions and habits of previous times are still significant in shaping life trajectories for both White people and, more importantly, for African Americans. Another main concern would be with how progress can be made toward equalizing the opportunities that African American citizens experience. This quest for a reduction in the impact of social strata in ways that are unfair or oppressive takes up a good deal of space in the U.S. psyche. Significant also to theorists is an understanding of the ways that African American experiences of contemporary culture express this troubled and complex social and cultural transition to a society that is supposedly progressing toward one less stratified by race/ethnicity. Perhaps most poignant to social stratification theorists is an examination of the complex and difficult experiences of stratification that African American women face in adapting to and succeeding in contemporary society given the dual difficulty of the remnants of subordination for race as well as gender. Social stratification can help explain the racial tensions, conflicts, and even rioting that can occasionally erupt when members of traditionally subordinate strata (African Americans) perceive intolerable levels of unequal and unjust treatment in communities and by government and government agencies. Such conflicts show that strongly held and enduring perceptions of inequality and injustice still exist and that there is much work to be done on this issue of promoting a society less grounded in unequal social stratification and more grounded in equality and social justice.

Cultural Studies

Inspiration for contemporary versions and applications of social stratification theory draw on postcolonial and postmodern examples, experiences, and concepts. Most notable for cultural studies is, perhaps, work that links issues of social stratification to the performance of class and class distinctions through consumption. Read one way, consumption choices based on class-based taste, styles (clothing, cars, interior-design choice), and sensibilities can be seen as everyday habits of constructing oneself within a particular class or prestige framework. Consumption based on particular name brandings, for example, might be viewed as a semiotic strategy for constituting a hierarchically class-based identity around exclusivity. That is, styles stand in place of—or symbolize—cultural superiority, or membership of upper social strata such as being middle class. Other forms of consumption choices such as musical taste and related (particularly youth) subcultural memberships have also been read as cultural performances of identity based largely on class that may be either middle or lower class, or grounded in racial identity, depending on the stylistic choices made. In either case, style and its consumption are intimately linked to the constitution of class-based identities.

Contemporary cultural analyses that are based on social stratification principles have produced valuable critical questioning of, and insight into, the ways that class and other stratifications (race, gender) affect people's lives. For example, social strata have been used to help account for the variability of

governmental and community preparedness and response to emergencies and disasters such as hurricanes. A key question involves asking if there is a link between race/class and the speed at which help in such emergencies is mobilized. Are communities, or parts of communities that have members of different social strata treated differently in such events? Another example of a contemporary application of social stratification principles would be within so-called post-Fordist or postmodern workplaces in which hierarchy and divisions based on status are supposedly minimized. A key question is whether there is a link between age, gender, disabilities, and so on, and the way that people are hired, treated, or promoted in contemporary workplaces. Other examples relate to questioning the variability of health care as it relates to status of the health care recipients. A key question here is if and how race and class have a significant impact on the quality of health care provided in communities of differing social status. More examples of applying social stratification principles have to do with understanding the various ways that social status, class, prestige, and so on affect educational institutions—particularly regarding the experiences of students in schools. Key questions relating to stratification have to do with ways that identities of students are affected by class membership, subcultural groups such as gangs that are in competition with other groups, the impact of race on access to and quality of educational training in schools, and the impact of more traditional and hierarchically gender-based prejudices relating to subject specializations and related career trajectories such as examining how young girls are socialized away from or into science and mathematics. Social strata can be seen to permeate and be reproduced in many more ways in these and other institutions (schools, government, health care, etc.) and affect the impact of these institutions on the practices of everyday life.

Pulling together the central threads across the various branches and developments of social stratification theory, some defining assumptions and characteristics are particularly important for understanding the relationship between social strata, people, and their individual and collective identities. First, social stratification has been important in promoting the understanding of the impact of hierarchy of various types on people's lives. Specifically, it can be seen through many examples that the hierarchical organizing of people primarily into classes, as well as other characteristics such as race, gender, and sexual orientation, can have significant and enduring implications for the lives that people live and the often conflicted relationships between people in different social strata. Second, social stratifications can and do change, and individuals can move between social strata such as class in some societies. Strata can be reorganized effectively, especially if there is sufficient energy and persistence in managing such change, and especially if change is linked rhetorically to progress, fairness, and social justice. It is possible to address steps to make sure members of different social strata receive the same consideration and treatment during disasters, for example. Third, change is complex in that people's assumptions, perceptions, and ways of being often change more slowly than they might appear to. Racism and sexism still echo quite loudly through many societies—even the most progressive. Systems have a tendency to try to preserve themselves and the status quo, and those with higher social status and prestige will naturally support that status quo unless there is an overriding will toward equality. Finally, the understanding of social strata is a key to understanding human behavior within the context of all social and cultural systems where particular groups or human characteristics are valued more highly than others.

Peter M. Kellett

See also Class Identity; Conflict; Political Economy; Status; Structuration

Further Readings

Beeghley, L. (2000). *The structure of social stratification in the United States* (3rd ed.). Boston: Allyn & Bacon.

Massey, D. (2007). *Categorically unequal: The American stratification system.* New York: Russell Sage Foundation.

O'Brien, J., & Howard, J. A. (1998). *Everyday inequalities: Critical inquiries.* New York: Blackwell.

Rose, S. J. (2007). *Social stratification in the United States: The American profile poster.* New York: New Press.

SOCIETY AND SOCIAL IDENTITY

Identity and its equivalents in languages other than English may currently be among the most used nouns in the world. They can be encountered in all kinds of contexts, referring to all kinds of phenomena. Gender, family, nationality, ethnicity, race, politics, place of residence, religion, age, sexuality, occupation, employment, consumption patterns, musical tastes, sporting allegiances, and leisure activities apparently all have something to do with the expression *identity* and are, for some people, foci for identification. That this could easily have been a longer list suggests genuine contemporary significance. But what does it actually mean, this word *identity*?

Before addressing that question, however, a few remarks about *society* and the *social* are necessary. To turn to *society* first, although it is a word in everyday use, what it might *be* is often frustratingly unclear. Are small, face-to-face groups societies, or do only the biggest and most abstract collectivities qualify? From a different perspective, does *society* refer to a generic dimension of the human repertoire—which might as easily be call *sociality,* perhaps—and to the fact that we are not solitary creatures and need our fellows to become competent human beings at all?

To narrow the focus somewhat, does the fact that the conventional sociological model of a society is based on the modern nation-state—an organized unitary group, characterized by definite boundaries and definite, if not exclusive, criteria of membership, with a hierarchical division of labor and some capacity for collective mobilization—imply that there were no premodern societies? No. And does this nation-state model actually fit all societies, as they are discussed today, anyway? Probably not: Just think about a *building society* (what is known as a savings-and-loan in the United States), a *society for the protection of animals, industrial society,* or *high society,* and the point is made. The word is imprecise.

Society is also a notion that is sometimes invoked in implicit or explicit contrast to *culture,* the one being patterns of human *behavior,* the other the *meanings* of that behavior. Looked at closely, however, society and culture depend on each other—one without the other is unthinkable—and, in many of the ways in which they are used, particularly to talk about collectivities, they seem to have more in common with each other than not. Once again, certainty about what one is actually talking about when using these words seems to be elusive.

Accepting these reservations, perhaps the best thing to do is to use *society* and *societies* as, at most, general words referring to the varieties of human collectivity, and the generic sociality on which they depend. They are certainly not words that encourage greater precision in their definition or use. This may be one of those cases in which strategic imprecision, which does not foreclose on the complex variety and routine fuzziness of the everyday human world, is necessary to achieve the greatest possible clarity.

This brings us to the *social* and to *social identity,* in particular. The adjective *social* is arguably redundant here, although it is probably now a fact of contemporary life. Human beings learn all that they know and most of what they can do directly *from,* or indirectly during dealings *with,* other humans (and this does not refer just to socialization in childhood and youth, nor does it ignore individual creativity and innovation). Identities are no different, and are definitively social: Their production and reproduction depends on interaction with other humans, with some of whom they will be in some senses shared.

Taken with the arguments of the previous paragraphs, this suggests that we should not attempt to distinguish too rigorously between social and cultural identity. More critical, however, is the need for skepticism about the distinction between *personal identity* and *social identity* that is a staple of the social identity school of social psychology. In this social psychological model, which derives from the pioneering work of the late Henri Tajfel, *personal identity* refers to that which distinguishes a unique individual from other, equally unique, individuals; *social identity* is the internalization of shared, frequently stereotypical, identities. In this tradition, social identity is often seen as the more influential in the shaping of behavior.

In the spirit of the discussion so far, however, personal identity cannot really be anything other than social: Personality is expressed in language, behavior, and things, which all draw on more-or-less shared human repertoires. The *content* of that expression may be somewhat idiosyncratic from

person to person, but *total* idiosyncrasy is an unlikely prospect, and difficult to imagine. Nor is it, in fairness, what the social psychologists seem to have in mind. Individuality is actually a matter of combining elements of shared repertoires. Bearing this in mind, it perhaps makes most sense to distinguish between *individual* and *collective* identity and identification, each of which is utterly social.

This may look like mere quibbling over terminology. However, the real-world implications of taking the meaning of words seriously can be seen in U.S. sociologist Rogers Brubaker's recent critique of social science analyses of ethno-nationalism. He argues that "groups" as defined by social scientists—and what he has in mind is basically the nation-state model of society, discussed earlier—are illusions. Worse, they are social theoretical versions of, and only reinforce, the images of collectivity conjured and manipulated by political entrepreneurs, for their own, typically nefarious, purposes. Groups as such have no substantive reality: All that is real, Brubaker argues, are individual actors, organizations, and a shared, socially constructed sense of "groupness," by which he means identification with a particular set of people.

Brubaker may partly be tilting at windmills here, because one accepted social scientific understanding of groups defines their reality exactly with reference to a shared sense of membership (i.e., "groupness"). However, his argument highlights two important themes. First, identity is not just a matter of academic debate. It continues to be a game of serious consequences for many people. Second, whether they agree with Brubaker or not, social scientists must, in their use of words if nothing else, beware of carelessly appearing to bestow unwarranted substance on collectivities and identities—such as "the Serbian people," "the African American community," or "gays and lesbians," to offer three random examples—the reality of which may be primarily rhetorical. When discussing a certain "identity"—or indeed "society" or "group"—social scientists must perpetually be on guard against carelessly assuming that these terms designate actual collective entities.

Knowing Who's Who

So, what is identity? Put most simply, it is a matter of who people are, or, rather, who they are seen to be, by themselves and by others. Identification is the complex generic human capacity to work out who's who, individually and collectively, in the human world—the multidimensional mapping of a human world that is in perpetual motion, of our place in that world, and of the places of others. This capacity is fundamental to the ongoing daily creation and recreation of the complex human world(s) in which we all live. Without knowing who's who, it is impossible to work out what's what. Mutual identification is, indeed, a basic prerequisite of society (and, as discussed earlier, the same is true vice versa).

It is probably not overstating the case to say that the first response of any person, on entering any situation—even a familiar situation, such as dinner with the family—is to do the identificatory work required to establish who's who and what's what. Identification is so routine, and usually so quick, that it only becomes obvious when there is a question or a problem. All day and every day, we draw on verbal and nonverbal communicative and interpretive repertoires to identify others and identify ourselves to others, who are engaged in the same business, at the same time. The most common of these repertoires are based on either language or the body:

- *Linguistic repertoires* draw on individual and collective naming, speech patterns (language, dialect, ecolect, idiolect), and the disclosure of further personal details (whether orally or in writing).
- *Embodied repertoires* draw on physiology (sex, skin color, etc.), nonverbal behavior (posture, facial expression, gesture, etc.), clothing, adornment, body modification (from cosmetics to amputation), smell, and touch.

This does not exhaust the possibilities, but in its emphasis on communication and interpretation, it suggests a further conclusion. Identity is not a thing that people have, it is something that they do—identification—a process that, in principal at least, is always open to some flexibility and variation. Although we should not overestimate the degree to which change is possible—it is one thing to take a new name, for example, but quite another to embark on gender reassignment—nor should we claim identity as a fixed, essential, and imperative

aspect of either individual or collective being. The observable realities of human life tell a somewhat different story. In this respect, Brubaker's argument that we should banish *identity* from the social science lexicon, replacing it by *identification,* may be unrealistic, given existing accepted usage, but it is understandable. The concern here is with *processes* of identification, for which *identity* is simply a shorthand term.

Apropos those processes, identification is an interaction, between how we identify ourselves and how others categorize us, between self-image and public image: This is what has elsewhere been called the *internal-external dialectic of identification.* One of the things that this means is that there can be no privileging of self-identification. Another is that identities, rather than being anchored on individuals, should be understood as distributed within networks: Identification is a process that in a real sense takes place *between* individuals. Finally, this also means that the product of the interaction, identity, at least partly depends on power relations, particularly on whose definition of the situation counts most. Identity can thus be imposed, something to which this entry returns later.

Similarity and Difference

Identification, before it is anything else, is a process of classification, drawing on criteria of similarity and difference. These criteria of comparison are the logical principles of all classificatory systems, and each depends on the other for classificatory work to be possible. Thus, to be an A is in some respects to resemble all other As, but it is also, and necessarily, to differ from Bs, Cs, Ds, Es, and so on; to be an English vowel, however—an A, an E, an I, an O or a U—is to be like other vowels, but different from the English consonants.

Human collective identification works in the same way. Being Danish, for example, is apparently to differ from the near neighbors, Swedes and Norwegians. Linguistically, however, Danes closely resemble other Scandinavians, the Swedes and Norwegians, but not Finns or Icelanders. Nonetheless, in other contexts, other classifications of culture and political system come into play, and Danes, Swedes, Norwegians, Finns, and Icelanders all become Nordic together.

Even with something as apparently clear-cut and definite as sex/gender—which, before it is anything else, is a matter of identifying individuals—the distinction between men and women depends as much on putative similarities within each category as on, equally putative, differences between them. What is more, the category-of-similarity "human," denoting our differences from other primates, provides the broader classificatory sense within which the distinction between men and women is made.

So difference in one context may become similarity in another. What is more, neither similarity nor difference can make any sense without the other. This is a more profound point than mere logic. Difference on its own would result in a world of incomparable individuality; similarity if pursued far enough would create a universe of homogenized, abstract monotony. Neither option is humanly plausible: Similarity and difference play off each other in the creation and attribution of meaning.

This argument becomes particularly important when considering much of the recent social science of identity. For the last 20 years or more, many of the most dominant voices in this field have emphasized difference. Under the signs of various mutations of postmodernism, postcolonialism, and poststructuralism, a fashionable orthodoxy has developed that emphasizes difference as the most important theme of identification in the contemporary world. Even those authors who recognize a distinction between identity (sameness) and difference seem to prioritize difference as the more significant.

The intellectual and political sources of this approach to this subject are not hard to see. In no particular order of significance, these include French philosopher Jacques Derrida's critique of structuralism and his notion of *différance*, psychoanalytic models of identification as early dissociation from significant others, hostility to universal (often Eurocentric) grand narratives, attempts to come to terms with globalization's subversion of old national certainties, the realities of extensive long-distance migration, the left's gradual move away from class politics, and, not least, campaigns for equality and rights by women, ethnic minorities, gays and lesbians, and disabled people. The unifying theme, such as it is, amounts to a celebration and defense of difference and diversity.

Under these circumstances, it is probably not surprising that this perspective has never amounted to a cohesive school of thought, but is rather a diverse, and loose-knit, network of broadly liberal and left-of-center intellectuals and commentators, who share some common points of agreement, but also disagree on many issues. Where there is a bedrock of broad agreement, some of this common ground is helpful if we want to understand how identification works: First, there is an insistence that identity is not fixed or primordial (although this is a theoretical wheel that has merely been reinvented) and, second, a healthy skepticism about political universalism, with its tyrannical implications of compulsory homogeneity.

In at least two respects, however, the difference model can be seen as a formidable obstacle to understanding identity and how identification works. The first issue is the privileging of difference as the driving force of identification. However, if we pay attention to difference alone, even if we just emphasize difference, we will find ourselves at odds with the observable realities of the human world. If nothing else, the significance to humans of collective belonging—*community*, for want of a better word, although we might also talk about kinship, friendship, faith, or other idioms of *we* and *us*—cannot easily be comprehended by this approach. Many difference theorists do acknowledge belonging, in its many forms. There is, however, a tension between that acknowledgement and the counter argument that identity politics is predicated on the creation and maintenance of difference.

The recognition of difference per se is not the issue here. The issues are, rather, the placing of differentiation on an analytical pedestal as the fundamental principle of identification; the failure to grasp the necessary and simultaneous interdependence of similarity and difference, each producing and informing the other; and mistaking how the world *ought* to be for how the world *is*. The latter may be the underlying concern: Celebrating the positivities of diversity and promoting mutually tolerant recognition are political positions that many doubtless support, but political programs, no matter how progressive, do not make for good theory, and wishful thinking is generally bad social science.

The second issue concerns history. Difference is seen as the dominant side of the equation and perceived to be something that is relatively new, a script for the times in which we live. This is the grand historical narrative that underwrites the analytical privileging of difference. It is worth a section in its own right.

Modernity and Identity

An image of difference and diversity as historically relatively novel—whether modern, late modern, or postmodern is beside the point—emerges in the work of many difference theorists. One example, from Stuart Hall, on the more moderate wing of difference theory, may make the general point: "Cultural diversity is, increasingly, the fate of the modern world" (p. 8). It is as if cultural diversity is either new or somehow on the rise. On the one hand, everything that we know about the past tells us that the cultural landscape, whatever else it may have been, has always been a panorama of diversity; on the other hand, the historical consequences of imperialism, ethnocide, nation-state building, and globalization are at least as likely to push us in the direction of greater homogeneity. Cultural diversity has always been the state of the human world.

Nor is it just difference that is at issue. A more general argument asserts that identity has become more salient in the modern world. There are three distinct elements to this argument: first, that identity today is chosen or achieved rather than ascribed; second, that identity has become a more pressing existential issue of selfhood than it was in earlier times; and third, that life is less stable and change more rapid and overwhelming than in previous eras. Each of these is discussed in turn.

To what extent, then, is identity in the modern human world chosen or achieved? The immediate answer is that identity is, to a large extent, mutable for some people. A marked degree of social mobility, which has no obvious historical precedent, is characteristic of modern capitalist industrial societies. It is the long-term result of economic expansion, democratic revolutions between the 17th and 20th centuries, the transformation of peasantries into proletariats, the impact of women's movements and mass-mobilized warfare on gender roles, expanded educational opportunities, and changing attitudes with respect to class (in approximate historical order). In addition, capitalists

learned long ago to use appeals to identity as a marketing strategy, so today the market place encourages and caters to all kinds of "identity projects," from youth lifestyles, to trophy child-rearing, to middle-aged adventurism, to post-retirement reinvention. One of the most important nexuses of identification has become money: If one can afford it, there are all kinds of possibilities.

The "for some people" is crucially important. Not everyone has access to the resources—economic and educational, in particular—that are required to either choose, or reject, particular identities. Despite increased affluence, this remains true for large numbers of people in democratic industrial societies because class stratification has not gone away. It is even more true for many millions of people in the poor countries of the world. Merely staying alive may be the most urgent identity project that there is.

What's more, for many people, the experience of being authoritatively categorized in the course of being "processed" by more powerful others and by organizations is an everyday, consequential fact of life about which they can do little: welfare claimants, disabled people, homeless people, and those who are confined in hospitals, prisons, refugee camps, asylum seeker detention centers, and similar institutions are only the most obvious. The labeling perspective in the sociology of deviance reminds us that this external categorization may become internalized as self-identification. Children and young people are in a particular situation in this respect. Lacking competence and the formal and informal rights of adulthood, categorization by others is simply a routine fact of life for them, and, indeed, an important and necessary part of socialization. So not everyone can choose who they are, or who they will become.

Disability has been mentioned already, but embodiment—or physiology—is important in other respects, too. It sets limits to what can conveniently or easily be achieved with respect to identity change. Gender reassignment, for example, is possible, but, by virtue of its bodily nature, no one can just *do* it, unilaterally. In addition to economic resources, the process requires the approval and participation of authoritative significant others—surgeons and possibly psychologists—and the everyday interactional cooperation of loved ones, friends, and a more distant audience. Race is even more obstinate: passing (identifying oneself as a member of race to which he or she does not belong) may be possible, depending once again on the limits set by embodiment, but it is unusual.

Less dramatically, the magazine racks of affluent societies are eloquent testimony that many of us are dissatisfied with our bodies: We may want to be taller, heavier and more muscled, thinner, or generally better looking. Despite the cornucopia of remedies on offer, however, individual bodies set real limits to how far we can change them. With respect to physiological embodiment, the world is not everyone's oyster.

Moving on, what can be said about the existential weight of identity, the pressing imperatives of selfhood and its realization that apparently characterize modernity? Does the fact that there is so much talk about identity today reflect anything other than the relatively recent adoption of a specialized term for something that was always part of the human repertoire? The most well-known sociological account of the contemporary existential significance of identity comes from British sociologist Anthony Giddens, who argues that *reflexive self-identity*—identity as a conscious project of self-improvement and personal development, as part of the "examined life"—is in some sense definitive of late modernity and is distinctly late modern. Reflexive self-identity, understood in this way, enables individuals, with the help of the expert knowledge of counselors, therapists, and the like, to write scripts for their lives that allow them much-needed senses of personal agency.

Much depends here on Giddens's narrow definition of *reflexive self-identity,* as a matter of planned personal growth rather than as a generic characteristic of all human beings. The latter may be a more defensible definition sociologically, not least because the former seems, simply by definitional fiat, to exclude most humans, throughout most of the long haul of human history, from the scope of the argument, implicitly dismissing them as incapable of reflecting on their lives or even, perhaps, knowing who they were. The most cursory look at the historical and ethnographic records suggest that Giddens's argument may say more about the conceits of modernist social theory than about selfhood.

Even taking Giddens's definition of reflexive self-identity at face value, however, the argument can be considered problematic for two reasons. First, there is simply too much evidence—not least in the religions of personal redemption, from the Buddhist scriptures to St. Augustine's *Confessions*—of premodern attitudes toward the self that at least somewhat resemble Giddens's reflexivity and the examined life. Second, Giddens's projects of reflexive selfhood, far from being definitive of modernity, are at most the preoccupation of a minority of relatively educated, relatively well-off people in the affluent capitalist industrial societies. Many other people in those societies, affluent or educated or not, do not spend too much time cultivating projects of the self in the manner that he describes: They have more urgent, if not better, things to do. This is essentially to revisit the argument about choice, earlier; these bear reiteration, however, and suggest the need for a political economy of identity.

To take the point further, and move away from Giddens, it is impossible to know how one might begin to assess empirically the claim there is a greater need "for a sense of who one is" today than there was in the past. All that can be said with any confidence is that society and sociality are, and have always been, matters of humans interacting with each other in mutually meaningful ways, for which a sense of who's who—with respect to self and others, individuals and collectivities—is necessary. How, or why, could that basic human need have become more urgent or pressing?

This is precisely the question that the argument about social change addresses. There can be little doubt that the pace of social change has speeded up during the 20th century (although the speed-up started earlier). The motors of change include capitalism, the spread of democratic government, the greater speed and volume of transportation, migration, successive revolutions in communications media, and the establishment of public health and welfare regimes. Many other factors could be mentioned. It is less certain, although it is plausible, that as a consequence of this array of changes, the nature of everyday human experience has changed. This, for example, is at the heart of the concept of globalization: Most humans are now believed to know, experientially in their everyday lives, that they live in a nonlocal, globalized world.

However, this does not mean that we can assume that there has been dramatic change in the networks and groups within which people live their lives and engage in mutual identification. Humans are adaptable and deal with change—indeed that may be one of the keys to understanding the global dominance of the species—but the continuity of human experience should not be ignored either. For most people, the basic contexts of everyday life and identification are family and kinship relations, friendship networks (whether face-to-face or online), neighborhood life, economic activity, spiritual or religious communion, and the institutions of authority or government. With respect to these facts of the human world, the more things change, the more they stay the same.

Nor does it necessarily mean that, in terms of identification, there is more to make sense of, or that sense making has become more difficult (although, depending on local circumstances, it may have become more complex, which is not always the same thing). Diversity is as diversity is experienced, rather than something than can be calibrated and measured, and too little is known about how diversity was experienced in the past to draw conclusions with confidence. However, then and now, some social settings and places were or are experienced as more or less diverse, and complex multicultural societies are not definitively modern. If anything, modernity has been characterized by the attempts of nation-states to discourage diversity in the pursuit of public cultural homogeneity.

Although identification in the modern world may, in some respects, be distinctive, that distinctiveness is not necessarily a matter of greater diversity or the greater significance of self-identification. Another—perhaps more plausible—view in this respect is that diversity, belonging, and everyday identification processes are, and have always been, generic characteristics of human life. They are part of what it is to be human.

What may be distinctively modern is the everyday significance of categorization by powerful others, and by organizations of power. This point was made compellingly by French social theorist Michel Foucault in his book *Discipline and Punish*. The process began in earnest with the state registration of populations for the purposes of taxation, which can be traced back to the ancient world. It gathered pace as the nation-state became the geopolitical norm, taking shape in population censuses,

passports and identity cards, fingerprinting, and bureaucratized internal political and criminal surveillance. With benign progressive intentions, the process spread into voter registration, public health monitoring, and state welfare distribution. Capitalists got into the act because marketing became ever more sophisticated, targeting individuals as members of consumer categories. Most recently, the process has expanded exponentially as new technologies have been developed—from cheap computing, to spy satellites, to electronic eavesdropping, to closed-circuit television in public places—and grounds for using them, such as the "war on terror" and "reclaiming the streets," have become available.

The broad historical direction of travel has been from population monitoring to individual surveillance. Today, we are recorded and categorized in ways that are often not visible to us. This categorization is always *potentially* consequential, and those consequences may be significant indeed, from the refusal of welfare or other benefits to the imposition of financial or other penalties. The power of states and corporations today comes at least as much from knowledge, specifically identificatory knowledge about individuals, as it does from the barrel of a gun or from money (not that there is any contradiction between these options).

Generic human identification is an ongoing interaction between self-identification and categorization by others, and individuals and groups will continue to assert their own identifications, to resist categorization in whatever ways they can. Where the balance will eventually be struck remains to be seen.

Richard Jenkins

See also Difference/Différance; Modernity and Postmodernity; Self; Social Identity Theory

Further Readings

Benhabib, S. (1996). Introduction: The democratic moment and the problem of difference. In S. Benhabib (Ed.), *Democracy and difference: Contesting the boundary of the political*. Princeton, NJ: Princeton University Press.

Brubaker, R. (2004). *Ethnicity without groups*. Cambridge, MA: Harvard University Press.

Foucault, M. (1979). *Discipline and punish: The birth of the prison.* Harmondsworth, UK: Penguin.

Giddens, A. (1991). *Modernity and self-identity: Self and society in the late modern age.* Cambridge, UK: Polity Press.

Gilroy, P. (1997). Diaspora and the detours of identity. In K. Woodward (Ed.), *Identity and difference.* London: Sage.

Hall, S. (1992, June). Our mongrel selves. *New Statesman and Society, 19,* 6–8.

Howard, J. A. (2000). Social psychology of identity. *Annual Review of Sociology, 26,* 367–393.

Jenkins, R. (2008). *Social identity* (3rd ed.). London: Routledge.

SOCIETY OF THE SPECTACLE

The writings of Guy Debord, and the idea of a society of almost total commodity-based *reification*—the society of the spectacle—is likely to remain the most significant legacy of Situationist thought. Debord's major work, *The Society of the Spectacle,* published in 1967, is a critique on the nature of the individual's identity in French society.

Debord was born in Paris in 1931 and grew up in the Mediterranean city of Cannes. He dropped out of the University of Paris, where he had been accepted to study law, to become a poet, revolutionary writer, and filmmaker. He founded the Lettrist International (perhaps most famous for disrupting the Cannes Film Festival in 1951) with Gil J. Wolman. This is a postsurrealist group of poets and writers that seeks the destruction of bourgeois cultural ideas and values by reducing its language—symbolized by the written word—to onomatopoeic syllables. The Lettrist ideas and interventions are represented by the journal *ION.* From 1957, Debord determined the actions of the Situationist International (SI), an activist movement that sought to set itself up as "the only contemporary power against the forces of the past." At the founding meeting, Debord presented a programmatic text titled "Report on the Construction of Situations," in which he outlined the strategies of the SI in relation to the cultural avant-garde. In the 1960s, Debord took the leading role in the SI movement and was a supporter of the Paris uprising of 1968. His major written work is the SI-inspired *The Society of the Spectacle.* In the 1970s, he disbanded the SI movement, and continued with filmmaking supported by the financial backing of Gerard Lebovici. Debord's two major films are the *Society of the Spectacle* of 1973, and the autobiographical *We Turn in a Circle at Night and We Are Consumed by Fire* (*In Girum Imus Nocte et Consumimur Igni*) of 1981. Debord committed suicide (shooting himself through the heart at his cottage in Champot) on November 30, 1994.

The SI is a political and artistic movement that centered on Debord's ideas and interventions. The movement is represented by a journal of the same name published between 1958 and 1969. Debord and his colleagues attempt to create a series of strategies to engage in Marxist class struggle by reclaiming a sense of individual autonomy from the pervasive embrace of the *spectacle:* "All of life presents itself as an immense accumulation of spectacles" (*The Society of the Spectacle,* p. 12). These strategies include the most-cited neologisms *dérive* and *détournement,* and draw on the traditions of the historical avant-garde, Dada, and surrealism in particular. *Dérive* might be described as a productive wandering, a Situationist drifting through the city to map the pyschogeography of different communities. Rather than being imprisoned by the daily routines of life, Debord urged citizens to follow their emotions in such wonderings and reconsider the urban spaces in which they and others live and work; this idea allies with Henri Lefebvre's call for *the Critique of Everyday Life.* Such wanderings led Debord to the belief that cities and their modes of spatial organization control populations through their design (the notion of spatial politics). *Détournement* suggests diversion, deflection, or hijacking for prohibited or political purposes. In this strategy, an artist reuses well-known elements to create a new work with a different, often contrary, message. This notion is anticipated by Marcel Duchamp's ready-mades, Bertolt Brecht's understanding of *Umfunktionerung,* and Dada photomontages. This strategy is also practiced contemporarily, as in Andy Warhol's Coca-Cola bottles, Brillo boxes, and Campbell's soup cans, in which consumer gratification is mimicked and appropriated, or in the work of the Brazilian artist Cildo Meireles, who silk-screens political messages onto empty glass Coca-Cola bottles and then "reintroduces" them into the capitalist system. Such strategies, in the hands of the Situationists, attempt to confront the power of the *spectacle* with its own commodity detritus. Capitalist products thus subvert capitalism itself.

The collection of writings that constitute *The Society of the Spectacle* is divided into 221 theses; Debord's discussion sets itself against the ruling conditions of contemporary French society. The book maintains its ground in relation to each single thesis, but seen as a whole, the work is significantly fragmentary and ambiguous. Nevertheless, it represents a powerful critique of the nature of the individual's identity in French society. Debord and Michel Foucault described two different ways of criticizing visual culture in terms of what is widely called the *scopic regime*. Foucault focused on the normalizing effect of being the object of the *gaze*, and Debord and the Situationist emphasized the dangers of being the subject of that gaze. For the Situationist, the seductive political manipulation of images is far more pernicious than is Foucault's concept of uncanny surveillance (brought to a head in contemporary closed-circuit television observations). In the French language, *spectacle* also refers to a theatrical presentation, that is, a suspension of belief, a situation analogous to the situation of the commodified consumer. According to Debord, in societies where the modern conditions of production prevail, all of life presents itself as an immense accumulation of spectacles. Everything that was directly lived has moved away into mere representation; all that was once solid melts into air. It is a world of vision and image, which has become completely objectified. Debord's point is that the image (TV images, advertising images, images of popular culture and of celebrity, newspaper images, film, and so on) is not at fault as such, images simply act as mediators among the people of a society. The real issue is the denigration of the way in which images mediate between those individuals. Debord argues that the spectacle, and its hypnotic, anodyne mediation, separates and alienates the individual—thus preventing any political engagement, any dialogue and consensus about class structure and class struggle within a society. According to this scenario, those who consume visual culture in passivity are suspended in a dream world of capitalist fantasy.

The commodified or *reified* individual (a situation where individuals themselves are reduced to commodities in capitalist cultures) no longer asks these images, or their systems, for knowledge or to provide some purchase on reality. The consumers of these images expect nothing of them but a continuation of a limitlessly productive game; one image after another, one commodity after another. In this schema, the individual subject is dealing with an explosion of signs without meaning, and without a means of exit. Society as a whole has been reduced to a giant spectacle, in which the images of the commodity (commodity fetish) totally occupy everyday existence, thus uniting capitalist production and consumption in a perfect dance. In *The Society of the Spectacle*, Debord describes a vast and meaningless game of meanings: Images lead only to other images and consume themselves in ever more rapid production, no deeper significance or object hides behind them, and they are entirely superficial. This is a simulation of reality or, as Jean Baudrillard would have it, a *simulacrum* of reality. That is, a condition arrived at when the distinction between representation and reality, between signs and their significations, dissolves. It was hoped that the strategies of *détournement* and *dérive* would go some way to break the pattern of reciprocal alienation Debord identifies as underpinning the relationship between the spectacle and the real (the real in this case being historical materialism). Debord is highly critical of the conventional practice of art because it is recuperated by capitalism (museums, collectors, the art market, critics, and historians) as a means of conditioning, "brain washing," the wider population. Asger Jorn, a founding member of SI, resigned from SI in 1961 in response to increasingly hostile criticism of art from the group around Debord, and in 1962, SI disqualified art from consideration as a legitimate site of revolutionary struggle.

Peter Muir

See also Artistic Development and Cognition; Collective/Social Identity; Modern Art; Propaganda

Further Readings

Debord, G. (2004). *The society of the spectacle*. New York: Zone Books.

Lebovici, G. (Producer), & Debord, G. (Writer/Director). (1973). *La société du spectacle* [Documentary]. Paris: Gaumont.

Lebovici, G. (Producer), & Debord, G. (Writer/Director). (1978). *In girum imus nocte et consumimur igni* [Documentary]. Paris: Gaumont.

SOCIOMETER HYPOTHESIS

The *sociometer hypothesis* is rooted in the historical tradition of psychology explaining the existence of self-esteem. According to this hypothesis, self-esteem acts as a gauge that measures the quality and state of an individual's relationships with other people. The foundational premise for the hypothesis states that people are pervasively driven to possess and maintain meaningful interpersonal relationships and group memberships. It would then follow that some type of mechanism would evolve that could monitor the status of relationships for individuals so they could then adjust accordingly to maintain their standing within social settings and not risk ostracism. This mechanism— the *sociometer*—constantly assesses cues from the social environment to determine the extent to which an individual is successfully maneuvering through his or her interpersonal relationships.

Psychologists have historically examined self-esteem because it has been seen as an important psychological construct. Researchers have identified two distinct types of self-esteem: *trait self-esteem* and *state self-esteem*. Trait self-esteem refers to an individual's general understanding of his or her value in the individual's social world, and *state self-esteem* refers to the situational fluctuations a person may experience in relation to his or her worth within the individual's social settings. Originally, the sociometer hypothesis was criticized for not considering these differentiated states of self-esteem; however, further clarifications of the hypothesis revealed that both states were accounted for by the sociometer hypothesis. Regarding the hypothesis, state self-esteem could easily be considered a baseline level self-esteem that has accounted for a lifetime's worth of evaluations of relational standing for an individual. State self-esteem, however, offers an evaluation of the current situation for an individual that can lead to fluctuations from the baseline trait self-esteem level depending on whether an individual encounters cues that relay high or low relational standing.

If one considers the sociometer to be a gas gauge in a car, where the needle rests, on average, represents the trait self-esteem of a person, and the movement of the needle represents the state self-esteem that is affected by the inputs received from the social cues in an individual's environment.

Considering the sociometer hypothesis attempts to explain the functional existence of self-esteem, other theories have come forward to offer opposing views. One of the most prominent alternative theories is *terror management theory*. This theory concludes that self-esteem exists because it helps distract people from the fear of death, which is a uniquely human experience because humans are capable of considering their own mortality. Terror management theory has been offered as a more cogent theory to explain self-esteem in contrast to the sociometer hypothesis, and several articles have examined the differences and similarities in their ability to explain the function of self-esteem. However, the authors of the sociometer hypothesis have summarized their own positions on this matter because each theory is useful in explaining certain domains of social behavior.

From *social identity theory*, people join groups to gain positive self-esteem based on comparisons with other relevant groups. Therefore, it would be most useful to have some mechanism in place that could monitor self-esteem. Also, within social identity theory, *self-categorization theory* argues that people within any given group will evaluate the characteristics of other group members to determine whether individual members are doing enough to maintain group membership. Based on this information, the sociometer serves an important function because it allows people to understand if their behaviors and attitudes are acceptable to the rest of the group. If the member successfully displays the appropriate behaviors and attitudes, he or she would experience positive self-esteem because his or her standing with in the group would be secure. However, if he or she does not properly display behaviors and attitudes indicative of the group, the individual would experience low self-esteem because this would communicate that he or she was in jeopardy of being ostracized and isolated.

Since its development, the sociometer hypothesis has been tested and shown to exist when people are given the choice of joining a new group. People low in self-esteem were more likely to join groups if they knew there were no conditions on acceptance. Meanwhile, people high in self-esteem showed no preference for group membership based on whether they were guaranteed acceptance from other group members. These findings have been replicated in other nations and while controlling for other variables that might have mediated the relationship between self-esteem and social acceptance.

The sociometer hypothesis stipulates that self-esteem is used as a mechanism for monitoring social cues that give information about acceptance in interpersonal relationships and group memberships. As self-esteem fluctuates around a general baseline state of self-esteem, it conveys specific information about an individual's standing within social settings. For example, low self-esteem conveys the message that an individual is at risk of being ostracized and isolated. However, having high self-esteem provides the information that a person has little need to change attitudes or behaviors because all social cues indicate that his or her social standing is secure. This means the person would have a good balance of enough *individuation* while displaying the necessary social markers for maintaining strong group identity. The sociometer is an evolutionarily important mechanism that is believed to have developed to monitor the social cues necessary to determine social standing through fluctuations in self-esteem.

Jason E. Rivera

See also Collective/Social Identity; Group Identity; Individuation; Self-Esteem; Self-Monitoring; Social Identity Theory; Terror Management Theory

Further Readings

Hogg, M. A., Hohman, Z. P., & Rivera J. E. (2008). Why do people join groups? Three motivational accounts from social psychology. *Social and Personality Psychology Compass, 2/3,* 1269–1280.

Leary, M. R. (2004). The function of self-esteem in terror management theory and sociometer theory: Comment on Pyszcznski et al. (2004). *Psychological Bulletin, 130,* 478–482.

Leary, M. R., & Baumeister, R. F. (2000). The nature and function of self-esteem: Sociometer theory. In M. P. Zanna (Ed.), *Advances in experimental social psychology* (Vol. 32, pp. 1–62). San Diego, CA: Academic Press.

SOVEREIGNTY

Sovereignty is a characteristic of a political entity that, within a defined geographical area, possesses and exercises power that is the highest in that area. The sovereign entity's decision is both generally applicable throughout the area and, although extraneous matters such as public or world opinion are not typically disregarded, the sovereign entity acts independently. Sovereignty has, since the European Renaissance, been an important characteristic of the modern state, assisting in the development of national identity. Initially, sovereignty operated within a state, establishing where power resides. Eventually, sovereignty functioned more within the context of international relations, distinguishing one state from another and thereby defining exclusive areas of political power as well as separable national political identities. Both political thought and political realities since the Renaissance have complicated both the intrastate and international applicability of the concept of sovereignty, however.

Sovereignty in Domestic Affairs

Within any geographical area, entities compete for power. When the concept of sovereignty developed in the Renaissance, there was competition between ecclesiastical and secular entities. Today, the competition might be between transnational corporate and secular entities. The concept of sovereignty assumes that there is a winner in any competition. This winner would possess the highest power and be able to exercise it independently of other entities. This victor's decisions would govern affairs throughout the area and would be final. This victor would be said to possess sovereignty.

The concept was defined well in Jean Bodin's *Six Books of a Commonwealth* (1576) and reiterated in Thomas Hobbes's *Leviathan* (1651). Both Bodin and Hobbes assumed a strong state, one that in their time would have been associated with a strong ruler such as a monarch. In the next hundred or so years, John Locke, Montesquieu, and Jean-Jacques Rousseau challenged the assumption that sovereignty rests in such a ruler. They instead invested power in the people or, at least, in a governmental body thought representative of the people. Although the concept of sovereignty and the idea that the state possesses this characteristic survived this challenge, these philosophers generated more democratic thinking, further texturing the concept of identity and democracy.

For example, if the sovereign state is said to possess the highest power, how can that be if the people are ultimately superior, especially if they can demonstrate that superiority by either voting the governors of the state out of power or by reversing the governors' decisions by referenda? Furthermore, if the people as voters have this ultimate power and if those who govern are aware of its existence as they act, how can the governors' decisions be said to be truly independent? Are not the decisions to some extent swayed by public opinion?

Many of the emerging democratic governments featured a system of checks and balances among those engaged in ruling the state. If an elected assembly's will can be overruled by an elected executive's veto, then is not that assembly's sovereignty at least qualified? Furthermore, if that assembly's will can be overruled by a court engaged in judicial review, is not that assembly's sovereignty still further qualified? The answer, in cases such as these, may well be to hold the government in its totality sovereign or to posit that a document such as the U.S. Constitution is sovereign, possessing power that is higher, more final, more generally applicable, and more autonomous than any governing body or agent that the document may establish and define.

Democracy, insofar as proponents assume popular sovereignty or features checks and balances, is not the only complication to the idea of sovereignty. The size and resulting complexity of the modern state also complicates the concept. In such a state, there is typically a distribution of power. In such a diffuse system, few acts are as generally applicable as are those of a monarch or despot. Furthermore, in such a state, there are typically layers of power. Final power may be distributed horizontally throughout the system based on jurisdiction as well as vertically based on whether the decision is thought to be trivial or important. Where the highest and final authority rests may well depend on what the matter under consideration is.

Despite these complications, the concept of sovereignty has endured. Theorists seem to grant popular sovereignty, checks and balances, and the diffuse, layered modern government while adhering to the assumption of the sovereign state initially articulated by Bodin and Hobbes. Political realities require qualifications but not a revision of the fundamental concept.

Sovereignty in International Affairs

As the names of the philosophers already mentioned suggest, sovereignty is a Western political concept. In the less-developed world, the concept has taken hold and is still functioning much as it did in the Renaissance: as a way to resolve competition for power among entities within a state. In the developed Western world, however, the concept is now functioning less within a state and more among states. In this larger context, sovereignty allows states, however they might be governed, to exercise the highest, the final, and the most all-encompassing power over their internal affairs without interference from other entities. The United Nations (UN) charter, for example, in Article 2, paragraphs 1 and 7, establishes this concept of sovereignty as a basic assumption for the conduct of international affairs in the post–World War II period.

Already implicit in that charter, however, is a complication that undercuts this concept of sovereignty: The charter recognizes the right of the global community to act under certain circumstances—for example, if human rights are being violated. That concern was important in the post-Holocaust environment in which the charter was written, and that concern has incrementally increased in the decades since. Joining it has been a concern for the common resources of air and water as well as the presumably common frontier of space. If the supposed sovereign state is violating human rights or fouling the commons, the international community should be able to act in some manner to overrule that state's internal decisions. Is, then, the international community—or some international organization such as the UN—sovereign? Most would say no, for UN edicts can be ignored by the state. Of course, the renegade state then tempts the UN to enforce its position militarily. Such action, however, would not be viewed as an affront to the state's sovereignty but, rather, an extraordinary response to a sovereign state's affront to internationally recognized standards of conduct that transcend sovereignty.

International law has long wrestled with the conflicting idea of sovereignty and the need to deal with the many matters that either do not stay neatly situated within a state's boundaries or require international intervention on moral grounds. Commerce, of course, was the primary example of boundary-crossing activity after the Renaissance. Initially, those involved could be clearly associated with one sovereign state or another, thereby providing international law as a starting point. Today, the globalization of commercial activities has created an environment in which the individual players are not necessarily under a single sovereign state's jurisdiction but are transnational. Under whose authority are they? Or do they possess power that transcends and perhaps surpasses that of the individual state? If so, perhaps these corporations, as well as other international entities, might be said to possess sovereignty.

Again, despite these complications, the concept of sovereignty and the assumption that it inheres in the state have endured. Theorists seem to admit both the sanctity of the sovereign state in the international arena and the circumstances under which this sanctity might have to be violated. They furthermore grant the many ways in which the autonomy of the state is increasingly a functioning myth. Again, political realities require qualifications but not a revision of the fundamental concept of sovereignty.

The concept of sovereignty then endures. It is, however, the subject of a considerable body of writing. That theorizing attempts to reconcile the fundamental notion found in Bodin and Hobbes, which presumes one kind of state, with newer political realities in many if not most states. Furthermore, that theorizing attempts, first, to modify the concept from one defining power within a state to one useful in defining the terms of relationships among states and, second, to adjust this modified concept to fit newer political realities in international affairs. In this literature, some have suggested that the concept of sovereignty has limited value in contemporary government and international relations. The prevailing opinion, however, seems to be that the concept, although it must be modified to fit contemporary political realities, offers a valuable if somewhat fictitious basis for defining power relations within a single state and among several.

Theodore F. Sheckels

See also Political Identity; State Identity; Transnationalism

Further Readings

Bull, H. (1977). *The anarchical society: A study of order in world politics* (3rd ed.). New York: Columbia University Press.

Dicey, A. V. (1959). *Introduction to the study of the law of the constitution* (10th ed.). London: Macmillan.

Held, D. (1989). *Political theory and the modern state.* Palo Alto, CA: Stanford University Press.

Hinsley, F. H. (1986). *Sovereignty* (2nd ed.). Cambridge, UK: Cambridge University Press.

Jouvenal, B. de. (1957). *Sovereignty: An inquiry into the political good.* Chicago: University of Chicago Press.

Kelsen, H. (1949). *General theory of law and state.* Cambridge, MA: Harvard University Press.

King, P. (1974). *The ideology of order: A comparative analysis of Jean Bodin and Thomas Hobbes.* London: Allen & Unwin.

Laski, H. J. (1917). *Studies in the problem of sovereignty.* New Haven, CT: Yale University Press.

Merriam, C. E. (1900). *History of the theory of sovereignty since Rousseau.* New York: Columbia University Press.

Morgenthau, H. (2005). *Politics among nations: The struggle for power and peace* (7th ed.). New York: McGraw-Hill.

Stankiewicz, W. J. (1976). *Aspects of political theory: Classical concepts in an age of relativism.* London: Collier-Macmillan.

SPECTACLE AND THE SELF

The history of the *spectacle* is tied to the politics of illusion, seduction, fantasy, and exaggeration. The spectacle's main function is to promote passivity and confusion by manipulating the perception of events in such a way as to obscure their true nature. Under different social formations, it emerges in different forms. Under late capitalism, what constitutes the modern spectacle is a complex network of ideological and material conditions. These conditions now play an increasingly significant role in the formation of the sociopolitical sense of identity and self that panders to a subjectivity that is narcissistically concerned with its own development in the name of self-fulfillment. As such, the common good is built on the promise of symbolic rather than material satisfaction; the contested territory of competing political solutions gives way to culturally defined niche markets and other distractions.

In the early 1960s, Guy Debord—the experimental filmmaker and the principle theorist for the Situationist International (SI), a rag-tag, ad hoc assemblage of self-proclaimed revolutionary intellectuals and avant-garde artists sporting surrealist, Marxist, Maoist, and Frankfurt school beliefs—first identified the qualitative change taking place in the character of capitalist society. In his book *The Society of the Spectacle* published in 1967, Debord advances the thesis that capitalism (both its liberal democratic and autocratic state forms), to cement its grip on all spheres of private and communal life, was turning society into an object. The condition of an all-encompassing social and economic system that promises the satisfaction of all individual needs is built on a kind of schizophrenia inherent in the taxonomy and idealism of Western society.

Though Debord was decidedly a Marxist in the 1960s at the time he identified the emergent spectacularization of society, he held the unique view that capitalism as an institution and a system had culturally co-opted its antithesis in the form of Soviet communism. Consequently, his critique of the spectacle as a totalizing environment of immediacy and manufactured values, rather than being rooted in a specifically class-based analysis, is premised on a model of difference and agency. From this perspective, reason, autonomy, individuality, self-representation, and self-determination are achieved and sustained only by resisting the distraction of capitalism's field of manufactured possibilities and opportunities, which are tied to its hegemonic ideology. The only true contradiction that exists within the society of the spectacle therefore is the one between imagination (creativity) and standardization (conformity). This critique builds on Walter Benjamin's view of the image world being created in the 1920s to 1930s by Hollywood in the United States as akin to the Nazis in that both used mass media to motivate and control their audience's imagination.

By attracting attention to the unpleasant, unusual, or ridiculous, the spectacle gives cohesiveness to reality by manipulating every subjective value and criteria until it has no other alternative but to become its opposite. This is then supplemented by a vision of cultural redemption in which it is proposed that neither group identity nor self-reflexivity are any longer necessary—and that these long-held goals just might be the cause of our present unhappiness. The Lacanian political theorist Slavoj Žižek envisions this phenomenon resulting from a condition he dubs "the passion for the real," which leads one to become fascinated by violence and those agents who express raw rage without apology. This repressed admiration for the other becomes an all-consuming fantasy of destruction, annihilation, transcendence, mutation, and apocalypse that dominates popular culture. In turn, Žižek urges us to protect ourselves against our own protective capacities, which form the prohibitions that simultaneously perpetuate institutional, economic, ecological, social, and other injustices. Afraid of its self and all others, the resulting self this dynamic produces is vulnerable to the growing role that machination and manipulation play in assuring us what we truly desire is a more controllable world to which no alterity might be imagined. The power of the spectacle, therefore, resides in its ability to represent our fantasies as if they were always already real.

Though test marketing and psychological research consume significant amounts of resources, the spectacle is not so much the outcome of conspiracies by the military/industrial complex, or a cabal of monomaniacal capitalists; rather, it depends on exploiting existent habits of thought. Consequently, the spectacle is not something imposed on society but a condition that arises from its motivating forces and desires; the spectacle is not reducible to the effects of the mass media. Although today the media are an all-important component of the spectacle, due to the media's ability to turn everything—sports events, breaking news and the weather, the lives of celebrities (those who are famous for being famous)—into heavily dramatized occurrences whose sole effects are to attract, distract, and influence its audience day after day.

Disseminating a dizzying array of conflicting messages of desire and fear, optimism and uncertainty, as well as promises of fulfillment and empowerment, mass media provides models for emulation, which in turn drives capital's economy. As a mechanism of cultural control, the spectacle as employed by capitalists infiltrates and organizes the private sphere in the name of convenience and profit, by creating demands for consumable novelties, which play on our sense of insufficiency, limitation, and fear. Inversely, in seeking ever-new content, the cultural venues that persist in producing or sustaining the notion of quality, innovation, or difference come to be appropriated so that they can be repackaged and commoditized. Therefore, the terror of the spectacle consists of the constant threat of loss, boredom, or inefficiency. This is reinforced by the collective experiences and confusion that comes from the dissemination of information from standardized sources and formats. This culminates in a failure to be able to differentiate between fact and fiction, between individual and collective experiences.

Aware that this power makes the public uneasy, the claim advanced is that the contents circulated reflect what the public wants and demands. This democracy of the marketplace masks the insidious nature of consumerism, which buttresses the tendency for profit to win over the social good. Beyond the proliferation of mass media as a way to realize profit and control, modern science and psychoanalytic theory—which proposes that the objective world is only the raw materiality from which we construct our reality—also plays an important role in society's spectacularization. The Western concept of subjectivity that these disciplines build on hypothesizes that the real is what it is thought to be and the individual is self-defined by what he or she thinks and feels. The interaction of the social, economic, and cultural spheres as ordered by the logic of capitalism results in an impossibility of determining who or what acts on what, which effectively turns the populace into spectators who view from a distance the events that circumscribe their lives. This results in an inability for broad sectors of society to autonomously differentiate their selves from the conditions of production and reproduction that the spectacle represents as the essence of their reality. This instrumentality, which conceals the real

implications of being inundated 24 hours per day by the interminable amount of information that is filtered and distributed through an ever-increasing network of mediated outlets functions to prevent the formulation of a political critique.

As we evolve an "experience-based economy," a designation that references the micromanaged zones of commerce that project ambience (or a kind of branding) around products, all aspects of daily life—from the way we are managed at work, to the lifestyles we consume—are being designed, standardized, and anesthetized. These messages differ from market to market, fragmenting society into competing groups whose self-interest is based on cultural affinities rather than on those of politics and economics, the latter of which once were the primary sources of both individual and group cultural identity. The intent is to lead the consumer to believe that his or her relationship to business, government, and even one to another is little more than that of client to a service provider of both individuated and common experiences. The constant dissemination of bourgeois values embedded in the seemingly neutral space of leisure time and personal consumption transforms subjectivity itself into an object of aesthetic experience. In these moments, feelings and thoughts are reconstructed, producing a simulated self, which is in turn experienced and affirmed as mutable in its wants, but as essential in its content. This manifestation of an essential self presents itself as an "as if" metaphor in which the self is regarded "as if it" were an object, and "as if it" were an autonomous subject. This leaves us with a vision of ourselves in which consciousness and the moment-to-moment restatement of self appear to be something potentially cruel, a cause for long-lasting pain by making the things that seem most important look futile, obsolete, and negligible. The ultimate effect of this is the redirection of the political impulse onto a marketplace of potential fulfillment ordered by the relative liberty of a judgment-free choice of lifestyles and diversion.

The political implications of creating a cultural environment that absorbs all and has no demonstrable borders rather than a political environment is that it creates an illusionary territory in which all issues may be resolved in a truly democratic manner. So in the place of the political, the ideology of consumerism has created a condition in which we no longer believe that we might realize ourselves in our ability to produce effect, but instead only on our ability to consume. The consequence of this process was the continuous seeking of reasons to apply technology to those territories of human activity that either had eluded colonization or been liberated. This process takes idealized forms and their contents, exchanging them for those of commerce and technology. All the products of the culture industry, not just the advertising, are committed to making us susceptible to this process by showing how the traits that lead to greed exploitation, manipulation, and dominance are also those of self-liberation and leadership. The resulting sense of self is that of being an autonomous subject existing in a world in which the public and private, political and economic, alternately disconnect and conflate into the cultural.

Susan Buck Morse, in discussing Benjamin's statement concerning aesthetics and politics, points out that the goal was to anesthetize the individual's experience of everyday life, therefore subsuming and disorienting him or her. Debord identifies this same process as having become an intrinsic aspect of capitalist society, wherein individuals' experiences are constructed and encoded for them as both a form of diversion and social and economic management. The objective of this process is not to direct us—but to addict us. Consequently, the reality of the spectacle is at first nuanced and complex; however, it is also less layered, varied, and concrete as the glut of un-ordered information closes the gap between the plausible, the improbable, and the existent. In this environment—a situation in which the distinction between past, present, and future is blurred—everything appears to be equally relevant, or worthless, foiling our attempts to make informed judgments. Inversely, the ongoing interaction between the technological, social, and cultural deeply embedded in an ideology of subjectivity and self-realization becomes a confusion of facts, fictions, and ersatz experiences sustained by the appeal of pragmatism, positivism, and passivity. Within this environment, the self is made susceptible to the permutations and changes in the symbolic values that come to be promoted as substantive content. It is no wonder that conspiracy theories concerning all aspects of government and business emerge alongside the enthusiastic promotion of computers, interactive games and the promise of virtual realities—as something that will fulfill what has become our neurotic need not to be idle or alone.

The dynamic that underlies the spectacle is multigenerational and continues to resonate with the cold war rhetoric that revolved around the representation of the individual's freedom to choose a lifestyle as constituting a political choice. This dynamic is indicative of this ideological shift. Accompanying this state of affairs was the additional promise that the resolutions of the conflicts and inequities inherent to capitalism would be resolved in the marketplace of cultural offerings. In the West, even those who opposed this schema have contributed to the successful dissemination of it by adhering to an idealized vision of individual, material, and conceptual wants and desires that are derived ideologically from the Enlightenment and then modernism. With poststructuralism's critique of the master narratives that made up these systems, the idea of the spectacle took on greater theoretical importance because its effects had become all pervasive. Jean Baudrillard proposed that the world of symbolic representation had become an "empire of the sign" in which the economy of images and meaning also carved out a new dematerialized reality in which signs and images precede the real. Within this field of cultural transformation, the constituent parts of a new collective sense of a virtual self were ultimately founded on the premise that biotechnology and nanotechnology were propelling the human species toward a post-human state. This sense of self rests on the notion that identity is little more than a construct of experiences, concepts, and social models, which are often at first thought to be inauthentic and then become real.

Postmodern individuals seek self-affirmation in their own distinctive personalities, to which they may give self-expression. Viewed in this frame, the political aspiration of various sectors of the society come to be represented as nothing more than a list of scripted positions awaiting to be fulfilled. At present, these scripts are more rightist than leftist and more emotional than intellectual given capitalism's successful appropriation of postmodernism's critique of how history and reason are used to advance a model of reality in which objects (such as freedom, progress, equality) can be prescribed, while allowing them to be subjectively interpreted as conditional terms. Within this schema, everything appears to be a disconnected component, whose value only resides in our ability to formulate a hierarchy of values permitting us to imagine and then assemble them into an integrated sensible whole. This awareness, rather than producing what once was identified as a state of emancipation, instead generates its antithesis. The fascistic nature of the spectacle lies in that its representations do not just displace the symbolic world of order, control, and meaningfulness but actually dissolve it into a sequence of externals that exist beyond our control—not as simulacra of the real, but as a condition of the environment in which all things come to exist.

Saul Ostrow

See also Frankfurt School; Simulacra; Society of the Spectacle; Visual Culture

Further Readings

Adorno, T., & Horkheimer, M. (1979). The culture industry: Enlightenment as mass deception. In T. Adorno & M. Horkheimer (Eds.), *Dialectic of enlightenment*. London: Verso.

Althusser, L. (1971). Ideology and ideological state apparatuses. In L. Althusser (Ed.), *Lenin and philosophy and other essays*. New York: Monthly Review Press.

Baudrillard, J. (1994). *Simulacra and simulation*. Ann Arbor: University of Michigan Press.

Bell, D. (1979). *The cultural contradictions of capitalism*. London: Heinemann.

Benjamin, W. (1992). *Illuminations* (H. Arendt, Ed., & H. Zohn, Trans.). London: Fontana. (Original work published 1936)

Debord, G. (2004). *The society of the spectacle*. New York: Zone Books.

Giroux, H. A. (2006). *Beyond the spectacle of terrorism: Global uncertainty and the challenge of the new media*. Boulder, CO: Paradigm.

Kellner, D. (2005). *Media spectacle and the crisis of democracy: Terrorism, war, and election battles*. Boulder, CO: Paradigm.

Merish, L. (1996). Cuteness and commodity aesthetics: Tom Thumb and Shirley Temple. In R. G. Thomson (Ed.), *Freakery: Cultural spectacles of the extraordinary body* (pp. 185–203). New York: New York University Press.

Virilio, P. (1989). *War and cinema: Logistics of perception*. London: Verso.

Warner, M. (1992). The mass public and the mass subject. In C. Calhoun (Ed.), *Habermas and the public sphere* (pp. 377–401). Cambridge: MIT Press.

STATE IDENTITY

State identity generally refers to the body of interests, values, self-understandings, and orientations from which states act in the world. As a term, *state identity* posits that it is meaningful to understand the political community of a state as having a collective identity or sense of itself at a highly generalized, but nevertheless important level. The body of interests, values, and self-understanding that makes up state identity is rooted in a country's history and cultures, human and physical geography, economy and underlying strategic context. At the same time, state identity is shaped by the state's experience of the process of international interaction through time.

A number of fundamentally important features of the concept of state identity flow from this. Although complex and multilayered, a state's identity has considerable stability. This gives the concept real analytic value because analysis can be framed in a way that appeals to general principles (of international politics in particular) while being sensitive to the dense particularity of specific states. Even though state identity is relatively stable, however, it is also flexible and evolving. Many of the elements in which state identity is embedded, or their significance, are changing through time—cultures are dynamic, the economic or strategic value of resources can change, and so on. Thus, the concept does not demand an essentialist or ahistorical account of identity. Moreover, as with individual or group identity, the ongoing development of state identity occurs to a significant extent through interaction with other states and international actors. This gives the concept of state identity particular relevance to questions of foreign policy as well as to efforts to theorize the nature of international politics.

The idea of state identity is closely associated with one of the leading contemporary theories of international relations: constructivism. As the name implies, constructivists understand states' identities as constructed through the process of international interaction. Conversely, the nature of the international sphere is constituted through the character of states' identities and actions. This emphasis contrasts with the other theoretical perspectives dominating mainstream international relations theory: neorealism and neoliberalism. In the words of Alexander Wendt, a leading exponent of constructivism, "anarchy is what states make of it"—that is, the international arena is as conflictual or as cooperative as states determine through their interactions over time. This is a dynamic, interactive grasp of international politics, which gives self-directed human action (or agency) a central role in shaping the character of international politics while providing a way of conceptualizing the complexity and difficulty of change. The concept of a socially constructed state identity also gives constructivists a way of understanding meaning and value as well as power and material interests as drivers of action in the international arena. This capacity to account for change, in ways that give norms and values a potentially significant role without being idealist, has given constructivism considerable appeal as a practical reflection on international politics.

Conceptual Frameworks

The concept of state identity in international relations theory provides a relatively complex, nuanced way of understanding a state's actions in the international arena. In this sense, state identity makes the category of the state as that category is understood by the preeminent neorealist schools and to a lesser extent by neoliberalism (liberal institutionalism) problematic.

The state is the primary international actor for neorealists, neoliberals (compared with earlier iterations of liberalism), and constructivists. In the 1970s, realism and liberalism were significantly influenced by rational choice theory, particularly in the United States, contributing to a refocusing for both orientations. As a consequence, both orientations conceptualized states more tightly as rational egoists; both also intensified their commitments to empirically driven social science research agendas. For both approaches, the international arena, as the context within which states act, is characterized by the lack of any compelling, overarching authority— that is, by international anarchy. For neorealists,

the fundamental feature of anarchy is the ever-present threat of conflict; to ensure survival, states are driven to seek security by maintaining or maximizing their relative power and resources. Although cooperation occurs, it is not the most salient reality of the international realm, which is fundamentally a self-help system, defined by each state's need to rely on its own resources to protect its own interests. Anarchy thus establishes the nature of the international system (as conflictual and competitive) and states pursue their interests, which necessarily revolve around calculations of security and relative power, within it. Though accepting the proposition of anarchy, proponents of liberal institutionalism are concerned with understanding the conditions under which cooperation is possible because cooperation as well as conflict characterize international interaction. States pursue interests, but these include interests in absolute (not only relative) gain that may result from cooperation. Neoliberalists consider that states can learn, but neoliberalism does not provide a conceptually integrated basis upon which to theorize the ways learning occurs.

Constructivism takes a different approach to the state, as the primary form of agency. The emergence of constructivism since the late 1980s (with scholars including Nicholas Onuf, Peter Katzentein, Frederich Kratochwil, and John Ruggie) reflected long-standing debates in social theory about the nature of society, human agency, and the state and about the best ways to seek to understand them (that is, methodological or epistemological debates). Rather than investigating social reality as an already established set of given "facts" (positivism) or the state as a set of fixed institutional arrangements peopled by individuals understood as rational calculators of interests (instrumental rationalism), constructivists drew on interpretive approaches to social theory. In particular, they were influenced by sociology of knowledge in the 1960s (notably Peter Berger and Thomas Luckmann) and sociological institutionalism in the 1970s. These approaches emphasized the ongoing work of collective human activity in constructing social reality and the close relationship between the ways we make reality and the ways we make sense of it.

Constructivists applied these approaches to the analysis of international politics. The idea of state identity points to states as having interests and identities through which interests are filtered; moreover, these identities are complex and evolving. Whereas "self-interest" or "self-help" in analyses of international relations can function as a closed box—fundamental categories that allow only narrow lines of investigation—state identity potentially opens the self of the state to further questioning and analysis. Thus, it becomes possible to explore what self-interest might mean for a particular state and how or why that may have changed beyond explanations offered by the analysis of strategic and economic opportunities or threats. What a state values can change how it construes its interests. The self-interest of security, for example, while remaining fundamental, could be understood and sought in radically different ways. State identity in principle at least provides a conceptual bridge for closely integrating analysis of the internal domestic and the international dimensions of why states act as they do.

Constructivism does not presume the pre-given identity or fixed system of exchange that is embedded in the rational egoist model of state interaction. The identities of states evolve to a significant extent through participation in international and transnational relations over time; they may become more pro-social and collective or more egoistic, or more or less confrontational, collaborative, or withdrawn. The character of the international arena can also shift in turn, albeit not readily. Identity generates motives and orientations and is the basis of interests, but interests are in turn defined and redefined through interaction; shifts in interests and their pursuit will cumulatively have an effect on self-identity and the perception of others. Identity is thus sustained or transformed through the inter-subjective processes of pursuing interests and dispositions, of planning, action, and experience in a world shaped by the dynamics of exchange. The idea of state identity thus provides a means for conceptualizing and exploring the ways by which states might change beyond the explanations offered by behavioral adaption to changing circumstances or an account cast purely in terms of individual leaders' decisions. Identity is nevertheless relatively stable and not readily changeable. More emphatically than neoliberalists, constructivists argue that

states learn. The notion of state identity, moreover, provides a way of explaining how learning takes place.

The idea of state identity is part of a process and practice-oriented view of identity, at least insofar as the international arena is concerned. In this view, international life is ordered not by natural systems but by socially constructed institutions, understood as cultural frameworks and deeply embedded cognitive practices or ways of knowing and being. This means that systems and norms develop across histories. For example, two of the key concepts structuring much international relations theory—the security dilemma (that is, entrenched cycles of competition driven by insecurity) and the balance of power—are understood as institutions, if deeply entrenched ones, not as systemic reality. Interests, identities, and institutions—process and structure—are thus understood as constitutive of each other.

The idea of state identity has been applied in an increasing number of ways. Some applications endeavor to render the concept more sharply defined, scientific and testable. Other applications emphasize the social interpretive dimensions. State identity has been used to analyze national security policies by considering cognitive frames and cultural and normative factors; it has also been expanded beyond the state to examine regional identities, international norms, and changes to the character of international interaction around particular issues. Some German constructivists have incorporated theories of mutual deliberation and dialogue (communicative action theories) into their approaches. The idea of the socialization of states has been enthusiastically embraced by theorists of global civil society and transnational advocacy networks because the idea of state identity allows norms and values a genuine, though not necessarily preeminent, place in this understanding of international politics. This flexibility enables constructivists to address both the dynamics of conflict and power and the conditions under which cooperation takes place. Some constructivists then, argue that constructivism occupies a pivotal position between neorealism and neoliberalism because constructivism can work with the intellectual project of either approach. Constructivism is also sometimes put forward as a bridge between these mainstream approaches to international relations and the more critical or reflectivist approaches.

Critiques

As various scholars have noted, the constructivist concept of state identity also has limitations, at least in its more prominent conceptualizations. State identity remains shaped by the conceptual division between inside and outside the state, despite its efforts to "bring society back in." The construction of state identity remains significantly located in the sphere of international interaction. Despite some focus on popular views (of national security orientations, for example), examination of the state as a political community tends to remain limited. Although state identity can open valuable avenues for understanding international politics, the political, social, and economic dynamics within or across states—that is, the processes of state formation that might produce and shift state identities from the "inside" or by mechanisms other than states—can remain obscured from view. Although some simplification of the object of study is necessary, this bifurcation imports unexamined and highly problematic assumptions into the study of state identity and weakens the concept's ability to be used to explore the production of collective meaning and action. In important respects the state continues to be taken as a given. (Wendt, for example, explicitly distinguishes between an established corporate identity inside the state and social roles constituted by international interaction.) Despite the potential of the concept, then, analyses using state identity can rely on overly simple characterization of states, by using an homogenized image of national identity, that is, of what is important to "Germans" or "Americans" and so on.

Inside the state can become in practice identified with policy makers or elites or what can be ascertained by social surveys; although in themselves important foci of study, these seem insufficient grounds for a conceptualization of state identity. Finally, constructivist renderings of state identity tend to assume an ideal model of the state based on the experience of the Global North, that is, on states not struggling fundamentally with the formation of political community. There is an assumption that states form relatively coherent political units and that these units are represented by governments. This reduces the relevance of the concept, at least as it is currently and predominantly applied, to a significant proportion of the world.

M. Anne Brown

See also Civic Identity; Nationalism; Social Constructionist Approach to Personal Identity

Further Readings:

Guzzini, S., & Leander, M. (Eds.). (2006). *Constructivism and international relations: Alexander Wendt and his critics.* London: Routledge.

Smith, S. & Owens, P. (2008). Alternative approaches to international theory. In J. Baylis, S. Smith, & P. Owens (Eds.), *The globalization of world politics: An introduction to international relations* (4th ed., pp. 174–191). Oxford, UK: Oxford University Press.

STATUS

Status refers to social rank defined in terms of prestige or esteem. Status is one of the most important variables governing the lives of social animals, human beings included. Although status is not the same thing as power, the two are closely related. Status tends to stem from power, and vice versa, because status elicits respect and deference. This simple case illustrates that status is of interest as both a dependent variable (an outcome of social-psychological processes) and an independent variable (a cause of social-psychological processes). Thus, this entry considers the dynamics of status, including how it is gained, maintained through its effects on social interactions, and resisted.

Gaining Status

Groups are seldom arranged along entirely egalitarian lines. Illustrating this point, the Harvard sociologist Robert F. Bales convened small decision-making groups of undergraduate students and found that typically within the first hour-long meeting, a hierarchy of status had developed. Usually, these status hierarchies formed quickly and smoothly. Where power struggles did occur, this postponed but did not cancel the development of a stable, unequal status hierarchy.

Status within these hierarchies can be earned or *achieved* by one's actions, or it can be assigned or *ascribed* on the basis of inherited characteristics, such as the status of one's family, race, or gender. This distinction is reflected in *expectation states theory* by Joseph Berger, in which the status granted to an individual depends on how much he or she is expected to help realize group goals. Individuals with characteristics that are *task-relevant*, such as expertise and talent, will tend to be granted high status. Individuals who are proto-typical of the group are also seen to be likely to further its interests and are granted status and, indeed, power as a result. But *diffuse status characteristics* such as family, race, and gender also influence group members' perception that an individual may assist the group. Therefore, these characteristics influence the status awarded to an individual. Indeed these traits are often more apparent than task-relevant characteristics in the early stages of group formation. These characteristics may therefore have an unduly powerful influence on the initial assignment of status.

This process, sometimes referred to as *status generalization,* illustrates how individuals' status outside the group affects their status within the group. It means that similar people tend to occupy high- and low-status positions within groups, even when the formation of each group is entirely independent. For example, when groups are composed of both men and women, men tend to occupy the high-status positions, be those groups political, cultural, religious, or economic. Thus, status hierarchies within local groups tend to enact and replicate global status hierarchies.

Diffuse status characteristics need not be social. For example, tall people tend to have higher status than do short people. This effect seems reliable in both experiments and in field studies, which show for example that CEOs are taller than average and tall job applicants are more likely to be successful. The link between status and height is implicit in the etiquette of many cultures, in which low-status individuals bow, curtsey, or even sit or kneel to confirm the higher status of high-status individuals.

Metaphors such as "social climber," "upper class," and "ideas above one's station" also reflect an implicit cultural equation of social status with physical height or elevation.

Maintaining Status

Research since Bales's pioneering studies has shown that once status hierarchies are formed, they tend to be reinforced and legitimized by group processes. A person's status characteristics influence the size of the contribution to the group's goals that the person will make. When a large contribution is expected of an individual, he or she tends to be given every opportunity to make one. These people are given opportunities to contribute earlier than other members are. Identical contributions are evaluated more favorably if made by a high- rather than low-status individual. Higher-status members are also rewarded more richly: Rewards within groups are assigned as a legitimizing marker of status independently of the value of a person's contribution to a group. The case of spectacular bonuses awarded to executives of failed corporations seems to illustrate this point well.

Status also tends to perpetuate itself by moderating the character of interpersonal relations. Across all known human cultures, people use deferential forms of address for strangers and those who are high in status (e.g., Madam, Sir, or *vous* in French), but not for familiars and persons of low status (where first names will do, or in French, *tu*). Any relaxation in formality is usually suggested by the higher-status communicator: A doctor is more likely than her patient to suggest a switch to first names. So, being high in status confers the privilege of control over intimacy.

Further, compared with lower-status persons, those high in status gaze more into the eyes of their conversation partners while talking, touch others more, stand in a more erect posture, interrupt more often, are more likely to direct who takes the next turn in a conversation, and criticize more frequently. High-status people are also likely to receive more flattery and more measured and mitigated forms of critical feedback, and are likely to benefit from others' attempts to ingratiate themselves. In some settings, low-status speakers tend to use more polite and tentative language. Consistent with expectation states theory, this phenomenon is most likely to manifest itself when lower-status people talk to those higher in status, and where the basis of status (e.g., gender, race, occupation, or class) is perceived to be relevant to the goals of the conversation.

Status can also be seen as a self-perpetuating form of social capital, allowing individuals to achieve their goals by enhancing their influence over others. Several studies show that compliance is more likely to requests made by higher-status individuals, and representatives of higher-status organizations. One of the most famous demonstrations of the effect of status on compliance was provided by Stanley Milgram's studies of obedience. In these studies, participants were asked to deliver an apparently life-threatening dose of electricity to an innocent stranger. The higher the apparent status of the experimenter (e.g., an Ivy League professor versus an employee of a shadowy research company), the more participants acceded to his requests. Similarly, high-status sources are more persuasive than are low-status ones.

People's status helps them win influence within a group and may help them enter a group in the first place. Groups are often keen to recruit individuals with high social status because they perceive these individuals to be able to assist in the realization of their aims. For example, the recruitment of high-status individuals allows groups to bathe in the associative glow of their prestige. High-status individuals may be able to employ their enhanced capacity for social influence to enhance ingroup cohesion and to successfully negotiate with external parties in the interests of the group.

Resistance to Status Hierarchies

Social psychological theories offer differing perspectives on the how people respond to their position within their group, and to their group's status within an intergroup hierarchy. According to both social dominance theory and authoritarian theories, many people prefer contexts in which there is a clear status hierarchy of groups to situations where groups have equal status. Social dominance theory also suggests that people actively seek a dominant position for their group, and support measures that might further this aim. In contrast, right-wing authoritarianism is thought to lead to acquiescent or "yielding" responses to low status.

In contrast, just-world and system-justification theories are premised on the idea that people generally prefer to see the intra- and intergroup hierarchies that they occupy as fair. This means that if individuals occupy low-status positions within their group, they are apt to perceive themselves as deserving of that status. Reductions in self-esteem and especially perceptions that one is lacking in status-relevant attributes such as competence tend to follow. Similarly, members of low-status groups may be prone to "outgroup favoritism" in an unconscious attempt to justify their collective position, endorsing negative stereotypes of their own group and seeing higher-status groups as superior to their own on key traits such as competence.

According to these theories, how people feel about their personal status is more or less the same as how they feel about their group status. In contrast, social identity theory postulates a subtle interplay between people's perception of the status of themselves and their group. For example, members of low-status groups are less likely to take action to improve their collective lot if they perceive that group boundaries are permeable, and that their personal status may therefore improve. They are also less likely to take action if they perceive the low status of their group to be legitimate, and if they are unaware of alternative social contexts in which their group may have higher status. If status relations between groups are seen as illegitimate and alterable, then social identity is said to be "insecure." When social identity is insecure, individuals are likely to take action to address the low status of their group.

One such class of strategies is known as social competition, in which groups collectively strive to better rival groups on the dimensions on which they are currently perceived as inferior. Another is "social creativity." These strategies include attaching positive value to attributes that were hitherto seen as negative, choosing other attributes as the basis of comparison with the outgroup, and choosing to compare themselves with other outgroups. The specific strategy that group members may use to enhance their status depends on contextual factors such as what is practical in the circumstances and how other groups react.

The status of one's own group in relation to others is not merely of symbolic importance, relevant only to collective self-esteem. Often, as recognized by social identity theory, group status determines what groups can do to each other. According to Susan Fiske's stereotype content model, group members are motivated to know what other groups can, and want to, do to their group. This means that they are particularly interested in two types of traits, namely competence (is the group capable or not?) and warmth (do they mean well or ill?). High-status groups tend to be seen as competent but cold, whereas low-status groups are often seen as warm but incompetent. These stereotypes are likely to help observers justify inequality and to cope with conflicting information (e.g., prevailing negative representations of an outgroup on the one hand, but a normative ban on prejudice on the other hand). Also, the stereotypes tend to explain how the high- and low-status groups got where they are.

Conclusion

Status is a precious, contested, and to some extent self-perpetuating social resource. Consensus has yet to be reached on key problems, for example, on when high-status groups exhibit more prejudice and ingroup favoritism than low-status groups do. Nonetheless, status is a crucial variable at the intra- and intergroup levels of human behavior. Given all the social benefits that status confers, it is not surprising that it is also beneficial to physical well-being. A number of studies link status to health and longevity, even when related factors such as wealth are controlled for. One of the most striking and well-publicized examples was uncovered by the University of Warwick economists Andrew Oswald and Matthew Rablen in 2005. They found that Nobel laureates in physics and chemistry lived 2 years longer than did the peers who were "merely" nominated for a Nobel Prize. The number of nominations received by scientists was not predictive of their life span, and neither was the size of the monetary award given to each laureate. As Oswald noted in an interview subsequent to the publication of this research, winning the Nobel Prize per se seemed to confer "a kind of health-giving magic."

Nonetheless, we probably do not need to appeal to magic to explain this finding. Researchers have observed immediate physiological responses to social status in human and nonhuman animals alike. For example, animals that are experimentally locked into a low-status or "subdominant"

position display endocrinologic changes, involving elevated levels of harmful, stress-related chemicals in their blood. Low status therefore appears to be an aversive and unhealthy state for many social animals. In some animals, however, these effects disappear once status hierarchies have been established and each animal settles into its place in the regime. In these cases, animal behavior is reminiscent of some of the patterns predicted by the social psychological theories we have reviewed.

Robbie M. Sutton

See also Forms of Address; Group Identity; Political Psychology; Social Comparison Theory; Social Movements; Stereotypes; Voice

Further Readings

Hogg, M. A. (2001). A social identity theory of leadership. *Personality and Social Psychology Review, 5,* 184–200.

Kroger, R. O., & Wood, L. A. (1992). Are the rules of address universal? IV: Comparison of Chinese, Korean, Greek, and German usage. *Journal of Cross-Cultural Psychology, 57,* 416–425.

Levine, J. M., Moreland, R. L., & Choi, H. (2001). Group socialization and newcomer innovation. In M. A. Hogg & S. Tindale (Eds.), *Blackwell handbook of social psychology: Group processes* (pp. 86–106). Oxford, UK: Blackwell.

Marmot, M. (2004). *Status syndrome: How your social standing directly affects your health and life expectancy.* London: Bloomsbury.

Ridgeway, C. L. (2001). Social status and group structure. In M. A. Hogg & S. Tindale (Eds.), *Blackwell handbook of social psychology: Group processes* (pp. 353–375). Oxford, UK: Blackwell.

Ridgeway, C. L., & Smith-Lovin, L. (1999). The gender system and interaction. *Annual Review of Sociology, 25,* 191–216.

Turner, J. C., & Brown, R. (1978). Social status, cognitive alternatives and intergroup relations. In H. Tajfel (Ed.), *Differentiation between social groups* (pp. 201–234). London: Academic Press.

STEREOTYPES

A *stereotype* is a social construct, a textually based assertion of what a given type of individual should be. A stereotype is also a representation. Whenever something is represented, something is always left out of the account, and this discontinuity is central to the meanings we derive; however, a stereotype leaves so much out of the account it operates more as a fiction than a reliable portrayal of an identity. The discontinuity in a representation leads to a desirousness to retrieve lost reality and to fill in what has been left out of the account, resulting both in readings that occur despite what has been left out of the account, and in misreadings *because* of what has been left out of the account. The more left out, the greater the scope of possible misreadings and the more likely the emergence of stereotyped understandings and oversimplifications based on the preponderance of absences. Stereotypes hew closely only to the most obvious regularities and irregularities of human body type and behavior.

Stereotypes are literary- and image-based texts based on sensory data, typifying and creating narratives of identity around harshly delimited sets of identity markers to stigmatize some and normalize others. Constituted thusly, a typecasting of sensory impressions can represent the whole panoply of stigmatizing social stories and mythologies with which it has been qualitatively associated. Normality itself is a social construct, comprising stereotypes and confirmed by contrasting stereotypes. A norm is constructed systematically, organizing only the most apparent and atypical textualizable regularities of human bodies and behaviors to make problematic any traits that do not coalesce in uniformity with those textual identifiers constructed as central to prevailing social hierarchies.

Stereotyping constructs some to be ugly, some to be beautiful, some to be heroes, and some to be monsters—oversimplifications rendered as texts that secure and extend a base of power and influence in social arenas. Regimes of influence that shape social identities and individual behavior employ stereotypes to caricature one group of people as insignificant, foolish, or dangerous in the eyes of another group of people. Dominant groups stereotype those they oppress; marginalized groups also stereotype those who dominate them; however, dominant groups also possess the means to institutionalize their stereotypic representations through the various media of mass communications.

In Western scientific discourse, one invariably encounters medians, averages, likelihoods, and patterns constructed as binary axes, polarities of understanding, *normal distributions,* and *standard deviations.* Stereotyped narratives of identity have converged with scientific discourse in several ways. The concept of establishing norms has a statistical derivation advanced amongst Western industrialists during the early 1800s. Adolphe Quetelet elaborated a conception of the "average man" with the bourgeoisie standing in at the mean position of a rational order of things. Quetelet believed that any middle-class individual epitomizing all the qualities of the average human was also invested with all the purported greatness, beauty and goodness imagined to be present at the center of society.

Within the dispensation of a rule of averages, this implies that the norm must somehow comprise the majority of the population. In a society where, for instance, the concept of "able-bodiedness" as a norm is in operation, the desirability of normalcy is further entrenched if every deviating or limited body is made problematic as a societal defect and marginalized as a repository for social angst and uncertainty. Public opinion and common sense can, however, generate a tyranny of normalcy when averages are corporealized through the media as stereotypes of desirability, while differences are measured either as natural deviations from the desirable, or as tragically acquired disabilities that cripple conformity to agreed constructs of beauty and well-being.

The propaganda of normalcy, and correlating acts and declarations of stigmatization, fixes the desirability of normalcy in the public opinion by systematically stigmatizing alternative behaviors and appearances. Because behavior patterns are fair predictors of future behaviors, the manipulation of public attitudes—such as legislated penalties for nonconformity to norms, public schooling using normalizing and stigmatizing textbook narratives, the media advertisement of desirable behavior and appearances and social rewards for adherence to those models, and the segregation of deviants and undesirables into marginalized social arenas, communities, and vocational tracks—have all served as masking strategies, leaving the spotlight only on the norms Western societies continue to hold central.

It is a useful fiction that some are normal citizens of the state, and others are marked as exemplars of a tragic failing, still yet to emerge from savagery and the natural, prelingual, irrational, amoral, and primitive state imagined so vividly in the seminal texts of Enlightenment mythology. This fiction makes possible the emergence of the normal and the invisibility of those who deviate from publicly accepted norms of beauty, speech, and lifestyle. Paradoxically, the representation of disabled figures in culture and literature as beings that wear lesser-than-normal masks simultaneously buttresses stereotypes of a normative identity and shapes a narrative of difference excluding those whose bodies or behaviors do not measure up to prevailing norms.

When a citizen is marked with the stigma of invalidity, that citizen is also weighed down with a mantle of illegitimacy regarding his or her contribution to history or the common sense regarding the known world. A bastardized identity nullifies the claim of equal partnership and shared citizenry in the discourse of nation building. When an identity is so stereotyped, its familiar humanity is masked from public gaze and rendered irrelevant to its interpretation; the stereotyped body is transformed by the normalizing/stigmatizing language game into something akin to a corporealized fingerprint, that of a cartoon character, not a human being. However, the stereotype of identity is interpreted as nothing less than "real" in the court of public opinion where the language game plays out.

The majority population within a diverse citizenry sets the norms of social discourse as well as the spokespersons of its norms, and the majority population's point of view establishes accepted boundaries of significance and normalcy and the power to confer stigmatization or "abnormalcy" on those who do not compare favorably to those in the center—the denizens of positions that fall beyond acceptable boundaries. As Western Europeans have constructed the story of progress of civilizations, the tale that has been told has been described by political psychologist and social theorist Ashis Nandy as a worldview that believes in the absolute superiority of the human over the nonhuman, the historical over the ahistorical, the masculine over the feminine, the adult over the child, and the modern or progressive over the primitive; the West has nevertheless shown impartiality in its belief in the monsters beyond the bell curve of Western normality. Western theology equated the gods of the Indian religions with the devil. Europeans also categorized Africans as heathen, and their folklore and religions as the spawn of the devil. The powers of the Indian shaman to cure or to kill, African idolatry, and the European belief in magic and witchcraft all blended into a fear of the uncontrollable as a power that must either vanquish or be vanquished. Anomalous identities and worldviews unfamiliar to Westerners were reduced to widely disseminated and destructive stereotypes.

The idea that the anomalous is synonymous with danger and evil has also been characterized in Western literature and film through symbolic depictions of disability, indigenous cultures, and dark-skinned peoples. In his poem *The White Man's Burden*, Rudyard Kipling stereotypes those lesser-than-normal bodies newly subject to colonialism as new-caught sullen peoples that were half-devil and half-child—the racialized depiction of a daunting confluence of congenital physical, spiritual, intellectual flaws, and deviances that would certainly doom all non-Europeans to live in poverty and ignorance were it not for the beneficence of the ruling empire.

Operating within the currency of what disabilities studies specialist Lennard J. Davis has termed the "hegemony of the normal," the history of the U.S. government is replete with instances wherein the proximity of subaltern bodies was meliorated by schooling or institutionalization as the initial or primary means for the corrective address; one of the more egregious of these instances is perhaps the U.S. "ugly laws" of the 19th and 20th centuries, which banned visibly disabled people from appearing in public places.

Norms tell stories both of favor and desire; deviations from the norm are always predicated on those stories. Western society strives to make beliefs of what it sees or thinks it sees with its own eyes, and ideates the preponderance of its constituents as representing the core of those beliefs and ideologies. Norms reflect the majority of instances falling within a particular "bell curve" of empirical sightings. In his video titled *Representation and the Media*, cultural studies professor Stuart Hall suggests that the supplanting of media stereotypes with new representation requires revisiting and reentering the stereotyped representation, inhabiting the territory that has been glutted by fixed and closed representations, thereby turning the stereotype against itself, permeating the sanctity of its borders with disruptive self-same reinterpretations. Any such interrogation of what was once a closed set of meanings serves as a fenestration of the authorial enclosures of those who have exercised the power to name. Perforating the names that bind us opens up window-like "micro-becomings," new possibilities for identity.

An enclosure constructed to normalize a set of meanings that it is no longer able to enclose is thereby un-named. Enclosure thus becomes a transitional space. A stereotype is constructed to enclose a set of meanings so they cannot migrate and, like animals in contemporary zoo enclosures, make it appear as if those meanings were absolutely natural to the setting of that particular enclosure—as if it were inconceivable that those meanings might be otherwise born free, born to mean something else altogether. A stereotype that can no longer enclose is a norm that can no longer capture, restrict and define—and is thus opened to poststructural renovation. Stereotype thereby becomes a site of inquiry, a transitional space awaiting the assignment of new meaning.

James Haywood Rolling Jr.

See also Orientalism; Stock Character; Xenophobia

Further Readings

Brunner, D. D. (1998). *Between the masks: Resisting the politics of essentialism.* Lanham, MD: Rowman & Littlefield.

Davis, L. J. (1995). *Enforcing normalcy: Disability, deafness, and the body.* London: Verso.

Goffman, E. (1963). *Stigma: Notes on the management of spoiled identity.* New York: Simon & Schuster.

Jhally, S. (1997). *Representation and the media* [Featuring a lecture by Stuart Hall, Professor, The Open University]. New York: Insight Media.

Nandy, A. (1983). *The intimate enemy: The loss and recovery of self under colonialism.* Oxford, UK: Oxford University Press.

Pieterse, J. N. (1990). *White on Black: Images of Africa and Blacks in Western popular culture.* New Haven, CT: Yale University Press.

Taussig, M. T. (1986). *Shamanism, colonialism and the wild man: A study in terror and healing.* Chicago: University of Chicago Press.

Thomson, R. G. (1997). *Extraordinary bodies: Figuring physical disability in American culture and literature.* New York: Columbia University Press.

STOCK CHARACTER

The phrase *stock character* refers to one-dimensional characters in literature, theater, and film who are constructed based on archetypical or stereotypical representations that inform their speech, mannerisms, style of dress, personality traits, or behavioral patterns, which are easily identifiable to a particular audience. Some examples of stock characters include the following: the hero, the villain, the damsel in distress, and the ingénue. Stock characters are beneficial to writers because they allow the author an opportunity to introduce familiar figures into a storyline who require little to no explanation. More often than not, the one-dimensional construction of the stock character lends itself to parody. However, it must be noted that the stock character is also a rather controversial figure, as one-dimensional representations of specific social and ethnic groups are said to influence identity politics and culture. This entry provides a brief historical overview with examples of stock characters, a critique of stock characters, and a discussion of the persistence of stock characters today.

Historical Overview

Stock characters can be traced back to the ancient Greeks. Comic playwright Aristophanes is considered the first to have posited the construction of stock characters in his work in Old Comedy. His plays are the only surviving examples of this genre. Aristophanes's work tended to focus on political satire. His plays often employed three character types: the alazon/imposter, the eiron/opponent, and the bomolochos/buffoon. Each character used a dialect and donned individual costume pieces to suggest characterization. However, in Aristophanes's writings is found the emergence of other stock characters who later figured greatly into the stock character type. For example, in *The Clouds,* the character Socrates functions similarly to the mad scientist.

The notion of character type was expounded by Greek philosopher Aristotle who in the *Nichomachean Ethics,* his text on virtue and moral character, is said to have drafted the basis for specific character types through the development of traits, which he termed *virtues.* He lists the following virtues: liberality, prodigality, magnanimity, modesty, amiability, sincerity, wit, and magnificence. These traits provided ancient Greeks terminology to assist them in the creation of characters with a variety of virtues and flaws that could be introduced into storylines. For example, one may have found the presence of the magnificent man who went out of his way to show off his wealth contrasted with the liberal man who would give all his belongings for the sake of the noble and just.

However, not until Aristotle's student and successor Theophrastus used his observations from Athenian life to create the text *The Characters,* sometimes translated as *Ethical Characters,* were the beginnings of contemporary explorations of the stock character seen. Some argue that Theophrastus borrowed from Aristotle's theories and used them to more specifically define character types who would later serve as the basis for all stock characters. With his work that is now classified as New Comedy, Theophrastus was able to identify the following character types: the ironical man, the flatterer, the garrulous man, the boor, the complaisant man, the reckless man, the chatty man, the gossip, the shameless man, the penurious man, the gross man, the unseasonable man, the stupid man, the surly man, the superstitious man, the grumbler, the distrustful man, the offensive man, the unpleasant man, the man of petty ambition, the mean man, the boastful man, the arrogant man, the coward, the oligarch, the late learner, the evil speaker, the patron of rascals, and the avaricious man.

Each character possesses an unattractive trait that dominates him. In *The Characters,* Theophrastus reflects on offensive traits that manifest as superficial patterns of behavior. Theophrastus' work served as the source for character development during the time when characterizations began to shift to more relatable characters who dealt with ordinary issues. This transitional period classified its work as Middle and New

Comedy, which are often referred to as the ancient Greeks' version of the comedy of manners—a genre of comedy popularized during England's Restoration period.

With the emergence of the celebrated playwright Menander, the most noted author of New Comedy, one finds a revisiting and fleshing out of the stock character. In New Comedy, the emphasis turned primarily to stock characters within everyday situations. Most New Comedy plays relied on recognizable Athenian types such as the angry old man and the trickster servant. Most common in new comedy were stories generally involving a romantic conflict between young lovers—a rich man and a poor girl. The interaction of the character types generates humor and creates urgency within the work. This is quite evident in Menander's *The Dyskolos/The Difficult Man* or *The Grouch,* where a rich young man falls for the daughter of a surly old farmer. One can certainly see more evidence of the stock characters in the titles of other new comedy works, such as *The Farmer, The Flatterer,* and *The Ship's Captain.* New comedy influenced much of Western European literature and specifically the work of William Shakespeare and Ben Johnson. However, the introduction of commedia dell'arte during the Italian Renaissance created a larger range of stock characters than had previously been seen; these remain visible in present-day literary and dramatic forms, which range from musical theater to situation comedy.

Commedia dell'arte, sometimes referred to as Italian comedy and loosely translated as comedy of the professional players, was popularized in Italy during the 16th century and marked the height of the stock character in performance. The commedia dell'arte acting troupes consisted of 10 to 12 actors who played stock characters that were easily recognizable to audiences because of the mannerisms, the personality traits, and the behaviors of the portrayers. The characters were fixed, although the stories were largely improvised. Actors in the performance troupe would wear masks or costuming that would have clearly identified their character type to the audience. The stock characters, Commedia dell'arte's best-known feature, were easily divided into three groups: the lovers, the masters, and the servants. Considered by many as popular art, which was less refined than the art found throughout Western Europe at the time, commedia dell'arte went on to become one of the most popular theatrical forms of all time.

Listed here are some of the popular commedia dell'arte stock characters:

- Harlequin/Arlecchino is a clown and a member of the Zanni. He is a simpleton who evolves into a sophisticated man. He generally wears a black hat and carries a slapstick—the origin of the term *slapstick comedy.*
- Pantalone is the rich elderly miser. He usually has a young wife or an adventurous daughter.
- Isabella is usually Pantalone's daughter. She is a prima donna who is flirtatious and headstrong.
- Brighella is a villain who would do anything for money.
- Il Capitano is the captain. He is a seemingly macho but cowardly military man.
- Scaramuccia is seen as the Italian Renaissance's "Robin Hood."
- The Innamorato and Innamorata are the handsome and fashionable young lovers.
- The Zanni represent the sly servants.
- Il Dottore is the pompous doctor.
- Pulcinella is a humpback with a crooked nose who chases pretty girls.
- LaRuffiana is the old woman or village gossip.
- Pedrolino is the dreamer or clown.

Although stock characters experienced their heyday during the Italian Renaissance, remnants of these characters persist in literature and theater.

Critique

Although stock characters serve a distinct purpose in the literary and dramatic arts, they also have been viewed as problematic representations. Even Menander was criticized for the lack of depth that his stock characters displayed. However, the presentation of stock characters becomes most problematic when they are presented through a certain racial or cultural lens. A case in point is the uniquely U.S. theatrical tradition of minstrelsy, which was the most popular form of entertainment during the 19th century. Minstrel shows told the stories of Blacks in the United States, although the shows were most often performed by Whites. With the application of burnt cork to their faces, actors were able to don the mask known as blackface to suggest racist archetypes. The stories were told by stock characters such as Jim Crow, Jim Dandy, and Zip Coon. Other characters included the mammy, the old darky, and the mulatto wench. These characters were one-dimensional representations that deliberately distorted the image of Blacks by presenting characters who were often buffoonish, lazy, ignorant, or grotesque. These characterizations aided the shaping of White America's perception of Blacks, while playing into the curiosity that Northern Whites had about Black people and their culture. Although the popularity of minstrelsy soared during the 19th century with even African Americans playing some roles in blackface, the presence of such ill-informed stock characters created much tension. These problematic representations continue to have an affect on African Americans today, making the discussion of characterization and the role that imagery plays in constructing identity a widely debated discursive practice.

Persistence of Stock Characters in Popular Culture

Stock characters have become an integral part of our dramatic experiences. In theatrical mediums such as theater and television, these character types persist. Different genres thrive on the presence of stock characters. For example, when viewing westerns, one always finds the hero, the villain, and the sidekick. For example, in the short-lived television series *Deadwood,* one finds the hero in Timothy Olyphant's Sheriff Seth Bullock and the villain in Ian McShane's Al Swearengen. In soap operas, often one will find the lovable rogue, the tart with a heart, the con man, the fussy widow, and the villain. Situation comedies have what some have termed the shrew and the slob. A clear example of these types could be in seen in the once-popular *Married With Children.* Ed O'Neill's Al Bundy fit nearly perfectly the type of the slob, and Katey Sagal's Peggy Bundy exemplified the shrew. In other genres such as science fiction, one often finds the mad scientist and the absent-minded professor. Even reality shows feature stock characters: the good girl, the jock, and the troublemaker. Stock characters continue to factor into our everyday reality. One need not look far to find remnants of historical figures that were drafted centuries ago and now fulfill a well-established role in our collective conscience.

Kamesha Jackson

See also Archetype; Discourse; Minstrelsy; Stereotypes; Trickster Figure

Further Readings

Aristotle. (350 BC). *Nicomachean ethics.* Retrieved December 28, 2008, from http://classics.mit.edu/Aristotle/nicomachaen.4.iv.html

Brockett, O. G. (Ed.). (1992). *The essential theatre.* Orlando, FL: Harcourt Brace Jovanovich.

Jebb, R. C. (1870). *The characters of Theophrastus.* Retrieved December 28, 2008, from http://www.eudaemonist.com/biblion/characters

Jones, J. B. (2004). *Our musicals, ourselves.* Hanover, NH: Brandeis University Press.

Rudlin, J. (1994). *Commedia dell'arte.* New York: Routledge.

Worthen, W. B. (Ed.). (2007). *The Wadsworth anthology of drama* (Brief 5th ed.). Boston: Thomson Wadsworth.

STRUCTURATION

British social theorist Anthony Giddens's theory of structuration presents some key insights about the extent to which social structures (organizations, social networks, societies) are influenced by human interaction. Giddens's theory addresses the debate about the complex relationship between individuals and society. On the one hand, one may argue that human action is influenced and even constrained by the rules, norms, and institutions that are central in human social systems. On the other hand, it may be argued that creative human action and human will are central in the creation of human social systems. According to communication scholar James Olufowote, Giddens's theory rejects both of these conceptual polarities.

Olufowote argues that in understanding structuration theory, one has to understand Giddens as proposing three fundamental axioms: first, Giddens argues that social structure is constituted by creative and knowledgeable human agents. That is,

the social actors who are engaged in regular interactions are aware of their social worlds and their surroundings and often act intentionally in these contexts. Second, Giddens argues that knowledgeable human creation is itself informed by social structure, and third, he claims that both structure and agency are mutually constituted in human social practices. In this third axiom, Olufowote argues, Giddens is positing that human social practices are the fundamental unit of social analysis. This third axiom also comprises what Giddens conceptualizes as the duality of structure.

Giddens posits that human interaction is the central force in constructing and maintaining social practices while producing and reproducing social systems and structures. Social structures are, therefore, both the medium and outcome of social interaction. The structuration perspective is useful to explicate the relationship between the production and reproduction of social structures and human interaction, and to underscore the perspective that social actors do not exist independently from the social structures that influence—and sometimes constrain—them.

Scholars have used structuration theory to research communication, culture, and identity issues. This entry first explores the conceptual framework of structuration theory and then examines the use of structuration theory in communication and culture and identity research. Finally, this entry discusses critiques of the theory.

Conceptual Framework

Three key concepts are important to understanding structuration: practices, systems, and structure. The theory of structuration argues that *practices* are human activities that are consistent, repeatable, and meaningful to the persons who do them; they can be small-scale activities, such as going to the store, or they can be large-scale activities such as the management of a supermarket or some other commercial enterprise. In structuration theory, *systems* are defined as observable relational patterns as manifested in various practices. *Structure* represents the rules and resources that social actors draw on as they partake in various system practices. Communication scholars Marshall Scott Poole and Robert McPhee define *rules* as principles or routines that guide people's actions. Poole and

McPhee describe a *resource* as anything people are able to use in action, whether material (money, tools) or nonmaterial (knowledge, skill).

The key argument of structuration is that drawing on rules and resources to enact social systems of practice results in the reproduction of the system and its structure. Poole and McPhee argue that reproducing the system does not necessarily imply that the system continues to exist without any changes; rather, change and transformation of the system can be thought of as reproduction, but in a new direction. In structuration, all actions and individual sequences of interaction produce important practices and reproduce the system and its structure either as changed or as stable. The key insight here, according to Poole and McPhee, is that structuration theory explains the system itself as the product of human actions operating in a duality in which structures are both the medium and the outcome of the actions. Human actors create social structures that are produced and reproduced in human interaction, so the implication for issues of identity is that communication is deeply consequential and fully implicated in the creation and maintenance of human social systems.

Structuration Theory and Communication Research

There has been significant communication scholarship during the past two decades that draws on Giddens's work to articulate concepts related to communication theory. Communication scholars such as Olufowote, Poole, and McPhee have set out to categorize the kind of scholarship that has developed in the communication field using structuration principles, and they have also sought to articulate the ways in which structuration provides fertile ground for more complex analysis of the role of communication in understanding the relationship between individuals and society.

According to Olufowote, during the past two decades, structuration theory has been used to frame investigations in communication subfields such as small group theory, organizational politics and culture, and organizational-group technology. Olufowote posits that structuration theory's popularity is partially explained by the breadth of its ideas and its openness to researchers operating in various traditions. Olufowote proposes four central

elements to the theory of structuration, elements that can be used to understand the wealth of communication research that has been conducted using this perspective. These four elements also constitute a model for understanding how communication researchers have come to analyze and explain the process of structuration and situate it in the context of theories and concepts of communication.

Olufowote argues that first, the fundamental unit of analysis in structuration is situated social practices. By this, he means that scholars' explanation and analysis of human social systems is based on a scholarly review of the routine practices engaged in by social actors with the aim of providing comparison of the nature of the routine inherent in these practices. The second element he proposes is the idea that structures partially explain why routines sustain themselves. He describes these structures as deeply sedimented or macrosocially shaped. By this, he means that structures are stable and predate and outlast the social actors who continually help to shape and re-shape them. Examples of these kinds of structures can include various kinds of communities, legal systems, and organizations. The history and stability of these structures are factors that are crucial to their analysis.

Third, Olufowote posits that structures are influenced by and are implicated in the interactions between real-life human beings who set out to reproduce or change the social systems of which they are a part. In other words, the interactions of human beings with various structures matter, and the communicative processes that are the foundation of these interactions have a significant impact on these structures. Fourth, he posits that the interaction between social actors and various institutions may result in various outcomes—some of which are intended and some of which are unintended. These outcomes are influential in the subsequent series of interchanges and interactions between social actors, which are then influential for affecting structures into the future. In using these categorizations, Olufowote set up important criteria for evaluating and contextualizing the scholarship that has been developed using structuration as a theoretical framework.

Poole and McPhee argue that scholars who treat organizations as social systems find structuration to be useful for analyzing how organizations are created and sustained by human interaction. Structuration theory also provides useful perspectives for understanding how organizations can be changed. Organizations are not, therefore, treated as static, implacable entities that are uninfluenced by the human beings who populate them.

Poole and McPhee also argue that because the theory charges scholars to closely examine the processes that underlie and undergird the social reality of organizations, it provides fertile conceptual ground for scholars to analyze the role of power and domination that may be inherent in the structuring processes that create and sustain organizations. Poole and McPhee argue that there is much utility in the interpretive and cultural perspectives inherent in this theory, and they provide a review of the literature that analyzes how scholars have applied the principles of the theory in communication studies that have examined organizational issues at the individual, group, and organizational levels of analysis.

Structuration, Culture, and Identity

Scholars who focus on issues of culture and identity across different communication research contexts also use structuration to investigate the interrelationship between human social actors, human social systems, and social identity. Anne Nicotera, Marcia Clinkscales, and Felicia Walker use structuration perspectives to examine the complexities of social identity and cultural negotiation that occur when organizational members who share predominantly African-based ancestry make up the numerical majority in an organization that is predominantly European in form, structure, and design, and that is situated in the primarily Anglo-European influenced national culture of the United States. The work of Nicotera and her colleagues reinforces our understanding of organizations as being embedded in complex relationships within national cultures, and underscores that organizations and their internal cultures cannot be understood separately from the cultural peculiarities of the societies in which they exist. As Nicotera and her colleagues point out, the concept of the modern organization is, in part, the result of the production and reproduction of an organizational form and design that is linked to cultural and scholarly discourses emanating from Western

Europe at the turn of the last century. Social interactions that include varying socialization processes such as orientation seminars, training workshops, and business school curricula have continually reproduced the modern organizational design and form conceptualized by European thinkers such as Frederick Taylor and Max Weber. These social and scholarly discourses have thus created and our social interactions routinely reproduce the notion of an organization as a White, Western European construct.

Other scholars such as Olufowote and Erika Kirby and Kathleen Krone have used structuration perspectives to examine how hidden, taken-for-granted meaning systems and discourses in organizations influence, for example, the use and meaning of informed consent procedures in health care contexts, or employees' decisions of whether to take maternity leave. These scholars have used structuration perspectives to argue that organizational and societal cultures are largely discourse-driven and have, therefore, made analysis of social discourses central to their analysis.

Critiques

Some of the critiques of structuration as outlined by Poole and McPhee focus on the fact that Giddens overemphasizes action in that he gives too much power to human agents and therefore oversimplifies human agency in the process of social change. Other critiques argue that structuration does not adequately provide an account of how social and organizational change can be both conceptualized and implemented. In this sense, Giddens is regarded as a social critic who does not fully account for the extent to which inequality and domination are pervasive features of many modern human social systems. Giddens seems to pay scant attention to capitalist exploitation, gendered and racial inequality, and the pervasive, lingering effects of the processes of colonization. Poole and McPhee provide thoughtful rebuttals to many of these critiques, arguing that structuration provides a framework for research using critical perspectives, and they point out that the field is open for more communication scholars to pursue such research.

Maurice L. Hall

See also Culture; Identity Politics; Organizational Identity

Further Readings

Giddens, A. (1976). *New rules of sociological method.* Palo Alto, CA: Stanford University Press.

Giddens, A. (1979). *Central problems in social theory: Action, structure and contradiction in social analysis.* Berkeley: University of California Press.

Giddens, A. (1984). *The constitution of society.* Berkeley: University of California Press.

Giddens, A. (1989). The orthodox consensus and the emerging synthesis. In B. Dervin, L. Grossberg, B. O'Keefe, & E. Wartella (Eds.), *Rethinking communication: Vol. 2. Paradigm exemplars* (pp. 53–65). Newbury Park, CA: Sage.

Kirby, E. L., & Krone, K. J. (2002). "The policy exists but you can't really use it": Communication and the structuration of work-family policies. *Journal of Applied Communication Research, 30,* 50–77.

Nicotera, A., Clinkscales, M., & Walker, F. (2003). *Understanding organization through culture and structure: Relational and other lessons from the African American organization.* Mahwah, NJ: Lawrence Erlbaum.

Olufowote, J. (2003). *Structuration theory and communication research: Developing and applying an organizational-evaluative framework.* Paper presented at the Annual Convention of the International Communication Association, San Diego, CA.

Olufowote, J. (2008). A structurational analysis of informed consent to treatment: Societal evolution, contradiction, and reproductions in medical practice. *Health Communication, 23,* 292–303.

Poole, M. S., & McPhee, R. D. (2005). Structuration theory. In S. May & D. K. Mumby (Eds.), *Engaging organizational communication theory and research: Multiple perspectives* (pp. 172–195). Thousand Oaks, CA: Sage.

STYLE/DICTION

Diction describes word choices in written and spoken communication. Correct diction includes appropriate and accurate word choices. A writer or speaker must make careful, well-informed word choices to communicate effectively with the intended audience. Diction also extends to proper arrangement of words, including grammatical concerns, such as subject-verb agreement, and to mechanics, such as punctuation and spelling.

Mastery of diction establishes the purpose, tone, and accessibility to any written or spoken work. In the discussion of writing, diction is synonymous with *style.* When describing spoken communication, diction more commonly refers to the ability to articulate and enunciate words clearly. This ability is more rooted in vocabulary, pronunciation, and tone than in word choice and style, as is connoted by the term *diction* in written communication.

Diction in written work varies with such factors as regional dialect, but the term generally describes the writer's distinct choices in vocabulary and the style of expression. William Strunk Jr. and E. B. White, authors of *The Elements of Style,* suggest that writers base their style on the fundamental rules established by Standard English.

In written and spoken communication, two basic types of diction exist: formal and informal. Formal diction strictly follows the rules of Standard English, whereas informal diction deviates from these rules and vocabulary. Whether in text or speech, the style best suited for a particular audience's level of understanding emerges through word choices that are either general or specific.

Using proper diction helps writers establish credibility; conversely, lax or sloppy diction can confuse the reader and diminish the writer's trustworthiness. Speaking with good diction focuses on controlling volume, pace, and enunciation, any of which may distract listeners from the message and risk a negative perception of the speaker.

When undertaking a written work, the writer must consider the readers for whom the information is intended. For example, even where identical terminology is used, the diction choices made in writing a textbook about finance will differ depending on whether the book is to be read by sophomores in a high school consumer economics course or by students in a master of business administration program. The vocabulary and sentence structure in the graduate-level text would be greater in complexity, befitting the sophistication of someone in a college course. Similarly, the formality or informality of style changes the way information is imparted and received, again depending on the reader.

Along with word choices that collectively construct either formal or informal diction, the writer must discern the best use of abstract and concrete words throughout the text. The writer's relationship with readers relies heavily on the ability to execute these choices effectively. Vague language can be interpreted as imprecise thinking. Diction, then, contributes to a speaker's or character's identity.

Formal

In the United States, formal diction follows linguistic rules known as Standard English. These rules were cultivated by certain cultural leaders and taught to and perpetuated by English speakers both native and foreign. Standard English is thought to be normative for educated native speakers. The structure includes guidelines for grammar, spelling, syntax, vocabulary, and pronunciation. Formal diction is commonly used for professional and academic communication in both written and spoken forms, including textbooks, scientific articles, political speeches, and government documents.

Formal diction acts as a base for communicating with a diverse audience. Readers and listeners alike may be interested in the subject at hand, but a lack of formal diction in a written work may obscure, rather than communicate clearly, the writer's message. To avoid shortfalls in interpretation, it is best to address the audience formally.

In an article published in the *New England Journal of Medicine,* Julie R. Ingelfinger uses precise word choices to explain the contamination of infant formula in parts of Asia. Ingelfinger wrote that more than 294,000 children in China were reportedly affected by melamine poisoning stemming from tainted infant formula. At the time, more than 50,000 were hospitalized, and at least 6 died. In her research on the matter, other reports indicated that children in other parts of Asia—such as Taiwan, Singapore, and Vietnam—were also affected because they ingested melamine-contaminated powdered infant formula. In efforts to stop the further spread of contamination, the 22 brands that were implicated were taken off the market.

The facts of the epidemic are clearly stated: the number of children who have been reportedly affected, the countries where the contamination has spread, the action steps taken to avert further contamination. The writer demonstrates her knowledge of the subject and offers the reader enough information to understand the depth of the issue. From this article, the reader can assess the problem without being influenced by the writer's personal opinions or colloquial language.

Standard English, when applied to formal oration, allows a speaker's words to truly influence the listener. In the delivery, the proper pronunciation and tone will persuade the audience of the speaker's knowledge and conviction. For example, U.S. Representative Shirley Chisholm, Democrat of New York, gave a speech in support of the Equal Rights Amendment on August 10, 1970. Although she spoke to her peers and colleagues, Chisholm chose words not typical in casual conversation; she thus established formal diction. In her address, without using first-person speech, she listed her reasons for supporting the resolution. Chisholm declared the amendment would provide equality under the law for both men and women against the "subtle and pervasive" institution of prejudice in the United States. The use of precise language suggests the importance and gravity of the subject at hand.

The use of formal diction thus underscores certain qualities of the subject, typically excluding the identity or attributes of the writer or speaker. In general, formal communication is void of the writer's voice, though the writer is able to shape and direct the text through the choice of words and information. This indirectly creates a vehicle or subtext through which the writer's own influence may pervade the text or speech.

Informal

In speaking with friends or family, people commonly use informal language. In prose fiction, informal language typically occurs through character voices. This informal diction gives the character a distinct voice separate from that of the writer. It also offers the reader clues to help situate a character by identifying the character's level of education, social status, regional influences, and other characteristics that can be associated with certain word choices. For example, a character says, "I was really happy." Another character says, "I felt undoubtedly exultant." The reader may infer that the second character has a better vocabulary, and therefore is probably older and more educated than is the first character. In another text, when the main character speaks of his private jet being repaired, the reader can assume that he is wealthy. When another character refers to the United States as "the mainland," the reader can deduce that she is from Hawai'i, Alaska, or one of the insular areas in the Caribbean.

The autobiography of Claude Brown, *Manchild in the Promised Land,* exemplifies how diction and identity are inextricably linked through informal diction. Brown grew up in Harlem in the late 1940s. In one section, he has just returned to his neighborhood after a stay in the hospital, where he was recuperating from a gunshot wound in his stomach. The virtue of Brown's character is emphasized when he discovers that he has missed a riot and returns to the neighborhood in the aftermath of the incident. He seeks details from police officers and friends alike. The police officers reject his inquiry and tell him to go home. When he talks with his friends, Brown shows himself to be unfamiliar with the concept of a riot, but the idea that people were stealing things clearly entices him. The reader can use this information to help in more precisely identifying young Claude's origins, his values, his habits, and his influences.

The types and degrees of informal diction are most typically exhibited in colloquialisms, slang, and jargon. According to the *Modern Writer's Handbook,* colloquial language is the conversational and everyday language of educated people. Colloquialisms are the words and expressions that characterize this language. Although not as informal as slang, colloquialisms are nonetheless generally too casual to be used in formal writing. Examples follow:

Formal: He had fun at the party.

Colloquial: He had a ball at the party.

Slang exists at another, more esoteric level of casual communication. An extremely informal style of speaking, slang can be trendy and often is humorous, ironic, or both. Words such as *snazzy, chillin',* and *teenybopper* are informal terms. More undignified or flippant slang terms such as *bimbo, lush,* and *twerp* can also evoke a response from the audience. Slang often is highly exaggerated and short lived. Subject to differences in connotations, it may be misunderstood. Despite these drawbacks, however, slang, used judiciously in formal writing, can communicate effectively.

Jargon is used to communicate with listeners who have related technical or professional backgrounds. It is frequently professional, highly specialized, and esoteric in meaning. These terms are used in addressing a knowledgeable audience of people with specific technical or professional knowledge. As a result, this highly specific language may exclude those outside the profession. Consider the following jargon related to photography: dpi, TIFF, ISO, and F-stop. Although people outside of this knowledgeable group may be aware of these terms, they may not know the origins, exact definitions, and particular meanings of such technical terminology. Their comprehension of the material in which these terms occur will therefore be limited.

General and Specific

It is the writer's responsibility to use precise language to communicate effectively with any audience. General words will "tell" the reader, but specific words "show" the reader. Consider the example: "He entered the room." This general statement serves the basic purpose of placing a character in a room. The statement does not indicate whether he entered the room on an electric stand-up scooter, in a pair of house slippers, or on the shoulders of an acrobat. To vividly depict the scene, the writer might use specific terms such as *sauntered, burst,* or *floundered.*

Abstract terms refer to general ideas or concepts and have no physical referents. *Love, success, democracy,* and *feminism* are all abstract terms. Writers must caution themselves to avoid general or vague words when the idea at hand is specific. Selecting concrete terms will create a clearer image in the mind of the reader. Words such as *spoon, hot,* and *mask* are concrete terms that refer to objects or conditions that can be captured by the five senses; readers can easily identify such terms in familiar, specific ways. The closer the words are to the reality of the subject, the clearer their meaning becomes to the audience. Without these precise distinctions, the writer's words could be misinterpreted in countless ways and clarity diminished.

Rashida S. Restaino

See also Dialect; Figures of Speech; Idiomatic Expressions; Intonation; Profanity and Slang; Reflexive Self or Reflexivity; Voice

Further Readings

Brown, C. (1965). *Manchild in the promised land*. New York: Signet.

Chisholm, S. (1998, April). *For the Equal Rights Amendment* (M. E. Eidenmuller, Ed.). Retrieved December 26, 2008, from American Rhetoric.com http://www.americanrhetoric.com/speeches/shirleychisholmequalrights.htm

Harris, J., & Cunningham, D. (1997). *The Simon & Schuster guide to writing* (2nd ed.). Englewood Cliffs, NJ: Prentice Hall.

Ingelfinger, J. R. (2008). Melamine and the global implications of food contamination. *New England Journal of Medicine, 359,* 2745–2746.

O'Hare, F. (1986). *The modern writer's handbook*. New York: Macmillan.

Strunk, W., Jr., & White, E. B. (2000). *The elements of style*. New York: Longman.

SUBJECTIVITY

Subjectivity refers to one's conscious and unconscious feelings, beliefs, and desires regarding experiences and relations to the world (i.e., to objects). Subjectivity addresses both individual experience and the shaping of those experiences' meanings; thus, subjectivity is the ground on which identity is constructed. Subjectivity implies a degree of thought and self-awareness about identity, while allowing myriad unconscious constraints on our abilities to understand our own, or others', identities.

Most contemporary philosophy of subjectivity is a reaction to Enlightenment thinking, where the subject was a rational and autonomous agent, the origin of all knowledge and experience. The self became the point of connection between all cognitive impulses (as in René Descartes's famous "I think, therefore I am"). The *I* was an active agent, encountering the world outside it in a way that generated a unified self. Enlightenment thinkers such as Descartes, John Locke, and Jean-Jacques Rousseau encoded a sense of agency in which one could remake and perfect oneself through methodical action. They valorized the "natural self," viewing persons as possessing an essential nature and potential, which could become entrapped by society.

Several critics suggested that the Enlightenment view ignored irrationality, emotionality, and the unconscious while de-socializing the subject. Friedrich Nietzsche, for instance, asserted that the subject was a grammatical fiction, not a real entity existing in the world. Martin Heidegger followed, questioning the nature of consciousness and subjectivity by arguing that being-in-the-world makes us *of* the world, not merely placing us *in* it. He charged that Enlightenment thinkers failed to question the character of experience and the need for an openness to being. These themes are developed in the five streams of thought most commonly drawn on in contemporary humanities and social science scholarship.

Freud

Sigmund Freud initiated a radical rethinking of subjectivity. Freud replaced the Enlightenment's autonomous and rational subject with a complex self directed by deep psychological drives obscured from the person's own awareness. Subjectivity is neither innate nor determined, but constituted by gender relations and sexual identifications forged in early childhood, particularly in the nuclear family. Freud suggested that children move through stages in early life where desires corresponding with body regions (oral, anal, genital) are either met or frustrated. Prominent among his concepts is the *Oedipus Complex,* which operates through the child's recognition of male and female genitals and fear of the father's power; it leads children to identify with either the powerful father (and to imagine sex with the mother) or with the mother and her role as the object of the father's sexual desire. In either case, said Freud, Oedipal desire is understood as inappropriate and is *repressed:* It is placed into the unconscious to avoid its effects. But repressed drives animate dreams and guide our experiencing, such that adult compulsions and identifications are shaped by unconscious gender associations, repressions of the libido, and projections of hidden and irrational sexual desires. The inner world is thus transparent to the self, yet one can grasp and control these unconscious forces with the objectifying assistance of the psychoanalyst.

Lacan

Not long after Freud, Jacques Lacan modified the former's claims through the application of

Ferdinand de Saussure's linguistic structuralism. Saussure held that language was a system of differences in which the arbitrary relation between the signifier and signified are held together in one's mind. From this, Lacan reasoned that the unconscious is structured like a language, and that if we are to understand subjectivity, we must understand linguistic human communication.

His most compelling notion along these lines is the *mirror stage,* the point at which an infant recognizes itself as being separate from the persons and objects around it, perhaps through seeing its reflection in a mirror. Such an image presents itself to the infant as undivided and, therefore, conveys a sense of mastery over the body. But this *imaginary* image is contradicted by the child's experience of fragmentation, disconnection, and powerlessness. Both image and experience are represented by signifiers repressed into the unconscious. This is accompanied by immersion in the *symbolic order,* where the stark distinctions of language provide an external definition of wholeness. The problem, then, is that the subject cannot define itself except in terms of the symbolic order's imaginary unitary identity. The subject is consequently *decentered,* and our sense of self, our identity, is generated from a *misrecognition,* a subject's misunderstanding of the unity of the ego alongside the accompanying alienation from oneself.

An important implication is that the subject seeks in the symbolic order—the apparently objective world we inhabit—the imaginary unity of the image in the mirror, and hence is driven by an unconscious *desire* to compensate for separateness and lack. And though we identify with the seductive objects of language to secure unity, the symbolic realm's basis in arbitrary linguistic distinctions and logical reason simply cannot provide that coherence. No object can replace the forever-lost unity and, in time, desire becomes its own object.

In his consideration of the symbolic domain, Lacan retained a Freudian attention to masculine domination. Freud saw the child's developing subjectivity as hinging on the possession (or lack of) a penis and a fear of the father, as controller of its possession. Lacan, however, emphasized language over anatomy. The father served as the *transcendental signifier,* marking the symbolic domain as a phallocentric order where meaning, reason, and truth reside. This line of thought later became

central to thinkers influenced by both psychoanalysis and feminism.

Althusser

Louis Althusser moved beyond Lacan in theorizing the subject as a social construction, suggesting that subjectivity is a consequence of power-laden practices. Althusser's contribution is based on a reading of Freud's unconscious and Lacan's mirror phase to produce a conception of the power of *ideology.* Althusser argued that ideology, and capitalist reproduction, is based on *ideological state apparatuses* (ISAs)—institutions such as religion, education, the political and legal systems, mass communication, culture, and the family— that *interpellate,* or hail, subjects (as when police on the street yell "hey, you!" and persons, guilty or not, recognize the call and turn) by appealing to their unconscious fears and desires. These ISAs generate submission to the rules of the established order because they are supported by public-domain *repressive state apparatuses,* that function by force. Drawing on these notions, Althusser argued for the impossibility of existence outside of ideology, while displaying how individuals enter the subject position they inhabit. In his thinking, individuals are interpellated by ideology as free subjects in a manner that leads them to freely accept their subjection and, concomitantly, perform the requisite gestures and actions on their own volition. From this, he suggested that the notion of subject refers both to the thinking, feeling person at the center of experience—the subject of action and the location of experiences, and to the person as an object of power, as in a citizen who is "subject of" a monarch.

The ruling ideology is powerful precisely because it can provide subjects an image of identity coherence and ontological security in an uncertain world. It involves a *misrecognition* that differs from Lacan's: Here, subjects believe themselves to be the source of meanings when they are, actually, the *effects* of those meanings. With such claims, Althusser's view appears to present a deterministic model of domination, but the picture is somewhat more complicated because (a) Both the dominated and dominators are interpellated into their positions because submission is required for all; (b) the functioning of ideology and subjectivity limits the degree to which a dominant group can smoothly reproduce itself; (c) the subject's recognition of the ISA's role in constructing its identity can lead to a critique of these institutions; and (d) by showing the multiplicity and overdetermination of ISAs, he helped show how "articulations" between practices and structures can become sites of struggle over meanings and associations among elements.

Foucault

Michel Foucault, a student of Althusser, developed a unique conception of subjectivity based on a denial of any ontologically given "nature" to the subject. Strongly influenced by Nietzsche, Foucault argued that discursive formations, or regimes of truth, *created* the concept of subjectivity to exert control over persons. Once the person is defined as a center of experience and responsibility, discursive formations classify and regulate subjects according to particular conceptions of knowledge and truth while providing materials to shape themselves. Subjectivity, then, cannot be an authentic expression of "who you really are," but rather is a contingent *effect* of power (or, more appropriately, of power/knowledge regimes). Foucault suggested that key in the construction of contemporary forms of subjectivity was the human sciences, which did not exist until "man" was constructed as an epistemological category in the 18th century. Akin to Freud's unconscious and Althusser's ideology, the discursive formation in Foucault positions and "disciplines" subjects in the appropriate means of expression and self-construction.

Power, for Foucault, is not the top-down authority of a unitary logic or a sovereign entity. Instead, it is "capillary," infusing all sorts of micropractices and entering into the deepest recesses of the individual. Thus, power does not remain external to the subject, but occupies the person's interiority; power produces the procedures by which we observe, analyze, interpret, and act on ourselves, and is not merely coercive.

Feminist Poststructuralists

Several of the preceding theorists see gender as central to the formation of subjectivity, but they tend to either portray it in deterministic terms that cannot conceive of woman except in the negative (e.g.,

Lacan's phallocentric order) or fail to theorize it explicitly (Althusser and Foucault). Dissatisfied, feminist thinkers produced novel views of gender, sexuality, and subjectivity, usually based in some fashion on Simone de Beauvoir's claims about "woman" being the "Other," perpetually defined and classified only with respect to "man."

Although many lines of theorizing follow from this, two are of particular interest. The first consists of work by French feminist psychoanalysts, including Hélène Cixous, Julia Kristeva, and Luce Irigaray. Irigaray, in particular, sought to deconstruct Lacanian phallocentrism. She argued that women's subjectivity cannot be captured in traditional terms because it is both multiple and decentered; thus, female subjectivity cannot be reduced to the converse of the male. Attempting to fit this version of subjectivity has forced women to replicate a male language that erases the feminine. In its place, she advocated developing a "female imaginary," fostering language and experience that is fragmented, nonlinear, and polysemic. The result would not be a subjectivity built on a female "essence," but instead would be open-ended, ambiguous, and destabilizing—and, in turn, would generate new possibilities for selfhood. Kristeva (as well as Cixous) took a similar stand, seeing the feminine as occupying a distinct mode of language. From this perspective, subjectivity is fundamentally and always *in process*, and desire is seen as an outcome of ongoing changes and contradictions in that subjectivity. Moreover, in Kristeva, the subject never considers herself stable and knowable, even to herself, and therefore cannot be fully captured by patriarchy's efforts to secure a controllable unity.

Also important here is Judith Butler and her conception of *performativity* as the basis of subjectivity. Butler argued that gender, sex, and sexuality are not the outcomes or implications of a (distinct) linguistic code, but are objects in a system of normatively governed and iterative performances, not all of which are under our control. These performances, always scrutinized for gender appropriateness, present themselves to subjects as both natural and authentic presentations of self. Their repetitiveness emphasizes the ritualized character of subjectivity but, at the same time, displays indeterminacy in that each iteration awaits its enactment and can never provide precise duplication. Performativity, therefore, assumes a potential for resistance to regulative discourses, sometimes unintended or unperceived by the actor herself. Recently, Butler argued that self-narratives are necessarily incomplete and that subjects are insufficiently aware of Others' claims on their subjectivities; accordingly, assertions about ethical obligations are always based on limited knowledge of self, implying an interrogation of regulative discourses as essential to ethical interaction. Butler, thus, retains a conception of agency, constrained though it may be, in her view of subjectivity, accompanied by a desire to shape ethical accountability. She does not subscribe to Irigaray's vision of a distinct female imaginary, preferring to seek destabilization and examination of all models of subjectivity to keep selfhood open.

Subjectivity and Identity

These five lines of thought present rather different conceptions of subjectivity, forming dramatic contrasts with Enlightenment thinking and, for several, creating the basis for social-political action. They address the unconscious, language, and the social world to varying degrees, and, with respect to identity, theories of subjectivity help us investigate how, when, why, and from where identity is constructed. Subjectivity thus concerns the nature of the self as well as the relationship between individual and collective—persistent and central concerns across the human sciences.

Timothy Kuhn

See also Critical Theory; Cultural Studies; Gender; Language; Modernity and Postmodernity; Philosophy of Identity; Self-Consciousness

Further Readings

Althusser, L. (1971). Ideology and ideological state apparatuses (B. Brewster, Trans.). In *Lenin and philosophy and other essays*. London: New Left Books.

Butler, J. (2005). *Giving an account of oneself*. New York: Fordham University Press.

Foucault, M. (1970). *The order of things: An archaeology of the human sciences*. New York: Pantheon.

Foucault, M. (1982). The subject and power. *Critical Inquiry, 8*, 777–795.

Hall, S. (1985). Signification, representation, ideology: Althusser and the post-structuralist debates. *Critical Studies in Mass Communication, 2*, 91–114.

SURVEILLANCE AND THE PANOPTICON

In its simplest sense, *surveillance* is the act of observing or the condition of being observed, and it has always existed in some form. The term *surveillance* is generally used, however, to mean the act of watching or being watched in a systematic and focused manner. The Panopticon is a prison structure designed by Englishman Jeremy Bentham in 1785, which allows one guard to observe all the prison cells from a central tower that provides a view into each prison cell. The Panopticon is often used to illustrate the ways in which surveillance can discipline the individual. Surveillance strategies can have a specific impact on racialized and gendered identities that are often targeted in specific ways by surveillance. This entry looks at the impact surveillance technologies have had on the entertainment industry, the importance of surveillance in a post–9/11 world, the ways in which data collection constitutes a form of surveillance, the details of Bentham's Panopticon prison, Michel Foucault's influential ideas about surveillance, the impact of surveillance on racialized and gendered identities, and the development of a new field of scholarship, surveillance studies.

In the past few decades in Western countries, sophisticated surveillance technologies have been developed that make it possible to monitor the activities of just about anyone or to put oneself under observation for the purview of others. Although surveillance has traditionally been understood to be the act of watching someone without that person's explicit knowledge, with the proliferation of surveillance technologies in public spaces (cameras in elevators and closed-circuit televisions to monitor public spaces, for instance), people are now often aware that they are being watched or that there is a possibility that they may be watched. Additionally, surveillance now includes collection of information about the activities of an individual and is thus no longer understood as an exclusively visual activity.

Surveillance activities are particularly relevant to the modern age because they can be used to monitor workers in industrial and bureaucratic institutions. Such institutions can improve productivity and maximize effectiveness by tracking and collecting information about the movements and activities of workers, for example. More recently, in the era of globalization and corporatization, surveillance has become a vital consumer marketing tool. A Web site such as amazon.com, for example, stores information about purchases made and products viewed by a consumer and uses this data to pitch products to the consumer based on his or her individual tastes and habits.

Surveillance and Entertainment

Surveillance technologies are increasingly being employed for entertainment purposes. Reality TV uses surveillance technology to gather footage of real people doing real things, often putting willing participants under constant 24-hour surveillance for an extended period. This footage is then used to create a television show. The popularity of reality TV signals a noticeable shift in perceptions of surveillance. The phrase "Big Brother is watching you," for example, originally referred to the invasive and controlling gaze of a totalitarian government that monitored inhabitants in the fictional Oceania of George Orwell's novel *1984*. In the reality TV show titled *Big Brother,* on the other hand, a group of people willingly agree to be confined to a house for several weeks to have their every move caught on camera and broadcast to paying viewers on the World Wide Web with select segments broadcast on national television. This show illustrates the shift from a view of surveillance as an ominous activity that monitors and controls a population to a comfort with surveillance and a perception of it as nonthreatening.

The use of surveillance to create entertainment products has extended to cyberspace as well with the explosion of online blogging that allows others to learn about the private parts of a person's life and the proliferation of Web sites where people put themselves on display doing any number of activities in front of a webcam. What is unique about the use of surveillance for entertainment purposes is the willingness of people to put themselves on display, to be monitored, to be under surveillance.

Surveillance Post-9/11

Surveillance became a hot topic after 9/11. Governments in many Western countries view surveillance as crucial in preventing acts of terrorism, shoring up national borders and protecting against potential security threats. The USA PATRIOT Act, signed into law by President George W. Bush on October 26, 2001, is largely about increasing the ability of government agencies to use surveillance techniques to track the activities (e-mail, phone conversations, bank transactions, medical records, and so on) of U.S. citizens as well as foreigners located in or wishing to gain entry to the United States. Surveillance here has the mandate to track the activities of individuals identified as potential threats to the nation and to intercept these individuals before their plans are carried to fruition.

Dataveillance and Cybersurveillance

Although surveillance has typically relied on visual observation, there has been a proliferation of technologies for dataveillance and cybersurveillance, that is, gathering nonvisual data to monitor an individual's activities (Web sites visited, online purchases made, physical location, and so forth). *Dataveillance* involves gathering information about an individual's activities through his or her use of information technology—collecting data from electronic tracking devices (GPS systems), cell phones, or online activities, for example. *Cybersurveillance* is a more specific term referring to the monitoring of an individual's actions in cyberspace—Web sites visited, activities performed on these sites, online purchases, and so forth.

An important aspect of dataveillance and cybersurveillance is that they produce a data persona rather than an embodied self. Additionally, surveillance practices increasingly focus on consumption practices: what people buy, how, when, and where. This produces an ideal consumer—that is, a consumer whose habits, tastes, likes, and dislikes can be tracked and catered to. Dataveillance and cybersurveillance enable mass individualization of advertising. Hence, a tool such as Gmail, the e-mail technology by Google, can electronically scan a user's e-mail for keywords that can then be used to advertise specific products to that individual: Ads are displayed on a sidebar when the user opens e-mail, each user seeing a different set of ads tailored to him or her based on data collected from the e-mail account.

Bentham's Panopticon

Bentham's prison was designed to lower operating costs by creating a structure requiring fewer guards to watch over and discipline prisoners. Bentham's panoptic prison is circular, with a tower at the center and several stories of prison cells surrounding and facing the tower. A prison guard sits in an observatory located in the tower, its windows covered by venetian blinds. This means the prisoners cannot see into the observatory, but the guard can see into any of the prison cells. Because a single person in the tower can observe all the prison cells, only one prison guard is needed at any given time. The ingenuity of the structure is that the threat of being watched by someone with the power to punish can make the prisoners behave as if they are always being watched (when in fact they may never be, may always be, or may only be once in a while). The fear of being observed breaking the rules of the prison results in obedient behavior, all this without the use of overt force. In other words, the specter of surveillance disciplines the behavior of prisoners.

The panoptic structure makes explicit some of the ways in which the threat of being under surveillance—being watched, observed, monitored—can be powerful. The terms *panoptic, panopticism,* and the *panopticon* suggest a structure, situation, space, or setting in which an individual's movements may be tracked either by real people through observation (visual or with the help of technology) or by monitoring his or her activities. The terms also express the power that knowledge of the potential of being monitored can exert on the individual.

Foucault, Discipline, and Docile Bodies

Bentham's Panopticon also serves as a metaphor for the power that institutional forces can exert. This metaphor was first used by French theorist Foucault in his 1975 work *Discipline & Punish*. Panopticism creates what Foucault calls "docile bodies," that is, bodies that self-discipline without explicit force being exerted upon them and that self-regulate according to the demands of their context. Foucault looks at the social and structural apparatuses undergirding changes in Western European society during the modern age, an age marked by industrialization and bureaucratization.

In his examination of the emergence of the penal system in the section of the book titled "The Birth of the Prison," Foucault explores the origins, implications, and productive powers of panopticism—how the threat of punishment can discipline the individual, how people learn to self-discipline to become ideal citizens for a given context. The need for docile bodies, Foucault argues, emerges in the modern industrial age with its factories, schools, military, medical institutions, and so forth that require the orderly and disciplined conduct of bodies. These institutions need individuals who can master particular tasks and excel at the training for such tasks. The discipline of bodies through institutional—panoptic-like—power is instrumental for this purpose. The exemplar of the type of institution that might generate these bodies is Bentham's Panopticon, which produces a body that internalizes the discipline needed to survive in this context without overt external force.

Race and Gender

Race and gender often define our identities, shaping how we interact in the world and how people perceive and treat us. They are thus important in assessing how surveillance practices affect the individual. Surveillance practices that rely on visual observation—looking and being physically visible to others—are especially relevant when it comes to how gender or race can make an individual more or less visible, more or less prone to attracting the look of others.

Historically, women and people of color have been subject to surveillance in particular ways. For instance, as art critic John Berger outlines in his 1973 book *Ways of Seeing,* women have become accustomed to perceiving themselves as always on display—on television, in film, in photographs—so much so that they look upon themselves in this manner, possessing a profound understanding that their physical appearance is integral to their identity. In her influential article "Visual Pleasure and Narrative Cinema," film theorist Laura Mulvey argues that women in film are constantly on display and subject to what she terms a "male gaze," that is, that they are filmed from the perspective of an imaginary masculine spectator who objectifies the women on screen. This suggests that women may experience visual surveillance as particularly stressful because of the existing focus on their physical appearance and the emphasis in much popular culture in putting women visually on display. Additionally, research has shown that some men who operate surveillance devices use them to objectify women for their viewing pleasure, by focusing a closed-circuit camera on a woman's body parts, as Kevin Haggerty notes in his research on the topic. Thus, a person's gender can affect how an individual experiences surveillance and how it is directed at him or her.

People of color are watched with particular attention in certain circumstances. For example, when it comes to crime, surveillance of people of color is especially intense: Areas with dense African American populations tend to have more surveillance cameras than other areas do because these are considered places with higher crime rates. Concomitantly, African Americans are likely to be watched more often in stores because of the suspicion that they will shoplift. As Haggerty again highlights, this can result in a disproportionate amount of surveillance (closed-circuit cameras, for instance) directed at certain racial groups. A person's race can have a particular impact on how he or she experiences surveillance and how it is directed at him or her.

The ability to willingly put oneself on public display—through the use of a webcam or a blog, for instance—can also offer a rebellious, liberating, and important outlet for people who have traditionally been oppressively put under the gaze of surveillance because it provides an opportunity to appropriate the means of surveillance and control its use.

Surveillance Studies

In the past two decades, surveillance studies has surfaced as an area of research in academia, resulting in work such as the online journal *Surveillance and Society* and the Surveillance Project at Queen's University in Ontario. This scholarship is concerned with the implications of the use of surveillance technologies and techniques. The research has grown alongside developments in new technologies and the changing social infrastructures around the practice of surveillance. The work is multidisciplinary, looking at the emergence, implications, effects, occurrences, and theories needed to understand how surveillance is used. Broadly

speaking, this work can touch on issues of democracy, privacy, freedom, and oppression, and look at the implications of the use of surveillance on politics and policy.

Rachel E. Dubrofsky

See also Voyeurism

Further Readings

Berger, J. (1973). *Ways of seeing*. New York: Penguin.
Foucault, M. (1995). *Discipline & punish: The birth of the prison*. New York: Vintage Books.
Haggerty, K. D. (2006). Tear down the walls: On demolishing the panopticon. In D. Lyon (Ed.), *Theorizing surveillance: The panopticon and beyond*. Devon, UK: Willan.
Mulvey, L. (1975). Visual pleasure and narrative cinema. *Screen, 16*(3), 6–18.

Symbolic Interactionism

Symbolic interactionism is a sociological perspective rooted in the philosophy of pragmatism, especially as it was developed by the philosopher George Herbert Mead, who taught social psychology at the University of Chicago in the early 20th century. His student, Herbert Blumer, who named the perspective "symbolic interactionism," asserted the three basic precepts that have defined the interactionist approach. First, people act in and toward the social world—its people, situations, social roles, goals, ideas, institutions, and material things—on the basis of meaning. Second, meaning is not fixed or immutable, but arises in concrete situations of social interaction, in the give and take of everyday life as people pursue their aims in cooperation and sometimes conflict with others. And third, meaning is used, and often transformed, in an ongoing process of interpretation in which self-consciousness plays a major part. The symbolic interactionist approach to identity rests on these ideas.

The Nature of Meaning

Human beings are symbolic creatures, for whom linguistic symbols are the principle basis for constructing, experiencing, and acting meaningfully on their worlds. A symbol is anything—a word, an image, a gesture—that stands for something else. National flags symbolize "patriotic" attitudes and feelings; certain hand gestures or facial expressions signify the user's contempt or disdain for another; names and labels identify people by their social roles, group memberships, and personal characteristics and thus establish expectations for and limits on their conduct. Of the various kinds of symbols, those carried in language are the most important for human conduct. People live in a world of named objects, and people's capacity to act successfully rests on learning the possible and expected ways of responding to or acting toward these objects.

Symbols enable people to coordinate their conduct because they arouse shared responses. The person who uses a symbol evokes thoughts, feelings, and ideas about possible actions in the minds of others who see or hear it, as well as in his or her own mind. For example, an announcement that building is on fire arouses in all who are present—announcer as well as listeners—a set of ideas about the dangers of fire in an enclosed space as well as how to respond to it. Likewise, derogatory words lay a shared basis for thoughts and feelings, and ultimately, actions toward others. The responses aroused by symbols are not identical from one person to another, but they are sufficiently similar to allow the individual to assume (at least initially) that others are responding to the situation in more or less the same way he or she is responding.

Meaning is thus a social rather than merely an individual phenomenon. It is the individual, of course, who learns and uses the meanings provided by the language of his or her community. Yet to use a word is to bring into public view a part of the individual's state of mind at a particular time and thereby to communicate it to others. To speak of "fire," for example, is to indicate to others (and to oneself) that one believes there is danger and is prepared to act on it, that the others should define the situation and act in a similar way, and that collectively they are seeking escape or rescue from a dangerous situation. To invoke a racial or ethnic stereotype in a conversation is to invite the other to view the member of a racial or ethnic outgroup in the same way as the speaker, and implicitly (though not necessarily immediately) to act toward

the outgroup member on the basis of that attitude. Meanings thus shape both the individual's conduct and that of others.

Meaning and Interaction

The symbols, and thus also meanings, available to the members of a society or one of its subgroups may seem fixed and immutable, but they are not. Linguistic symbols—words—do have relatively stable meanings, in the sense that they have dictionary definitions and, more significantly, because they are used more or less consistently by those who speak a given language. It might seem, therefore, that human beings are confined by a linguistic straightjacket, able only to respond to a given and more or less fixed set of symbols and to enact the lines of conduct they make possible. A cry of "fire" in a public place, in this view, could only lead to more or less well or badly coordinated efforts to escape.

Meaning is not a fixed quality, however, but an emergent one. Human conduct and the meanings on which it depends are situated. People form their conduct as they interact with others, use and hear symbols, define the situations in which they find themselves, construct lines of conduct for themselves, and influence the conduct of others. In this process, new meanings emerge and shape conduct, previous meanings prove not to be useful, and unexpected events transform meanings, whether subtly or drastically, and lay the basis for new conduct. In other words, people use meanings to organize their conduct and respond practically to the situations they face. They adopt new symbols and discard or transform others as circumstances dictate or make possible.

Consider conflict between an adolescent and his or her parents over the young person's freedom to come and go as he or she pleases. "Independence" is a principle goal of the young in U.S. culture and a matter of concern to and often resistance by their parents. Middle and high school students expect increasing degrees of freedom year by year, and their parents, concerned (realistically or not) about the dangers of drugs, alcohol, cars, and sex, are often inclined to hold their children close and resist their quest for independence. Many arguments thus begin with established cultural meanings—"independence," "freedom," "rebellion," "danger." But the conduct of the disputants—what they say and what they do—arises in the situation and not simply and automatically from fixed cultural meanings and scripts. Who did what to spark an argument? How did participants define those actions? Was staying out past curfew, for example, seen by the adolescent as a declaration of independence or by his or her parents as an act of rebellion? Or was it taken as an unintended but avoidable mistake? Likewise, to grasp how an argument became more heated or how it cooled, we must examine how participants interpreted one another's words and deeds. Did a parent, for example, recognize his or her own adolescence in the son or daughter's actions and therefore decide to be more accommodating? Did the adolescent come to regard overt resistance as futile and thus decide to present a more contented self while finding more secret means of rebellion? Established meanings provide a framework for interaction, but the process of interaction often yields fluidity and change.

The Self

Because human beings are symbolic creatures, they are necessarily also self-conscious. Humans live in a world of named objects and are capable of acting toward themselves as objects, much as they act toward any object. Individuals have names, just as other objects—houses, chairs, cars—have names. To name something—whether it is a new Lexus or a newborn infant that is called by such relational names as "son" or "daughter" as well as by an individual name, "Jacob"—is to assign it a place in the social world and to invoke shared ways of acting toward it. A new luxury car invokes shared ideas about social standing or wealth; a new infant invokes shared ideas about how girls and boys should be treated or about an ancestral "Jacob" whose qualities it is hoped will be shared by his namesake. Cars do not hear or use their names, but people do. "Jacob" learns his name and, along with it as socialization proceeds, he learns his "meaning" in the eyes of others. He learns the attitudes they hold, the expectations they have of him, the ways they are prepared to act toward him. In thus becoming an object he can himself name, think about, develop feelings about, and act toward, he acquires a self.

In the symbolic interactionist perspective, the essence of the self lies in reflexivity—that is, in the capacity of the person to be conscious of his or her own past, present, and future actions from the imagined perspective of other people. Infants are born into a relatively small world of caretakers such as parents, siblings, and other kin whose relationships to one another they gradually grasp and, as they acquire language, name. The social world expands—to the extended family, neighborhood, village, town, city, nation—and as it does, the individual develops a cognitive map of that world and his or her various roles in it. The child learns he or she is "son" or "daughter," and later "Black" or "White," "college student" or "worker." The social roles that others enact provide the perspectives from which individuals imaginatively see and respond to themselves. The "son" sees himself as son by adopting the perspective of others, particularly of "mother" and "father."

This reflexive capacity to see oneself from the point of view of the other enables people to transform meanings rather than merely respond automatically to fixed meanings. When people act, they indicate meanings to themselves. For example, they tell themselves that they are angry, that their parents are trying to exert too much control over them, or that their protests are only making things worse. In other words, in forming their conduct people consider themselves—their own thoughts, feelings, and actions—as a part of the situation in which they find themselves. They imagine how they appear to others and how their impending actions will affect how others see and act toward them. And as they indicate alternative meanings, they also lay out alternative lines of conduct for themselves, and thus lay the basis for choosing one act instead of another. And when individuals find themselves defined in ways they do not like because of their actions, they seek to repair damage to the conceptions others have of them by excusing or justifying their conduct. In any case, self-consciousness makes it possible to sort, sift, and consider various meanings, and to replace one set of meanings with another.

Identity

Although Mead did not use the term, the concept of *identity* has become central to the symbolic interactionist analysis of the self. *Identity* refers to the individual's location in social life, and it is established by the thoughts, feelings, and actions of others as well as those of the individual. Identity is therefore inherently a social process rather than simply an individual possession. A person "has" an identity—as a parent or child, as an African American or a Jew, as a Roman Catholic or a Lutheran, as a friend or enemy, as brilliant or intellectually slow—when the individual's *announcements* of identity correspond with the *placements* made by others. Every act announces an identity of one kind or another. Approaching a sales clerk in a store with a confident sense that one expects the clerk's attention is an announcement of one's identity as a customer. The executive who disdainfully ignores a janitor or other service worker announces an identity of "superior" and assigns the other the place of "subordinate." When the clerk attends to the customer, he or she places the other in the customer identity. When the service worker avoids eye contact and attends only to the work at hand rather than to the executive, he or she places the other in the claimed position.

Identities vary along two major dimensions—*social* versus *personal* and *situated* versus *biographical*. People announce and are placed in a variety of identities that depend on group, organizational, and demographic memberships or affiliations: familial, occupational, educational, age related, political, ethnic, religious, and the like. These social identities locate the individual in a social world whose map is shared and understood by its members. Some of these social identities acquire a more central place in the self than others do—the individual may be chiefly identified by others and identify himself or herself as a professor, for example, or an African American, or a woman. These social identities are announced when people enact the social roles on which they are based, as when the professor enters the classroom and begins to teach. They are also announced in other situations, as when an individual is introduced to someone at a cocktail party as "Professor Smith."

Social identity is a key part of the person's sense of self—and for some people, the most important part—but it does not fully define the self. People also construct personal identities that reflect their particular life histories or accomplishments rather than only their group memberships and social roles.

Some individuals—Apple Computer CEO Steve Jobs is a good example—develop such distinctive personal identities that their names alone establish their place in the social world. They truly "need no introduction" and their actions are interpreted as manifestations of "themselves" rather than of their social roles or group memberships. Their personal identities nonetheless depend as much on the acts of others as on their own actions. Steve Jobs is "Steve Jobs" because of his announcements and because of his placement by others as a unique individual with a particular history of accomplishment.

Identity is both situated and biographical. In any given social situation, the individual typically acts on the basis of a particular identity—for example, mother, professor, physician—and does so in relation to particular others—son, student, patient. Situated identities are established largely on the basis of role relationships, and when the person departs the situation, the situated identity is left behind, to be replaced by an identity relevant to the next situation. The son leaves for school and becomes a student; the mother leaves for work and becomes a professor. But people are not merely participants in situations, with their actions merely governed by role requirements. They are creatures of biography. That is, they have life histories, a series of experiences with a variety of situations and roles, and they think of themselves—and are thought of by others—as having a reality beyond the boundaries of the particular situation. Sometimes the biographical sense of self is mainly founded on particular social identities that they experience repeatedly, such as occupational or familial ones. Other people emphasize personal attributes or accomplishments. In either case, and in various mixtures of the social and the personal, the person has a life history and his or her identity is founded on a biographical narrative announced to and accepted by others. We use the stories we tell about ourselves to locate ourselves in the social world.

Identity provides a major basis for motivation and action. People see the world from the vantage points of their various identities. As Catholics or Jews; Blacks, Whites, or Hispanics; or as Steve Jobs, they define their circumstances and opportunities for action on the basis of their identities. The actions people take within the groups to which they belong or in the roles they enact as well as their relationship to the members of other groups and occupants of other roles are shaped by their identities. People act on the basis of meanings provided by their identities and by interaction with others in terms of identity norms. Individuals explain their actions in terms of their identities. Thus, for example, the professor in the college classroom sees that microscopic social world as a professor—he or she views the others present as "students," responds to their questions or lack of questions as indicators of professorial success or failure and, at least in theory, does not pay attention to gender, race, or other characteristics that are presumably not relevant to the student identity. Taking "professor" as the essence of the self in that situation, his or her perception of self and others is that of a professor.

The motivational significance of identity, however, can be complex. If a student in a classroom makes a comment that the professor and others regard as racist, for example, the roles and identities of all present are challenged and may be temporarily transformed. Instead of "professor" and "student," those present may find themselves interacting as "tolerant" and "intolerant" or as "condemners" of a "bigot." Even within defined and relatively stable situations, therefore, roles and identities can be somewhat fluid. In contemporary life, many people are conflicted about which identity should claim most of their time and energy, as when a demanding occupational role interferes with a parental role. Moreover, announcements and placements do not always agree. Members of an ethnic group may be more interested in placing an individual among them and eliciting identification with the group than the individual is in announcing a group affiliation and identifying with it. An individual's identification with a group may be met with indifference or rejection by group members. In such circumstances, we cannot really say that the individual simply "has" a particular identity. Nonetheless, identity is a motivating element in his or her conduct, whether it promotes an effort to reconcile the demands of work and family or to resist a group's pressures or to overcome its resistance.

John P. Hewitt

See also Collective/Social Identity; Identification; Impression Management; Looking-Glass Self;

Narratives; Reflexive Self or Reflexivity; Self; Self-Presentation

Further Readings

Blumer, H. (1969). *Symbolic interactionism: Perspective and methods*. Englewood Cliffs, NJ: Prentice Hall.

Hewitt, J. P. (2007). *Self and society: A symbolic interactionist social psychology* (10th ed.). Boston: Allyn & Bacon.

Mead, G. H. (1964). *On social psychology* (A. L. Strauss, Ed.). Chicago: University of Chicago Press.

Reynolds, L. T., & Hermann-Kinney, N. J. (Eds.). (2003). *Handbook of symbolic interactionism*. Walnut Creek, CA: AltaMira Press.

SYMBOLISM

Symbolism is a technique used widely to convey a deeper message, substitute for language when language is not shared, and enhance the intended message. Symbolism occurs in literature, religion, politics, and many other disciplines, academic and beyond. What makes symbolism so diverse is that people often use this technique to enhance communication. Identity often depends on symbols, thus symbolism and identity are inextricably linked. Both symbolism and identity operate beyond the individual. Identity studies scholars recently refocused their attention from the study of "me" to include the collective and the political implications that result from the interaction of the collective.

Signs on buildings, streets, and other venues use symbols to represent establishments, provide directions, and send messages. Symbolism transcends language and cultural barriers that, at times, impedes communication. Tourists often rely on symbols to identify landmarks and other essential places when in a land where language is not shared. Mathematicians rely on symbols as road maps to solve equations. Symbolism may be universal, that is, widely recognized. Often symbolism is universal even when the symbol is culturally specific. A symbol is loosely defined as an object that represents or suggests something else, and symbolism has various universal and contextual applications. This entry explores several of these applications.

Literature

In literature, symbolism is often contextual in that specific symbols develop meaning only in the context of the literary work. Writers rely on symbolism to elicit the reader's prior knowledge, bring a deeper meaning to the words that transcend the textual description, and, as a creative art form, to use language and style. The key component of symbolism is that symbols, words, or pictures are used to represent something other than the actual definition of a word. The intent is to give words deeper or profound meaning. For example, in Charlotte Perkins Gilman's "The Yellow Wallpaper," the yellow wallpaper represents many arguable issues in the story. Each detail of the wallpaper represents an idea or conflict between the protagonist and the setting. Thus, the wallpaper itself represents or suggests something else, and the character's identity hinges on her interpretations of the symbols.

Other literary genres rich in symbolism are poetry and drama. Symbolism is systematically weaved through the fabric of a poem. Some poets strategically place symbols in their poems, and others use symbols as the primary language of the poem. The reader is able to identify the voice, tone, and mood by the use of symbols throughout the stanzas of a poem.

Drama depends greatly on the use of verbal communication. Language is filled with symbolism and stresses the identity of the author and the characters. Like other language-specific techniques, spoken language reveals much more than the rhythmic sounds and blends of letters. The listener is able to identify the speaker's origin, culture, and many other details. In addition, language uses tonal shifts to communicate emotion and emphasize meaning. Drama uses symbolism as a necessary tool for communication. Many dramatists use symbolism to assist the actor in bringing the words to life. Additionally, this technique is used to help the reader envision every element that assists the words in painting a picture in the reader's mind.

Religion

The use of symbolism is a large part of religion. Many religions embrace the idea that believers walk by faith and not by sight. The hope of reward at the end of life serves as motivation to adhere to the tenets specified by a governing book, spirit, and so forth. Many religions share the belief that as reward for people's "good works" during their mortal days, their eternal life will be spent in a place free from iniquity and filled with divinity. This idea is reinforced by using symbols of heaven, such as purely clad angels maneuvering harmoniously through clouds and playing harps. Many people use religious symbols to identify themselves as believers of those specific tenets. Biblical texts inscribe symbols to reinforce ideals and "prove" that the consequences or rewards exist. Examples emerge in the book of Revelation as it foretells the occurrences of the last days. Unnatural weather conditions are among the many occurrences mentioned in the text. Some Christians viewed Hurricane Katrina as a symbol, for they attributed its devastation to those references in the book of Revelation. Hurricane Katrina became a modern-day symbol of the wrath of God and his communication with the earth. Although the weather phenomenon was itself a hurricane, and there was scientific evidence to substantiate this occurrence, some people relied on symbolism inscribed in the book of Revelation.

Another common religious symbol is the number seven. In 2007, the world witnessed the occurrence of July 7, 2007, or 07/07/07. Deemed the luckiest day of the century, July 7, 2007, became the day couples exchanged vows, parents induced labor, and casinos ushered in crowds, all in the name of the divine and complete number. Christianity, Judaism, and Islam share a divine connection to this number, which is identified as sacred and complete. Islamic texts relate the number seven to sacred rituals, heaven, and creation. Christian texts relate the number seven to heaven, creationism, sin, and virtue.

Those who believe in religion as a governing source rely on symbols to identify deeper meanings in religious texts. Many people wear religious symbols to identify themselves as members of a specific belief system and to identify with others who share the same belief system. Historically, people have relied on symbols in almost every area of human existence.

Politics

Politicians use symbols to identify with potential voters and pledge their allegiance to change the status quo in the name of progress. In a period of unbalanced budgets and sagging economies, political promises hinge on the idea of change and economic stability. Many political analyses refer to a stronger economy and a balanced budget as symbols rather than are actual achievable goals. Politicians themselves often become symbols of hope and representatives of the people who identify with their messages and goals.

The use of symbolism to identify with potential voters is a key component of any political campaign. As potential candidates tour the country in an effort to garner support for election, they seek effective ways to engage the people. The use of patriotic colors, images, paraphernalia, and words symbolize the candidate's political rhetoric. For constituents, words such as *hope* and *change* symbolize the promise of a better tomorrow.

Constituents often look for symbols as they consider which candidate they will support. Many seek candidates who proffer symbols of hope. Interestingly, the most effective political symbols are ambiguous in nature. Constituents respond to symbols that appeal to their sense of self rather those with concrete definitions.

Race

One of the most sensitive referrals to symbolism and identity is race. Even more sensitive is the exploitation of a race with the use of a symbol. History reveals that the idea of superiority divides people. The idea of superiority presupposes that one group is superior and another group is inferior. Historically, symbolism has been used in reference to race identification. Differences in skin color, nose width, and hair texture have affected the degree to which different groups interact. Symbolism is often used to evoke fear and send disturbing messages to people of various races and cultures.

Recently, a small town in Louisiana gained national attention when a group of White students hung a rope from a tree. The rope was looped around itself to form a circle. The rope became a noose. Once the object changed from rope to noose, it evoked a long history of racial inequality and physical abuse. The noose, then, resulted in symbolic violence. During the days, weeks, and months that followed, people from different races and cultures united and divided around the issue.

Once an object becomes a symbol, its historical and current meanings have the potential to inflict pain, cause joy, or galvanize a community. Like the noose, the Confederate flag holds the same dark history. Although the Confederate flag is the historical flag of the South, it also represents the dark days of slavery that was primarily practiced in the southern region of the now United States. Many believe that those who continue to hang the confederate flag are doing so to show their support of a caste system that dehumanized a race of people. A symbol has the same impact as words or, perhaps, a greater impact than words.

Symbolism, then, hinges on the use of objects as themselves, but those objects carry an implied meaning. In an attempt to maintain the idea of race, physical attributes that may be consistent with a race of people are often used as symbols. Groups of people with certain physical characteristics have been persecuted for centuries. Identity is greatly influenced by public reaction to specific symbolic characteristics of race and culture. People often go to great lengths to change these characteristics with the hope of changing their identity.

Identity

Human existence and experience are inextricably linked. A symbol has the potential to evoke a range of responses with varying intensities. Based on the origin of the symbol and its implied meaning, a symbol has the potential to bridge gaps in communication and culture or further create a wedge. Symbols that are culturally specific and associated with pain are usually the symbols that have the most potential to either separate or unite a people. Still, people rely on symbols to identify with belief systems and society-at-large. Furthermore, identity itself is symbolic. Identity uses symbolism to further its "we" agenda. Inextricably linked, identity and symbolism offer society a mechanism for forming a collective. Key questions related to symbolism, such as how meaning is assigned and how meaning is rooted in experience, clearly reflect identity.

Symbolism has the greatest potential to offer society a mechanism for change and unity. The greatest contribution that symbolism can make to identity is to emphasize likeness and respect diversity while building a strong and sound collective.

Although this task has not been attempted, it is possible. Once groups find similarity, the potential for unity is greater. Symbolism can offer unity in the name of identity.

Concetta A. Williams

See also Cultural Representation; Symbolic Interactionism

Further Readings

Cobb, J. (2008). The noose. *Ebony 63*(3), 110.

Cohen, A. (1979). Political symbolism. *Annual Review of Anthropology, 8*, 87–113.

Duster, T. (2007). How to read a noose. *The Chronicle Review, The Chronicle in Higher Education, 54*(11), B24.

Fogelin, L. (2007). The anthropology of religious ritual. *Annual Review of Anthropology, 36*, 55–71.

Fonrobert, C. E. (2005). The political symbolism of the Eruv. *Jewish Social Studies, 11*(3), 9–35.

Gilman, C. P. (1973). *The yellow wallpaper.* New York: Feminist Press. (Original work published 1892)

Goud, N. H. (2001). The symbolism identity technique. *Journal of Humanistic Counseling, Education, and Development, 40*(1), 114–121.

Spears, A. K. (Ed.). (1999). *Race and ideology: Language, symbolism, and popular culture.* Detroit, MI: Wayne State University Press.

Turner, V. (1975, October). Symbolic studies. *Annual Review of Anthropology, 4*, 142–161.

SYNCRETISM

Syncretism describes the mixing, blending or combining of beliefs, practices, and traditions from one religion to another, or in certain cases between multiple religions, that result in the creation of complicated individual and group religious identities. *Syncretism* has become a term used almost exclusively in religious studies, although it may also exist in culture, politics, and philosophy. Syncretism is often a way for religious identity to grow or expand, sometimes without official sanction of religious authorities, and finds its greatest expression in such practices as saint veneration, mysticism, and folk belief and practice.

Before the rise of more or less strictly monotheistic religions (Judaism, Christianity, and Islam) that believed in one god to the exclusion of others, nearly all religions had a marked syncretistic character. For example, Greek and Roman religions in the Greco-Roman period (about 332 BCE to 640 CE) borrowed from each other and the varied cultures with which they had contact. The native Greek and Roman religions adopted practices, beliefs, and dogmas from Egyptian, Persian, and Near Eastern religions, among others. Local religions, such as the worship of Isis in Egypt, reached the scope and level of Mother-Goddess worship found in most ancient Mediterranean cultures, and had a wide appeal throughout the Roman Empire. Mithraism, a religion from Persia, was adopted by Roman soldiers and carried all throughout the empire, where it picked up elements from different religions. Isis worship and especially Mithraism, which were both deeply syncretistic religions, had some influence on the rise of Christianity and the shape it took.

Yet, syncretism has not been confined to ancient religions and has influenced the monotheistic religions of Judaism, Christianity, and Islam. For instance, syncretism played a vital role in the formation of early Christianity. Members of early Christianity, or the Jesus movement, moved increasingly away from their Jewish roots in the 1st and 2nd century of the Common Era, and syncretism was one of the factors that helped the new religion expand its reach. For example, early Christians borrowed heavily from their rival religions, including Mithraism, and even adopted Mithra's birth date in December as Christ's. Ancient Roman religions also helped give form and substance to early Christianity, making it more appealing for Greek- and Latin-speaking peoples. Christian identity in its formative years was deeply syncretistic, borrowing heavily from the rich and diverse range of Greek and Roman religions and philosophies, even as they supplanted those same religions and philosophies to become the official religion of the Roman Empire in 380 CE.

During the long periods both before and after the destruction of the Second Temple in Jerusalem in 70 CE, Jews adopted and adapted their faith as they traveled to new lands. For example, for much of their recorded history, the Jews of Morocco venerated Jewish saints, a practice not widely found in other Jewish communities. Moroccan Muslims also venerated saints, and the custom probably dates back to the practices of the pre-Islamic, Berber native religions. Moroccan Jews made pilgrimages to saints' shrines to venerate, feast, and pray. The shrines were usually in semi-isolated places, and their locations were most often near prominent rocks, trees, or wells, which also points to the pre-Islamic origin of Jewish saint veneration: The rock, tree, or well was once the sacred object of the pilgrimage, and the Jews of Morocco simply adopted the local landmark into their version of Judaism, creating an overlay of syncretistic identities by blending elements of Judaism, Moroccan Islam, and the nature worship of native Berbers.

Syncretism is also found in many elements of Islamic practice and theology and in the many regions of the world where Islam is observed. Perhaps no varieties of Islam are more powerfully syncretistic than Sufism, or the mystical orders of Islam, and the folk expression of Islam, or the Islam practiced by people with little or no religious training or education. A powerful example of syncretism in Islam can be found in the Balkan region of Europe. In the 13th century, the Ottoman Turks began their invasion of the Balkans, and eventually conquered much of the region. They brought with them a variety of Islam heavily influenced by Sufism, which encompassed a range of mystical movements developed early in the history of the religion. Balkans Sufism was quite pliant, and the preachers and Sufi masters who converted Slavic Christians to Islam were not averse to retaining many of the old Balkan native folk practices already found in Balkan Christianity—as well as those Christian practices and beliefs. Balkan Islamic identity was deeply syncretic. Balkan Muslims often venerated Christian saints, kept Christian holidays, and baptized their children in the belief that it would protect them from disease. The form of Islam created and spread in the Balkans borrowed heavily from Greek and Roman Christianity, Balkan folk beliefs, and Sufi pantheistic tendencies (the belief that God exists not as one entity, but is the world or the universe) to create a unique form of religious identity.

Scholars of religion have recently criticized the term *syncretism* as too broad. They argue that changes and developments in a religion are an expected process in its growth, and cannot be clarified by so wide a concept as syncretism. Syncretism has been viewed as too reductionist, or useful for little more than breaking apart the component elements of a religion and labeling them according to their individual origins. Those who wish to study religion more holistically oppose this view, and see religious identity as the more or less fluid working of systems of belief and practice. The concept of syncretism has also been accused of belittling religions of less developed areas or peoples, and insulting their identity as impure or debased forms of some parent religion. Cases in point are Afro-Caribbean religions such as Santeria and Haitian Vodou or Voodoo. All these criticisms point to the need to use the term *syncretism* carefully and precisely, and with fine variations.

Eric Maroney

See also Acculturation; Clan Identity; Fundamentalism; Globalization; Multiculturalism; Pluralism; Religious Identity

Further Readings

Leopold, A., & Jensen, J. (2005). *Syncretism in religion: A reader.* New York: Routledge.

Maroney, E. (2006). *Religious syncretism.* London: SCM Press.

Steward, C., & Shaw, R. (1994). *Syncretism/anti-syncretism: The politics of religious syncretism.* New York: Routledge.

T

TAG QUESTION

A *tag question* is a form of indirect communication consisting of a short question appended to a declarative statement. It often is used in polite speech to soften or weaken a statement's impact (e.g. "The meetings would run more smoothly if we e-mailed the documents to everyone in advance, *don't you think?*"). Throughout this entry, tag questions are italicized.

The tag question has many functions. For instance, it may (a) help prevent the speaker from appearing pushy and thereby help circumvent conflict; (b) confirm information of which the speaker is nearly but not totally certain ("The meeting is at 2 p.m., *is that correct?*"); (c) intimidate or coerce courtroom witnesses being interrogated under oath ("You *did* have time to hide the gun after you shot your brother, *didn't you?!*"); (d) show empathy ("That's a shame about the company's closing, *isn't it?*"); (e) enhance camaraderie and humor among speakers of African American Vernacular English ("Obama ain't playin', *o-kay?*"); (f) express sarcasm in colloquial fashion ("Governor Sarah Palin could focus a little less on lipstick and a lot more on foreign policy, *ya think?*"). Robin Lakoff also provides an example of frequent colloquial use of tags by teenagers: "So I went to see her, *OK?* And she was all—*y'know?*—'What're you doing here,' *right?*"

In this entry, discussion of the tag question is set within the broad context of scholarly discourse about women's language use, differences in men's and women's communication styles, features of African American and hip-hop women artists' language use, and impact of the credibility and context of a speaker on persuasion. Use of the tag question in various professional and social arenas is also explored. The concept has relevance in matters as diverse as social education of boys and girls, court interpreting for foreign-language defendants, authenticity in advertising, communication between nurses and physicians, and the political communication style of women elected officials, among other issues. Tag questions can reveal identity status among speakers, as well as power differentials among different identities.

Tag Questions and Women's Language

The tag question long has been viewed as a feature of women's language, which traditionally is more deferential and indirect than men's because of socialization. Since the late 1960s, much has been written about the tag question, often considered an element of powerless or overly polite speech of those lacking agency.

Generally, women and girls are socialized to communicate in ways that avoid conflict and preserve relationships, whereas men and boys often are culturally programmed to dominate, control, and take charge. As Daniel Distelhorst notes, when women and men work together in groups, these issues of deference and dominance can create frustration for women and hinder overall group effectiveness and collaboration.

Women's socialization results often in their abandoning direct speech, along with the assertiveness and self-confidence connected with it.

Examples of indirect communication strategies frequently used by women (and generally by persons in subordinate positions professionally or socially) include use of *qualifiers* ("*Perhaps* you might consider . . ."); use of *disclaimers* ("*This is probably a stupid idea,* but what about . . ."); use of *tag questions* ("That was a fine performance of *Othello, don't you agree?*"). Groundbreaking work by Lakoff in the early 1970s suggested that women's language is typically marked by three characteristics: propriety, hesitancy, and verbal excess. Hesitancy often is expressed by circumlocution, the use of hedge or filler words (such as *um*), and tag questions.

Barbara Stern suggests that feminist critics, led by Lakoff, have studied the impact of *place* on woman's language, focusing on such things as word choice, sentence structure, and organizational flow, to determine how women select, combine, and use words in their daily lives. This language is the direct result of covert messages that women receive from the culture about their "proper" place. Cultural imperatives require women to communicate in ways that are nice, polite, and ladylike, and that show concern for others' feelings. By contrast, cultural signals to men permit them to be rough, tough, powerful, and intellectual in speech. Such male speech habits are learned on athletic playing fields, in the military, and in industrial and other blue-collar work settings. Deborah Tannen refers to these distinctive male and female ways of speaking as *genderlects*.

Thus, women often complain that they make a suggestion during a meeting and it is not accepted, but then a man in the group makes the same suggestion a bit later and it is enthusiastically received. This is because men do not take a tentative, hesitant approach seriously. Daniel Distelhorst suggests that when women, seeking not to appear overly aggressive or to jeopardize relationships, use tag questions to present an idea ("That would be a good way of going about it, *don't you think?*"), men hear it through their own language culture, one of tough, direct talk and one that values projecting oneself, and dismiss whatever is being proposed. When the same idea is presented later in a more direct way by a man, the men in the group hear it and connect with it.

Stern and other marketing experts discuss the need for verisimilitude in human behavior and speech depicted in mini-dramas or dramatic scenarios used to sell products and services in print advertisements and in radio and television commercials. To be profitable, ads must show the "culturally approved" version of femininity and masculinity. Marketing research gives attention to the use in advertising devices of women's language features described here, including use of the tag question. Debate persists regarding the degree to which advertising serves as an agent of change with respect to societal norms for men and women versus the degree to which it actually perpetuates or concretizes societal norms of men's and women's behaviors and features of communication.

Social Education of Boys and Girls

Kathryn P. Scott stresses the need to understand sex-based language differences and argues that to be professionally successful, both boys and girls need to be socialized to balance skills of *leadership* (assertiveness—typically associated with males) and *nurturance* (typically associated with females). She posits that boys should be taught the same skills of interpersonal sensitivity as girls, and that girls should be socialized to be more self-confident and assertive like boys. For girls, such social education would involve close attention to communication strategies employed, and would call for instruction in direct communication. Use of direct speech involves eliminating the use of qualifiers, disclaimers, and tag questions. It also involves making requests directly ("Please close the door," rather than, "Would you please close the door?"), and not smiling when expressing a negative or challenging viewpoint. To this list of direct communication strategies one also might add the need to not use the inflection of a question for statements ("He seems as if he is really not interested?").

Nurse-Physician-Patient Communication

Others such as Linda Lindeke and Ann Sieckert, who have written about nurse-physician collaboration and communication, also suggest the elimination of tag questions by nurses when expressing a difference of opinion with doctors about patient care. They suggest that there is a direct correlation between some aspects of collaboration between these health care professionals, who have an unequal power relationship, and the quality of patient care. Although doctors tend to bring more money to hospitals and, thus, often receive more respect from bottom-line-oriented administrators, nurses are critical to patient care and must be respected. Creation and maintenance of an atmosphere in which nurses are free to disagree with physicians' decisions is critical. To be more assertive in making patient care recommendations, Lindeke and Sieckert stress the need for nurses to refuse to use disclaimers that rob them of credit for their contributions and suggest the elimination of tag questions, which often deprive them of respect. Frankness, along with flexibility and open-mindedness, are urged to improve communication and overall collaboration with physicians in the interest of patients' well-being. However, use of tag questions with patients by doctors, nurses, or any other health care professionals likely would show empathy ("That spot is a bit swollen and tender, *isn't it?*"), and thereby enhance the patient-caregiver relationship.

African American Vernacular English and Hip-Hop Language

So-called powerless or self-effacing speech often has been attributed to African Americans as well as women. From the time of slavery until the Black Power Movement in the late 1960s, survival often depended on deferential communication with Whites. Rosina Lippi-Green, Geneva Smitherman, and others have written extensively about the African Verbal Tradition (AVT) and its unique African American Vernacular English (AAVE) intonation, address systems, rhetorical features, discourse strategies, sermonic tone, and use of tag questions. Here are two examples of AAVE tag question use: "Naw, they gots to go, *know what ah'm sayin'?*" "The Bears bettah be on they A-game Saturday fo' I lose my shirt, *ya heard me?*" Of note, scholars in this field of linguistics stress that although some view AAVE speakers as mostly poor individuals with limited education, highly educated, prominent African Americans who are bidialectal also are AVT speakers, not because they use the morphology, phonology, or syntax traditionally associated with AAVE, but rather because they make use of certain intonations and discursive techniques that are connected with it.

Marcyliena Morgan and other scholars indicate that during slavery and Jim Crow segregation, speech expressing subservience and subordination was necessary for Black survival. Such speech featured the overuse of tag questions and other elements of female speech to help ensure that a White person to whom one was speaking would not be provoked to anger. Under those historical circumstances, use of linguistic agency that provoked White anger could lead to brutality and cruelty—to beatings, maiming, castration, and lynching.

Since the civil rights and Black power movements of the 1960s, however, both Black men and women have increased the use of direct speech with Whites. With the heightened popularity of urban hip-hop music and culture in the 1980s and 1990s has come the advent of "in-your-face," sometimes threatening, sometimes sexually explicit verbal directness of Black women hip-hop artists. Per such scholars as Angela Davis, these women take their cues from earlier, bawdy blues women. Hip-hop women strenuously reject societal expectations both for women's (people-pleasing) speech, which basically focuses on helping others keep their turn during conversation, and for what they consider subservient, slave discourse, with its tag questions and other forms of hesitancy.

The bolder language has replaced former deferential speech, often considered "Uncle Tom" speech used by those possessing a slave mentality or filled with self-hatred. The new discourse style confronts White supremacy and evidences a sense of entitlement by the speaker.

Court Interpretation and Interrogation

After the 2000 census, the United States boasted some 47 million citizens who spoke a language other than English, and some 2,000 different languages spoken in U.S. homes. Thus, the issue of interpretation of court proceedings for non-English speakers has gained much attention in recent years and has resulted in legislation requiring that interpreters be assigned to all those identified as foreign-language defendants who need them, to help ensure their Constitutional right to a fair trial. Specifically, the Fifth, Sixth, and Fourteenth Amendments guarantee due process of law and related rights.

Elena de Jongh has written comprehensively about the issue of court interpreting and the concepts of *linguistic presence* versus *linguistic absence* during criminal legal proceedings. Courts have determined that it is not enough for a criminal defendant to be *physically* present in the courtroom. Rather, he or she must be *meaningfully* present. One who has no *linguistic presence* (i.e., does not understand the language and does not have assistance in the courtroom of a qualified foreign-language or sign language interpreter) is not meaningfully present, and his or her constitutional rights may be abrogated as a result. Examples abound of instances involving wrongful imprisonment or extended jail time because of language miscommunication during trial.

False cognates and tag questions often are the source of misunderstandings. For instance, the English word *crime* should not necessarily be translated as the Spanish word *crimen*. The former refers to any illegal activity, whether a misdemeanor or a murder. The latter Spanish term, however, refers to the most serious crimes—those that might secure the death penalty or long imprisonment. The Spanish term *delito,* which means any violation of law, would be a more appropriate translation for the word *crime* when lesser offenses are involved.

De Jongh asserts that in U.S. English, tag questions, which she defines as interrogative fragments added to a statement to elicit agreement or disagreement, require a negative answer to deny an accusation (e.g., "You vandalized the equipment, *didn't you?*" "No, I did not.") In Spanish and many other languages, however, tag questions can be answered either negatively or affirmatively with no change in the meaning of the response.

The potentially coercive nature of tag questions in legal proceedings already has been mentioned. Lakoff has written about the use of tag questions in the interrogation of Anita Hill during the Senate confirmation hearings for then-Supreme Court Justice nominee Clarence Thomas in fall 1991, and how answering these can sometimes go against a witness's interests. In a related study, Norma Mendoza-Denton notes that Hill was asked significantly more tag questions than was Thomas (27% vs. 17% of the total), and addressed with many more declaratives functioning as questions. Through use of tag questions, the questioner forces a response, and thereby can highlight (a) the inappropriateness of a woman speaking in public at all;

(b) the inappropriateness of her accusations against a man; (c) her weakness, incompetence, and possible prevarication (for she must respond, but has to be prompted to do so).

Source Credibility and Women's Political Communication

Recent scholarship by Kevin L. Blankenship and Traci Y. Craig highlights the role of *context* in which tag questions are uttered and the *credibility* of the source or speaker. Issues such as power relationships and status come into play. The tag question, often viewed as a form of powerless speech that diminishes persuasion, may not be viewed as such if the source or speaker is in a power position or considered knowledgeable on the topic at hand.

Much research exists about the perceptions of competence, credibility, and persuasiveness of the messages of women elected officials, research that buttresses the insights of Blankenship and Craig. For instance, Arla Bernstein, Margaret Andersen, and others suggest that women politicians are viewed as most competent and credible when they address issues traditionally of concern to women (such as child care and education), and are viewed as less competent where they address so-called masculine issues (such as prison reform, defense, and the economy). The research also indicates that women are associated with warmth and expressiveness, but men are associated with rationality and competence, as if the two were somehow mutually exclusive.

Scholars in the field of women's political communication often speak of the backlash that can occur when women politicians use a communication style perceived as "masculine," thereby violating the societal expectation that women's speech should be deferential. They experience a decrease in persuasiveness. Scholars such as M. S. Leeper suggest that even given this, if the candidate's issue position is unambiguous and assertive, persuasiveness is enhanced and the use of gender cues in evaluation of candidates is minimized.

In their research examining the possible moderating role of source credibility on the persuasive effects of tags, Blankenship and Craig conclude that use of tag questions by persons perceived as experts on their topic do not reduce persuasiveness of the message. If used by a noncredible source, the use of tags indicates to listeners that the speaker is not knowledgeable and lacks confidence or certainty about his or her message. Persuasiveness is then adversely affected. Listeners who consider why a credible source uses a tag question, however, are unlikely to decide that the speaker is lacking in confidence or knowledge. Rather, they deem the use as an indication of the speaker's anticipation of an affirmative response from hearers.

Brenda Eatman Aghahowa

See also Communication Competence; Communication Theory of Identity; Ethnolinguistic Identity Theory; Gender; Language

Further Readings

Andersen, M. (1997). *Thinking about women: Sociological perspectives on sex and gender* (4th ed.). Boston: Allyn & Bacon.

Bernstein, A. G. (2000). The effects of message, theme, policy explicitness, and candidate gender. *Communication Quarterly, 48*(2), 159–173.

Blankenship, K. L., & Craig, T. Y. (2007). Language and persuasion: Tag questions as powerless speech or as interpreted in context. *Journal of Experimental Social Psychology, 34*(1), 112–118.

De Jongh, E. M. (2008). Court interpreting: Linguistic presence v. linguistic absence. *Florida Bar Journal, 82*(7), 21–32.

Distelhorst, D. (2005). Dominance and deference: Status expectations of men and women. *The Diversity Factor, 13*(2), 24–28.

Lakoff, R. T. (2001). *The language war.* Berkeley: University of California Press.

Lakoff, R. T. (2004). *Language and woman's place* (Rev. exp. ed.). New York: Oxford University Press.

Lippi-Green, R. (1997). What we talk about when we talk about Ebonics: Why definitions matter. *Black Scholar, 27*(2), 7–11.

Morgan, M. (2005). Hip-hop women shredding the veil: Race and class in popular feminist identity. *South Atlantic Quarterly, 104*(3), 425–444.

Scott, K. P. (1986). Learning sex-equitable social skills. *Theory Into Practice 25*(4), 243–249.

Stern, B. (1997). Advertising to the "other" culture. *National Forum, 77*(2), 35–43.

Tannen, D. (1994). *Gender and discourse.* New York: Oxford University Press.

TECHNOLOGY

Technology refers to scientific knowledge, manifested in the form of artifacts, ideas, techniques, and dispositions, which can be used in some kind of productive capacity. *Information and communications technologies* (ICTs) facilitate virtual interaction and the flow of information between individuals who need not be physically copresent. Given the tendency among scholars to regard the self and its relation to others as formed primarily through face-to-face contact, the capacity to circumvent such interaction using ICTs undermines many traditional ideas about identity. This entry provides a conceptual overview of recent developments in the relationship between identity and technology, reviews early claims about the impact of ICT-mediated interaction on individual and collective processes of identity formation, and presents several important critiques and theoretical implications of these claims.

Conceptual Overview

Identity, the enduring sense of who I am and who others perceive me to be, is socially constructed through our everyday interactions with others. According to symbolic interactionism, this is a complex process in which claims about identity are made and verified through the continuous exchange of meaningful symbols. Individuals form images of themselves, modeled on their own self-perception and on how they feel they are perceived by others, which they convey to others via cues that have context-specific meaning. Those who bear witness to these self-presentations interpret them and respond in ways that either affirm the identity claims being made or question them. The latter scenario is likely to occur whenever there are seen to be discrepancies between the cues that an individual provides. As a result, the extent to which individuals freely construct this image of themselves is tempered by a need to consider their anticipated audience; a shared agreement on identity is *negotiated* between the interacting parties. The meanings social actors attach to the symbolic cues they exchange during this process are context-specific, and reflect the broader discourses that structure relations of power and identity across society. Recent technological innovations shape this process in two important ways. First, the boundaries that delineate contexts of social interaction, which thereby specify the meanings and discourses applicable to those contexts, have begun to erode. This has been made possible by transportation and communication networks that foster interconnectedness between people and places across the globe. As flows of information within and between societies accelerate, space is less bounded by time and distance, and decisions in distant regions shape events in one's own backyard. Meanings that were once specific to certain contexts acquire broader applicability because it is no longer clear where one kind of setting ends and another begins. This expands the repertoire of meanings on which individuals draw when they present themselves to others and interpret their responses, thus adding a degree of flexibility and ambiguity to the identity process.

The second way in which technology affects identity consists in the use of communications media to conduct the symbolic exchanges that underpin identity formation. The concept of *virtual space* has emerged as a kind of generalized "place" whose distribution across multiple physical spaces is sufficiently entrenched and widespread for it to be thought of as a new category of space. The spread of ICTs, especially the Internet, creates a virtual space where people may interact without being physically copresent. In face-to-face settings, people make and verify claims about identity by exchanging cues that are primarily physical; this makes it difficult for people to consistently present images of themselves that conflict with their physical appearance because this discrepancy in cues is always visible to others. In a virtual environment though, self-presentation is not bound by the same physical constraints as in face-to-face settings. Furthermore, as the boundaries between these settings erode, those who interact virtually must grapple with an expanded array of meanings, and they must learn to couple these with a new symbolic repertoire of text and imagery to construct their identities online.

ICT-Mediated Interaction and Identity

The implications of these developments for individual and collective processes of identity have been the subject of extensive debate, especially in the literature dealing with the social and psychological effects of ICT-mediated interaction. Much of the preliminary research into Internet usage relies on qualitative techniques, such as participant observation in chatrooms and bulletin boards, to illustrate the nature of online interaction and explore its links to postmodern ideas about identity. According to this view, the modern notion of self as a fixed, unified, and hierarchical entity lying "behind" every action, has merit only insofar as it describes the kind of identities that arise in a face-to-face context. Individuals who interact anonymously online are not bound by physical constraints or, therefore, by the inscribed meanings and discourses that order spatial settings according to relations of power. People are free, it is argued, to construct personae that reflect the different aspects of their personalities that are ordinarily suppressed in such contexts. Without physical cues, individuals must author the narratives or biographies of these personae for those with whom they interact, employing the symbols at their disposal. Identity, under these conditions, is decidedly postmodern—a flexible, decentered assortment of multiple selves or identities that an individual cultivates and cycles through depending on the context in which they find themselves.

Alongside their claims about individual processes of identity, postmodern theorists contend that the experience of online interaction challenges assumptions about the categories that are used to socially construct identity. These binary categories, which distinguish between various modes of collective experience such as masculine/feminine or Black/White, enable people to pair certain meanings with the symbols that are exchanged during interaction. In face-to-face exchanges, the relationship between these meanings (i.e., masculine) and their usual physical cues (i.e., firm handshake) appears "natural" and necessary. Yet when individuals author their online identities, it appears they have a choice—to maintain these associations or to subvert them. How people choose to deploy identity categories is thus revealed as a contingent process, and one that reproduces a specific hierarchical ordering of power relations between social groups on the basis of their characteristics. Furthermore, it is claimed that the sorting of those characteristics into dichotomous categories (i.e., male/female) denies and excludes the existence of an array of meaningful social experiences that fit neither category (i.e., transsexual), but which individuals are able to express online when they appropriate the symbols with which to do so. The Internet, along with other ICTs, is thus portrayed as enabling individuals to "be themselves" and interact with others in ways that traditional social settings and conventional discourses often do not allow.

As a result, it has also been argued that ICTs facilitate the rise of a new form of community. Unlike traditional communities, where being a member often entails satisfying some form of physical criteria, virtual communities arise spontaneously out of interaction between diverse clusters of people pursuing common goals and interests. To the extent that they reconcile individuals from a wide range of geographic locations and social backgrounds, these communities have been viewed as promoting a more inclusive sense of collective identity. For this reason, ICTs are often hailed as having the potential to halt and reverse declining levels of social capital within traditional communities, to give marginalized individuals access to valuable information and social support, and to enhance participation in all areas of society.

Critiques and Theoretical Implications

Early literature on ICT-mediated interaction and identity has been criticized as lacking empirical support for its theoretical claims, and for its failure to situate the online experiences of ICT usage within the offline context of everyday life. Subsequent research, which has begun to develop more sophisticated sampling techniques and a broader range of qualitative and quantitative methods, has shown a number of these claims to be problematic. For example, the ability of individuals to "freely" construct online identities that circumvent the physical constraints of face-to-face interaction appears conditional on the relative proximity of their audience. If, as evidence suggests, our most regular online interactions involve people with whom we also interact offline, then our claims to identity will be assessed on the basis of both the physical and the virtual cues we give. Having to physically face up to the expectations

of one's audience, in this sense, ensures that discourses in everyday life still influence how individuals present themselves online.

On this note, more recent studies have shown how ICTs extend the existing capacity of individuals to conceal and emphasize aspects of themselves as they negotiate identity. By exploiting the ambiguous, disembodied nature of interaction online, ICT users are able to manage more effectively the impressions others have of them in the flesh. However, some also argue that for the remaining portion of online interactions—those involving complete strangers—this ambiguity poses an obstacle to the symbolic exchanges through which identity is formed. Although individuals may be able to make any identity claim they wish online, including ones that fall outside of traditional identity categories, this does not mean others will verify those claims. On the contrary, the increased possibility for deception and identity fraud has been shown in some cases to engender skepticism and distrust about such claims, and ultimately, to reinforce the use of stereotypes to make sense of identity.

The view that ICTs foster a new and more inclusive sense of collective identity has also been criticized for several reasons. First, this claim assumes that simply because ICTs afford people the capacity to interact with others to whom they have little or no relation, they will exercise this capacity. Yet, as noted previously, the ambiguity of disembodied interaction represents a major obstacle for individuals as they attempt to negotiate identity with anonymous others. As a result, it is unclear whether ICT-mediated social networks are any more immune to the effects of *homophily*, the tendency for individuals to associate with similar others, than are ordinary face-to-face networks. Second, the idea that the goal-directed nature of virtual communities would constitute a shift toward more heterogeneous social relations has itself been questioned. Critics argue that the grouping of individuals into communities of interest may simply create new and more pervasive forms of social exclusion, based on more specific and individualized identity criteria, thereby increasing homogeneity. Third, underpinning many such claims about the social impact of ICT is a kind of technological determinism, where technology is portrayed as a neutral force that transforms society while remaining unaffected by it. In reality, individuals and groups vary in their access to, and use of, technology, and these variations are reflected in how technologies are designed to be used. As such, values, behaviors, and identities are not shaped *by* ICTs as much as values, behaviors, and identities are shaped *through* ICTs, according to broader processes that structure how individuals and groups interact.

To fully understand the relationship between technology and identity, it is therefore necessary to situate claims about the role of ICT-mediated interaction within a theoretical context dealing with the changing nature of contemporary society. Many scholars argue that in late modern society, the influence of traditional structures and processes has waned, rendering identity less embedded in the structural realities of society and more open to reflection and self-appraisal. As they reflexively construct their own life narratives, individuals move more freely between the spheres of everyday life, forming relationships with others that circumvent geographic region and social background. The spread of ICTs, which facilitate such relationships, is thus seen as accelerating these processes of *deinstitutionalization* and *reflexivity*. This coheres with preliminary claims about ICT-mediated interaction and identity that emphasize the potential for individuals to construct online personae and to interact with others in ways that were not possible within a physical setting. However, as critics of this early research have pointed out, identities acquire shared meaning when there is a reciprocal exchange of symbolic cues, and although online interaction might provide a new symbolic repertoire with which to present oneself to others, it offers no guarantee that presentation will be interpreted as intended. Such ambiguity likely hinders ties between strangers online and reinforces bonds between those who are already familiar offline. This means individuals who construct identities online are still constrained by the structures and discourses to which they are subject in their interactions in face-to-face settings. Yet this also means that as the boundaries between such settings erode, individuals encounter diverse new ways of constructing and interpreting identity. Increasingly, ambiguity and flexibility feature in the symbolic exchanges that underpin identity in everyday life; ICTs simply extend the existing ability that all individuals have to seize on such ambiguity as they endeavor to manage the impressions others have of them.

Jonathan F. Smith

See also Modernity and Postmodernity; Reflexive Self or Reflexivity; Self; Society and Social Identity; Symbolic Interactionism

Further Readings

Castells, M. (2004). *The power of identity: The information age—Economy, society and culture.* Oxford, UK: Blackwell.

Cerulo, K. A. (1997). Identity construction: New issues, new directions. *Annual Review of Sociology, 23,* 385–409.

Rheingold, H. (2000). *The virtual community.* Cambridge: MIT Press.

Turkle, S. (1995). *Life on the screen: Identity in the age of the Internet.* New York: Simon & Schuster.

Zhao, S. (2005). The digital self: Through the looking glass of telecopresent others. *Symbolic Interaction, 28*(3), 387–405.

TERRORISM

Although not a new phenomenon, the incidence of terrorism in the present age has several elements that make it distinctly different from previous experiences. Contemporary terrorism generally has several expected elements: It is egregious violence, perpetrated against innocents, for a political agenda. Furthermore, contemporary terrorism is typically staged before an audience for maximum multiplication of psychological effect. As former British Prime Minster Margaret Thatcher noted, publicity is the oxygen of terrorism. It is often is undertaken by a nonstate actor (NSA). Terror and fear are the intended result. Globalized mass media and the Internet greatly magnify these results.

State-level actors do use terror for their interests and may be the invisible forces behind transnational terrorist groups doing their bidding. But state sponsors of terror run the risk of international opprobrium and sanctions, and can have state-centric remedies applied against them, including war. The disastrous example of Serbia and the Black Hand's assassination of Austro-Hungarian

Archduke Franz Ferdinand in Bosnia-Herzegovina in 1914 is a prime example. States that employ terror as a matter of policy—as in ethnic cleansing and human rights abuses—are subject to the aforementioned sanctions and perhaps war crimes proceedings. The application of terror by NSAs has garnered the most attention.

There exists no agreed upon definition for terrorism within the international system. The United Nations has been unable to draft a summary definition despite shepherding more than a dozen international conventions (treaties) on many aspects of terrorism. Moreover, the argument is continually restated that what one nation may view as a terrorist act, another will see as legitimate resistance. Despite the requests of its close ally, the United Kingdom, the United States refused to name the Irish Republican Army (IRA) as a terrorist group for many years. Likewise, the United Kingdom allows the Islamic Movement of Uzbekistan (IMU) to operate openly in its borders despite the pleas of many of its allies. Consensus on definition, to say nothing of identity, remains elusive in this area. This entry, therefore, addresses several questions that are often asked about terrorism.

What Motivations Exist for Terrorism?

The modern global community has passed through four significant eras of terrorist activity. The anarchist period of the late 19th and early 20th centuries sought to overturn the international order. Post–World War II to the mid-1960s saw the liberationist and nationalist motivation for terrorism as many societies strove for political mastery of their destinies. Ideological motivations for terrorist activity, especially of the leftist sort, characterized the 1960s through the late 1980s. The latest division has been the religious period, which describes many groups since the late 1980s. In addition, motivations for terrorist activity can range from outrage over social and economic conditions for the attackers to inhuman policy decision making on the part of the terror masters who carry out their attacks.

Martha Crenshaw has surveyed terrorist motivations and mapped its motivation this way: terrorism has a certain logic. It can be both effective and satisfying to the terror perpetrators. Robert Pape, studying the worrying trend toward suicide bombers as the weapon of choice in modern terror, describes this as a strategic logic. Although an immediate, existential defeat of its target opponent may not be possible, the terrorist movement is resilient and attractive because at a certain level it is successful, especially against a superior enemy military force. Terrorism is attractive because it works in the right circumstances where other methods have not worked. The apparently unstoppable Oslo Peace Process between Israel and the Palestinians was stalled—perhaps stopped—by a cascading barrage of suicide bomber attacks from several organizations which claimed thousands of Israeli lives. Attacks against Madrid commuter trains in 2004 seemed to convince Spain to withdraw its troops from Iraq. Moreover, such attacks—and suicide bomber attacks are just the most dramatic—are both economic and effective. Relatively small investments in time and personnel net huge media attention, demoralizing civilian casualties in the target population, and can be countered only with great difficulty. The security measures necessary to arrest terror attacks can become so autarkic that the terrorist group wins a strategic victory merely by destroying the opponent's public square and denying its people a normal life. The open society that is always on guard against a terror attack does not long last as an open society.

Who Becomes a Terrorist?

A comprehensive study commissioned by the U.S. government and published in 1999 profiled terrorists as generally poor and uneducated, with limited training and operational capability. Although there were notable exceptions—especially among suicide bombers—this view has described the dominant profile for terrorist identification. Recent research has pointed to a different picture, at least for terrorists motivated by religion. This new wave of terrorist descriptors finds them well educated, middle income to better in wealth, generally mid-twenties in age, religiously motivated, socialized toward violence, and alienated from the norms of their surrounding society. Their identification with radicalized agendas often leads them to exclusive associations that Marc Sageman terms "ingroup love and outgroup hate." This includes recruitment efforts as well as terrorist cell maintenance. Members are motivated strongly to self-sacrifice and personal bravery out of devotion not just to their cause, but also to the friends and associates in their group. Likewise, these attachments—so strong internally—are matched by a vigorous rejection of those outside, especially the named enemy. He further delineates their associations as that of friendship, kinship, and discipleship. Thus, most contemporary terrorist groups are recruited and are close social groupings related by ties of friendship or blood. Relatively few are knit together by other ties, such as meta belief systems. They may share these beliefs ultimately, but personal associations bring them into membership initially. Ultimately, the group becomes self-reinforcing, admits no external contradiction, and becomes difficult to disassociate from because this means abandoning friends, perhaps even family.

How Can Terrorist Violence Be Possible?

Security video files of the November 2008 attacks on India's financial center of Mumbai by Lashkar e-Taiba showed quite ordinary looking young men coldly, almost joyfully killing large numbers of people with hand-held weapons. It is difficult to assess the psychological topography that would permit such acts of violence within an integrated personality. A consistent vein running through the literature on terrorism studies holds that acts of terror are usually rational acts—often requiring notable amounts of premeditation, planning, and even technical expertise. Although vast portions of the world's populations would find such violence against civilians (at least) repellent, the terror masters do not. Part of this dynamic may be revealed in the insights of Sageman and his description of ingroup love, outgroup hate. This form of ingroup love and outgroup hate can both acknowledge and question the existence of another human being. Such extremes render the possibility of deliberate elimination of another's personhood. Once the victim is marginalized as irretrievably different, the Other, he or she can be treated in summary fashion. They become nonbeings. Worse, they can be, as Hannah Arendt noted for the Nazis, beneath human and a rallying point for many inchoate angers. One can find in the rhetoric of Al Qaeda, for example, characterizations of their target societies as being descendents from monkeys, dogs, unclean, and so forth. The Italian Red Brigades,

the German Baader-Meinhof Gang, and the U.S. terrorists Timothy McVeigh and the Unabomber left significant written testimonies of the moral alienation they felt toward their target-victims. The utility of hatred as a lightning rod for violence and an excuse for violence is the theme of Italian psychologist Franco Fornari, who observes that warfare and violence are useful for exorcizing internal fear (which he terms the *pantocrastic terrifier*) by slaying those who have been branded as the personifications of that evil. Thus, frequently, the terrorist is not killing innocents, but something alien to the human condition—or at least something inimical to the human condition as it is conceived by the terrorist's worldview.

Is Terrorism Synonymous With Religious Identification?

The nature of a religious identity for a broad swath of terrorist activity in the present day seems to argue for some affective connection. Successful religious organization closely parallels the structures successful terrorist movements must produce, and so a terrorist group that can assimilate a religious system—or more commonly—emulate religious systems, can be formidable. Several connectors between the two present themselves. Both movements tend to see their struggle in Manichean terms—a relentless, zero-sum competition between what is good and what is evil. Both tend to rely on self-regimented idealists who willingly follow charismatic, inspirational leadership. Each depends heavily on self-sacrifice, and self-sublimation. Both offer a sort of paradise prize: one a perfect spiritual world where evildoers are punished, and the other a perfect social-political world where evildoers are punished. This offers the benefit of instantly bending an already functioning infrastructure to the goals of the terror group. Most major religious systems can successfully resist the splinter into violence. But where the co-option is successful, it can be a devastatingly effective synchronicity. As in the case of the Japanese millennial cult Aum Shinrikyo, the movement may resort to terrorism after its salvific message has been delivered—and rejected—by its wider audience. But where religious messages are combined with terror tactics, the religious system rarely begins with terror as its tactic, much less its end.

Ethno-Nationalistic Terrorism

Occasionally, the terrorist movement may have purely secular motivations—or have religious identifications that are synonymous with ethnic or national identity. Such groups can be highly cohesive, and add the further binding agent of language or ethno-identity to the exclusivity of membership. These movements operate in many of the same lanes as religious groups, but also add several distinctive features of their own. Generally, ethno-nationalistic groups have a vitriolic image of their enemies, and a redemptive image of themselves; they believe their extremes of violence are justified by the vicious history of oppression they themselves have suffered at their targets' hands. Furthermore, this leads to a fantastic self-image of victimhood that brooks little historical criticism or redaction by the facts. The sense of justification by being wronged usually grows with time. This reinforces their determination to see justice done and justifies their extreme violence. The target in turn responds to this crescendo of violence with—in the eyes of the terror group—more outrageous actions. This fuels the pejorative image of the other, vindicates the use of extreme violence, and buttresses the iron triangle of hate, violence, and destruction.

Insurgency, Guerillas, and Terrorists

These three groupings tend to segue into each other in tactics in popular conception and media eyes. But they are distinctly different. Although they borrow from each other, the three represent different elements of asymmetrical warfare. Insurgencies are organized, disciplined military actions seeking to overthrow an established government. They have a set political agenda and often a strong political philosophy. These groups—from Tito's Yugoslav Partisans to Ho Chi Minh's Vietminh—often are successful in defeating and overthrowing far greater powers. Others, such as the Liberation Tigers of Tamil Eelam in Sri Lanka, may struggle for decades and make no headway against their governmental opponents. *Guerillas*—a term coined to describe the nonuniformed soldiers of Spain's resistance to French occupation during the Napoleonic era—are several stages below the insurgency level. They are irregular warriors with no immediate chance at confronting their governmental opponent in the open, let alone toppling the state. Their political and philosophic program may or may not be sophisticated enough to motivate large numbers of the wider society. But their relative popularity with some section of the masses, success in asymmetrical warfare, and their small numbers makes them difficult to target and eradicate. Sendero Luminoso in Peru and the Armed Islamic Group (GIA), as well as other groups, in Algeria during its civil beginning in 1991, are cases in point. Both insurgencies and guerilla movements may employ terror as a tactical element of their combat. As a result, it is easy to conflate them into terrorist typologies.

Terrorists lack the comprehensive military capacity of an insurgency, as well as the broader social or political support of the guerilla movement. Terror movements are by definition weak. If their political, social, or religious messages were universally attractive, their extreme violence would be unnecessary. Alternately, in the case where their agenda has a coherent ethnic following or definite political goals—such as the Kurdish Parti Karkerani Kurdistan (PKK) battling the government in Turkey—there already exists a sovereign state with a well-established national identity resisting them. Therefore, apropos of Crenshaw's strategic logic, the terrorists employ the egregious violence that—magnified by a globalized media—leverages their relatively small abilities into national and even international impact. Occasionally—as in the cases of the World Trade Center attacks on September 11, 2001, and the Bali disco bombings on October 12, 2002, in Indonesia—the shockwaves can be massive, global, and deeply effective.

Transnational Insurgencies

It is useful to identify a new metastasis in the terrorist canon: the evolution of a globalized, sophisticated structure of terror cells operating at several levels and capable of challenging not just a state level opponent but perhaps the international system itself. To achieve such success, the movement would need to employ violence outrageous enough to earn the terrorist moniker, but be popular enough to enjoy transnational support to facilitate its operations on a global scale. The anarchist movement of the 19th century may have been a candidate for this description, although its central direction, by obvious definition, made such control moot. Nonetheless, some 600 major national and international leaders were killed by the anarchists' hands from about 1880 to 1920. In recent years, however, only the Al Qaeda organization and Hezbollah would fit this description. They are different entities and have quite different goals. Nonetheless, both employ terror tactics with considerable success, have international reach heretofore unseen in such groups, and have a staying power that is beyond many smaller states. More significantly, both have managed to directly challenge—and as of this moment survive—much more powerful military opponents. Yet, despite their characterization as terrorist organizations, both Al Qaeda and Hezbollah retain important support from various populations in the world.

The advent of such global insurgencies may be a new phenomenon to the international system. Their effectiveness is amplified by all of the strategic theater enjoyed by successful terror groups, as well as the growing lawlessness of fragile and failed states that becomes useful safe areas for training, recruitment, and logistics. Opinions differ about the gravity of their threat to the state-centric world system. But they have a resiliency and attraction that has been successful in defying their more potent state-level antagonists.

Terrorist and Criminal Identities

Terrorist and criminal enterprises have traditionally been assumed to be separate, pathological behaviors. The trend in recent years has been for a nexus between the two to become increasingly advantageous. Many terror groups—especially local terror cells—have become self-financing through highly profitable crime. The globalized world and the Web have permitted identity theft to be a vast profit center for even small cells. Other criminal formats from counterfeiting to credit card fraud to the illegal drug trade have allowed terror groups to thrive. In addition, in important instances, criminal and terror networks have become symbiotic. Al Qaeda is closely linked to the heroin trade in Central Asia and Europe. The Revolutionary Armed Forces of Colombia (FARC) in Colombia has been the security apparatus for the cocaine cartels there for decades.

Should the State Negotiate With Terrorist Movements?

The state may see the terrorist violence as so *obligatory* that such groups do not merit the dignity of negotiation. On the one hand, negotiating with the terrorists has several risks: It lends their cause recognition, provides them with a platform for their views, potentially legitimates them as equals to the state, might seem like appeasement, and could alienate allies of the government. On the other hand, some benefits may accrue should such discussions be held. Negotiations with terror movements—assuming such are possible with a particular group—can provide the terror groups with an alternative to violence for political action, split their own cadres into moderates and hard-liners, give insight into their mind-sets to their opponents, and show that the state has a human face. Saudi Arabia's *Counseling Program,* which uses religious scholars teaching from the Koran to answer the arguments of captured Al Qaeda members, has an audience far beyond them. The Good Friday Accords of 1998 were possible in no small way because the British government did what had not been publicly possible before: sit down and speak with Sinn Fein, the ostensible political front for the IRA.

How Do Terrorist Groups End?

A small sample of the overall movements is successful in their violent methodology and the target society agrees to their agenda. Most groups are either destroyed through coercive measures, or co-opted by gradual political programs by target populations that undermine their effectiveness. Time, and some political or economic accommodation, can undercut the vital social underpinnings that allow terrorist elements to move like fish through sympathetic social water. Welsh (United Kingdom), Süd Tyrol (Italy), and Quebecois (Canada) groups were ultimately undone by a minimum of force and a methodical application of cultural and political concessions. Unlike the state, which has durable resources, terrorists groups do not generally have the ability to sustain lengthy campaigns. Of those that do, such as in Ireland, Spain, and Greece, their life spans can be measured in scores of years. Terrorist groups closely tied to national insurgencies can take decades to defeat, or in some cases, achieve victory for their causes.

John Sawicki

See also War

Further Readings

Combs, C. (2009). *Terrorism in the twenty-first century* (5th ed.). New York: Pearson/Longman.

Crenshaw, M. (1998). The logic of terrorism: Terrorism behavior as a product of strategic choice. In W. Reich (Ed.), *Origins of terrorism: Psychologies, ideologies theologies, states of mind*. Washington, DC: Woodrow Wilson Center Press.

Ganor, B. (2006). *The counter-terrorism puzzle: A guide for decision makers*. New Brunswick, NJ: Transaction Publishing.

Howard, R. D., & Sawyer, R. (Eds.). (2009). *Terrorism and counterterrorism: Understanding the new security environment* (3rd ed.). New York: McGraw-Hill.

Kegley, C. W., Jr. (2003). *The new global terrorism*. Upper Saddle River, NJ: Prentice Hall.

Nacos, B. L. (2008). *Terrorism and counterterrorism: Understanding threats and responses in the post-9/11 world* (2nd ed.). New York: Pearson/Longman.

Pape, R. (2005). *Dying to win: The strategic logic of suicide terrorism*. New York: Random House.

Sageman, M. (2004). *Understanding terror networks*. Philadelphia: University of Pennsylvania Press.

Schmitt, M. N. (2003). *Counter-terrorism and the use of force in international law*. Garmsich-Partenkirchen, Germany: George C. Marshall Center for European Security.

TERROR MANAGEMENT THEORY

Terror management theory (TMT) offers a social psychological and empirical framework for examining such questions as "What is the psychological function of culture?" and "Why do people need self-esteem?" The theory suggests that existential concerns associated with the awareness of mortality underlie a pervasive need for meaning imparted by the culture and value derived from living up to cultural standards. In short, cultural worldviews impart a context for deciding what is meaningful and setting the standards through which individuals can perceive their lives as significant. To the extent that individuals obtain self-esteem by perceiving themselves as valuable members of a meaningful reality, they can obtain a sense of symbolic (i.e., feeling that they can live on by being part of something larger, more significant, and more enduring than their own individual lives) or literal (i.e., promise of an afterlife) immortality, and thereby manage existential concerns. This framework provides an account of how existential motivation can affect a great deal of human behavior, including how a person forms and maintains identity.

This entry begins by detailing the history of TMT. Next, this entry discusses empirical support and extension of the theory. Last, this entry explores the implications of TMT on identity.

Theory and Background

In the early 1980s, while graduate students studying social psychology at the University of Kansas, Sheldon Solomon, Jeff Greenberg, and Tom Pyszczynski met often and pondered these questions about the function of culture and self-esteem. Shortly thereafter, the trio discovered Ernest Becker's Pulitzer Prize–winning text, *The Denial of Death*. In this book, Becker postulates that the human species faces a unique existential dilemma. On the one hand, humans share with other animals instincts aimed at biological survival, yet, on the other hand, humans' cognitive capabilities render them aware of the inevitably of their own death. This awareness, agued Becker, posed the potential to paralyze people with terror. However, rather than experience the terror, argued Becker, humans used these same cognitive capabilities that render them aware of the threat to contrive a solution: To the extent that individuals can conceive of themselves as beings of value in a symbolic world, rather than animals fated only to obliteration upon death, they can ameliorate the existential terror. The psychological insights of Becker's ideas were apparent to Solomon, Greenberg, and Pyszczynski, thus they went on to develop TMT to provide an empirical framework to test these ideas in the context of social psychological research.

In developing TMT, Solomon, Greenberg, and Pyszczynski began with two fundamental assumptions. First, Becker's perspective implies that faith in a worldview and maintenance of self-esteem should buffer anxiety and protect people from death-related concerns. The TMT team called this the *anxiety-buffer hypothesis* of TMT. They further deduced that if, as Becker indicated, worldviews and self-esteem provide protection against death-related concerns, then reminding individuals of death should increase their need for these structures. This was labeled the *mortality salience hypothesis,* because to test it, thoughts about mortality would have to be rendered salient. In conjunction with numerous colleagues, the trio tested these, and other, propositions, resulting in one of the most prolific programs of theory-driven empirical research in all of social psychology.

Empirical Support

The first basic hypothesis of TMT, the anxiety buffer hypothesis, suggests that faith in one's worldview and self-esteem should buffer anxiety and protect people from death-related concerns. Research has supported this hypothesis by demonstrating, for example, that boosting people's self-esteem in the context of an experiment (with favorable personality feedback) reduces the anxiety that they experience in anticipation of a painful electric shock. Other research has found that high self-esteem is particularly protective in the context of death-related concerns. In addition, research recently conducted by Jeff Schimel and colleagues demonstrates that threatening people's worldview (for example, presenting pro-creation participants with an anti-creation essay) brings thoughts of death closer to consciousness. These represent just a few of the ways in which research has tested, and provided evidence in support of, the anxiety-buffering properties of culture and self-esteem.

The lion's share of TMT research, however, has tested variations of the mortality salience hypothesis. In this research, thoughts of mortality are rendered salient (mortality salience) in several ways. The most common manipulation entails presenting participants with open-ended questions concerning the thoughts and feeling associated with their own deaths. This is then followed by some kind of delay and distraction (for example, a puzzle task or short essay to read), so that thoughts of death are activated, but not conscious, when participants respond to the dependent measures.

Alternatively, some research has manipulated mortality salience with subliminal death primes, or naturalistic events, such as walking by a funeral home or viewing a car crash. Notably, mortality salience has been shown to produce defensive reactions distinct from a variety of other aversive topics, such as giving a speech, failing an exam, intense physical pain, becoming paralyzed, social exclusion, or uncertainty, suggesting that these effects result specifically from thoughts of one's own mortality rather than general negative affect or threats to self.

Most research testing the mortality salience hypothesis has focused on the effects that reminders of mortality have on individuals' efforts to conform to and defend their cultural worldviews. In one study, mortality salience led participants to express more hesitancy when an experiment called for using a culturally cherished artifact, such as a U.S. flag or crucifix, in an inappropriate manner (hammer a nail with the crucifix). Perhaps the most frequently replicated finding in all TMT research is that people to respond more positively to others who support their worldview and more negatively to individuals who threaten their beliefs (sometimes by merely holding different ones) after a reminder of death. For example, Christian participants reported liking a person more when the person was purported to be a fellow Christian after being reminded of death, but when the same person was described as Jewish, reminders of mortality led participants to like this person less. More recently, Iranian researcher Abdolhossein Abdollahi joined forces with Tom Pyszczynski and the rest of the TMT team to demonstrate how prejudiced attitudes exacerbated by mortality reminders can contribute to aggressive tendencies. Their research showed that Iranian students become more supportive of martyrdom (suicide bombing) and U.S. students of extreme military interventions when mortality was primed. Thus, TMT depicts how fears associated with mortality can underlie prejudice and its consequences.

People seek validation of their cultural worldviews in response to mortality salience, and they seek validation of their standing within the cultural context; thus, they strive to bolster their self-esteem. For example, people for whom the physical body is an important source of self-worth respond to mortality salience by indicating that the body is a more central aspect of the self. As another example, people who derive self-esteem from driving fast have been shown to drive faster on a driving simulator when mortality is primed. Notably, this research demonstrates that efforts to manage mortality concerns do not necessarily coincide with that which would be most likely to facilitate survival (driving carefully), but rather, with psychological defenses aimed at reducing the potential for anxiety associated with awareness (rather than the actuality) of mortality.

Extensions

Beyond the basic model, TMT has been extended in numerous directions. For example, Jamie Goldenberg joined forces with the TMT team to investigate the pervasiveness of anxiety surrounding the body and sex. The researchers speculated that the sheer physicality of the body threatens the symbolic modes of defense (worldview and self-esteem) against death anxiety. It follows that confrontations with physical aspects of the body can pose a psychological threat, at least under some conditions, and that people should be especially motivated to imbue the physical body with symbolic meaning when thoughts of death are salient. In support of this, research has shown that presenting people with "disgusting" bodily products and activities causes thoughts of death to become more accessible to consciousness. In addition, priming mortality salience causes people to report less interest in the physical aspects of sex and to avoid physical sensations (such as a foot massage). With her colleagues, Goldenberg applied this framework to specific aspects of women's bodies (pregnancy, lactation, menstruation), and other research spearheaded by Mark Landau shows that mortality salience leads men to deny attraction to women who arouse lustful feelings in them.

Researchers Mario Mikulincer, Victor Florian, and Gilad Hirschberger have also suggested that, in addition to worldviews and self-esteem, close relationships function as a death-anxiety buffering mechanism. Close relationships help people feel that their lives are meaningful and that they are valued, and they may also provide a fundamental source of comfort regarding the threat of death because of the psycho-evolutionary mammalian importance of attachment to close others.

In support of these ideas, a substantial body of research has shown that mortality salience heightens the motivation to form and maintain close relationships and increases appreciation of one's romantic partner. In addition, thinking about the dissolution of important relationships brings death-related thoughts closer to consciousness.

In another recent extension of TMT, Jamie Goldenberg and Jamie Arndt developed a terror management health model (TMHM). Building on research that indicates that the type of symbolic defenses characterizing worldview and self-esteem defenses occur when thoughts of death have been activated but are no longer conscious, in contrast to more direct (and intuitive) defenses that occur in the context of conscious death thought, TMHM suggests that health behaviors will be motivated by different factors (self-esteem compared with health protection) as a function of the consciousness of death. One implication is that to the extent that a health appeal highlights the fatal consequences of a health risk behavior, once thoughts of death fade from focal attention, people's health decisions should be guided more by the need for self-esteem than by health protection. Thus, research reveals that people become more, rather than less, likely to engage in behaviors that convey both self-esteem and health risk (e.g., tanning, smoking) when thoughts of death are nonconsciously activated.

Implications for Identity

The TMT conceptualization of culture and self-esteem has clear implications for the ways in which people form and maintain senses of identity. Individuals' identities are based largely on the cultural worldview into which they are socialized. Beyond that, identities are shaped by the desire to sustain a sense of significance within the context of that worldview. Thus, TMT posits that people strive to emphasize aspects of their personal identity, and their identification with others, in ways that enhance their own perception of significance (similar to other theories, such as Henri Tajfel and John Turner's social identity theory). TMT suggests that these motives are fueled by mortality concerns, thus reminders of mortality lead people to manage their identities to optimally enhance them.

The previously described research depicting self-esteem striving in response to mortality salience supports this position. Recall that people drove faster and placed more importance on their physical bodies as a function of mortality salience and the centrality of these values to their identity. Moreover, research conducted by Jamie Arndt, Mark Descene, and others demonstrates that in response to mortality salience people dis-identify with important aspects of their identity (even their own gender and ethnicity) when these aspects are portrayed to reflect negatively on the individual. In addition, building from the ideas of Otto Rank, and in psychology, Brewer's optimal distinctiveness theory, research conducted by Linda Simon and colleagues indicates that reminding participants of their mortality leads them to identify relatively more or less with others depending on feedback they are given about their distinctiveness. This research, and the TMT framework more generally, provides insight into the origin, maintenance, and function of personal and social identity.

Jamie L. Goldenberg

See also Culture; Optimal Distinctiveness Theory; Self-Esteem; Worldview

Further Readings

Becker, E. (1973). *The denial of death*. New York: Free Press.

Goldenberg, J. L., Pyszczynski, T., Greenberg, J., & Solomon, S. (2000). Fleeing the body: A terror management perspective on the problem of human corporeality. *Personality and Social Psychology Review, 4*, 200–218.

Greenberg, J., Solomon, S., & Arndt, J. (2008). A basic but uniquely human motivation: Terror management. In J. Shah & W. Gardner (Ed.), *Handbook of motivation science*. New York: Guilford Press.

Landau, M. J., Greenberg, J., & Solomon, S. (2008). The never-ending story: A terror management perspective on the psychological function of self-continuity. In F. Sabio (Ed.), *Self-continuity: Individual and collective perspectives*. New York: Psychology Press.

THEORY OF MIND

In developmental psychology, *theory of mind* (ToM) refers to the normative capacity for humans to understand the intentions of another person.

With early aspects of ToM apparent in 3- to 4-year-olds, the mind begins to understand that one's own knowledge and intentions differ from those of other people. As ToM becomes more sophisticated as the child becomes increasingly social, this cognitive ability is the first step in associating personal characterizations of another person's self: their patterns of goal-directed behavior and general autonomous agency. These ToM identity files for others are then followed with the emerging adolescent's own social skill of being able to display a personal identity that is a calculated plan to represent a chosen set of characterizations. Thus, the foundation of identity involves representing in your mind an expectation for how another person will perceive your chosen characterizations. Within this research, identity does not exist to express basic innate beliefs about one's own self, but rather, it primarily functions as a social skill to importantly gain more social resources. This aspect of cognition is also related to evolutionary psychology in that it is a second phylogenetic step (after primary consciousness) toward advanced neurological identity. In an evolutionary model, ToM emerged from the need to display trustworthiness to one's social group. ToM became increasingly sophisticated and adaptive as humans could reasonably predict the desires (agency) of other group members, especially whether they are advantageous or harmful regarding both the self and the collective good of the group.

The term was originally coined by David Premack and Guy Woodruff in 1978 at the University of Pennsylvania to illustrate how chimpanzees infer the mental status of their fellow chimpanzees and was broadly understood as the ability to attribute mental states, intents, desires, and knowledge to oneself and others. Grounded in the neurosciences is an innate potential cognitive process in humans, which enables humans to see others as intentional agents, to develop a "theory" about another person's mind, different from our own. For one modern and basic example, consider the experience of driving behind another driver whose turn signal is on for an extended time. With ToM, you predict that the first driver is not planning to turn and is unaware that the turn signal is activated. Of course, ToM may be incorrect. The driver may be experiencing trouble and have the caution lights on with one side of the signal broken, or the first driver may activate a turn signal long before most other drivers would choose. At other times, ToM also stimulates not one but a set of cognitive scenarios in which a person will hold to a group of interpretations until further information is gained. For example, a couple walks out of the restaurant they just dined in, the wife turns and runs back in. The husband wonders why: Maybe his wife was *looking* for something she *wanted* to retrieve, and she *thought* it was in the restaurant. Maybe his wife *saw* someone familiar in the restaurant, and *wanted* to say hello to that person. Maybe his wife *intended* to grab another beverage, but in her haste to leave the restaurant, she *forgot*. In knowing that his wife has a mind and that her behavior has purpose, the husband is using ToM.

Research in developmental psychology has shown that cognitive functions associated with ToM begin to appear in children at about 3 to 4 years of age. Considered a basic standard in developing ToM, the *false belief task* is the ability of a child to understand that another person may hold an incorrect belief. In a typical scenario, Sally has two boxes and sees a person place a marble under one box. Sally leaves the room, and the person moves the marble to the other box. Then Sally returns. After witnessing this scenario, the researcher asks where Sally will look for the marble. Without ToM, young children and those with nonnormative cognitive development will not be able to understand that Sally will be wrong (false belief) about where the marble will be. Without ToM, individuals can only represent their own thinking and thus they know that the marble was moved and everyone else, including Sally, should know this. It is thought that the lack of ToM is the key deficit in autism. Children with affective disorders such as autism cannot comprehend that people have minds or feelings; such deficiencies may be detrimental to the child's social, communicative, and imaginative abilities. In Asperger's syndrome, children show a higher level of cognitive functioning and may excel in math and science, but may be socially deficient; they are incapable of understanding the feelings of others.

There are two categories of ToM: instrumental ToM and affective ToM. Instrumental ToM allows humans to make predictions about another person's behavior to achieve a specific goal; we may try to influence another person's behavior to meet that goal. One might conclude that deceit is an important aspect of instrumental ToM and is necessary for many human activities, such as war, politics, and business. There is a tendency when using instrumental ToM to assess behaviors attributed to the whole when only part of that behavior is observed; this incomplete assessment of behaviors can lead to inaccurate ToM.

Affective ToM refers to the cognitive process involved in understanding another person's emotional state. This process takes into consideration how another person might feel now and predict how another person might feel in a particular situation. Empathy is the hallmark of affective ToM. Affective ToM requires internalizing and feeling another person's emotional state. And subsequent to empathy is compassion, another cognitive ability that gives us the drive to alleviate or reduce the pain and suffering of other people.

Self-perception and ToM are related in that one's theories of self stem from one's ability to make theories about others. One's identity is created through social interaction with others, including one's other's perceptions and understandings of others as intentional agents, and the two aspects are interconnected in a way that reinforces one another through interactive experiences.

Christopher See and David M. Bell

See also Development of Identity; Evolutionary Psychology

Further Readings

Brune, M., & Brune-Cohrs, U. (2006). Theory of mind-evolution, ontogeny, brain mechanisms and psychopathology. *Neuroscience and Biobehavioral Reviews, 30,* 437–455.

Carey, S., & Gellman, R. (1991). *The epigenesis of mind: Essays on biology and cognition.* Hillsdale, NJ: Lawrence Erlbaum.

Drubach, D. (2008). The purpose and neurobiology of theory of mind functions. *Journal of Religious Health, 47,* 354–365.

Wellman, H. (1990). *The child's theory of mind.* Cambridge: MIT Press.

THIRD CULTURE BUILDING

Third culture building (TCB) denotes a process by which two parties, through protracted interaction, consciously decide that they would like to share perspectives, negotiate values, test beliefs, or proceed in a direction that leaves both of them permanently changed. TCB therefore implicates relationships, business transactions, cultural exchanges and home stays, and intercultural or interracial communication in general. TCB's premises include that the interactants must be willing to change themselves during the interchange and that neither party should dominate from a position of greater power or lay out preconditions for participating in TCB. Actual interactions over an extended period are measured against these expectations.

TCB moves from a unilateral process to a bilateral one, and from an intrapersonal to interpersonal to rhetorical to intercultural one. If it successfully proceeds, it leaves both parties with a new and enduring identity. This entry explores the process of TCB.

Unilateral Awareness

One prospective interactant develops awareness and interest in another. The other's unfamiliarity requires the first party to consider variations in language and cultural preferences and values to refine some motivation to initiate contact. Initiation of contact proceeds following investigation into the state and nature of perceived differences between the parties. A motive such as curiosity or the need for some form of business exchange may be modified in light of the findings of the process of unilateral inquiry. The ideal TCB mind-set examines both the self and the other before initiating contact.

Interpersonal Contact

The first interactant makes some contact with the prospective partner, directly or through a third party, in person, or through electronic means. The first interactant represents a stranger to the other, and the mutual uncertainty among the parties will begin to be reduced with the assistance of information that was learned by the first interactant during the stage of unilateral awareness. The interpersonal contact may continue indefinitely for as long as both parties are able to identify some benefit to continuing the contact. At this stage, elements of the identity of the self and the other become more evident to both parties.

Persuasion Stage

The parties gain a more thorough understanding of one another. To move toward achieving the goals they have identified as worthy of pursuit, they engage in perspective taking and negotiation, first of material aspects of the negotiation and subsequently of their perceptions about cultural realities. Some aspects of the cultural preferences of the other become attractive, and elements of one's own cultural approach are placed under closer scrutiny and evaluation. Partly because of the need to address a new social reality that stems from the contact between the parties, new ways of defining and addressing social needs develop. These alternative approaches are tested, then adopted, then dropped, or retained by the parties. In those cases where new and overlapping behavioral repertoires develop for both parties, identity changes in accordance with the demands of the new requirements.

Intercultural Stage

Once the parties find a reason to prefer cultural behaviors of the other or to develop behaviors that were native to neither party as their new primary means of communicating, their altered preferences may be institutionalized in rules, protocols, adjusted languaging, or behaviors. Because the new pattern of communication behaviors represents a change from previous practice, and because the changed behavior has proven to be adaptive, the new behaviors are passed along to others as preferred behaviors. The relationship, the business, the offspring of the union, move to form a generalizable mode of conduct. By linguistic analogy, a pidgin has become a creole, and an identity emerges that is neither that of one nor the other interactant but, rather, represents some fusion of both interactants.

The TCB model represents an idealized process. Enslavement, colonization, and hegemony represent one-way processes that seek personal and unilateral benefit at the expense of the other. Motives to engage in the TCB process may be the same or they may be complementary, but both parties must continue to perceive a benefit in following the rules and conventions of the hybridized identity.

To this extent, the TCB model encounters skepticism from those who believe that nature always presents hierarchies and that self-interest always places the needs and wishes of the self over those of another interactant. Given the belief in hierarchies of power, those in power might fear any relinquishing of their authority. Apart from its use as an ideal state toward which parties might aspire, TCB could be made to work more effectively through the inputs offered by third parties to the interaction. The prospect, of allowing third parties to influence the interpretation or the course of TCB interactions, has not yet been explored in the literature.

Double-Emic Analysis

The two interactants start with a native or *emic* understanding of social realities. The TCB process moves them gradually or precipitously toward some *double-emic*, or comparative perspective. As the process proceeds, it moves toward a new synthesis at some higher level of generality and awareness.

Third culture building seeks ways to de-anchor persons from their native perspective, and to lead persons, companies, and governments to a more global sense of community. That broadened community may be known as an international market, a human ecosystem, a world at peace, a regional or religious heritage, or some other prospective community of interests. The native way of seeing things inevitably gets redefined when some broader vision expands the scope of action. This emic view may be expanded and refined under conditions of mutual need and benefit.

Before moving to a broader horizon, to a wider vision, the parties each assert their own parochial ways of acting on the world. For this reason, a world event, or anything that takes place outside the usual scope of one's own native heritage, inherently gets pictured in a combination of two ways: by applying the native view of the sending community, and by applying the native view of the receiving community. Each community has its enculturated meanings for the event, as well as its sense of what is in the interest of the community itself. Taken in isolation, the two emic views may be the subject of cultural analysis.

Treaties, cultural exchanges, competition for a share of a world market, ecological concerns, academic collaboration, the wish for intercommunity harmony, and others may increasingly place the discourse of one emic perspective before the eyes of some other emic community. Messages in an Internet era can no longer be counted on to remain within the circles of one's own discourse community.

The double-emic perspective occurs when a member of one community sizes up the messages from someone of another community. If the communities have been relative strangers to one another, and in the absence of historical antipathies, such interaction becomes a matter of *culture learning*. The interactants are aware of differences and may realize a need to work through these differences through self-edification to share the same intellectual and psychological space. Area studies and language learning, home stays, tourism, comparative literature, lectures, films, and ethnic events and cuisine may be avenues to learning about the unfamiliar culture. This effort might be mutual, but often it is unilateral. As globalization occurs, it becomes more likely that more and more persons will learn at least something new about unknown populations. This knowledge is filtered through existing perceptions, so such knowledge may resemble or not resemble the interpretations offered by the other native community of its own discourse and actions.

More often, given that some motivation was present to encourage or to force one native to hear the words of some other, the two interactants hold some prior impressions or knowledge of the other party, and of that party's community. That motivation may stem from a sense of historical similarity, or the belief that the two parties share some interest such as religion or business needs. Or it may arise out of a perceived competition for the same scarce resources.

Actions based on the perception of competitive difference or threat seldom reach a stage of disinterested inquiry or goodwill that mark the idealized case. In the face of conflict, the parties may find the need to deal with the other in the interest of preventing warfare or of lowering the level of hostilities between the communities. In this latter case, a third party enters the equation.

The Roles of Third Parties

At the level of the critic, a third party may investigate the comparative views that members of the respective cultures hold of an event or piece of discourse. The critic starts by delineating what was said, and then offers a plausible interpretation of how the message might be parsed within the respective native communities. Aiding the critic may be the interpretive investigation of the way the message has been received by members of the communities. Also, the creating of a collaborative research team that combines both professional expertise and the cultural insiders' knowledge can place the critic(s) into a position that speaks more meaningfully to the differences in perspective that are derived from the multiple communities than might review by single critic of one or the other native community. Thus, increased clarity and objectivity should result from the interpretation of the double-emic critic. The public should be able to better grasp how those of the respective communities size up the discourse generated by the other community.

A second double-emic perspective deals with cases where the native parties seek to intercommunicate on a less acrimonious and a more cooperative basis. This moves toward what might be considered as intercultural listening, and it defines a role for someone who is conversant with the rival views of social reality to facilitate interaction among the parties. The two parties begin from incompatible understandings of the social world, and may start from the idea that the gains of one community correspond to the loss of the other, so a third party who can rise above the alternative perspectives to promote conciliation and inter-understanding among them becomes the means to achieving higher social, political, and intellectual aspirations. Such a third party must be tolerated or respected by members of both of the native communities for authentic intercultural listening to be promoted.

Third parties may adopt a number of perspectives and represent differing levels of familiarity or institutional authority. Their role may be constructive vis-à-vis the goals of third culture building, or detrimental to the achieving of those ends. It seems probable that some parties find a benefit to maintaining perceptual differences and frictions among defined cultural communities, perhaps for political or economic gain, whereas other parties may organize to promote greater understanding and

smoother contact between those of different communities (e.g., the "Teaching Tolerance" initiative of the Southern Poverty Law Center). Whether the third party is a relative or neighbor, a counselor or facilitator, a business or government, the positionality of the party and the interpretation of the motives of that party will be of paramount importance in determining the influence that party can exert in defining and guiding the parties toward some mutual goal.

Third Culture Building, Intercultural Listening, and Identity

Though the literatures on intercultural communication, interracial communication, third culture building, culture learning, training, intercultural rhetoric, intercultural competence (particularly intercultural sensitivity), international listening, relationships, and intercultural training draw from different sources and move in diverse directions, at their core they deal with common questions of identity. Persons or businesses, ethnic groups and linguistic communities, the privileged and those excluded from power, partners in bicultural relationships, and diversity trainers face questions of identity on an ongoing basis. These questions appear to be partially contingent on the choices of others because the assertion of one's own identity hinges in some measure on the assertion of the identity by the other. Although this diversity of possible identities might be regarded as a luxury or as a source of synergy, in practice it often produces competition. Attempts to avow an identity are offset by attempts by some other to ascribe an identity for the community and to proscribe its content.

The TCB process supposes that a relationship can be developed to promote the examination, testing, and exchange of elements of identity in an environment that is voluntary and mutually rewarding. The negotiation of identity, and with it the formation of a third culture, takes place longitudinally. TCB requires a sustained, ongoing, conscious, and mutual effort to survive. The TCB process can lead to the birthing of a culture that is new in content, insofar as it is the result of protracted exchange of cultural impressions, their testing, their adoption or rejection, and their possible transmission to a new generation. As framed, the thrust of TBC is toward cooperation, inter-understanding, and the amelioration of frictions that occur when those of different native views first start to interact across difference.

William J. Starosta

See also Acculturation; Intercultural Personhood; Third World

Further Readings

Chen, G.-M., & Starosta, W. J. (1997). A review of the concept of intercultural communication sensitivity. *Human Communication, 1,* 1–16.

Chen, G.-M., & Starosta, W. J. (1998). *Foundations of intercultural communication.* Boston: Allyn & Bacon.

Chen, G.-M., & Starosta, W. J. (2004). Communication among cultural diversities. In G.-M. Chen & W. J. Starosta (Eds.), *Dialogues among diversities: Intercultural and international communication annual.* Washington, DC: National Communication Association.

Starosta, W. J. (1971). United Nations: Agency for semantic consubstantiality. *Southern States Speech Journal, 36*(3), 243–254.

Starosta, W. J. (2000). dual_consciousness@USAmerica.white.male. In M. W. Lustig & J. Koester (Eds.), *AmongUS: Essays on identity, belonging, and intercultural competence.* New York: Longman.

Starosta, W. J., & Chen, G.-M. (2005). Intercultural listening. In W. J. Starosta & G.-M. Chen (Eds.), *Taking stock in intercultural communication: Where to now? Intercultural and international communication annual.* Washington, DC: National Communication Association.

Starosta, W. J., & Chen, G.-M. (2005). Where to now for intercultural communication: A dialogue. In W. J. Starosta & G.-M. Chen (Eds.), *Taking stock in intercultural communication: Where to now? Intercultural and international communication annual.* Washington, DC: National Communication Association.

Starosta, W. J., & Coleman, L. (1986). A case study of rhetorical interethnic analysis: Reverend Jackson's "Hymietown" apology. In Y. Y. Kim (Ed.), *Interethnic communication: Current research* (pp. 117–135). Beverly Hills, CA: Sage.

Starosta, W. J., & Olorunnisola, A. (1995). *A meta-model for third culture development.* Pittsburgh, PA: Eastern Communication Association.

THIRD WORLD

The label *third world* as it relates to identity highlights issues of national cohesiveness, authority, epistemology, and cultural and social roles. The rank of *third* is currently designated to and associated with a country's general economic condition and the difficult circumstances that result. These include widespread poverty, susceptibility to disease and natural disasters, and disorganized governance. The etymology of the term *third world* is found in an article written by Frenchman Alfred Sauvy and published in *L'Observateur* on August 14, 1952. In this article, Sauvy coined the term *third world* stemming from the medieval notion of the *third estate,* a term that described the common man as distinguished from nobility and clergy. The relationship of third world identity to the historical third estate contextualizes critiques of first and second world ideological and cultural domination through military and political power. It also creates a historical underpinning that connects third world identity to imperial domination, ethnocentric politics, and arbitrary geographical and ideological boundaries.

The Third Estate

The meeting of Eastern and Western thought clears a field in which to revisit the historical contexts of third world and its etymological origins. Both the historical understanding of third estate and the reality of colonialism influence interpretations of human dependency and necessity within contemporary third world identities. These conditions are perpetuated with international aid programs and international political, economic, and juridical bodies. The third estate during the Middle Ages was dependent on both the clergy and the nobility to fulfill certain needs: the clergy spiritual, and the nobility political and judicial. The lack of equality and the abuse of power between these three estates or three worlds is as problematic now as it was then. The relationship of third worlds to this historical social classification does, however, texture the historical genealogy of present global circumstances that continue to affect individual interpretations of human experience. A most significant aspect of the medieval third estate, even though grouped together as common, was the particularity of profession and skilled labor, exemplary of social multiplicity and diversity. The people of the third estate were artisans and craftspeople, the social class being responsible for much of the physical legacy that exists from the medieval period.

Colonialism

One of the more important historical trends that influences characterizations of third world identity is imperial colonialism, generally assigned a time period between the 15th and 20th centuries. Colonialism, originating and perpetuated for many different reasons, has had a significant and lasting impact on economic and social structures in contemporary third worlds. Colonialism is also a phenomena that textures the meeting of the proverbial East and West, where commonly more industrial, capitalistic nations exploited less industrially developed nations, mining their natural and their cultural resources. Colonized countries were used as centers of production but not necessarily for industrial development. Often when imperial interests diminished, countries were left in varying levels of social, political, and industrial disarray. These centuries of exploitation have had lasting effects on the formulation of indigenous third world governments that are not sufficiently representative of the multiplicity of ethnic groups that persist in third world contexts.

Colonialism also marks a shift from social and communal divisions to nationalized divisions indicative in the creation of national borders based on imperial control and conquest. The borders created in the African continent or the partition of the Indian subcontinent in 1947 demonstrates the attempt by colonial or imperial powers to create boundaries ideologically without attention to human relationship, resource, and necessity. These events leave a lasting impression on current third world identities as different indigenous or displaced parties fight against borders that test a more fluid experience of time and space in third world mentalities. Warfare over sacred ground or porous borders cannot be understood without paying attention to the strong resilient connection in third world identities between the immanent and transcendent qualities of human identification. This reality places third world identity in direct relationship with the two other historical estates in the Middle Ages that completed a social structure with national and social roles.

Other visible factors include the slow development, or decay, of reliable transportation infrastructure that prohibits easy travel between different regions in third world countries. This lack of infrastructure has perpetuated a certain degree of provinciality that has been classified as exotic or exemplary of a radical alterity compared with the universal power and purpose attributed to first world countries. Although it would be an exaggeration to say that alterity in third world counties can be directly associated with provinciality and physical isolation, these attributes do factor into third world mentalities regarding nationalism. In these terms, third world identity can be considered more particular and local, oriented toward communal and familial concerns.

The epithets of radical alterity and particularity as common or characteristic of third world mentalities have been criticized as representative of thoughtless attempts to perpetuate notions of extreme or incommensurable difference. These appositional cultural differences are interpreted as magical, as demonstrated in the generic classification of novels that describe third world experience through *magical realism,* in which stark contrasts are made between the tragic reality of third world poverty and hardship, and miraculous events taken in stride by the characters in the story. Authors that exemplify this interpretation include Louis de Bernieres and Gabriel García Márquez. Both authors, while representing first and third world authorial origins, describe unfortunate events common to less developed countries, interspersed with supernatural episodes that are often unexplainable through the lens of realism. This is the presumption that anything can happen in places like these.

Authority and Epistemology

The magical interpretation of third world identity highlights the significant contrast in third world and first world understandings of authority and epistemology. Third world ideas of authority are greatly influenced by the history of colonialism that influences political and national, as well as intellectual and artistic identities. The authority of imperial powers over less developed nations is proven through the use of mechanics, method, careful administration and technical prowess. The authority of Western thought and art is demonstrated in the ranking of progress as industrial, spurred on by scientific discovery and in art as the extension of formal boundaries. The significance of authority in the third world is determined by longevity and adherence to forms of class and tradition. These forms in third world identity transcend the industrial focus of first world authority, in which religious mentalities compete with scientific methods for the realm of knowledge. First world epistemology is derivative of industrial ideology, specifically the scientific method, in which knowledge is developed and maintained through careful scrutiny and measured doubt is developed in things that present no physical evidence. Epistemological credibility in third world contexts is often asserted through less quantitative means, determined much more on the basis of traditional, historical, and class qualities.

The issue of epistemological authority highlights foundational characteristics in third world identity linked to religion and timelessness. A third characteristic of third world authority and epistemology relates directly with ideology itself. Ideology, often a common way to trace the development of first world countries, has less interpretive cogency when applied to third world contexts. Religious positions still hold sway in third world identities, positions that have in some ways been replaced by ideological concerns in first world mentalities. This again highlights the dichotomous interpretation of third world identities as largely disconnected or beyond real because time and space is interpreted from different experiences of natural and supernatural distance and a person's relationship to his or her surroundings and circumstance.

The meeting of two significant figures in Western and Eastern histories acts as an exemplar of this division. A conversation that occurred on July 14, 1930, on the nature of truth and reality between Albert Einstein, considered to be one of history's most influential scientists, and Rabindranath Tagore, a Nobel-Prize-winning poet from Bengal, reveals, at first, apparent differences, the bridging of incommensurable alterity, and the magical reality that characterizes interpretations of third world identity. Tagore, adhering to a Platonic understanding of

science, describes the world as appearing, and only having meaning and truth in its relation to human interpretation. Einstein, alternatively, understands truth as existent outside of human space and time, giving it an objective quality. Einstein's first question follows the characteristic dichotomy of first world mentalities: "Do you believe in the Divine as isolated from the world?" He ironically concludes the conversation by stating, "I am more religious than you are!" Situating truth outside human interpretation indicates the significance of ideology in first world identities as individual, not relative to existential circumstances but to the capabilities of human cognition. Tagore interprets truth as dependent on the human interpreter, and on his position in the world. This perspective aligns itself with the physical attributes of third worlds that are not peripheral to identity but serve as its lens. The third world's depletion of necessary physical resources by a history of colonization creates circumstances in which dependency is a daily mode of existence. All aspects of human life and experience are reflected through the lens of daily necessity and dependence on familial and cultural fidelity. Einstein's statement that he is more religious than Tagore in his understanding of truth and reality reveals the ideological bases of his position, which are linked to a notion of an ideal, the separation of human sociality from the existential limits of human dependence and necessity. Third world identities instead demonstrate the combination of both, of the magical and the real, which is not an ideological mysticism but rather grounded, embodied position that is too close to necessity and dependence to allow a total transcendental isolation or ideologically independent experience.

The possibility of a distinct third world identity therefore depends on its relation or dependence on other nations with first and second ranking, whether it is economic, political, or ideological. Although in some instances, the defining characteristic of the third world is its stated difference and alterity, in others, the defining characteristic is its necessary or circumstantial relationship with other national figures of authority, epistemology, and ideology. Critics of the epithet *third world* make the claim that the designation is arbitrary and rhetorical. *Third world*, instead of classifying a distinct type or category of nation or economy, defines a third removed rank preventing identification with other world nations. Postmodernity as a theoretical structure and globalization as an economic reality have questioned the clear divisions that are often made between first, second, and third worlds. In an expanding world economy, and the union of multiple nations into cooperative governing bodies, the physical and political boundaries that were once the means of distinguishing alterity in world identities have lost some of their distinctive clarity. Singular or universal ideological boundaries have lost their efficacy to legitimate colonial imperatives, making the line between East and West and North and South tenuous. Third world perspectives do in some cases accept these limiting boundaries as a way to understand necessary relationships and existential dependencies that form the framework for both social and national identities. Notions of authority and epistemology are derivative of purported limitations, for it is often in relation to difference and rank that another position, whether first or third, becomes possible. From these existential lived boundaries, third world identities emerge and flourish.

Joel S. Ward

See also Collective/Social Identity; Colonialism; Nationalism; Transnationalism

Further Readings

Larrain, J. (1994). *Ideology and cultural identity: Modernity and the Third World presence.* Cambridge, UK: Polity Press.

Tagore, R. (1931). *The religion of man.* London: Allen & Unwin.

TRANSCENDENTALISM

The subject of transcendentalism and transcendental argumentation generally are a major part of the claims of professional philosophers to a distinct and autonomous, nonempirical, area of inquiry, clearly distinguishable from the natural and social sciences. In the continental European tradition, the term *transcendental philosophy* covers a wider range of philosophical approaches

than just the philosophy of Immanuel Kant, from whom that term originated. Transcendentalism is a systematic way of doing philosophy that includes writers from Johann Gottlieb Fichte, G. W. F. Hegel, and Friedrich Schelling to Edmund Husserl, Martin Heidegger, and Jean-Paul Sartre, as well as the field of hermeneutics. Transcendentalism includes the social phenomenology of Alfred Schutz and the "proto sociology" of Peter L. Berger and Thomas Luckmann in the 1960s. Transcendentalist scholars described the basic parameters of the historical process, whereby objective social reality comes to be confronted by a human subject. These parameters were held to be nonempirical, universal structures, a priori, rather than a description of any specific society. These structures were said to find expression in human history and were to be given content in empirical inquiries by sociologists into particular, concrete societies. Transcendentalism plays a role in present-day studies of identity, where debate has focused on whether identities are fixed or adaptable. This entry explores the two types of transcendentalism, their criticisms, and their relevance to the study of identity.

Two Types

There are two main kinds of transcendental inquiry in philosophy, both dealing with something universal, conceived as either (a) above and beyond the universe or (b) in the human cognition of nature and society. Variants of these two can be found, adapted, and blended with social data and concepts widely in sociology and social theory.

Transcendental thinking of type (a) is in evidence where the focus of a study of social processes relies on postulated ideal states of affairs existing as a potential in society, or when employed as a universal yardstick for social criticism of the present (e.g., in Karl Marx, and versions of Marxism). Type (b) informs conceptual schemes that express the preconditions that make society or cultural forms possible or knowable (e.g., in Georg Simmel, Max Weber, Alfred Schutz, Talcott Parsons, Michel Foucault). Few major thinkers in the sociological tradition have escaped the tacit absorption from philosophy of premodern transcendental motifs into their theoretical and empirical work. A notable exception is Norbert Elias, whose work was founded on an abandonment of philosophy as such, including all forms of transcendentalism.

Transcendence as Potentiality

Type (a) inquiries in philosophy conjecture about a deity or deities or perhaps a spirit world or the enigma of Being itself. In this sense, the term *transcendence* preserves an uplifting, sometimes visionary, tenor and contrasts with its opposite, *immanence,* which is evocative of what is actually existing in the less inspiring, mundane world. The utopian writings of Marx and later Marxists are essentially secularized and politicized, social-scientific versions of this kind of thinking, involving a transformation of Hegel's notion of the "concrete universal." Hegel argued that universals such as pure freedom or justice or the "absolute ethical life," were actually embedded in the finite and imperfect world. This conception provided Hegelians with an absolute evaluative standard for the critique of present society. Against them, Marx wanted to transform society to make it, in practice, what it could ideally be. This accent produced the characteristic contrast in later Marxist work between society as it *is* (capitalism) and society as it could *ideally* be (communism). The latter stage of human society was said to be embedded in the present society as its *telos,* or transcendental potential, yet to be realized by the revolutionary action of the proletariat.

Writing in the 1920s, the Marxist writer Georg Lukács, in a sophisticated example of transcendental reasoning of type (a), distinguished between the actual and imputed consciousness of the proletariat. He argued that these two forms of consciousness represented two truths. The transcendent, imputed class consciousness existed on a higher philosophical plane from the actual consciousness of the proletariat that could be empirically ascertained. Lukács argued that even if the Marxian hypothesis were proved wrong empirically, it would not affect the higher truth of the potential proletarian class consciousness.

Once the possibility of proletarian revolution faded with fascism, the critical theory of the Frankfurt School (Theodor Adorno, Max Horkheimer, Herbert Marcuse) sought to preserve the transcendental truth of communism and freedom in theory as a possibility. Adorno and others

talked of the "utopian moment" or "horizon." Later, theorists such as Jürgen Habermas, Karl-Otto Apel, and Zygmunt Bauman have looked for new models of the unrealized utopia to provide a defensible yardstick for social criticism of inequality and injustice in the present. These have taken the form of Habermas's and Apel's ideas about distorted communication and the presupposed "ideal speech situation" or "speech community," and Bauman's speculations, drawing on the philosopher Emmanuel Lévinas, about a "pre-social," transcendent responsibility for others implicit in the human being-in-the-world.

One drawback of this kind of inquiry is evident in Bauman's conception of the present global society as a condition of "liquid modernity." This viewpoint systematically undervalues the present reality as producing unremitting anxiety and uncertainty. This negative diagnosis is made, typically, by comparison with the ideal of a pure state of democracy, freedom, and equality, which exists as a continual, nagging possibility. From this point of view, it is difficult to assemble an inventory of progressive human achievements that must be preserved. Type (a) inquiries in general, when applied to the nature of modern society, as in the case of Bauman, tend to devalue the identity experiments and preferences of ordinary people (e.g., lifestyle groups or mass entertainment). They are implicitly and sometimes explicitly, presented as a "lower" form of social life, compared with the "higher" form of communal life that *could* be achieved in a future society.

Transcendence as Conditions of Possibility

Type (b) inquiries seek to establish a different kind of universality or truth, by focusing on the nonempirical conditions of possibility of valid knowledge, society, or cultural forms. Transcendental philosophy in this sense was inaugurated by Kant in the 18th century as an enterprise occupied not so much with the objects in the world, but with the *mode* of our knowledge of them. This mode of knowledge makes it possible for us to know objects at all. But we can never know the objects themselves, as such. He attempted to establish as a universal mode of knowledge a priori (prior to experience) certain *categories of the understanding* (such as space, time, cause, number, etc.) that were said to be the conditions of possibility—sometimes called the limits—of all experience.

In various adaptations, reasoning of type (b) is common in the mainstream sociological tradition. It has been well-established that the work of many of the key writers in the classical tradition of sociology (e.g., Émile Durkheim, Simmel, Weber, Parsons) was fundamentally shaped by principles derived from the philosophy of Kant, as developed by various 19th and early 20th century neo-Kantians such as Charles Renouvier, Rudolf Lotze, Hermann Cohen, and Heinrich Rickert. Weber's ideal-types, for example, were formal constructs related to reality by the principle of "objective possibility." They were heuristic, regulative postulates, used to connect the objects of experience, otherwise deemed to be structure*less*. Simmel's forms of sociality play a similar role as a mode of a priori knowledge that makes possible for individuals the experience of society or other social regularities. Parsons's notion of the importance of the central value system in the maintenance of social order posits—against Utilitarian individualism—the transcendental normative conditions of ordered economic life. This viewpoint also lies behind Durkheim's insistence that economic individualism is made possible by the prior moral categories that inform and enable it.

Critique of Later Variants

The Kantian transcendental method has also been adapted more recently to provide analyses of the conditions of possibility of many cultural items, practices, and activities. These include, for example, Claude Lévi-Strauss's demonstration of invariant structures across the contents of many myths and Michel Foucault's epistemological organization of the main discursive practices (e.g., political economy, psychology, law) of a particular epoch as an episteme, or historical a priori. The transcendental approach of the two authors shapes research into the production of synchronic, static inventories of the invariant features that make possible whatever is the focus (myths or discursive formations in these cases). Transcendental sociology often also provides *analytically* distinguished subsystems of action (personality, culture, politics, etc.) as the preconditions for the possibility of a

social system, as in, for example, the work of Parsons. This approach appeared in a new form in the 1980s with Giddens's theory of structuration. This comprises an analytically elaborated metatheory of action, depicting the preconditions necessary for the reproduction of society as a system by the intentional actions of those it constrains.

Some writers, including Lévi-Strauss, Parsons, and Foucault, have openly acknowledged their Kantian inspiration, whereas other social scientists are unaware of its presence. This is partly because the transcendental dimensions of the theoretical frameworks that they have inherited and find available in disciplines in university institutions have been forgotten or only partially understood. Parsons and Giddens are not so much concerned with actual actions of real people as with the conditions that enable action as such. This feature points to one of the drawbacks of sociology conducted in this manner, that is, over-abstraction and an attenuation of social reality. There is also a problematic relationship between analytically distinguished static preconditions (say subsystems in a determinate hierarchy, as in Parsons, or the forms of sociation in Simmel's or Giddens's conditions of system reproduction) and the real world. Factual evidence and examples can be cited in relation to these, but they will not disconfirm them because of their transcendental status. They are not a description of the real world, nor a testable theory. Nor, by their nature, do they contain a dynamic conception of social development.

A further example of this problem from the sociology of identity is Giddens's analysis of the "pure relationship" in sexuality, marriage, and friendship. This is presented as an ideal-type construct and said to be one that can guide empirical investigations. This model lists the features of intimacy, commitment, and reflexive organization and posits an entirely internally self-sufficient relationship, driven by mutual and equal effort bargaining. It is said not to be linked externally to the economic system because the identities of both partners are now assumed to include the possibility of either one being a possible breadwinner—unlike in former times, when in heterosexual marriages invariably the man was the breadwinner.

Interview research has shown, however, that there is no evidence that this model of relating is becoming predominant in heterosexual partnerships, in particular. Strictly speaking, though, this evidence does not affect the conceptual integrity of the analytic model. It cannot be changed by it. The author could legitimately neutralize the empirical findings by saying that the model is only an ideal type, a regulative principle, so may not necessarily correspond entirely to all cases or contexts. It is a regulative principle, an idealization. An unresolved issue is the desirability of proceeding in this transcendental fashion in the first place. The method carries the further disadvantage that because the individual theoretician creates the construct, there is no control over the selection of the dimensions included. There is little to prevent the smuggling in of assumptions based on the author's convictions as to how society and relationships *ought* to be organized.

Beyond Transcendentalism

Much debate has taken place in the sociology of identity as to how far people today can adopt identities at will and how fixed are the clear identities of male and female. Attention has been drawn to a spectrum of "we" identities of varying strengths, including those relating to family, social class, community, neighborhood, region, ethnicity, gender, religion, language group and nation, which can vary in intensity as part of the rise and fall of tensions *between* opposing or socially adjacent groups defined by these dimensions. More transitory group attachments have also been put forward as being typical of the so-called postmodern world—for example, Michel Maffesoli's theory of neo-tribes, which draws on transcendental motifs from Friedrich Nietzsche and Durkheim. These affinity groups are diverse, including youth subcultures and style groups and many more groups such as golf clubs, rock festivals, coffee mornings, and supporters of sports teams, as collective identity responses to modern political, economic, and consumerist individualism.

Norbert Elias's figurational or process sociology is notable because it has explicitly expunged all traces of transcendentalism and thus provides a useful counterpoint. Elias pointed out that in the age of extensive individualization, most "we" identities within what he calls the "We"/"I" balance have correspondingly weakened, with the exception of national and ethnic identities. These appear to have strengthened as the result of the geopolitical repercussions following the fall of the Soviet empire dominated by Russia, and the subsequent end of the polarized superpower tension of the cold war.

Abram de Swaan's theory of widening circles of identification, drawing on Elias, provides a longer view of the contemporary debates about identity. He shows how the scope of "we" identifications has become wider and wider throughout human history, from those based on kinship and proximity, such as villages or neighbors, to broader forms based on clans, dynasties, military affiliations, monastic orders, and medieval guilds. An enlarging and unifying momentum can be observed, from primary survival groups right through to nation-states, culminating in substantial "we" identifications with social classes, religions, and nations. Nation-states are the largest and most persistent, large-scale survival units.

Harbingers of possible higher, continental, and global integrations of nations can be observed in the current period. The highest possible "we" identity would be with humankind as a whole, although this does not carry at present the same emotional charge as the "we" identity of national or ethnic consciousness. This is partly because national identities are bound up with people's survival in wars between nation-states in recent centuries, which continue unevenly until the present day. This entire process can be seen to have a demonstrable structured direction of widening scope, but in this framework, no *telos* or end-state of a unified, global humankind is assumed.

Richard Kilminster

See also Being and Identity; Critical Theory; Frankfurt School; Social Identity Theory

Further Readings

Berger, P., & Luckmann, T. (1967). *The social construction of reality*. London: Allen & Unwin.

Elias, N. (1991). *The society of individuals*. Oxford, UK: Blackwell.

Kilminster, R. (1998). *The sociological revolution: From the Enlightenment to the global age*. London: Routledge.

Kilminster, R. (2007). *Norbert Elias: Post-philosophical sociology*. London: Routledge.

TRANSNATIONALISM

Simply defined, *transnationalism* is the continuous communication and exchange of ideas as well as transaction of relationships that occur across spaces of separation. Transnationalism can be understood as the ways in which immigrants, or members of diaspora cultures, import idioms, conventions, and resources of communication to continue to maintain the identity that they acquired in their home countries even as their identities are open to the vast unknown of identityscapes in their new country of settlement. This entry discusses the conceptual framework of and debates surrounding transnationalism.

Conceptual Differences and Theoretical Framework

To understand transnationalism in the most precise ways, one must distinguish it from colonialism, postcolonialism, nationalism, and globalism. *Colonialism* was and is a process by which different countries and cultures came into assault by a foreign power known as an empire. This resulted in a state of siege for those experiencing colonial relations. Colonialism can be said to have resulted in the erosion of culture, language, symbolisms, and psychic unity of those who experienced its traumatic effects. However, colonialism also resulted in uprisings, revolution, and transformation of colonial oppression into conditions for freedom and liberation. A clear-cut example is British rule in India and the subsequent nonviolent freedom movement spurred by Mohandas Gandhi and his followers. The ways in which people who were formerly colonized expressed their sense of liberation as well as critique of colonialism can be called *postcolonialism*. The possible continuation of former process of domination and subordination also falls under the rubric of postcolonialism. An extensive and exhaustive undertaking of this concept is beyond the scope of this entry. Postcolonialism is associated with the spaces of colonialism, the vigorous transformation of home turned colony to nationhood.

Nationalism is the construction and constitution of identity through processes of nation building as well as the ideologies and discourses that constitute nationhood. Nationalism is not a unified construct but rather an imagined one of unification. Nationhood can be rife with the conflicts and tensions that accompany it, such as gender, race, class, and ethnicity, as well as religion. Nevertheless, insofar as nation building in a postcolonial context was a response to the excesses of colonialism, it can be said to be an identity-conferring process, a means by which individuals and groups come to identify under the umbrella of nationhood.

Although these are broad brushstrokes of the building blocks of a conceptual and theoretical framework within which to understand transnationalism, it is important to grapple with the historical processes of change undergone by individuals living under colonialism and its aftermath. Postcolonial individuals may engage in migratory behavior as a means to seek better opportunities for themselves and their families in an ironic sense in the metropole or centers of capitalism and commerce. However, it has become evident that immigration is not a unidirectional movement. It is not about leaving never to return, though this option is limited to those who leave under voluntary conditions rather than forced circumstances of exile. In the process of keeping ties with the home country as well as countries to which fellow migrants emigrated to, individuals can be said to have spawned a wide variety of communication practices that connect home and abroad. A key factor in establishing continuity is media. This includes both conventional and new media. Conventional media can be exemplified, for instance, by the concept of Bollywood. There has been much research done on the effects of Bollywood movies on Indian immigrants to the United States. Immigrants turn to Bollywood as a means of defining and redefining space, particularly the concept of home and abode. Immigrants find Bollywood a means to connect with the home country, albeit in a fantastic way. Bollywood offers them a sense of space and familiarity that is not available where they reside in the host country.

Therefore, transnationalism begins to take root as the expansiveness of nationalism, a means to bridge two countries at the same time. The imagined ways in which national identities begin to take hold of the psyches and sensibilities of the audiences across the spectrum of oceans can be understood as transnationalism. Another source of transnationalism is travel. The back-and-forth dynamic that accompanies immigrants the world over is what continues to sustain and foster transnationalism. When immigrants return to their home countries, they may feel reverse culture shock or a feeling of nonadaptability because of profound changes to their identities. Yet, their return is accompanied by a strong yearning for the feeling of recreating a home where they live. Catching up with their lives, that of their extended families, the friends they have left behind, politics, culture, and so forth gives birth to a discursive sense of transnationalism. In addition to the psychic and discursive, there is institutional transnationalism. Institutional transnationalism takes the form of attending such institutions as places of religious worship as well as building organizations that crosscut boundaries and borders between home and abroad. These organizations are fluid and permeable spaces where culture, belief systems, and affinities flow back and forth. Transnationalism is then a splitting of the concept and experience of nationhood. What occurs elsewhere occurs here, so to speak, though the nature and quality as well as feel of that occurrence may differ considerably between there and here.

Debates

Several debates underlie transnationalism, and these merit consideration. The first of these revolves around the concept of essentialism. Is transnationalism an essentialist concept? Some would disavow any connection between essentialism and transnationalism, essentialism being the idea that there is some universalizing force that unites and confers some kind of sameness and uniformity to all members of a culture, race, or ethnic group. Transnationalism is not an offshoot of sameness. In this sense, it anticipates a different debate that is space, place, and time.

Transnationalism is an experience that accompanies relocation. It is not the exclusive preserve of members of a culture to experience transnationalism. Transnationalism can be experienced and enjoyed by members of an associative culture as well. For example, two friends who may be differentiated on basis of place of origin and citizenship might still savor each other's trajectories of transnationalism. The key seems to be degree of participation and alertness as well as attentiveness to the connectors and stressors that accompany

relocation to a different place. So even if an individual claims a transnational identity on basis of being from a certain country or culture, those around him or her can still experience its effects and benefits. Cyberspace is an example of how different individuals can tune into the dimensions of transnationalism. Anyone can enter the interlocking set of vectors that constitute transnationalism to increase one's awareness of the factors that propel, push, and pull together individuals from different countries who are separated from one another by great oceanic distances.

Another example of the contested terrain of transnationalism shares an intellectual border with globalism. Is globalism a homogenizing and flattening tendency? Does globalism threaten to wipe out differences and create a singular world subject? Such debates are equally applicable to transnationalism. In values, attitudes, and ideologies crisscrossing the oceans at great speed, does the transnationalist subject become the subject effect of such destinies rather than find a way to carve out a path, or pathways, for himself or herself?

One could argue that transnationalism is about finding difference-in-sameness. There is no logical explanation for why individuals would lose their specific places in the world because of the various influences that span the oceans. If anything, transnationalism has an element of volition in it. An individual or even group can choose to be influenced by certain elements that attend their separation from their home countries. Similarly, an individual can be constituted by variegated influences from many different countries that have become a home to their fellow citizens from their birthplace. Therefore, identity becomes a kaleidoscope of an infinite possibility of existence rather than some one-dimensional aspect that is the function of being exposed to the same influences from the same place. Similarly, a transnationalist individual can be exposed to a multitudinous set of influences from many countries both in a contiguous and noncontiguous sense. These proliferate the possibilities for identity rather than limit them.

Another crucial debate that cuts through transnationalism is that of longue durée (literally, "over the long term") or temporality versus space and place. Each of these concepts of space and place themselves constitute a debate. The debate regarding space and time is a timeworn one, yet it is critical to consider if transnationalism is one or the other. Transnationalism is a temporal concept insofar as it is galvanized by relocation. From the time an individual relocates from one country to another and begins to connect with the home country, a variety of factors are activated. When and to what extent these are a source of change, transformation, and reconstitution of identity is a matter of time. Yet, transnationalism is a spatial concept as well. Transnationalism is the recreation of the concept of home and the distance between there and here through conventions and idioms of familiarity. For transnationals, home is not some readily identifiable artifact that one can point to and say it is theirs or mine. Instead, a whole host of imaginary and fantastic acts constitute this space of home. This takes us to a critical distinction between place and space. On the one hand, place can be said to be a physical topographical entity, something readily identifiable as solid matter. Space, on the other hand, is a set of practices that constitute a surrounding or milieu. Therefore, transnationals can be said to be a composite of both space and place. Immigrants, for instance, have physically relocated to a different place, and this place has a huge impact on their quests for identity. Navigability of this place through the imaginative and creative resources of transnational building is definitely a spatial exercise. It takes a whole range of practices to put into motion the aspect of transnational identity. To reiterate, it requires renewed social relations, redefining conventional and new media, travel, and in general an openness to what is occurring to members of the home country the world over. This is a spatial exercise, an exercise to create, build, and rebuild space.

Finally, the debate about transnationalism's limits and boundaries is not complete without a foray into ideology. Is transnationalism ideological, and as such, does it promote retrograde concepts of nationalism and anti-cosmopolitanism? In other words, does transnationalism limit individuals' endeavors to begin to fit into their host country by tending to hold onto their roots tenaciously despite spread of globalization? Transnationalism, like other forms of nationhood, is loaded with ideologies of gender, religion, and class as well as nationhood writ large. Let us look in particular at gender and sexuality. The ideologies surrounding gender and sexual expectations and norms in the home country can exert a tremendous power over those who leave. Gender is subjected to the intersecting demands of patriarchy and religion, and in this sense, these norms can be viewed as restrictive and prohibitive. At the same time, these norms can also be productive, generating different ways to be a woman or man. The conceptions of femininity that emerge and circulate in the circuits of transnationalism can be rigid, however, lacking motility and mobility. Many films of the diaspora suggest just this, that transnationalism can generate oppressive and repressive images of Indian gender and sexuality. Ideologies can be contested and transformed into progressive notions of gender. For instance, many domestic violence support centers have developed because of the realization of the transnationalist connections between ideologies of dependence, reliance, and self-effacement and the need to change them toward empowerment of women in transnational spaces. These are some of the debates about transnationalism—a concept and experience whose time has come, is here to stay, and can be said to have fundamentally changed the world into one of difference.

K. E. Supriya

See also Colonialism; Diaspora; Hegemony; Hybridity; Nationalism

Further Readings

Mendez, J. B., & Wolf, D. L. (2001). Where feminist theory meets feminist practice: Border-crossing in a transnational network. *Organization, 8,* 723–750.

Rocco, R., & García Selgas, F. J. (Eds.). (2006). *Transnationalism: Issues and perspectives.* Madrid, Spain: Editorial Complutense.

Smith, M. P., & Guarnizo, L. E. (Eds.). (1998). *Transnationalism from below* (Vol. 6). New Brunswick, NJ: Transaction Publishing.

Transworld Identity

The term *transworld identity* is often discussed in the discipline of philosophy as an individual's identity across possible worlds. This is rooted in the idea that a person's identity exists in more than one possible world, including the world in which he or she currently lives, which is referred to as the actual world. According to the philosopher David Lewis, there is no objective difference in status between an actual world and a possible world. The possible world is a place similarly "real" to an actual world and the difference in one's identity in either world is one of interpretation. Lewis, for instance, suggests that the playwright Bertrand Russell could be a playwright in his actual world, but a philosopher in a possible world. Russell could inhabit simultaneously the identity of a playwright and a philosopher depending on when, where, and by whom he was being perceived. This entry discusses transworld identity as an individual's coexistence in multiple possible worlds, relying on a few key concepts from postcolonialism and the related area of cosmopolitanism.

The Process of Identification

Interpretive researchers are interested in transworld identity because it implies an understanding of identity as a process that is dynamic, unstable, and constantly in emergence in temporally distinct spaces and geographies. Recently, academic discourse on identity has shifted from discussions about the self as a stable entity to the self as a socially produced subject that, as Stuart Hall points out, is neither simple nor stable. Referring to it as a structure that is split, Hall proposes that identity can be many things at many different times as a "process of identification." Our selves are influenced to a great degree by people with whom we choose to identify and this can mean that we can simultaneously reside in different worlds.

Such approaches to identity have become commonplace in postcolonial and cosmopolitan studies where scholars have focused their attention on transworld identity in related ways. Postcolonial theory is a term that refers to cultures—in the Americas, Africa, and Asia—affected by the imperial process from the moment of colonization to the present. Postcolonial theorists are interested in examining how the colonial epoch affected education; language; geographic borders; religion, institutional, and governmental structures; and cultural values; and how these influences are lived and indeed embodied by individuals in the present. This theory makes complex any simplistic understanding of identity, especially among individuals born and raised in postcolonized countries or those who moved to the colonial metropoles after decolonization movements. Hybridity and liminality are two identity-specific concepts that are central to postcolonialism.

Multiplicity

Homi Bhabha defined *hybridity* as the condition of identity of persons who live between colonial pasts and postcolonial presents. Bhabha identifies three spaces along which a postcolonial identity may be understood. The first space is identification with the colonizer. The second space is identification with the colonized. The third space is where a postcolonial identity resides because the postcolonial identifies with yet feels outside of first and second space identifications, thereby residing in an in-between or liminal third space. For instance, for a person from India, which is a former British colony, identity could reside in-between Englishness and Indianness—a third space that is neither here nor there but in-between. Hybridity exemplifies the complex and multiple ways that people are located within contingent realities and affiliations.

Cosmopolitanism

In the past few decades, it has been argued that *hybridity* can refer to most individuals and not just persons from postcolonized nations because the world is witnessing a period of constant reterritorialization and replacements driven by powerful forces of globalization, capitalism, wars, and so forth. Contemporarily, power can be understood in more complex ways than as merely the simple binary opposition between colonial subjugation and domination.

Given these trends, contemporary scholars within the area of cosmopolitan studies have been proposing the idea of "the cosmopolitan"—a person who views himself or herself as belonging to the world and thereby of obligations that exceed any one community, religion, ethnicity, or nationality. Cosmopolitanism dates back to the Cynics of the 4th century BCE, who are credited with coining the expression that means "citizen of the cosmos." The movement was a rejection of the conventional view that human beings belong to one community among communities. Instead, a cosmopolitan was a person who straddled many communities within the universe; thus, his or her identity was spread across worlds. Although cosmopolitanism as a movement went in and out of popularity, it has seen resurgence in the humanities and social sciences. For those interested in understanding identity in complex ways, cosmopolitanism entails universality plus difference and suggests that we can and do belong to various worlds and so have disparate identity affiliations. Alongside, we are all universally connected and have obligations to each other. Cosmopolitanists oppose the solitarist approach to identity that implies that human beings are members of merely one group. Such an approach is unable to capture the complexity of alliances and choices that a person encounters in contemporary life. A cosmopolitan identity is a transworld identity because it entails a person who belongs to many groups, and even though these groups may or may not agree with each other, they include the person in their midst.

As understood by social researchers, a transworld identity suggests human identities that are spread across worlds are based on our affiliations with different groups, that are affected by geopolitical, social, and economic developments, and most importantly, that implicate universality plus difference.

Devika Chawla

See also Cosmopolitanism; Diaspora; Hybridity

Further Readings

Appiah, K. A. (2006). *Cosmopolitanism: Ethics in a world of strangers*. New York: W. W. Norton.

Bhabha, H. (1994). *The location of culture*. London: Routledge.

Hall, S. (1991). Ethnicity: Identity and difference. *Radical America, 23*(4), 9–20.

Lewis, D. (1986). *On the plurality of worlds*. Oxford, UK: Blackwell.

Sen, A. (2006). *Identity and violence: The illusion of destiny*. New York: W. W. Norton.

TRICKSTER FIGURE

The *trickster figure* appears in the myths and folktales of nearly every traditional society. In the study of mythology and folklore, the trickster character may be a god, goddess, man, woman, spirit, or animal. There are significant differences between trickster characters in different traditions. They may be cunning, comic, or foolish, but in African and now in African diasporic literature, they usually perform an important cultural task. The roots of the African American trickster figure can be traced to fundamental terms maintained through mnemonic devices peculiar to the African oral literary tradition that continue to function now both as meaningful units of New World belief systems and as traces to their origins. These cultural fragments were not obliterated but retained major elements that survived the Middle Passage. African American folklore derives from the trickster figure of Yoruba mythology known as Esu-Elegbara. He is known in African American literature as Exu, Echu-Elegua, Papa Legba, and Papa Le Bac. Esu-Elegbara of the Yoruba people in Nigeria speaks to the aspects of culturally retained epic memory that manifests itself in African New World literary traditions. Because these individual tricksters are related parts of a larger, unified figure, they are usually referred to collectively in the United States as Esu (also known as Eshu), or as Esu-Elegbara. These variations on Esu-Elegbara speak eloquently of a continuous metaphysical presupposition and a pattern of figuration shared through time and space among certain Black cultures in West Africa, South America, the Caribbean, and the United States. The trickster figure is relevant to identity and identity studies because it embodies an African worldview and contributes to one's understanding of the significance of connecting early African American writing to the oral African tradition.

Esu as trickster informs and becomes the foundation to locate, reassemble, and then theorize complex diasporic fragmented experiences unique in the west. Additionally, Esu is complementary—that is, he connects truth with understanding, masters the elusive, and works to dispel the mystical barrier that separates the divine world from the profane. Much of Esu's literature concerns the origin of nature and the function and interpretation of language. Esu can be seen as the indigenous Black metaphor for the literary critic or as the study of methodological principles of interpretation itself, or what the literary critic does. Using the trickster figures as a historical or cultural center ensures that the entire analytical process remains located in the culture that produced the work. Other trickster figures can be identified in Legba "the divine linguist" from the Fon people of Benin; also as Exu in Brazil, Echu-Elegua in Cuba, Papa Legba in Haiti, and Papa La Bas in the Ioa of Hoodoo in the United States.

In 1988, Henry Louis Gates Jr. presented the concept of the signifying monkey in *Signifying Monkey: A Theory of Afro-American Literary Criticism* based on the functionality of the divine Esu trickster figure. The text examines the origins of the African American cultural tradition of "signifying" and ties that tradition back to West African oral traditions. Gates noted how the trickster figure had assimilated into the ordinary dimensions of African American life and that African ancestors continued to make their presence felt in African American literature. Gates's use of the monkey figure can be traced back to the Yoruba myth of the origins of interpretation that is relevant to the use of Esu as the figure of the critic and is helpful in explaining the presence of a monkey in Latin American versions of their primal myth. The presence of the monkey in Yoruba myth, repeated with a difference in Cuban versions, stands as the trace Esu in African American myth, a trace that enables us to speculate freely on the functional equivalence of Esu and his African American descendant, the signifying monkey.

Following in this tradition, Esu's various characteristics are gleaned from several sources: what the Yoruba call the Oriki Esu, the narrative praise poems, or panegyrics, of Esu-Elegbara: the Odu Ifa, the Ifa divination verses; the lyrics of Esu song; and the traditional prose narratives in which are encoded the myths of origin of the universe, of the gods, and of human beings' relation to the gods and their place within the cosmic order. Much of Esu's literature concerns the origin, nature, and the function of interpretation and language use beyond that of ordinary language. Esu is the Yoruba figure of the meta-level of formal use, of the ontological and epistemological status of figurative language and its interpretation. The Ifa consists of philosophical and ethical teaching texts of the Yoruba people—Esu acts as the translator. The importance of the trickster figure to literary theory can be summarized in three related ways.

First, the characters function as focal points; the vernacular or "folk" tradition names the opposition of its formal literary counterpart. Second, using a trickster figure enables the creating tradition to define the role of the figurative, placing agency within the culture that produced the work ensuring cultural fidelity. And finally, the trickster figure confirms the importance indeterminacy of interpretation; that is, the trickster figure underscores the relationship of some common assumptions of literary theory. In the Americas, the trickster figures displayed an early understanding of the way cleverly manipulated language can dismantle restrictive hierarchy.

In earlier writings, the trickster figure was referred to as primitive and childlike; however, now in the light of Afrocentric scholarship, trickster figures are viewed as linkers of cultural transformation, personal history, and social change—suggesting that the spirit of the trickster figure is critical to human and social maturation.

V. Nzingha Gaffin

See also Aesthetics; Afrocentricity; Agency; Diaspora; Language; Mythologies; Narratives; Signification; Worldview

Further Readings

Baker, H. (1971). *Black literature in America:* New York: McGraw-Hill.

Baker, H. (1984). *Blues, ideology and Afro-American literature.* Chicago: University of Chicago Press.

Gates, H. L., Jr. (1988). *The signifying monkey: A theory of Afro-American literary criticism.* New York: Oxford University Press.

Holloway, K. F. C. (1992). *Moorings & metaphors: Figures of culture and gender in Black women's literature.* New Brunswick, NJ: Rutgers University Press.

Hynes, W. J. (1988). *Mythical trickster figures.* Tuscaloosa: University of Alabama Press.

McDermott, G. (1996). *Zomo the rabbit: A trickster tale from West Africa.* San Diego, CA: Harcourt Brace.

Pelton, R. D. (1989). *The trickster in West Africa: A study of mythic irony and sacred delight.* Berkeley: University of California Press.

Smitherman, G. (1977). *Talkin and testifyin: The language of Black America.* Detroit, MI: Wayne State University Press.

UNCERTAINTY AVOIDANCE

Cross-cultural investigations based on *uncertainty avoidance* enlighten research on identity and its role in behavior and communication. Geert Hofstede developed uncertainty avoidance in 1980 as one of four dimensions of national culture on which people vary in their thinking because of their different cultural values. Hofstede points out that uncertainty avoidance is the extent to which people attempt to avoid experiences that they perceive as unstructured, ambiguous, or unpredictable by maintaining strict codes of behavior through laws and rituals and beliefs in absolute truths. This is similar to *xenophobia.*

Different cultures vary in the degree to which they value uncertainty avoidance and fall on a continuum between weak and strong uncertainty avoidance. Weak uncertainty avoidance can be found in Hong Kong, Sweden, and the United States, and countries with strong uncertainty avoidance include Greece, Japan, and Argentina. The following entry describes the conceptual framework of strong and weak uncertainty avoidance, controversies and support for this construct, and the relationship of uncertainty avoidance to identity and cultural facework communication.

Conceptual Framework

Uncertainty avoidance is an important predictor for understanding national differences. Studies of cultural dimensions such as uncertainty avoidance tend to focus on the differences between societies. Such studies help bring into focus the workings of the global world. Hofstede describes cultures with strong uncertainty avoidance as security seeking, nervous, intolerant, aggressive, and emotionally expressive.

For example, when a person enters a store in a strong uncertainty-avoidant culture, the store owner feels nervous because of being uncertain about what the person will do. So if, for instance, a customer picks up a piece of merchandise and handles it, the security-seeking owner may feel intolerant of this person, preferring to stand over the customer to make sure that nothing unpredictable is done. If the customer should become bolder and start to try out a mechanical piece of merchandise, the store owner may become intolerant and aggressive and insist that the potential customer put down the merchandise. The storekeeper may even become irate and insist that the customer leave the store.

In contrast, people from cultures with weak uncertainty avoidance are typified by subjective feelings of well-being, strong achievement motivation, calmness, and risk taking, and tend to be less emotional, less aggressive, more relaxed, more accepting of personal risks, and relatively tolerant. Consequently, store owners in weak uncertainty-avoidant cultures do not mind if customers try out merchandise, handle it, or even break things (they will call someone to clean up the mess), and may even not charge people for breaking the merchandise that they handle.

Cross-Cultural Controversies and Conceptual Support

Although a number of research articles employ Hofstede's conception of uncertainty avoidance, there is a shortage of research using uncertainty avoidance compared with Hofstede's other cultural dimensions. This could be a result of a controversy that arose when Hofstede and M. H. Bond revealed a fifth dimension of culture, *long-term orientation* (LTO). Specifically, when LTO was discovered, a debate ensued about whether LTO had replaced the uncertainty avoidance dimension in Asian samples. Later, however, Hofstede affirmed that the uncertainty avoidance dimension characterizes whether organizations are tightly controlled (e.g., structured) versus loosely controlled (e.g., open). Support for uncertainty avoidance as a predictor of national differences was also found regarding such concepts as expectancy violations and self-assessed fears.

Despite this support, another controversy arose about whether Hofstede's overall approach to studying culture via cultural dimensions should even be considered altogether. Also, authors of a study carried out with airline staff found it hard to interpret uncertainty avoidance results because they were so highly intercorrelated with Hofstede's power distance dimension of culture. A final point of controversy questions whether one can generalize Hofstede's findings to other contexts at all, given that his original study used a single IBM organizational sample. Despite this viewpoint, however, claims have been made that Hofstede's findings are applicable to other contexts such as the mental health field and the airline industry.

Uncertainty Avoidance and Identity

The underlying anxiety associated with strong uncertainty avoidance is connected to a person's cultural identity or *self*. A person's self is reflected in his or her *face*. According to Erving Goffman, face is the public self-image that a person effectively claims for himself or herself. One's face expresses the self through interactive *facework*. During the process of facework, one's face resides in the flow of the events of an encounter. People from cultures with strong uncertainty avoidance

perform facework nervously seeking security and could possibly become inappropriately aggressive or emotionally expressive if they feel a threat to their faces during interactions. In contrast, during public encounters, people from weak uncertainty-avoidant cultures do not feel terribly threatened by the ambiguity inherent in meeting strangers who are different from themselves. Actually, the more distinct people are, the more potentially interesting they may seem. Thus, face threats are perceived differently depending on an individual's level of uncertainty avoidance.

This difference in perception can be further explained by understanding B. Aubrey Fisher's *psychological perspective*, which demonstrates how communication takes place in the individual. According to the psychological perspective, after a message is presented, an internal mediational state that acts as a filter is stimulated in the mind of the receiver. This filter affects the meaning of the message as *noise* that intervenes between the message and the receiver. Thus, the psychology of the receiver is a type of noise or filter that determines, or colors, what the receiver perceives.

A person's psychology is affected by his or her culture, and cultures differ in emotional perceptions and the attribution of meaning to a message. This process becomes relevant when, for whatever the reason, we try to communicate interculturally and want to make an impact on a recipient in a strong uncertainty-avoidant culture. To make an impression, we need to have the receiver's attention. Yet, if our recipients are from cultures with strong uncertainty avoidance, they receive others' messages through a filter. First, they must reduce uncertainty. Only after that can they attend to the message. If there is too much initial uncertainty present, they will not be able to focus on our message at all because they are too concerned with their perceived face threat and consequent heightened anxiety during unpredictable meetings. Hence, strong uncertainty avoidance is implicitly expressed during intercultural interactions, and affects facework behaviors because such cultures have a low tolerance for ambiguity in perceiving others.

Cultures vary widely in their beliefs about the nature of uncertainty and what to do when encountering it. Members of strong uncertainty-avoidant cultures have a strong need for clarity. In such cultures, people's underlying beliefs about uncertainty lead to measures for escaping from ambiguity. One way such cultures manage to reduce situational uncertainty is through the use of rules or rituals.

Internally, when doubt replaces basic trust in the way of life of one's social group or in one's place in it, one's sense of identity can be undermined. Therefore, one's social group and its corresponding communication rituals take on a great importance to culture members with strong uncertainty avoidance. This is because the violation of social communication rules could possibly lead to a loss of face.

During an interaction to establish control, receivers of ambiguous messages also aim to impart their communication rules. In strong uncertainty-avoidant cultures, rules or rituals are explicitly conveyed to the uninitiated to prevent the uninitiated from engaging in unpredictable communication that might violate their trust.

Clear *low-context messages* are characterized by spelling things out and tend to be the expression of choice by strong uncertainty avoidant culture members. Helen Mer Lynd points out that there is a natural tendency to feel a kind of security with language where meaning does not alter. Communication that includes free verbal play with its inevitable risks of misunderstanding is something to be feared by people from strong uncertainty-avoidant cultures, but the same encounter for people from weak uncertainty-avoidant cultures could be seen as inviting. Strong uncertainty avoidance calls for a conception and sense of the world that implies and depends on an exact definition of words because without this armor of verbal specificity there is no feeling of security in one's thinking. Therefore, along with strong uncertainty avoidance come formal rules for interaction that are in place to avoid face-threatening uncertainty. These formal rules often take the form of predictable ritualistic practices.

In particular, research findings have shown that strong versus weak uncertainty-avoidant culture members report using more ritualistic and aggressive facework strategies and fewer harmonious ones. Numerous cultural implications could emanate from this conceptualization. For example, if someone from the United States is having a business meeting with someone from Japan, the U.S. citizen must pay careful attention to Japanese communication rituals (e.g., the exchange of business cards). Although rituals may seem trivial to U.S. citizens (weak uncertainty avoidance), this is not the case with the Japanese (strong uncertainty avoidance). To the strong uncertainty-avoidant Japanese, a violation or mishap relating to the carrying out of rituals sets up an internal alarm message that causes Japanese people to be guarded to prevent further mishaps that could possibly cause a loss of face. Furthermore, after a communication mishap, there may be a communicative response from the Japanese of silence and stonewalling to express their anxiety to the U.S. business partner. What's more, if after the silence, the U.S. business partners still display no cultural sensitivity to the required rituals of the Japanese business partners, the Japanese party could become aggressive and remove themselves entirely from the face-threatening situation.

Thus, uncertainty avoidance is an important predictor for understanding cross-cultural facework. As a part of facework, after experiencing a response to the face presented, individuals determine whether to amend their strategies or not. Thus, a person presents his or her face and, based on the responses received, then negotiates his or her face further when intermingling with people. Those who have strong uncertainty-avoidance are afraid of experiencing a loss of face so they won't be caught off guard in front of others. This is true for those with weak uncertainty avoidance as well, but to a much less significant extent. Although there are cross-cultural differences in how much uncertainty avoidance people experience, a universal cultural similarity is that all people need to save face. It is essential to keep this universal need in mind during intercultural interactions by striving for clarity and certainty as much as possible if one wishes to develop global relationships.

Rebecca S. Merkin

See also Face/Facework; Rituals; Values; Xenophobia

Further Readings

Arrindell, W. A., Eisemann, M., Oei, T. P. S., Caballo, V. E., Sanavio, E., Sica, C., et al. (2004). Phobic anxiety in 11 nations: Part II. Hofstede's dimensions of national cultures predict national-level variations. *Personality and Individual Differences, 37,* 627–643.

Burgoon, J. (2005). Expectancy violations and interaction adaptation. In W. B. Gudykunst (Ed.), *Theorizing about intercultural communication* (pp. 149–171). Thousand Oaks, CA: Sage.

Fisher, B. A. (1978). *Perspectives on human communication.* New York: Macmillan.

Goffman, E. (1955). On face-work. *Psychiatry, 18,* 213–231.

Goffman, E. (1967). *Interaction ritual.* New York: Doubleday.

Helmreich, R. L., & Merritt, A. C. (1998). *Culture at work: National, organizational, and professional influences.* Aldershot, UK: Ashgate.

Hofstede, G. (2001). *Culture's consequences: Comparing values, behaviors, institutions, and organizations across nations.* Thousand Oaks, CA: Sage.

Hofstede, G., & Bond, M. H. (1984). Hofstede's cultural dimensions: An independent validation using Rokeach's value survey. *Journal of Cross-Cultural Psychology, 15,* 417–433.

Hoppe, M. H. (1991). *A comparative study of country elites: International differences in work-related values and learning and their implications for management training and development.* Unpublished doctoral dissertation, University of North Carolina at Chapel Hill.

Lynd, H. M. (1958). *On shame and the search for identity.* New York: Harcourt Brace & World.

McSweeney, B. (2002). Hofstede's model of national culture differences and their consequences: A triumph of faith—a failure of analysis. *Human Relations, 55,* 89–118.

Merkin, R. S (2006). Uncertainty avoidance and facework: A test of the Hofstede model. *International Journal of Intercultural Relations, 30*(2), 213–228.

Shackleton, V. J., & Ali, A. H. (1990). Work-related values of managers: A test of the Hofstede model. *Journal of Cross-Cultural Psychology, 21,* 109–118.

VALUES

Values are our important and fundamental beliefs about what we consider to be good or right. As such, they are necessarily broad and prescriptive in nature. They are closely related to attitudes that also have an evaluative component; however, attitudes relate more toward specific objects whereas our values are broader life-orienting principles. Being prescriptive in nature, they also relate to our norms about what one should and should not do. However, norms are also more context specific. This entry looks at the relationships between our values and our social identities. The values we share with others form part of our social identities. Our socialization into specific groups and broader society involves internalizing their associated values and norms, as part of performing our various social roles within those social groups and broader society.

Values associated with social identities can be distinguished from values associated with personal identities. Both our social and personal identities contribute to our self-concept. However, our social identity derives from membership of our social groups whereas our personal identity derives from our unique personal characteristics and traits, as well as our unique interpersonal relationships. The relative importance of personal and social identities varies between social contexts from the perspective of social psychology. However, from the perspective of symbolic interactionism, even personal identities are ultimately social constructions because they can only be formed within the context of social exchanges and shared meanings. Nevertheless, this entry focuses on values relating to social identities derived from social group memberships and broader society.

The first section in this entry examines our values as derived from our social groups. This section comes from the perspective of social psychology, which focuses on how individuals are influenced by the actual or implied presence of others. The remaining two sections come from a broader sociological perspective. The second section examines our values as they relate to our different social classes and class cultures in society. The third and final section takes a more national and international perspective by examining how countries differ on two broad values: (1) traditional values versus secular-rational values, and (2) survival values versus self-expression values. This entry finishes with a short summary.

Values, Social Identities, and Social Groups

Values become linked to social identities because we internalize the values of social groups to which we belong. We tend to positively value the attributes of our social groups because we are also motivated to view ourselves positively and wish to represent ourselves positively to others. These social values influence how we evaluate ourselves and how we evaluate others. Generally, we evaluate ourselves and others within our social group with a positive bias (i.e., ingroup favoritism and ethnocentrism), and similarly we tend to evaluate those in other social groups with a negative bias. In this way, intergroup comparisons (ingroup versus outgroup) can contribute to our self-esteem, based on our social group memberships.

As well as the social groups we join voluntarily, our social identities are also based on our ascribed social characteristics, such as sex, ethnicity, and nationality. Social identities relating to our ascribed characteristics are interesting because our ascribed characteristics are not chosen; however, we are nonetheless motivated to value them positively. This often leads to creative strategies in the social construction of social identities relating to these ascribed social characteristics.

For example, Nigel Edley and Margaret Wetherell in 1997 described a study of male students aged 17 to 18 years at a single-sex school. These male students negotiated the meaning of being masculine in the context of being students in a lower-status group because they did not play rugby. Rather than accepting the less manly and negative social identity relating to not playing rugby, these students reconstructed masculinity in their own discourses so that masculinity was related more to *mental* agility and toughness rather than to *physical* agility and toughness. They then attributed more mental agility and toughness to themselves and so favorably compared themselves to the dominant rugby group.

Our social comparisons with others tend to be positively biased because we do not consider both favorable and unfavorable comparisons in equal measure. Although we have a need to evaluate ourselves by comparing ourselves with others according to social comparison theory, we are also motivated to make comparisons that enhance our social identities. This results a range of innovative cognitive strategies such as selecting favorable dimensions of comparison, making comparisons with lower-status groups, and changing the meaning of evaluated characteristics.

These cognitive explanations of how values relate to social identities are part of the social cognition paradigm within social psychology. Social psychology usually focuses on individuals in small group contexts—in particular, how an individual's values, attitudes, and behaviors are influenced by the actual or implied presence of others. Sociology, however, is more concerned with examining how we are influenced by larger social structures and institutions. The rest of this entry focuses on the larger societal context.

Values, Social Classes, and Class Culture in Society

Different values and cultures have been associated with different social stratifications in society that are themselves hierarchical social orders based on wealth, status, and power. Stratification research commonly focuses on social classes (e.g., lower, middle and upper classes), though other dimensions of inequality also exist such as gender, race, ethnicity, and age, which are often neglected and marginalized in stratification research.

Although relationships between social classes and values do exist, the relationships are not straightforward in that social classes will share some values and will vary on others. For example, Melvin Kohn and colleagues have found that both working- and middle-class parents value honesty, consideration, obedience, and dependability in their children. However, working-class parents generally placed more importance on obedience and compliance, and middle-class parents generally placed more importance on consideration of others and self-control. These value distinctions have been found in both U.S. and Italian cultures and are linked to aspects of the father's occupation: the degree to which the father's work was supervised or self-directed, and the degree to which the father worked with things, other people, or ideas.

Even though some values may be more associated with some classes, there is no clear correspondence between particular class identities and class cultures. This may be partly because our social class identity is not always salient or easily identified. For example, working-class identity is made more salient under oppressive working conditions that stimulate values of solidarity and loyalty toward organizations such as trade unions and associated political parties, as in the classic study in 1956 of Yorkshire coal miners by Norman Dennis, Fernando Henriques, and Clifford Slaughter called *Coal is Our Life*.

Such instances are case specific, however, and often identifying one's class is frequently not straightforward. For example, with the increasing affluence of workers in Western countries, many in traditionally working-class employment identify with the middle class; however, they may still have lower education levels and cultural traits normally associated with the working class. These affluent workers may be accommodated within a traditional Marxian class framework by defining subclasses such as lower-middle class (or petty bourgeois). However, this only accounts for the economic dimension of class. Pierre Bourdieu, in his 1984 classic *Distinction,* enriched the study of class, culture, and values by introducing another dimension of discrimination in addition to economic capital: the discrimination between social groups based on different lifestyles and tastes (i.e., cultural capital).

Bourdieu explains that social discrimination is also marked by social symbols of what constitutes good taste, which can be implicitly and unconsciously acquired through living in one's particular social milieu. The objective characteristics of one's social milieu he calls "fields" and the subjectivity experience of living in those fields he calls "habitus." Our own fields and habitus shape our aesthetic experiences, preferences, knowledge, and tastes. According to Bourdieu, the dominant higher classes have the power to define the preferences of lower classes as being of lesser taste, and thus higher classes tend to have more cultural capital. Also, there is a natural barrier for the lower classes in acquiring more cultural capital because the most authentic way to acquire the sensibilities of higher classes requires growing up in their field and habitus.

With the example of affluent "workers," social mobility into the middle class is hampered by lower cultural capital, even if more economic capital is acquired. Bourdieu argues that acquiring more cultural capital through education is only partially effective because such scholastic knowledge is considered lesser than the more authentic and naturally acquired knowledge gained through living in and growing up in the higher classes.

Bourdieu's shows that cultural capital (e.g., good taste in manners, music, food and other cultural goods) is largely constructed, that cultural capital is largely inherited from one's social milieu, and that it does not necessarily align with economic capital when determining one's class identity. However, Bourdieu's work has some limitations. Any innate aesthetic sensibilities are downplayed. More importantly, Bourdieu does not explain how higher classes dominate what is considered good or bad taste, and he does not address how what is considered good or bad taste changes over time.

Values, National Identity, and International Comparisons

At a national and international level, Ronald Inglehart and his colleagues have identified two main value dimensions from the World Values Survey (an international study of values in contemporary societies) along which all countries can be measured: (1) traditional values versus secular-rational values and (2) survival values versus self-expression values. On the first dimension, traditional values are associated with religious beliefs, nationalistic pride, and conformity among other things, whereas secular-rational values are associated with less conservative values toward issues such as divorce, euthanasia, and international collaboration. On the second dimension, survival values are concerned with gaining income, material, job, and economic security and self-expression values give more importance to issues such as the environment, friends, leisure, imagination, and free choice.

Using 18 years of data from the World Values Survey, Inglehart and Wayne Baker in 2000 published evidence supporting their thesis that national values change as countries develop economically, which is also reflected in generational changes in values. They theorized that as countries move from agrarian-based to industrial-based economies, national values on the first dimension change from more traditional values to more secular-rational values. This occurs with a declining dependence on the vicissitudes of nature and increasing human control over physical environments. Also, national values on the second dimension change from more survival values to more self-expression values as countries move from industrial-based economies to postindustrial economies with higher levels of employment in the professional and services sectors. This theory is actually a sociological extension by Inglehart of Abraham Maslow's theory describing a hierarchy of needs at the individual level.

Inglehart argues that in postindustrial economies, younger generations generally grow up in affluent circumstances and so national values shift from concerns about survival and security to concerns about self-expression and quality-of-life issues. Thus, the move from industrialized to postindustrialized countries is generally associated with a shift from materialist to postmaterialist values. However, the strength of any generational shifts in values may also depend on political factors such as presence and ability of minor parties and social movements to legitimize postmaterial values.

There are differences between individuals within the same country in their values on these two dimensions. For example, in the study by Inglehart and Baker in 2000, different values were associated with different religions within countries. Nonetheless, the value differences between religions within countries were less than the value differences between religions across countries. This suggests that societal institutions and economic development are more important than are religious institutions in promulgating values on these two dimensions.

Countries often share religious and cultural histories, and these countries tend to cluster together on the two value dimensions (see the Inglehart-Welzel Cultural Map of the World on the World Values Web site). However, these clusters are fairly loose, and two countries with different religious and cultural histories could have similar values on these two dimensions (e.g., Poland and India). Thus, countries with otherwise distinct national identities can share similar national values on these two broad dimensions (i.e., traditional/secular-rational values and survival/self-expression values).

In summary, our social identities are socially constructed and our associated values are derived from the social groups and societies to which we belong. These social identities and values influence how we see ourselves and others, often in biased ways. They influence how we evaluate ourselves and others, what we consider is good and bad taste, and our concerns with economic security and self-expression. We are often unaware of these social influences.

Rod McCrea

See also Class; Society and Social Identity

Further Readings

Berger, B. M. (1986). Taste and domination. Review of *Distinction: A social critique of the judgment of taste*
(Pierre Bourdieu). *American Journal of Sociology*, 91(6), 1445–1453.

Devine, F., & Savage, M. (2005). The cultural turn, sociology and class analysis. In F. Devine, M. Savage, J. Scott, & R. Crompton (Eds.), *Rethinking class: Culture, identities & lifestyle*. New York: Palgrave Macmillan.

Edley, N., & Wetherell, M. (1997). Jockeying for position: The construction of masculine identities. *Discourse & Society*, 8(2), 203–217.

Inglehart, R., & Baker, W. E. (2000). Modernization, cultural change, and the persistence of traditional values. *American Sociological Review*, 65(1), 19–51.

Pearlin, L. I., & Kohn, M. L. (1966). Social class, occupation, and parental values: A cross-national study. *American Sociological Review*, 31(4), 466–479.

Vaughan, G. M., & Hogg, M. A. (2008). *Introduction to social psychology* (5th ed.). Frenchs Forest, New South Wales, UK: Pearson Education.

World Values Survey: http://www.worldvaluessurvey.org

VELVET MAFIA

The *Velvet Mafia*, or *Gay Mafia*, is an imprecise term that refers to either a secret cadre of powerful gay elites believed to control the fashion and entertainment industries or the amorphous collection of lesbian, gay, bisexual, and transgender (LGBT) rights and advocacy groups that work to repeal discriminatory laws and change social attitudes toward LGBT people. No one claims to be a member of the social group Velvet Mafia or Gay Mafia; rather, the Velvet Mafia or Gay Mafia is largely a pejorative category invoked by people who have an anti-gay bias.

This aim of this entry is threefold: First, it outlines two key assumptions on which the concept of a Velvet or Gay Mafia rests. Second, it discusses the historical, social, and cultural conditions from which the term *Velvet Mafia* emerged. Third, the term's circulation and political relevance within the wider culture is tracked.

One cannot engage in a discussion of sex or gender nonconformity in Western culture without engaging with a wider debate about the etiology of LGBT identities, whether these identities are inborn or acquired. The search for the cause of homosexuality has dominated scholarly writing in the West since the coinage of the term in the early 19th century. Alongside this tendency is the notion that homosexuals have unique intrinsic aesthetic or artistic sensibilities, codified in the early writings of sexology and psychiatry in the 19th century. An in-depth recounting of this history is beyond the scope of this entry, so the reader is referred to Camille Paglia's recent reiteration of this long-standing cultural trope. Paglia argues that gay men are born with an artistic gene, which is the root cause of homosexuality. Within this logic, gay men would be both predisposed to aesthetic competency and, with this genetic advantage, dominate the field of aesthetic production.

Sometime in the 1990s, *Gay Mafia* replaced *Velvet Mafia* as a term of choice, but neither term is taken seriously in reputable scholarship, though it continues to have currency in the popular arena. The concept of a Gay Mafia is commonly mocked within LGBT circles, and at least one comedy troupe has adopted it as its stage name. A widely circulated quip begins by announcing the Gay Mafia broke into a home the previous evening. The punch line is that the Gay Mafia did not steal anything, but they had redecorated. This joke successfully exploits the contradictions in the term, juxtaposing the audience's conception of the "Mafia" and its implied violent behavior with common stereotypes of gay men who are often believed to be overly concerned with aesthetics and interests culturally defined as "feminine" and nonthreatening.

The term *Velvet Mafia* was coined by journalist and author Steven Gaines in a *New York Daily News* article in the 1970s, in reference to influential captains of the entertainment and fashion industries. This coincided with a more visible gay presence in U.S. cities, the result of the emergence of gay rights movement. Gaines also deployed the moniker in a thinly disguised novel called *The Club* about the infamous Studio 54 and the influential gay powerbrokers who routinely patronized that establishment. This "mafia" was more or less rumored to include fashion magnates, media moguls, artists, and playwrights.

At this time, U.S. culture in general was struggling to come to terms with a newly emerging visible LGBT subculture that historians argue took root in its cities after World War II. The massive

mobilization and urbanization that occurred after the war laid the groundwork for the formation of gay neighborhoods. Some soldiers coming home from the war who had discovered their homosexual orientation opted not to return to the farm and preferred the anonymity and freedom that the cities offered, where they might live their lives free of familial interference. Although a gay subculture existed in U.S. coastal cities such as New York and San Francisco, after the war, most of the gay establishments were owned by the established "Mafia," or organized crime syndicates. Many such establishments, though illegal, remained open through bribes paid to the police. The Stonewall Inn (the gay bar where the infamous Stonewall riots took place, which is commemorated every year as the start of the modern gay movement) was actually a Mafia-owned bar. The rise of the gay liberation movement led to the emergence of businesses that catered to a gay clientele. Thus, "gay" sections of cities formed, much like ethnic and racial neighborhoods. Furthermore, LGBT political organizing also borrowed from the successes of the civil rights movement, and adopted a racial or ethnic model for political organizing. Within this model, homosexuality is an inborn, essential identity, much like conventional ideas of race and ethnicity.

The Velvet Mafia, in Gaines's conception, was probably intended in a camp, ironic way, and not meant to describe a dangerous threatening mob; it was an attempt to understand and describe emerging visible gay populations. Within this logic, the Velvet Mafia organized around sexual orientation, whereas crime syndicates organized around ethnic and racial identity. The increased visibility of ethnic/racial crime syndicates in popular culture (for example, *The Godfather* trilogy of films) coincided with increased LGBT visibility. The shift from *Velvet* to *Gay Mafia* has implications, however. In dropping *velvet* and its juxtaposition with *Mafia*, the ironic or tongue-in-cheek elements of the term were lost. The trope of the Gay Mafia deployed later by those opposed to the LGBT movement served to delegitimize LGBT advocacy organizations and their efforts. Standard tactics employed by social activists such as lobbying, protests, and product boycotts become reconfigured as "mafia tactics" construed as intimidating and threatening.

The tactic of "outing"—the process of revealing one's privately held gay status—figures prominently in any discussion then of a Gay Mafia, whether one's usage of *Gay Mafia* references political action groups or connotes a secret cadre of elites believed to control media and politics. Employment discrimination has always been an issue for sexual minorities, much as for ethnic and racial minorities. Soldiers can still be discharged from the military (in the United States) if their homosexual identity is discovered. Homosexuals have been the target of such Mafia tactics as extortion and blackmail since the 19th century, where they were threatened with having their secret sexual orientation revealed. Gay people themselves first used the tactic in the late 1980s. The emergence of the HIV/AIDS pandemic raised the stakes, and secretly gay politicians who either did nothing to help gay causes or, at worst, voted against bills that would assist people living with HIV, had become unacceptable. With the new pandemic, these issues were far from trivial but, rather, matters of life and death. Gay activists were no longer willing to keep closeted politicians' homosexuality a secret when they supported anti-gay causes. Critics of outing sometimes referred to gay activists who engaged in the practice as a "Gay Mafia." Thus, the term *Gay Mafia* shifted from describing a group of influential but closeted gay men to LGBT journalists and activists who would expose closeted politicians for their hypocrisy.

The practice of outing is also relevant because a major component of the concept of the Gay Mafia is that powerful elites control media and politics. Yet these individuals were actually the targets of outing precisely for promoting anti-gay agendas in both the political arena and in the popular media by circulating insulting and demeaning stereotypes of LGBT people.

Recent same-sex sex scandals involving Congressman Mark Foley (R-FL) and Congressman Jim Kolbe (R-AZ) and teenage congressional pages, as well as Senator Larry Craig's (R-ID) conviction for soliciting an undercover police officer for sex in a Minneapolis airport bathroom led some television news commentators to speculate that there might be a Republican "Gay Mafia" in national politics. In 2006, the *New York Times* ran a front-page article exposing this Republican

"Velvet Mafia," (their term) and noting the "presence of homosexuals, particularly gay men, in crucial staff positions has been an enduring if largely hidden staple of Republican life for decades, and particularly in recent years." Highlighting their alleged power and influence, the *Times* noted that gay Republicans "have played decisive roles in passing legislation, running campaigns and advancing careers."

However, congressional leaders, specifically Kolbe, Foley, and Craig, did not support gay-affirmative legislation; voted against hate crimes legislation aimed at ensuring that crimes against sexual minorities received fair sentencing; voted against the Employment Non-Discrimination Act (ENDA) that would make it illegal to discriminate in employment on the basis of sexual orientation; opposed efforts for civil unions for same-sex couples; and supported legislation such as the Defense of Marriage Act (DOMA) that defined marriage as a union between a man and a woman and did not require other states to legally recognize same-sex marriages, even if they were recognized legally in the states they were performed. Thus, little evidence suggests that collectives of hidden gays conspired to promote any unified "gay" agenda, and much evidence suggests the opposite.

The notion of a Gay Mafia still circulates within the political realm and news, but is also salient and perhaps more elaborated within the realm of "reality" television. Reality television consists of supposedly unscripted dramatic situations, or documented actual events, that usually feature ordinary people rather than professional actors. The implicit assumptions that underlie the notion of a Gay Mafia are the accepted taken-for-granted working assumption of reality television programming staples like *Queer Eye for the Straight Guy* (Bravo Network) and *Project Runway* (Bravo/Lifetime). Within these shows, homosexuality is normalized and features openly gay people in their presumed "natural habitat," in fashion and aesthetics. *Queer Eye* features five openly gay men tasked with providing a makeover for an aesthetically challenged "straight" (heterosexual) presumably in an effort to woo a female love interest. Each of the gay men, or "fab five," are responsible for increasing the straight man's cultural capital, by redecorating his living space, instructing him on appropriate dress, updating his coiffure and instituting "proper" grooming regimens, expanding his epicurean boundaries, and assisting him in acquiring upscale aesthetic tastes. The fab five stand in judgment as the arbiters of "taste."

In *Project Runway,* contestants (some of whom are openly gay) compete to win the top honors as a fashion designer. The premise of such shows is the assumption that being victorious in the series will secure for the lucky winner entrance into the fashion industry and a prominent, coveted place within it. Openly gay fashion guru Tim Gunn functions as a gatekeeper to this world, making decisions about what is good and what is bad, who in allowed in, and who is cast out.

These programs take for granted that gay men are imbued with an aesthetic sensibility intrinsic to their sexual orientation: a "queer eye" presumably inaccessible to heterosexual man. When examined critically, the supposed prominence of gay men within the world of aesthetic production, if it has any resonance with reality, arose out of more complex historical, cultural, and social formations than biological markers. Although the term *Gay Mafia* may also embody some "positive stereotypes" for gay men—for example, that gay men are artistically talented or aesthetically gifted—like all stereotypes, it is a double-edged sword. Although the term *Velvet Mafia* could imply that gays are gifted in aesthetics production, the homophobic other side is that gays control fashion, and entertainment seems to be inextricably embedded in the term.

Stephen Hocker

See also Aesthetics; Identity Politics; Self; Sexual Minorities; Social Movements

Further Readings

Becker, H. (1982). *Art worlds.* Berkeley: University of California Press.

D'Emillio, J., & Freedman, E. (1988). *Intimate matters: A history of sexuality in America.* New York: Harper & Row.

Gross, L. (1993). *Contested closets: The politics and ethics of outing.* Minneapolis: University of Minnesota Press.

Leibovich, M. (2006, October 8). Foley case upsets tough balance of Capitol Hill's gay Republicans. *New York Times.* Retrieved December 26, 2009, from http://www.nytimes.com/2006/10/08/washington/08culture.html

Marotta, T. (1981). *The politics of homosexuality.* Boston: Houghton Mifflin.

Murphy, P., & Stout D. (2007, August 8). Idaho senator says he regrets guilty plea in restroom incident. *New York Times.* Available at http://www.nytimes.com/2007/08/29/washington/29craig.html?_r=2&oref=slogin

Paglia, C. (1994). *Vamps and tramps: New essays.* New York: Random House.

Popkin, J., & Roston A., & NBC News Investigative Unit. (2006, October 13). Feds probe trip that Kolbe made with pages. *NBC Nightly News,* msnbc.com. Retrieved December 26, 2009, from http://www.msnbc.msn.com/id/15249733

Russo, V. (1987). *The celluloid closet: Homosexuality in the movies.* New York: Harper & Row.

Sender, K. (2004). *Business, not politics: The making of the gay market.* New York: Columbia University Press.

Top Gunn. (n.d.). *Entertainment Weekly.* Retrieved December 26, 2009, from http://www.ew.com/ew/article/0,,1217353_2,00.html

Zernike, K., & Goodnough, A. (2006, September 30). Lawmaker quits over messages sent to teenage pages. *New York Times.* Retrieved December 26, 2009, from http://query.nytimes.com/gst/fullpage.html?res=980CE4DA1730F933A0575AC0A9609C8B63

VISUAL CULTURE

For many people around the globe, life in contemporary times is mediated through the swirl of visual imagery. Television, film, the Internet, medical imaging devices, cell phone cameras, satellites, newspapers and magazines, and a host of other multimedia devices enhance our sight, represent ideas, and help human beings see and be seen. Attempting to understand this cultural condition, its material and symbolic manifestations, and the effect on our individual and collective identities is the project of *visual culture.* As a hybrid enterprise recently formed through the convergence of a variety of theories and methodologies, visual culture examines relationships between individuals, societies, and images. Visual culture is the characterization and examination of meaning making through the visual—how we see, what we see, what we can't see, what we are not allowed to see, and so on—beyond traditional disciplinary boundaries.

Beginning in the early 1990s, scholarly texts, professional journals, new course and program descriptions, and conference proceedings specifically focusing on the concept of visual culture began to flourish across disciplines. These disciplines included art education, art history, cultural studies, English, and media studies. There are three interrelated definitions of visual culture woven through the literature emerging from these areas. The definitions suggest that visual culture is (1) a cultural condition in which human experience is profoundly affected by images, new technologies for looking, and various practices of seeing, showing, and picturing; (2) an inclusive set of images, objects, and apparatuses; or (3) a critical field of study that examines and interprets differing visual manifestations and experiences in culture. The three definitions often overlap, converge, and inform one another. In some cases, scholars use the term *visual culture* to mean all of the definitions simultaneously. The potential source of confusion notwithstanding, all three definitions of visual culture deal largely with the process and pressures of constructing individual and collective identity.

Visual Culture as a Cultural Condition

The term *visual culture* can connote a shift or turn in society where the increase in production and consumption of imagery in concert with technological and economic developments has profoundly changed the world and the context in which awareness of that world and one's identity in it is rooted. Visual culture is thus defined as a shift in reality and a present-day condition where images play a central role in the creation of knowledge and the construction of identity. Although one could argue that the "visual" has always mediated an understanding of identity, experience in much of the world today is deeply affected by an abundance of visual imagery in a variety of global contexts, in a different respect than the past. For example, images flow across borders to convey information, offer pleasure, and initiate and reinforce values and beliefs. These circulating signs affect the formation of individual identities and inter-individual power relations in ways unimaginable for many even a few decades ago.

The relationship between humans and their experience in visual culture is engendered by what some describe as an endless placement and displacement of meanings through the proliferation of imagery, as well as the negotiation of social relationships through images and the process of imagining. Like the postmodern condition, identity in visual culture depends largely on images and the tendency to visualize ourselves and others as pictures in our imagination. On the one hand, these pictures come together in our minds with purpose and direction. On the other hand, we unconsciously learn to look and practice interpreting meanings of images around us on a daily basis.

For many human beings around the globe, visual culture is how the feeling of life in contemporary times is toned, colored, and textured. The increased visual stimuli in the mediated through constructed instruments help forge identities. These identities include notions of ethnicity, race, nationality, sexuality, friendship, family life, independence, and citizenship. In this new cultural condition, visual representations and their mediating resources do more than "represent" a world already out there; they shape and limit visions of the world and are constitutive of identity itself.

Visual Culture as Stuff

When the term *visual culture* is used to describe a cultural condition, it often emphasizes the identities that are constructed through culture. Although images cannot be easily separated from the values and beliefs they imbue, another definition of visual culture focuses on the substantial things of culture— the "stuff." Scholars who use the term *visual culture* to describe the substance of culture offer examples of images, objects, sites, and instruments. This register of stuff includes, for instance, advertisements, architecture, artworks, automobiles, computer games, fashion, films, graffiti, Internet sites, landscape design, malls, magazines, medical images, newspapers, packaging, performances, photography, popular images, satellite images, scientific illustrations, simulation rides, tattoos, television programs, textiles, toys, and videos. Although some of the things mentioned in the attempts to catalog visual culture's constituent parts include fine or high art, most of them come from outside of the art world—outside the museum realm.

When describing visual culture as stuff, scholars also refer to new technologies designed to enhance biological vision. In recent years, for example, apparatuses for monitoring and tracking individuals, such as surveillance cameras, global positioning systems, spy-cams, thermal imaging devices, and biometric machines have become visual *objects of interest*. These things are of particular interest to scholars writing about identity in a time of global "permanent war." Some theorists, however, focus less on technology and more on "natural" objects and scenery. Examples of these things include landscapes, geographic conditions, outer space, and animals. Although these forms may seem to fall outside things that are culturally mediated, they are in most cases encountered by individuals who have been affected consciously and unconsciously by previous representations of nature and the entire history of imaging nature in a particular society. All natural objects and sites are part of visual culture when people bring cultural knowledge to bear on their experience with them.

None of the substantial parts of visual culture are exclusively visual. Applying the term *visual culture* to a thing does not exclude the multimedia aspects of that thing. Using the term *visual culture* to describe a particular image, for example, does not negate the fact that images appear in a variety of contexts and are viewed in different situations. These specific contexts and situations—whether watching television, playing a video game, leafing through a magazine, or standing in a museum—affect the available senses to one degree or another. Although one representational register may be more acute than another, usually we cannot voluntarily immobilize all other senses and view an image in complete optical isolation. Therefore, our experience with visual culture, similar to our identity in general, is also always situated and incomplete. For most scholars of visual culture, however, the content for study is not simply "things." The experience of human subjects interacting with the substantial parts of visual culture is of primary concern to visual culture when defined as a field of study.

Visual Culture as a Field of Study

Besides referring to a cultural condition or suggesting a range of images and objects, visual culture can be defined as a field of study. As a critical set of projects, visual culture attempts to interpret the wealth of visual (multi-mediated) experiences in culture and the visual practices of a culture—the interactions between viewers and what is being viewed. Some theorists prefer to use the term *visual culture* to refer to a field of study, but other scholars prefer to deploy the term *visual culture studies* or *visual studies*. For those who prefer to use *visual culture* to connote the project, the term is usually employed as a field of study not abstracted from its substantial content (stuff) and historical presence (cultural condition). For others, the attempt to extricate formations of the visual from the cultural is mainly based on the belief that the term *visual culture* is a potential source of confusion. Either way, whether one uses the term *visual culture, visual cultural studies*, or *visual studies*, there seems to be no categorical formations or fixed components of the field. However, two general themes seem to cut across most scholarly writing around the subject of inquiry and methodological process. One is the *contextualizing of visuality in everyday life* and the other is the notion of *transdisciplinarity*.

Contextualizing of Visuality in Everyday Life

For many scholars interested in visual culture, the subject of inquiry and methodology for their project is often determined around issues that stem from the conditions of everyday life. The concept of everyday life is important because meanings and identities are created and contested through the seemingly endless array of visual images we encounter on a daily basis. The questions involved in the study of visual culture may be determined by the circumstances created by this proliferation of visual representations that function within public and private spaces everyday. When the inquiry turns to specific forms of visual culture, such as artwork or film for example, understanding the context of production and reception is vital. Context includes the cultural purposes of the development, production, distribution, and regulation of images. Context also includes the sociopolitical, economic, environmental, and historical conditions around the production and reception of images.

Although many scholars of visual culture often refuse to adopt a predetermined methodology, there are central questions around visuality that seem to be common across disciplines. For instance, these questions may revolve around how identities have been fashioned through the visual in the past and how they are being refashioned in present. Other questions may deal with the politics of identity as constituted through social categories of seeing, spectatorship, gazing, and glancing. In addition, there may be questions of what it means to be looked at, seen, not seen, or made invisible. In this sense, the project may focus on who is privileged as producers of images and as consumers of images, what aspects of history circulate as visual representations, and who is empowered and who is subjugated through visuality. Here, visuality refers to the socially constructed character of vision, and the politics and ideology of specific visualizing practices that may serve the needs of particular identities.

Other inquires in the field of visual culture revolve around the concept of vision as a totality, the ubiquity of vision in a particular era, or how images play a central role in representing certain parts of the world. Additional questions may focus on differences and similarities between so-called high and low culture, or between fine art and vernacular images. Although these questions and issues can be understood as part of a larger rubric of inquiry, as stated earlier, the methodologies to engage these issues are usually quite fluid.

Visual culture's methodological fluidity is connected to and depends on its ability to destabilize traditional notions of disciplinarity—the legitimate knowledge base of a discipline. Therefore, visual culture is transdisciplinary by crossing and challenging disciplinary boundaries to provide a useful set of provisional theoretical collaborations. Transdisciplinarity can be understood as a gleaning of knowledge and practice from a myriad of disciplines while pushing against and permeating the rigid boundaries of those disciplines. Visual culture as a transdisciplinary field of study does not negate disciplinary areas of inquiry—it merely refuses to remain confined to restricted parameters defined by experts in a given field.

The following disciplines and areas of study are usually implicated in the field of visual culture: anthropology, archaeology, architectural theory, art criticism, art education, art history, Black studies, critical theory, cultural studies, design, feminist studies, film studies, linguistics, literary criticism, Marxism, media studies, philosophy, postcolonial studies, poststructuralism, psychoanalytic theory, queer theory, semiotics, and sociology. Scholars interested in visual culture work in these fields and appropriate ideas from them. They reject doctrinal disciplinary foundations and patch together whatever works for the study of visual culture.

Conclusion

Visual culture is used to describe a social and cultural condition (historically and contemporaneously) where visuality and visualizing practices have a profound effect on individual and collective identities. Visual culture is also a way of referring to the images, objects, and instruments tangled up in the complex process of understanding what it means to see and be seen, and to picture something or someone—including ourselves. In addition, visual culture is a transdisciplinary field of study that attempts to recognize, theorize, and interpret, in all of their contextual richness, the interactions between subjects and objects, and viewers and what is being viewed.

Kevin Tavin

See also Gaze; Scopophilia; Simulacra; Spectacle and the Self; Visuality

Further Readings

Barnard, M. (1998). *Art, design, and visual culture.* New York: St. Martin's Press.

Darley, A. (2000). *Visual digital culture: Surface play and the spectacle in new media genres.* New York: Routledge.

Elkins, J. (2003). *Visual studies: A skeptical introduction.* New York: Routledge.

Mirzoeff, N. (Ed.). (1998). *The visual culture reader.* New York: Routledge.

Mitchell, W. J. T. (2002). Seeing showing: A critique of visual culture. *Journal of Visual Culture, 1*(2), 165–181.

Sturken, M., & Cartwright, L. (2001). *Practices of looking: An introduction to visual culture.* Oxford, UK: Oxford University Press.

Walker, J., & Chaplin, S. (1997). *Visual culture: An introduction.* Manchester, UK: Manchester University Press.

VISUALITY

Visuality refers to the intersection of text and image, or more precisely, the relationship between the verbal and the visual within a social and ideological context. W. J. T. Mitchell, professor of English and art history at the University of Chicago and editor of the interdisciplinary journal *Critical Inquiry* since 1978, is strongly associated with visuality, its relation to cultural and social identity, and the emergent field of visual studies (or visual culture). His book *Picture Theory* (and other subsequent works) has been significant in establishing visual culture (a term often associated with, and perhaps analogous to, postmodernism) as a field of critical inquiry in the humanities. Because of his work, and the work of others of like mind, this field now has a recognizable institutional profile, with a number of associated journals and university programs functioning internationally. This entry provides an overview of the concept of visuality and the discipline of visual studies.

In *Picture Theory*, Mitchell proposes that a verbal image is a picture in logical space. This is a proposition that he explores over a wide range of visual material, including an analysis of Michel Foucault's significant 1968 essay on the relationship between words and image, *"Ceci n'est pas une pipe"* ["This is not a pipe"]. The essay considers the complexities of the appearance of words (language) in René Magritte's 1929 image *Les trahison des images*. Foucault's text can be interpreted as challenging the self-understanding and the social positioning of the autonomous and unified self in modern society. The picture, Foucault's text, and by association poststructural visual criticism, are interpreted as an attempt to destabilizes self-identity (the stable Cartesian self) and dominant ideology by exploring the complex and circuitous transaction between the picture, the text, and the observer. Mitchell explores this complex relationship, here and throughout his writing, as he attempts to expand the field of what constitutes visuality.

In 1995, Mitchell was invited to present his intellectual perspective in the journal *Art Bulletin*, the long-established, and some might say, the conservative voice of the College Art Association of America. An association that had already awarded *Picture Theory*, the Morey Prize for a book of special distinction; further, in 1996 in a special issue (No. 77), the poststructuralist writers associated with the journal *October* (Rosalind Krauss, Yve-Alain Bois, Hal Foster, Annette Michelson, and Benjamin Buchloh) initiate a discussion that brings to the surface the crucial tensions between the discipline of art history and the emerging discipline of visual culture. These writers suggest that visual culture avoids dealing with the aesthetic specificity of works of art, concentrating instead on images that are mediated by mass culture and, therefore, open to the processes of commodification and reification. This is a challenge to visual studies' integrity that Mitchell responds to by proposing a cluster of arguments and neologisms.

Mitchell suggests that Western culture has consistently privileged the spoken word as the highest form of intellectual pursuit, and seen visual representations as mere "illustrations" of ideas. According to Mitchell, visual culture as a subject of study contests this hegemony, developing what he calls *picture theory*. In Mitchell's view, Western philosophy and science now use the pictorial, rather than the textual, for making models of the world. This marks a significant shift in understanding and presents a challenge to the notion of the world conceptualized as a written text. A position that has dominated contemporary intellectual discussion in the wake of the linguistic-based movements: structuralism and poststructuralism (Jacques Derrida, Jacques Lacan, Roland Barthes, Michel Foucault, Rosalind Krauss, and others).

In exploring the conditions that enable the life of images, Mitchell attributes a crucial role to their "medium," which he understands as an expanded field of study, as a "habitat" or "ecosystem," in which images circulate. By doing this, Mitchell questions the received notion of medium specificity. Emphasis on medium specificity as an internal and constitutive characteristic of modernism fulfills the Greenbergian stipulation that "purity" in art consists in the acceptance of the limitations of the medium of the specific art. For Mitchell, the notion of the medium is much more than a material or limitation that is specific to a particular art form. According to Mitchell, the medium now includes the entire range of practices that make an image possible in the world. This represents a much wider notion of the visual as a social field.

This is one of Mitchell's most important contributions to the emerging field of visual studies.

Those writers who promote visual studies against traditional forms of art history, a model of inquiry that concentrates, for example, on developments in medium and style, would do so by saying that the material groundings and fixed notions of quality or historical and aesthetic specificity so important to that discipline have never been lost; they have, in the postmodern period, simply migrated from one system to another: that is, visual studies. Those defending this emerging phenomenon in the humanities would argue that the "history" now involved is that of the viewing subject (the previously silenced voice of the beholder that simply received the images presented). It might be suggested that such a new discipline is not organized around its "objects" of study, rather, the theories and methodologies by which it considers those objects.

In the 2002 article "Showing, Seeing: A Critique of Visual Studies," Mitchell charts the expanding territory of visual studies, and its character as dangerous supplement, as well as the possible ramifications of its de-disciplinary effect. According to Mitchell, visual studies stands in an ambiguous relation to art history and aesthetics. It functions as an internal complement to traditional fields of art historical study and is a way of "filling in a gap" between the disciplines. If art history is about visual images, and aesthetics about the senses, then it can be proposed that a subdiscipline might evolve that concentrates on the notion of visuality as such. Mitchell suggests that this discipline would link, or integrate, the field of aesthetics and art history around the conceptual problems of the visual experience. For example, issues concerning light, visual apparatuses of various kinds (for example, the camera and the mirrors), optics in general (microscopic and macroscopic), and optical experiences, the eye, notions of the scopic drive, and so on. As noted, Mitchell tells us that the problematic issue arises when this supportive or complementary function of visual studies threatens to become what Derrida calls *supplementary* (the supplement transfigures what has been previously interpreted as a site of wholeness and authenticity). In this aspect, visual studies might be understood as threatening the internal coherence of aesthetics and art history because these disciplines have somehow failed to pay attention to consider the most central material in their own domain.

Mitchell is reflecting a position adopted by many contemporary writers and critics who deal with an expanded field of culture and visuality, for example, Kobena Mercer, Richard Dyer, Simon Watney, Isaac Julien, John Grayson, Judith Baine, Teresa de Lauretis, Tom Waugh, Cindy Patton, Richard Fung, and Stuart Marshall. One might suggest that these writers feel that cultural and social identity, which include sexual and race identities, has not been sufficiently theorized or understood by the academic world. Within contemporaneous social determinates, their writing, along with Mitchell's, attempts to coordinate issues and practices concerning the exercise of power, ideology, the aesthetic marginality of race and gender, and psychological self-division (homosexuality and lesbianism) in relation to contemporary philosophies of consciousness and selfhood. Others would warn that such interpretations might lead to a type of fetishism that focuses too much on difference and not enough on human commonality and solidarity.

Peter Muir

See also Society of the Spectacle; Visual Culture

Further Readings

Mitchell, W. J. T. (1986). *Iconology: Image, text, ideology*. Chicago: University of Chicago Press.

Mitchell, W. J. T. (1994). *Picture theory: Essays on verbal and visual representation*. Chicago: University of Chicago Press.

Mitchell, W. J. T. (2005). *What do pictures want? The lives and loves of images*. Chicago: University of Chicago Press.

VISUALIZING DESIRE

Vision plays a key role when one thinks of desire. Although vision in and of itself is a synesthetic activity involving the interrelations of all the senses, it is the primary sense when we think of the way desire, *unconscious* desire in this case, is mobilized. Desire, as conceptualized within psychoanalysis, is central to the construction of identity. Desire is sex/gendered when looking, and hence, the discourse of psychoanalysis has attempted to expose its difficulty, given that the desire of the subject who looks is not confined to biological sex alone. To illustrate visualizing desire, this entry first turns to Jacques Lacan and then to the discussions of desire that surround the art of French painter René Magritte as interpreted by several feminist critics.

Lacan develops the notion of unconscious visual desire in his seminar, *The Four Fundamental Concepts of Psychoanalysis*. In his lecture, "What Is a Picture?" he recounts the story told by Pliny to demonstrate the generation of desire when looking. It seems that one day, Zeuxis and Parrhasius were having a painting contest to determine who could best paint nature in all its verisimilitude. Zeuxis went away and painted grapes that were so lifelike that birds came and began to peck at them. Overjoyed, he thought that he had won the mimetic prize. Parrhasius, on the other hand, painted a picture of a curtain. Zeuxis came over to see what Parrhasius had painted behind the curtain. When he tried to pull it away, he realized that he been fooled. But it was not the quality of the curtain (in Latin, *linteum* is translated as "veil") that fooled Zeuxis. Neither birds nor man need an exact representation to be drawn in. Such gestalts could vary widely in quality and yet serve their purpose. Birds merely required a crude stimulus to be attracted, and Zeuxis was not deceived so much by the representation of the veil (curtain) itself, as by his gaze that had lured him into searching for the fantasy—the fascination for a presence beyond the absence. *He had been seduced by desiring to know what lay behind the curtain.*

From such a tale, many feminists have written about imagination's desire for that ideal closure— the hidden picture that fulfills fantasy, the final signifier, so to speak, to fulfill the perpetual "lack" that lies beyond our grasp, but paradoxically doesn't exist. The enigma of a heterosexual woman as an unconscious desire for a heterosexual man conceals that there is nothing to conceal. There is "nothing" behind the mask, nothing behind the veil, but another displaced signifier, another veil ad infinitum. With visual desire, we are all caught by appearances as we project the fantasy into the object its ability to make us feel satisfied and

whole. In the remainder of this entry, this complexity of visualizing desire is illustrated by the critical reception of two of René Magritte's paintings by feminist critics.

Elizabeth Wright: *Le Viol*

Elizabeth Wright develops the machinations of visual desire in her examination of René Magritte's picture *Le Viol* (The Rape). The subject of the picture is apparently a face surrounded by hair in what was then a consciously fashionable manner. On closer inspection, however, the viewer sees that this is an illusion: The eyes become nipples, the nose is a navel, and the mouth becomes the woman's pubic hair. If the hair is removed, the naked torso is made plainly visible, suggesting yet another level of reading of *Le Viol* that Wright overlooks. Removing the hair through an intentional act of the imagination, the viewer rehearses the removal of hair from painting of classical nudes, exposing the scopophilic unconscious imagination. Hair, after all, is a sign of virility. Its removal adds to the passive quality as an objectification of flesh that infantilizes women. At the same time, it eroticizes looking and feeling, certainly for the hetero male. Magritte's *trompe l'oeil* effect, however, mitigates such a possibility by forcing a misrecognition to take place.

Mary Ann Caws: *Les Liaisons Dangereuses*

Mary Ann Caws, like Wright, sees the potential disruptive possibilities of Magritte's oeuvre in terms of sexual desire. She draws on Rosalind Krauss's analysis of surrealist photography for its transgressive potentials as the "denial of presence." According to Krauss, within surrealist photography, the doubling of the signifier produces a paradox that exploits what we think is real. Caws explains how this same "doubling" of vision is possible so that the singularity, the unifying experience of looking, is ruptured and destroyed. The viewer is caught looking at his or her own looking. Here, we have an example of the copy as a double, as simulacra functioning in its capacity for disruption. Magritte's painting *Les Liaisons Dangereuses* (1936) serves as Caws's example of the denial of presence. Paraphrasing Caws's description: Here a woman is shown down to her ankles with her head bent down in profile. She is holding a mirror exactly in the middle of her body. Portrayed in the mirror is a side view of her nude. It is reversed in the center of the image, parts of her hair in the mirror do not match her hair outside it, nor does the lower part of her body match her thighs that are outside the mirror. This deformation can be read as central to the self; the woman divided is also watching herself, but without seeing us see her from behind. The narcissistic glance in the mirror is reversed. *Les Liaisons Dangereuses* stages a ruination of sexual desire. The look that captures the gaze is thwarted.

Caws's interpretation of "dangerous meetings" as the loss of presence of the self borders on the belief in a humanistic subject that Magritte wanted to avoid; namely, as if the model could "read" herself (as "natural frontal beauty") in a mirror provided that she had been properly painted in perspective. Another way to read *Les Liaisons Dangereuses* is to take the pun of the title seriously: The self should not be confused with the mirror image of the self. In other words, desire of the self should not be confused with the object that proposes itself to satisfy the desire, namely, the mirrored image. A dangerous meeting happens when this is forgotten. That may be why Magritte painted a side view of the nude in the mirror. It is an anamorphic projection, a mirror within a mirror, or *mise-en-abyme*, which sets up the acknowledgment of a "split subject," a subject who "is" only insofar as it is *not where it thinks it is* as Lacan might say.

Susan Gubar: *Le Viol*

Susan Gubar, whose antipornographic stance is well-known, gives an entirely different reading of Magritte's *Le Viol*. She maintains that Magritte's "body parts" are indicative of the historical degradation of women that pornography has wrought. After presenting the contradictory readings of *Le Viol*, including the radical disruptive possibilities of Magritte's surrealist rhetoric developed earlier, she settles for a more conservative reading: Magritte's imagery is a vindictive mockery over his mother's suicidal drowning while he was still an adolescent. Sadistic desire is at work. The rejection of his mother leads to rejecting the feminine part of himself.

Gubar returns to the "scene/seen" of the crime playing a familiar psychoanalytic card. The ambiguity surrounding the interpretations of surrealist art and Magritte in particular (Is it art? Is it pornography?) comes down to *Le Viol* as a projection of Medusa, the ambiguity involved in the male's pleasure and horror of seeing women's genitals, a direct result of castration anxiety. Magritte's *Le Viol* is a decapitation of his lost phallic mother, who, having drowned, remained omnipotent and now needs a proper burial so that Magritte may reduce the threat to his own vulnerability. Magritte's desire of loss is now appeased through this painting.

Given that *Le Viol* suggests a male face (according to Gubar), and given that there are many paintings of absent men pictured in empty suits, or with missing heads throughout Magritte's oeuvre, Gubar suggests that Magritte has also been castrated, made impotent. *Le Viol* now becomes an inverted portrait. If that is not enough, *Le Viol* becomes a fearful portrait. According to Gubar, by re-creating in his own image the woman who created him, by repossessing through fantasy the woman who had to be relinquished, by punishing the woman whose separateness was itself experienced as a punishment, and by eroticizing the woman whose eroticism was taboo, Magritte coverts his greatest trauma into his greatest thrill, a fact that explains why the perusal of pulp magazines and the communal showings of stag films function like *rites de passage* for so many adolescent boys. Visualizing desire in Magritte has now become a semi-pornographic and sadistic act in the eyes of Gubar confirming that—in the eyes of the beholder—desire plays with what is hidden as Lacan's lesson on Pliny's story indicates.

These interpretations of *Le Viol* range from being an art of rupture to a pornographic sadistic art of domination. Historically situated, Gubar claims that the surrealist image reflects the masculine anxiety of the World War I and the breakdown of heroic individualism. Magritte, once a hero, has been broken. His images of corporeal absence are now balanced by his disgust of the female subject. Deconstructed, he has joined the ranks of *porno-artgraphy*, that "third" term that avoids assimilation in the opposition art/pornography, a realm between art and pornography where artists are buried who searched for revenge on their mothers.

In defense of Magritte, one might consider Magritte's title, *Le Viol*, which translates as violation or desecration. Magritte linguistic theories made the naming of things through his puns and play of the signifier problematic. Reversing just two letters and adding an "e," one arrives at "*Le Voile*," or veil, and is thrown back to Parrhasius's curtain. In this sense Gubar, Caws, and Wright are like Zeuxis, reading their own desires to articulate what's behind the veil when there is nothing there except another veil (the canvas). There is another interesting aspect of this title. In German, Magritte's *Le Viol* translates as *Vergewaltigung*—literally, a misuse of power. Freud took advantage of the German language to present these parapraxes (errors and slips in speech) of everyday life. In German, the prefix *ver* performs an anamorphic function, a displacement to the side, calling up the unconscious. *Vergewaltigung* means a violence coming from the unconscious; the desire to remove the veil of the woman and forcibly possess the thing she hides without her permission. Magritte is providing us with an anamorphic view, a "looking awry" as Slavoj Žižek would put it, of this form of masculine desire. As mentioned earlier, the title refers to the male's *failure* at possession.

This discussion of Lacan's reading of Pliny and the reading of masculine desire in Magritte's paintings by Wright, Caws, and Gubar is meant to illustrate the difficulty of unconscious desire when looking that directly draws on the notion of what is sanctioned by a societal gaze. Most problematically, that gaze has been identified as being masculine and patriarchal; however, Magritte turns that gaze around, confounding the looking and placing masculine desire in doubt through his clever images and punning titles. The ambiguity of reading desire in his work by Caws and Gubar testify to Magritte's ability to have his images (appearances or simulacra) play a devilish role for us spectators.

jan jagodzinski

See also Gaze; Scopophilia; Simulacra

Further Readings

Caws, M. A. (1985). Ladies shot and painted: Female embodiment in surrealist art. In S. R. Suleiman (Ed.), *The female body in Western culture: Contemporary perspectives* (pp. 262–287). Cambridge, MA: Harvard University Press.

Gubar, S. (1987, Summer). Representing pornography: Feminism, criticism, and depictions of female violation. *Critical Inquiry, 13*, 712–741.

Krauss, R. W. (1985). *The originality of the avant-garde and other modernist myths.* Cambridge: MIT Press.

Wright, E. (1984). *Psychoanalytic criticism: Theory in practice.* London: Methuen.

VISUAL PLEASURE

Visual pleasure refers to the enjoyment one feels when viewing an object of desire. Visual pleasure is a common topic in feminist theorizing, including the role it plays in the formation of women's individual and social identity. It has also been the subject of an article by British feminist film theorist and filmmaker Laura Mulvey. This entry focuses on Mulvey's article "Visual Pleasure and Narrative Cinema" and its relevance to feminist intervention, film theory, and psychoanalytic concepts of identity.

Central to Mulvey's ideas on visual pleasure is the notion of the unconscious in patriarchal society being structured around inequality: an inequality that positions women as the inferior "other." In a short article written in 1973, "Fears, Fantasies and the Male Unconscious; or, You Don't Know What's Happening, Do You, Mr. Jones?" Mulvey reviewed the work of the British Pop artist Allen Jones. This article, along with her essay "Visual Pleasure and Narrative Cinema," established Mulvey's engagement with Freudian and Lacanian psychoanalytic thinking. Christian Metz and Jean-Louis Baudry had already tried to configure psychoanalytic ideas in relation to the theorizing of the cinema, but Mulvey's essays begin a specific historical intersection of feminist intervention, film theory, and psychoanalysis.

Mulvey's article "Visual Pleasure and Narrative Cinema" does not engage with any empirical research in relation to film audiences. Instead, Mulvey make a political use (in the sense of gender politics) of Sigmund Freud and Jacques Lacan, adapting some of their concepts to argue that classical Hollywood cinema positions the spectator (male or female) as masculine and the figure of the woman on screen as the "object" of desire. Mulvey's influential study links different types of looking and the pleasure derived from them to notions of gender, society, and difference. The emphasis in her work in the 1970s is placed on how these different forms of looking express inequality and oppression within capitalist society, but more particularly, patriarchal society. One approach to artworks is from the standpoint of aesthetic experience, but the other, adopted by Mulvey and others, involves treating artworks as heuristic devices that can teach us about the world and human identity. Such psychoanalytically inspired studies do not investigate the viewing practices of individuals in specific social contexts, but instead consider how subjects' positions and identities are constructed by ideology.

The primal scopic scene considered by Mulvey in "Visual Pleasure and Narrative Cinema" echoes the search for identity through the intermediary of the image and conforms to Freudian and Lacanian paradigms; that is, models that center on the castration fear of the male viewer. This fear of castration invokes a crisis between the conception of the subject (the self) and its authentication. Mulvey points to a relationship between the young boy's horror of castration (in the *Symbolic* phase of development) symbolized by the metaphorically castrated body of the female, and the subsequent implications of the male viewers' projection of that primal horror as a threat to his psychic coherence. According to Mulvey's thesis, when viewing filmic images of the female, two possible resolutions to this scopic crisis present themselves: either to disavow the fear of castration through a fetishization of the female body, or to avow the female by a certain disparagement of her symbolically mutilated form; in other words, the viewer can either reenact the original trauma by continually "investigating" the woman (the feminine) in an attempt to demystify her (which is counterbalanced by a devaluation of the woman) or else completely disavow the castration by substituting a fetish object or turning the represented figure itself into a fetish. In this way, the feminine body becomes reassuring rather than dangerous. This strategy can lead to an overevaluation of the female, producing, for example, the cult of the female star. This second avenue—fetishistic scopophilia—amplifies the physical beauty of the feminine object, transforming it into something satisfying in itself.

According to the choice of disavowal through the evocation of fetishism, part of the female anatomy or an item of feminine clothing becomes the focus of desire to compensate or substitute for the penis, which is symbolically missing. The avenue of avowal has another result: instead of displacing or deflecting desire away from one part of the body to another, it moves the focus from the woman's "cosmetic outside," to her "abject interior"; an interior as it were, unknown and primal. The female is understood as being inferior, which can be traced back to her own interior/internalized nature. The resolution of the male viewers' anxiety (male in the sense of the type of active looking, not necessarily in relation to gender) permits "him" to move to a position of superiority; that is, away from the "other" (female) who is a mutilated and uncanny figure. Thus, Mulvey describes the female body as a spatial metaphor for the structural division between surface allure and concealed decay as well as a metaphor for structured inequality in human relations (thus engaging with a politics of identity). The cosmetically finished surface of the body must conceal the abject matter of the interior of the female body. In psychoanalytic terms, this cosmetic surface conceals the wound or void left in the male psyche when it perceives sexual difference.

Mulvey considers that in patriarchal societies pleasure in looking has been split between the active/male and passive/female. This is reflected in dominant forms of cinema as well as many other representations. Conventional narrative films in the classical Hollywood tradition typically focus on a male protagonist in the narrative and assume a male spectator. In "Visual Pleasure and Narrative Cinema," the viewer (male or female) occupies a specifically masculine position—a position that provoked strong reactions to Mulvey's text, and a position that she later reevaluated. The viewer identifies with the *gaze* of the male, experiencing his anxiety of castration and, at the same time, the pleasure and desire of the neutralization of that anxiety through the two methods of avowal and disavowal already described. In terms of the nature of the scopophilic gaze, Freud isolated scopophilia as one of the component instincts of sexuality that exist as drives quite independently of the erotogenic zones. At this point, he associates scopophilia with taking other people as objects, subjecting them to a controlling and intrusive gaze. This position describes the moral paradox faced by a woman when viewing another woman. The female viewer can either betray her (the viewed female) and identify with the masculine point of view (the male gaze) or, in a state of accepted passivity, adopt a masochistic/narcissistic attitude to identify with the object of the masculine gaze (the desired or complete woman). Mulvey argues that certain features of the cinematic apparatus and experience allow viewing conditions (e.g., dark and essentially private) that facilitate both the voyeuristic process of objectification of female characters and the narcissistic process of identification with an ideal version of the self projected on the cinematic screen.

According to Mulvey (and other feminist writers), the meaning of woman is ultimately sexual difference, the absence of the penis is visually ascertainable, the material evidence on which is based the castration complex essential for the organization of entry into the symbolic order and the law of the father. What this sense of feminine castration entails is the woman's exclusion from the symbolic power articulated by her passivity: The woman's gaze, according to this thesis, is partial, passive, and flawed. She is left without a voice, silenced by the patriarchal symbolic order. Mulvey's argument in "Visual Pleasure and Narrative Cinema" is that the pleasure derived from these films reinforces the oppression of women. As a response to this repression, she advocated a radical experimental cinema that renounces the standard pattern of fascination built into establishing filmic forms. In this way, Mulvey calls for a total negation of the plenitude of the narrative fictional film. A major criticism of the essay is that, although Mulvey believes that classical Hollywood cinema reflects and shapes the patriarchal order, the perspective of her writing actually remains within the heterosexual order that she seeks to expose as oppressive. The radical claims of the article are, thus, a perpetuation of patriarchy. The basis of this criticism is that Mulvey's article presupposes the spectators' identity to be a male, heterosexual. Thus, it was posited that she denied the existence of lesbian women and even heterosexual women.

Sixteen years after the publication of "Visual Pleasure and Narrative Cinema," Mulvey's 1991 essay on the artist Cindy Sherman "A Phantasmagoria of the Female Body" articulates a modified position. As in "Visual Pleasure and Narrative Cinema," Mulvey is concerned with what images can tell us about popular culture, specifically the images of women circulating in modern capitalist societies. The artist Cindy Sherman is considered noteworthy because she is thought to have found a way of representing woman that achieves a "critical effect." Mulvey argues that it is significant that the women depicted are always Sherman herself; Mulvey sees the images as important because together they constitute a kind of glossary of pose, gesture, and facial expression that characterize the "construction" of feminine identity (anti-essentialism). Sherman's work, then, performs a crucial role not by refusing the dominant images or trying to produce something new, but by compulsively reiterating the existing images of women. Mulvey thematizes this argument by suggesting that Sherman's photographs constitute "infinite varieties of the masquerade." The notion of the *masquerade* has been developed by the psychoanalyst Joan Riviere, who suggests that femininity—womanliness—is a kind of performance. In this argument, femininity is not the real condition of women; rather, women wear femininity as a kind of cultural mask, and masks hide or obscure the identity of the wearer. Cosmetics and cosmetic rituals offer a useful metaphor for this role. A number of feminist theorists have developed this idea along with Mulvey, suggesting that femininity is a heavily ironic mode—a hyper-femininity as it were, preceding the representational character of gender difference—that enables women to occupy the role inscribed for them in patriarchal culture while managing to keep a psychological distance from it. Because gender identity is considered a role to be played, different performances can be imagined. This argument plays a key role in the development of theories of performative subjectivity and the construction of gender, cultural, and racial identities. "A Phantasmagoria of the Female Body" represents a key shift from "Visual Pleasure and Narrative Cinema"; the account of the masquerade allows Mulvey to conceptualize female subject positions as more than ventriloquized versions of masculine fantasy. Mulvey reads Sherman's work as a gradual movement from the exteriority of woman-as-fetish (based, as previously described, on male castration anxiety) to the interiority of what is hidden behind this mask in terms of the defetishized female body.

Peter Muir

See also Gaze; Scopophilia

Further Readings

Mulvey, L. (1975). Visual pleasure and narrative cinema. *Screen, 16*(3), 6–18.

Mulvey, L. (1991). A phantasmagoria of the female body: The work of Cindy Sherman. *New Left Review, 1*(188), 136–150.

Mulvey, L. (2005). *Death 24x a second: Reflections on stillness in the moving image.* London: Reaktion.

VISUAL POLITICS

See Embodiment and Body Politics; Extraordinary Bodies; Ideal Body, The; Otherness, History of; Propaganda; Stereotypes

VOICE

Literature depends a great deal on the manner in which the identity of the author, narrator, or speaker is perceived by the reader. *Voice* is the literary term for this presence. Sometimes the author speaks without pretense as the author; sometimes he or she adopts a persona—that is, a mask of some kind. Sometimes he or she creates a narrator who has a distinctive voice of his or her own separate from the author; sometimes the narrator is simply a mouthpiece for the author. Sometimes there is apparently no narrator or authorial presence at all.

The voice of a work may be difficult to perceive because often it lies behind the story itself. However, it may be inferred through tone and mood. *Tone* measures the author's attitude toward the reader; *mood* measures the author's attitude toward the subject matter. As an example, Harriet Beecher Stowe, who is quite outspoken in *Uncle Tom's Cabin,* is earnest in tone as she reveals the evils of slavery to her audience and argues for its abolition; her mood is a combination of bitter sarcasm and sympathy: She is sarcastic toward those who profit from slavery or compromise with it, and she is sympathetic toward the slaves.

There have been several famous misappraisals of voice that have led to misinterpretation of intentions and even punishment for authors. Daniel Defoe's *The Shortest Way With the Dissenters* was an ironic mockery of the intolerance of Anglicans toward dissenting Protestants that landed him in jail for sedition, neither side in the controversy having much patience with the subtleties of voice in his work. The letters of Johann Wolfgang von Goethe's *Sorrows of Young Werther* so inspired young men to suicide pacts that Goethe was asked to preface the second edition of the work (ostensibly in the voice of Werther himself) with a warning for young men *not* to follow his path to suicide.

A master of using voice was Frederick Douglass, who used two voices for rhetorical advantage in his famous Fourth of July speech. He began in a conciliatory tone searching for common ground between him and his audience, then abruptly changed course and, emphasizing the vast distance between him—a slave—and the audience—free men and women—denounced the present generation of Americans for their sloth in not fighting for freedom as their ancestors once had.

The use of voice in fiction and poetry is multifaceted. Wayne Booth's *The Rhetoric of Fiction* categorizes the many forms that the author's voice can take in novels and stories. In one of the earliest novels, Henry Fielding's *Tom Jones,* the author is a reliable commentator who speaks boldly in his own voice to provide facts, describe scenes, or summarize action. He is reliable in that the reader can trust that his words are truthful. Such commentators can be used to mold beliefs as well. Jane Austen establishes moral norms in her novels and then, usually in an ironic mood, shows characters stumbling over them. A later author, Kate Chopin, establishes an unconventional moral norm in "The Storm," one in which extramarital affairs need not have any more consequence than a thunderstorm that cools and freshens the summer air.

Sometimes the reliable voice is a character who narrates the action. In *Great Expectations,* an older and wiser Pip is able to guide the reader's impressions of the younger, mistake-prone Pip as he misapprehends the source of his expectations. Likewise, Robert Hayden in the poem *Those Winter Sundays* looks back on his uncomprehending younger self with a mature understanding of the lonely and disciplined love of his father.

It is particularly challenging to discern the author's presence behind unreliable narrators. Toni Cade Bambara's Sylvia narrates "The Lesson" and affords no respect at all for Miss Moore, her mentor; yet, through the haze of Sylvia's childish prejudices, Bambara still manages to reveal the remarkable benevolence of Miss Moore and the essential lesson she tries to teach a group of underprivileged children. Likewise, in Robert Browning's dramatic monologue *My Last Duchess,* the arrogant duke is unaware that he is ruthless and self-centered, but the reader soon understands that Browning intended his audience to see him in precisely this manner. In each case, the author grants readers enough clues so that they can infer his or her attitude toward the subject.

With the realist and naturalist movements in the latter half of the 19th century and modernist movement that followed, fictional narration became more impersonal. Innovative artists—such as Gustave Flaubert, Henry James, and James Joyce—wished to avoid unrealistic, extraneous, and overt commentary. To avoid it, for example, James sought a way to dramatize commentary, thus effacing the author as much as possible. Rarely does any story completely accomplish this, but a hallmark of modern fiction is the extent to which the reader is left to struggle alongside characters in confusion without help from a guiding authorial or narrative voice. Voice in such novels as *Madame Bovary, The Ambassadors, Ulysses,* and *As I Lay Dying* reinforces the modernist stance that individuals are disconnected from their fellows, lonely, and confused by shifting conceptions of truth.

In the past, even with an implied author, there could be collusion between reader and author. For instance, the reader of *The Adventures of Huckleberry Finn* could enjoy with Mark Twain the King and the Duke's making a hash of their performance of Shakespeare even though none of the characters in the novel, including narrator Huck, got the joke. But in a modernistic work such as Ernest Hemingway's "Hills Like White Elephants,"

the authorial voice is silent. Hemingway's preference for a dramatic point of view—that is, presenting essentially a scene or dialogue between characters with little or no narration—effectively eliminated the authorial voice.

In poetry, a radical change in the use of voice came with the romantic movement. Whereas classical and neoclassical authors saw the poet's voice as a learned one speaking in a poetic diction that was dignified and heightened above the common, Romantics argued for new criteria. The voice and language of poetry, said William Wordsworth in his "Preface to the *Lyrical Ballads,*" should be common to all of humankind. The poet's identity should not be an artificially poetic one, separated from ordinary persons, but one that was down-to-earth and accessible for all to understand. The U.S. poet Walt Whitman adopted such a voice in *Song of Myself,* a poem spoken by a kind of U.S. everyman in a universal voice resonating with the romantics' sympathy for political democracy.

As with modernist fiction writers, modernist poets, such as T. S. Eliot, Wallace Stevens, William Carlos Williams, and Marianne Moore, gravitated more and more toward impersonal voices even as their subject matter became increasingly personal and introspective. A notable exception to this increased self-reflexivity was African American poetry. Concerned like the romantics with finding an authentic voice that would connect with common people, African American poets attempted to incorporate the distinctive voices of the blues, spirituals, Black preaching, and other cultural expressions to articulate a vernacular culture common to all African Americans.

Voice varies greatly from work to work and period to period and has a wide range of purposes. Although harder to define than such elements as character, plot, theme, and setting, voice is particularly important as a way of measuring the interaction between readers and authors. The identity of an authorial voice may be as essential to a reader as a story well told or a character well drawn; in more modern works, understanding the author's intention of communicating with a severely limited voice or his or her effort to speak in a communal voice serve ultimately to enrich the experience of literature.

William L. Howard

See also Discourse; Language; Masking; Narratives; Rhetoric

Further Readings

Booth, W. C. (1983). *The rhetoric of fiction* (2nd ed.). Chicago: University of Chicago Press.

Brown, F. P. (1999). *Performing the word: African American poetry as vernacular culture.* New Brunswick, NJ: Rutgers University Press.

Doreski, W. (1995). *The modern voice in American poetry.* Gainesville: University Press of Florida.

Wolosky, S. (2001). *The art of poetry: How to read a poem.* Oxford, UK: Oxford University Press.

VOYEURISM

The term *voyeurism* is etymologically derived from the French word *voir*, which ultimately comes from the Latin word *videre*, both meaning "to see." *Voyeurism* describes in general the behavior of a voyeur or a voyeuse, suggesting a secret spectator who experiences satisfaction in the sexual activity of others. To look at or to observe other persons—secretly or openly—can be a way to generate one's own identity by reflection, by contrast or stimulated by the wish for visual participation.

Numerous examples of voyeuristic depictions and subjects are found in the art of all eras in Western art as well as beyond the Occident, in Chinese and Japanese art for example. It is important to note that voyeurism is not an exclusively male phenomenon as is often suggested. Numerous females, including artists such as the U.S. photographer Merry Alpern, work purposefully within the constructs of the voyeuristic gaze.

The definition and use of the term *voyeurism* customarily recurs in association with the fields of psychoanalysis and psychology. Jean-Paul Sartre's and Jacques Lacan's examinations of voyeurism drew on the theories of Sigmund Freud. In Freud's theories, voyeurism is assessed as a perversion in which the "passive" party is perceived as a victim, and "active" exhibitionism plays only a secondary role. Defining *voyeurism* as a form of victimization without fully considering the role of the "passive" party continues to stigmatize the voyeuristic act as a "perversion," resulting in prejudicial and moralizing reflexes. This one-sided and negative assessment of voyeurism may have to be analyzed or reversed.

Religious moral traditions play a role in the issues and debates surrounding voyeurism. However, it may be possible to dispense with rigid moralizing around the phenomenon of voyeurism when one considers it as *one* of many legitimate possibilities for appropriation in a visual world. Nevertheless, it should be understood that the phenomenon of voyeurism cannot be delimited to occurrences within the world of art, which is only one of the places it has manifested itself.

This entry first discusses the roots and chronological frame of voyeurism. Next, this entry presents the primary types of voyeuristic depictions. Finally, this entry examines the implications of voyeurism in today's global environment.

Roots of Voyeurism

The roots of voyeurism are closely connected with undiscriminating visual curiosity, a basic human quality. On one hand, visual curiosity is a compelling drive and is necessary in the formulation of research and science. On the other hand, visual curiosity is fundamentally an amorphous longing, directed toward all aspects of an individual's experience and surroundings, both the existing and nonexisting, visible and invisible, obvious and obscure.

Hierarchically speaking, the eye or the act of seeing is allocated first place in human sensory functioning. In a grand sense, the operation of curiosity can be focused equally on areas considered as either legitimate or deviant. Seeing, both as an active sense and as a matter of principle, tends to disregard frontiers, to ignore them, to cross over them, or to obviate them. The growing number of regulations and frontiers, restrictions and bans, avoidances and exclusions to viewing what we are socialized to treat as invisible or accept as taboo makes collisions with our desire to see inevitable.

At its roots, voyeurism does not distinguish between sexual interest and other kinds of curiosity, between eros and insight. The threshold between prurience and platonic curiosity remains thin even after determining a rationale for their separation; therefore, there continues to be a fluent transition between the desire to view either the illicit or the irreproachable.

Chronological Frame

Even though the term *voyeurism* is relatively young (it left its mark primarily in the 19th century) the phenomenon is not. Documents of voyeurism go back so far and are so closely connected with the development of human civilization that one may speak of the phenomenon as an anthropological constant. A relatively large number of voyeuristic depictions have been preserved from Greek and Roman art. Examples are repeatedly to be found in wall paintings in Pompeii and in the imagery of the Warren Cup, a silver cup with relief decoration of homoerotic scenes in the British Museum in London (c. 1–20 CE). Typical in this imagery is that spectators and eyewitness are in many respects hard to distinguish and that moral assessments about the appropriateness of viewing do not yet seem to play a role.

The earliest figurative depictions of voyeuristic scenes of the post-antique eras are to be found in Carolingian book illumination but pieces of circumstantial evidence suggest that the roots of voyeuristic practice go back even further. The connections between voyeuristic practices and mythical traditions that revolve around visual prohibitions within sacred contexts also speak for this. Veils or curtains, and acts of covering and unveiling, often play a central role. An example of this is the revelation of the "naked truth"; as an allegory in the form of a naked woman it exemplarily combines eros and insight. The mergers between the emperor cult traditions of Antiquity and early Christian rites reveal a deft ability to generate visual euphemisms for both dignity and inviolability.

Early illustrative examples for this practice are the variations of the hole-boring motif in the late Carolingian and Ottonian book illumination. They show how the scribe of Gregory the Great uses his stylus (writing implement) to pierce the curtain that separates the saint to observe through a peephole the inspiration of the Holy Spirit in the form of a dove. He becomes in a double sense the eyewitness of the divine origin of Gregor's words and voyeur.

Emerging from the Middle Ages, depictions of biblical topics have entered the visual arts canon as certain archetypal scenes, such as King David's voyeuristic attraction to Bathsheba (2 Samuel 11), or the two old men who lusted after Susanna as they secretly watched her daily walking to work in her husband's orchard (Daniel 13:7–14). Such scenes are depicted in numerous variations, in almost all techniques and styles up to the 21st century. Characteristically, they appear in religious contexts emphasizing an unambiguous morality. However, the motives of the artists depicting these subjects were far more ambiguous, as they are frequently only pretexts to depict attractive female nudes, erotic scenes, or the culturally charged dialectic of unveiling and covering.

The flux between sacred topics and profane topics with voyeuristic motifs that since the late Middle Ages have often used the same picture schemes is of particular note. An example for this is the scheme of the "window observer," common to both sacred and profane imagery. This continuity is reflected, for example, in the popular appeal in producing and contemplating "deputy" portraits, in which the observer in the picture represents the observer in front of the picture. Nevertheless, tradition and the history of voyeurism in the fine arts reveal certain fashions or economies of voyeuristic motif to be revisited in increasing numbers.

Between the Middle Ages and the 19th century, fine artists developed a great number of voyeuristic topics, exploring variations from the lustful complicity of the viewer to the tragic dissipation of the protagonist in the carnal drama. Since the 18th century, there seems to be evidence of an increasing frequency of voyeuristic depictions in painting and graphic arts in particular. The growing number of depictions correlates to the increasing proliferation of images of all kinds in modern and postmodern visual culture. It has been long acknowledged that the invention of photography and the efficiency of other mechanical forms of reproduction have contributed considerably to the spread of visuality. Just as would later prove to be the case in film, video, and newer digital forms of media reproduction, photography is a technique that makes distance, secrecy, and anonymity possible merely by the preconditions concerning the use of the apparatus—each an important criterion contributing to the voyeuristic gaze.

It is not by chance that the voyeuristic gaze through the viewfinder is similar to a look through the keyhole—and to the look through the peephole in the peep show. The motif of a person looking through the keyhole was especially popular from the late 18th century until the early 20th century. The keyhole can be described in its characteristic form as a hole or passage in a frontier (curtain, door, wall, etc.) and be compared with a small window. Once prevalent, the keyhole has nowadays disappeared as a framing device for paintings or an image-matting schema, imitating a window-like visual passage. However, it continues to be used as a trope of secret visual participation in one's surroundings, or of the acquisition of intimate knowledge or erotic insight that is at the same time forbidden—and it also owns modern-day equivalences to minimally invasive "keyhole surgery." As such, it remains a popular design motif in magazines, book covers, and works of art. The artists René Magritte and Mel Ramos repeatedly painted variations on keyhole paintings and other voyeuristic motifs.

The work of Pablo Picasso is a treasure trove of voyeuristic motifs. In numerous early drawings and paintings, Picasso tackled the voyeuristic; in his late work, however, he increases the erotic intensity of the voyeuristic scenes into burlesque and the absurd. In Picasso's 1903 painting *Self-Portrait, Making Love,* he includes himself in the imagery and thus reveals in an unabashed openness himself as artist for whom seeing means life. William Hogarth's engraving *Boys Peeping at Nature,* originally created in 1730, draws on ancient myths of fauns, sagas involving putti, and legends of Mother Nature into one image involving the secret behind the curtain and the unity of eros and insight for the depicted as a metaphor of the search for natural truth. In this image, however, the old curtain or veil as it often appeared in Renaissance and later periods of art has become the skirt of a woman—in this case, the skirt of Artemis or Diana of Ephesus, the classical personification of "Mother Nature." The identity of the skirted figure alters in different successive versions of the etching, varying between an antique sculpture and a living female figure.

Typology

In principle, at least three types of voyeuristic depictions can be distinguished in the fine arts. The first type is the most popular variation, which only shows the secret male or female observer but excludes the object of his or her desire, occurring often in caricatures; what he or she can see or observes remains omitted and is left to the fantasy of the viewer in front of the picture frame. An example representing this first type is an erotic print titled *The Impatient Adulterer* (1896), one of a series of a pen-and-ink drawings created by Aubrey Beardsley as illustrations to the *Sixth Satire of Juvenal;* this image leads into the world of theatre and shows us a half-naked masturbator no different than any other actor before the beginning of the performance as this man peeks through the theatre curtain. But whatever he witnesses and whatever excites him to fiddle with his foreskin in impatient expectation, as Beardsley himself describes in a private letter, can only be revealed by the reading the text of the play.

The second type comprises the depiction of voyeuristic constellations that allocate the role of the voyeur to the observer in front of the picture frame. Depending on the viewer, this may happen reluctantly and with no small embarrassment, or in a passionate and accepting way. The first viewer of the captured image is of course the artist himself. Thus, artist and observer are identified one with each other, or the artist lets the observer look through his eyes, so to speak, and allocates to him or her a role that originally belonged to the artist. This typically leads to a bipolar constellation wherein the viewer in front of the picture frame is like an outsider, observing the scene or the events captured in the image as if through a window, and sometimes literally looking through a window into a closed room. The persons shown within the picture frame consider themselves to be unobserved. Three completely different examples of this include Jean Auguste Dominique Ingres's famous late work *The Turkish Bath* (1862), in which the round shape of picture becomes a peephole. Edward Hopper's painting *Night Window* (1928) can be considered an iconographic exemplar of voyeuristic looking, taking a point of view across the street from a trio of open upper-story windows in an unidentified apartment building. The viewer looks into a wide-open room with the occupant, a partially clad woman bent over slightly with her back to the window, unaware that she is being watched. The Polish artist Katarzyna Kozyra used a hidden camera to secretly film and observe the public versus private behavior and hygiene rituals of men and women visiting the nude bathhouses at the Hotel Gellert in Budapest.

The result of Kozyra's voyeurism consists in almost monumental projections of highly aesthetic value. Is it, nevertheless, the objective acquisition of the "male gaze"? Critics found fault with the violation of the privacy of the women observed, particularly as their identities are not obscured for the camera. The manner in which Kozyra filmed the male counter piece—by disguising herself as a man, using fake body hair, and covering her breasts by using a towel draped strategically over her shoulders—does nothing to refute the objection that that those being filmed were also in a real way being violated.

It is not uncommon that the observed figure in the picture is given the illusion of awareness of the observer in front of the picture frame. This picture strategy allocates to the observer the role of an accomplice. As such, he or she can take on this role consciously or refuse to do so: The observer can accept it with pleasure or can be made accomplice against his own will. This is usually revealed by the fact that figure being gazed upon also looks out on the world outside the frame of the picture inviting onlookers with a gesture, with spoken words, or with some other form of body language inviting participation. The protagonists of such images and the forms their depictions take are thus applied to the observer. So a dialogue-like synergy develops that possesses the possibility of a theoretically unlimited duration. A classical example for this invitation is Jacob van Loo's erotic painting *Le Coucher à L'italienne* (c. 1650).

This painting represents the third type of voyeuristic depiction; in it, van Loo adapts a well-known painted subject that he reduces to just the central figure, the nude wife of Candaules, king of Lydia. Jacob Jordaens's *King Candaules of Lydia Showing His Wife to Gyges* (c. 1646) at the National Museum of Stockholm concerns the classical ménage à trois that includes the observer as the fourth participant and as eyewitness. This exemplar reveals the primary characteristic of the third type of voyeuristic depiction: the observed observer. In this form, of voyeuristic depiction the observer in front of the picture becomes witness of how the observer in the picture secretly observes.

It concerns a two-sided voyeurism, so to speak. In this third voyeuristic type, Sartre's reflections on voyeurism and shame, which play a crucial role in his main philosophical work *L'être et le Néant: Essai d'ontologie phénoménologique* [Being and Nothingness: An Essay on Phenomenological Ontology], may well have their starting point.

Distance and the Global Implications of Voyeurism

The voyeuristic gaze is characterized by distance. Distance may have disadvantages when it is too vast, making it too difficult to see or too dangerous to negotiate the illicit gaze without risk of retribution or being revealed. The advantages of distance, however, are not to be overlooked: the avoidance of contact, odorless, faceless, anonymous, imperceptible, and above all harmless, as is the gaze of the hunter through his binoculars. The voyeuristic eye is able to bridge the distance actively as well as passively. It needs only to be supported by a growing arsenal of assistive instruments.

A classic example of the assisted voyeuristic gaze—and at the same time an exemplar of the cinematic voyeurism—is the 1954 Alfred Hitchcock film *Rear Window,* which was also jokingly called a "backyard peep show." The cinema is often regarded as the prime voyeuristic medium. Numerous films work with voyeuristic effects or motifs make voyeurism a direct subject of discussion. An example is the film *Peeping Tom,* produced and directed by Michael Powell in 1960, the title referring to the old English legend of Lady Godiva and Peeping Tom. (In the English language, *peeping tom* is a synonym for *voyeur.*) Television series such as *Big Brother* have popularized the interest in voyeuristic forms of media, inviting the participation of a large audience on a new level. Most recently, film, television, and video have had new competitors to their potential as voyeuristic media such as webcams and cybersex.

As a symbol of transparency and in relation to contemporary possibilities of glass construction, voyeurism can also become an aspect of modern architecture. The glass house is an architectural metaphor. The connections between transparency and secrecy, clarity and "We've nothing to hide" sincerity, frankness, and identity, which all are suggested by glass houses, are surprisingly complex and versatile. Life, similarly to glass architecture, so to speak, often takes place in a shop window. The visual participation in other people's lives afforded by glass architecture and the like also demonstrates socially performed identity: By showing what you have, you show who you are.

Traversing previously proscribed visual frontiers with newfound ease and detachment characterizes the increasing proliferation of contemporary voyeurism. French multimedia and performance artist Orlan purposely co-opts the technical possibilities of medical image production and uses them for the worldwide transmission of cosmetic operations of her own body. New theoretical analogies and correlations follow. Techniques for watching people that did traditionally exist before have been expanded in various ways because of present-day realities of mass electronic and satellite surveillance. Thus, it is justified to speak tendentiously of a global voyeurism.

Voyeurism is advancing as a global phenomenon. Increasingly, we live in glass houses; what was once kept secret is now open to public scrutiny. It is fair to ask whether a world characterized by total transparency is at the cusp of a new utopia or an inevitable insurrection and the grassroots abolishment of voyeurism as we know it today.

Peter Springer

See also Gaze; Scopophilia; Visualizing Desire

Further Readings

Bonnet, J. (2006). *Die Badende. Voyeurismus in der abendländischen Kunst* [The (female) bather. Voyeurism in Western art]. Berlin: Parthas.

Clarke, J. R. (1998). *Looking at lovemaking: Constructions of sexuality in Roman art 100 B.C.–A.D. 250.* Berkeley: University of California Press.

Levin, T. Y., Frohne, U., & Weibel, P. (Eds.). (2002). *CTRL [SPACE]: Rhetorics of surveillance from Bentham to Big Brother.* Cambridge: MIT Press.

Öhlschläger, C. (1996). *"Unsägliche Lust des Schauens." Die Konstruktion der Geschlechter im voyeuristischen Text* [Unspeakable sensual pleasure of looking. The construction of gender in the voyeuristic text]. Freiburg, Germany: Rombach Verlag.

Springer, P. (2008). *Voyeurismus in der Kunst* [Voyeurism in art]. Berlin: Reimer.

WAR

War, which can be broadly defined as armed conflict between groups of persons, has been a perennial feature of the human condition. Yet, despite its ubiquity and importance, the true nature of war is complex. Though the "total wars" of the 19th and 20th centuries have prompted many to think of war solely in terms of pitched battles between massive, technologically sophisticated armies, many scholars of warfare contend that such a style of war making is actually only a relatively recent phenomenon in world history. Today, new forms of warfare—terrorism, guerilla insurgencies, genocide, or even large-scale police actions to combat piracy or organized crime—are transforming how and why people fight each other, with important strategic and human consequences. This entry provides an overview of the current debate concerning the nature of warfare framed by the classic work of the Prussian general Carl von Clausewitz, describes the importance of just war theory in understanding armed conflict, and suggests ways in which war influences the understanding of identity.

Clausewitz and Beyond

In *A History of Warfare,* the British military historian John Keegan argues that war is not a monolithic phenomenon but a diverse practice that is both culturally and historically situated. People have fought each other throughout human history, but combatants' understandings of the nature and purpose of war, the technologies that they have had at their disposal, and the ways in which they have conducted themselves in battle have contributed to profoundly different approaches to fighting. Wars fought between states are different from those fought between ethnic groups, for instance, and wars of national survival are different from wars fought for primarily ceremonial reasons.

Keegan's work emphasizes the need to recognize the importance of these differences and to encounter military theorists and their theories as reflective of particular cultural and military traditions. For the Israeli military historian Martin van Creveld, these traditions can be engaged by asking five interrelated questions: *By whom is war fought? What is war all about? How is war fought? What is war fought for?* And, finally, *Why is war fought?* In asking these questions, van Creveld draws attention to the ways in which the nature of war can change depending on the involvement of professionalized armies or irregular forces; the fundamental assumptions and norms that guide the conduct of war; the strategies, tactics, and technologies deployed; the interests or reasons that are understood to justify war; and the sense of meaning or overarching purpose that inspires combatants to fight.

Such perspectives encourage readers to encounter texts like Sun Tzu's *The Art of War* through the eyes of its ancient Chinese author instead of their own preconceptions. The corporate executives and military strategists who currently read *The Art of War* to position themselves against the threats in their midst may be startled to find a Confucian military theory that is often at odds with Western expectations. Though its 13 chapters certainly address topics that have since then become the stock-and-trade of military strategy—building strategic advantage, strategic deception, and so on—Sun Tzu encourages generals to harmonize themselves and their forces within the *tao* or "way" of battle through the careful balance of their strengths and weaknesses. Keegan notes that this emphasis on harmony, which is described through natural metaphors, contributes to an unexpectedly conservative approach to conflict, in which destroying the enemy's forces always comes second to preserving one's own. In many ways, *The Art of War* is not the art of combat but the art of developing and using one's strategic capacities to avoid combat and bloodshed altogether.

Clausewitz's *On War,* perhaps the definitive statement of the modern war-making tradition, rejects Sun Tzu's ideal of bloodless warfare as naive. Drawing from the experience of the Napoleonic wars and the intellectual foment of modernity, Clausewitz places armed conflict within the context of the burgeoning mass societies of industrial Europe. For Clausewitz, war making is a fundamentally political phenomenon that constantly triangulates among what he describes as the *strange trinity* formed by the government, the military, and the people. Much like Machiavelli, whose recovery of the classical war-making tradition also emphasizes the importance of military power attached to the state, Clausewitz believes that warfare is always conducted by the army in pursuit of the state's rational political self-interest, even as the more irrational forces of public opinion may seek to force the war's strategic direction in one way or another. By understanding and negotiating the relations and calculations of these overlapping sectors of society, *On War* sees armed conflict not as an aberration of social life but as something inextricably connected to—and a necessary consequence of—human life together.

Van Creveld argues that Clausewitz's contention that war is a product of mass society leads almost necessarily to the conception of total war, in which all of a society's resources become focused on achieving victory in what Clausewitz understands to be a zero-sum game. For Clausewitz, the concentration of forces necessary for such strategic victory is an organizational and technological problem, in which bureaucratic organization and constant technological advancement play important parts in developing the rationalized efficiency necessary to achieve overwhelming strategic advantage. As a centralized strategic planner, the commanding general and his staff become the animating consciousness of a vast military machine, minimizing instances of inefficiency—which Clausewitz describes through the metaphor of *friction*—and gathering the mathematical, geographic, and statistical information necessary to reduce the inherent uncertainty of war. In contrast to Sun Tzu's emphasis on the limitation of casualties and fighting, Clausewitz contends that the general and his staff must approach their task with grim indifference toward those under their command. Whether through a series of direct blows or a war of attrition, he contends, war is an inherently bloody endeavor that must be prosecuted ruthlessly in pursuit of the state's political self-interest.

Whether or not one agrees with its conclusions, Clausewitz's *On War* is a foundational text in the study of modern warfare, and the connections it makes between military force and political self-interest remain essential to contemporary debates in power politics. Yet, given the experiences of the 20th century, in which massive displays of military force led to two catastrophic world wars and a cold war that placed humanity on the brink of mutually assured destruction, many military historians have come to question the importance that has been placed on the text. B. H. Liddell Hart, a British historian and army officer during World War I, blames Clausewitz's militarism and emphasis on direct combat for almost single-handedly causing the horrors of the trenches. Other critics, however, are more nuanced in their approach. *On War* captured the 19th-century imagination, Keegan contends, because Clausewitz's understanding of warfare spoke directly to conditions that were already present in European culture, which was steeped in nationalistic fervor, committed to unfettered technological progress and bureaucratic rationality, and enamored with military valor. Keegan's reading of Clausewitz's classic text has important practical implications. Keagan argues that for all its emphasis on rational objectivity and pretensions of definitiveness, *On War*'s conclusions about armed conflict are not absolute but conditioned by the demands of a particular historical moment and that, as conditions change, our understanding of armed conflict will change as well.

Even as Clausewitz remains important in the fields of military planning and defense policy, scholars such as van Creveld are rethinking Clausewitzian orthodoxy to meet the emerging threats of the 21st century. In response to Clausewitz's emphasis on technological development and massive concentration of force, van Creveld contends that the massive concentration of nuclear and conventional forces—which, he notes, has led to 95% of the world's military might being confined to only a handful of nations—has made the armies of advanced nations *less* relevant on the world stage than ever before. As Clausewitzian military planners seek to expand their already massive technological superiority to meet what van Creveld describes as *high-intensity conflicts,* other threats, particularly terrorism, guerilla insurgencies, genocide, and violent criminal activity, have emerged in spaces that have historically been ignored. Van Creveld describes these threats as *low-intensity conflicts,* not because they are less violent but because they occur in less developed regions without the professional armies or sophisticated weapons systems deployed by advanced nations. Low-intensity conflicts are not only extraordinarily costly in terms of human life—van Creveld describes them as "warre" in the Hobbesian sense—but also extraordinarily difficult, if not impossible, for Clausewitzian armies to meet successfully. Sophisticated and expensive weapons systems designed to fight professional armies are suddenly useless against enemies that readily use civilians as cover, and armies designed to serve the political wills of nation-states are easily frustrated by transnational threats.

Most important, van Creveld notes how low-intensity conflicts disturb the very foundation of Clausewitz's definition of war, which assumes that war can always be reduced to rational political interests and that conflicts can be resolved by appealing to those interests. When modern states encounter low-intensity conflicts like acts of terrorism or genocide that are driven by deep-seated ethnic hatreds, religious differences, or ideologies that seem "fanatical," the result is typically a mixture of bemusement, confusion, and military failure. Such reactions are not unusual. Indeed, Keegan notes how Clausewitz reacted with horrified confusion when he encountered the Cossacks, whose marauding warrior culture was categorically different from the staid, professionalized military tradition of European armies. In such a moment, advanced, "high-tech" militaries are increasingly called to move beyond Clausewitzian orthodoxy to discover new ways of meeting these emerging, "low-tech" threats.

Just War

Both Keegan and van Creveld note that war occurs for any number of reasons, only a few of which have anything to do with Clausewitz's emphasis on political "interests." What is more, a society's understanding of what war is and what armed conflict should achieve places important restraints on fighting. Wars fought for primarily ceremonial purposes, for instance, may cease as soon as there is bloodshed, and wars fought for the sake of glory may be restrained by strict codes of honor.

In the Clausewitzian conception of war as an extension of politics, war is limited by political calculation, ending only when the enemy is destroyed, when fighting is not in the state's strategic interest, or when some other objective is achieved. As both Keegan and van Creveld note, the Western intellectual tradition before Clausewitz understood war not as an extension of *politics* but as an extension of *justice.* Understanding war as justice by other means limited combat by placing it within the framework of what is known as *just war.* Though just war theory began with the reflections of Christian thinkers like Augustine and Thomas Aquinas, it developed into a broad tradition of religious and secular ethical reflection about warfare and its possible limitations. Political philosopher Michael Walzer observes that because war inevitably involves killing and the destruction of property, proponents of a just war framework recognize that armed conflict is always a grave moral matter. Just war theorists proceed by determining whether or to what extent a particular conflict meets certain publicly acknowledged criteria or "tests"; this allows just war theorists to assess the relative "guilt" or "innocence" of the warring parties and the justifiability of their responses before, during, and after hostilities.

The standards of just war are high. At the outset of hostilities, for instance, parties must show proper grounds for going to war (*jus ad bellum*), and once hostilities begin, they must adhere to certain standards of military conduct (*jus in bellum*). For van Creveld, parties seeking to establish the justice of their cause must show that the war is being fought with the legitimate authority of a government that has the support of the people; that the war is being fought with the intent of addressing a specific and appropriate grievance, such as keeping the peace or addressing a clearly justifiable wrong; and that the military prosecuting the war uses force that is proportionate to the threat. Walzer's treatment of just war, however, suggests additional criteria. Because, according to just war theory, armed conflict must always be the course of last resort, parties must establish (a) that they have exhausted ordinary means of resolving the conflict, (b) that the war would have tangible benefits that outweigh the harms that it will inevitably inflict, and (c) that the parties would have a good chance of attaining their objectives. Furthermore, parties must show that the safety of noncombatants has been respected and that the war has resulted in a "just peace" acceptable to all sides.

In an age of nuclear weapons and other weapons of mass destruction, the notion of just war and its various tests have become controversial. Walzer notes the ways in which policy realists dismiss the framework of just war as irrelevant—indeed, Clausewitz summarily declares such strictures to be nonsense—while pacifists reject the notion of a "just" war altogether. The terrorist attacks of September 11, 2001, and U.S. involvement in Iraq and Afghanistan have further tested the criteria of just war by raising important questions about the proper response to enemies who reject the conventions of just war, the problems of "preventative war" in response to uncertain intelligence reports, and the proper treatment of those detained during military action. Though these questions present significant and difficult challenges to just war theory, van Creveld contends that the notion of just war continues to remain relevant, because the men and women who fight and die in war always need to establish that the justice of their cause outweighs their sacrifice. As the challenges of war change, reflection continues to be necessary to establish the conventions and criteria that make armed conflict intelligible, legitimate, and limited.

War and Identity

Scholars of warfare universally recognize that war is an extreme environment that has important and far-reaching effects on those touched by it. Indeed, the methodical training and discipline that Clausewitz demands are intended to help soldiers caught in the middle of battle to survive the trauma of combat. Yet war and the effects of war are not confined to combatants alone. Today, the mass migrations of refugees, humanitarian crises, and programs of ethnic cleansing emerging from low-intensity conflicts have significant political, cultural, and psychological implications that extend far beyond those immediately involved in the fighting.

Warfare also has more indirect effects on society and culture. Perhaps the subtlest effect emerges in how military metaphors have come to penetrate the everyday conversation of the postindustrial marketplace, as executives consult Sun Tzu in developing business plans, the military language of "strategies" and "tactics" predominates in corporate discourse, and the business world matter-of-factly expects the same level of strategic aggressiveness and calculation that Clausewitz expects of his generals. The interrelationship is not accidental. Observers of Clausewitz's military theory often note the interrelationship between his understanding of the creation and deployment of military force and the broader development of bureaucratic organizations and technological progress that occurred throughout the 19th and 20th centuries. Clausewitz sees strong parallels between warfare and the competition between business interests, which he understands to be an essential part of the political life of states. At the same time, however, this subtle interrelationship also has significant ethical and social implications that can go unnoticed by those embedded in it.

Scholars have also noted the important implications of war for our understanding of gender. For instance, Keegan shows how much Clausewitz's understanding of warfare both reflected and informed the European understanding of masculinity that was predominant during the 19th and early 20th centuries. For generations of European men, Keegan contends, war and military service were understood to be vital rites of passage, the crucible where honor and courage were simultaneously tested and forged. Van Creveld notes the forgotten place of women in this cult of masculinity—a fact that is especially true of Clausewitz's text, which contains no reference to women at all—and he observes that war remains a deeply gendered phenomenon, an area of human existence in which men and women are still kept separate. For military studies, this omission is particularly tragic, not only because it ignores the heroic contributions of the women who have fought and died in war but also because women and their children are particularly vulnerable to the effects of war, including displacement, starvation, and rape. For van Creveld, acknowledging the presence and contributions of women in war is an essential but nevertheless missing part of military theory, as women increasingly become active participants in war and increasingly face the consequences of low-intensity conflicts that directly target noncombatants.

In his cultural history of war, Keegan raises a provocative question that has important implications for those who seek to understand the human person: Is war an inevitable part of human nature? Are people naturally warlike or naturally collaborative and peaceful? Keegan finds no easy answer to that question, suggesting instead that warfare, while perhaps not intrinsic to human nature, is a *habit* that has become so ingrained that it has become second nature to human life. For this reason, he concludes, although war will always exist and armies of some sort will always be necessary, war itself—how it is fought and understood—remains a habit that can, and perhaps must, be changed.

C. T. Maier

See also Conflict; Terrorism

Further Readings

Clausewitz, C. von. (1971). *On war* (O. J. Matthijs Jolles, Trans.). New York: Random House. (Original work published 1832)

Keegan, J. (1993). *A history of warfare*. New York: Knopf.

Liddell Hart, B. H. (1991). *Strategy* (2nd rev. ed.). London: Meridian.

Sun Tzu. (1993). *The art of warfare* (R. T. Ames, Trans). New York: Ballantine.

van Creveld, M. (1991). *The transformation of war: The most radical reinterpretation of armed conflict since Clausewitz*. New York: Free Press.

Waltzer, M. (1992). *Just and unjust wars* (2nd ed.). New York: Basic Books.

WHITENESS STUDIES

As an academic field, *whiteness studies* began in the 1990s for the purpose of critically examining what it means to be White in the United States. Black writers such as James Baldwin and W. E. B. Du Bois wrote about whiteness much earlier. Du Bois defined whiteness as ownership of the earth. David Roediger defined whiteness as a destructive ideology exercising political force despite its discrediting as a culture, meaning that though many White people do not recognize that they have a race, they have been given profound systematic advantages. In fact, Ruth Frankenberg found that her research participants experienced being White as unmarked and unnamed. Christine Sleeter wrote that characteristics of whiteness include ravenous materialism, competitive individualism, and a way of living characterized by putting acquisition of possessions above humanity.

Because naming White as a racial category with advantages was not previously included in the academic curriculum, whiteness studies is considered a suppressed history. Though whiteness studies is often traced to the writings of Black intellectuals as early as David Walker's *Whites as Heathens and Christians* in 1830, its inclusion in the academic curriculum was spurred by mostly White writers and intellectuals who study history, literature, labor movements, economics, popular culture, identity development, and communication. Because of its interdisciplinary nature, whiteness studies has no specific journals, professional associations, book series, or academic departments in the United States, though a professional association exists in Australia. Nonetheless, the field has offered provocative scholarship exposing the problem of whiteness. There is an international whiteness studies movement with scholarship coming from

Canada, the United Kingdom, and Australia as well as the United States. This entry focuses on whiteness studies as it pertains to the United States.

The Beginnings of Whiteness Studies

Black writers were the first to write about whiteness. Du Bois offered that though the degradation of others is as old as humankind, Europe discovered the eternal worldwide mark of meanness—color. Baldwin wrote that White people realize that the history written by White people is mythic but that White people do not know how to release themselves from the myth. Subsequently, White people suffer from the incoherence of claiming to be perpetuators of justice and democracy while being appallingly oppressive. Whiteness studies offers a means for White people to release themselves by naming and recognizing their ancestors' role in past oppression and their current benefits as a group and as individuals from these acts.

In addition to Roediger, Noel Ignatiev is consistently associated with whiteness studies. Roediger wrote that the field's foundational texts would include Alexander Saxton's *The Rise and Fall of the White Republic: Class Politics and Mass Culture in Nineteenth-Century America*, written in 1990, and Toni Morrison's *Playing in the Dark: Whiteness and the Literary Imagination*, published in 1992. Acknowledging the field's impetus, Roediger's 1998 edited book *Black on White* offers examples of what Black writers had to say about White people.

Current Concepts in Whiteness Studies

The body of literature encapsulating whiteness studies includes the intersections of the social construction of race with antiracist consciousness-raising and the analyses of the culture of whiteness, immigration to the United States, and economics of labor practices. Because whiteness studies cannot be described without an understanding of the literature that defines it, overlapping themes of whiteness studies are described here along with a few examples of authors and their works. These are not exclusive categories of themes but rather porous intersections of topics that are common throughout the field of whiteness studies.

Social Construction of Race

The cornerstone of whiteness studies is the understanding that race is socially constructed. Race is not a natural phenomenon but rather was created by White men to advantage themselves and disadvantage others. Means of separating humans into racial groups is based on social models that represented scientists' biases and attitudes of the time rather than on biological fact. Current-day biologists and anthropologists agree that there is no organic fact of race. Means used today to identify human groupings, such as through antibodies and DNA, have no correlation with racial groupings. However, there are profound historical and current-day social implications of race. Ignatiev wrote that Africans were not enslaved because they were Black; rather, they were defined as Black because they were enslaved.

Ivan Hannaford's 1996 *Race: The History of an Idea in the West* is a detailed historical account of how early Greek philosophical writings planted the seeds for the creation of the idea of race that was nourished by European scientists in the 1500s and refined in the 1700s into racial groupings we can recognize today. Frankenberg's edited book *Displacing Whiteness* contains essays that expose current-day repercussions of the social construction of race.

Attention has also been paid to the *role* that place or geography has had on the social construction of race. For example, Joe Kincheloe and William Pinar, in several essays as well as in a 1991 edited book, explore the significance of the U.S. South as a place of slavery, a place under attack, and a place where people are longing for atonement.

Antiracism

When they first hear of whiteness studies, some people perceive it to be connected to White supremacy groups, when in fact whiteness studies exposes the detriments of White supremacy to all people. A goal of whiteness studies is the erasure of racism and other oppressions from society. This can occur first through the recognition that racism exists. Raphael Ezekiel's 1995 text *The Racist Mind* is an account of extreme racism from inside neo-Nazi and Ku Klux Klan groups. However, more numerous antiracist works are memoirs of

White scholars reflecting on their lives in White communities where extreme racism, as well as more subtle forms of racism, was rampant. These include Melton McLaurin's *Separate Pasts: Growing Up in the Segregated South* (1987), Mab Segrest's *Memoir of a Race Traitor* (1999), Timothy Tyson's *Blood Done Sign My Name* (2004), and Tim Wise's *White Like Me: Reflections on Race From a Privileged Son* (2005). These books offer personal experiences of the emotional and psychological cost of racism on both people of color and White people. These authors expose how they were influenced by those around them to continue racist practices and also to become antiracist activists.

Joel Kovel's *White Racism: A Psychohistory* (1970), Roediger's *Towards the Abolition of Whiteness* (1994), and Benjamin Bowser and Raymond Hunt's edited volume *Impacts of Racism on White Americans* (1996) analyze the costs of racism to White Americans and to their institutions and organizations.

It is one thing to read about whiteness and quite another to discover how one can and should act once knowing about whiteness. Subsequently, there is an application aspect to whiteness studies. Several authors have addressed the "so what now what" aspect of whiteness studies. They include Allen Johnson's 2006 book *Privilege, Power and Difference,* in which he offers a chapter titled "What Can We Do?" Paul Kivel's book *Uprooting Racism: How White People Can Work for Justice,* written in 1995, also advocates for ways in which people can fight racism. There is also novel work being reported in the area of ally development in higher education. Allies are those people who work to confront oppression when they are not the targets of that oppression. In their study on racial justice ally development, Robert Reason, Elizabeth Roosa Millar, and Tara Scales found that college students were more likely to become racial justice allies when they were invited to participate in opportunities to reflect on their racial identity. This was especially the case in structured experiences such as in coursework and activities that involved people of color. Opportunities to work with other allies encouraged students to continue to be not only allies but mentors for allies. These researchers found that their study participants responded to specific and concrete opportunities for action.

European Immigration

Roediger and Ignatiev, as well as others, have written about how immigrants to the United States considered race both before coming and after having arrived. It has been noted that one of the first aspects of American life learned by new immigrants is the "n" word. In instances of several immigrant groups from Europe, the abandonment of their national identity and complicit joining of a White racist identity allowed for a higher status above people of color. Ignatiev's 1995 work, *How the Irish Became White,* follows Irish immigrants as they left a country opposed to slavery and became supporters of a slavery state. Ignatiev noted that the misery of the Irish in the United States in the 1850s was severe. The life expectancy was only 6 years after arrival. Efforts of the Irish to gain rights similar to those of other White men conflicted with the efforts by free Blacks to maintain their right to work. Karen Brodkin's book *How Jews Became White Folks and What That Says About Race in America* (1998) and Roediger's 2006 book *Working Toward Whiteness: How America's Immigrants Became White: The Strange Journey From Ellis Island to the Suburbs* also expound on the racial mutation of immigrant groups.

Du Bois exclaimed that the public and psychological wage of whiteness led to many workers defining themselves as White, yet at a cost. Authors of whiteness studies acknowledge whiteness as a prize but verify that it comes at a cost of sacrificing the moral self and an ethnic heritage.

Culture of Whiteness

Several articles on whiteness studies proposed that there were two disagreeing camps within whiteness studies. One camp promotes the existence of a White culture and White subcultures. Writers in this group include cultural critics such as Fred Pfeil, who, in *White Guys* (1995), analyzed White rock and Wild West cultures. In 1997, Matt Wray and Annalee Newitz edited *White Trash,* which illuminated cultural characteristics of poor Whites. Ignatiev advocates for the abolition of whiteness, which necessitates the resistance of the perks that come with being White. Ignatiev claims that without privilege, there would be no significance to White as a racial marker. In fact, he wants to destroy the meaning associated with race. For many years, he edited a newsletter and later a journal called *Race Traitor,* which carried the motto "treason to whiteness is loyalty to humanity." Today there is a "Race Traitor" online journal.

Class and Labor Studies

How race influences socioeconomic status and labor practices in the United States and around the globe is another theme of the genre that is whiteness studies. The struggles of poor White people and their perception of race against the mainstream myth that the poor in the United States are solely Black and urban is a reoccurring topic of analysis. According to Roediger, whiteness scholarship reflects Marxist commitments to social problems. In her book *The Politics of Whiteness* (2001), Michelle Brattain examined how racial discrimination and hence occupational segregation contributed to the definitions of race. She maintains that jobs are important representations of racial identity. This mirrors the notion of Black feminist scholar Patricia Hill Collins that White people are their work, whereas Black people do their work.

Tensions Within Whiteness Studies

In addition to the disagreement over the existence or nonexistence of White culture, there also is tension over other aspects of whiteness studies. First, why might it be that though early Black authors wrote about whiteness, it took White authors writing about whiteness to move the field into academia? White authors had to legitimize whiteness studies in order for it to gain entry as a field. This phenomenon is exactly what whiteness studies authors are trying to expose and eliminate: the privilege and advantage of White people.

Moreover, by writing about whiteness, White authors are accepted as genuine contributors to the multicultural and social justice paradigm in ways they were not previously. Paradoxically, the bulk of what traditionally was taught in schools and colleges was the history, literature, and experiences of White people. However, it was not labeled as such, but rather as universal scholarship. The European American experience had been studied for quite some time and without critique. Whiteness studies offers a critique of the mythic America where people succeed based on merit alone. However, in adding whiteness studies to the curriculum, it adds more in the curriculum about White people. At least now it is a critical look.

There is also a concern from whiteness studies authors of generalizing too broadly about the experiences of White people. Some authors fear that offering too generalized a picture of whiteness does not adequately express the complexities of society and lived experience. Whiteness studies attempts to offer complexity to its interdisciplinary subjects—history, economics, psychology, and education about poor and rural White people as well as those who are rich, middle class, and suburban. In addition, where might the new scholarship on multiracial people and their experiences be placed? Proponents of White racial identity models and ally identity development models promote the notion that advocating for social justice is a developmental task, emphasizing that descriptors of White people (like all people) should be nuanced and multifaceted. Educators and psychologists believe that through individual customary cognitive development, in addition to educational efforts, racist attitudes and behaviors can be eliminated.

Lastly, if the purpose of whiteness studies is to eliminate the notion of whiteness, does writing about it help achieve this intent, or does whiteness become more legitimized by holding whiteness up to the microscope? Most whiteness scholars would concur that exposing and problematizing whiteness are necessary. Before a social problem can be eliminated, it must first be exposed, defined, and dissected. This process then allows society to begin to forge a way to enact solutions without its racist underpinnings.

Criticism of Whiteness Studies

Such provocative scholarship as whiteness studies has received intense criticism from outside the field. *Newsweek* magazine reported in 2003 that Ignatiev was one of the 10 most dangerous minds in the United States. Whiteness studies has been called a leftist philosophy, a derogatory term for Western civilization, and important only to those who think ethnic studies has not made sufficient progress in challenging Anglo-American bias, Roediger wrote that whiteness studies has become a lightning rod for critics. This is partly because whiteness studies is not specialized but rather crosses several disciplines; a cursory glance often misses its broad narratives and impact. It is also the case that whiteness studies questions some of our most profound assumptions about U.S. society. The existence of criticism suggests that whiteness studies is taken seriously.

Jan Arminio

See also Culture, Ethnicity, and Race; White Racial Identity

Further Readings

Bailey, P. (2003, July 14). World without "white." *Newsweek*, p. 7.

Baldwin, J. (1998). On being White . . . and other lies. In D. R. Roediger (Ed.), *Black on White: Black writers on what it means to be White* (pp. 177–180). New York: Schocken Books. (Original work published 1984)

Breines, W. (2006). *The trouble between us: An uneasy history of White and Black women in the feminist movement*. Oxford, UK: Oxford University Press.

Collins, P. H. (1991). *Black feminist thought: Knowledge, consciousness, and the politics of empowerment*. New York: Routledge.

Du Bois, W. E. B. (1998). The souls of White folks. In D. R. Roediger (Ed.), *Black on White: Black writers on what it means to be White* (pp. 184–199). New York: Schocken Books. (Original work published 1920)

Fears, D. (2003, June 20). Hue and cry on "whiteness studies": An academic field's take on race stirs interest and anger. *Washington Post*, p. A01.

Frankenberg, R. (1993). *White women, race matters: The social construction of whiteness*. Minneapolis: University of Minnesota Press.

Goldstein, E. (2006). *The price of whiteness: Jews, race, and American identity*. Princeton, NJ: Princeton University Press.

Ignatiev, N. (1995). *How the Irish became White*. New York: Routledge.

Jacobson, M. F. (2006). *Roots too: White ethnic revival in post–civil rights America*. Boston: Harvard University Press.

Negra, D. (2006). *The Irish in us: Irishness, performativity, and popular culture*. Durham, NC: Duke University Press.

Reason, R. D., Roosa Millar, E., & Scales, T. C. (2005). Toward a model of racial justice ally development. *Journal of College Student Development, 46*, 530–546.

Roediger, D. R. (1994). *Towards the abolition of whiteness*. London: Verso.

Roediger, D. R. (Ed.). (1998). *Black on White: Black writers on what it means to be White*. New York: Schocken Books.

Roediger, D. R. (2006, July 14). Whiteness and its complications. *The Chronicle of Higher Education*, p. B5.

Sletter, C. (1996). White silence, White solidarity. In N. Ignatiev & J. Garvey (Eds.), *Race traitor* (pp. 258–265). New York: Routledge.

Talbot, M. (1997, November 30). Getting credit for being White: Porn theory and queer scholarship were last year's college news. The latest academic trend: Whiteness studies. *The New York Times Magazine*, pp. 116–119.

Yemma, J. (1997, December 21). "Whiteness studies": An attempt at healing. *Boston Sunday Globe*, pp. A1, A40.

WHITE RACIAL IDENTITY

White racial identity refers to how White people conceptualize their sense of self as members of the White race. A person's racial identity is influenced by a complex mixture of environmental forces (e.g., familial attitudes, geography), individual attributes (e.g., cognitive development), and personal life experiences. For many White individuals, an extremely influential aspect of racial identity is being a member of the numerical majority and the socioeconomic and political dominant group. White racial identity models have been created as a way to understand how White people could escape the effects of living in a racist society. Two theorists who are most connected with White racial identity development are Janet Helms and Rita Hardiman. Both began their work within the same 5-year period (1979–1984) but did so independently. Both models propose a progression toward a personal responsibility and abandonment of racism. The discussion here focuses mostly on the work of Helms because she has attempted to verify the model through empirical research.

Though initially considered a stage theory, whereby a person moves through a linear process of increased acknowledgement of racism and consciousness, Helms replaced her initial concept of "stage" with "statuses" to better communicate that people can act and have attitudes at all levels simultaneously but have one status from which to behave most comfortably.

Progression Through Helms's White Racial Identity Development

According to Helms, there are two phases of White racial identity development: overcoming racism and developing a positive sense of self as a White person. The statuses in the abandoning racism phase are contact, disintegration, and reintegration. The statuses of pseudo independence, emersion, and autonomy lead one to a positive sense of self as a White person.

Contact

Contact is the status of White people who are becoming aware that different racial groups exist. Depending on where an individual lives, this could occur at a very young age or not until early adolescence. Television has allowed White people in secluded areas to become more aware of people of other racial groups at an earlier age than in the past. Racial naïveté could be a simple description of contact. Even if people realize that people of other races exist, people in contact do not believe that there are consequences of belonging to a particular racial group. Common contact statements include, "I'm color blind," "I don't see race," or "I belong to the human race." All the while, this person is benefiting from racism. Consequently, this person remains satisfied with the racial status quo and judges people of color according to White cultural criteria. The longer the person remains segregated from people of color, the longer he or she will be most comfortable in acting from a contact perspective.

Disintegration

Through socialization with people of color, White people usually discover that not all people are treated equally and that differences in treatment are often determined by racial group. For example, a White person may notice how often a colleague of color is stopped for speeding, asked to speak on behalf of his or her race, or singled out because of his or her race. The person may begin to feel guilty and anxious about such realizations. As these negative feelings increase, White individuals may attempt to alleviate the guilt and anxiety by avoiding any occasion to witness these inequities or by beginning to blame people of color for them. Moreover, the desire to be accepted by one's own White racial group influences one's racial belief system.

Reintegration

In this status, sometimes referred to as the "racist" status, to avoid guilt and anxiety, White people consciously acknowledge a White identity where they idealize people of their own race and grow intolerant of people in other racial groups. From the status of reintegration, they not only believe that bad things happen to bad people but that perhaps bad things should happen to people of color. Individuals in this status believe that White culture is superior and that White people are superior. Helms noted both a passive and an active aspect of reintegration. Reintegration behavior does not only entail outrageous and criminal behaviors such as joining hate groups and attending cross burnings (active reintegration) but also subtler behaviors, such as telling racist jokes, not welcoming people of color into one's community, only reading literature of one's cultural group, and only advocating for one's own needs (passive reintegration).

Pseudo Independence

Many White people can come to see, act, and behave beyond reintegration often through witnessing racist events or connecting racism to their own experiences of oppression (i.e., sexism, homophobia, classism, ableism). Through these connections, White individuals begin to understand the reality of oppression. This reality often occurs first as an intellectual exercise. People often begin to read about race and racism, attend lectures, and contemplate racial issues as they pertain to society at large. However, because at this point the White person has few White social justice mentors, he or she may want to help people of color become more like White people, rather than desiring to change the racist beliefs of White people.

Immersion/Emersion

In this status, White people begin to understand their individual responsibility in creating a more just society and the ways they personally benefit from racism. They begin to reflect upon their racist behaviors and those of people around them as well as the systematic nature of racism. They read biographies of White people who are antiracist activists, find mentors who are antiracist activists, and join groups that promote antiracist work. In addition, they assess their individual actions and contemplate how they must change their behaviors to create a more just society. Such individuals learn skills to confront others' racism and, in doing so, begin to take on a positive racial identity. Some feel liberated from previously held distortions of themselves and other racial groups. In this status, White people dive into (immersion) learning about their racial group and subsequently learn to work with other racial groups, diving from one's own group (emersion).

Autonomy

Though autonomy is a difficult status from which to behave consistently, people in this status work collaboratively with others to eliminate individual and systematic racism. To act in autonomy means to go against the status quo of White superiority. It means to confront racist practices, including those of supervisors, family members, friends, and teachers. One's commitment to confront racism can be measured by what one is willing to risk on behalf of it; in autonomy, White individuals take risks. In doing so, they feel positive about being White.

People use internal standards for defining themselves. They take advantage of opportunities to learn from other racial groups and become increasingly aware of the oppression of other stigmatized groups in addition to racial groups. Autonomy requires ongoing learning and action.

Application

White racial identity models were created as a way to understand how White people could escape the effects of living in a racist society. One of the foundations of White racial identity development is that as a result of socialization, it is difficult for White people to be immune to racist tendencies.

White racial identity development not only describes a model by which a White person can overcome racist attitudes and behaviors and come to have a positive White identity, but it also provides a means to better serve clients and students in a variety of settings. Because we live in an increasingly diverse society, and because making social justice reality requires cultural cohesion across differences, there is a need for the general population to become multiculturally competent.

Interactive Dyads

Helms created an interaction application model to demonstrate how the racial identity development of counselor and client dyads influences the counseling process. This model is based on the framework of parallel, regressive, and progressive relationships. A progressive relationship—the interaction dyad with the largest potential for growth—is a relationship in which the person with the most influence (i.e., the counselor, supervisor, or teacher) has developed a more complex racial identity than the person with less power (the client, student, or employee). For example, this would occur when a counselor is most often behaving from the status of autonomy and the client is most often behaving from the status of contact, disintegration, or reintegration in White racial identity or encounter in Black or people-of-color racial identity. Racial identity theorists believe that progressive relationships lead to a stronger counselor–client relationship, are more likely to not end prematurely, and offer the most potential for client growth.

A regressive relationship occurs when the person with the most influence or power in the relationship has a less complex racial identity. In this relationship, the client's growth is stifled. Because people of color typically learn about race and racial consequences earlier than do White people, it is not uncommon for the White "helper" to have a less sophisticated racial identity than the student or client of color. These relationships can be stifling if not harmful to clients of color.

Lastly, a parallel relationship is when the client and counselor share a racial identity worldview. It is the least contentious of the three types of interactions, but there is little potential for growth. The counselor, teacher, or supervisor is unable to challenge the client, student, or employee to think more complexly about race. This interaction model could also be helpful in other interactive dyads, such as in trying to understand and mediate conflicts.

Theory Validity

When Helms first proposed her model, the reintegration aspect of her model, in particular, was criticized. Some White people rejected the idea of reintegration because they did not join hate groups, burn crosses in lawns, or use racist language. However, it is argued that they failed to consider the subtler and more common forms of racial bias as behaviors and attitudes encompassed in reintegration. Subsequently, more authors and researchers have acknowledged the validity of both active and passive reintegration.

Whereas Helms's model is readily accepted by researchers, the instrument most associated with measuring White racial identity, the White Racial Identity Attitudes Scale (WRIAS), has come under scrutiny for psychometric reasons. When tested using factor and component analyses, the WRIAS scales do not consistently hold up independently, and the factors do not correspond to the theory. Other research indicates that the WRIAS has yielded adequate reliability estimates to measure factors such as White superiority/segregationist ideology, cross-racial competence and comfort, and interest in racial diversity. In essence, though the WRIAS has psychometric problems in measuring White racial identity development, it does measure important constructs of the theory. Furthermore, there is debate over whether White identity development is a theory of what White people should do and feel or rather what they are meant to do.

Some theorists question the conceptualization of Helms's White racial identity theory in that it was formulated on similar grounding as William Cross's Black racial identity development. Regardless of the psychometric concerns, the theory has had a major impact on the identity development expectations of White people.

Jan Arminio

See also Being and Identity; Culture, Ethnicity, and Race; Development of Identity; Development of Self-Concept; Whiteness Studies

Further Readings

Carter, R. T. (1997). Is White a race? Expressions of White racial identity. In M. Fine, L. Weis, L. C. Powell, & L. Mun Wong (Eds.), *Off white: Readings on race, power, and society* (pp. 198–211). New York: Routledge.

Cross, W. E., Jr. (1971). The Negro-to-Black conversion experience: Toward a psychology of Black liberation. *Black World, 20,* 13–27.

Hardiman, R. (2001). Reflections on White identity development theory. In C. L. Wijeyesinghe & B. W. Jackson III (Eds.), *New perspectives on racial identity development: A theoretical and practical anthology* (pp. 108–128). New York: New York University Press.

Helms, J. (1990). *Black and White racial identity.* Westport, CT: Praeger.

Helms, J. (1995). An update of Helms' White and people of color models. In J. G. Ponterotto, J. M. Casas, L. A. Suzuki, & C. M. Alexander (Eds.), *Handbook of multicultural counseling* (pp. 181–199). Thousand Oaks, CA: Sage.

Tatum, B. D. (2003). *Why do all the Black kids sit together in the cafeteria? And other questions about race.* New York: Basic Books.

Wing, L., & Rifkin, J. (2001). Racial identity development and the mediation of conflicts. In C. L. Wijeyesinghe & B. Jackson III (Eds.), *New perspectives on racial identity development: A theoretical and practical anthology* (pp. 182–208). New York: New York University Press.

WOMANISM

Womanism is a form of feminism that focuses on the perspectives and experiences of women of color. As a term, it has an often-quoted genealogy. In 1983, Alice Walker coined the term with a four-part definition in her text *In Search of Our Mother's Gardens.* The first part of the definition emphasizes the importance of women's handing down their wisdom from one generation of women to the next. The second part of the definition stresses communal thought and action. The third part of the definition critiques the standards of beauty Black women are subjected to. Finally, womanism is a critique of the limitations of White feminist thought and activism and its shortcomings in dealing with race and class. This etymology is the birthplace of *womanism* as a term but not as a tradition. In this entry, the etymology or history of the term is mentioned, but the focus is on the ways in which womanism functions as a theory, method of inquiry, and framework for identities.

Theorizing womanist rhetoric is about locating the cultural and theoretical narratives that place Black women at the center of their own narrative. This has been the overarching goal of womanist scholarship since its inception. This goal recognizes that for centuries, women in general and Black women in particular have been the oppressed subjects of "universalizing" European academic discourse.

Womanist scholars bring to academic theorizing their own historic locations and cultural, social, and political knowing. This knowing is born out of a place of liberation rather than a constant dwelling on the limiting discourse of oppression. This opens womanist scholarship up to new possibilities for theorizing. For womanists, theorizing happens primarily outside of the academy as a result of finding solutions to the problems that persist in the communities of women of color. Through womanist theorizing, scholars have created a paradigm and a discourse shaped as much by experiences as raced, classed, and gendered as by identities aligned as sexual, professional, or national.

The strength of womanist theorizing lies in the privileging of multiple identities in a singular body. This means that the womanist is understood to be gender/race/class/sex/family/friend/worker/nation. These are not mutually exclusive identity constructs that exist as boxes on shelves like so many pairs of shoes. Identities, unlike shoes, can be worn 40 at a time. Womanist theorists may be inclined to delete the slashes in this construct, preferring instead to argue that the strength in the theory is the ability to reveal the world as an interlocking narrative of genderraceclasssexfamilyfriendworkernation. Without punctuation to separate identities that are mutually informative and totally encompassing, womanists utilize all the cultural scripts available to investigate the world and articulate modes of change. The cultural scripts used to construct a worldview that gives moral agency to Africana women can be spiritual, academic, religious, literary, music, personal narrative, or all of these. The creation of womanist knowledge is mapped from local spaces to academic places. Walker's definition and coining of the term *womanism* came at a critical juncture for Black women

scholars who have developed a theory of womanism that privileges multiplicity in identity. The naming of the cultural identity *womanist* allowed for the construction of theory and theology that lead directly to epistemological centeredness.

Womanist Epistemology

Editors Marsha Houston and Olga Davis introduce the volume *Centering Our Selves* with the idea that in the daily lives of African American men and women, there is an acknowledgment of a cultural knowledge of survival. This cultural knowledge is expanded daily with the embodied narratives and performances of individuals within a given community. Coming out in a variety of ways in womanist scholarship, cultural knowledge appears in the womanist consciousness and informs narratives of self presented within this text. This section explores the ways in which the theory of knowledge is articulated as womanist ways of knowing, which are authenticated through communal discourses, both formal (academic) and informal (daily cultural interactions), by womanist scholars.

As a centralizing work that focuses on the ways in which social knowledge is constructed in African America, Patricia Hill Collins opens her text with a positioning of the discourses of Black women. For her, central to a discourse on Black feminism is that it be understood not as an offshoot of White feminist theories or movements but as a vital movement and theory that is unique. She recalls, in part, Walker's fourth part of the womanist definition, which critiques White feminist thought and activism. Collins is but one example in a long and varied list of scholars who use Walker's definition of *womanist* to center a formal epistemology of Black womanhood.

The use of Walker as a central access for womanist epistemology allows for a relational discourse of Black women's theories that centers her narratives as a valued part of the discourse. Collins begins the historical account of womanist thought with Maria Stewart, one of the first African American women to be granted an itinerate minister's license. This move locates womanist rhetoric as a semiotic relationship between race, class, and gender oppressions and predates Walker's use of the term. In hailing past discourses, womanist scholars create tangible links to cultural ways of knowing that exist outside of the formal structure of academe yet influence the ways in which theory is articulated within that context.

Womanist ways of knowing often begin in the informal cultural discourses that shape daily life. In the modern era, one could argue that womanist ways of knowing are informed as much by hip-hop as by the Bible. History and personal narrative are coconstructors of womanist knowledge in local and global ways. By using scholars, preachers, domestic workers, and political workers, womanist scholars articulate the variation in interpretations of womanist. What is most important is the diversity from which knowledge is created. Womanist takes on the notion that knowledges are created, shared, and maintained through various methods. We engage in information sharing in classrooms, living rooms, boardrooms, and chat rooms. Knowledge produced and perpetuated through and by the academy carries cultural weight; yet at the same time, localized knowledge is perhaps the most valuable to womanist scholars as they seek to ensure their communities survive and thrive.

Womanist Theology—Defining a Discourse

As part of the process of womanist theorizing, practitioners become a transparent and an active agent within the text. This does not mean that there is a rampant self-disclosure without reflection. Rather, it requires that the scholar consider herself or himself as both speaker and hearer of the text presented. In this way, one remains consistently engaged. In terms of womanist theology, this is particularly evident in the scholars who take on the definition of womanism and immediately put it to use in the American Academy of Religion. In the 25 years since these women first began to engage in womanist theology, there have been significant changes in the landscape of theological education. Much of that change is owed to the work of foundational womanist theologians. As scholars, these women and men expanded the academic space in which theologians of color could function. The contribution of womanist theology to womanist identity discourse is of central import. Most women of color find their primary institution of daily interaction outside of employment is with the church. As the number of seminary-trained preachers

increases, the influence of womanist theology on the daily lives of women also increases.

Womanist theologians define womanist theology as a theological tradition with sermonic roots that far extend its own short history. Womanist readings of the Bible support a narrative of Black women that is positive and productive for them and their communities. Three foundational theological texts were written between 1984 and 1995. Each text explores the questions of race and gender as identity constructs that influence the practices of religion. Each work of early womanist theology also served as a response to feminist theology and liberation theology, which are unique theological perspectives that deal with justice, race, gender, or all of these, as elements of a Christian hermeneutic.

As outsiders within, African American women engage in a process of theology building that takes on a critique of the limits of both feminist and liberation theologies. What is unique about their critique is that there is a legitimacy granted to both feminist and liberation hermeneutics, while at the same time African American women work toward a legitimating space of their own that centers the narrative of Christ in the experience of Black women.

In the introduction to *Katie's Canon*, the definition and development of womanist theology brings about a new methodology by which to view the work of African American women in the American Academy of Religion and the Society of Biblical Literature. Cannon comes to her explanation through some frustration with the limiting responses she received from other theologians who attempted to delegitimize Black women's voices. She developed a discourse of womanist theology that located the narrative of Christ and the redemption of the church within a space where African American women could thrive without apology or constant reminders of oppression. She argued that womanist theology provides a Christology that centers the salvation of women of color within the redemptive discourse of Christ. This means reading Christ as the savior of all and not the savior of the few.

The work of womanist theologians met with early resistance. Some read Walker's all-encompassing definition of *womanism* as one whose secular origins were not suitable for identity work within the narrow parameters of theology. Others insisted that it was time that theologies expand to allow the voices of a new generation of scholars and readers, each of whom may explore the meanings of religious text for an ever-expanding identity politic that looked at identities not as singularities but multiple actions and discourses. This meant necessarily interrogating dichotomies of theology, such as feminist (White) versus womanist (Black), while providing a critical response.

Some scholars, including Jacquelyn Grant, argue that womanist theology is more closely aligned with liberation theology. They demonstrate that womanist theology serves the purpose of liberating Black women from forms of Christology that subjugate and marginalize women of color. Grant explains that where feminist theologists might ask how or if Jesus can be the savior of women, womanist theologists look at why he is the savior of everyone, particularly those oppressed in society. What becomes central to Grant's argument is the humanity of African American women. Citing from the Old Testament through to contemporary movements by which Africana women experience firsthand the voice of God, Grant estimates that if God includes Africana women in his earliest works, then their humanity cannot be denied. She troubles the claim that it was only as slaves that Africana women had biblical significance, by calling the reader's attention to the number of wives and mothers whose Africanness is central to the teachable moments of the Holy Spirit. She argues that even as Christian slavery and its psychological residue attempted to erase or misrepresent the roles of biblical Africana women, the centrality of their existence in basic biblical narratives is so apparent that it becomes the theme of contemporary Black women's identity within the body politic of Jesus Christ. In this way, womanist theology becomes a continued discourse in the lives of women of color. It is these narratives that are then preached from pulpits around the world, that provide libratory moments.

Womanist Ethics and the Location of Authentic Voice

Womanist theology functions as a theory and method of inquiry. Similarly, womanist ethics provides contemporary womanist scholars with a means to discuss womanist identity politics. The ethic of voice in the womanist context is understood in terms of the speaker and the cultural community. Voice is the authentic telling of truth and knowledge that is agreed upon between the scholar and cultural community. Each possesses voice, and the ethic of voice is constituted by and through each person's presence.

Womanist ethics as theory and method centers the ethical and moral choices that Black women make as foundational discourse. Womanist ethics sets forth the argument that Black women are capable of, and engaged in, ethical behaviors and discourses. Womanist ethics speaks directly to the images, discourses, and actions, upheld by normative ethics, that support a racist ideology against Africana women. As a theory advanced in scholarly arenas, womanist ethics is grounded in the daily practices and talk of women who, in their lived experiences, speak back to normative ethics that seek to discount them.

The backbone of this ethic is a clear understanding of Black women's daily applications and interventions in a contemporary moment. The test of such theorizing, however, is the ability of a group of people to live the ethic of the community over time. Like womanist theology, womanist ethics and womanist rhetoric are rooted in the lives of Africana diaspora women in literary, historic, biblical, and present-day narratives. Karen Baker-Fletcher argues that only through the telling and hearing of women's stories are women's experiences articulated and that storytelling is the singular construction of womanist theological and ethical discourse.

It is through the telling of the personal past, both triumph and tragedy, that a Black woman develops an ethic of voice. Central to her ability to share her story is a womanist appeal to her moral center and the morality of her community. Next is her authority as a speaker. For an ethic of voice to be effective, a speaker must be viewed as having authority to speak with knowledge and discernment. This requires the speaker to be able to tap into her own narrative and locate that narrative within the cultural knowledge of the larger community. In this way, womanist theo-ethicist Stacey Floyd-Thomas argues for a method of doing womanist ethics research. This method uses several elements, including sacred text—both biblical and literary sources. She acknowledges that the systematic analysis of such sources is strictly an academic pursuit, yet the analysis is not foreign to the communities of Africana women. She argues that as women employ these sacred texts in their daily lives, they draw on the narratives as a source of strength, identity, and method through which to articulate resistance.

What is unique to womanist ethics is the idea that voice and narrative are central constructs for identity and community. As such, a woman is judged ethical through the way in which she tells her narrative and that of others. It is through discourse, as much as through action, that one is ethical. A primary example is seen in Toni Morrison's *Beloved* when Sethe tells of her choices in providing liberty to her children. Morrison presents a character who, when judged by normative standards, is unethical. However, in light of the unethical rules of slavery that make a body not human but property and yet also humanly and morally responsible for the act of murder, which is unethical, one sees the illogical demands of an impossible bind. Morrison's character sought her own narrative of ethic voice, one that understands the conundrum of multiple identities and the need for an ethic that privileges an ultimate truth: Only God can judge. Through the telling of the narrative, the character establishes an ethic of voice that allows the narrative of choice, liberty, and discernment to be of central importance. Womanist ethics is ultimately focused on the ways in which narrative choices give rise to ethical discourses that are practically and theoretically confirmed by the culture in which they exist.

Womanist Rhetoric

Womanist rhetoric is used as an umbrella to discuss the various formal and informal discourses entered into by African American women. These conversations center on the mental, physical, and spiritual health, wealth, and vitality of African American women and their community. This includes an active discourse about the roles of race, class, gender, and sexuality as normative social constructs. Critical to womanist rhetoric are authentic womanist voice, gendered cultural knowledge, and ethical discourse for salvation.

Authentic womanist voice creates an oppositional discourse to normative social constructs. The identities constructed through normative discourses function in both historic and contemporary frameworks to demean, exploit, and destroy Black bodies. Womanists employ an authentic womanist voice to privilege their standpoint as social agents. Womanist rhetoric seeks out the injustices within and outside of the Black community. Womanist social agents attempt to find humane and equitable solutions for the good of the whole community rather than simply the good of women.

Womanists employ gendered cultural knowledge as a way to contextualize the world around them. This is done through the use of narratives that contain gendered verbal, nonverbal, and paralinguistic cues. Central to gendered cultural knowledge are the ways of knowing that come through the narrative of Black women. Womanist intellectual tradition exists in and outside of the academy. As a narrative, womanist rhetoric is identifiable by its concern and search for equitable solutions to the problems of liminal identity discourses that play themselves out within and outside of the African diaspora. Gendered cultural knowledge is used to organize the narratives of Black women as solutions to the problem of normative identity discourses that exclude them and their unique ways of knowing.

Finally, womanist rhetoric contains an ethical discourse for salvation. Ethical discourse for salvation focuses on the ways in which Black women organize their narratives to privilege their salvation. This discourse is a response to normative Christology that does not articulate a way for Black women to attain salvation. Womanist social agents engage in ethical discourse for salvation through daily discourse, sermons, personal narratives, novels, and other forms.

Spaces for Men and Non-Black Womanists of Color

One of the most interesting and powerful aspects of womanism is its usefulness to theorists and practitioners of various identities. Where feminists tends toward exclusionary identity politics, limiting theoretical and practical space to those who share in a gendered female identity, womanists tend toward an open gender policy. Likewise, although the earliest womanist definitions tended to focus specifically on African American women, this has not limited the use of the theory to only women and men who choose to mark their bodies within the racial constructs of blackness.

There are spaces for practitioners of womanism that are not identified by the etymology of the term. African American womanist scholars have included the diverse intellectual traditions of race, class, sexuality, and gender in their inquiries. It is perhaps for this reason that scholars such as Gloria Anzaldúa, Eric King Watts, Wenshue Lee, Bernadette Calafell, Ronald L. Jackson II, and others are comfortable working from womanist paradigms of inquiry. Rather than be excluded from this location of inquiry, scholars who share the epistemological goals of womanism are encouraged to share in the intellectual work of equitable justice and discourse espoused by the womanist identity construct.

Toniesha Latrice Taylor

See also Afrocentricity; Diaspora; Gender; Language; Liberation Theology; Worldview

Further Readings

Baker-Fletcher, K. E. (1994). *A singing something: The literature of Anna Julia Cooper as a resource for a theological anthropology of voice.* New York: Crossroad.

Cannon, K. G. (1995). *Katie's canon: Womanism and the soul of the Black community.* New York: Continuum.

Collins, P. H. (2000). *Black feminist thought: Knowledge, consciousness, and the politics of empowerment.* New York: Routledge.

Floyd-Thomas, S. M. (2006). *Mining the motherlode: Methods in womanist ethics.* Cleveland, OH: Pilgrim Press.

Grant, J. (1989). *White women's Christ and Black women's Jesus: Feminist Christology and womanist response.* Atlanta, GA: Scholars Press.

Morrison, T. (1987). *Beloved.* New York: Penguin.

Walker, A. (1983). *In search of our mother's garden: Womanist prose.* New York: Harcourt Brace Jovanovich.

WORLD SYSTEMS THEORY

World systems theory (WST) is an interdisciplinary theoretical approach that advances an integrated framework for examining the development and evolution of the modern world under the transformative cultural, political, and economic effects of capitalism. Founding theorist Immanuel Wallerstein (1974) defined a world system as

> [a] social system, one that has boundaries, structures, member groups, rules of legitimation, and coherence. Its life is made up of the conflicting forces which hold it together by tension and tear it apart as each group seeks eternally to remold it to its advantage. It has the characteristics of an organism, in that it has a lifespan over which its characteristics change in some respects and remain stable in others. . . . Life within it is largely self-contained, and the dynamics of its development are largely internal. (p. 347)

Four fundamental conceptions are at the heart of WST. First, a world system is one social system with many interlocking parts. Contemporary polities are not societies, but pieces of one socioeconomic system expanding in the interests of capital. Second, a world system is characterized by economic conflict between varying polities, with the market as the chief stratifying force. Polities vie for access to, and control over, goods and services, while their uneven positions within the market produce distinct political and cultural effects. Third, a world system is structured by a core, semi-periphery, and periphery. The core consists of advanced liberal democratic societies that are industrialized, whereas the periphery remains underdeveloped and exploited for its labor and natural resources. The semi-periphery lies between the core and periphery and has more access to necessary goods and services but little control over the division of labor and flow of power to the core. Fourth, cycles of growth, contraction, contradiction, and crisis affect the evolution of a world system. Eventually, the world system of today will give way to an alternative social order.

WST's methodological approach draws from the fields of history, sociology, economics, and area studies. It has become a popular tool among scholars interested in the large-scale and long-term conceptions of historical development of global society, critical understanding of the evolution and plight of developing nations, and identity and identity formation within the social sphere. This entry discusses the rise of the modern world system, the theoretical influences and criticisms of WST, and the role of WST in identity and identity formation studies.

The Rise of the Modern World System

According to WST, there have been three social orders in human history: mini-systems, single-polity world empires, and multipolity world economies. Wallerstein located the origin of the modern multipolity world economy (i.e., the "modern world system") at the start of early European capitalist mercantilism. With the spread of capitalist hegemony, distant geopolitical entities were incorporated into a singular market-based economy characterized by a global division of labor. Unlike world empires—societies dominated by extensive political networks beholden to one political center—the capitalist economy produced a system in which multiple polities flourished under the expansion of a singular economic order. In this system, economic stratification became society's principle structuring factor.

World systems theorists argue that in the modern world system, society's core is made up of polities that established strong centralized governments, bureaucracies, armies, and cultural identities that allowed them to take part in the Industrial Revolution and colonialism. These states developed technologies and social networks that allowed them to produce and distribute complex goods and services and attain an economic edge over others. Over time, they fabricated diversified regional economies marked by cutting-edge information and service industries. Core states continue to have stable political orders that facilitate long-term economic planning and management while providing insulation from external political intervention. Conversely, polities that were previously colonized or did not make the agrarian-to-industrial transformation (states located in what many today term the *Global South*) have consistently been forced to supply natural resources that constitute those goods and services and provide free or cheap labor. Many continue to be exploited by foreign entities in conjunction with local ruling classes. These polities are internally polarized with respect to income, education, and citizen life chances, and the majority live far below the standards of core states. Some nations have entered the semi-periphery by way of gain or loss of stability in their political systems, alterations to the level of diversification in their local economies, or changes to the integrity of culture and quality of education within their borders. These nations may set trade policies with the core or periphery that benefit themselves, but they continue to contribute to the dominance of the core.

World system theorists recognize the United States as the elite core polity. Wallerstein delineated three types of economic dominance: productivity dominance (the ability to produce cheaper and better products for a lower price), trade dominance (the ability to sell more goods on the global market), and financial dominance (the ability to amass greater wealth and control the system's financial markets). Related to these types is military dominance, which, according to world systems theorists, can cause polities to lose wealth and status in the global economy. Wallerstein, for example, believes that the United States is losing its dominance as a result of costly and unpopular postwar military exploits.

Theoretical Influences

WST emerged at the nexus of Marxism, development theory, cyclical economics, and the Annales School of historical studies. Along with Marxism, WST takes a totalizing approach to humanity and human history. Within this grand social history, world systems theorists maintain that economic conflict is the driving factor of social formation, order, and change, and they consider social class as the dominant social structure. Thus, WST adheres to the historical materialist principle that describes social evolution as divisible by material (as opposed to ideal) stages of development. WST analyses are expressed in Marxian dialectical terms.

With Marxism, WST also focuses on the increasing alienation and estrangement of human labor, proletarianization, and the commodification and festishization of goods via an ever-expanding division of labor. World systems theorists agree that society's division of labor is best characterized by a ruling capital class (the core), which dominates a subordinate, exploited class (the periphery and semi-periphery). World systems theorists use the language of surplus value, capital accumulation, and uneven exchange to discuss social dynamics within the system. World systems theorists also draw upon Lucácsian and Gramscian notions of class consciousness and hegemony in order to reveal the powerful role ideas play in the world economy. Foremost, world systems theorists advocate for a socialist solution to the ills of the modern capitalist order.

Following brands of development theory popular at its emergence, world systems theorists oppose theories of modernization that assume the nation-state is the main agent in the struggle for modernization and that there is one trajectory that all polities must follow. Instead, world systems theorists view varying polities as interdependent and in flux. Likewise, they emphasize underdevelopment as a form of avertable socioeconomic exploitation. World systems theorists adopt the language of dependency theory—terms that highlight the uneven social relations between core and peripheral states. However, they augment traditional dependency theory with recognition of a liminal state that core and periphery move in and out of (the semi-periphery).

Finally, WST is drawn from major concepts in cyclical economics and Annales School historical studies. World systems theorists are particularly indebted to Joseph Schumpeter and Nikolai Kondratiev, two economists focused on rise-and-fall intervals pertaining to seismic economic shifts, for their critical expansion/constriction view of social history. WST is a combination of Schumpeter and Kondratiev's long-term cyclical perspective and an Annales School *longue durée* historiographical approach, wherein local events are portrayed in terms of broader historical dynamics and regional socioeconomic transformations are analyzed with an eye to larger systematic shifts.

Recent Debates

Economists, sociologists, and historians alike have criticized WST. Neoliberal and conservative economists have criticized WST primarily for its negative characterization of capitalism and globalization, its prediction of the eventual rise of socialism, and its characterization of core states as hegemonic entities. Sociologists have suggested that world systems theorists too often focus on elite institutions and dominant discourses. Many have, likewise, opposed the foregrounding of economic, as opposed to political or cultural, concerns. Historians have rejected specific historical evidence provided by WST analyses. In particular, broad characterizations of political booms and declines have come under fire for failing to prove the dominance of one or another polity in the drive for capitalist accumulation.

Internal theoretical and empirical debates also permeate the discourse. Some points of contention include what countries have constituted the core, semi-periphery, and periphery at a given time; exactly when the transition from world empire to world economy took place and who was at the helm of that change; whether the cycles of growth and decline are appropriate units of analysis for describing social change and, if so, how they map out over time; what constitutes hegemonic dominance in a modern world system; what constitutes growth or decline; what the relationship between colonialism and capitalism is and how processes between colony and metropole have informed broader systemic change; and what contemporary dynamics reveal about previous models.

Relationship to Identity

WST has inspired many scholars to criticize the uneven relations between advanced liberal democracies and less developed nations. It has provided a framework and language for analyzing local and historically particular instances of exploitation in terms of a larger humanistic picture. WST has become a popular tool for those writing revisionist histories and sociologies. One example is Eric Wolf's *Europe and the People Without History*, which drew together histories of local colonial economies to make a systematic critique of capitalism under colonialism. Histories of colonial contact and postcolonial effects are common themes in WST. Together, these critical studies promote a space for scholars to think relationally about identity, identity formation, and the categorical dichotomies that permeate today's social sphere. In particular, WST's focus on grand-scale intercontinental processes permits a critical viewpoint on the formation of racial concepts, the evolution of racial theories, and the effects of concepts and theories in the racial identities people assume today.

Catherine Bliss

See also Class; Colonialism; Globalization; Hegemony; Political Economy

Further Readings

Abu-Lugod, J. (1989). *Before European hegemony: The world system A.D. 1250–1350.* New York: Oxford University Press.

Chase-Dunn, C., & Grimes, P. (1995). World-systems analysis. *Annual Review of Sociology, 21,* 387–417.

Chirot, D., & Hall, T. D. (1982). World-system theory. *Annual Review of Sociology, 8,* 81–106.

Goldfrank, W. L. (2000). Paradigm regained? The rules of Wallerstein's world-system method. *Journal of World-Systems Research, 6,* 150–195.

Wallerstein, I. (1974). *The modern world system I: Capitalist agriculture and the origins of the European world-economy in the sixteenth century.* New York: Academic Press.

Wallerstein, I. (1984). *Politics of the world-economy: The states, the movements, and the civilizations.* Cambridge, UK: Cambridge University Press.

Wolf, E. (1982). *Europe and the people without history.* Berkeley: University of California Press.

WORLDVIEW

To posit a discussion of identity and worldview is to explore philosophical constructs of time, place, and culture. The components of a definition of oneself (*self* being a commonly accepted synonym for the *identity* of the human) change depending on the habitat of the human, the historical era in which he or she lives, and the culture to which his or her community subscribes.

One's worldview encompasses not only one's particular and individualized perspective on the common, mundane, and ordinary comings and goings of daily life but also a comprehensive and usually personal conception of the collective self, humanity in all its pluralities.

The word *worldview* comes from the German word *Weltanschauung.* It was first used in 1858 to denote a broad idea of the world, especially from a specific point of view. The term *worldview* can be further organized into perspectives on identity related to place (physical location on the globe), time (historical era), and culture. The intersections of identity, worldview, and culture are the centerpieces of this entry. The entry explores the roles played by the interpretations of religions, genders, politics, languages, fashions, and leisure activities in the formation of both individual and collective worldview identifications of self. It examines whether any of these constructs act as identity exemplars, as metaphors or similes for worldview identities of self.

Worldview, Identity, and Definitions

In the interest of understanding the conceptual frameworks of this discussion, operant definitions of *worldview* and *identity* must be established. A beginning point for the establishment of such definitions can be found in religious philosophy. Religion in this context is broadly and universally defined as the attention paid to the existence of metaphysical forces. And it is to this word *self* that religion, again in its broadest and most universal aspects, addresses it*self.* Believers in these metaphysical forces are assured that to know one*self* is indeed a prime directive. The *self,* as commonly defined in religious terms, refers to the essence of the human being. The study of self, as defined in this way, can be seen as part of the science of hermeneutics. For the quest for identity is indeed universal and subject to interpretation, oftentimes in terms of morality, values, and distinctions between the black and white philosophical poles of right and wrong. These subjects, of course, are the major axes along which religious thought is promulgated.

A survey of various dictionary definitions of *self* leads to the concepts of intention, knowledge, and cultural norms. As one unpacks these definitions, one learns that the self is essentially a singular, inner awareness of the human being. The self connects with the world, forming a singularly individual worldview, through its interpretation of its existence within a particular time frame, a discreet era in history. These periods or ages of human history (time) are characterized by unique circumstances of existence of specific cultural, philosophical, or religious mores. The self may even be projected onto the world stage in a futuristic way as is depicted in the popularity of science fiction. In summary, worldview meets identity in the focusing of the lens through which one envisions the world. Worldview is an aggregate set of values, an individual prism for interpreting reality. It is the outcome of thinking about the way things were, the way things are, or the way things could or should be.

The passage of time, whether counted in centuries or months, has a profound impact on one's individual worldview. Identity is extended to individuals at birth. Where, when, and even how one is born have lasting effects on the sense of self and what is possible for the self to achieve and to do. A 16th-century British royal female has in common only the country of birth with a 20th-century phenomenon like Princess Diana. Low-birth-weight, premature babies endure dreadful struggles to achieve and maintain the state of well-being held by full-term infants.

Worldview, Identity, and Time

Central to a discussion of worldview, identity, and time is an examination of what time is and when and how time began. How time is regulated is also significant. It is generally accepted that time has both metaphysical and scientific attributes. According to Jan Faye, Uwe Scheffler, and Max Urchs, time is essentially the interaction of temporal relations with other logical connections and operators. To begin a review of the philosophy of time is to begin with Aristotle and Immanuel Kant. In *De Interpretationes,* 4th-century Greek philosopher Aristotle described time as an aggregate of motions or actions counted sequentially and fixed in place onto a continuum, a decidedly linear and Western view of the cosmos. History is cast as a slide rule against which people may calculate their place in time. History informs them about their personal realities. Kant, the 18th-century German philosopher, on the other hand, relates time to the observer's subjective analysis, a more metaphysical approach. But it is Aristotle's contemporary Augustine, an important Latin church father, who relates time to the identity of humans, through a comparison with God.

Augustine is giving the believers a model of identity to which they are exhorted to strive. As created things/beings, the believers both have and do not have the identity of God. This conundrum is the legacy of free will. But to define *worldview, time,* and *identity* in terms acceptable to the religious and nonreligious alike, the concept of time seems to be a basic organizing principle, a necessary prerequisite to understanding ourselves and the world in which we live.

The accident of birth at a particular time causes the formation of identity in a particular manner—a manner that is married to the particular moment in time when the birth occurs. In the previous example of the two British princesses, outside of birth in England and gender, the two royals have nothing in common. As we are seeing in the 21st century, even concepts of gender identification have changed dramatically. The march of time orders the world, demarking human behaviors, cultures, and conditions.

Grant McCracken, in his book *Transformations: Identity Constructions in Contemporary Culture,* gives us a startling perspective on how the passage of time affects the definition of both the individual and collective self as each seeks identity. In one example, he contrasts the collective life spans of humans as hunters and gatherers with the changes that have occurred in life experiences over an astonishingly shorter period of time.

He presents a ratio of movement and achievement across a backdrop of time, putting into perspective the stasis of the earliest human identity (diggers with sticks), even as it juxtaposes the remarkable and miraculous achievement of the human race as a fraction of time. Whereas McCracken's theory is based on a linear and decidedly Western concept of time, the African-centered concept of time is circular. This entry on worldview, time, and identity accepts the Western and the African, the linear and the circular concepts of time.

Issues of identity repeat themselves and resurface as the human progresses through time. For example, the righteous yet benign "noble savage," an object of literary studies in the early 19th century, reemerges as a member of the beat generation of the mid-20th century. While primarily seen as other, apart from society, there was a significant evolution of this modern noble savage. Identity struggles, both individual and collective, which had taken place over the passage of time, served to empower the beatniks. Their influence on the arts was far-reaching, explosive, and long lasting.

A couple of additional examples underline the importance of time as an agent of identity and worldview. In the 18th century, society was constructed along fairly rigid and castelike lines. Any movement across the lines was achieved only through an extraordinary change in individual circumstances. This change, or upward mobility, came with prima facie identity reformations in fashion, language, domicile, and community. But these exemplars of changing identity were unable, in the 18th century, to establish this new identity on their own. Contrast this state of affairs with the current, postmodern time, when identity and the assumption of it has become an individualized activity, almost by definition. It is the identity as destiny school of thought.

Worldview, Identity, and Space/Place

If, in examining identity, worldview, and place, one divides the spaces and places occupied by humans into rural and nonrural, suburban and urban, across the continuum of time, one finds both similarities and differences in the formation of the self. This bifurcation of identity can be brought into clear focus using the optic of contemporary United States in the context of its global citizenry. In contemporary times, those who were born in the United States are hardly culturally distinguishable from those who acquire citizenship through a legal process. In fact, it is not really even necessary to live in the United States to live the cultural life of an American. U.S. popular culture is pervasive: Euro Disney, Starbucks in Russia, and the popularity of Oprah worldwide. *E Pluribus Unum,* the motto on the U.S. Seal and translated as "Out of One, Many," has become the keyword phrase for U.S. culture.

An interesting sidebar to the discussion of a globally colored U.S. identity is analysis of the climate of the post–9/11 United States. H. V. Savitch looks at identity in a time of terror by tracing the connections to space and place of so-called jihadists and religious extremists and the important functions of place in terms of support for individual identity. The formations of identity would appear to apply as well to domestic terrorists like Timothy McVeigh, the D.C. sniper, and the Son of Sam. These men are examples of youthful males untethered to any one cultural community and only loosely tied to those with similar philosophies. As these agents of twisted identity roam their neighborhoods and the world, the impact has been a shrinking of the perception of available, safe space within U.S. cities. Space is physical and outlined by a sense of personal boundaries. The self operates freely within the confines of those boundaries. Some cite the Homeland (place) Security Act, a direct outgrowth of 9/11, as having significantly altered the U.S. self-concept by collapsing the boundaries of personal space.

Worldview and Cultural Formations of Identity

The historical review of worldview and identity formation has focused on formations not necessarily individualized or achieved as a matter of individual effort. Upward mobility and the resultant change in self-concept required at least tacit approval of society at large. Even then, such self-definitions could carry a negative valence, for example, the difference between the newly rich and old money. The stories of unsuccessful attempts of immigrants to recast themselves are analogous to the continuing saga of the Black man in the United States. For example, one of the legacies of slavery, in North America in particular, has been the remnant of identities formed by the slave masters. Throwing off the jacket tailored with hostility and hate has proven to be very difficult.

Assimilation, integration, cultural rites of passage, even the study of archetypes—as agents of identity transformation, all require a modicum of collective will. The ascendancy of the self as its own creator is a relatively recent phenomenon (given the vast timeline of human existence presented at the beginning of this entry). But the definition of *self,* by self, seems to be growing exponentially. There are hundreds of dictionary definitions of words beginning with the prefix *self, self* being defined equally as the essence of the individual, the survival instinct, and moral character.

We are now situated in the era of "to each his or her own." We are cocooned inside our individual cars, listening to our own personal theme music created for us by the iPod shuffle, and wearing jeans to work on Friday in honor of "dress down day," an acquiescence to a collective of individual identities: no uniforms for us. We are almost slavishly beholden to popular culture. Entertainment icons define and transform us into specific types and orientations. Pervasive use of the World Wide Web has made it possible for individual identities to meld with like minds, sending viral messages of "come fly with me" seamlessly and effortlessly, seeking to effect a more perfect "brave new world." People everywhere are in chat rooms, on blogs and social networks, gaming and reinventing themselves. Culture in the 21st century is breeding an individualistic orientation to the world, which seems to know few limits. Leaving traditional ways of the world in defining *self*, McCracken offers a postmodern construct that defines the self in terms of worldview. He posits that the individual is actually a multiplicity with distinct assignments for its parts. A global self is the result of interactions between the world and this individuated self. Achievement of a global self is the purpose of life. The postmodern exemplars of identity are those who are in the vanguard of world movements.

McCracken offers two cultural formations of identity that are globally present today and that will likely extend into the near future. The first is the *swift self*, and the second is the *radiant self*. Each can be seen as aspects of the global self. The swift self is an outgrowth of a need for change. The advent of computer technology is an example of what happens when a need is met with the ability to effect a change. In less than 50 years, computers have revolutionized almost everything. Their presence in the market has affected the worldwide economy and the stock market, the language, the spaces we inhabit, the way we communicate, and the way we have come to define business. The computer industry morphed into a wealth of information technology architects and engineers, who work to invent smaller and smaller gadgets, until our bodies are literally and figuratively wired for sound and action. All of this happened, and is changing at the speed of thought, simultaneously across the globe. It is a transforming or transformation phenomenon that is producing transformational selves. The swift self is a product of this movement of change. The swift self stands ready to sacrifice all to better its own environment. Swift selves are about refashioning reality.

The swift self stands apart from another modern identity formation, the radiant self. One of the casualties of the Age of Reason was a turning away from the metaphysical, a rebuke of the mythical and magical, a repudiation of the third

eye, fifth dimension, and supernatural powers of man and woman. In postmodern times, we have seen a massive return to what McCracken calls "Re-enchantment" New Age teachings; feng shui, iridology, and the healing powers of touch and crystals now inform the lifestyles of not only the rich and famous but also the ordinary mother, father, and child. The radiant selves lead the charge toward all things new. The radiant selves are global selves responsible for raising global consciousness on a variety of critical issues: the environment, genocide, and clean energy, for example. Momentum is not all, but exploration of possibility and hope is paramount. Some see the election of Barack Obama as president of the United States as a result of a call to the radiant selves of the world. His challenge to believe in change is in alignment with the quintessential character of radiant selves to concretize possibility.

There is, however, another school of thought as relates to McCracken's transformational construct, which poses the possibility that, at least in the United States, this acceptance of all things global leads to the nondevelopment of self. In *Death of the Grown-Up*, Diane West argues that we (continental Americans) are undergoing an identity crisis that has to do both with our split personality as the world policeman and world villain and what she calls unbalanced attention to multiculturalism. Far from embracing the global self, West is holding out for some emphasis on distinctly U.S. ways and means. She rejects the reticence to choose one's own way of being, to the exclusion of others, in the name of multiculturalism. To her way of thinking, some cultural practices, especially when defined in terms of identity, should be subjected to a standard of acceptability. Without such judgments, without such an absence of so-called political correctness, West argues that our children are being taught to be so accepting of others as to become members of a nation of people afraid and unable to speak plainly or in a forthright manner, an ability essential to maintaining a contained sense of self.

No matter which cultural formation of identity one subscribes to, as we move deeper into the 21st century, a fierce sort of individualism is pervasive throughout the world, forming the neural network of our senses of self. This individualism is unique to this time, but not to space, place, or national culture. This individualism is a world culture that reinforces identity. Fueled by a worldwide and seemingly unceasing desire for change and augmented by a longing for the mystical and mythical, the postmodern sense of identity is in a perpetual state of recareering. McCracken calls it "the switching of hats." The citizenry of the earth is now engaged in phenomenal changes in consciousnesses and self-management. In fact, change appears to be the hallmark of 21st-century constructions of identity. The global self is a complex personality, feeding on the synergy of its multiple selves and astonishing in its ability to meld its various faces. The global self, an identity crafted in line with universally held tenets of belief, is a transformational self. And like the popular toys known as transformers, which reassemble themselves from one form to another, in a process akin to the transformation of the caterpillar into the butterfly, assumption of identity, when subject to prevailing worldviews, produces creatures of magnificence, flexibility, and utility.

Lydia Brown Magras

See also Archetype; Cultural Studies; Gender; Identity Change; Philosophical History of Identity; Religious Identity; Self

Further Readings

Faye, J., Scheffler, U., & Urchs, M. (Eds.). (1997). *Perspectives on time*. Dordrecht, the Netherlands: Kluwer Academic.

Gates, B. (1999). *Business @ the speed of thought. Using a digital nervous system*. New York: Warner Books.

McCracken, G. (2008). *Transformations: Identity construction in contemporary culture*. Bloomington: Indiana University Press.

Muhammad, E. (1965). *Message to the Blackman in America*. Chicago: Muhammad's Temple Number 2.

Peters, T. (2003). *Re-imagine!* London: Dorling Kindersley.

Savitch, H. V. (2007). *Cities in a time of terror. Space, territory, and local resilience*. Armonk, NY: M. E. Sharpe.

Spiro, P. J. (2008). *Beyond citizenship. American identity after globalization*. New York: Oxford University Press.

XENOPHOBIA

Prejudice is one on the most common forms of conscious injury perpetuated by humans on one another. Ethnicities and cultures of mass proportions all have their own interpretation of prejudice, although the general consensus is that all people have their own prejudices. People are composed of essential characteristics that are unique to their own ethnic groups. People do not all share the same belief system, skin color, or history, and traditions. Whether one is the object or subject of prejudice, the challenge lies in having mutual respect and tolerance for those who are different from oneself. The *xenophobia* phenomenon is one form of prejudice, the term derived from the Greek word *xenos,* which means "stranger" or "foreigner," and *phobos,* which means "fear." The concept of xenophobia can be traced back to historical, evolutionary sources. Its manifestations are distinctly rooted in the impression that individuals have a thoughtless discomfort with strangers. It is based on the idea that the target of prejudice is directed toward people who are different from oneself. The term *xenophobia* is typically used to describe the irrational fear or hatred of strangers or foreigners. One's attitude toward different ethnicities and the intent to carry out acts of xenophobia classifiy one as a xenophobe.

Xenophobia tends to have two main objectives. The first objective, based on phobia, is to exclude or maltreat a group that is not considered part of a specific society. Those who are considered nonmembers of the society are often deemed as immigrants, and xenophobia is regularly directed toward them and in some cases toward a population of people that has existed in the country for centuries (i.e., Native Americans or First Nations people in the United States). This form of xenophobia can manifest into outright violence and hostility or, in extreme cases, genocide. Acts of genocide are committed with the intent of mass expulsion of a population of sorts. The second objective relates to the purification of a culture or language. This manifestation of xenophobia is primarily cultural; hence, the targets of the phobia tend to be toward aliens. Aliens are individuals who reside in a country other than their birthplace without obtaining citizenship. In essence, all cultural groups have the potential of being subjected to cultural xenophobia, which is narrowly directed. For example, many countries are exhausting their efforts and resources to try to implement English as an official language. Xenophobia can take on various forms; one can be socially xenophobic referring to a fear or hatred toward a particular social group. One can also be xenophobic toward cultures and belief systems—all of which can potentially manifest into acts of violence, hate crime, race wars, religious prosecution, and ethnic cleansing, to name a few.

Externalization of xenophobia can be demonstrated in two forms: *projection identification* and *projective identification.* One is classified as a fearful type, and the other is a hate-filled type. Projection identification often precedes projective identification in that projections flood individuals' conscious in a given experience. Projection is prevalent in various forms, and many of our projections shape many of our actions and feelings. For example, many high schools seniors will project their fear of going to college so they don't necessarily need to experience this fear. By displacing or projecting this fear, they are released from admitting to themselves that they have this fear and its accompanying feelings. Projection (identification) is one of the first defense mechanisms developed early on in childhood.

The second type is projective identification, which is related more to hatred. During an interaction between a stranger (subject) and a xenophobe (object), the xenophobe will first suppress the rejected parts of the stranger, and then the suppressed rejected parts will be projected on the stranger. For example, if I as a xenophobe think members of a certain culture are inherently non-intellectual, then I will project this perception onto them and suggest they always tend to make poor choices or underperform in school. I will seek out cases where that is true and use that as verification of my belief that is, of course, shaped by my xenophobia. To completely prevent the fear, the xenophobe will need to rid his or her conscious of having an encounter with the stranger—this is the premise of projective identification. The concept of projective identification involves the impulse of xenophobia either repressed incompletely or not at all. With the repressed thoughts still present in one's conscious, the projection invokes the thoughts, feelings, or behaviors projected. Simply put, the xenophobe is consciously aware of his or her own impulses even though he or she has projected them upon the subject. Typically, this results in a delusional, distorted, even schizophrenic view of reality. Projective identification is a self-fulfilling prophecy in that the person believes something to be false, and then behaves in such a manner as to make the belief true. Another example of projective identification would be a paranoid person developing the delusion that he or she is being pursued by the police. A total fixation on the fight against the pursuer (police) would result in the paranoid person behaving in such a manner that raises suspicion that he or she has committed a crime. Consequently, the police would presume that he or she has engaged in criminal activity, thus making the belief true.

The xenophobia phenomenon is not a concrete ideology in that it takes on various patterns such as faces, agendas, and forms of establishment. In various contexts, xenophobia has been interchangeably used with ethnocentrism and often racism; however, the ideology is completely different from both phenomena. Ethnocentrism is an orientation toward one's own ethnic group and tendency to elevate one's own culture above others, and racism is an enacted prejudice about a race that is managed by someone who has the power to influence a collective in any given society. As indicated earlier, xenophobia takes on various patterns whereas racism is solely based on race. One particular pattern or concept of the xenophobia phenomenon is *unmentalized xenophobia*. Unmentalized xenophobia is the act of a profound disinterest in those who are culturally, racially, or religiously different and have a heightened sense of self. Furthermore, one who exhibits unmentalized xenophobia is not attracted to the idea of educating himself or herself about those who are racially, culturally, or religiously different from him or her. Unmentalized xenophobics also fail to seize any opportunities one may gain by having such knowledge to and lacks knowledge of them. Socially, unmentalized xenophobics are restricted to those of their own kind, resembling a lifestyle of loyalty to his or her group. Xenophobia is one of the most dangerous types of hatred potentially causing mental, physical, emotional, and epistemic violence.

Ronald L. Jackson II

See also Clan Identity; Cultural Contracts Theory; Culture, Ethnicity, and Race; Etic/Emic; Eugenicism; Self-Monitoring

Further Readings

Jackson, R. L. (2006). *Scripting the Black masculine body: Identity, discourse, and racial politics in popular media.* Albany: SUNY Press.

Kupe, T., Worby, E., Verryn, P., & Abad, D. (2009). *Go home or die here: Violence, xenophobia and the reinvention of difference in South Africa.* Johannesburg, South Africa: Witwatersrand University Press.

Roemer, J., Lee, W., & Straetan, K. (2007). *Racism, xenophobia, and distribution: Multi-issue politics in advanced democracies.* Cambridge, MA: Harvard University Press.

Index

Entry titles and their page numbers are in **bold**.